# MASTERPLOTS II

## SHORT STORY SERIES
### REVISED EDITION

# MASTERPLOTS II

## SHORT STORY SERIES
### REVISED EDITION

# Volume 6
Ora–Sho

*Editor, Revised Edition*
**CHARLES MAY**
*California State University, Long Beach*

*Editor, First Edition*
**FRANK N. MAGILL**

**SALEM PRESS**
Pasadena, California    Hackensack, New Jersey

*Editor in Chief:* Dawn P. Dawson

*Editorial Director:* Christina J. Moose     *Assistant Editor:* Andrea E. Miller
*Project Editor:* R. Kent Rasmussen     *Research Supervisor:* Jeffry Jensen
*Production Editor:* Cynthia Beres     *Acquisitions Editor:* Mark Rehn
*Copy Editor:* Rowena Wildin     *Layout:* Eddie Murillo

Some of the essays in this work originally appeared in *Masterplots II, Short Story Series*, edited by Frank N. Magill (Pasadena, Calif.: Salem Press, Inc., 1986), and in *Masterplots II, Short Story Series Supplement*, edited by Frank N. Magill and Charles E. May (Pasadena, Calif.: Salem Press, Inc., 1996).

∞ The paper used in these volumes conforms to the American National Standard for Permanence of Paper for Printed Library Materials, Z39.48-1992 (R1997).

**Library of Congress Cataloging-in-Publication Data**
Masterplots II : Short story series / editor Charles May. — Rev. ed.
    p.   cm.
    Includes bibliographical references and index.
    ISBN 1-58765-140-8 (set : alk. paper) — ISBN 1-58765-146-7 (vol. 6 : alk. paper) —
    1. Fiction—19th century—Stories, plots, etc. 2. Fiction—19th century—History and criticism. 3. Fiction—20th century—Stories, plots, etc. 4. Fiction—20th century—History and criticism. 5. Short story. I. Title: Masterplots 2. II. Title: Masterplots two. III. May, Charles E. (Charles Edward), 1941-
PN3326 .M27 2004
809.3′1—dc22

                2003018256

First Printing

# TABLE OF CONTENTS

# TABLE OF CONTENTS

# TABLE OF CONTENTS

# MASTERPLOTS II

## SHORT STORY SERIES
### REVISED EDITION

# THE ORANGING OF AMERICA

*Author:* Max Apple (1941-    )
*Type of plot:* Satire
*Time of plot:* The 1920's through the 1960's
*Locale:* Throughout the United States
*First published:* 1974

> *Principal characters:*
> HOWARD JOHNSON, founder of the motel and restaurant chain
> MILDRED "MILLIE" BRYCE, his secretary
> OTIS BRIGHTON, his chauffeur

*The Story*

The story opens with a historical retrospective of what Howard Johnson, his secretary, Mildred Bryce, and his chauffeur have been doing for the last forty years: traveling throughout the United States in a Cadillac limousine, visiting Howard Johnson's motels and restaurants and scouting out new sites for future facilities. They are continuing their long-time practice of tasting new ice cream from their tidy ice-cream freezer, in which there are always at least eighteen flavors. Howard eats only vanilla, and Millie rarely indulges in ice cream because of her recurring stomach problems. Their African American chauffeur, Otis Brighton, has become the primary taster for any new ice-cream flavors. In the back seat, Howard keeps an eye on the rearview mirror to observe Brighton's reaction to new flavors of ice cream. The itinerary they have followed for six months of each year has been determined by the bright orange dots on their travel map indicating existing Howard Johnson motels and restaurants and the white dots indicating future sites.

The first part of the story ends at the Los Angeles airport with Howard Johnson departing for New York City because his board of directors is planning new strategies for the company. Millie senses that their idyllic world may be coming to an end, but she is also experiencing greater pain from her bleeding ulcer.

Millie financed Howard Johnson's original investment from a $100,000 inheritance that her father left her when he committed suicide. She is thus the real power behind the throne and has grown immensely wealthy as a result. Howard Johnson has an almost mystical gift for locating prospective building sites: He often suddenly asks Otis to stop the car and then wanders into a field until he feels a secret vibration. Millie once had a similar experience, being inexorably drawn to a desolate spot in the Palestinian desert where she felt they must build a Howard Johnson's motel. Both Howard and Millie began to see themselves as pioneers rather than businesspersons.

The trio began their journey into the great American West as Howard suggested they turn right at Cairo. Twenty years later, Millie finds herself a wealthy woman living in a luxurious apartment building in Santa Monica, owned by bandleader Lawrence Welk. Although Millie is only fifty-six years old, she is beginning to feel that her life may be winding down toward death and looks into the possibility of being frozen and placed in a cryonic capsule rather than being buried in a cemetery. After she visits the Los Angeles Cryonic Society home office and views the resting places of several famous people, she decides to pay the necessary fees to preserve her body in a frozen state for eternity.

Howard Johnson returns from New York after four months. He has been named his company's chairman emeritus and has been given the job of traveling to Florida to sell homeowner franchises to the thousands of people moving there, to provide motels for the emerging giant called Disney World. Howard considers this the greatest challenge of his life—his inevitable confrontation with the king himself, Walt Disney. Millie decides that her health is too tenuous to embark on such a venture and worries that she would be too far from her cryonic cylinder. She and Howard muse over their accomplishments. They have transformed the drudgery of travel into a celebration of comfort, and Millie has changed the motel from a place people had to be into a place they wanted to be. The orange Howard Johnson signs that cover the nation have become a symbol of an Edenic oasis awaiting the exhausted traveler. Millie recalls the day she introduced Howard to the poet Robert Frost. It was sunset of that day, a few miles from Frost's home, that Millie recalls: "The feeling we had about that orange, Howard, that was ours, and that's what I've tried to bring to every house, the way we felt that night." Howard presents Millie with a specially designed, twelve-foot, orange cryonic U-Haul—her own personal crypt—attached to the limousine, so she will never be more than a few seconds from her own immortality. She changes her mind and decides to accompany Howard in his battle with the giant, Walt Disney.

*Themes and Meanings*

This subtle satire by comic short-story writer Max Apple caricatures the so-called American Dream. It parodies a number of motifs, such as rugged individualism, the power of money to attain comfort in life as well as in death, and the inability of Americans to deal with death in a realistic fashion. Howard Johnson, Millie Bryce, and Otis Brighton are modern versions of Huck Finn and Jim floating down the Mississippi in search of the freedom that the United States should offer all its citizens. It is also a gentle parody of the Western movement, in which pioneers sought new lives and possibilities. This capitalist trio, though, is searching for new materialistic ventures as they "orange" the United States with their restaurants and motels, and as they direct their imaginations toward the creation of an infinite variety of ice-cream flavors. As new pioneers, their goal is to transform the drudgery of travel into a new quest for comfort, which is both Millie's and Howard Johnson's favorite word. Mythically, they are involved in regenerating the drab old motels of a previous era into Edenic oases—homes away from home. At the end of Millie's western journey, she has established her own Edenic home on the eighteenth floor of an apartment building owned by none other than Lawrence Welk himself.

Because Millie is not religious and has no discernable spiritual life, it becomes vitally important to her to preserve her body because that is what life is exclusively about. Motifs such as ice cream, cryonics, and Vaseline Petroleum Jelly cohere into a major symbol of Americans' desperate attempts to preserve themselves from the onslaughts of time and mortality and to practice their peculiar form of denial. Denial is the principal theme of this highly entertaining story, but a kind of denial that shows itself in its ability to "orange" America—that is, to transform it according to the sentimental dreams of the rich and powerful.

### Style and Technique

"The Oranging of America" employs parody and caricature throughout. Apple caricatures an actual person in this story—Howard Johnson—but he satirizes more than the character of that one man. He directs his satire at the all-consuming materialism on which the United States has built its values. Apple subtly invites the reader to compare the spiritual quest of Huckleberry Finn—to define his own salvation—to the financial conquest that Howard and Millie are pursuing across the American landscape. Both Howard and Millie undergo spiritual epiphanies on their travels, but the genesis of those experiences comes from their gigantic wealth, though they view those visions as some kind of divine manifestation.

Apple also invites comparisons with other travel stories, such as Jack Kerouac's "On the Road" (1957). "The Oranging of America" is the rugged individualist's and consumerist's "On the Road," complete with spiritual visions in the middle of Iowa cornfields in which Howard Johnson falls into a kind of trance that leads him to the spot where he must erect the first air-conditioned motel in the United States. This brilliant story satirizes many of the entrepreneurial heroes who spent their lives modifying the face of the United States to reflect their own personal values and visions of what it should become.

*Patrick Meanor*

# ORDER OF INSECTS

*Author:* William H. Gass (1924-    )
*Type of plot:* Psychological
*Time of plot:* The late 1950's
*Locale:* Suburban United States
*First published:* 1961

> *Principal characters:*
> THE NARRATOR, a homemaker with children
> HER HUSBAND, also unnamed

## The Story

The first-person narrator was once a typical homemaker, terrified by the fast-moving roaches in the family's previous house and concerned only with her motherly and wifely duties. Then she notices the dead bugs that appear daily on the living-room carpet, and as self-punishment for mistreating the children one evening, she forces herself to examine the bugs carefully.

Initially, she reacts predictably and normally, in her opinion, by withdrawing in disgust from the ugly insects. Strongly and unaccountably to her, however, she later begins to study the bugs in intimate detail, noting their shape, color, appendages, and the subtle differences between the adult and nymph bugs—slightly different size, degree of transparency of their legs, and color. At this stage, she seems to examine them because they daily intrude into and disrupt the meticulously closed and orderly life she leads. Later, however, she becomes very curious about them, especially about how they move when alive because she never sees one alive. Her dilemma begins when she feels disgust about her own interest, saying the study of bugs is not for a woman.

She vacillates throughout the story between intense interest in the bugs and embarrassment about her interest, but with the interest becoming fascination and her embarrassment steadily lessening. She admits later that the bugs are interesting because they are a novel experience, and acknowledges her gratitude for this experience. She then admits to beginning serious study of the bugs, using a text a friend gives her, and she reaches new understanding of the orderliness of the insects' physical nature. Noting this new knowledge and her mixed feelings, she is no longer disgusted with the orderly insects but believes that they are still not a fit subject of a woman's interest.

Despite the internal conflict, the narrator admits that her life has been fundamentally changed by studying the bugs. She develops new insight into human reality by analogizing human behavior to that of the bugs, for example, that humans tend to love the external, physical person rather than the intangible, spiritual qualities, with the human body analogous to the empty, dry shells of the dead bugs. She also develops new energy and enthusiasm, as well as vividness and freedom of imagination, and acknowledges a heightened understanding that is like the perspective of a god. She begins to see beyond conventional knowledge reflected in accepted language, noting the inaccuracy of her previous reference to herself as innocent in relation to the dead bugs. She has realized the power of humans in controlling other species, even insects, and by the end of the story has begun to protect various types of insects from the insecticides used by her husband. In fully comprehending the orderly beauty of the insects that she once regarded as ghastly, she notes that she has penetrated to comprehension of the world's dark soul—the godlike perspective. This causes her to act in ways that disturb her children, who fear her frighteningly probing eyes, and shows her the limitedness and lack of fulfillment of her life as a housewife. That life interferes with her growth, her learning, and the spiritual and psychological satisfaction her learning provides, creating her psychological dilemma. She has studied the insects with masculine-like commitment, but she is still "the wife of the house, concerned for the rug, tidy and punctual, surrounded [trapped?] by blocks."

*Themes and Meanings*

Although a complex story, "Order of Insects" is unified by a single thematic focus that derives from William H. Gass's training as a philosopher at Cornell and his career as a teacher of philosophy, primarily at Washington University. The story dramatizes the fundamental dichotomies of the Platonic idealist point of view, with the obvious, easily perceived, apparently real world as actually an insignificant reflection of a deeper, more important reality. The narrator's seemingly orderly and complete life as a housewife and mother is exposed as insignificant, incomplete, and confused compared to the order and beauty that she finds in the world beyond herself—in the bugs in her carpet. She admits that she once believed that love meant chaos and that life was inherently tumultuous and confusing. Both beliefs are descriptive of her housewife's life, but the world's larger reality, epitomized by the bugs, shows her that she could take control of her life, and discover peace and orderliness in all things, if she could devote herself totally to study and appreciation. Thus she could transcend her physical being (false reality) for the life of the mind (true reality of spirit and intellect). She feels like Galileo in her intellectual discoveries but admits that her physical self struggles against the mental joys and tires of the intellectual effort.

The bugs represent this inverted reality, too: Their bodies, although splendidly intact with the Egyptian permanence of mummies, are presented as only light, empty cases lacking the heaviness—the fundamental realness—of their souls. Similarly, the narrator notes, humans tend to value the temporary, the unreal in others: the external features, comprising muscles, water, and adipose tissue, which are proven least real, least substantial, because of how rapidly they deteriorate. Human bones, more real, last much longer, and the human soul, the least tangible and least obvious, is most real and is, in fact, eternal. Thus, through study beyond the surface or superficial, the narrator pierces to the real, the world's dark soul, which casts a large shadow over the superficial housewife's reality. Because she is still trapped in the unreal, her body, the narrator cannot escape to the reality of pure mind. Despite feeling shell-like as her imagination roams in the wonders of the intellectual universe, the narrator is still trapped in the duties of her earthly role as wife and mother. This is her psychological dilemma.

Gass's story illustrates that progress toward that Platonic reality is possible via intellectual development, that the special, godlike human quality of mind allows humans fleetingly, at least, to comprehend the wonderful order, completeness, and spirituality of the universe. Gass suggests that the struggle to achieve such comprehension is what living a meaningful, fulfilled life is really about, whether one is Stephen Hawking studying black holes and the universe's origin, or Jane Doe keeping the carpet clean and the baby's diapers washed.

*Style and Technique*

"Order of Insects" is so emotionally and intellectually absorbing that it is easy to overlook the technical artistry with which it is written. The most important means by which Gass achieves the great impact is by use of a first-person narrator whose relating of the events and her feelings is so intimately and painstakingly done that she comes powerfully to life as a character. As Gass has noted in "The Concept of Character in Fiction," in his collection of critical theory and practical criticism *Fiction and the Figures of Life* (1970), character creation is an especially exciting and important aspect of successful fiction writing because characters are the fundamental entities to which everything else in fiction relates and because they are the most energized components of stories. "Order of Insects" succeeds primarily because of this realistic narrator. The reader never learns her name, but such superficial realness is omitted appropriately because the story operates on a much more intimate level than that of human names. It is nearly stream-of-consciousness in its intimacy, with the narrator talking more to herself than to a companion or distant reader.

Although this intimate type of first-person narration is by no means original, Gass's narration is technically masterful, the character becoming so lifelike that thoughts about an author's controlling hand quickly fade. Even the story's symbols and images are so closely tied to the narrator's consciousness that they seem perfectly natural extensions of her perspective, such as when she notes her being surrounded by blocks at the story's end. She clearly perceives the blocks as symbolic of her familial trap, the insight not seeming to be foisted on her by an intrusive author. Likewise, the story's similes and metaphors reflect the narrator's increasingly imaginative perceptions, as she goes from the rather commonplace comparison of dead bugs on the carpet to dead earthworms in the road after a rain, to the creative comparison of seeing the intensity of the bugs' shells as similar to the intense stare of South Sea islanders in Paul Gauguin's paintings. Such increasing creativity realistically dramatizes the narrator's psychological change, keeping the reader absorbed in the most dramatic and mysterious reality of all: the human mind.

*John L. Grigsby*

# THE ORDINARY SON

*Author:* Ron Carlson (1947-    )
*Type of plot:* Domestic realism, coming of age
*Time of plot:* Summer, 1966
*Locale:* Houston, Texas
*First published:* 1999

> *Principal characters:*
> REED LANDERS, the narrator
> DUNCAN LANDERS, his father
> GLORIA RAINSTRAP, his mother
> CHRISTINA ROSETTI, his older sister
> GARRETT LANDERS, his younger brother

*The Story*

Reed Landers is the ordinary son in an extraordinary family of geniuses. Looking back from the perspective of adulthood, Reed narrates the story of his family and several key incidents in the summer of 1966. Reed's father is Duncan Landers, a National Aeronautics and Space Administration (NASA) scientist who has changed his last name from Lrsdysksz to Landers to accommodate the public relations department at the agency. Reed's mother is Gloria Rainstrap, a poet and social activist who spends most of her time traveling around the country and giving poetry readings and speeches on behalf of migrant workers and other disadvantaged groups.

Life at the family home in suburban Houston, Texas, reflects the idiosyncrasies of a household of geniuses, each of whom is preoccupied with his or her own intellectual pursuits. Duncan works at a drafting board in the front hallway of the house, and Gloria is constantly on the road trying to advance social causes. The family survives on a diet of sardines and crackers in a house that lacks a telephone, television, or automobile. The daughter leaves home to study chemistry at the Massachusetts Institute of Technology but later joins her mother's social crusading. Meantime, Reed waits for the spark of the family's genius to strike him.

In the summer of 1966, when he is seventeen, Reed is finally freed from the expectation of following in the inspired footsteps of his parents and sister when his little brother Garrett manifests the signs of genius. Reed realizes that the family's genius has passed him by and pursues a more normal life. Reed buys a car, a green Plymouth Fury III, and goes to work doing odd jobs at the San Jacinto Resort Motel. His best friend, Jeff Schreckenbah, works next door at Alfredo's American Café. He starts buying fashionable clothes for himself and living the life of a typical American teenager.

While working at the motel, Reed has a pivotal experience that opens up the new world of ordinary life and reveals his own special gifts. One day, while on break, Jeff and Reed are engaged in a typical male adolescent conversation about sex. Recognizing Reed's total lack of experience and knowledge of sexual matters, Jeff decides to enlighten his ignorant friend. Mr. Shinetower, a permanent resident of the motel where Reed works, has an extensive collection of pornography. While the old man is having his lunch at the café, the boys sneak out and break into the man's room. Jeff picks up one of Mr. Shinetower's magazines and opens it to a closeup of female genitalia. Looking for the first time at these pictures of the female body, Reed has a near epiphany. He gazes at the photograph like an explorer. Mr. Shinetower returns early from his lunch, and the boys barely escape without being discovered.

Reed begins to enjoy his new life as a non-genius. His work is simple, involving landscaping, sweeping the parking lot, cleaning the pool, and general light maintenance. It is a far cry from the advanced studies and avocations of the rest of his family, but the money he earns provides a new sense of freedom and opens up a life radically different from what he has known before. At Jeff's house, Reed becomes acquainted with life in a normal household. They help Jeff's father work on race cars in his shop. The boys also go on regular excursions to fish in the surf near Galveston. Smoking cigars and drinking beer, Reed and Jeff build a fire on the beach and fish all night.

After his genius is discovered, Reed's brother Garrett moves out of the house to study at Rice University. Reed goes to visit his brother in the dorm where he lives with other child prodigies. Watching the children in the lunchroom, who have to be encouraged to eat by the adult monitors, Reed begins to understand the destructive effects that the gift of genius has on children like Garrett and on families like his own. After eating lunch with Garrett and his friend Donna Li, Reed takes them outside to admire his Plymouth Fury III, which still smells of half-rotten shrimp bait from a recent fishing trip. The children are amazed by the size and power of the car, which is so different from their surroundings in a world of geniuses. As Reed drives away, he hopes that his brother and the other children will be able to find their way to the simple happiness of a normal life.

### Themes and Meanings

In "The Ordinary Son," Ron Carlson contrasts the nature of genius with the notion of an ordinary life. He portrays Reed's quest for normalcy against the backdrop of life in a family of geniuses. Each of the individual members of the Landers family portrays a different aspect of genius. The father, Duncan, the NASA scientist, is the typical lone genius. He works at a drafting table in the front hallway, which literally blocks the entrance to the house. His only contact with his son is a brief exchange of words as Reed maneuvers past the table on entering the house after work.

Reed's mother, Gloria, the poet, has directed her genius into her work for social causes. She spends her time traveling across the country to give readings and lectures on behalf of various disadvantaged groups. Because she is absent from the house for weeks and months at a time, she leaves notes of advice on the bottom of things like shoes and jars in order to share her wisdom and insight with her children.

The daughter, Christina, shows great promise in the field of chemistry. Instead of expanding the periodic table of elements, she drops her studies and joins her mother on the road. She represents a mind that is unable to cope with its own genius and seeks escape from the pressures of research and intellectual production.

The youngest child, Garrett, is the model of the child genius. Taken away by experts to live and work with other youthful prodigies at Rice University, Garrett is forced to leave his childhood and his home behind because of his special gifts. In a single day, he goes from a typical boy drawing pictures to a wunderkind writing out complicated mathematical formulae. In contrast to each of the other family members, Reed shows no special aptitude for engineering, chemistry, physics, or literature. Instead he acquires the special gift of being able to live an ordinary life. While Garrett is confined to a dormitory of genius children, Reed discovers the personal freedom of earning money, buying clothes, hanging out with friends, and driving a car.

*Style and Technique*

Carlson's stories signal a return to the tradition of realism in American short fiction. The author describes ordinary people who struggle to maintain their balance in unusual circumstances. "The Ordinary Son" is the story of a seventeen-year-old boy born into a family of geniuses who must learn how to live a normal life when he realizes that he is the only family member who possesses no extraordinary gifts or aptitudes. Many of Carlson's stories are concerned with the issues of growing up. As in "The Ordinary Son," the narrator is typically an adult reflecting back across time on key periods in his adolescence. For Reed Landers, the summer of 1966, when he takes his first job and buys a car, is the pivotal season of his life.

Reed's remembrances of that summer coalesce around four incidents that mark his discovery that the family curse of genius has passed him by and the beginning of his attempts to embrace the freedom and possibilities that life as a non-genius is offering him. In Carlson's story, these four episodes acquire a sharp clarity of focus that makes them stand out from Reed's recollections of his family and his home. The first incident is Reed's realization that his brother Garrett has begun to manifest signs of genius. Walking into his brother's room one day, Reed finds Garrett writing out complicated mathematical formulae for rocket trajectories on sheets of white butcher paper spread across the floor. With the knowledge that the family trait of genius has passed him by, Reed is liberated to pursue a new kind of life. The second key incident of the summer is the awakening in Reed of the typical male adolescent sexual interest. The third is a fishing trip Reed takes with his buddy Jeff. During this first summer of freedom, the two high school students drive down to Galveston to fish in the nighttime ocean surf. Reed's narrative captures the full range of sensations of struggling to land a large catfish: the fish's frenzied motions on the end of the line, the feel of the warm gulf waters, and the light of the bonfire on the beach, the sting on his hand of the sharp gills as he removes the hook. The fourth incident is Reed's visit with his brother Garrett at Rice University. Looking at the other children, preoccupied with their interests and pursuits, Reed comes to see Garrett's life and genius itself as a prison. The story ends with Reed driving away on a road that leads to freedom and an ordinary life.

*Tony Rafalowski*

# THE OTHER PARIS

*Author:* Mavis Gallant (1922-　　)
*Type of plot:* Social realism
*Time of plot:* The early 1950's
*Locale:* Paris
*First published:* 1953

> *Principal characters:*
> CAROL FRAZIER, the young protagonist, an American living in
> Paris
> HOWARD MITCHELL, her fiancé, an American also living in Paris
> ODILE PONTMORET, Carol's Parisian acquaintance
> FELIX, Odile's young lover, a mid-European refugee in Paris

*The Story*

One late spring afternoon, Carol Frazier, the twenty-two-year-old protagonist, is concluding a visit with an acquaintance, Odile Pontmoret, to a Parisian dressmaker, Madame Germain, who is making Carol's wedding gown. Odile disapproves of the traditional, "unoriginal" gown that Carol chooses. Moreover, to Carol's annoyance, Odile blabs to the dressmaker that Carol fell in love at first sight with her fiancé, Howard Mitchell, an economist, who, with Carol and Odile, works in a U.S. government agency in Paris. Odile is aware that Carol, perceiving Paris to be the city of romance, wants to believe in the magic of the moment of falling in love. As they leave the dressmaker's apartment, Carol realizes that Odile is making fun of her romantic notion. This realization occasions a review of the preceding winter months, beginning with her engagement to Howard.

Her engagement and her subsequent relationship with Howard are actually quite prosaic. Three weeks after she met him he proposed to her, not in a romantic setting but at lunch, over a tuna salad. She is not really in love with Howard, but common sense, buttressed by college lectures on marriage, dictates that they have the proper basis for marriage—that is, a similar social and economic background. In choosing Howard, Carol herself dispenses with "the illusion of love," but having decided that he is the right person for her, she feels the urge to be a part of romantic Paris. She therefore sets about "the business of falling in love" with Howard.

Postwar Paris, with its drab streets and shabby people, is not conducive to this plan, but she persists. Believing that befriending the French would help, she approaches Odile, Howard's secretary, a thirty-year-old woman. Odile, shabbily dressed, money-conscious, and resentful of American materialism, hardly evokes romantic Paris, nor does Odile's relationship with her twenty-one-year-old lover, Felix, which Carol considers distasteful. Felix, a mid-European, lost his family at the end of the war; he is in Paris without a passport or a work permit, and he may well be involved in black-marketing. The romantic in Carol finds him fascinating and mysterious, but the realist perceives him to be lazy and parasitic.

Carol, still hoping to experience the elusive charms of Paris, persuades Howard to accompany her to hear the carol-singing in the Place Vendome. This, too, is a disappointment. The affair is artificially staged for the media; the weather is wet and miserable. Later, when Howard tells his friends about the evening, he is able to make it "an amusing story," and as Carol listens to him, it strikes her that accounts of experience "could be perfectly accurate but untruthful," an observation reiterated toward the end of the story.

Soon after this, Odile invites Carol and Howard to the concert debut of her sister, Martine. Carol is quite excited, believing that she finally is to be allowed into the other life of Paris. Once more she is frustrated. The audience is devitalized; the theater is falling apart. After the concert, Carol and Howard observe Felix waiting outside the theater for Odile; Odile's family evidently does not accept him. Carol momentarily becomes hysterical and rants against Odile's snobbery, Felix's laziness, and their distasteful love affair. Her emotional outburst is cathartic. After the concert, she stops "caring about Paris" and believes that "she has become invulnerable."

At this point, the past comes abreast of the present, as the narrative returns to Carol and Odile leaving the dressmaker's apartment. Carol reluctantly agrees to accompany Odile to Felix's apartment. Carol is appalled at Felix's dirty room and embarrassed by Odile's and Felix's unabashed intimacy. Odile falls asleep, and Carol decides to leave. Felix accompanies Carol to the Metro. There, declining his offer to buy her a drink, she reprimands him for not working and advises him to migrate to the United States, where he could start afresh. As Felix explains to her the practical and emotional difficulties involved in this, Carol becomes aware of Felix's and Odile's love for each other. For a fleeting moment she wants to share in this romantic love that has been denied her. She draws back, however, refusing to accept that "such a vision could come from Felix and Odile," two shabby individuals spending hours together "in that terrible room in a slummy quarter of Paris."

As she returns to her apartment, she convinces herself that the passage of time will allow her "a coherent picture, accurate but untrue" of her experience in Paris. "The memory of Felix and Odile and all their distasteful strangeness would slip away; for 'love' she would think, once more, 'Paris,' and after a while, happily married, mercifully removed in time, she would remember it and describe it and finally believe it as it had never been at all."

### Themes and Meanings

In a journalistic piece written in 1947 for *Standard Magazine* entitled "Is Romance Killing Your Marriage?" Mavis Gallant refers to the anthropologist Margaret Mead's theory that the myth of romantic love was responsible for the increasing collapse of marriages in North America. Those seeking romantic love, Gallant states, affirming Mead's observation, will find that it does not exist. This idea reappears in "The Other Paris," but although the article is a categorical rejection of romantic love, the story, in portraying the intense emotional and mental conflict of an individual forced to come to grips with a possible need for romantic love, has a richly ambiguous tone.

Young Carol learned at college that "the illusion of love was a blight imposed by the film industry, and almost entirely responsible for the high rate of divorce." However, during her first stay in Paris, she experiences the tug of romantic love and is caught between her romantic yearning and her realistic perception. She is attracted to Felix, who, dispossessed, world-weary, and mysterious, exhibits the trappings of the romantic hero. She is momentarily tempted to abandon the evident staidness of her world for the apparent excitement of his. However, she resists, persuading herself to believe that what "she and Howard had was better." She compromises herself. In doing so, however, she evades or at least eases the tormenting inner conflict caused by her indulgence in romantic love.

The omniscient narrator, whose presence is evident throughout the story, neither condemns nor sanctions Carol's decision. The reader is invited to consider whether it would have been better for her to choose Felix's world, which is romantic but contains aspects that are abhorrent to her; whether, given Carol's particular sensibility, she has chosen what is best for her; and whether, in not risking a romantic relationship, Carol has robbed herself of a richer emotional life.

It is possible to see the story as an account of a Jamesian American innocent in Europe, or of the comforting nature of memory, or of the interplay between illusion and reality, or of the relative truth of art, or of the differences between American and European mores. All of these are evident in "The Other Paris," but they are ancillary to the main study of Carol's confrontation with romantic love.

*Style and Technique*

Gallant points up the inner conflict of her protagonist, who is caught between antithetical perceptions of love, by employing a pervasive pattern of opposites. The two time sequences reveal this pattern: The past is characterized by the bleakness and darkness of winter; the current time sequence by the buds and light of spring, the advent of which is "like coming out a tunnel." The past episodes show Carol consciously striving for romance and are set against the immediate incident that reveals her confronting the possibility of romantic love without deliberately seeking it.

Gallant's characterization also exhibits the counterpointing principle at work. Although Odile, who has romance, worries about financial security, Carol, who is materially comfortable, yearns for romance. Odile's stock observations of New York are compared with Carol's fixed expectations of Paris. Also, Felix is a perfect foil to Howard.

A subtler form of contrast that helps to keep before the reader Carol's fluctuation between reality and fancy is that between the actual and the desired suggested by the frequent use of "as if" constructions. At one point, for example, the narrator says: "Her heart leaped as if he, Felix, had said he loved her." There are at least a dozen such phrasings in the story.

The story constantly and subtly shifts between two voices, Carol's and the omniscient narrator's, which offer contrasting perceptions of Carol's experiences. The protagonist's assessment of herself is narrow; the narrator's of her is inclusive. Carol's elicits sympathy; the narrator's is occasionally ironic but never mocking, for the narrator recognizes the honesty as well as the limits of Carol's self-assessment and makes the reader aware that she is no worse than the other characters, such as Odile, who is biased in her view of others, has questionable expectations, and compromises as well.

This is an early Gallant story, but her skills as a short-story writer are recognizable. Besides this appropriate pattern of opposites, there are her graphic but economical portrait of postwar Paris, her structural skill, her subtle tone, and her grasp of the complex and the elusive in examining the individual's ordinary experiences.

*Victor J. Ramraj*

# THE OTHER SIDE OF THE HEDGE

*Author:* E. M. Forster (1879-1970)
*Type of plot:* Fantasy
*Time of plot:* About 1904
*Locale:* Paradise
*First published:* 1904

> *Principal characters:*
> THE NARRATOR, a man who believes in progress and science
> HIS GUIDE
> HIS BROTHER
> MISS ELIZA DIMBLEBY, an earnest and hard-working woman

*The Story*

The story opens with the narrator resting by the side of a seemingly endless road. Although others on the road jeer him for stopping his walk, and the energetic Miss Eliza Dimbleby exhorts him to persevere, he subsequently collapses and thinks of his brother, who had collapsed a year or so earlier after wasting his breath on singing and his strength helping others. The narrator lies prostrate from exhaustion until a faint breath of air from a thick hedge alongside the road revives him. After glancing around to ensure that he is unobserved, he musters his remaining strength and fights through the dead branches of the hedge, although he has no idea what he might find on the other side. Just as he feels he might die from his exertion, he falls through the undergrowth into a moat. He nearly drowns but is rescued by a man who becomes his guide to the world on the other side of the hedge.

This guide, who looks fifty or sixty years old but has the voice of an eighteen-year-old boy, shows the narrator through the park, which is of indeterminate size but of definite beauty. Unlike the dusty and dry road, the park teems with vitality and is filled with images of pastoral happiness: flowers covering the green hedge, fish swimming in the moat, people singing and working contentedly in the fields. The narrator, however, is disenchanted to learn that the residents of this paradise have no need for science or machines. After arguing that a society must progress or else it is worthless, he states his intention to leave this world—beautiful as it may be—to return to the competition of the road. Before he can leave, his guide shows him two gates. The first opens outward and is made of ivory: It is the gate through which earliest humanity walked when first taken with the idea of leaving the paradise to explore the outer world.

As the narrator and his guide walk away from this gate, the narrator believes he sees Miss Dimbleby with her feet in a fountain. Although his guide confirms that it is she, the narrator rejects the sight as an impossibility because her earnest demeanor would never allow such laziness. He then asks to leave the park immediately. His guide reluctantly shows him a second gate, made of half-transparent horn and opening in toward the park. Through its translucency, the narrator can see the dusty, dreary road flanked by dead hedges that he left earlier. When he hesitates, a man passes by with a can of liquid. Suddenly seized by an uncontrollable thirst, the narrator snatches the can and drinks from it. He starts to lose consciousness but hears his guide say that this second gate is the one through which all that is left of humanity will pass on its return to the paradise. The man whose drink he has taken catches the narrator as he collapses. Slipping into a deep sleep, the narrator realizes that he now lies in his brother's arms.

*Themes and Meanings*

In his brief introduction to *The Celestial Omnibus, and Other Stories* (1947), E. M. Forster points out that each of the six stories in his collection are fantasies, meaning they are more far-fetched in plot and characterization than his novels usually are, even though both often deal with similar themes. This generalization about the stories holds especially true for "The Other Side of the Hedge," a dreamlike parable that uses heavy-handed symbolism to condemn modern, mechanistic society.

As in Forster's other fantasies in *The Celestial Omnibus, and Other Stories*, "The Other Side of the Hedge" exemplifies the value of a pastoral society in which men and women can ignore the pressures of a modern world. Unlike the other fantasies, this story is overtly allegorical and is to be read symbolically. The dusty road, for example, represents life; the reader should understand that when the narrator—who is anonymous because he is an Everyman—stops walking along this road he is contemplating suicide rather than continuing his monotonous trek. He has already dropped many of the tools of civilization but has kept his pedometer and his watch, obvious symbols for the mechanistic society in which he lives.

The narrator's trip through the hedge and consequent immersion into the moat symbolize his physical rebirth into a new world, one in which neither his pedometer—which still reads "twenty-five" and thus suggests his age—nor his watch functions. The narrator has left his dreary existence for a perfect utopia, although he fails to realize this fact and stupidly seeks to escape from it. Consequently, the latter two-thirds of the story are about the narrator's psychological rebirth, his tortuous inner growth toward the realization that he can attain happiness only by rejecting the modern world, which places so much emphasis on progress.

The success of the narrator's realization hinges on his acceptance of the symbolism of the two gates. According to classical mythology, false dreams enter into one's consciousness through gates of ivory; in Forster's story these are the gates that lead from the other side of the hedge into the modern world. True dreams, however, come through gates of horn, and it is these gates that lead into the world hidden beyond the hedge. It is at these gates that the narrator loses consciousness in his brother's arms and finally surrenders himself to a new life. Here the reader comes to understand the crucial role of the narrator's brother.

The narrator's brother is first mentioned in the second paragraph, after the narrator collapses by the side of the road. The narrator states that his brother similarly left the road after devoting his time to such things as singing and helping others; it is clear from his sarcasm that he regards such pursuits as frivolous wastes of time. At the end of the story, after the guide is beginning to make him doubt the worth of a life of conformity on the road, the narrator realizes that his brother did not waste his time because he had lived a life of individuality and freedom.

Forster does not advocate suicide in this fantasy but suggests that people should examine their lives carefully to ensure they are not so caught up in the modern world that they fail to appreciate the imaginative qualities of life. As in his other stories in *The Celestial Omnibus, and Other Stories*, Forster suggests here that people balance their world of experience with the too-often forgotten world of innocence. Rather than condemning themselves to identical lives of conformity, they should never hesitate to strive for individuality.

*Style and Technique*

Critics often praise Forster's fiction for its understated tone, and "The Other Side of the Hedge" does not deviate from this standard. Rather than use extravagant descriptions, Forster adds just enough telling details to allow readers to imagine the scene. An example of his subtlety occurs when the narrator contrasts the vast sky above the paradise on the other side of the hedge with the limited sky above the road: As he emerges from the moat, he notices that the "blue sky was no longer a strip." This sort of light touch throughout the story is effective, especially because the story's symbolism can be heavy-handed at times.

A typical Forster story, such as "The Road from Colonus" or "The Celestial Omnibus," both of which appear in *The Celestial Omnibus, and Other Stories*, is built around a central symbolic image; once a reader grasps that image, a subtle theme emerges from the story because the other images are subordinated to the primary image. Although "The Other Side of the Hedge" has the hedge as its central image, Forster burdens his story with so many other major symbols that they compete with one another for prominence, and attempts to discover an overriding theme can be frustrated.

*Jim McWilliams*

# THE OTHER TWO

*Author:* Edith Wharton (Edith Newbold Jones, 1862-1937)
*Type of plot:* Wit and humor
*Time of plot:* The early twentieth century
*Locale:* New York City
*First published:* 1904

*Principal characters:*
MR. WAYTHORN, a Wall Street broker
MRS. ALICE WAYTHORN, his wife
HASKETT, Alice's first husband
GUS VARICK, Alice's second husband
LILY HASKETT, Alice's daughter

*The Story*

A successful New York investor named Waythorn and his twice-divorced bride, Alice, cut short their honeymoon because her twelve-year-old daughter, Lily, has fallen ill with typhoid. Awaiting them at home is a letter from the lawyer of Alice's first husband, Haskett, requesting that his weekly visitation rights be continued at the Waythorn household because Lily cannot be moved. Waythorn reluctantly agrees but, not wishing an embarrassing scene, leaves early the following day for work. While on a crowded train, he runs into Alice's second husband, the well-connected but boorish Gus Varick, who asks for his help with an important business transaction. Waythorn's partner Sellers has been handling it but is currently ill with the gout. Despite the awkwardness of the situation, Waythorn agrees. A few hours later, at lunch, he spots Varick at a nearby table, pouring cognac into his coffee cup. Eschewing direct contact, Waythorn wonders whether Varick ever was put in embarrassing situations with Haskett while married to Alice.

That evening, Waythorn inquires about Haskett's visit. Alice replies that the nurse showed him in, implying, to Waythorn's relief, that she had no direct contact with him. After dinner, Alice pours liqueur into his coffee cup, just as Varick had done at lunch. When Waythorn exclaims that he does not take brandy, she blushes.

Ten days later, with Sellers still ill, Waythorn confers with Varick, who is pleasant and even alludes to past financial problems that, rumor has it, caused his rupture with Alice. Meanwhile, as Lily recuperates, Waythorn grows less uneasy about Haskett's visits, although a chance face-to-face encounter is awkward for him. Although Haskett seems unimpressive and undistinguished, wearing a "made-up tie attached with elastic," Waythorn comes to respect his concern for his daughter's welfare. When Haskett complains about Lily's French governess, Waythorn resents the criticism but has the servant dismissed.

The increased contact with Haskett and Varick causes Waythorn to scrutinize and analyze his wife's behavior. He learns, for example, that, despite her denial, she conversed with Haskett during his first visit. At a ball, "wandering through the remoter rooms," Waythorn comes on Varick and Alice sitting together. "She colored a little, and faltered in what she was saying; but Varick nodded to Waythorn without rising, and the latter strolled on." Later, however, when Waythorn expresses surprise that she talked to Varick, she claims that it has not happened before and will not again, if he so desires. Wearily, he replies, "It's better to speak to Varick."

Thereafter, Alice's behavior is irreproachable, as she neither initiates nor avoids contact with Varick at social functions. Observing his wife's tactful behavior, Waythorn comes to appreciate the bizarre humor in the situation.

One afternoon, finding Haskett in the library awaiting a meeting with Alice, Waythorn offers him a cigar. Their blended smoke creates a symbolic bond of intimacy. Soon Varick joins them, and then the footman brings in a tea table. Finally Alice enters the room and nonchalantly proceeds to serve tea with such ease and charm that "the situation lost its grotesqueness." After the "other two" accept cups, Alice glances at Waythorn, and he takes the third cup "with a laugh."

*Themes and Meanings*

This comedy of manners satirizes the sensibilities of a New York aristocrat trying to cope with an extremely awkward situation. Until his infatuation with Alice, Waythorn had lived—by choice and temperament—a rather "gray" life. Unhappy with his "womanish sensibility," which caused him to "suffer so acutely from the grotesque chances of life," he married a woman whose charms sparked in him a "thrill of boyish agitation" but whose past divorces were unwanted baggage. Alice is Waythorn's opposite: imperturbable, lighthearted, composed, with perfectly balanced nerves. As the story unfolds, Waythorn comes to see her in a changing light—no longer uniquely his but as "a shoe that too many feet had worn." In each marriage, he realizes, she had "left hanging" a "little of the inmost self where the unknown gods abide."

Nevertheless, Waythorn becomes more tolerant and less judgmental. Instead of imagining Haskett as a brute or Varick as a heel, he recognizes that there must have been an aspect of their personalities appealing enough to have lured Alice into marriage. Wharton sums up the meaning of this comedy of manners when she writes of Waythorn that "habit formed a protecting surface for his sensibilities."

In the opinion of Lewis, "The Other Two" is "the most nearly perfect" short story Edith Wharton ever wrote. Published in *The Descent of Man* (1904), her third volume of short stories, it deals with beliefs and illusions, ethics and aesthetics. Like so many of her works, "The Other Two" examines the stresses and forced adjustments of married life. Perhaps Edith Wharton's own unfulfilling marriage led her to use this motif as a symbolic battleground on which to explore the perplexities of human nature.

Angry at criticism that her fiction was a pale imitation of Henry James, Edith Wharton started work on *The House of Mirth* (1905), her most brilliant novel, soon after completing *The Descent of Man*. In both works she proved herself to be an unrivaled satirist of New York society during a time of transition—its mannerisms, social gestures, habits of speech, and patterns of dress as well as its fears, foibles, and taboos. Unlike Lily Bart, the heroine of *The House of Mirth*, Alice is not ostracized by society for her marital indiscretions. Although heads turn and tongues wag, her behavior is forgiven, even defended. Indeed, hostesses seem to delight in inviting the Waythorns and Varick to the same social function.

### Style and Technique

Wharton wrote with such precision that every phrase seems fitting—Varick's "handsome overblown face," Alice's "rosy-pale dress," Haskett's "made-up tie" and "air of mild obstinacy." Reading "The Other Two" is like entering a crowded room where every artifact seems perfectly in place and appropriate to the setting. The dialogue is terse but pregnant with implications, as when Waythorn says to Alice, referring to Haskett's visit, "You didn't see him, of course?" Wharton is a master of the nuance, the "scarcely perceptible" glances, the various shades of red to measure embarrassment. Writing in the classic style of the nineteenth century drawing room, she blends realism with elements of satire and parody.

Although "The Other Two" is quite short, the main characters are fully rounded. Alice is so composed that, as much as she loves her daughter, when she "did all she could for Lily, [she] would not be ashamed to come down and enjoy a good dinner." The reader senses the discomfort of the aristocratic Waythorn on the crowded train as he feels "crushed between two layers of pendulous humanity." On the other hand, there is a comic flavor to the way he chooses his after-dinner cigar.

In *The Writing of Fiction* (1925), Wharton declared that in short stories, in contrast to novels, situation is more important than character development, and an illuminating incident or moment of truth should accentuate the story's inner meaning. Such a moment occurs when Waythorn is debating whether to ignore Varick's smile of recognition. Seeing it was impossible to do so anyway, he concludes: "And after all—why not?" There is a progression of such incidents related to the question, "Why not?"— beginning with Waythorn's discovery that Alice has not been candid with him about seeing Haskett, continuing with his intruding on Alice and Varick at a party, and culminating with the serving of tea in the library.

In a 1934 article on permanent values in fiction, Wharton asserted that great works of fiction contain two elements: living characters and some general law of human experience. Similarly, in *A Backward Glance* (1934), she declared that enduring literature provides "a little ray through the fog" that "helps humanity to stumble on, and perhaps up." Wharton believed that morality manifested itself in one's willingness to sacrifice personal gain and even be ready to reject social conventions that were frivolous and stultifying. Waythorn's learning to live with life's absurdities and unavoidable embarrassments is a sign of his spiritual growth, as is his acceptance of Haskett's parental demands, Varick's idiosyncrasies, and his wife's past experiences. In the end, he learns to accept the principle of "Why not?"

*James B. Lane*

# THE OUTCASTS OF POKER FLAT

*Author:* Bret Harte (1836-1902)
*Type of plot:* Regional
*Time of plot:* 1850
*Locale:* The gold-mining camps of the Sierra in California
*First published:* 1869

*Principal characters:*

MR. JOHN OAKHURST, a gambler with a strong sense of honor
THE DUCHESS, a prostitute with a heart of gold
MOTHER SHIPTON, another prostitute with a heart of gold and a
  sharp tongue to go with it
UNCLE BILLY, a thief and a drunkard
TOM SIMSON, "THE INNOCENT OF SANDY BAR," a youth who is
  running away to seek his fortune
PINEY WOODS, Simson's fifteen-year-old girlfriend, who is
  accompanying him to Poker Flat to get married

*The Story*

Mr. John Oakhurst notices on November 23, 1850, that there is a change in the moral atmosphere of Poker Flat, a California gold-mining settlement. His premonition is correct, as a secret committee has determined, in its local prejudice, to rid the community of certain undesirable people. Two men are executed, and four alleged reprobates are banished, including Oakhurst. The other exiles are two prostitutes, known as the Duchess and Mother Shipton, and a thief called Uncle Billy.

After an armed escort abandons them on the outskirts of the settlement, with a warning never to return, they decide to head for Sandy Bar, a camp that has not yet experienced the regenerating influences of Poker Flat. It is a long day's journey through the mountains, and by noon the Duchess declares that she will go no farther without a rest. Although Oakhurst advises against stopping, the others, under the influence of liquor, refuse to move. The gambler does not drink, because he believes that it would interfere with his profession. For the first time since he became a gambler, he is lonely and depressed. He studies his pathetic companions, now sleeping, but he does not abandon them.

Oakhurst's reverie is broken by the sound of his name. Tom Simson, a youth known as The Innocent of Sandy Bar, ascends the trail, followed by Piney Woods. They are on their way to Poker Flat to get married and to seek their fortune. Simson knows the gambler because he was once in a poker game with him. Oakhurst won the youth's entire fortune, but he returned it with the advice that Simson should never gamble again. The kind act won for the gambler a devoted friend.

The Innocent reports that he has an extra mule with provisions, and that he has located a roofless cabin. Despite Oakhurst's protest, the others decide to accept Simson's offer, and they make camp in the cabin. It snows during the night, and in the morning Oakhurst discovers that Uncle Billy has absconded with the mules and most of the supplies. The snow forces the group to take refuge in the camp. A roof is made of pine boughs, and the wait for the end of the storm begins. Simson provides an accordion and a copy of Alexander Pope's translation of Homer's *Iliad* (750 B.C.E.; English translation, 1611) for entertainment.

The snow, however, does not abate, and the food supply dwindles. On the tenth day of being snowbound, Mother Shipton, thought to be the strongest of the party, weakens. She reveals to Oakhurst that she has saved her share of the rations from the last week so that the girl, Piney Woods, will have a better chance to survive, and then she dies. The gambler assumes that they will all die soon unless something is done. He sends Simson on the difficult journey to Poker Flat in an attempt to get help. Oakhurst accompanies him for part of the way, and the Duchess and Piney Woods are left alone in the cabin. They fall asleep in each other's arms. That is the way they are discovered by a tardy rescue party several days later. The third body is found under a tree at the head of the gulch. A note, printed on the deuce of clubs, is pinned to the tree with a bowie knife. It states that John Oakhurst had a streak of bad luck and handed in his checks on December 7, 1850. He had been shot by his own gun.

## Themes and Meanings

The pretentiousness of the Poker Flat community is contrasted with the essential goodness of the exiles. The hanging of two men and the banishment of four people are tactics associated with vigilantes of the Old West. In their attempt to establish their own brand of law and order, the people of the town are hypocritical. The gambler and the prostitutes serve as scapegoats for the collective guilt of a community that is trying to look respectable while its sole purpose for existing is the pursuit of gold. History illustrates that gambling and prostitution thrived in places such as Poker Flat. The author emphasizes the communal hypocrisy, then, by creating an honorable gambler and prostitutes with the proverbial hearts of gold.

Oakhurst is a heroic protagonist whose inclusion among the exiles is a matter of revenge rather than justice. Some members of the committee had urged hanging him as a means of getting back the money that they had lost to him, but they were overruled by those who had managed to win. He is merely banished, then, but Oakhurst takes the punishment philosophically. His profession has prepared him to accept bad luck. Oakhurst emerges as the leader of the exiles, who, had they taken his advice, probably would have survived. One of his former noble deeds is related when Tom Simson arrives. The compassion he has shown for the youth in returning his money sets him apart from ordinary mortals. Oakhurst commits suicide when he assesses the hopelessness of the situation. Like Mother Shipton's death, it is a sacrifice that gives the others a better chance to survive. Although it does not work that way, it is his final noble act in the game of life, which, in the gambler's terms, no one wins.

The prostitutes also work at an unrespected trade, but, like the gambler, they possess noble qualities. The love they show for the young Piney Woods puts them morally above the people who have banished them. They are victims of a town that has temporarily decided to enforce a narrow view of virtue. Like Hester Prynne in Nathaniel Hawthorne's *The Scarlet Letter* (1850), they grow in a moral sense, in contrast to their tormentors. The prostitutes have hearts of gold; the townspeople are striving to obtain pockets of gold and the respectability that goes with wealth and social position. Of the four exiles, only Uncle Billy deserved the punishment, which leads to the question of the guilt or innocence of the men hanged by the committee. The gambler and his two women compatriots seem to be superior to the vigilantes.

Bret Harte, in this story, is thematically in the mainstream of American literature. His most famous predecessors and contemporaries dealt with the archetypal theme of society forcing its value system on all its members. The tyranny of the community in punishing those who fail to conform to its narrow standards is illustrated in the works of contemporaries such as Mark Twain, Henry James, and William Dean Howells. Nathaniel Hawthorne and Herman Melville, the most famous precursors of Harte, championed the individual who was wronged by society—Hawthorne most notably in *The Scarlet Letter*, "The Artist of the Beautiful," and "The Minister's Black Veil," and Melville in *Moby Dick* (1851) and *Billy Budd, Foretopman* (1924). Harte moved the setting to the West but continued the literary struggle against local prejudice and the people who organize secret committees as a means of protecting their own interests. The real villains are the ordinary people, not the outcasts, of Poker Flat.

*Style and Technique*

Bret Harte is usually labeled a local colorist. The local-color, or regional-realism, movement hit its peak in American literature between 1870 and 1890. It was fiction that emphasized the speech, dress, mannerisms, and values of a particular region. Literature of this type was usually more concerned with surface presentation of the characters than with probing their psychological motivations. The characters are more likely to be representatives of a specific place than clearly defined individuals, and the stories often descend to the facile conventions of hack writing. Harte never quite transcended this genre, but he became one of the most famous practitioners of local color, along with the early Mark Twain, Hamlin Garland, Kate Chopin, Sarah Orne Jewett, George Washington Cable, and Joel Chandler Harris.

Two aspects of local color that help illustrate the attributes of a locale and its people are humor and hyperbole. Harte uses comic scenes, dialogue, and descriptions to offset the tragedy of the story and to keep it from turning into melodrama. Much of the humor is based on hyperbole—language that is exaggerated or overstated for the situation. Sometimes this is reversed to understatement, in which the words seem too insignificant for the occasion. The language is often a parody of romantic or sentimental fiction. Also involved in balancing the tragedy is the gambler's stoical approach to life. Outwardly impervious to pain or anger, Oakhurst faces life as if it were a game of cards, and his attitude is defined in language associated with gambling. The ridiculous or pathetic aspects of the others are contrasted with the dignity of Oakhurst.

The opening pages are filled with language that seems too grand for the events. Oakhurst notices that there is a change in the "moral atmosphere" of the town. There is a "Sabbath lull" in a community "unused to Sabbath influences." Poker Flat is experiencing a "spasm of virtuous reaction" to the crimes that have been committed. The secret committee rids the town "permanently" of two alleged criminals, while it "sits in judgment" on the "impropriety" of the "professional ladies" it decides to banish. The gambler is saved from hanging caused by "local prejudice" only because of a "crude sentiment of equity" in the breasts of several townsmen who had been lucky enough to win from him.

For a brief period in the story, Uncle Billy serves as a foil to Oakhurst. When the "deported wickedness" of the town is abandoned by the vigilantes, Mother Shipton uses some bad language, but Uncle Billy explodes a "volley of expletives" at his tormentors in an attempt to gain revenge through the colorful use of words. Billy then directs his attention to his fellow expatriates and condemns them in a "sweeping anathema." When Tom Simson arrives, Billy, at the threat of a kick from Oakhurst, stifles his laughter while listening to the youth talk about how he is going to Poker Flat to "seek his fortune." He can barely restrain himself when Simson refers to the Duchess as Mrs. Oakhurst. Billy has to retreat from the group until he can "recover his gravity," but not before he "confides his joke" to the trees with leg-slapping, face contortions, and the "usual profanity." As he returns and surveys the "sylvan group," Uncle Billy formulates his plan of desertion.

In contrast, Oakhurst sees the situation from the stoical viewpoint of a gambler who has not unexpectedly fallen on hard times but who has to make the best of it in an honorable way. He tries to hide Billy's treachery from the others by suggesting that he and the mules only got lost in the blizzard, but their morale is damaged by the loss of the supplies. Only Simson enjoys the "prospect of their forced seclusion," and he tries to entertain them with "square fun," including tales about Homer's "Ashheels" (or Achilles). Oakhurst, however, concerns himself with the "losing game before him." When he sees that there is no hope left, he "hands in his checks" to conclude his "streak of bad luck." His acceptance of death has been learned from his "pariah trade," and his suicide note is written on the deuce of clubs, the lowest card, to symbolize that his luck and life have run out.

The tone of the story, though, is essentially humorous. Life is cheap in the Old West, where gold is more important than morality. However, with his objective method of telling the story, the author is able to make his social commentary unobtrusively. The story is, first of all, entertaining.

*Noel Schraufnagel*

# THE OUTLAWS

*Author:* Selma Lagerlöf (1858-1940)
*Type of plot:* Fable
*Time of plot:* The Middle Ages
*Locale:* Sweden
*First published:* "De fågelfrie," 1894 (English translation, 1899)

Principal characters:

BERG, an outlaw wanted for killing a monk
TORD, a young outlaw accused of stealing a fishing net
UNN, a beautiful woman for whom Berg has killed the monk

*The Story*

Berg, a handsome well-built man, the strongest and tallest man in the country, kills a monk and flees to the woods. Living in the forest so increases his strength that he is eventually called a giant by the villagers, who cannot capture and punish him for the murder. Another outlaw, Tord—accused of stealing a fishing net—escapes to the forest, where he and Berg share a cave. Berg, the giant, comes from a respected Christian family, the wealthiest peasant family in the area, but Tord, a slight boy of sixteen, has a pagan thief for a father. Tord's mother is a witch who eats parts of human bodies that she finds in the sea. When the outlaws first meet, Tord serves and honors Berg as a god, but Berg merely ignores Tord, considering him a weak, petty thief.

Each man survives in the wilderness by fishing, hunting, and gathering. After Berg learns that Tord's father, not Tord himself, stole the fishing net, he begins to appreciate Tord's services. When Tord falls ill, Berg nurses him to health; afterward, they become friends. On a fishing expedition, they travel to a swampy lake high in the mountains, where steep walls of rock encircle the water, from whose surface pine roots emerge like snakes. On an island in this lake, the men fish, but they show no interest in their catch; instead, they daydream. A green light enters their brains, allowing them to imagine a Nixie, a half-human, half-fish creature sleeping in the water. While the men are lost in reverie, Unn, a beautiful young woman, rows past—her skin is white like water lilies, her eyes and hair are dark, and her skirt is blue with a wide red hem.

That night Tord dreams of Unn, the beautiful woman, and of a drowned man. The following day Berg tells him that Unn was the woman for whom he killed the monk. Berg explains that his wife became jealous of the attention that he paid to Unn, a rich and unconventional woman. Berg's wife invited a monk to their Christmas feast, hoping that his spiritual advice would end Berg's affair with Unn. Instead, Unn's anger at the monk's speech caused Berg to kill the man. When Tord congratulates Berg for performing such a heroic deed in the service of a beautiful woman, Berg explains Christianity and the concept of sin. This conversation affects Tord powerfully, causing him to realize that Berg has actually committed a grievous sin, an act for which he must atone, or for which he will be damned.

Later, as Tord walks through the woods alone during a storm, he thinks that he hears an elf, then he imagines that the fallen, blowing leaves are sinners following him. This vision intensifies until Tord convinces himself that a monk is trailing him, a dead monk with a bleeding gash caused by an ax blow. As the storm persists, Tord is certain that God is talking to him, commanding that Berg must surrender and be punished. This experience causes Tord to run to the valley, where he reveals Berg's hiding place to the villagers. When he returns to the cave, Tord begs Berg to confess his sins and to surrender to a priest. When Berg refuses, Tord admits that he has revealed Berg's cave. As Berg reaches for his ax, Tord throws his own at Berg, killing him with a wound to the head, leaving a gash like that which Tord envisioned on the monk. Somberly, Tord announces to the villagers that whereas Berg killed a monk for Unn, he has killed Berg for justice; he asks that they communicate this news to Unn.

*Themes and Meanings*

Throughout this story several reversals occur. First, the outlaws are exiled from their friends, family, and community to the forest, where they must live like animals. The relationship of Berg and Tord is hierarchical—Tord initially serves Berg as he would serve a god, while Berg ignores him as a worthless suppliant. Later, when Tord becomes ill, this relationship reverses and the two men become friends. Within a friendship, there exists a state of equilibrium, a state in which Berg ceases to think of Tord as a weak, petty thief, and in which Tord ceases to serve Berg as a god. This period of friendship begins with Tord's illness and climaxes during their time on the lake fishing. After the appearance of Unn, a final reversal occurs. After Tord learns about Christianity, he considers himself to be better than Berg. Tord still wishes Berg well and sincerely begs Berg to confess, but he feels compelled by the invisible chains of justice to kill Berg, thus sacrificing their friendship for an abstract sense of morality.

In her most famous book, *Gösta Berling* (1891; *The Story of Gösta Berling*, 1898; also as *Gösta Berling's Saga*, 1918), Selma Lagerlöf recounts the adventures of a disgraced minister, a man who, like Berg, is handsome and well liked, but who has sinned. This book ends with Gösta Berling saying that there is a riddle in life: How can a person have fun and be good too? Unable to solve this riddle, Gösta attempts to redeem himself numerous times, but he always falls from grace. For a Christian this becomes a dilemma, a dilemma that Berg also cannot resolve; instead of resolving it, he lives as an outlaw in the woods. For Tord, a pagan, such a conflict is not a dilemma until Berg teaches him Christianity. After learning about sin, Tord becomes a zealot who is willing to sacrifice both friendship and pleasure for justice, for doing good. This becomes the final reversal, and when this occurs the two men may no longer maintain their friendship. Tord commits a murder for the cause of justice; however, in an ironic conclusion, he wishes the knowledge of his deed communicated to Unn, as though this action will bring him fame and earthly pleasure. Tord, not unlike Judas who delivered Jesus to his enemies, betrays his previous lord for an abstract ideal and for the admiration of the villagers.

*Style and Technique*

Although "The Outlaws" has been translated from Swedish, its simple, direct prose is notable even in English; it is the prose of myths and legends. The characters themselves are mythical figures. Berg is described as a giant, a person who can catch spears thrown at him and outrun any enemy. Lagerlöf is noted for this simple mythical style—she wrote about a number of legends both Christian and pagan, and these stories commonly contain an element of the supernatural. "The Outlaws" originally appeared in a book titled *Osynliga länkar* (1894; *Invisible Links*, 1899), and the supernatural elements of the story symbolize these invisible links to family, to morality, to justice, to pleasure, and to passions, forces that compel humans to act in ways that they cannot control and that they may not understand.

"The Outlaws" alludes to the split between Christians and pagans. Tord mentions that Berg's family has a hall built before Saint Olaf's time. In 1030, Saint Olaf, the first Christian king of Norway, was slain in a battle by his pagan subjects. Thus, Lagerlöf sets this story in a period when some people, such as Tord, are still pagan and Viking traditions and values still exist. Like Saint Olaf, Berg is killed by a pagan subject, but Tord is a pagan subject who, ironically, has converted to Christianity.

This characterization of one man as a pagan and the other as a Christian becomes symbolic; Lagerlöf wrote this story at a time when there were no longer Vikings, pagans, or witches. The story's symbolism nevertheless represents a conflict that modern humans face, the same conflict that Gösta Berling stated: How can a person enjoy life, seek pleasure, and be good? On one level, the pagan tradition represents hedonism: humans enjoying life and seeking pleasure. On the same level, the Christian religion symbolizes morality and justice, humans being good: doing what is correct.

Unlike traditional fables and myths, however, "The Outlaws" does not offer a simple solution to this conflict, no clear moral appears at the end to guide one's future action. Instead the symbolism moves to a second level, one on which the pagan and the Christian characters represent the conflicting impulses within each human being; thus the characters become psychological symbols of a split within everyone. *Gösta Berling's Saga* ends with a riddle, a riddle with which each human must struggle, a riddle for which there is no solution: If Tord ignores Berg's sin, he is not behaving morally, but in order to force Berg to justice, Tord must murder his friend.

*Roark Mulligan*

# AN OUTPOST OF PROGRESS

*Author:* Joseph Conrad (Jósef Teodor Konrad Nałęcz Korzeniowski, 1857-1924)
*Type of plot:* Adventure
*Time of plot:* The late nineteenth century
*Locale:* Central Africa
*First published:* 1897

*Principal characters:*
  KAYERTS, the chief of the trading post
  CARLIER, his assistant
  MAKOLA, also called Henry Prince, the worker in charge of the
    storehouse
  GOBILA, chief of the neighboring villages
  THE DIRECTOR, head of the Great Trading Company

*The Story*

From the first lines of "An Outpost of Progress," the reader knows that the two main characters are comical and pathetic, thrust into circumstances that will first humiliate and then destroy them. As different as they are in appearance—Kayerts is short and fat, while Carlier is tall and birdlike—both of these men embody the arrogance and stupidity that are the distinguishing marks, according to author Joseph Conrad, of the white European men who set out to make themselves rich by spreading commerce and civilization to black Africa. The fate of the two new administrators of the trading post, the "outpost of progress" ironically referred to in the title, is prefigured early in the story: Even their boss, the mysterious director of the trading company, thinks of them as hopeless "imbeciles," and the most prominent landmark in the trading post is the grave of the previous administrator, marked by a huge cross. There is little doubt that before long Kayerts and Carlier will suffer through the same "fever" that killed their predecessor.

The first few months pass by rather uneventfully. Although they are generally fearful and begin to cling to each other more out of desperation than out of any feelings of affection or respect, both Kayerts and Carlier imagine themselves to be in a kind of pastoral scene: As the legitimate masters of the area, at least in their own eyes, they simply sit back and wait for the "ignorant savages" to bring them piles of valuable ivory. They are indeed well served by Makola, their employee, who actually takes care of the details of managing the entire operation. Makola is a crucial figure in the story. He possesses a great deal of power and dignity, and his "uncivilized" qualities—the musical tones of his speech, his impressive physical stature, and "worship of evil spirits"—provide a contrast to the impotent refinement of the civilized men.

Unlike Makola, Kayerts and Carlier are almost completely blind to the effects of the surrounding darkness and mystery, symbolized best by the impenetrable jungle.

There is not much action in part 1 of the story, as Conrad attempts to describe their obliviousness and present a kind of psychological portrait of their increasingly futile attempts to "think better of themselves" and maintain their sanity. Like modern Europeans in general, Conrad suggests, Kayerts and Carlier lack "all independent thought, all initiative," and once they are taken from the customary social rituals and institutions that support them, they are powerless. They fall back on a self-serving ideology of imperialism, but Conrad never lets the reader forget that this is the refuge of scoundrels. As the days pass and it becomes clear that even their own company has temporarily abandoned them, they look over old newspapers and have long discussions about "Our Colonial Expansion" and the "sacredness of the civilizing work" they are doing.

For all the high seriousness of their arguments, Conrad skillfully shows that these spokespersons for progress are buffoons: When they meet with Gobila, the chief, to spread their civilizing influence, they behave like clowns, lighting matches and passing around an ammonia bottle to thrill the villagers, while Gobila acts with great dignity and intelligence. Kayerts and Carlier simply cannot overcome their basic incompetence and impotence, for by the end of part 1, they are physically wasting away and slowly coming to an awareness that they are threatened by the circumstances they claimed to have mastered.

Throughout most of part 1 the dangers of which Kayerts and Carlier are barely conscious are described in vague, moody, portentous language: The jungle, for example, is a place of "throbbing life," and the trading post is only a tiny clearing surrounded by "immense forests, hiding fateful complications." In part 2, though, these abstract threats take on violent physical forms. A group of armed people visits the trading post, confers with Makola, and arranges to return later that night, bringing ivory in exchange for the indigenous men working at the station. In the commotion at nighttime, one of the men resisting is shot dead, and after this episode, there can be no escaping the fact that trade and "progress" are based on theft, violence, and oppression.

Kayerts and Carlier do not engineer this trade of men for ivory, but they are nevertheless complicit; they quickly rationalize the incident, saying, "It had to be done." The price of their greatest economic success is thus complete moral collapse and, as a direct consequence, fear and utter isolation. Gobila and his people withdraw from all contact with the trading post, the steamship from the company fails to appear, and Kayerts and Carlier begin to treat each other with the contempt that has marked their treatment of the indigenous people. Short on supplies and, perhaps more important, plagued by an "inarticulate feeling that something within them was gone, something that worked for their safety, and had kept the wilderness from interfering with their hearts," they begin to quarrel, and even a trivial disagreement quickly becomes murderous. In a faint gesture to maintain discipline, a last vestige of civilization, Kayerts rations their last bit of sugar, and when Carlier objects, their argument escalates into a bizarre chase that concludes with a scene that is as comical as it is frightening: "They came into violent collision. Both shouted with surprise. A loud explosion took place between them." Carlier is killed, absurdly and unintentionally, by a man who is basically incapable of willful action.

The ease with which Kayerts rationalizes this murder is only momentary. Although Makola is perfectly ready to report that Carlier died of the fever, it is in fact Kayerts who is feverish, feverish unto death. A dense fog envelops the trading post, evoking his mad confusion, and the loud shrieking noise he hears is simultaneously his own tormented voice and the whistle from the steamboat, calling out to him in the name of "progress." When the Managing Director finally comes ashore, he is met by a grotesque scene: Kayerts has hanged himself on the cross over the grave of the previous manager of the outpost, "and irreverently, he was putting out a swollen tongue at his Managing Director." This is perhaps a symbol of defiance—Kayerts may well have experienced a moment of mad illumination—but most of all his shocking suicide, a parody of a crucifixion as he hangs from a cross, is a powerful emblem of not only the inevitable destruction but also the inevitable self-destruction prompted by those who base their notion of progress and civilization on a shallow understanding of their own weakness and wickedness.

*Themes and Meanings*

In a letter describing this story, Conrad said that it expressed his "indignation at masquerading philanthrophy," a continuing theme throughout his work. Although he was by no means a political radical, he was appalled by abuses of power and wrote with great insight about the mechanisms of imperialism during the late nineteenth and early twentieth centuries. As exaggerated as they may seem, the Managing Director and the Great Trading Company (which Conrad wryly renames the "Great Civilizing Company") that hover behind the action of "An Outpost of Progress" accurately picture the ruthlessly ambitious businessmen and powerful economic conglomerates (in England and Belgium especially) that set out to colonize non-European countries for their own profit. All this was advertised as a well-intentioned attempt to spread civilization to the undeveloped parts of the world, but Conrad points out clearly that such a notion of progress originates not in piety and compassion but in racism, brutality, and greed. The veil is irreparably torn from the gospel of "progress" when Carlier suggests that "exterminating" the indigenous people is a necessary part of the civilizing process, and throughout the entire story, Conrad shows that when the colonizing Europeans move into central Africa, the "heart of darkness" they discover is their own.

Conrad is also deeply concerned with psychological as well as political issues in this story. Kayerts and Carlier are not only exploitative colonizers but also examples of the kind of "mass man" created by modern society, "two perfectly insignificant and incapable individuals," loveless, unimaginative, and alternately paralyzed and volatile. As long as they are within a highly structured society, controlled by habits, rules, and rituals, they can function satisfactorily, but once they face the abyss of the jungle, they lose the qualities one normally thinks of as "human" and become capable of any atrocity. In this respect, the story is not only an adventure set in Africa but also an existential fable about the frailty and precariousness of human life: The jungle is, after all, not the only place where one experiences the blank mystery of being and alienation.

*Style and Technique*

Conrad is known as one of the great stylists of modern fiction, and "An Outpost of Progress" displays many of his characteristic techniques to full advantage. He uses a certain amount of realistic narrative, but for the most part, the story is filled with ominous and moody passages that create a haunting landscape that is not only the background for Kayerts and Carlier but also a disturbing projection of their minds. The purposely vague and melodramatic descriptions of the jungle and the river, for example, place the trading post in a setting that is impenetrable and unintelligible. Kayerts and Carlier never see anything clearly or have anything firm to hold on to, and it is inevitable from the start that they will be overwhelmed by mysterious forces that they have no hope of controlling.

The story is also effectively structured. There are, for example, repeated contrasts that make the reader aware of the key alternatives or conflicts being dramatized: Europe versus Africa, the trading post versus the jungle, "civilized" white men versus indigenous society, and so on. Furthermore, Conrad uses highly charged symbols to suggest that he is writing not an action story but a philosophical and moral parable: The storehouse, for example, is called a "fetish" and stands as a mock-shrine for the worship of material goods that characterizes European civilization. Finally, Conrad keeps his tale from becoming ponderously serious by interjecting grotesquely comic moments: Kayerts and Carlier, the ambassadors of civilization, are more laughable than imposing, although their absurdity does not make them any less destructive.

The most important technique used throughout the story, however, is irony, and its effect is especially noticeable when one reads "An Outpost of Progress" as an implicit parody and critique of traditional adventure stories by Rudyard Kipling and Robert Louis Stevenson that glorify adventurers and colonizers. From beginning to end Conrad's corrosive irony undermines the pretensions of the would-be civilizers by showing that their notion of "progress" leads only to decay and murder, that the culture they disrupt is wiser than their own, and that the jungle and all the forces it symbolizes may yet win out over all attempts to banish darkness from human life.

*Sidney Gottlieb*

# THE OUTRAGE
## A True Story

*Author:* Aleksandr Ivanovich Kuprin (1870-1938)
*Type of plot:* Social realism
*Time of plot:* 1905
*Locale:* Odessa, Russia (now in Ukraine)
*First published:* "Obida (Istinnoe proisshestvie)," 1906 (English translation, 1916)

*Principal characters:*
NINETEEN JEWISH LAWYERS
THE ORATOR, the leader of a delegation of thieves
YASHA, one of the thieves

*The Story*

On a sultry summer day in the Black Sea port of Odessa, nineteen Jewish lawyers gather to determine who is responsible for the latest pogrom against the Jewish population. The day is getting late and the heat is intolerable when seven men demand to be heard by the lawyers. To the lawyers' amazement, these men represent the United Rostov-Kharkov-and-Odessa-Nikolaev Association of Thieves. The lawyers are even more surprised when they learn the reason for their visit. The smartly dressed leader of the group proceeds to give a long speech, even though he promises to be clear, simple, and brief because of the lateness of the day and the heat. He wants to voice his protest against the press reports, planted by the police, as he points out, that the thieves, along with other dregs of society, instigated the pogrom.

In addition to passionately denying the accusation, the orator takes advantage of the opportunity to explain the philosophy and rationale of his thieving profession. The gist of his arguments is that the thieves not only are not wrong, but actually help right wrongs in the society. For example, when a lazy, ignorant, degenerate idiot of a son inherits a vast wealth, which in turn has been acquired on the backs of many hardworking people, it is the thieves who correct the excessive accumulation of wealth in the hands of undeserving individuals, as a protest against all the hardships, abominations, arbitrariness, violence, and negligence of the human personality—all the monstrosities created by the bourgeois capitalist society. Such unjust social order will inevitably lead to a revolution, and they will all perish in it.

Leaving aside the philosophical, social, and economic sides of his arguments, the orator points out another important aspect of his profession, the artistic one. More than mere property-seeking and greedy individuals, the thieves are also inspired, inventive, ambitious, and hardworking people, always perfecting their science. Waxing sentimental about the virtues and dexterity of the thieves, who find beauty in risks and dangers, he likens them to foxes and society to a chicken-run guarded by dogs, and he sees genius and inspiration in the thieves' creations. At the same time, their occupation is by no means easy and pleasant; it requires hard work and long practice. To prove his last point, the orator orders his companions to demonstrate their skills such as opening a locked door in seconds, picking pockets, and showing card tricks.

After portraying his companions as talented and artful—although little appreciated by society—the orator comes to his main point: How would they, the lawyers, feel if they were unjustly slandered as criminals?—exactly what has happened to the thieves. They have been falsely accused of participating in the pogrom by people who are themselves anything but honest; for example, they knowingly buy stolen goods. The truth of the matter is that, living among the lower strata of the society, the thieves feel the injustice of the pogroms much more keenly than others. Moreover, operating underground, they know that the police have organized the pogroms. Hating the police even more than others do, how can they be accomplices of the hated enemy? By voicing a final reprimand of the lawyers themselves for holding such principled people as thieves in contempt, the orator pleads for understanding and for rejecting the clever machinations of the true perpetrators of the pogroms and other evils.

Impressed by this oration, the lawyers shake hands with the thieves as a sign of understanding and agreement, and leave. However, one of them cannot find his hat until the orator yells at Yasha to return the stolen hat. Explaining that one of his people mistook it for his own hat, Yasha apologizes profusely and disappears in the street.

*Themes and Meanings*

At first glance, Aleksandr Ivanovich Kuprin's "The Outrage" may be seen as a humorous story, a parody, or even a farce in which thieves lecture lawyers about justice and legal matters. On a second reading, however, one finds much more to it than first meets the eye.

Kuprin wrote the story immediately after the bloody demonstrations in St. Petersburg, Russia, in January, 1905, known as "Bloody Sunday"—an event considered as the start of the first of three revolutions in Russia at the beginning of the twentieth century. Although the demonstrations were not prompted by pogroms, they underscored the desire of the Russian people to protest openly against injustices perpetrated on them by the insensitive authorities. The phenomenon of pogroms against the Jewish people in Russia fits into the overall picture of an unjust society.

Kuprin was a liberally minded intellectual who, along with many others, often voiced his disagreement with government policies. The utterly unjust and inhumane treatment of the Jews as ready-made scapegoats for any misfortune, be it natural or otherwise, but mostly as a transparent excuse for the government's own mistakes, caused many writers to voice similar protests. As an artist, Kuprin believed that the most effective way to voice his displeasure was a story that could be easily and unmistakably understood. At the same time, instead of attacking frontally, he opted for allegory as a more powerful artistic device. The subtitle "a true story," though a ruse, underscores the gravity of the matter. To make his point even stronger, he chose a paradoxical situation of thieves speaking up for justice and legal order.

Another reason for choosing the allegorical approach lies in Kuprin's wish to attack the social injustices on a broad scale, reflecting a general abhorrence, his own and that of all liberal intellectuals, of unjust government. The thieves, unsavory though they may be, are nevertheless entitled to a humane treatment according to the principle that one is "innocent until proven guilty," which was frequently absent in dealing with them. Kuprin believed that if thieves were treated fairly according to law, all other segments of the society, including the Jews, would be assured of justice. Human dignity and its preservation are Kuprin's foremost concerns, even when the not-so-pristine members of the society are involved.

Another way of bolstering his argument is seen in his choice of characters: If even thieves must protest against being linked with the instigation of pogroms, when every intelligent person knew that the police were the real culprits, the despicable nature of such practices is made all the more flagrant.

*Style and Technique*

The greatest artistic merit of the story lies in the author's success in preventing a potentially dry and didactic matter from ruining the artistic truth of his story. To prevent his story from being little more than thinly veiled social criticism, he imbues it with a hefty dose of comedy. An illustration of this occurs when the thieves' leader makes an impassioned plea for understanding, compassion, and plain justice, while Yasha plies his trade in the very room in which the plea is being made. When the lawyers and thieves leave the building after the thieves' leader has convinced the lawyers of their right to be treated as "honest" citizens, Yasha again succumbs to natural impulses: He cannot resist swiping a hat from a volunteer. By skillfully using paradox, allegory, and humor Kuprin achieves his main purpose: to castigate the ruthless authorities assisted by the hypocrisy of the "respectable" members of the society.

An effective approach is a wry humor with which he endows the leader, Yasha, and other thieves. Speaking with a straight face, they make sly, witty remarks about the "honorable" society in which they live, and by which they are judged, which in turn makes even those being criticized accept the criticism in good humor.

Another effective method applied by Kuprin is the straight realistic approach to the story, despite its allegorical connotations. Both the thieves and the lawyers speak in a clear language, expressing easily comprehended thoughts. Even though the orator sometimes embellishes his speech with jests, allusions, and even sarcasm, his ideas come across well. Most important, however, the absurdity of the entire situation is clearly understood by the reader as an allegory, not just as an amusing story. In this way, Kuprin added his voice to a long line of Russian writers who spoke as a conscience of their people throughout centuries.

*Vasa D. Mihailovich*

# OUTSIDE THE MACHINE

*Author:* Jean Rhys (Ella Gwendolen Rees Williams, 1894-1979)
*Type of plot:* Psychological
*Time of plot:* The mid-twentieth century
*Locale:* A clinic near Versailles
*First published:* 1960

> *Principal characters:*
> INEZ BEST, the protagonist, a poor young English woman who is hospitalized for an operation
> MADAME TAVERNIER, a kindly old lady in the next bed
> PAT, a young dancer in another bed
> MRS. MURPHY, a suicidal girl at the clinic

*The Story*

The story is divided into five parts, all told from the point of view of Inez Best, who lies in a clinic in pain, awaiting an operation. The cold, institutional nature of the clinic is established on the first page in an exchange with the matron, who criticizes Inez for bringing her makeup with her. Inez is weak and bewildered, a sympathetic figure.

Madame Tavernier, an old woman, strikes up a conversation from the next bed. She tells Inez about her two husbands, now deceased, and shows herself to be a woman of feeling and sentiment, although Inez is somewhat skeptical of her glowing description of the good husband. Inez and Madame Tavernier watch two English matrons chatting across the ward, both of whom appear "aggressively respectable." Inez perceives one of these women, who stares at her sharply, as one who has set the machine in motion.

The next day, Inez watches the nurses on their morning rounds and sees their smooth, accustomed routine as part of the machine. She has a fantasy that, because she is "outside the machine," they might pick her up and toss her on a rubbish heap to rot. Inez falls into a conversation with Pat, a pretty, saucy English dancer on the bed on the other side, who tells spicy stories of her life as a chorus girl. Inez observes that even Pat has her place in the machine, which increases her own sense of isolation.

When a clergyman comes to the ward to give a sermon, Inez looks forward to hearing a male voice and longs for a bit of comfort or a spark of humor, but the sermon turns out to be a recitation of platitudes. His trite morality leaves her in even greater despair.

Under the influence of a morphine injection preparatory to her operation, Inez has the sense of floating away. She looks down to see herself being led across the floor with streaming tears, for which the nurse reprimands her. When she awakens three days later in bed, she looks in her hand mirror and is horrified by her appearance, which she considers her "principal asset." She tries to amend this by putting on makeup, but after she has applied it Pat tells her that she looks even worse.

Inez grows accustomed to the hospital routine while convalescing from her operation and finds it almost soothing. Although she suffers vague anxieties about the future, she tries to push these away and watches a mysterious girl on the ward who does not seem to be suffering from an illness. She feels worse than she expected to feel and worries over whether she will be allowed to stay another week, although she has not paid for it. However, she is so terrified of being refused that she postpones asking the matron.

One day in the washroom, Inez sees the mysterious girl, Mrs. Murphy, leaning over the sink, apparently unwell. The girl opens her sponge bag, but several nurses rush in to rescue her from what is an assumed suicide attempt. Mrs. Murphy breaks into sobs and begs to be left alone, while Inez creeps back to bed. When the others learn of the suicide attempt, Pat and the respectable English woman across the ward discuss Mrs. Murphy in a contemptuous way, passing her off as "neurasthenic and neurotic." They believe that because she has a "perfectly good husband and kiddies," she has no reason to be unhappy. Inez tries to protest, but Pat responds with the admonition to "stop always trying to be different from everybody else." Inez sinks back into her own misery.

When Mrs. Murphy comes into the ward with one of the nurses to help make the beds, Pat speaks to her cruelly. Inez attempts to defend the unhappy girl but succeeds only in attracting verbal abuse to herself. The scene is interrupted by the entrance of the doctor and nurse on their rounds. Inez starts to ask them if she can stay another week, but she realizes that no one is listening to her.

Finally, the day arrives when the nurse tells Inez that she must leave after lunch. Desperate now, Inez asks the nurse if she can stay a bit longer, although it is apparent that she has no money to pay for another week. The nurse informs her that she has waited too long to ask; all the beds are filled, and Inez must go home to finish recuperating. Inez is terribly upset and imagines that she will attempt suicide like Mrs. Murphy.

After the midday meal, Inez reflects on the fact that she has no place to go. She puts on her clothes in the washroom and leans against the wall, crying and thinking of Mrs. Murphy. Eventually she returns to the ward, intending to lie on her bed until they throw her out.

Her misery is suddenly interrupted by a request from Madame Tavernier to come to her bed. She compliments Inez on her dress, tells her not to mind the others, and slips her some money in a linen handkerchief. Inez stops crying but feels vaguely degraded because she does not trust women and has never accepted money from one before. The two women have tea together, and when the old lady asks for a kiss before she departs, Inez kisses her and thanks her warmly.

In the final scene, Inez drives to the station in a taxi but wishes that she were back in bed in the ward with the sheets over her head. The story ends on a bitter note, as Inez reflects that "you can't die and come to life again for a few hundred francs. . . . It takes more, perhaps, than anyone is ever willing to give."

### Themes and Meanings

Inez Best is an embodiment of the typical Jean Rhys heroine who first appeared in *Quartet* (1928) and who is the central character of her first four novels, although her name and minor details of her life vary from volume to volume. The typical Rhys heroine lives a passive, aimless existence, at the mercy of the whims of strangers, and often in a foreign country. Any effort to save herself seems beyond her energies. These heroines may reflect Rhys's own experiences during the 1920's, when, married to a Dutch poet, she led a rootless, wandering life on the Continent, mainly in Paris and Vienna.

The theme of the outsider who is alienated from society is neatly captured in the title, "Outside the Machine." As each character appears in the story, she is immediately identified as either belonging to the "machine," that is, society, or as being an outsider. The doctor, the nurses, the "respectable" English women, the dancer, all belong to the machine. Madame Tavernier also seems to belong to the machine, but through her attributes of compassion and kindness she can respond to those outside.

Mrs. Murphy, the suicidal girl, is clearly "outside the machine," and it is with her that Inez identifies most closely—so closely, in fact, that when Mrs. Murphy attempts suicide, there is a clear suggestion that Inez will attempt suicide as well. It is significant that Inez is saved from her predicament of having no money or home by the sudden generosity of Madame Tavernier. This incident illustrates the terrible dependence on the whims of others that is typically suffered by Rhys's heroines.

Although Inez receives enough money to solve her problem temporarily, there is no suggestion that she will ever gain control over her own life. Rhys does not offer much hope for her heroine.

*Style and Technique*

The power and success of this story can in part be attributed to the strictly controlled viewpoint of the heroine. Although the story is told in the third person, the author switches to internal monologue at times, so that the reader is privy to Inez's most secret thoughts. This internal monologue is sometimes indicated by italics, sometimes by parentheses; sometimes it is not marked at all.

Description is minimal and usually seen through Inez's eyes. Because she is in an extreme state of mind, the descriptions are sometimes distorted, which gives them a psychological, if not objective, reality. At one point, for example, the ward is described as "a long, grey river; the beds were ships in a mist."

Characters reveal themselves primarily through dialogue, of which there is a large amount, and it is in their comments about one another that they give themselves away. The character of the suicidal Mrs. Murphy is skillfully used to reflect Inez's own state of mind, adding tension to the story.

In addition to the major symbol of the machine, a gold ring carved with two roses worn by Madame Tavernier achieves symbolic significance. The ring fascinates Inez, and she dwells on it each time she looks at, or thinks about, the old lady. It is noted that the petals of the two roses are touching, which perhaps indicates the ability of kindly Madame Tavernier to touch the lives of others.

Irony is important in the story, primarily in the difference between the viewpoints of those inside and those outside the machine. All these stylistic techniques work together to enhance the story's meaning.

*Sheila Golburgh Johnson*

# THE OUTSTATION

*Author:* W. Somerset Maugham (1874-1965)
*Type of plot:* Realism
*First published:* 1924
*Locale:* Borneo
*Time of plot:* The early 1920's

> *Principal characters:*
> MR. WARBURTON, a colonial official
> MR. WARBURTON'S HEAD BOY
> ALAN COOPER, Mr. Warburton's assistant
> ABAS, Cooper's servant

*The Story*

A narrative of personality and class conflict in an exotic setting, this story opens with Mr. Warburton, the Resident, anxiously awaiting the arrival of his new assistant, Alan Cooper. For twenty years, Mr. Warburton has been the only Englishman within many miles, but at the station, work has increased to the point that an assistant is needed. As he steps off the boat, Cooper disconcerts Mr. Warburton by greeting him with a breezy informality. After showing Cooper to his bungalow, the Resident invites him to dinner.

Although the dinner is for two, Mr. Warburton has arranged a formal table with a continental menu prepared by his excellent Chinese cook. As always, he dons his formal dinner jacket and tie. Thus he is taken aback when Cooper arrives in the same soiled shorts and shirt that he wore on the journey. The dinner confirms Mr. Warburton's perplexed conclusion that Cooper is no gentleman. A colonial born in Barbados, he received an indifferent education and was an enlisted man during the war. The conversation becomes strained as Mr. Warburton gives Cooper some pointers about dress and manners. After dinner, Cooper asks Mr. Warburton to find him a new servant because his previous boy unaccountably disappeared during the journey upriver.

As the narrative makes plain, Mr. Warburton's character and background differ markedly from Cooper's. At twenty-one, he inherited a fortune that enabled him to move with ease and grace among the highest London society. A popular young man, unfailingly generous and polite, he preferred the company of noblemen, not for their wealth but for their titles. He became known as a snob, though his extravagance and generosity made the fault appear minor. He was also passionately fond of gambling and speculation, activities that led to his financial ruin at age thirty-four. After paying off his debts, he did what English gentlemen in his situation usually did: He went out to the colonies to seek a living. Now fifty-four, he retains many habits and attitudes from his London days, but he has gradually changed. During his annual visits to England, he now feels uncomfortable and out of place. He has developed an affection for

Borneo and its indigenous people. His will, though no one knows or even suspects it, orders that he be buried there.

At a second dinner on the following Sunday, Cooper arrives in proper dress, and Mr. Warburton wonders whether his first impression might have been severe. For Cooper's servant, Mr. Warburton has selected Abas, a nephew of his own head boy. Feeling relaxed and congenial, he entertains Cooper with stories of his association with dukes and princes. Cooper, who has heard of Mr. Warburton's snobbery, listens with wry amusement. Though he speaks little, he makes it plain that he is glad that the power of the aristocracy is broken. At one point, he angers Mr. Warburton by alluding to snobbery, never realizing how great an offense he has given.

A few weeks later, Mr. Warburton's anger changes to hatred through a seemingly trivial occurrence. Having been called away from headquarters, he leaves the management to Cooper. When he returns, he finds copies of his London *Times*, which arrived during his absence, disordered and scattered as Cooper had left them after he searched for details of a murder case. The Resident views the spectacle with anger and dismay. Normally, copies of the *Times* reach him in a large bundle several weeks after publication. He carefully dates and numbers each paper without tearing the wrappers, so that every morning at breakfast he opens the issue dated six weeks earlier. It gives him the illusion that he is still connected with London society and represents a tie to civilization. Cooper, lacking any understanding of such matters, storms out of the room after Mr. Warburton confronts him.

Thereafter the two avoid each other's company except when their duties bring them together. However, several episodes involving Cooper and the Malays, for whom he has contempt, require Mr. Warburton's intervention. When Cooper's servants leave him because of his harsh and tyrannical treatment, the Resident orders them to return. At one point, Cooper violates regulations by requiring prisoners to work overtime, and Mr. Warburton countermands his order. Following an angry confrontation over this matter, the Resident writes to the sultan asking that Cooper be transferred.

The reply comes from the sultan's secretary, whom Mr. Warburton knows. It suggests that Mr. Warburton is too much impressed by social distinction and emphasizes that Cooper's energy and industry are valuable. Rebuffed, Mr. Warburton feels discouraged and weary with life. When the head boy learns that Cooper will not be transferred, he startles Mr. Warburton by intimating that there will be a misfortune. All of Cooper's servants have abandoned him except Abas, whom he has kept by withholding his wages.

The Resident ruefully observes that Cooper has no understanding of the Malay character and inclination toward vengeance. The idea of finding him dead with a knife thrust into his back strikes Mr. Warburton as an appropriate outcome, and he is tempted to let events take their course. However, his sense of duty requires him to warn Cooper. The warning falls on deaf ears, for Cooper only sneers contemptuously.

Without servants, Cooper finds that, over several months, nervousness, irritability, the extreme heat, and poor food take their toll, and one day he goes too far. When the boy Abas confronts him to demand his wages, Cooper strikes a savage blow to his head, knocking him down. Afterward, he realizes his rashness, but vanity prevents his seeking help from the Resident. When Mr. Warburton hears of the incident and again decides to warn Cooper, the raucous sound of Cooper's phonograph deters him from going to the bungalow. The next morning he is awakened by the calls of his head boy. Summoned to Cooper's dwelling, he finds Cooper lying face down on the bed, a kris in his back, the body quite cold.

Mr. Warburton immediately takes all the necessary steps. After he orders the arrest of Abas, his head boy tells him that witnesses can place Abas elsewhere. Mr. Warburton curtly dismisses the alibi, and the head boy temporizes, cautiously inquiring whether Abas will be hanged. The Resident acknowledges that the provocation was great. Abas will be sentenced to serve a term in prison. In a short time, he will be paroled and taken into the Resident's house as a servant. His uncle can teach him his duties. Mr. Warburton intimates that Abas should surrender to him soon. He turns to his breakfast and ruffles the pages of the Times. Lady Ormskirk has at last given birth to an heir. He must send his congratulations at once.

## Themes and Meanings

The story represents the powerful conflict between two characters with contrasting values, temperaments, and personalities. When two characters so unlike are brought together, even minor matters can lead to animosity. Beyond character differences, however, the story touches on two more general themes. The first is W. Somerset Maugham's ambivalent attitude toward the English upper class and aristocracy. On the one hand, he finds them in decline and failing as leaders; they cling to illusions and are too proud and aloof to be effective. On the other, as in the story, they still possess admirable qualities—industry, resourcefulness, courage, aplomb, perseverance—and in a crisis, often acquit themselves well. Thrown among the indigenous people, Mr. Warburton experiences a deepening of his character. While retaining his reserve, dignity, and ties with civilization, he develops affection and respect for the Malays. Intuitively, he knows how to treat them so as to assure their cooperation. Ironically, the English snob fares much better in a primitive, exotic setting than does Cooper, a capable worker inept in human relationships.

A second general theme, colonialism, emerges through the characters. Mr. Warburton's view of colonial matters is not tinged with idealism. Tolerant of the Malays' weaknesses, he wants their assistance and does not care to change them. His assumptions are commonsensical and pragmatic; he considers efficient work and management beneficial to both the Malays and the English. Colonialism, thus, is depicted as a system of getting things done, not an evil exploitation or an idealistic mission. This view contrasts sharply with the same theme in other English authors—Joseph Conrad, Rudyard Kipling, and George Orwell.

## Style and Technique

In "The Outstation," Maugham avoids his narrator-character, or the Maugham persona, that appears so often in his fiction. The narration is from both the omniscient author's and the limited character's point of view; the latter occurs both for dialogue and for the character's inner thoughts. Maugham's narrative often shifts the point of view imperceptibly from the omniscient author to a more limited character perspective. The following passage describing Mr. Warburton is a good example: "The great whom he adored laughed at him, but in their hearts felt his adoration not unnatural. Poor Warburton was a dreadful snob, of course, but after all he was a good fellow." In the first sentence, one hears the voice of the omniscient narrator. That voice quickly changes, however, to an unnamed representative of the upper class, "the great," speaking to others of the same class in a decidedly colloquial tone.

One encounters in the story Maugham's usual fluent, lucid, and idiomatic English prose. The structure relies on familiar dramatic episodes from Maugham's fiction— scenes in which two opposing viewpoints are argued out at dinners or during other brief encounters. Ironically, the intense conflict between the main characters contributes only indirectly to Cooper's death.

*Stanley Archer*

# THE OVERCOAT

*Author:* Nikolai Gogol (1809-1852)
*Type of plot:* Satire
*Locale:* St. Petersburg, Russia
*Time of plot:* The 1830's
*First published:* "Shinel," 1842 (English translation, 1923)

> *Principal characters:*
> AKAKY AKAKIEVICH BASHMACHKIN, a government copying
> clerk
> PETROVICH, a tailor
> A PERSON OF CONSEQUENCE, a member of high society

*The Story*

A lively narrator with his comments on the events of the plot—and his digressions from it—is one factor that makes "The Overcoat" so entertaining. As in other Gogol stories such as "The Nose," the plot combines fantastic elements with narrative simplicity in the manner of a folktale. A lowly copying clerk sacrifices greatly to purchase an overcoat, which is a necessity in the harsh winter of St. Petersburg, located in northern Russia. Shortly afterward, the coat is stolen by thieves, and in despair, the clerk goes to powerful people in St. Petersburg to request help in its recovery. Because of the self-centeredness of these powerful people, the request is not handled properly, and the clerk dies as a consequence of exposure and despair. Unfairly treated, the clerk returns as a ghost to haunt St. Petersburg. In particular, the ghost seeks revenge on those powerful people who did not help him when he was alive.

However, this story is more than entertainment. On one level, it is an attack on the nature of bureaucracies, and appropriately enough, the narrator opens the story with a discussion of why the particular department in which the story occurs must remain unnamed. The narrator declares that there is nothing more touchy than a department, a regiment, a government office, or in fact, any sort of official body. The narrator does, however, name the clerk who is the protagonist—Akaky Akakievich Bashmachkin—in a long discussion of how Akaky was christened this particular name. The name itself establishes the lowly nature of this clerk, since "kaky" in Russian is associated with fecal matter, and "bashmak" means "shoe." Akaky is a hardworking clerk whom the other clerks tease and insult. A peaceful man, he harms no one, while others take advantage of him, making him the butt of the office jokes.

Akaky, however, can withstand the insults of his fellow workers; year after year, he continues at his job of hand-copying written documents, doing his work without errors. It is when his old overcoat wears out that his problems begin. The coat is so thin and threadbare that his fellow clerks term it "the dressing gown." On Akaky's low salary, a new coat—which would cost more than a quarter of one year's wages—would seem to be beyond his means. Yet after Petrovich, the tailor, convinces Akaky that his old coat cannot be remade, Akaky realizes that he must save to buy a new one. He undergoes hardships to squeeze all available savings from his already meager life: He does without candles in the evening, does not wear his copying clothes at night so that he may cut down on the laundry bill, walks the streets "almost on tiptoe" so as to spare shoe soles. These privations, however, give Akaky a great sense of purpose, and instead of feeling deprived, he feels spiritually nourished by his ordeal. The uncertainty and indecision that characterized his previous life now vanishes as he contemplates the beauty of the coat he shall wear.

At last, after more than a year of such hardship, Akaky orders the coat made. When the tailor delivers it, the coat's beauty and warmth make this day the most triumphant in Akaky's life. At the office, his supervisor, the assistant head clerk, insists on having a party at his house in honor of the occasion, and that evening, filled with pride, Akaky walks across town to attend the festivities. At midnight, after a wonderful evening of eating and drinking, Akaky starts his walk home. It is then that disaster strikes: Out in one of the large squares of the city, two men overwhelm Akaky and steal his coat, leaving him unconscious in the snow. When he wakes, he begins screaming, and runs to a police officer's sentry box on the other side of the square for help. The officer tells him that nothing can be done now, that Akaky should report his loss to the police inspector the next day.

When Akaky arrives home in his distraught state, his landlady advises him to go the next morning directly to the police commissioner, because the police inspector might deceive him. So, the next day, Akaky goes to the house of the official, but instead of providing assistance, the man questions Akaky on what he was doing out at such a late hour, and Akaky leaves, more confused than ever.

The next day, when Akaky arrives at work in his "dressing gown," the clerks take up a collection for him, but very little money is raised—the clerks simply do not have much left over from their wages. One of the clerks, however, urges Akaky to appeal for help to some person of consequence. The clerk knows the name of such a person, and he gives Akaky that name. Akaky does go to this "Person of Consequence," but the results prove disastrous. The Person of Consequence has only recently assumed his position, and when Akaky calls, he has an old friend for a visitor. To impress his friend, the Person of Consequence uses his most supercilious manner on Akaky, and Akaky flees the interview in complete confusion. Dazed, he stumbles around the streets of St. Petersburg in a snowstorm, and the next day comes down with pneumonia. Within a short while, Akaky goes into delirium, curses the Person of Consequence, and dies.

Several days after his death, a ghost begins to haunt the neighborhood, stripping the coats off passers-by. Orders are given to catch the ghost "regardless of trouble or expense, dead or alive, and to punish him severely, as an example to others." The impossible nature of this order—as a ghost cannot be caught, and to punish him is ridiculous—couched in these bureaucratic terms illustrates the satiric nature of this story. One late night, the Person of Consequence is crossing town in his sleigh when the ghost confronts him, grabbing his coat collar and declaring, "It's your overcoat I want; you refused to help me and abused me into the bargain! So now give me yours!" The ghost then strips the horrified Person of Consequence of his coat and leaves him disoriented and frightened. His revenge complete, the ghost disappears forever.

The story ends with the final point of the incident making such an impression on the Person of Consequence that he never again abused the clerks under him in such a manner as he had abused Akaky.

## Themes and Meanings

The theme of the common man suffering insult and injury because of the circumstances of modern life became such a central concern of nineteenth century Russian literature that a whole school of subsequent writers are viewed as being, in Fyodor Dostoevski's words, "out from Gogol's overcoat." Although Akaky is portrayed as a somewhat grotesque, humorous figure, Gogol will not allow the reader to lose sight of his humanity. On its deepest level, the story is concerned with the basic theme of people's inhumanity to other people. To emphasize this point, early in the story the author relates an incident in which one of the new young clerks observes the others teasing Akaky. In a state of compassion, the new clerk refuses to take part in the activity:

> And long afterward, during moments of the greatest gaiety, the figure of the humble little clerk with the bald patch on his head appeared before him with his heart-rending words: "Leave me alone! Why do you insult me?" and within those moving words he heard others: "I am your brother." And the poor young man hid his face in his hands, and many times afterward in his life he shuddered, seeing how much inhumanity there is in man, how much savage brutality lies hidden under refined, cultured politeness.

Gogol explores this theme of people's inhumanity to others with a brilliant, cutting satire that holds up people's behavior for the reader's critical examination.

## Style and Technique

Gogol's use of the grotesque and the fantastic to portray his characters in his attacks on society's ills recalls Charles Dickens on the one hand, and on the other, his use of a narrator with his continual digressions and comments on the expectations of readers recalls Laurence Sterne. Like both Dickens and Sterne, Gogol delights in the use of language for its own sake: idiomatic phrases, phonetic and etymological puns, wordplay in general. The names of his characters, the little idiosyncrasies of their behavior, and the oddities of their physical appearance become major elements in the controlling tone of his fiction. Gogol does not deeply explore complex human motivation; rather, his method is to identify the flaws in people's social behavior and to hold that behavior up for critical examination. Because his method focuses on people's social actions, it is not surprising that Gogol also is the author of one of the world's great comic dramas, *Revizor* (1836; *The Inspector General*, 1890), a satire that also examines men's actions in bureaucratic organizations. Gogol, who worked as a bureaucrat himself, also wrote an epic novel of satire, *Myortvye dushi* (1842, 1855; *Dead Souls,* 1887), which examines provincial avarice and which is based on a bureaucratic flaw in the method of counting serfs for taxing purposes on pre-emancipated Russian estates.

His satiric approach is finally so effective because of his underlying concern with people's inhumanity to others. In the character of Akaky, Gogol gave the world its first modern common man, a man who is overwhelmed by the complex bureaucracy of which he is a part.

*Ronald L. Johnson*

# THE OVERCOAT II

*Author:* T. Coraghessan Boyle (Thomas John Boyle, 1948-     )
*Type of plot:* Parody
*Time of plot:* The 1980's
*Locale:* Moscow
*First published:* 1982

> *Principal characters:*
> AKAKY AKAKIEVICH BASHMACHKIN, a clerk in the Soviet
>   bureaucracy
> PETROVICH, a tailor
> STUDNIUK, a resident of Akaky's apartment
> RODION IVANOVICH MISHKIN, Akaky's chess partner
> ZHARYENOYE, an inspector with the Security Police

*The Story*

Akaky Akakievich Bashmachkin, an anonymous clerk in the Soviet bureaucracy, lives for his work, has no outside interests, has no time for anything but waiting in endless queues for items that may not even be available when his turn finally comes. Even though he shares a four-room apartment with fourteen others, the only dissatisfaction he finds with his life is the cheap, tattered overcoat that does nothing to protect him from Moscow's below-zero weather. Akaky bought the coat only because a Central Department Store clerk ridiculed the quality of Soviet-made products and tried to sell him a black-market overcoat in an alley.

Akaky takes his problem to Petrovich, a tailor, who assures him that the coat is beyond repair and offers to make him an overcoat "like they wear in Paris" for 550 rubles, nearly three months' salary. Akaky's younger coworkers, who wear black-market blue jeans and leather flight jackets with fur collars, make fun of his appearance and drape his pathetic coat over the life-sized statue of Lenin in their office. Akaky loses his temper for the first time during his twenty-five years there and tries to stir them with an oration about comradeship, only to be greeted by a "rude noise."

Akaky is upset because he sees himself as "a good man, true to the ideals of the Revolution, a generous man, inoffensive, meek: why did they have to make him their whipping boy?" Old Studniuk, one of those living in his apartment, tells him that he is foolish for continuing to believe in the Party, that he must wheel and deal on the black market to get everything he can because there "ain't no comrade commissioner going to come round and give it to you." Studniuk explains that Akaky's fellow clerks despise him because, in his sad overcoat, he acts as if he considers himself a saint.

Because Akaky has, for twenty-two years, sent half of his meager salary to his invalid mother in the Urals, he has to exhaust his savings and sell his television set to pay Petrovich, but the beautiful camel's hair overcoat with a fox collar is worth it.

Akaky is overwhelmed by its beauty and warmth, thinking that it makes him look like a member of the Politburo or the manager of the National Hotel.

His coworkers are equally impressed but suspicious. Rodion Ivanovich Mishkin, Akaky's lunchtime chess partner, says, "so you've finally come around." Akaky ignores the implications of such remarks, especially when Mishkin invites him home for the first time. On the way to Mishkin's home, Akaky experiences another first, being approached by an attractive young prostitute, but he runs away, "hurtling headlong up the street as if a legion of gypsy violinists and greedy yankee moneylenders were nipping at his heels."

After having one of the best times of his life with Mishkin, Akaky walks into snowy Red Square "thinking how lucky he was," only to have two men beat him and steal his beloved coat. After a day of waiting in lines, Akaky is brought before Inspector Zharyenoye of the Security Police. The police have recovered his coat, but his joy is short-lived when Zharyenoye removes the collar lining to reveal that the coat was made in Hong Kong. Akaky is fined one hundred rubles for receiving stolen goods, and the coat is confiscated.

Akaky finds that everything in which he has believed has been betrayed. He goes home, develops pneumonia, and dies. Everyone who has known him soon forgets him. After some initial guilt, Inspector Zharyenoye wears the coat proudly because "people invariably mistook him for the First Secretary himself."

*Themes and Meanings*

"The Overcoat II" is an updated version of Nikolai Gogol's 1842 classic "Shinel" ("The Overcoat"). Parody is a favorite genre for T. Coraghessan Boyle, with such stories as "I Dated Jane Austen" and "Rupert Beersley and the Beggar Master of Sivani-Hoota," a Sherlock Holmes spoof, and his 1981 novel *Water Music*, a send-up of travel books and Victorian novels.

Boyle uses Gogol's story primarily as a means of satirizing contemporary Soviet life, as he does in "Ike and Nina," in which President Eisenhower and the wife of Premier Khrushchev have an affair in 1959. Gogol's Akaky dies from the despair of losing his coat; Boyle's Akaky dies from losing something even more irreplaceable: his belief in the Soviet system.

Akaky is disgusted by the black-market dealings of his coworkers and neighbors; he is perfectly willing to wait in line for hours for shoddy goods. He is willing because "he knew how vital personal sacrifice was to the Soviet socialist workers' struggle against the forces of Imperialism and Capitalist Exploitation. He knew, because he'd been told. Every day." Akaky believes what he reads in *Pravda* and *Izvestia*. He even clips and saves articles; one about cheese production in Chelyabinsk proves how much progress his nation has made since his grandmother had to make her own cheese. Boyle's satiric target is not only the Soviet system but also propaganda in general and anyone foolish enough to accept any ideology without question.

"The Overcoat II" is full of examples of the incompetence, absurdity, and corruption of the Soviet system. When Akaky tries to telephone his office, he gets Kropotkin's Laundry; the telephone system rarely works. He has to fill out an extensive police form that asks for his mother's shoe size. His mother's entire village has been relocated because of some "mysterious calamity" about which Akaky is not even curious. Gogol's story ends with the clerk's ghost gaining revenge on those who have wronged him; Boyle's reflects a much more cynical age: Zharyenoye profits from Akaky's naïve belief in the system that exploits him.

The story, however, is not simply satiric. It is also about loneliness. Akaky only imagines sharing comradeship with his fellow citizens, but ironically, the illicit coat allows him to make some human contact for once. He feels gratitude toward those at Mishkin's party for treating him as an equal, as a human, making him realize how much he has been missing. However, in Boyle's paranoid world, regardless of the setting, such moments cannot last; some unexpected, uncontrollable force is out to get the individual, and only those as cynical as their societies can survive.

*Style and Technique*

Whether Boyle's fiction is set in Africa, South America, India, or Northern California, he seems to pride himself on veracity. The details of daily Soviet life in "The Overcoat II" include Akaky's antiquated Rostov Bear typewriter, his eating a dry sandwich of raw turnip and black bread for lunch, and the almost constant intoxication of almost everyone but Akaky. The miniature of Misha the Olympic bear on Akaky's desk helps set the time of the story, establishes further Akaky's nationalistic pride, and reminds the reader of the American boycott of the 1980 Moscow Olympics because of the Soviet invasion of Afghanistan.

The most consistent stylistic element in Boyle's fiction is his excessive reliance on similes, which he uses to make descriptions more vivid and to establish and maintain his comic tone. Some of the similes in "The Overcoat II" are predictable: a police officer's head is "as heavy and shaggy as a circus bear's." Some are distinctively Russian and ironic: Akaky's "throat was raw and his eyelids crusted over by the time he flung himself into Petrovich's shop like Zhivago escaped from the red partisans." Frequently, Boyle takes what could be simply a cliché and expands it: One of Akaky's fellow clerks has a voice "like a great whirring mill saw bogged down in a knotty log." Others are simply colorfully comic: Akaky's woolly black hat clings to his head "like an inflated rodent"; Studniuk's nose has been broken so often it looks "like a question mark." Boyle's energetic fiction occasionally borders on the overblown and sophomoric, but the sheer vitality of his style overshadows any such defects.

*Michael Adams*

# THE PACIFIC

*Author:* Mark Helprin (1947-    )
*Type of plot:* Psychological
*Time of plot:* World War II
*Locale:* California
*First published:* 1986

> *Principal characters:*
> PAULETTE FERRY, a young woman working in a defense factory
> LEE FERRY, her husband, a Marine Corps officer

*The Story*

A factory dedicated to the production of war materials is located in an idyllic rural landscape on the edge of the Pacific Ocean in California, north of Los Angeles. It is World War II and most of the factory's assembly-line workers are women, many married to soldiers who are far across the Pacific waging war against the Japanese.

One worker is Paulette Ferry, a young woman in her mid-twenties, originally from South Carolina. Her husband, Lee, is a Marine officer. While training on the east coast, Lee commented to Paulette that after the war, if he returned, they should go to California, where, because of the light, it would be like living in a dream. They did not have to wait until the war ended, however. Lee was assigned for further training at Twentynine Palms, in the desert outside of Los Angeles. With help from their parents, Paulette was able to accompany him, and they crossed the country by train, in perfect weather and north light, committed to embracing the experience as something to seize and remember in the event there was no future to share.

During the six months that Lee was at Twentynine Palms, Paulette worked in a defense factory south of Los Angeles. When Lee received his final embarkation orders, she moved north to the small town where the newly constructed factory was located. At the edge of the continent, where she would have a small house and a garden to till, only the air and the sea separated her from Lee.

Paulette, with her small hands, is a precision welder. Her factory produces altimeters used on American aircraft above the islands where Lee and his Marine comrades are fighting for their lives. One evening, Paulette takes on additional work when one of her coworkers on the assembly line becomes ill. She continues the double duty, telling her supervisor that she can work twice as fast as before. Everyone wonders how long Paulette can keep it up, but she does not falter.

Although physically spent when she returns to her small home in the early morning hours after her ten-hour shift, Paulette refuses to succumb to sleep. Instead, she sits in a chair, staring over the Pacific and trying not to sleep. While Lee was still in training, he told Paulette about the time when his company marched for three days and nights without rest, and afterward, while the rest of his company slept, he was assigned sentry duty despite his exhaustion. If he failed and fell asleep, he could be courtmartialed and sentenced to death. Just as he did his duty, Paulette now does hers.

Lee and Paulette exchange letters, but Lee does not want to hear about her life on the assembly line, or even about her garden, but only about her—what she thinks, what she eats, and how she looks. He asks for one of her barrettes as a keepsake, and he vows to come home. He is fighting for his life while she lives among golden hills on the edge of the Pacific where the clear sunlight "seemed like a dream in which sight was confused and the dreamer giddy."

In late 1943, Paulette learns that Lee and his Marine division are engaged in brutal combat on the island of Tarawa. Each day she scans the casualty lists in the newspaper for Lee's name. Her work is an escape—she cannot think about anything else under the pressures of the assembly line—but so long as she does her work and so long as Lee stays alive, she senses some sort of justice and equilibrium. Now instead of writing, she speaks silently to him. On the assembly line, she pushes herself faster and faster, all for him and for love, in the unstated hope that by so doing she can create a miracle that will keep Lee alive far across the misnamed Pacific. The story closes with the simple statement that the miracle "was not to be hers."

### Themes and Meanings

Mark Helprin frequently uses the circumstances of love and war in his writings, both in his short stories and in his novels. "The Pacific" combines those two primordial themes. Sometimes Helprin writes of actual fighting, but often his stories are concerned less with the physical act of war than about the effects of war on both soldiers and noncombatants. For example, in the short story "Martin Bayer," set in 1916, the future death and destruction of war are glimpsed by a young boy in the midst of an engagement celebration. In "A Room of Frail Dancers," an Israeli soldier, after the battles have ended and on the eve of his sailing to Europe, commits suicide.

"The Pacific" is a war story whose protagonist, Paulette, lives in a small town on the peaceful California coast, thousands of miles from the scenes of battle, but war infuses the story: Her husband Lee is fighting the Japanese, Paulette works in a defense factory that produces war materials, and she is living in the small coastal town so as to be as near to him and battle as the sea and air allow. It is her war, not just Lee's, and it has become her complete life: working twice as fast as anyone else on the assembly line and forcing herself to remain awake in the morning light as a sentinel because of her love for Lee and her hope for their future when the war is over and Lee returns—if he returns.

Light is a theme of many of Helprin's stories, including "The Pacific." There are many different lights: the north light visible from the train while crossing the country, Lee's belief that California's light is like living in a dream, the clear sunshine and California's golden hills contrasted with the cold colors of the Pacific Ocean. There is also the light produced by the welders on the assembly line: "Welders' light is almost pure. . . . The silvery whiteness is like the imagined birth of stars or souls." The various lights created on the assembly line by the working wives of soldiers fighting and dying across the ocean "assaulted the senses—by the scores, by the hundreds," and although the flashes from the welders' lights are beautiful, the lights' product is to be used in war, leading to pain and death. Implicitly, the flashing lights from guns and shells were doing the same on the islands and above them far across the sea.

The welders' light, like the birth of the souls it suggests, is transient, born to fade. Not dedication, not commitment, not working twice as hard as anyone else, not staying awake as on sentry duty after a night shift, not even love, can ensure permanence. Dreams end. The individual lights generated by the assembly line last but for a brief time, and like the love between Paulette and Lee, are destined to end in the carnage of war. Still, "the sharp burst of light is a brave and wonderful thing."

*Style and Technique*

Told in the third person, Helprin's "The Pacific" combines a straightforward story about two lovers parted by war with a quality of writing that—through the use of both tone and contrasts—raises the work to a different plane. Contrast is used often and effectively. The idyllic small California town contrasts sharply with the actions of the assembly line devoted to producing violence and to the distant war itself. The title, "The Pacific," is a contrast to the carnage of battle. Paulette's small hands produce items to be used on powerful fighter aircraft. To reach the defense factory at which Paulette had worked previously, she and the other workers walked silently through groves of orange trees to the war-making assembly line. The many contrasts between a physical setting of peace and beauty within the context of war and battle cannot fail to affect the reader.

The tone of Helprin's writing creates a dreamlike quality. Lee remarks that he wishes to go to California because the light there gives one the feeling of living in a dream. As Helprin's story follows Paulette, from the east coast to the west, from Los Angeles to the small town to the north, from the factory that will vanish when the war ends to her small house and garden, it is as if she exists, not necessarily passively, in circumstances that could make the "dreamer giddy." The reader, too, cannot help but get caught up in that dreamlike world of war and longed-for peace.

*Eugene Larson*

# THE PACING GOOSE

*Author:* Jessamyn West (1902-1984)
*Type of plot:* Fable
*Time of plot:* The mid-twentieth century
*Locale:* Vernon, Indiana
*First published:* 1945

> *Principal characters:*
> JESS BIRDWELL, a nurseryman and farmer
> ELIZA BIRDWELL, his wife
> ENOCH, the Birdwells' hired man
> SAMANTHA, the pacing goose

*The Story*

Winter is making its hasty retreat, and spring is making its entry. Farmer Jess Birdwell smells melting snow and wants to hasten winter's exit. He is in the mood to celebrate the rites of spring. Unhappily, he finds nothing new to celebrate either in nature or in his family; maybe there is nothing new under the sun, he reflects.

Jess is particularly worried about the geese that Eliza raises every spring. They are destructive: They mow down sprouting corn and level off rows of pie plants, and fences do not make good neighbors as far as the geese are concerned. The only good thing about geese is that they make good roast for the table. On the other hand, Eliza loves the geese. According to her, they are beautiful, lordly creatures who are far more productive than they are destructive; there is no better food than a fried goose egg for breakfast, according to Eliza's father. In fact, Eliza has already purchased eight goose eggs, without Jess's knowledge, from the Overby farm and has set them under a hen.

Jess is worried about his corn. Knowing that Eliza, as steady as a pump bolt, is determined to have her way, he decides to use devious means to scuttle Eliza's project. He hatches a plot by enlisting the help of Enoch, his hired man. He instructs Enoch to puncture all the eggs with a darning needle. Unwillingly, Enoch agrees, even though he is convinced that most of the eggs are bad.

On the thirtieth day, when the geese are expected to break their shells, Eliza finds that only one egg has hatched. She is happy and relieved. She is happy that she can have the new gray-gold goose for a pet; she is relieved that she does not have to raise geese for the table. She gives the gosling the name Samantha; she will call it Sam if the gosling turns out to be a gander, she announces.

The goose grows up well-rounded, as a pet, in the Birdwell household. She eats and drinks—especially tea—off the family table, to the joy of the Birdwell children. Though Samantha is a joy to behold, she is a sore sight to Jess, especially because she eats the pansies that he has planted at the base of the Juneberry tree.

One evening, Jess is happy and relieved to hear that Samantha has flown away to be with her goose clan at the Overby coop. Immediately, Eliza goes to the Overbys to claim her Samantha. The Overbys refuse to let Samantha go because Eliza has insulted them; Eliza has accused the Overbys of selling her seven bad goose eggs. The Overbys simply swear that they have only their forty geese and no more. Eliza loses her temper; Milt Overby is as stubborn as ever.

Jess can no longer bear to see Eliza and the children unhappy over Samantha. He decides to hire a lawyer to argue Eliza's case in the court of law—something Quakers abhor doing; they would rather settle disagreements amicably out of court. No sooner than he is hired, the lawyer secures a restraining order on the Overbys so that they cannot sell or kill the goose Eliza said was Samantha.

In mid-December, the trial is held. Eliza is ready for the day of reckoning. She wears her best clothes and is in the best of moods. A devout Quaker, Eliza refuses to take oaths or to address the judge as "Your Honor." However, she will affirm and address the judge as Friend Pomeroy. The young circuit judge is favorably impressed by the urbane civility and good manners of Eliza. The defendant, Milt Overby, is overbearing and frowns on the judge because the judge has asked him some naïve, elementary questions concerning the habits of geese. When the judge puts Eliza on the stand, she answers politely, sincerely, and truthfully the questions that the judge asks her. She can easily identify her goose from the Overby geese because Samantha is the only pacing goose in the flock. Judge Pomeroy is convinced: He knows the difference between geese that pace and that do not pace. Without much ado, the judge awards custody of Samantha to Eliza and dismisses the case.

As soon as the trial is over, the Birdwells and Enoch return home, with Samantha in the crate, in the horse buggy. During the ride home that winter evening, Jess has learned his lessons well: Eliza is always right; there is at least one pacing goose among all the walking geese of the world.

*Themes and Meanings*

Metamorphosis of the mind or a change of mind is the main theme of the story. Jessamyn West dwells primarily on the psychological conversion that Jess Birdwell experiences in his relationship with his wife. He learns a few fundamental truths about Eliza.

Because Eliza is steady and dependable, Jess does not have to worry too much about his wife. The dependability of the woman consists in her ability to change and give new life; she is like Mother Nature, who changes with the seasons and brings forth new life in spring, in spite of the ravages of time, the destructiveness of winter, and the depredations of the male and animal world on her. For example, two men, Jess and Enoch, try to sabotage nature's plan for new geese by puncturing the goose eggs. Eliza, however, salvages her life-giving project by giving life to a new goose and by raising her with love and tenderness—that is the art of life and the poetry of spring found missing in Jess's life.

Indeed, Eliza changes with the seasons by being productive and by nurturing new life. In this process, West implies, the woman changes even the man who refuses to change himself and who wants only to change the woman by making her in his own image and likeness. Jess admits at the conclusion of the story, "I learned first, dependability is woman's greatest virtue . . . don't try to change her. Not even in spirit . . . Don't need to waste any worry on the woman."

Jess also learns another truth about men: They are not as reliable as he thought they were. Not all men, however, would learn this truth. The Enochs of this world are not an extinct species.

*Style and Technique*

Because one of the purposes of the story is to teach men certain truths about womankind, West presents the story in the form of a modern bird fable, told from a woman's perspective. The simple moral of this modern fable is that the woman is more steady and dependable than the man.

In this regard, West is working in the fable tradition of the Greek Aesop, the Sanskrit *Panchatantra* (c. 100 B.C.E.; *The Panchatantra*, 1925), and Geoffrey Chaucer's "The Nun's Priest's Tale," one of his *Canterbury Tales* (1387-1400), about the rooster Chanticleer; the deliberate use of archaisms in the dialogue between Jess and Eliza confirms West's indebtedness to this ancient literary genre.

*Zacharias P. Thundy*

# THE PAGAN RABBI

*Author:* Cynthia Ozick (1928-    )
*Type of plot:* Psychological
*Time of plot:* The 1940's to 1960's
*Locale:* A large American city
*First published:* 1966

> *Principal characters:*
> SHEINDEL KORNFELD, a rabbi's widow
> THE UNNAMED NARRATOR, the deceased rabbi's friend

*The Story*

After Rabbi Isaac Kornfeld commits suicide in an obscure city park, the unnamed narrator, his lifelong friend, wants to know why the rabbi has hanged himself, and visits the site. The narrator explains that his father and Isaac's were nominal friends who were, in fact, scholarly enemies. Both Isaac and the narrator attended the same seminary, but the latter dropped out, earning the silence and the hatred of his unforgiving father. Although they remained affectionate, if distant, friends, the two young men were perfect opposites. Isaac became a brilliant Talmudic scholar, published widely, married a Holocaust survivor, and had seven daughters. The childless narrator never returned to the seminary, became a furrier and later a bookseller, and divorced his gentile wife.

The narrator visits Isaac's widow, Sheindel Kornfeld, hoping to learn the reason for the tragedy. What he finds is a contemptuous, tearless widow who queries the bookseller concerning Isaac's interest in books on plants. The narrator is shocked by Sheindel's bold declaration that Isaac was never a Jew. She then relates her husband's increasingly bizarre behavior: his sudden insistence on lengthy picnics, the numerous second-rate fairy tales that he wrote and later burned, and his seemingly inexplicable passion for public parks. The narrator's first visit to Sheindel concludes when she commands him to study Isaac's small notebook in order to solve the mystery. In effect, he becomes the scholar to Kornfeld's text.

The late rabbi's writing proves to be just as baffling to the bookseller as was the suicide itself. Written in Greek, Hebrew, and English, it contains mostly quotations from the Bible and Romantic poetry, the latter displaying a marked emphasis on English Romantic views on nature. The bookseller returns to visit Sheindel with the intention of eventually marrying her. Sheindel produces an even more perplexing document—Isaac's suicide note. She says that it is a love letter and proceeds to recite it to the reluctant narrator. The letter discloses an imaginative, even irrational human being who is wholly at odds both with his vocation as a rabbinical scholar and also with the tenets of Judaism.

The lengthy suicide note, which may more accurately be described as a tract, is the antithesis of the rabbi's scholarly work. Its affirmation of sylvan spirits and its denial of the possibility of idolatry account for Sheindel's dry-eyed demeanor and her bold declaration that her husband was a pagan. As the narrator follows Sheindel's recitation, his role shifts from the reluctant listener to that of the active participant: He seizes the note from her when she can no longer continue. The bookseller is incredulous as Kornfeld's note progresses from a rejection of Talmudic law to a celebration of nature imagery, characterized by such mythical beings as dryads, naiads, and oreads. The rabbi practiced abstinence with his wife in order to copulate with one of these spirits, and claims in the note that he has done so. This dryad, whom Isaac calls "Iripomoňoéià," declares a book-laden old man to be Isaac's soul. When the latter chastised Isaac for abandoning the Law, the rabbi seized the old man's prayer shawl and hangs himself with it.

The tale concludes with the narrator parting from the unforgiving widow for good.

*Themes and Meanings*

The key to understanding "The Pagan Rabbi" lies in a quotation from an early rabbi that precedes the story. Loosely paraphrased, it warns of the danger in trying to combine one's studies, presumably religious in content, with an appreciation of nature. Rabbi Isaac Kornfeld suffered precisely this fate, and could not live with the consequences. The rabbi's fall from grace may be viewed as a tragedy in the classical sense of the word: A brilliant Talmudic scholar, in the prime of life and at the top of his field, destroys himself through his own flawed character. Cynthia Ozick undercuts what otherwise would be a somber story through the ludicrous events that led up to Kornfeld's demise. His desperate obsession with picnics and his belief that he had sex with a dryad stand out in particular. In this sense, Ozick's tale may be said to be tragicomic. The message is not that one should avoid nature, and the author is certainly not condemning Orthodox Judaism. She is pointing out the risky nature of trying to serve two masters, attempting to reconcile polar opposites. In Isaac's case, it was nature and his religion. The consequence of the rabbi's plight was a split consciousness, one that pitted his romantic yearnings against tradition.

Although the rabbi's skill at explication was unparalleled, the story also points out that his imagination was so remarkable that he could "concoct holiness out of the fine line of a serif." Therein lay the danger in Isaac's life: By the end of the story, his fertile imagination is no longer compatible with the intellect of the scholar. His internal division is played out at the scene of his suicide, in which Ozick makes concrete the rabbi's moral dilemma. Isaac's soul, the embodiment of his life of study, laments the fact that he was abandoned by his owner. Kornfeld's romantic imagination, represented by the dreamy image of Iripomoňoéià, recalls the visionary works of the English poet William Blake. Isaac's radically splintered consciousness can no longer balance the narrow confines of a rigorous intellect with the freedom necessitated by a supremely romantic imagination.

In a larger sense, Isaac's plight can be seen to represent the timeless struggle between the constraints of tradition and the artist's need to transcend boundaries. Isaac's abortive attempts at writing certainly cast him in this role. His immensely imaginative mind simply could not find adequate expression in scholarship. When his imagination no longer found satisfaction in searching for textual meaning, he constructed a world of Pan and sprites in a decayed city park that reeked of excrement. Rabbi Kornfeld lost contact with reality.

*Style and Technique*

As befits a tale that explores a scholar's inner turmoil, Ozick's style is, by turns, lively, ironic, humorous, and, above all, calculated. From her imposing command of classical imagery to her dazzling use of figurative language, Ozick creates a text of depth and breadth that demands a close reading. Starting with the title of the tale, she addresses the central conflict in the story, Rabbi Kornfeld's divided nature. A "pagan" rabbi is an obvious impossibility, because it literally means a Jew who is not a Jew. This is precisely what ailed Isaac: It epitomizes his struggle.

The oxymoron in the title, with its combination of antithetical terms, is reflected in the separateness of the human relationships in the story. Just as the title represents a juxtaposition of opposites, so did Isaac's marriage. Although he exhibited an almost magnetic attraction for the imagination, his wife came to symbolize cold intellect. She was the astonishingly learned bride of seventeen, who entered life in a place of death—the concentration camp. While her birth occurred in the midst of destruction, Isaac's demise resulted when he sought the birth of his soul. Appropriately, Sheindel's asterisk-like scar symbolizes her association with the scholarship that ultimately proved to be the rabbi's undoing.

Ozick heightens this sense of division through the image of the lace runner on the dining table in Sheindel's apartment. The fact that the table is separated "into two nations" suggests irreconcilable opposites, not only within Kornfeld but between his widow and the visiting narrator. This effect is underscored when Sheindel sits across from the narrator "on the other side of the lace boundary line." Another salient division is the rift between the narrator and his own father. Just as an invisible barrier separates the bookseller and the widow, his rejection of the seminary creates one more antithesis—that of the apostate and the rabbi. There is one division in the story that does not hold and whose loss contributes greatly to Kornfeld's destruction: the separation between sanity and insanity.

*Cliff Prewencki*

# A PAINFUL CASE

*Author:* James Joyce (1882-1941)
*Type of plot:* Psychological
*Time of plot:* 1899-1903
*Locale:* Dublin, Ireland
*First published:* 1914

Principal characters:
JAMES DUFFY, an unmarried middle-aged bank cashier
EMILY SINICO, a married woman who becomes his friend

*The Story*

James Duffy, a middle-aged bachelor without family or friends, is a cashier in a private bank and lives a spartan existence in a Dublin suburb. He dislikes physical and mental disorder, ignores beggars' pleas for alms, and does not attend church. His only luxuries are playing Mozart's music on his landlady's piano and attending an opera or concert. At three such concerts, he sees Emily Sinico, the wife of a ship captain who has "dismissed [her] from his gallery of pleasures." The pair begin meeting for evening walks, but because Duffy objects to stealth, he convinces Emily to invite him to her home. Thinking that Duffy is interested in his daughter, Captain Sinico welcomes the visits. Now, for the first time in his life, Duffy has an audience for his political and social ideas, and he lends Mrs. Sinico books and explains them to her. A good listener, she also encourages him to talk about himself, but she fails to persuade him to publish his thoughts, for he eschews both competition and criticism.

Their solitary meetings, often in darkness, inevitably bring them closer together. A sense of companionship develops, and the union eventually begins to smooth the rough edges of his character and even "emotionalize[s] his mental life." At the same time, he continues to assert the soul's incurable loneliness, believing that every person is an island, which ultimately is alone. When one night Mrs. Sinico presses his hand to her cheek, he is surprised and disillusioned, and a week later breaks off their relationship—an action that greatly disappoints her.

Duffy reverts to his even way of life, but avoids concerts to forestall encounters with Mrs. Sinico. Four years pass, and one day he sees a headline in the newspaper: "DEATH OF A LADY AT SYDNEY PARADE." Subtitled "A PAINFUL CASE," it reports the outcome of an inquest regarding the body of forty-three-year-old Mrs. Emily Sinico, who was killed by a train engine while crossing the tracks at Sydney Parade Station. Captain Sinico and his daughter have testified, the former stating that his wife and he had been happily married until about two years ago, when she became rather intemperate of her habits, and the latter reporting that recently her mother had begun going out at night to buy spirits. The jury has exonerated the engine driver from all blame, the deputy coroner has called it a most painful case, and the news item closes with the statement that no blame was attached to anyone.

Profoundly affected, Duffy reads the story over and over again, at one point "moving his lips as a priest does when he reads the prayers *Secreto*." He is repelled by what he considers a commonplace, vulgar death, and thinks at first that by so dying Mrs. Sinico has degraded not only herself but also him: He sees the "squalid tract of her vice, miserable and malodorous." Is it possible that he has deceived himself so utterly about her? Later, he wonders if he is to blame and whether he should have acted differently toward her. He begins to appreciate how lonely her life was and admits to himself that he also is lonely and unlikely to be remembered after he dies. Feeling that his moral nature is collapsing and that he is an outcast from the joys of life, he wonders why he withheld life from her. He had met someone who had seemed to love him, but fears he had denied her life and happiness and sentenced her to a death of shame.

*Themes and Meanings*

*Dubliners* (1914) is a collection of fifteen James Joyce stories, of which "A Painful Case" is the eleventh. It follows "Clay," with which it shares the theme of lovelessness. Like all the works in the volume, "A Painful Case" dramatizes what Joyce saw as an emotional and moral paralysis afflicting his native city. Duffy's inability to admit changes into his daily routine or feeling into his life is the centerpiece of the story, which describes two painful cases: a man who denies love and a woman who vainly searches for it. Although Roman Catholicism was pervasive in Irish spiritual and temporal life at the time, its reach does not extend to these characters, and Joyce's comment that Duffy lives "his spiritual life without any communion with others" signals his rejection of the church. Among Duffy's books is Friedrich Nietzsche's *Also sprach Zarathustra: Ein Buch für Alle und Keinen* (1883-1885; *Thus Spake Zarathustra*, 1896), an anti-Christian tract about a self-sufficient superman who needs neither social interaction nor romantic love. Also, at one point in their relationship, Mrs. Sinico, with an almost maternal solicitude, becomes Duffy's confessor. In Catholicism, however, women cannot play this role. Such an ironic or inverted treatment of Ireland's religion is a recurrent thematic motif in other *Dubliners* tales.

Like all of these stories, "A Painful Case" progresses toward what the author called an "epiphany," a sudden realization or rude awakening to the truth about oneself or one's world. Duffy experiences such an enlightenment, but, as is typical in these stories, it is too late to do him any good. It comes in stages: His first reaction to Mrs. Sinico's death is disgust; then he experiences pangs of guilt; finally, he reaches the point of self-awareness. A wiser man, he also is infinitely sadder. Except for the brief time with Mrs. Sinico, he has lived alone and seemed suited to a solitary, adventureless existence; but after his epiphany, for the first time he feels alone, and what remains of his life indeed may be intolerable.

The consequences of Duffy's denial of Mrs. Sinico's instinctive passionate gesture are beyond his ken. Rather than reestablishing the reasoned order of his life, it sows the slowly nurturing seeds of its destruction. Further, the denial destroys Mrs. Sinico. Seeking love, she finds only temporary intellectual companionship, and when the interlude ends, her physical and emotional decline is aggravated by alcoholism. A normal person, according to an examining surgeon, would not have died of Mrs. Sinico's injuries; her death, he thought, probably was the result of shock and heart failure. Whether it was accidental or a suicide, she dies of a broken heart.

The last paragraph of the story starts with the rhythm of a freight train reverberating in Duffy's ears and concludes with utter silence, symbolizing his loneliness. The passage also suggests another theme, the failure of people to communicate, which Joyce develops throughout the story. For example, in the opening paragraph, Duffy is said to be an unpublished author, a closet writer; later, responding to Mrs. Sinico, he explains his reluctance to publish by speaking scornfully of potential audiences. In addition, her interpretation of his words disillusions him. On the night he learns of her death, Duffy goes to a pub, but the proprietor does not talk to him, even while serving him obsequiously. Duffy gazes at other men in the pub, but neither sees nor hears them.

"The Sisters," the first *Dubliners* story, begins "There was no hope for him . . . ," and the young narrator, looking up at a dying priest's window, says softly to himself the word "paralysis." Nor is there any hope for Duffy in "A Painful Case"; he suffers from the same emotional and spiritual paralysis that afflicts so many people in *Dubliners*, which ends with the aptly titled story "The Dead."

*Style and Technique*

"A Painful Case" and the other *Dubliners* stories are written in a realistic style with so much naturalistic detail about Ireland's capital that some critics consider the city to be the hero of the book. Because Joyce has a definite design in mind, however, the details not only heighten verisimilitude, but also are symbolically and thematically significant.

For example, the name of the Dublin suburb where Duffy lives—Chapelizod—recalls the tragic love story of the Arthurian prince Tristan and Irish princess Iseult. Joyce's description of Duffy's unpublished translation of Gerhart Hauptmann's play *Michael Kramer* (1900; English translation, 1911) in his desk also is highly suggestive. Joyce probably selected the play, which he himself once had translated, because both Hauptmann's hero and Duffy are aloof loners who are incapable of love and believe that artists must isolate themselves. The lack of color in Duffy's room; the brown tint that is both the color of his face and Dublin's streets; the shallow river and disused distillery near which he lives—all of these details are of a piece, creating a sense of sterility, drabness, and ineffectuality. The method is similar to that which Joyce utilizes at the start of "Araby," the third *Dubliners* story: Physical details signify inner qualities.

Joyce's narrative realism is combined with a simple plot whose few incidents culminate in a crisis leading to a personal revelation or recognition. The enlightenment that comes with this epiphany, something of a confrontation with reality, is illuminating but not rejuvenating, and indeed may reinforce prevailing inadequacies and paralysis. Joyce uses this technique, like his symbols, not only in "A Painful Case" but also elsewhere in *Dubliners* to give cumulative emphasis to his themes.

*Gerald H. Strauss*

# PALE HORSE, PALE RIDER

*Author:* Katherine Anne Porter (1890-1980)
*Type of plot:* Symbolist
*Time of plot:* 1918
*Locale:* A small town in the foothills of the Rockies
*First published:* 1938

> *Principal characters:*
> MIRANDA, a twenty-four-year-old woman from the deep South who works on a small-town newspaper
> ADAM, a twenty-four-year-old soldier from Texas who is stationed at a local army base before being sent to Europe

## The Story

The story begins in a first-person dream sequence with a southern gothic setting, complete with a five-times-removed cousin, a decrepit hound, horses used for fox hunting, and a "stranger" who will ride with the speaker at dawn. As the narrative shifts to the third person and Miranda wakes up to her dreary job on a small-town paper, her problems with adjusting to reality are shared by the reader, who is never given any clearer explanation of Miranda's past and its relation to her present situation.

Although both past and future are only suggested, the present is depicted in grimly realistic detail. Miranda's colleagues on the paper are a collection of semifailures, all haunted by a sense of inadequacy and badgered by a Liberty Bond seller who is not above real as well as moral blackmail. The war is the overpowering external reality, dictating proper conduct for everyday actions from drinking coffee to knitting.

Miranda's conflict with the external reality of the war arises from her attempts to establish and maintain an internal sense of personal order and priority. Her struggles are illustrated by encounters with the Liberty Bond salesperson, an actor whose performance she reviewed negatively, men at the hospital where she does volunteer work, and with Adam, the man with whom she is in love. Miranda's mind shrinks from the external reality of the war, but—as her internal sense of priorities is not firmly established—finds no other clear focus; thus, she always seems to be thinking about something other than the matter at hand.

The only exception to this is Adam, but even with him Miranda is overpowered by externals. She thinks more often of his "olive and tan and tawny" exterior, of his splendid and seemingly indestructible youth, than she does of her feelings for him or of their mutual plans. He is about to be shipped overseas, so their future is entirely dominated by the war. Miranda struggles against this but is at the same time aware that without the war, Adam would have remained in Texas and unknown to her. They both make a conscious attempt to live in and for the present, but the constant intrusion of war-related songs and situations and of the many funerals resulting from an influenza epidemic make this impossible. They had no time together in the past and they will have no time together in the immediate future, but their awareness of this seems to leave them no time in the present.

Miranda continually complains of feeling dizzy and disoriented, and the reader puts this down to her struggles with internal and external realities until a much more prosaic reality manifests itself: Miranda develops influenza. She is seriously ill, but because of the shortage of hospital beds, Adam tries to nurse her in the rooming house where she lives. Finally, at the insistence of her editor, two interns come to take Miranda to the hospital. They arrive while Adam is out buying more food and medicine, and she is later given a note saying that he will come to see her as soon as the doctors will allow it and that he loves her.

Miranda's fever dreams leave her (and the reader) confused about the following sequence of events. She is seriously ill for several weeks and in her dreams makes a series of choices that lead her back to reality and life with Adam. She awakes to the bells celebrating the Armistice. As she begins to recover, the nurse forces her to read her mail, which includes a note telling her that Adam died of influenza in the camp hospital. Miranda makes meticulously detailed plans to return to a world without war, without influenza, and without Adam, a world in which there is nothing but "dazed silence," the "dead cold light of tomorrow," and "time for everything."

## Themes and Meanings

The sense of foreboding established by Miranda's dream-choice of a pale gray horse to ride at dawn with the "stranger" on his gray horse never leaves the reader and builds as the narrative progresses. By providing so little external action in the story, Katherine Anne Porter focuses the reader's attention on the inner voice and the inner eye, and on the figure of Death always visible from the corner of that eye. For Miranda and Adam, death is not an ancestral memory or a future shadow; it is riding with them in the present moment, moving between them and an "ordinary" real life together and finally between them as individuals. There is no time for living; there is only time for death. As individuals, Adam and Miranda may think that they make their own choices—Adam keeps repeating that he wanted to fight in the war and Miranda chooses life in her dreams—but Porter presents death and its power as a reality that supersedes all others.

Porter's skillful combination of setting and allusion provides the framework within which she develops her theme. The end of the "war to end all wars" and the title's echoing allusion to Revelation 6:2 ("Behold a pale horse: and his name that sat on him was Death, and Hell followed with him") both balance the names of the main characters—Adam, the first man, and Miranda, William Shakespeare's heroine who learns of a "brave new world"—to create an alpha and omega, a beginning in which there is always and already an ending, a world in which there is no time because there is infinite time.

*Style and Technique*

Porter's style, like that of Flannery O'Connor and Eudora Welty, shows the strong influence of the oral tradition of storytelling. In this story, however, she draws from this tradition not as an end in itself, but as a way of clearing the ground for her other concerns. Her ability to summon an entire personality from a detail of description or an idiosyncratic action allows her to exercise a narrative economy that, in turn, leaves time and space for her experiments with stream-of-consciousness interior monologues. The first description of Adam, for example, captures the essence of both his appearance and his manner:

> He was wearing his new uniform, and he was all olive and tan and tawny, hay colored and sand colored from hair to boots. She half noticed again that he always began by smiling at her; that his smile faded gradually; that his eyes became fixed and thoughtful as if he were reading in a poor light.

Like William Faulkner, Porter opens the mind of her character not only for the reader's inspection, but also for the reader's participation—for example, the reader's confusion during the dream sequences is just as complete as is Miranda's. Like Virginia Woolf, Porter uses this technique to stop space and move in time (as in the opening dream) or to stop time and move in space.

*J. M. Walker*

# THE PAPERHANGER

*Author:* William Gay (1943-    )
*Type of plot:* Realism
*Time of plot:* The 1990's
*Locale:* East Tennessee
*First published:* 2000

> *Principal characters:*
> DR. JAMAHL, a successful doctor
> HIS WIFE
> ZEINEB, their four-year-old daughter
> BELLWETHER, the sheriff
> THE PAPERHANGER, a worker

*The Story*

"The Paperhanger" is a dark tale of the disappearance of a child, the resultant disintegration first of her parents' marriage and then of their lives, and of a shocking miracle engineered by the paperhanger, a strange dispassionate man. The story is told by an omniscient narrator who unfolds his yarn with consummate skill and a portentousness that vacillates between grim, almost biblical, wisdom and brutal irony.

The narrative opens with the assertion that the vanishing of the child "was an event so cataclysmic that it forever divided time into the then and the now" and proceeds to detail the events that immediately preceded the child's disappearance and the actions of the doctor, his wife, the authorities, and the paperhanger after the child vanishes. In the first pages, the doctor's wife quarrels with the paperhanger on the building site of a mansion being built for her and her husband. The child, Zeineb, is innocently playing with the paperhanger's long flaxen hair as the mother assails him for his shoddy work and for overcharging her. The paperhanger's insolent and sexually provocative response enrages the doctor's wife, and she verbally abuses him, whirls on her heels, and marches out of the house to her silver Mercedes. When she calls for her daughter to join her, there is no response. She goes back into the house and demands to know where her daughter is. No one knows; but led by the paperhanger, the workers search the house and grounds for the missing child. She is nowhere to be found. The sheriff is called, and the authorities search the house and grounds again as well as the vehicles of the workers. An extensive search of the woods behind the house is organized and continues long into the darkness. No trace of the child is found.

In the days that follow, Dr. Jamahl, a Princeton-educated Pakistani who returned to his own country to find a wife befitting his station and selected a woman on the basis of her beauty, begins to blame his wife for the loss of the child. The couple becomes increasingly despondent and estranged. Work ceases on the mansion, and in the days and months that follow, the doctor and his wife become immersed in alcoholic despair and mutual recrimination. Then one day, the doctor's wife and her silver Mercedes vanish. The doctor does not search for her; he sits passively stroking his cat and drinking scotch while his practice falls into ruin. Then after a botched operation during which a woman dies, he too disappears, driving off into the west in the middle of the night.

In the interim, the paperhanger is revealed to be a perplexing and somewhat menacing individual who, in fact, had had a previous confrontation with the doctor's wife. On an earlier occasion while working for the couple, he had responded to what he felt was sexually provocative behavior in a way that earned him a violent slap from the doctor's wife. When she hired him again, the paperhanger was intrigued not so much because he was sexually attracted to this foreign beauty but rather because her apparent fascination with him made her vulnerable to him and to his desire to humble this wealthy and arrogant woman. He expresses no sympathy for the bereaved parents but observes the search for the missing child with a dispassionate eye. He lives alone deep in the Harrikin, a vast dark and forlorn wooded area dotted with old mines and abandoned foundries and furnaces. He digs up a few of the graves in an abandoned graveyard and examines the bones and relics with cold curiosity.

A year or so after she drives away, the doctor's wife reappears, a shadow of her former self. She haunts the abandoned mansion, drinking vodka martinis and praying for the return of her child from the dead or even for the lesser miracle of the discovery of her child's body. When the paperhanger appears late one fall afternoon, she hires him to take her into the Harrikin, into the woods in which she believes her daughter vanished. He takes her to the abandoned graveyard and tells her a strange story about perhaps having murdered his unfaithful wife and buried her in a grave under an old coffin. The woman attempts to leave, but the paperhanger begins to molest her sexually; drunken and almost insensible with grief and despair, she offers no resistance. He is exultant not because of his sexual conquest but because he feels that she has fallen to his level.

Later that evening, the paperhanger awakens in his cabin with the doctor's wife sprawled beside him naked and deep in a drunken sleep. With terrifying insouciance and a philosophical air, he retrieves from his freezer the tiny body of the dead child whom he had seen as a clone of the mother, murdered in response to her mother's verbal abuse, and hidden in his toolbox. He arranges the body of the child in the sleeping mother's arms and drives away in her Mercedes, pleased with his ability to grant her one of the miracles for which she longed. He heads "west into open country, tracking into wide-open territories he could infect like a malignant spore."

*Themes and Meanings*

William Gay, like William Faulkner, is a writer whose stories are firmly rooted in his native soil (Tennessee in Gay's case), yet are not merely regional stories but haunting tales of human struggles in the beautiful but alien and perhaps malevolent world of modern times.

"The Paperhanger" may be viewed as a parable of the New South, here characterized by materialism, instability, and solipsism. The story depicts a world in which, in myth at least, there was once beauty, graciousness, and order, but now there is a desolate landscape of derelict mansions, ruined foundries, and abandoned graveyards. A landscape peopled by wealthy foreigners with no essential connection either to the land or to one another, obsequious building contractors, an unctuous and self-serving sheriff, and the paperhanger, a drifter with no apparent connection to any human being or any humane value. However, this is not a story about the South so much as it is a story about a nightmarish modern world of violence and disorder such as the one envisioned in "The Second Coming," a poem by William Butler Yeats that Dr. Jamahl calls to mind in his despair.

Gay depicts a society in which people have no real identity and are known only by their profession or position in society: the doctor's wife, the electrician, the backhoe operator, and the paperhanger. The only characters who are identified by name are the four-year-old child, Zeineb, who is too young either to have achieved or lost a real identity; the doctor whose foreign name identifies him as an outsider; and the sheriff whose name, Bellwether, denotes his status as a sheep and mocks his status as a leader of the flock for his "bell" sounds only self-serving notes. The human beings adrift in this impersonal world are lonely and estranged.

The world that Gay envisions is not merely characterized by the desperate loneliness and soulnessness of modern times but also by what seem to be truly malevolent forces. At the center of this world is the paperhanger, a creature of cold intellect without pity or conscience, whose murderous hatred of others, of beauty, of difference, and of innocence is ultimately instinctive rather than rational. Subtle but pervasive religious references suggest that he is a sort of demon. His hand snakes out like a serpent to snap the child's neck, he lives alone in a decidedly infernal landscape, he parodies resurrection by idly reassembling the bones of the dead, he sees the doctor's wife as a fallen angel as she yields to him, and he performs the perverse miracle of restoring the lost child to its mother.

Ironically and sadly in an age committed to self-interest and materialism, the existence of evil like that of the paperhanger seems natural rather than supernatural, and the religious references point not to the diabolical nature of the paperhanger but to the absence of Christian values and true miracles in this grim but recognizable world. The paperhanger's story is disconcertingly realistic, and his character is convincingly human.

*Style and Technique*

"The Paperhanger," like many of Gay's stories, is characterized by spare but eloquent prose; the descriptions of nature and of human beings and their words and actions are sharp and yet evocative. Gay is exceptionally skillful at depicting both the beauty and the menace of the natural world. There is no sentimentality in his appreciation of nature; he is sensitive to the alien, inhuman quality of natural beauty. His descriptions are vivid and realistic yet often carry a hint of impending danger or disaster. This mixture of realism and ominous mystery is characteristic of his technique. The prose is laced with shades of darkness; there are suggestions that the world is hostile to humankind and that evil forces actually walk the earth. However, these are not tales of fantasy or horror but rather realistic stories alive to the mystery and evil, the unpredictable and inexplicable in nature and in human conduct.

The spareness and darkness of Gay's language and the calm realism of his narrative voice are reflected in the lives of the people in his fictional world. For the most part, each is locked away in the cell of the self, closed to others. Even if these characters seem to long for some sort of intimate human conduct, they remain essentially remote from one another and communicate without revealing any personal truths, without giving up any insights into the inner self. The story is told in an impersonal and dispassionate voice that is appropriate to this world of the cautious, the self-serving, and the damaged.

"The Paperhanger" and other stories by Gay are filled with strangeness and mystery, not because of the bizarre quality of his vision but rather because life and people are endlessly unpredictable and surprising. The reader of these stories comes to expect calamity; there is calamity at the end of this story, but it is a calamity more startling, more disconcerting, and more real than whatever one anticipated. The poetry of the common, everyday disasters of human lives echoes hauntingly through Gay's fiction.

*Hal Holladay*

# PARADISE

*Author:* Edna O'Brien (1930-    )
*Type of plot:* Impressionistic
*First published:* 1968
*Locale:* An island abroad
*Time of plot:* The twentieth century

>        *Principal characters:*
>            SHE, the protagonist, mistress, and victim
>            HE, her lover and victimizer

*The Story*

She (the two characters in this story are referred to only by the use of the pronoun) has come to stay with her older lover on a beautiful island. Fields, trees, ocean, and especially the mountains, which "seemed to be made of collapsible substance so insubstantial," capture her interest. She has come out of love and desire for him, although their worlds are different. She "is an inland person," who likes "roses in a field, thin rain and through it the roses and the vegetation." He loves the ocean, loves to sail, fish, and hunt; discovery is what matters to him. For her, the "sea is dark as the shells of mussels, and signifies catastrophe." He surrounds himself with friends, of whom he is contemptuous but who amuse him. They watch her with curiosity, knowing, as does she, that in the past there have been other wives, other women for him.

He has arranged for her to learn to swim: An instructor has been brought in for this purpose. She is afraid of the water, but she knows that she must adapt to this new medium if she is to win him. Every day, she fearfully enters the water, at first holding the instructor's hands, then a board, and later, a rope, unwilling to give herself up to the water.

She is responsible for the supervision of the cooks; she must be nice to his friends, who cut her (and often one another) with their subtle malice; and she must prepare for the day on which she must demonstrate to him, and to his friends, her ability to swim. Slowly, she masters her new environment. She reads every day, looking for amusing anecdotes to tell his friends at table. She goes out on her lover's boat with him and his friends. The food for which she is responsible sometimes is quite good. She has stopped using contraceptives (she knows that he longs for a son). She endures his occasional sneers. Finally, she learns to swim.

The day comes for the demonstration of her ability:

> She went down the ladder backwards and looked at no face in particular. She crouched until the water covered her shoulders, then she gave a short leap and delivered herself to it. Almost at once she knew that she was going to do it. Her hands no longer loath to delve deep scooped the water away, and she kicked with a ferocity she had not known to

be possible. She was aware of cheering but it did not matter about that. She swam, as she had promised, across the width of the pool in the shallow end. It was pathetically short, but it was what she had vouched to do.

To celebrate her achievement, he plans a party, ordering Gypsies, flowers, caviar. She will not have to worry about the food—others will prepare it. He is proud. He will, he says, teach her to ride, or he will have her taught.

However, now that she has attained her goal, she is tired. She knows that her relationship with him is limited by his fear of love: "She knew that if he chose her that they would not go in the deep end, the deep end that she dreaded and dreamed of. When it came to matters inside of himself he took no risks." Her new dress, a gift from him, reminds her of a corpse.

She goes to the pool and enters the deepest water, submitting to it "in a great bountiful baptism." As she goes down, she thinks, "They will never know, they will never know, ever know, for sure." Later, she comes back to consciousness at the side of the pool. He has rescued her from her suicide attempt. She is alive. She is also free: She has rejected his world, and now he rejects her. His friends spurn her. She knows that "when they got back to London there would be separate cars waiting for them at the airport."

*Themes and Meanings*

"Paradise" belongs to Edna O'Brien's second phase, inaugurated by the novel *August Is a Wicked Month* (1965), to which this story bears a passing resemblance, and concluded by the publication of the novel *Night* (1972). The work of this period typically depicts female protagonists in states of rootlessness and sexual exploitation or anxiety. It would seem that the author's raw materials originated in the fashionable, but perhaps callow, world of filmmakers and their entourages: During this period, O'Brien wrote a number of successfully produced film scripts.

In contrast to her early fiction, "Paradise" and its companion pieces represent a marked departure from Irish settings and naïve gaiety. The author's fictional world may have broadened in her second phase, but her protagonists find authentic experience virtually impossible to attain in it. This wider world may be populated by the so-called (or perhaps self-styled) beautiful people, and not by crude provincial swains, but the jet-setters' beauty is barely skin deep. Their lives are a tissue of surfaces, objects, and locations. They lack depth and substance; thus, in the protagonist's view, though she is superficially one of them, they lack credibility. The story's muted, though nevertheless intense, conflict arises from the protagonist's need to attain credibility—first, in the eyes of her lover and the social milieu in which he feels at home; and second, and more significantly, more desperately, in her own eyes.

A central preoccupation of all O'Brien's work is with love—how to obtain it, how to retain it, its status in contemporary culture, and the pain and peril that attend it. Her invariably female protagonists seem to be conceived as emotional seismographs, registering helplessly the destruction of their social autonomy and moral integrity. The protagonist of "Paradise" spends her life menaced by a divided sense of her affair. Her one source of legitimacy in the world of the story is the affair. She is not independently wealthy and possesses none of the material props or behavioral savoir faire exhibited by the rest of the group. She seems to have no particular interests. Her past is not available to her in a meaningful way. She only has the overwhelming immediacy of her feelings; for that reason, it seems, her environment rejects her.

All the other characters in the story are, in contrast, strikingly complacent. They reveal little emotional range and no capacity for companionship or fellow-feeling. Participants in a charade of sociability, their collective presence has the ultimate effect of making the protagonist unbearably aware of her own distinctiveness. The most important embodiment of the scenario's predominant shallowness is the protagonist's lover. A patriarchal figure by virtue of his age and property, he seems to be a consumer of others' appetites and energies rather than a personage capable of acting out of a free, unconsidering emotional nature. The acquisitive nature of his response to the protagonist's question, "What interests you?" is a vivid reminder of his lack of depth.

The story's portrayal of superficiality and its psychic or emotional taxation is counterpointed by the vacancy of the physical environment. An empty sea under a cloudless sky, "beautiful but unreal" mountains, an absence of any sense of community or established local habitation—these are the essential constituents of the locale. The world is a postcard, and those desiring to inhabit it are apparently required to be similarly one-dimensional. Paradise ensues when these two manifestations of shallowness coincide. For those who cannot attain the degree of sublimation necessary to feel at home in this psychic lotusland, there is always the hell of their private emotional reality, denoted in the text by the protagonist's dream: "In the night she heard a guest sob. In the morning the same guest wore a flame dressing-gown and praised the marmalade which she ate sparingly."

In "Paradise," the story ironically belies the title. The discrepancy between the title's connotation of eternal reward and heavenly bliss and the psychological actuality of the story's contents enacts in conceptual terms the author's overall concern with differences between appearance and reality. The protagonist's failure to integrate herself with her ostensibly ideal environment is a critique of the paradisiacal elements of that environment. Moreover, her failure to integrate is replicated and felt most acutely on the personal level. The more intimate, the more sexually voracious she and her lover become, the more estranged from him the protagonist feels. Their being together is not an end; it is merely a preliminary to division and alienation.

To a certain extent, this story's thematic material covers familiar ground—ground mapped out originally by F. Scott Fitzgerald. By giving her story a focus in feminine responses, however, O'Brien manages to intensify the sense of waste and unfulfillment endemic to such material. The protagonist's desire for honesty and her inability to deny that she sees through the facade of politesse maintained by her companions give her a certain moral superiority. However, because of her condition of social dependence, she cannot act effectively in the name of that superiority—or rather, she can act only in ways that endanger herself. The protagonist's unusual dual status—she is both an insider and an outsider—gives the story its tension. The precariousness of that status is convincingly rendered by the plot's air of open-endedness, drift, and uncertainty.

Another aspect of the protagonist's distinctiveness is her evident faith in romance, her capacity to affirm passion and desire. Her ultimate lack of emotional fulfillment may be considered the predictable outcome of such a naïve disposition. The story suggests, however, that it is not romance that should be criticized, but those who spurn it. From the perspective of her own psychological reality, the protagonist again seems beset by a duality. In common with many contemporary female characters, the protagonist has a strong awareness of her body, yet she seems to be her body's prisoner. She is at once more physically present than the other, rather disembodied, characters, and at the same time more socially constrained and emotionally desperate than they are. Her swimming lessons may be seen as an elaborate metaphor for her physical and emotional floundering.

The protagonist's alienation from herself as well as from the rest of the characters may originate in her thwarted emotional integrity, but it is reinforced by the material circumstances of her world. It is these circumstances that, superficially, give the story its paradisiacal plausibility. However, not only does the protagonist fail to adapt to material ease, but also she seems innately incapable of comprehending it as an end in itself. In addition, she fails to perceive the codes appropriate to the social rituals of her world (dinner, for example), thereby antagonizing her lover. Here again, an immense disparity is evident between the norms of objective experience and the compulsions of subjective need.

*Style and Technique*

The style of "Paradise" is erratic and lacking in uniformity. Governed by a limited, unusually closely focused point of view, it succeeds impressively in conveying both the hollowness and immediacy of the characters' momentary existence. Just as the physical environment supplies a sense of a merely nominal context, the style provides a sense of existence being a tissue of moments, devoid of cumulative significance or relevant recall. This treatment of time is perhaps the story's most satiric implementation of standard expectations of paradise. (Because paradise represents an attempt to imagine eternity, conventional experiences of time do not apply there.) The story's time signature also underlines the manner in which matters such as direction of plot and development of character are made deliberately problematic. This aspect receives additional emphasis from the fact that the story's moments of experience bear a merely tangential relationship to one another.

By these various means, "Paradise" becomes a story of condition rather than of possibility. Thus, its style and form contribute by their nature to the overall sense of the protagonist's paralysis of will, or moral imprisonment. In turn, the story's tacit but insistent characterization of entrapment makes it an interesting variation on traditional, or at least pre-Freudian, fictional techniques for depicting sexual entanglements.

Perhaps the story's novelty will be more readily perceived by dwelling on its most satisfying artistic innovation, which is the imaginative suggestiveness latent in the protagonist's swimming lessons. These lessons perform a number of important technical functions. They confirm a sense of the protagonist's hapless, feckless situation. They reveal her difficulties with autonomy. They detach her from the group without making her aware of the value of doing so. These lessons invoke various, no doubt unworthy, but not entirely unhelpful, puns about the protagonist: Is she out of her depth? Will she sink or swim? (The latter seems to be actively invited by the author in the swimming-pool scene.) More important, the lessons provide a means of offsetting the tendency toward cliché contained in the protagonist's impulse to self-destruction. In all, the stressful charade of swimming provides the story with a structural and thematic depth that, elsewhere and otherwise, it ironically repudiates.

The variations in the style of "Paradise" between the tight-lipped and the open-eyed, its variations in tone between plangency and frustration, and the idiosyncratic continuities of its narrative structure all remove it from the traditional Irish short story, which is modeled on such authors as Ivan Turgenev, Anton Chekhov and Guy de Maupassant. O'Brien has successfully availed herself of this model on other occasions. As though to match its fashionable characters and setting, "Paradise" is a more modish piece of work. However, while it effectively internationalizes the author's fictional world, it also succeeds in reenacting her enduring preoccupation with the vagaries of love.

*George O'Brien*

# PARAGUAY

*Author:* Donald Barthelme (1931-1989)
*Type of plot:* Antistory
*Time of plot:* About 1970
*Locale:* The United States
*First published:* 1970

> *Principal characters:*
> THE NARRATOR
> JEAN MUELLER, his hostess
> HERKO MUELLER, Jean's husband

## The Story

"Paraguay" does not lend itself easily to a plot analysis because Donald Barthelme has not created a clear sequence of events. Nevertheless, the fifteen sections of the story, all but one with its own heading and most with only a tenuous relationship to the others, do add up to a recognizable journey to a bizarre country.

The opening section, narrated by an unidentified "we," describes an expedition, apparently in the Himalayas, making its perilous way up and down peaks and through passes. The tone is similar to that of dozens of other reports of its kind. Indeed, a footnote then identifies the passage, "slightly altered," as a quotation from a book published in 1906, *A Summer Ride Through Western Tibet*, by Jane E. Duncan. The alteration no doubt refers to the last sentence of the section: "Ahead was Paraguay," which is obviously not part of the original quotation. The second section, entitled "Where Paraguay Is," says that this country is not the one in South America. "This Paraguay," the narrator states, "exists elsewhere."

## Themes and Meanings

What and where is Paraguay then? Although Spanish phrases occur in several places, nothing else in the story suggests a distinctly Latin American setting. Rather, what ultimately emerges is a fantastic land that resembles more than anything else a setting in the United States at around the time the story was written. Although the various sections have little apparent relationship to one another, they are united by the mocking and whimsical tone used to satirize twentieth century civilization.

The first obvious target is the fine arts and their popular manifestations. The encounter in the section "Jean Mueller," which is the name of a woman who identifies herself as the narrator's host, suggests a parody of a trite scene in countless films in which the protagonist meets a mysterious woman early in the film who forebodes intrigue and adventure. The section entitled "Herko Mueller" introduces the character of Jean Mueller's husband, who is identified as a professional "arbiter of comedy." Barthelme uses him to caricature critics who make absurd and incomprehensible rules about drama. Art as a commodity is the subject of "Rationalization," a splendidly grotesque description of how art in Paraguay is treated as a business problem in production, shipping, and distribution. Furthermore, as the title of the section implies, art has been rationalized; that is, it has been diminished, its vitality and originality wrung out, as it is made quickly and easily available to all the citizens of Paraguay. Finally, "The Wall," which a footnote explains is a "slightly altered" version of a passage from Charles Le Corbusier's "The Modular" (1954), has been inserted, apparently to serve as a self-parody of architectural jargon and concepts.

Another major area for satire is science and technological progress. "Temperature," in describing how the activity of the citizens of Paraguay is controlled by temperature changes, is a burlesque of an elaborate scientific study that measures the precise effects of temperature changes on organisms. Sexual intercourse between adult Paraguayans living in the "silver cities," the section concludes, occurs between sixty-six and sixty-nine degrees. In "Herko Mueller," the narrator goes swimming and is surprised to discover a sand dollar under his shirt because he knows that the sand "is sifted twice daily to remove impurities and maintain whiteness." The narrator also is surprised because the ocean is "not programmed for echinoderms," an observation that makes fun of the application of computer technology in unlikely places. The section entitled "Microminiaturization" (a splendidly redundant term) pushes to an absurd extreme the modern technological thrust toward smallness: "Walls thin as a thought, locomotive-substitutes no bigger than ball-point pens, Paraguay, then, has big empty spaces in which men wander, trying to touch something." Finally, "Silence" points to the prevalence of noise in contemporary civilization.

Throughout "Paraguay" there are references that suggest a pervasive government guiding and manipulating society. "Error" specifically burlesques government ways of dealing with a mistake "resulting in the death of a statistically insignificant portion of the population." The mishap is thus handled: "A skelp of questions and answers is fused at high temperature (1400° C) and then passed through a series of protracted caresses. Amelioration of the condition results." Another area of concern to the government is skin. Paraguayans are obsessed with the removal of skin. Why skin removal is so important and, indeed, what the process entails are not clear in the story. Barthelme, however, seems to be more interested in satirizing narcissistic compulsions regarding the body, such as the application of cosmetics, deodorants, or tanning lotions. In language that emphasizes the intense gravity of the process, the narrator describes Jean Mueller, accompanied by lights and noises, doing exercises to loosen and remove her skin.

Two sections suggest that Paraguay is a civilization that values progress and is reluctant to ask basic questions that challenge the status quo or seek answers to nonpractical questions. In "Terror," Jean tells the narrator that explanations lead nowhere: "Therefore we try to keep everything open, go forward avoiding the final explanation." Similarly, in "Behind the Wall," the narrator and Jean discuss the significance of a field of red snow. The concluding sentence, however, suggests that questions of meaning are ignored in Paraguay: "It seemed to proclaim itself a mystery, but one there was no point in solving—an ongoing low-grade mystery."

There are some sections that defy unifying rational explanation. "The Temple," for example, strings together short observations on a grove of trees (an abandoned temple), drinking apple juice, and the sexual life of Paraguayans, who have devised some new words for erotic practices, such as "dimidiation" and "quartering," terminology that suggests something sinister or at least bizarre. In the last section, "Departure," Herko Mueller informs the narrator that he has been chosen to lead a column out. The last sentence emphasizes the fantastic nature of Paraguay: "We began the descent (into? out of?) Paraguay." It does little, however, to clarify the logic or details of the plot except to suggest that this bizarre and satiric journey has ended.

*Style and Technique*

"Paraguay" can be classified as an antistory because it deliberately flouts traditional techniques of fiction. Besides the lack of a conventional plot with events causally related to one another, the point of view remains vague. True, it is told by a first-person narrator who reports on the culture of Paraguay, but his identity, like that of Jean and Herko Mueller, remains unrealized and vague, and his connection to the story he is telling unclear. As in many stories by Barthelme, the characters remain fragmentary and undeveloped persons who fail to engage the emotions of the reader. The creation of such characters in much modern fiction represents a departure from one of the traditional central concerns of fiction—to endow an individual with personal identity, family, a place in society, and a history. Even the conventional sense of setting suffers in the story; Paraguay remains a shadowy and unrealized location. All these characteristics, then, contribute to the unsettling effect that antistories such as "Paraguay" have on many. Not only do they fail to meet a reader's usual expectations, but also they sometimes are impervious to common sense.

An important aspect of Barthelme's style, and one that also contributes to the bafflement of readers, is that he is interested in words as words; that is, words may be referential in that they point to some outer reality, but they are still things in themselves to be manipulated for the fun of it. Much of the antic charm of "Paraguay" lies in the arrangement and connections of words: the non sequiturs, the strange juxtapositions, the unexpected choice of words, the odd image, and the wry violation of the rules of plausible discourse.

Coupled with the emphasis on words themselves is the concern with the surface of things. "Paraguay" does not enter very deeply into the essential nature of the place it describes. It relies heavily on bits and pieces, on collages of details and impressions. Furthermore, there is little sense of what parts of the surface are more important than others; everything is treated on the same level of importance, and often the real is blended with the fantastic.

Ultimately, then, "Paraguay" offers little satisfaction to conventional readers, but it does provide a delightfully weird and satiric view of the American scene.

*Walter Herrscher*

# PARKER'S BACK

*Author:* Flannery O'Connor (1925-1964)
*Type of plot:* Realism
*Time of plot:* 1964
*Locale:* Georgia
*First published:* 1965

> *Principal characters:*
> OBADIAH ELIHUE PARKER, the protagonist, a tattooed man
> SARAH RUTH CATES, his wife

*The Story*

O. E. Parker, a profane and shiftless man, has married Sarah Ruth Cates, a plain-looking, self-righteous woman who was "forever sniffing up sin." Parker is unable to understand this marriage—why she stays with him, or he with her.

He had met Sarah Ruth one day when his truck broke down before her house. Sensing that the woman was watching him, Parker pretended to mash his hand in the machinery, swearing profusely. Without warning, Sarah Ruth appeared, striking him for talking filth. However, Parker noticed, beneath her severe countenance, that she had a curiosity in his tattoos, even though she denounced them as a "heap of vanities." Parker's fascination with tattoos began at age fourteen, when he saw a tattooed carnival man. Years later, he had got his first tattoo, then another, until now his front was almost entirely covered with serpents, eagles, hawks, and other animals. However, all these tattoos failed to make a coherent design, and his back had no tattoos at all.

Parker had not intended to marry any woman, especially not Sarah Ruth; he could not imagine why anyone would marry her. Nevertheless, he is married to her, and growing increasingly dissatisfied. Nothing will do, it seems, but to get another tattoo—something on his back, something religious, something forceful enough to "bring Sarah Ruth to heel."

A few days later, Parker is baling hay with a broken-down tractor. Distracted by thoughts of his tattoo, and by the fierce sun, Parker collides with an old tree that seems to reach out at him. Parker finds himself knocked out of his shoes, hurled high into the air, shouting, "GOD ABOVE." He watches, amazed, as the tractor and the tree burst into flames, consuming his shoes.

Knowing somehow that his life has been changed, Parker rushes immediately into town for that tattoo and demands a picture of God. Leafing backward through various pictures of Christ, Parker selects a stern, Byzantine Christ with fierce eyes. He insists that the tattoo artist begin immediately.

This tattoo of Christ requires two days to complete. Before returning home, Parker stops in a pool hall, where some of his friends beg to see his tattoo and taunt him for having "gone and got religion." Parker vigorously denies such accusations. Within himself, however, Parker knows that just as he has always followed his instincts in getting tattoos, he must now obey those all-demanding eyes tattooed on his back.

Driving home, Parker convinces himself that Sarah Ruth will be pleased with his tattoo, but he finds the door locked. Indeed, she refuses to open the door until he whispers his full name—Obadiah Elihue, a name he has always despised.

Parker removes his shirt and demands that she look at the tattoo, but Sarah Ruth does not recognize the picture. When Parker insists that the tattoo is God, Sarah Ruth becomes quite angry, beating his back with her broom, screaming, "Idolatry!" Parker, too stunned to resist, staggers out the door, weeping. Large welts cover the tattooed face of Christ.

*Themes and Meanings*

Obadiah Elihue is, as his biblical name suggests, a kind of prophet, mysteriously driven to bear the truth to his stubborn wife, Sarah Ruth. While he fails in his mission, he nevertheless discovers that the direction of his own life has been changed significantly.

Flannery O'Connor was a devout Catholic, whose religious faith consciously informed her fiction. The difficulty of her work, she once explained in a letter, is that many of her readers do not understand the redemptive quality of "grace," and, she added, "don't recognize it when they see it. All my stories are about the action of grace on a character who is not very willing to support it, but most people think of these stories as hard, hopeless, brutal."

In O'Connor's mind, Parker is an unwilling agent of spiritual "grace" who cannot understand what is happening to him until he is beaten and rejected by his wife. Sarah Ruth, not Parker, is the "heretic," O'Connor explained in another letter, for Sarah Ruth holds "the notion that you can worship in pure spirit." By refusing to see anything redemptive in Parker, or in his instinctive motivation to "please" her, Sarah Ruth is, in effect, doing nothing less than battering the face of God, embodied in the flesh of Parker.

Parker is clearly likened to other familiar prophets, Moses and Jonah. Like Moses, who encountered God in a burning bush and was ordered to remove his shoes, Parker is impelled to carry a message to an unreceptive audience; like Jonah, he seeks to evade his responsibility. He has not "gone and got religion"; rather, it has come and got him—first, through his instincts and his impulsive actions, and finally, through the all-demanding eyes of Christ at his back. By being true to these mysterious, inner forces, which he does not even understand, he serves to expose the falseness of his wife's arrogant religiosity and her own implicit idolatry.

*Style and Technique*

In almost all of her stories, O'Connor reveals her characters by their eyes. Here, Sarah Ruth has "icepick" eyes, and Parker's eyes are "the same pale slate-color as the ocean," reflecting "immense spaces around him." Consequently, when Parker gets the tattoo of Christ on his back, the significance of what he has accepted is revealed by the all-demanding, penetrating eyes, under whose gaze Parker feels transparent.

O'Connor's undisguised satire is apparent in Parker's turning backward through the pictures of Christ; he rejects the milder, "up-to-date" versions of Christ for the older, more compelling Byzantine Christ. Irony, too, is a favorite technique of O'Connor and is usually quite glaring. For example, Parker's shouting "GOD ABOVE" brings what he least expects—a response as surely as if his shout were a prayer.

The conclusion of "Parker's Back" is a model of O'Connor's economical storytelling and mythic vision. Parker, in the final scene, leans against the tree, beaten, rejected, "crucified," as it were; but his "crying like a baby" suggests at the same time a rebirth, a new direction, a new life.

*Thomas Becknell*

# THE PARSLEY GARDEN

*Author:* William Saroyan (1908-1981)
*Type of plot:* Coming of age
*Time of plot:* The early 1940's
*Locale:* Fresno, California
*First published:* 1950

Principal characters:
AL CONDRAJ, an eleven-year-old boy
HIS MOTHER, the "creator" of the parsley garden, an immigrant
farmworker
MR. CLEMMER, a Woolworth store manager

*The Story*

Explained nonchalantly by the need to "break the monotony" of one day in August and get a tool "to make something," young Al Condraj's casual pocketing of a small hammer at Woolworth becomes a traumatic and obsessive experience. He has no plan to break the law when he lifts the ten-cent object; his single-minded concern is to "make something" out of freely available wood and nails. Although he is released by the store manager, Al knows that "he had been humiliated and [is] deeply ashamed." The trauma of feeling humiliated and shamed gives way to hatred for adult authority. Al begins the process of maturing as he reflects on his position in society.

At first, Al decides to summon enough courage to take revenge on the young man who caught him, but he loses his nerve outside the store. He believes that because he was "made to feel like a thief anyway," he should at least get the hammer. He returns home "crushed," confused, and "bitterly ashamed." When he recounts what happened to his mother, his mother scolds him, offering him money to buy the hammer. Al refuses, saying that he really does not need the hammer.

Restless, Al finds no one with whom to discuss his plight: Johnny Gale, the worker who resembles a machine at Foley's Packing House, has no time to pay attention to him. An entire night is consumed by the problem of "adjusting the matter," filled with thoughts of murder and a life of crime.

When the mother and her neighbor return home at nine o'clock and prepare their supper, using vegetables from their garden, Al is in the process of constructing a bench. In the exchange between Al and his mother, the reader learns that Al has partly resolved his dilemma: He has worked all day at Woolworth, earning the hammer, but has also asserted his right to refuse the offer of a job from the two men he hates. Although puzzled that he would not accept a job that pays handsomely, his mother accepts his judgment. His satisfaction in his work and the smell of the garden purge him of humiliation, but not of the hatred for the two men, although he acknowledges that they did what they had to do.

## Themes and Meanings

In a society that is dominated by private ownership of the means of production—tools, land, factories—the freedom and dignity of human beings is constantly limited and threatened. As part of the immigrant working class, Al Condraj's family—note the father's absence—depends to a large extent on the labor of its members. Thus, the mother's summer earnings "had to keep them the whole year." There is no joy or spiritual gain derived from such alienating work. Johnny Gale, "the fastest boxmaker," has been reduced to a machine. However, Al's one-day job in the store, translated into a dollar, is an example of the alienating use of time and energy that, for the boy, becomes transformed into an occasion to redeem himself.

In the beginning, the youthful protagonist refuses to recognize the division of society into those who own and those who are deprived. He rejects this milieu of commodity and private ownership; he believes that he can get a hammer from the store because he needs it, just as he and his mother can pick vegetables from their garden for food. He suffers humiliation, anger, confusion, and bitter shame when he is ushered into a world where things and people are split into use-value (satisfaction of human needs) and exchange-value (profit realized through market operations). For Al, the hammer is useful as a means of making a useful object; for adults, the hammer is valuable as a commodity yielding profit.

What disturbs Al is not the charge of theft—he accepts the distinction between what belongs to him and what does not—but the humiliating treatment accorded him. The only way he can affirm his dignity is to become a worker for the store, the site of his humiliation, and subsequently to reject that position. Even though he has publicly redeemed himself, however, he continues to hate the men—symptom of a divided psyche that signifies that he still cannot accept the alienating world of money and dehumanized property relationships.

Opposed to the public sphere of managers, consumers, workers in Foley's Packing House, Woolworth, and Inderrieden are Al's mother, her neighbor Leeza, and the parsley garden. The mother represents the strong, independent, self-reliant woman. She accepts the necessity of the learning process that her son is undergoing. Her parsley garden symbolizes the realm of pleasure and fulfilling work: "Every night in the summer . . . she would sit at the table and enjoy the cool of the garden and the smell of the things she had planted and tended." When she and Leeza return home from a full day's work, they make supper with Leeza's home-baked bread and the harvest from the garden. The vivid description of the two women enjoying their supper, communing together, drinking Turkish coffee, smoking cigarettes, and exchanging stories, juxtaposed to the impersonal workplace and store, exhibits the freedom and humanity of these exploited immigrants.

It is after describing this warm solidarity between the mother and her coworker that the text establishes the communication between the mother and her son, their renewed bond, and his expression of a newly gained confidence and courage.

Associated with the values of natural innocence and life-generating creativity symbolized by the garden, Al's recounting for his mother of his crisis-ridden day may also be viewed as an attempt to show the control this child of immigrant workers is beginning to have over a world pervaded by cold, materialistic interests and calculating demands. Against it, the garden stands as warm refuge and fertile haven.

The central theme of the psychological crisis generated by the conflict between the alienating, money-centered society and the nurturant ambience of the garden is not completely resolved because the boy is not yet ready to assume his defined position as a worker in a business society. However, the narrative clearly manifests sympathy for the moral predicament of the boy, who is not yet fully aware of his complex situation. The garden and its organic life circumscribe the boy's unease, a momentary disturbance neutralized by the good fortune that the mother and Leeza read in the coffee grounds: "health and work and supper out of doors in the summer and enough money for the rest of the year."

*Style and Technique*

William Saroyan's use of the third-person point of view enables him to penetrate the mind of his main character, Al, and also to follow Al's mother on her daily routine. The narrative focuses on the boy's consciousness for the first seven pages, shifts to the mother, and then returns to the boy in the last two pages. A chronological sequence of events conveys to the reader the boy's wanderings, until the narrative switches to his mother's work, packing figs at Inderrieden. When Leeza leaves, the narrative presents a scene, analogous to the early scene with Al being questioned by the manager, Mr. Clemmer, in which Al recounts to his mother his productivity as a worker and his rejection of being reduced to money (exchange-value). In effect, Al tells the only sympathetic listener in his life the story of his growing up: his moral crisis and attempted resolution.

The reader is brought into the story not only by the structuring of the episodes and the use of the enticingly naïve but sensitive character of Al but also by the economy and restraint of Saroyan's style. As Saroyan confessed in "The Writer on Writing," the words of this story "only imply the real story."

Saroyan's diction and syntax appear deceptively simple and spare, reflecting the speech of the eleven-year-old boy and the immigrant mother. The narrative reproduces the broken English of the mother, contrasting with the law-encoded grammar and idiom of mainstream society as illustrated by the Woolworth employees. Actually, the pedestrian-looking sentences and the repetition of words tend to hide the complex ambiguities of thought and feeling with which the boy is grappling. Consider, for example, the strange logic of the boy's statement to his mother: "I won't take your money for something I don't really need. I just thought I ought to have a hammer, so I could make something if I felt like it." Terms denoting duty and obligation conjoin with a vocabulary of feeling and need to produce a contradictory discourse, just as the coalescence of shame, humiliation, anger, and hatred in Al's psyche makes him a site where the tensions and conflicts of everyday life are enacted.

An examination of the abrupt, harsh tone of the exchange between the boy and the Woolworth employees, in contrast to the moralizing tone of the mother (in the first conversation) and her supportive comments (in the second exchange), clearly shows the polarized value systems personified by the characters. This polarity is under-scored by the opposition already discussed between the Utopian realm of the garden and the depersonalized, market-oriented space of Woolworth, Foley's Packing House, Graf's Hardware, and Inderrieden.

When the boy lapses into the broken English of his mother in articulating his sense of revolt against the discriminating world of managers and police—"Because I hate the both of them"—and his mother pronounces her tender approval with "All right. . . . Shut up," this laconic reply (which exemplifies the narrator's often-cited sentimental celebration of human goodness) indicates the moral center of the test: the trust and comradeship of Al and his mother.

Saroyan himself regarded this story as "grave, commonplace, and satisfying." The loving descriptions of the mother's flourishing garden (her image as nurturing care-taker) and of such pleasurable activities as eating, gardening, carpentry, and affection-ate conversation are orchestrated with the boy's anxious circular walk around town and his anguished night to project a subdued initiation drama with a hopeful note of transcendence at the end.

*E. San Juan, Jr.*

# THE PASSING OF GRANDISON

*Author:* Charles Waddell Chesnutt (1858-1932)
*Type of plot:* Satire, regional, realism
*Time of plot:* The 1850's
*Locale:* A plantation in Kentucky and the North
*First published:* 1899

> *Principal characters:*
> DICK OWENS, the indolent heir to a southern plantation
> CHARITY LOMAX, the young woman he is trying to win as his
> wife
> COLONEL OWENS, his father
> GRANDISON, an apparently model slave who reverses expectations

## The Story

"The Passing of Grandison" is told in the third person and primarily limited to the consciousness of Dick Owens, the cynical and lazy young heir to a large plantation in Kentucky. His desire to win the hand of his sweetheart Charity Lomax leads him on a mission to accomplish something of humanitarian import. Given his character and the contradictions of the South, however, his efforts can have only an ironic result.

Set in the early 1850's just after the passage of the federal Fugitive Slave Law, the story begins with the highly publicized trial and subsequent martyr's death of an abolitionist who tried to help the slave of Tom Briggs, an abusive master and neighbor of the Owens and Lomax families. Charity wishes that her handsome but worthless beau would do something equally worthy. This leads Dick to vow to induce one of his father's slaves to run away.

Dick chooses to accomplish his task by going on a trip to the North accompanied by a personal body servant. At first, he selects a slave who he knows will want to run away at the first opportunity. The plan is complicated by Colonel Owens, who insists that he go with Grandison. The colonel believes that Grandison is loyal and abolitionist-proof, that is, immune from those who would entice him to run away. Indeed, the colonel quizzes Grandison, who assures his master that he accepts his subordination, is contemptuous of free blacks, and fears abolitionists. As an added inducement, Colonel Owens promises Grandison that he can marry his sweetheart on his return.

Although his plans are complicated by the choice of such a seemingly model slave, Dick repeatedly attempts to get Grandison to flee, only to see his plans comically backfire as the slave seems indifferent to freedom. Dick resorts to progressively more outrageous approaches to tempting his slave: giving him extraordinary amounts of free time, sending anonymous letters to abolitionists, taking him to Canada, and finally paying men to kidnap and keep him in Canada. Only the kidnapping works, or seems to work.

After Dick returns home without his slave, Colonel Owens is outraged, not at Grandison but at the abolitionists he is certain lured his slave away. Dick achieves his heart's desire. Charity marries him but not because she thinks his conduct heroic. She actually terms his actions absurd but believes his foolish behavior clearly illustrates that he needs direction from a right-thinking woman.

Four weeks later, Grandison, tattered and worn out, appears back at the plantation, having escaped from freedom and seeking his former slave status. Colonel Owens thinks this is further vindication of the southern way of life and another indication that slaves prefer to remain as dependents of kindly masters.

A few weeks later, Grandison, his mother, father, siblings, and new wife all disappear from the plantation. Their escape to Canada is so smooth that it has obviously been prepared in advance. The colonel pursues them and is last seen shaking his fist at the rapidly receding steamboat taking his slaves to Canada.

*Themes and Meanings*

Charles Waddell Chesnutt's depictions of the South make it fair to classify him as a regionalist writer of the American literary realism movement. His use of dialect, descriptions of local customs, and probing of the master-slave relationship all link him to that movement's concern with bringing the customs of specific regions of the United States to the reading public's attention. However, Chesnutt was not simply content to describe regional quaintness. Beneath the easygoing portraits of a comfortable southern culture lie the disturbing injustices of slavery, the power struggles between differing peoples, and the age-old desire for freedom.

In the story, two parallel themes shed ironic light on each other. The surface plot of Dick Owens's outrageous parody of the chivalrous wooing of a lady is governed by the comic theme, "What a man will not do to please a woman is yet to be discovered." However, an alternative theme to describe the hidden motives of Grandison might be phrased, what a man will not do to achieve freedom for himself and his family is yet to be discovered. Grandison bides his time until it is wise to act, and he acts only when he can free his entire family, not only himself. Thus, Grandison's unselfish behavior, patience, and seriousness of purpose are implicitly contrasted to Dick Owens's absurd, selfish, and cynical purposes. This contrast is further supported by the comment of Dick's mentor, Judge Fenderson, who states that Dick only needed "the whip of necessity, or the spur of ambition" to overcome his indolence. As a slave, Grandison is driven by both the necessity and ambition that Dick lacks.

An important historical issue in the story is the Old South's contradictory behavior. While it prided itself on its benevolent paternalism, embodied by Colonel Owens, Chesnutt suggests that its principles were suspect. Although every plantation owner in the neighborhood deplores the brutality of Tom Briggs toward his slaves, it is a matter of principle that the abolitionist who attempted to help one of those slaves be imprisoned for three years, while no charges at all are brought against Briggs. Chesnutt leads readers to the conclusion that the South's principles were as empty as Dick Owens's character.

The southerners' combination of arrogance toward and misunderstanding of the slaves is also a theme. Colonel Owens regards his slaves as sacred to him because they are indicative of his wealth and social status. He prides himself on being an expert on the black person's mind and a keen judge of character. However, his firm belief that blacks understand their inferiority to whites and prefer slavery to freedom is shattered when the seemingly perfect model of the contented slave, Grandison, proves to be both a shrewd dissembler and a skilled engineer of his and his family's freedom.

*Style and Technique*

Typical of Chesnutt's work is the use of irony to convey the contradictory aspects of life on the color line. In many of his stories, there is a discrepancy between what readers are expecting and what finally occurs. Grandison, for example, uses a thick dialect, refers repeatedly to Colonel Owens as "marster," and stresses his gratitude for all he has as a slave. His subsequent lack of interest in escaping suggests that he is exactly what Colonel Owens brags that he is. The surprise ending suddenly contradicts all that the characterization leads readers to believe, for Grandison proves to be devoted not to his master but to his and his family's freedom.

Chesnutt uses a double layer of irony at times. Knowing that his readers will be aware of the stories of escaped slaves using the North Star as their guide to freedom, he ironically describes Grandison leaving Canada for Kentucky with the North Star at his back. At first, this seems to reinforce the idea that Grandison is a model slave who literally turns his back on freedom. At the end of the story, however, it becomes clear that he has thought first of his family and planned for all their happiness even at the risk of losing his own freedom.

Another original technique in the story is Chesnutt's use of a hidden plot. No details whatsoever are supplied about the dilemmas and motivations of the slaves, and yet the ending suggests a whole dimension of activity of which the reader (and the Old South) is unaware. This untold story lying beneath the happy-go-lucky life of Dick and the delusional world of his father calls into question the superficial ruling class of the Old South and invests the titular hero with a shrewdness that suggests a complexity normally lacking in the portraits of African American characters in literature of Chesnutt's time. In the title, Grandison's passing refers both to his passing into freedom at the end of the story and to his ability to pass as the perfect slave even as he is planning a most sophisticated escape, the magnitude and audacity of which seriously undermine the South's representation of itself.

*William L. Howard*

# A PASSION FOR HISTORY

*Author:* Stephen Minot (1927-      )
*Type of plot:* Social realism
*Time of plot:* The 1970's
*Locale:* Nova Scotia
*First published:* 1976

> *Principal characters:*
> KRAFT, a liberal American intellectual, in his forties
> THEA, a Nova Scotian woman
> MR. McKNIGHT, Thea's father

## The Story

Kraft, an American historian, college lecturer, and writer, wants to escape the demands and distractions of his busy life. He has used the royalties from his book on the radical movement to purchase a large plot of land in rural Nova Scotia. The story begins at a boathouse, where Kraft is conversing with a young woman named Thea.

As they talk, Kraft is dismissive about his academic work, self-conscious that his work ostensibly compromises his professed radical values. Nevertheless, he is proud of the way he perceives and teaches history, emphasizing the lives of ordinary people, rather than kings. Trying to express this idea to Thea, he is condescending, repeating himself and overly simplifying as if he were talking to a child. He tells her that "history is people. Little people."

Immediately following this exchange between Kraft and Thea, the narrator backs away from the characters and presents another framed picture. A man and woman embrace and kiss, and the man begins to unbutton the woman's dress. As the narrator backs still farther away from the man and woman, the reader's view turns out on the surrounding environment—estuaries, river, sea, and Kraft's large house, which is a bit of an embarrassment to Kraft. Once again, his actions compromise his values. Owning a vacation home on nearly a thousand acres is inconsistent with his reputation as a radical.

Kraft usually retreats to this weathered old house in Nova Scotia with his family, but this spring he has come alone, ostensibly to work. As he proceeds to undress Thea, he thinks about his wife. He knows that she would consider his affair a serious transgression. He concurs, but this does not alter his behavior.

Thea's father approaches, interrupting the younger couple. Old Mr. McKnight has come to the house for coffee, after which he will go back out to scavenge on the beach. As Kraft considers McKnight, his mind moves back and forth between being present with this man as another human being and surveying him from an academic distance, putting him in historical perspective. He makes parenthetical notes about the wooden wheel of the barrow that the old man pushes and about scavenging as an economic necessity of a forgotten time in history.

Kraft's mind is always leaping to a point of historical perspective, and in this way he removes himself from the present moment and the real lives of Thea and her father. Thea observes that his constant backward glance will turn him to salt. Doubly binding him, Kraft is also either cursed or blessed—he is unsure which—with verbatim recollection of the observations he has written in his journal. He is bound not only by his historical perspective, but also in his recollection of his historical perspective. He tells himself that this "historical sense of reality" is necessary to keep his affair with Thea from seeming too complicated.

McKnight enters the kitchen where Kraft and Thea wait for him. The old man calls Kraft into a workroom to see the frame of a rowboat that he is making. McKnight moves Kraft's hand along the smooth keel. His boats are made only of wood—no nails, only pegs. He is proud of his Old World workmanship. Then he abruptly gets up from the table and leaves, off to see what the receding tide has deposited on the beach.

Alone again, Kraft broods over an imaginary sepia photograph of Thea that haunts him. He tells her that she must feel trapped, that there is nothing for her to do, nothing to read; however, she does not see her life in this way. She reminds him that she has her cleaning, mending, cooking, and gardening. When he tells her that she is isolated, she can only respond that now, at this moment, she is not alone. She lives in the present, and while Kraft admires and envies the simplicity and order of her life, he cannot understand it. He can see it only from his own perspective—from his own experience of modern American life.

As they resume their lovemaking, Kraft determines to stay mentally, physically, and emotionally rooted in this present moment. His wife and children will join him in a week, but this does not seem to bother Thea. They have the present, she says; they have a whole week. Kraft begins to unbutton Thea's dress. His determination to put his wife from his mind is futile—he foolishly promises Thea that he will not even think about her. However, just bringing up her name interrupts the moment, and Kraft cannot keep his mind in the present with Thea. Their lovemaking proceeds, but it is merely another of the pictures of Kraft's life.

Later, as Kraft climbs the hill toward his own house, he cannot resist the urge to look back at the McKnight house. What he sees is from a time in the future, which puts this moment in the long-ago past. He sees the boathouse in ruins. No smoke is coming from the sagging chimney, the roof has rotted, the windows are broken. There are no flowers. There is no life in this picture. It is all history.

*Themes and Meanings*

As suggested by the story's title, the protagonist, Kraft, has a passion for history. There is double meaning and irony in Stephen Minot's use of the word "passion," which is often associated with strong sexual or romantic feelings. Kraft himself is confused about his own passion: He mistakes the intense envy that he feels for Thea's simple, uncomplicated life for sexual desire. Significantly, he fails fully to unite with her sexually. His passion for history, his inability to stay focused and resist the pull to see their moment of lovemaking from a future moment, makes true sexual passion impossible.

Minot uses the three characters of the story to represent past, present, and future.

Old Mr. McKnight is the past, living "in the previous century." Thea is the present; as she tells Kraft, "Now is now." These two characters, free of historical perspective, are content in their place and time. They seem to accept their lives and their work, their belief in themselves undisturbed by outside opinion. Kraft, however, is tortured by his overarching perspective—one forever in the future that keeps him continually looking back. Because he is always in the future, he even looks "back" on the present. To him, every moment in time is either history or potential history. Thus, his erudition prevents his full embrace of life's moments. Rather than liberating him or enriching his experience, Kraft's historical perspective binds him to a point in time that is always removed from his present.

Finally, there is a darkness and an irony to Kraft's problem. He professes a philosophy that he fails to embrace. While he claims to value ordinary individuals—as opposed to the "big names"—who make history, he contradicts himself by condescendingly calling them the "little people." He regards Thea and Mr. McKnight as two of these little people and hopes to benefit somehow by spending time with them. Clearly, he does not see himself as he sees the McKnights. Illustrating another of his double standards, Kraft buys the large tract of land with the quaint old house that neighbors the McKnights' house. A vacation house on a thousand acres is hardly consistent with his espoused radical values.

## Style and Technique

The most significant stylistic device that Minot uses in this story is the narrative and structural "picture" segments. The movement in perspective from a close view of Kraft's present moments to a more distant view, in which the reader and Kraft see his life from afar, is not only described by the narrative voice, it is made a structural part of the story, doubly emphasizing this remove. These distant views are introduced by the italicized label "picture." These markers jar the complacency and mood of the story, just as the pictures jar Kraft's complacency and mood, making him unable fully to live and experience his life.

Significantly, Minot's story begins where the river, that archetypal symbol of the passage of time, joins the sea, which is the archetypal symbol of the source and end of all life. It is also significant that the point of view shifts ever so slightly, maintaining a stance that is sometimes close to Kraft and his own perspective and feelings, sometimes distant. In the opening "pictures" the perspective has an almost objective stance, describing a boathouse and the couple standing next to the boathouse.

The focus and the language move in until one realizes that the man in the second "picture" is Kraft himself. As the reader nears this protagonist, Kraft too comes closer to himself, first viewing himself from a distance and then slowly stepping inside his own skin and mind. He becomes conscious of being the actual person in the picture that he seemed to see from beyond, gaining an awareness of himself, his surroundings, his companion.

*Julie Thompson*

# A PASSION IN THE DESERT

*Author:* Honoré de Balzac (1799-1850)
*Type of plot:* Psychological
*Time of plot:* The late 1790's
*Locale:* An Egyptian desert
*First published:* "Une Passion dans le désert," 1832 (English translation, 1874)

*Principal characters:*
THE NARRATOR
HIS WOMAN FRIEND
THE SOLDIER, whose experiences are narrated to the woman
THE PANTHER, the object of the soldier's passion
MR. MARTIN, an animal tamer

*The Story*

The narrator and his woman friend are leaving a wild animal show. The woman wonders aloud how Mr. Martin, the animal tamer, is able to perform tricks with dangerous wild animals. The narrator, who has learned of Mr. Martin's secrets from a soldier, suggests that he can explain the mystery, but hesitates to do so verbally. He finally concedes, after much begging and solicitation, to write the solution out for her. The next day, he sends her a strange story about a soldier from Napoleon's invading army, who is fleeing from his Egyptian captors, searching for his regiment in the Egyptian desert. He stumbles into a cave to take refuge for the night. When a female panther returns to this cave after hunting, she snuggles up next to the sleeping soldier and prevents him from leaving as he had planned. Afraid that the panther will eventually kill him, the soldier thinks only of preempting its attack or of escaping.

After spending several days together, the soldier and the panther develop a mutual, erotically charged, affection. The soldier, for example, shows his amorous feelings by referring to the panther as his mistress and by calling her "Darling"—the nickname of his first lover. The soldier also caresses the panther, at one point causing her tail to stand voluptuously erect. Quickly understanding the positive effect of these caresses on the panther's temperament, the soldier redoubles his efforts until he is sure that her passions are completely sated, leaving him safe in her presence. The soldier can be assured of his success because as he finishes his caressing, the panther returns her affection and lets loose an orgasmic sound described as one of those purrs by which cats express pleasure.

Eventually, this imaginary love affair ends violently. The soldier plunges his dagger into the panther's neck when he suspects that she is about to devour him. The mortally wounded animal rolls on the ground, crying plaintively to the soldier; curiously, she shows no sign of hostility or vengeance. The soldier realizes he must have misinterpreted the panther's intentions, and he expresses his most profound sorrow.

## Themes and Meanings

In a second reading of "A Passion in the Desert," the love story between the man and the panther appears perhaps less exotic and more complex than on first reading. As is the case with many of Honoré de Balzac's tales, "A Passion in the Desert" is allegorical; clues of the narrative's deeper significance must be found in indirect, symbolic evidence, such as clusters of interrelated images or metaphors. When the narrative is reevaluated in light of its symbols, and when this symbolic evidence is situated within the broader historical and cultural context of early nineteenth century France, common themes emerge that readers familiar with both French history and Balzac's other writings can readily identify. Chief among these is the impact of the collapse of France's traditional Christian, monarchical, and patriarchal ideals on the human psyche. With the challenge to Old Regime ideals in 1789, and with their formal obliteration in 1830 (two years before the story was published), the French people suddenly had to sever their emotional ties to the old paternalistic, phallocentric social order and learn to adapt themselves to the secular, legalistic, and mercantile ideals promoted by the new post-revolutionary Napoleonic order.

This shift in emotional allegiance from the old to the new order is precisely the psychological drama that the reader sees the soldier undergoing while stranded alone in the desert with the panther. One can detect this drama in Balzac's use of phallic, monarchical, religious, and cutting imagery to portray the soldier's hallucinatory observations. One set of hallucinations is associated with a clump of date palms that the soldier observes standing in sharp contrast with the unmerciful immensity of the Egyptian desert. These date palms, which immediately become the focal point of the soldier's dream thoughts, are described, variously, as the columns of a cathedral, the king of the desert, and a dead parent's body, perhaps his father's—obvious symbols of the lost monarchical, phallocentric order. Even more significant is the soldier's desperate effort to cling to one of the phallic palms, which the reader later learns was infertile, as if he were attempting to hold onto a fleeting mirage of traditional, patriarchal France's foundational symbol: The soldier "wrapped his arms tightly around the date-palm as if it were a close friend's body. . . . Then he sat down and cried, contemplating with a profound sadness the implacable scene before him."

A second set of hallucinations is associated with the panther. The panther is the caretaker of a second clump of date palms, this time fertile, on which the soldier finds sumptuous dates to nourish his body. This symbolically demonstrates a reconfiguring of the soldier's emotional ties. One can detect this in the soldier's newfound love for the panther, who is described, like Napoleon, as imperial and royal. Eating the panther's dates causes the soldier's spirits to shift suddenly from somber desperation to an almost insane joy. Inspired by the panther's physical and spiritual nourishment, the soldier runs back to the infertile palms, knocks down the one referred to as a king, and strips it of its leaves "like an inheritor who does not grieve long over the death of a parent." This knocking down of the paternal, monarchical phallus symbolizes the soldier's willful renouncement of his past ideals and opens the way for the transferral of his allegiance to the new ideals.

The soldier's newly found faith is extremely precarious because it depends on his absolute devotion to satisfying the panther's every whim. One knows, at the thematic level, that the soldier risks being bitten if he fails to satisfy the panther's desires. At the symbolic level, one can also see that he risks a spiritual wound: The panther reminds the soldier of his first lover, who often threatened him with a knife; the panther's voice resembles the sound of a saw; and the panther's habitat in the desert glitters like a steel blade. These symbols of cutting associated with the panther indicate that the soldier's new faith is an all-or-nothing proposition. The soldier eventually renounces his new object of faith because he winds up destroying its external symbol, the panther. When the narrator asks for an explanation, the soldier responds: "It is God without men."

*Style and Technique*

The most important stylistic feature of this tale is Balzac's narrative strategy. Although Balzac is commonly thought to portray human reality in a straightforward, realist fashion, he often veils his ideas behind the cloak of a narrative mystery. In this case, he hooks the reader's imagination by making one desire to know the solution to the surface-level mystery surrounding Mr. Martin. This outer narrative frames a second narrative (the soldier's story) that is offered as the locus for resolving the issues of the frame narrative. Balzac frustrates the reader's desire, however, by encouraging the curious reader to reread his tale to discover a deeper mystery he has planted—the network of symbols and images used to portray the soldier's hallucinations. As one pieces together the various parts of Balzac's narrative puzzle, one discovers a sophisticated theory of the relationship between a cultural crisis and the psychological crisis of an individual.

What makes Balzac's narrative strategy especially rewarding is that he never tells readers what to think. Instead, he coaxes them to discover what he thinks. Although Balzac preordains their discovery of his ideas, his genius is to give them the illusion of making the discoveries themselves.

*Scott M. Sprenger*

# PASTORALIA

*Author:* George Saunders (1958-    )
*Type of plot:* Satire, science fiction
*Time of plot:* The early twenty-first century
*Locale:* A historical reenactment theme park
*First published:* 2000

> *Principal characters:*
> THE NARRATOR, an actor performing as a cave dweller at a theme park
> JANET FOLEY, his coworker
> GREG NORDSTROM, their supervisor

## The Story

"Pastoralia" is set within an imaginary historical-reenactment theme park, with its action occurring largely within the confines of an artificial cave. The primary interaction takes place between the two main characters, an unnamed man who plays the caveman, and Janet, who plays the cavewoman. The central difficulty experienced by the caveman actor arises from Janet's inability to play her part on a continuous, consistent basis, although she knows it is her livelihood.

The two actors live a life of routine. Each morning, they emerge from their separate areas and go to a dispenser called the Big Slot to obtain their food, usually a dead goat that they must skin and roast over a fire. The rest of the day is spent at such miscellaneous activities as working on cave paintings and hunting for imaginary insects to eat.

Soon after the story begins, the caveman actor rises and goes to the Big Slot, only to find a note apologizing for the absence of the goat. Janet complains aloud in English, while the caveman actor tries to maintain his role and grunts imaginatively. Attendance at their cave-dweller site has declined in recent weeks, and Janet's ability to stay in role has taken a downturn as well. Even so, the actor ends his day by faxing in his Daily Partner Performance Evaluation Form by answering questions concerning Janet's attitude and performance in the positive. Again, the next day, when no goat appears, the pair live off their backup supply of crackers, and again Janet complains, while the actor tries to maintain his role. When a goat does appear the third morning, Janet puts effort into her role once again, even though they have no audience to witness it.

The actors are occasionally required to leave their space, primarily to carry wastes to the disposal area. A nearby employee-only store is run by a couple named Marty and Jeannine. Marty's young son attends a private school and sometimes visits the couple at the store. When the caveman actor goes to buy a favorite drink for himself as well as mints and cigarettes for Janet, he learns that another actor, who played the

Wise Mountain Hermit, has been fired. The Wise Mountain Hermit is another "Remote," as are the cave dwellers. The next day, a note arrives about the firings called "Staff Remixing."

An unprecedented event then follows: A supervisor in the organization, Greg Nordstrom, invites the actor away from his cave for brunch. Over bagels, Nordstrom queries the actor about Janet and encourages him to tell the truth about her. Nordstrom knows that Janet is not doing well but needs a negative evaluation from her partner before he can fire her. Nordstrom emphasizes to the actor that the company simply wants him to tell the truth.

Through a handwritten note, the actor reveals to Janet that she is in trouble. Grateful, she promises to stick to her role, which she does for several days, despite the hardship resulting from a lack of goats from the Big Slot. One morning, however, Janet's son walks into the cave. The boy is in trouble for stealing and taking drugs, and his presence makes Janet break character. The caveman actor, however, still covers for her. He has his own preoccupations, with faxes arriving each night from his wife about their son's health and financial problems.

He continues covering for Janet until the day when visitors finally drop by to observe their reenactment. Janet interacts poorly with them, speaking in English and not altogether pleasant English. The caveman actor finds he cannot justify covering for her again and finally sends in a negative evaluation form. Nordstrom, approving, tells him to be absent from the cave the next morning when they take Janet away.

Afterward, the caveman actor is rewarded with food and drink. Then he receives a company memo about its attitude toward truth. Truth, according to the memo, "is that thing which makes what we want to happen happen . . . truth is the wind in our sails that blows only for us."

The story ends with the entrance of a woman. She is the new cavewoman. She is so dedicated to her role that she has had a high-brow ridge permanently attached to her face.

*Themes and Meanings*

"Pastoralia" concerns itself with the division between outer and inner worlds and with the difficulty of making the two mesh coherently. On the most obvious level, this division is expressed within the life of the actors, who not only must play their parts throughout the day but also must live on the set at night, albeit in private quarters. In private, they are able to speak and write in English, send faxes, and eat modern-day snacks, if they can get them. Throughout the day, however, they must act according to guidelines set for them by their employers. The organization controls their lives down to the smallest detail; they must even eat according to the dictates of their reenactment. Above all, whatever their internal thoughts, they are forbidden to speak them. As cave people, after all, they are capable only of grunts and gestures.

George Saunders first establishes the conflict between inner and outer worlds at a slightly deeper level, however. Within the first paragraph, the man playing the caveman considers his feeling of discontent but also states that he would never, or at least should never, verbalize the feeling, even in private, because of an injunction to think and speak positively. This injunction turns out to be an official directive from higher above in the organization of the theme park and is one of many features that tie the cave-dweller reenactment to life within the corporate cubicle.

Because the caveman actor's problems are caused by Janet's imperfect ability to play her part, his internal conflict becomes more intense when he is confronted by Greg Nordstrom, who represents the organization. Although Nordstrom does appeal to the actor's sense of duty to the organization, he appeals even more heavily to his sense of duty to himself. He wants the actor playing the caveman to tell the truth about Janet. Unless he tells the truth, the organization cannot get rid of Janet and replace her.

The character struggles within this complex situation. Within his private room, he has to act as a responsible father, responding with concern to faxes from his wife about their sick child. Within the cave, he has to be the caveman. Within the greater organization, he has to act true to its guidelines. In addition, that greater organization, which serves as the outermost layer of this story's layered world, is also calling on him to deal most deeply with his own internal being, in calling for his honest action.

In dealing with all these aspects of his situation, the caveman actor is alone. Despite the outwardly family-like nature of his role in the organization, he is ultimately an isolated soul.

## Style and Technique

Saunders adopts an informal, chatty, and sometimes slangy tone throughout the twenty-six short chapters of "Pastoralia." By this means, he creates an atmosphere close to that of the office place of the 1990's or later, even while the characters are busily roasting goats or banging stones together. He adds to this evocation of the business world in other ways, the most prominent of them being the repeated use of fax machines, memos, and notes. These appear regularly, unlike supervisors or family members, each of whom are represented by only a single physical appearance.

Despite its mechanical nature, the fax machine carries the messages in the story having the most emotional weight because almost all the interactions between the narrator's and Janet's family members take place by means of this device. In this way, the organization effectively stands between the main characters and their families. The only family member to visit, Janet's son, does so by slipping around corporate barriers without paying the entrance fee. In other words, criminal conduct enables personal contact.

Saunders also uses faxes and memos to underline the hypocrisy of the organization, in part through the use of irony. Apart from the supervisor's single visit, a series of communications from him reiterates his need to hear the truth from the caveman actor. The series culminates in a companywide memo about rumors, falsehood, and truth, which arrives after the caveman actor finally reveals the truth about Janet in his Daily Partner Performance Evaluation Form. The company memo makes clear its stance:

"Truth is that thing which makes what we want to happen happen." In other words, truth is provisional. The caveman actor learns that the company had never needed the truth from him. It needed only the truth of the moment.

The use of repetition is among the most prominent techniques employed in "Pastoralia" to establish the sense that the characters are living lives according to a dictated routine. These also help establish the rhythm of the overall work. The morning appearance, or nonappearance, of food from the Big Slot begins many of the story's sections, while the faxing in of the daily evaluation form brings many to a close. The repetitions are often exact in wording but not always. The end-of-day fax that brings events to a climax near the end is a decidedly different fax. The change from routine helps give the moment its impact.

*Mark Rich*

# PATRIOTISM

*Author:* Yukio Mishima (Kimitake Hiraoka, 1925-1970)
*Type of plot:* Psychological
*Time of plot:* February 28, 1936
*Locale:* Tokyo
*First published:* "Yūkoku," 1961 (English translation, 1966)

> *Principal characters:*
> LIEUTENANT TAKEYAMA SHINJI
> REIKO, his wife

*The Story*

Early in the morning on February 26,1936, about fifteen hundred officers and sol-diers from the Japanese army's First Division attacked the homes of the prime minis-ter and other officials and occupied parts of central Tokyo. After four days, the muti-neers surrendered to loyal elements of the army that were brought in to quell the uprising. Quick trials and executions of the ringleaders brought an end to the anarchy that had prevailed in the Japanese military since 1931. "Patriotism" glorifies the ritual suicide of Lieutenant Takeyama Shinji and his wife as he finds himself torn between loyalty to his unit, which has sided with the mutiny, and his loyalty to the emperor.

In Japan, seppuku, or ritual suicide, has been a time-honored means of escaping from capture or an irreconcilable conflict. More widely known in its vulgar form as hara-kiri (literally, belly-slitting) in the West, it is a painful way of dying meant to show the courage and tenacity of a samurai even in the face of defeat. Japanese culture does not have Christian prohibitions against suicide, so such a death can be seen as honorable, even admirable.

Only six months before the ill-fated mutiny, Takeyama married his twenty-three-year-old bride, Reiko. They lived in a modest house in Yotsuya, near central Tokyo. In Mishima's story, a fictionalized account of their double suicide, the young bride makes a pledge on their wedding night to follow Takeyama in death because she had become the wife of a soldier. She does this silently by displaying a prized dagger that her mother had given her.

The marriage is as brief as it is passionate. They make love at night and sometimes as soon as Takeyama enters the house, still in his muddy uniform. However, this pas-sion is depicted almost as a religious ritual, for even in sexual release "their hearts were sober and serious." Each morning the lieutenant and his wife stand at the house shrine and bow to a tablet from Shinto's most sacred shrine, Ise, and a photograph of the emperor and his wife.

Takeyama is not directly involved in the plot to overthrow the government. He is awakened on the snowy morning of February 26 by the sound of a distant bugle. He quickly puts on his uniform and rushes out of the house, not to return until late on the twenty-eighth. Reiko finds out about the mutiny on the radio and spends the two days preparing her personal belongings for death if her husband does not return. As the mutineers are isolated, the names of men in Takeyama's unit are denounced on the radio.

At sunset on February 28, Takeyama returns, pounding at the door. He is tired, wet, and dejected. His comrades did not let him in on the plot, and he fears being placed in an impossible situation: "I shall be in command of a unit with orders to attack them. . . . I can't do it. It's impossible to do a thing like that." The only resolution to his dilemma is suicide.

Reiko instantly recognizes his unstated decision. Both suddenly feel at peace as they realize what the other is thinking. They resolve to commit suicide that night. The rest of the story describes in vivid detail their careful preparations for a proper ritual suicide. It is important that no irregularity occur. Takeyama trusts his wife enough to know that he can die first, knowing that she will follow. A suspicious husband would kill his wife first.

First they take a bath and drink sake, filled with anticipation. Takeyama reflects that his death will be without glory, yet he will be on the "frontline of the spirit." In a very erotic scene, Takeyama notices Reiko's physical beauty for the last time, lingering over her naked body. She has smooth arms and delicate fingers, swelling breasts, and a soft but resilient stomach. As his kisses trace her body, she, too, wishes to have one last look at his body. Modesty has prevented him before, but now he surrenders himself to his wife. His naked skin glows as the muscles stand out, befitting a soldier of the emperor. Seeing his firm stomach, about to be cut open with the silent sharp blade of the sword, she covers it with kisses. They make unrestrained love for the final time, ecstasy and death blending into one emotion. Finally falling back from each other, Takeyama and Reiko lay on their backs with their fingers entwined.

They put on clean clothing and prepare their suicide notes. Takeyama writes boldly and simply, "Long Live the Imperial Forces." He then undoes his uniform collar for the coup de grace and exposes his bare stomach for the sword. Reiko watches in a bridelike white gown as her husband plunges his sword deep into his left side. He then slowly draws it sideways to his navel. Despite his agony, he continues until the entrails burst out, spilling into his lap with a raw smell. Reiko suppresses an urge to rush to his side. When he has trouble cutting his throat, she moves through the blood that has spilled out to loosen his collar. Finally the sword blade pierces his neck and Takeyama escapes his agony.

Reiko withdraws to tidy the house and herself, releasing the door bolt so their bodies will be discovered before they begin to rot. Placing herself by her husband's side, she uses her family dagger to slit her throat, choking on the warm blood and sharing his pain.

*Themes and Meanings*

Yukio Mishima was a writer who became obsessed by what he saw as the loss of Japanese traditional values, although he led a cosmopolitan and bizarre life. He used his writing success to fund a small private army, the Shield Society, to fight against

Communism and support a prewar vision of the emperor as the soul of the Japanese nation. However, he was also an exhibitionist inspired by violence and homosexuality. Sexuality and violence are combined in "Patriotism," in retrospect perhaps the most revealing of Mishima's works, because the author, like his protagonist Takeyama, committed seppuku.

On November 25, 1970, Mishima led a band of his private army to the headquarters of the Japanese Self Defense Forces, where he told the troops to show the "samurai spirit" to protect the "Imperial Way." These prewar sentiments were derided by the soldiers, who saw Mishima as a crackpot. Mishima then showed his sincerity by withdrawing from the balcony on which he was speaking and disemboweling himself. The nation was shocked at this spectacular and strange death of one of Japan's most popular writers. It is difficult to consider his writing without reference to his suicide.

In "Patriotism," written more than a decade earlier, one can see an early sign of Mishima's linking sex and death, or ecstasy and agony, in his version of the Takeyama suicide. The theme of this very tight story—the focus is on the suicide—is the honor and dedication of the lieutenant and his young and beautiful wife. They transcend the life-preserving spirit of most people to find peace in death. Their dedication to the nation and to the emperor is unsullied by selfishness: "The last moments of this heroic and dedicated couple were such as to make the gods themselves weep."

Mishima wanted to restore what in his personal vision were the traditional values of Japan, values that were deeper than the materialism of the 1960's. Many contemporary Japanese intellectuals worry that Japan's rush to economic success has left behind any real values other than an increasing gross national product and electronic gadgets. Like Mishima, some seek answers in Japan's military past, while others look to religion to restore a sense of values that transcend materialism.

Suicide is a sin in the Christian view, and the Western reader is likely to be repelled by the act if not by the motives of Takeyama and his wife. In Japan, however, there is a long tradition of the "failed hero," to quote Ivan Morris, in which admiration is given to the loser in a failed but just cause. In the feudal period, the losing hero could redeem himself by committing deliberately painful seppuku to show, quite literally, that he had guts. In Takeyama's case, he was ready to die rather than attack his comrades in revolt, who were supposedly acting in the name of the emperor, the nation, and the army.

Another theme is doing things in the proper way, even suicide. This becomes very clear as the couple prepare their bodies, home, clothes, and suicide notes in a ritualistic manner. The only new element that Mishima introduces into this tradition is the strong eroticism that describes the bodies and passion of Takeyama and his beautiful wife. Beauty and truth are seen as one, and pleasure and pain are integrated in this disturbing story.

## Style and Technique

Mishima is one of the best-known postwar writers, yet he uses few of the literary allusions that fill the pages of Jun'ichiro Tanizaki or Yasunari Kawabata. Mishima frequently read classical Japanese literature, and he was capable of writing in a variety of styles. He disagreed strongly with writers who wanted dialogue to reflect everyday speech, and he used a deliberately artificial style. Mishima was fond of ornate expressions. Frequent use of metaphor and a rich vocabulary is characteristic of his style. This gives his characters a quality that transcends the mundane concerns of the average person.

In "Patriotism," every act of preparation and the stages of the suicide are used to find meaning and to create a sense of understanding—an appreciation of the worldview of the young officer and his wife. Mishima's literary inspiration was often a real event such as the suicide of Takeyama, which he enhanced through use of convincing detail. In such a tightly constructed story, every action and gesture is fully drawn out for its meaning. Although Takeyama and his wife have a silent appreciation of the thoughts of each other, Mishima takes pains to ensure that these are clear to the reader; he wants the reader to know how dedicated they really are.

Mishima's finest work, *Kinkakuji* (1956; *The Temple of the Golden Pavilion*, 1959), like "Patriotism," is a work of fiction that tries to explain the meaning of the actions of a real individual. Perhaps all writers draw on real people to create their characters, but Mishima carries this further by creating feelings and motives to develop a strong persona for real people.

*Richard Rice*

# PAUL'S CASE

*Author:* Willa Cather (1873-1947)
*Type of plot:* Character study
*Time of plot:* 1905 or earlier
*Locale:* Pittsburgh and New York City
*First published:* 1905

> *Principal character:*
> PAUL, the protagonist, a high school student

## The Story

The story begins in industrial Pittsburgh at the height of American industrial expansion and at a time when wealth, power, and material values are supreme and dominate the thought and goals of the nation. Paul is a misfit in every way, and the reader is given a detailed description of his conflicts with school, home, and society. Paul is different from his peers. He dresses with a kind of dandified elegance, sporting fancy neckwear and a flower in his lapel. He is bored with school and hates his shabby room at home and his middle-class neighbors and the street where he lives. Paul's mother died shortly after his birth, and he has been reared by his father, who seems distant and preoccupied with money and hard work.

Paul's real love, his only true mental and spiritual life, seems to be realized in the glamour and color of the world of theater and music. He works part-time as an usher in Carnegie Hall, where concerts are held. There he loses himself in the music, the glitter of performance, and the fantasy of a world that is sensual and utterly removed from the prosaic day-to-day needs and routines of his domestic and school worlds. He wants to be noticed, to be important, and he seems to be devoid of the psychological equipment that enables others to accept the limitations and realities of their circumstances. Paul creates for himself a fantasy life that forces him to lie continuously.

Paul's conflict with the demands of the school curriculum, the learning of grammar, theorems, and history, reaches a point where the principal informs Paul's father that the conflict between his son and the school's teachers requires that some action be taken. The father takes Paul out of school, puts him to work as a "cash-boy" in a business office, and forbids him access to theaters or concerts. Paul's compulsion to be lost in a world of sensual experience, a life of elegance, leisure, and pleasurable sensation, finally confronts the pressures on him to work, conform, and obey the rules of his humble and prosaic background. His life is now intolerable. His need for the "fairy tale" world that he tasted "behind the scenes" drives him to a plan that seems obvious to him and not even a struggle for him as he executes it.

Paul steals a large sum of money from his employers and makes his way to New York. Here, for eight fantasy days, he resides in splendor at the Waldorf hotel, one of the great palace hotels of the turn of the century. Dressed in new finery, Paul wines and dines and goes to concerts, drives around in carriages, and loses himself in pleasure. Finally, just before Paul has exhausted his finances, he reads in the Pittsburgh papers that his father, having paid back the stolen money, is coming to New York to search for his son. Paul has a vision of home, his dingy room, the drab social life of a provincial town, and the prospects of no further escape. The contrast with the last few days of his fairy-tale life is too much for him, and he takes the final steps that lead to his suicide. Thus the author closes Paul's case.

### Themes and Meanings

Much of Willa Cather's writing develops an interest in the minds, ways, and lives of artists: This theme of contrast and discord between conflicting values is present in a number of ways in "Paul's Case." Although Paul is not an artist in the sense that he creates works of art, he has the kind of imagination that in a friendlier environment might have developed to enable him to convert the material of his real world into art. As it is, Paul's case is painful and hopeless. The author shows the reader a world that is blatantly materialistic. The predominant color is gray, while Paul longs for the richness of purple, of light-reflecting crystal. It is sad that for Paul, and indeed for his world, money seems to be the only means to experience the felt life, the excitement of performance. Paul is a spectator. He has no interest in books, which might have helped him to imagine other possibilities. His is a solipsistic vision, stimulated by music that acts like an addictive narcotic on his nervous system and produces an excitement from which he recovers in a state of severe physical and emotional deflation. Paul's teachers and family seem peculiarly insensitive to his condition, his needs, and his suffering.

In spite of the rather detached and clinical description of this conflict between Paul and his world, the author's distaste for the materialistic and rather coarse society she describes becomes evident. While Paul is clearly presented as emotionally disturbed and as almost pathologically lonely and isolated, he is also, in part, the victim of a society that is somewhat deadened in its imagination and finer sensibilities. Paul is like an aesthete for whom there is no place to belong, no home, and who finds no kindred spirit anywhere. Had he been able to find a group like Oscar Wilde's "art for art's sake" movement or the Bloomsbury group, both artistic cults that flourished during Cather's lifetime, he might have found a friendly haven in a bohemian subculture, part of an aesthetic minority group. As it is, he is simply a doomed misfit.

### Style and Technique

Cather writes here with characteristic restraint. She implies, she understates, she hints, believing that it is important to leave the reader to figure things out and become actively involved in "making" the story. The author purports to be writing a case history and thus aims for an emotionally detached quality in the style. She wants to let the facts speak for themselves, and she concludes without diagnosis or explanation. In spite of her desire not to appear to take sides or to prejudice the reader's judgment, the nature of this writing brings one close to Paul and not to anyone else. By making the reader intimate with Paul's thoughts, perceptions, and feelings, she draws the reader's sympathy to him. The author takes the role of omniscient narrator, so that when she says, "in Paul's world, the natural nearly always wore the guise of ugliness," she justifies Paul's need for artificial beauty. Paul may be deluded and extreme, but the author's facts about his ugly world are not to be disputed.

Cather also has a special talent for creating the visible, an eye for that detail or mood or scene that calls on her talent and experience as a journalist when she wrote for a Pittsburgh paper and later for *McClure's* magazine. She characterizes Paul's thoughts of home by "damp dish towels" and shows the reader the champagne in his glass at his hotel dinner as "cold, precious, bubbling stuff that creamed and foamed in his glass." By the use of such images and the vivid language conveying them, Cather is able to convey what Paul sees and feels and how intense the conflict must be that causes him to want to die rather than return to the flatness and drabness that he has managed to escape for a little more than a week.

It is interesting to note that the case history had become a vigorous form of psychological writing in the later half of the nineteenth century and has in the twentieth century established itself as a major story form, particularly in the genre of crime and detective fiction. Clinical case histories have escaped the confines of medical reports and obtained a wide, popular audience.

*Joseph Gold*

# THE PEACH STONE

*Author:* Paul Horgan (1903-1995)
*Type of plot:* Psychological
*Time of plot:* 1935 to 1941
*Locale:* New Mexico
*First published:* 1942

> *Principal characters:*
> CLEOTHA "CLEE" POWERS, a native of Weed, New Mexico,
> married for ten years to Jodey Powers, the hub of the Powers
> family
> JODEY POWERS, a native Texan but longtime resident of New
> Mexico
> BUDDY POWERS, the nine-year-old son of Cleotha and Jodey
> ARLENE LATCHER, Buddy's schoolteacher, who is
> psychologically and emotionally repressed

*The Story*

Using a point of view that shifts among the story's principal characters, Paul Horgan presents their inner experiences on a silent, four-hour automobile trip from their home near Hondo, New Mexico, to the town of Weed, New Mexico. Each character responds in some way to one or more of the other occupants of the car, as well as to the tragedy prompting the trip: the accidental death on the preceding day of the Powerses' two-year-old daughter. While playing near the back fence of the family's small ranch house, where tumbleweeds had been collecting that Jodey had been meaning to clear away, the baby had been caught in a fire ignited by some chance sparks from the kitchen chimney. Now the Powerses, accompanied by the town's schoolteacher for support, travel to the place where Cleotha was born and reared in order to bury the baby in Cleotha's family plot on the side of Schoolhouse Hill.

In the story's short closing section, after the arrival at Weed, the schoolteacher, Miss Latcher, briefly breaks down, and then the ceremony is held. Cleotha's notice of a tardy schoolboy's interest in the proceedings triggers her weeping, her first outward manifestation of grief that day, which causes the family to reunite around her after its short period of psychic fragmentation.

*Themes and Meanings*

In the silence of the automobile ride, each character undergoes a crisis and then emerges transformed, restored to emotional health by the power of love. Cleotha is healed by her gradual recognition of the beauty in all things living, which she has seen with new eyes on the trip, and in which the spirit of her infant daughter is reflected. Jodey, worried about losing Cleotha's love because of his partial responsibility for the infant's death, is comforted at the graveside when he senses that Cleotha is no longer emotionally distant from him and the others. Buddy, like his father, is also made anxious by his apparent loss of rapport with Cleotha but rejoices and regains his sense of security when, on arriving at Weed, she suddenly winks and smiles at him as well as slightly leaning toward him in the car. Finally, Arlene Latcher, who has been unhealthily shunning true emotional contact with others, now abruptly realizes her envy of the emotional ties of the Powers family and bursts into tears when contact is poignantly renewed between mother and son.

Related themes are fruitfulness and life versus barrenness and death, communication versus isolation and alienation, engagement with people and ordinary living versus disengagement, and forgiveness versus guilt. Against the apparent purposelessness and waste of the child's death amid the wastes of New Mexico and the symbol of their barrenness, the tumbleweed, the story counterposes Cleotha's awakening sensitivity to the orchards and new spring life all around her, Arlene Latcher's discovery of the sterility of her detachment from the people and world around her, and Jody's absolution from guilt through Cleotha's love and forgiveness. Just as the cycle of life continues in the seasonal change from winter to spring, which is emphasized in the story, so out of the child's terrible death the members of the funeral party are reborn psychologically and emotionally. Thus the child's death and the suffering it has subsequently caused have not been purposeless.

*Style and Technique*

The story's shifts in point of view enable juxtaposing two characters' thoughts in order to bring out similarities and contrasts. For example, Cleotha's observation of an orchard and her reverie on petals and peach stones contrast a faith opening up and out to the world with Arlene Latcher's musing on her education and a painting of virgin martyrs, which reveals a belief in withdrawal from people and experience. As Miss Latcher's reverie on the painting is escapist, so is Jody's mental review of his "fantastic scheme" for converting useless tumbleweed into salable fuel, these thoughts diverting his attention from the death of his daughter in the tumbleweed fire.

Horgan's manipulation of point of view is also notable in the cryptic use of often-italicized personal pronouns, especially "she," as well as in his concluding shift in verb tense. The former device helps convey Jody's guilty uneasiness for having been in part responsible for depriving his wife of their daughter. Thus, he tends to think of Cleotha obliquely as "she" and "her," until, when he is absolved at the story's close, Cleotha becomes "his wife" in Jody's thoughts. Also in the story's last paragraphs the startling shift into the present tense helps vividly actualize the narrative statement about the graveside mourners, that "Everything left them but a sense of their worship, in the present." The verb-tense shift thematically suggests the importance of heightened awareness of all of life, moment by moment.

The story is pervaded by symbolism. One symbolic pattern of imagery encompasses the repeated references to flora and fruitfulness. The journey's destination is the town of Weed, the name of which suggests the paradox that out of waste something productive may come. Similarly hinting at this paradox are the coverlet of cross-stitched flowers spread on the baby's coffin and the New Mexico white dust that settles over the car and its occupants in "an enriching film, ever so finely." Cleotha's meditations about her childhood notion that holding a peach stone long enough would cause its sprouting suggest again how hopeful belief and contact with the experiential world may bring life out of death. Further, Cleotha observes from the car an old blackened and twisted peach tree that with its one little top-shoot of green leaves affirms fertility in the midst of decay.

All the other occupants of the car are evaluated against this imagistic pattern as well. Buddy's youth, innocence, vulnerability, and worth are conveyed by the description of him as having plum-red cheeks and the smell of a raw potato newly pared. Arlene Latcher's struggle against the natural world is conveyed by the ironic metaphor of her summoning the "fruits of her learning" to keep from yielding to emotional involvement. Jodey's part-hopeful, part-pessimistic personality is suggested by his visionary tumbleweed scheme as well as by his jocular musing just before the accident about "how far along the peaches would get before the frost killed them all, snap, in a single night."

A final important symbolic strand is the religious or theological one, appropriate to a story exploring the meaning of life and death. The story's repeated references to ascent—the road ascends to Weed and the car's occupants must ascend Schoolhouse Hill at Weed—suggest the characters' spiritual ascent. (Indeed, all the characters have a kind of revelation at the significantly named burial ground, Schoolhouse Hill.) Cleotha's thinking that the peach stone tale was like a biblical parable about which she could preach a sermon recalls the synoptic Gospels' parable of the mustard seed, which similarly is about the productive power of faith and engagement. Arlene Latcher thinks about an enormous painting of the Roman slaughter of Christian virgins, which she ironically fails to realize should evoke her emotional response to the dead child. Last, the mysterious "ball of diamond-brilliant light" that the Powerses' car follows up the ascending road for some time, though revealed to be probably a reflection off the back of a truck in the glaring sunshine of New Mexico, inevitably suggests the guiding star followed by the Magi. As the Magi's journey ends, so does that of the occupants of the Powerses' car in revelation and spiritual rebirth.

*Norman Prinsky*

# THE PEACHES

*Author:* Dylan Thomas (1914-1953)
*Type of plot:* Sketch
*Time of plot:* About 1924
*Locale:* Gorsehill, a farm in North Carmarthenshire, Wales
*First published:* 1938

> *Principal characters:*
> DYLAN, a young boy spending the summer at his aunt and uncle's
> farm
> JIM JONES, his uncle, a Welsh farmer who drinks his farm's
> profits
> ANNIE JONES, his aunt, a timid but kindly woman
> GWILYM JONES, his teenage cousin, who is studying to be a
> Nonconformist minister
> JACK WILLIAMS, his best friend from Swansea
> MRS. WILLIAMS, Jack's mother, a wealthy and snobbish woman

## The Story

Dylan, a boy about ten years of age, is going to spend the summer holiday at his Uncle Jim and Aunt Annie Jones's farm. As Uncle Jim brings Dylan to the farm from his home in Swansea, Jim makes him wait in the cart in a scary dark alley while he goes into a pub to drink. They do not get home until midnight, much to Aunt Annie's annoyance.

The next morning, Dylan and his cousin Gwilym look at the pigs and discover that one is missing—Uncle Jim has sold it to get drinking money. Gwilym, who wants to be a Nonconformist minister, entertains Dylan by singing hymns to God and telling him stories about girls who died for love. He shows Dylan the chapel that he has fixed up in a dilapidated barn, and he officiates at a mock service, preaching a sermon and taking up a collection.

That afternoon, Jack Williams, Dylan's best friend from Swansea, is arriving for a visit. Aunt Annie makes Dylan put on his best suit, and she prepares a tea in the best room, a rarely used parlor. When Mrs. Williams arrives in a chauffeur-driven Daimler, Annie gives her an obsequious welcome, apologizing for her house. Mrs. Williams wants to drop Jack off and be gone, but Annie insists that she stay for tea and offers her tinned peaches that she has hoarded since Christmas for a special occasion. Mrs. Williams dusts the seat of a chair before sitting down, refuses the peaches, and leaves without finishing her cup of tea.

Dylan and Jack play cowboys and Indians all afternoon. They climb a tree and spy on Gwilym when he uses the lavatory, sitting on the seat with his trousers down, reading a book, and moving his hands. When they call out, Gwilym hastily pulls up his trousers and stuffs the book in his pocket. As the boys climb down the tree, they tear their jackets. Before bed, they go to the chapel with Gwilym. Gwilym tries to make Dylan confess his sins, but Jack gets scared and sobs on his way back to the house.

As the boys lie in bed at midnight, they hear Uncle Jim come home drunk. Jim asks Annie if Mrs. Williams has paid the thirty shillings to keep Jack. When Annie tells Jim about the peaches, he becomes furious and shouts, "Who does she think she is? Aren't peaches good enough for her? To hell with her bloody motor car and her bloody son! Making us small." When Annie tells him to stop or he will wake the boys, he continues shouting, threatening to wake them up and whip them. He yells that if Annie does not send Jack back, he will do it himself. This exchange, coming on the heels of the chapel scene, upsets Jack; he buries his head under the covers and refuses to listen.

The next morning after breakfast, Jack walks to the post office. Later, the boys play separately; Dylan tries to be friends but Jack ignores him. Mrs. Williams arrives at midafternoon to take Jack back to Swansea. Jack tells her that Jim threatened to whip him, that Gwilym took him to the barn in the dark and let the mice run over him, that Dylan is a thief, and that Annie spoiled his jacket. Annie comes to the door, curtsying obsequiously, as the car drives off. Dylan waves his handkerchief, but Jack sits still and stiff by his mother's side.

### Themes and Meanings

"The Peaches" rests on Dylan Thomas's childhood experiences of spending long holidays on his Aunt Anne Jones's farm, Fernhill, in Carmarthenshire. It is the opening story in a collection of autobiographical sketches, *Portrait of the Artist as a Young Dog* (1940), that describes life in South Wales during the 1920's and early 1930's. In "The Peaches," Thomas sensitively illustrates the nuances of personality within his family, focusing on their imperfections, but in a nonjudgmental way.

Three themes emerge from this sketch: the idyllic world of childhood, how powerlessness in the face of adults tempers that idyll, and how adults play false roles. Dylan, the narrator, appears on the surface to be detached from, and even oblivious to, the events that occur around him. He spends his days looking at farm animals and playing cowboys and Indians with his friend Jack Williams. Children are not unobservant or insensitive to their surroundings, however, and Dylan is aware of the undercurrents in the relationships between Uncle Jim and Aunt Annie and between Aunt Annie and Mrs. Williams.

Children, however, cannot control their unequal relationships with adults. The story opens with Dylan forced to wait in a dark alley, prey to the childhood terrors of clawed hands and demons. More terrible, perhaps, are Jack's fears. At first, his visit goes well, but in the evening he is scared by Gwilym's bullying in the chapel. Worse comes when he overhears a drunken Uncle Jim say mean things about his mother and threaten to beat him. Jack is threatened by this hostile and unpredictable environment, and he escapes from it by calling his mother. Dylan, however, is not threatened because he feels at home with his relatives, despite their imperfections.

The adults in the story play false roles and don masks to present themselves to the world and to one another. Gwilym plays at being a minister, preaching sermons, taking up collections, and interrogating his congregation, but the nature of his belief is ambiguous. The erotic feelings of a normal twenty-year-old have been diverted and suppressed. Hence his religion is heavily laden with cruelty, shown in his treatment of Dylan and Jack, and sexuality—his hymns are as much songs to girls as to God, and his mysterious behavior in the lavatory hints at masturbation. Aunt Annie plays the obsequious, fawning underling, curtsying to Mrs. Williams. Mrs. Williams is a caricature of the grande dame, displaying the airs of superiority but neglecting the graciousness of the true lady.

## Style and Technique

Thomas pays careful attention to the details of conversation and is a keen observer of physical detail. In this story, as in others, he uses thick descriptive images to create the atmosphere. He goes into meticulous detail when describing persons, for example, the people in the pub where Uncle Jim goes to drink, and places, such as the warm and homey kitchen, the best room where Mrs. Williams is entertained, and Gwilym's chapel.

Thomas also uses well-chosen analogies to depict character and behavior. Uncle Jim's red drinker's face, with bristling side-whiskers and a long, pointed nose, sometimes looks like a fox's, sometimes like a devil's. The narrator even imagines that the foxlike Uncle Jim eats piglets and drinks their blood. Gwilym, thin of body, with a flat square face, is like a garden spade. Mrs. Williams looks and moves like a ship. Aunt Annie, fussing, darting her head around, clucking, fidgeting, appears birdlike.

Most characteristic of Thomas's style is his use of the *hywl*, the passionate, singsong Welsh preaching style, shifting back and forth between whisper and shout. One can hear this style in Thomas's recorded recitations of his own and others' poetry, and one can hear it in his prose, for example, when the narrator describes his joy at playing cowboys and Indians:

> On my haunches, eager and alone, casting an ebony shadow, with the Gorsehill jungle swarming, the violent, impossible birds and fishes leaping, hidden under four-stemmed flowers the height of horses, in the early evening in a dingle near Carmarthen, my friend Jack Williams invisibly near me, I felt all my young body like an excited animal surrounding me, the torn knees bent, the bumping heart, the long heat and depth between the legs, the sweat prickling in the hands, the tunnels down to the eardrums, the little balls of dirt between the toes, the eyes in the sockets, the tucked-up voice, the blood racing, the memory around and within flying, jumping, swimming, and waiting to pounce.

This long sentence, piling up dependent clause after dependent clause, shows both Thomas's use of description and the rhythms of his prose.

*D. G. Paz*

# THE PEARL

*Author:* John Steinbeck (1902-1968)
*Type of plot:* Parable
*Time of plot:* The late nineteenth century
*Locale:* Baja California, Mexico
*First published:* 1945

> *Principal characters:*
> KINO, an Indian pearl diver
> JUANA, his common-law wife
> COYOTITO, their infant son
> JUAN TOMAS, Kino's brother

*The Story*

This long story (or short novel) follows five momentous days in the life of an Indian pearl diver living in La Paz, a small port on the Gulf of California. Though told by an omniscient author, the work most often limits itself to Kino's perspective as he suffers the gratuitous trials of an innocent tragic hero.

His sufferings begin when he witnesses a scorpion sting his beloved son, Coyotito, as the child lies happily in his cradle. Beside herself with terror, Kino's common-law wife, Juana, insists that they take Coyotito to the doctor because that individual has authority even though he "was of a race which for nearly four hundred years had beaten and starved and robbed and despised Kino's race." The doctor irresponsibly evades seeing the child, and Kino takes his first step in his tragic growth by challenging the unfair order of existence. He strikes the doctor's gate "a crushing blow with his fist." His knuckles give instead of the doorway, but Kino's gesture shows that he is prepared to become "a man."

That same day, he and Juana go to dive for pearls. Juana tries to bargain with her people's ancient gods and offers a prayer to the Christian God that they might find a pearl. Though she has made a better poultice of seaweed than the doctor could, she still feels the need for his magic and wants the wherewithal to force him to attend her baby. As if in answer to her supplication, Kino finds "the greatest pearl in the world." He begins to dream about the good the pearl will bring his family. He imagines being married now that they can pay for the service. He pictures a new harpoon and then dares imagine possessing a rifle. That last image is so defiant that he goes even further: He dreams of sending his son to school to learn to read, write, and "make numbers."

The people of La Paz have heard the news, however, and they intrude on Kino's dream. Even the priest comes to express his hope that Kino will not forget the Church. The doctor rushes over to force a powder down Coyotito's throat, one that will make him temporarily ill so that the doctor can pretend that the scorpion's poison is still working and he can "cure" the baby. The doctor also tricks Kino into revealing the place where he has hidden the pearl, and that night either he or his henchman returns to steal it. In defending his home, Kino draws his first blood. Still, the family begins the next day "with hope."

This optimism is quickly dashed. The pearl brokers, acting together (because they actually are agents for a single dealer), offer him a pittance. Kino refuses to sell and announces that he will take the pearl to Mexico City instead. His family—his brother, his sister-in-law, and his wife—stick by him, but they are worried. Juana urges him to crush the pearl between two stones and forget it, but Kino answers that he is "a man" and will not be cheated. He does not yet recognize the reversal his fortunes have taken.

The third day begins with Juana stealing the pearl and trying to throw it back into the gulf in order to avert the evil she senses is bearing down on her family. Kino stops her, but as he returns from the shore, he is attacked. Dropping the pearl, he slays his assailant. Juana finds the gem and submissively returns it to her man; she also urges him to flee to save himself from certain arrest. They go to get their canoe and find that someone has knocked a hole in its bottom. Then their brush house is burned by other searchers, the "dark ones." Taking refuge with Kino's brother, the family hides out all that day while Juan Tomas borrows provisions for their flight.

That night, the three head into the Sierra de la Giganta, planning to go to Lorento, a gulf town to the north, but trackers quickly find their trail. By the evening of the fourth day, Kino and his family are holed up in a cave while the trackers camp in the mountain cleft below them. Kino tries to sneak up on them to steal their rifle, but Coyotito whimpers, and one of the trackers, thinking (ironically, considering the baby's name) that it is a "coyote pup," idly shoots in that direction. Kino leaps too late. He kills all three men but finds that the top of Coyotito's head has been blown off.

Late in the afternoon of the fifth day, the two return to La Paz, carrying their dead child. They walk straight through the town to the gulf shore. There Kino pulls out the great pearl and offers it to Juana, but she declines, and it is he who returns the pearl to the sea. Because of its tragic dimensions, their story becomes forever one of the town's legends.

*Themes and Meanings*

In a work so rich, there are many themes that John Steinbeck explores: for example, the Creoles' mistreatment of the Indians, the cupidity of the Church, the survival and power of ancient religious beliefs behind a veneer of Christian rituals, the strength of the family unit in the face of adversity, the traditional view of women and the truth about feminine capabilities and understanding that it often conceals, humankind's position in the universal scheme, the transcendental quality of tragedy, and the ambiguous nature of good and evil. Steinbeck explicitly wants the reader to view his story as a parable, that is, as a moral or religious lesson. In the foreword, he writes that the story contains "only good and bad things and black and white things and good and evil things and no in-between anywhere." He continues, "If this story is a parable, perhaps everyone takes his own meaning from it and reads his own life into it."

Like his good friend Ed Ricketts, a marine biologist with whom he first visited the Gulf of California in 1940, Steinbeck saw human beings teleologically as part of the animal order. At one point, he describes La Paz affirmatively as "a colonial animal." Generally, however, it is Alfred, Lord Tennyson's "Nature, red in tooth and claw" that Steinbeck portrays: "Out in the estuary a tight-woven school of small fishes glittered and broke water to escape a school of great fishes that drove in to eat them. . . . And the night mice crept about on the ground and the little night hawks hunted them silently." Just so, Kino is physically attacked by a series of unknown assailants, while the brokers try to prey on his ignorance. In the mountains, he is hunted down by trackers described in canine terms. Kino "became curiously every man's enemy. The news stirred up something infinitely black and evil in the town; the black distillate was like the scorpion." However, Steinbeck also holds that humans can transcend their animal qualities, for humans alone can reason. Humans alone can understand parables.

What lesson, then, does the pearl teach? The answer is complex. For each positive contribution the pearl makes, there is a negative, and vice versa. The pearl is pure and capable of giving Kino and his family all sorts of economic advantages, especially an education for Coyotito, so that he can become free to rise above his "station." The pearl permits new and formerly impossible dreams, causing a dissatisfaction with the status quo of which Steinbeck approves; he calls it "one of the greatest talents the species has and one that has made it superior to animals that are satisfied with what they have." However, the pearl unaccountably brings evil to the family: "The essence of pearl mixed with essence of men and a curious dark residue was precipitated." Juana says, "The pearl is like a sin! It will destroy us." However, the pearl, by releasing new possibilities to Kino, has made him "a man," and when he drops the pearl during the struggle, Juana recognizes that she must restore it to him. At the same time, she urges him to flee La Paz (perhaps an ironic plea because the town's name means "peace"). The pearl finally seems "ugly; it was gray, like a malignant growth." However, it has proved the good in Kino's brother and sister-in-law, who have protected them. The resulting tragedy has also brought new dignity to Kino and Juana: "The people say that the two seemed to be removed from human experience; that they had gone through pain and had come out on the other side; that there was almost a magical protection about them." Kino and Juana have fallen from innocence; the Pearl of the World is akin to the Tree of Knowledge of Good and Evil. Their final tragic position somehow seems more worthy of respect than their earlier, untried ignorance.

In developing his parable, Steinbeck was possibly influenced by the medieval English allegory *Pearl*. Curiously, the pearl of great price described in Matthew 13:45-46 seems not to have affected him. The short novel is one with Steinbeck's other works, but it offers most interesting parallels with "The Great Mountains," the second part of *The Red Pony* (1937, 1945), and "Flight." In its use of quasi-allegory it anticipates *East of Eden* (1952), a more complex exploration of the Adamic fall from innocence.

*Style and Technique*

*The Pearl* grew out of an anecdote Steinbeck had heard during his visit to La Paz, which he recorded in the log section of *Sea of Cortez* (1941, 1951). An Indian boy discovered an exceedingly large pearl and saw in it a future of drink, many girlfriends, and, ultimately, personal salvation. He refused to sell the pearl for the ridiculously low price he was offered, and after he had been beaten and searched for two nights running, he angrily threw the pearl back into the gulf. Afterward, "he laughed a great deal about it." Steinbeck mused: "This seems to be a true story, but it is so much like a parable that it almost can't be. The Indian boy is too heroic, too wise." In developing *The Pearl*, Steinbeck tried to avoid the incongruities he had sensed in the original tale. He moved the story into a sort of timeless past and changed the happy-go-lucky boy into a responsible father and husband. In the process, the tone became tragic instead of comic.

From the beginning, Steinbeck had seen *The Pearl* as a basis for a film by the Mexican director Emilio Fernandez. Throughout the story run musical leitmotifs (which were actually used in the film), particularly three: the Song of the Family, which Kino hears each time he looks at his wife and especially his son; the Song of Evil, "the music of the enemy," which sounds every time they are threatened; and the music of the pearl itself. The story's visual sense is strong. The town, the gulf, and the sierra are described in sharp colors and high relief. Such scenes as Kino's dive into the sea, the flight into the mountains, and the daily life of the people demand cinematographic treatment.

Steinbeck's writing is deceptively simple, avoiding complexities of emotion and characterization. Only Steinbeck's occasional philosophical meditations and ironic asides could not be easily filmed. Shot on location by cameraman Gabriel Figuero with an all-Mexican cast, *La Perla* was premiered in 1946. To coincide with the film's release, the story was reprinted in book form under its present title and with illustrations by the great Mexican artist Jose Clemente Orozco, one of only three books he so honored.

*Drewey Wayne Gunn*

# THE PEASANT MAREY

*Author:* Fyodor Dostoevski (1821-1881)
*Type of plot:* Autobiographical
*Time of plot:* 1850 or 1851, with a flashback to 1830
*Locale:* A prison camp in Omsk, Siberia; a country estate near Moscow
*First published:* "Muzhik Marey," 1876 (English translation, 1919)

Principal characters:
THE NARRATOR (DOSTOEVSKI)
THE PEASANT MAREY

*The Story*

Fyodor Dostoevski spent the years 1850 to 1854 in a prison camp in Siberia, and in "The Peasant Marey" he recalls an episode in the camp that made him remember a still earlier incident from twenty years before. Thus, "The Peasant Marey" is a story-within-a-story, a recollection of two important experiences in the author's past.

The setting is Easter week in 1850 or 1851, and the prisoners are enjoying a rare holiday. The weather is pleasant, and the inmates are drinking and brawling. Violence and disorder prevail in a brutal atmosphere. A drunken prisoner named Tatar Gazin has been beaten senseless by six of his fellows, and Dostoevski is repelled by the bestiality that confronts him everywhere in the camp. At this point, he meets "a political prisoner called M." (The real M. was a Pole named Mirecki.) M. is as disgusted as Dostoevski is, and he snarls at Dostoevski in French, "I hate these bandits." Dostoevski returns to his bunk and lies down, but he is too agitated to sleep. As he lies there, his mind wanders over his past and fixes vividly on "an unnoticed moment in my early childhood when I was only nine years old."

He remembers a cool autumn day in 1830 on his father's estate in the country, a lovely day that made him dread returning to Moscow and French lessons. He is wandering through a thicket of bushes, close enough to the fields to hear a peasant plowing nearby. He is suddenly terrified by a mysterious shout of "Wolf!" At this, he runs shrieking to the peasant at the plow. "I don't know if there is such a name, but everyone called him Marey—a thick-set, rather well-grown peasant of fifty, with a good many grey hairs in his dark brown, spreading beard." Marey has seen no wolf and heard no shout, and he calms the child and convinces him that there is no wolf. When the reassured child leaves, Marey makes the sign of the cross over him and follows his progress up the ravine to the barn, where the child's dog greets him and makes him feel safe.

Dostoevski recalls that he soon forgot Marey but realizes that the meeting in the field "must have lain hidden in my soul, though I knew nothing of it." He remembers the "timid tenderness" of Marey and the "eyes shining with great love." His judgment of the event twenty years later is profound:

It was a solitary meeting in the deserted fields, and only God, perhaps, may have seen from above with what deep and humane civilized feeling, and with what delicate, almost feminine tenderness, the heart of a coarse, brutally ignorant Russian serf, who has as yet no expectation, no idea even of his freedom, may be filled.

After musing on the Marey experience, Dostoevski sees his brawling companions in a different light: "Suddenly by some miracle all hatred and anger had vanished utterly from my heart." He is overwhelmed with compassion for these unhappy victims of life's vicissitudes, seeing another Marey in each "shaven peasant, branded on his face as a criminal." Meeting Mirecki again that evening, Dostoevski feels sorrow for a man who has only hatred in his heart. What makes the difference between him and Mirecki, Dostoevski realizes, is that the Pole has no memories of Russian peasants to engender in him a love for humanity.

*Themes and Meanings*

The best interpretation of "The Peasant Marey" is given by Joseph Frank in *Dostoevsky: The Years of Ordeal, 1850-1859* (1983). The account given here follows Frank.

In January, 1876, Dostoevski had published the first installment of *Dnevnik pisatelya* (1873-1874, 1876, 1877-1881; *Pages from the Journal of an Author,* 1916), a corrosive critique of the decay he saw in Russian family life, noted for its endemic drunkenness and wife-beating. In this mood, he reverts to the bitterness of his early prison camp days, and "The Peasant Marey" is meant to mitigate the harshness of the first piece. The story is probably intended to sway his readers to sympathy with his own deep-rooted faith in the peasantry as the soul of Russia. Whatever his motive, the incident with the peasant Marey was enormously fructifying for Dostoevski's spiritual life and may be read as an important conversion experience.

Frank argues that "The Peasant Marey" does not recount a religious experience in the usual sense, however, because Dostoevski had never completely abandoned his Christian faith. Frank maintains that he never, as far as is known, subscribed fully to the atheism of the radical groups with which he associated. According to Frank, "He always remained much closer to the French Utopian Socialists, who, while rejecting official religion as embodied in their own Roman Catholic tradition, regarded their radical social ideals as the application of the divinely inspired Christian doctrine of love to the modern world." Dostoevski's conversion, then, is not from religious despair to religious faith, but from a feeling of humankind's hopelessness and degradation to "a faith in the Russian common people as, in some sense, the human image of Christ."

The circumstances of Dostoevski's life in the camp made him susceptible to a conversion. He suffered from the "divided self" identified by William James as vital to the state of mind that precedes conversion. He was unhappy and plagued by guilt over the revulsion he felt for the peasant-convicts—even though he knew it was wrong to detest his fellowman. Furthermore, he was living under extraordinary stress, physical as well as mental, creating what Frank calls "the perfect physical and psychological situation for a conversion to have taken place." Dostoevski also was having epileptic seizures at this time, and Frank believes that this illness would have increased his susceptibility to a profound religious experience.

Frank cites in James's own words his three characteristics of a conversion experience: "the loss of all worry," "the sense of perceiving truths not known before," and last, "an appearance of newness" in the outside world that "beautifies every object." Frank finds the first two phenomena clearly evidenced in "The Peasant Marey," and he asserts that even though Dostoevski did not mention the hallucinatory events often associated with the third characteristic, he did believe "that he could at last see through the surface of the world to a beauty hitherto concealed from the eyes of his moral sensibility."

The profound religious feeling that glows in "The Peasant Marey" should be understood in terms of Dostoevski's rejection of Westernism, especially as he perceived it in the contemptuous Poles in the camp, and his embrace of the Russian peasantry as the heart of the Russian national character. Because he identified the peasants with the Russian Orthodox Church, "his recovery of faith in the people was also a rediscovery of Orthodoxy, or at least an estrangement from his previous 'progressive' Christianity, whose doctrines he could well castigate as the fatal source of all his old illusions." Thus, "The Peasant Marey" is an extremely important document for anyone studying Dostoevski's sensibility.

### Style and Technique

Dostoevski's works are marked by an emotional intensity not found in many other writers, and this intensity is usually focused on themes of the utmost significance in theology and the individual's relationship to God and humankind. His concern with these harrowing topics is obsessive and gives his work great power, although in long stretches many readers will find him emotionally draining.

There is little that is distinctive about Dostoevski's style in the translation of "The Peasant Marey." He uses the convention of the flashback to frame the most important part of his tale. The story of Marey comes back to him in a reverie, almost a dream. The point of view is consistently first person, giving the account immediacy but limiting the reader's perceptions to what goes on in the narrator's mind. Dostoevski carefully builds the mood of the piece through accounts of the weather. He explains immediately that "the air was warm, the sky was blue, the sun was high, warm, bright, but my soul was very gloomy." This contrast between the weather and his spirits is effective, and he resorts to the weather again in describing his mood at the time he heard the cry of "Wolf." He recalls it was "a dry bright day but rather cold and windy." Besides describing the weather and noting the season, Dostoevski also develops the scene of his childhood experience with some attentive description of nature. He remembers, for example, collecting beetles and other insects, and he refers to his love of mushrooms and wild berries, as well as his fondness for the smell of dead leaves and birch wood in the open forest. All these touches contribute to the texture of his account and bring back the childhood experience vividly.

*Frank Day*

# THE PEDERSEN KID

*Author:* William H. Gass (1924-    )
*Type of plot:* Antistory
*Time of plot:* About 1961
*Locale:* A North Dakota farm
*First published:* 1961

> *Principal characters:*
> JORGE SEGREN, the young narrator and protagonist, whose
>     perceptions of the journey dominate the story
> PA SEGREN, his father, a brutal drunk
> BIG HANS, the Segrens' hired hand
> THE PEDERSEN KID, a neighbor's son
> A MURDEROUS UNNAMED INTRUDER, from whom the Pedersen
>     Kid escaped

## The Story

One stark winter morning after a snowstorm, Big Hans, the Segrens' hired hand, finds the unconscious body of the son of a neighboring farm family. After a ritualistic process of revival, the Pedersen Kid, still somewhat delirious, tells the strange, horrifying story of how a yellow-gloved stranger had broken into his house and forced the family into the fruit cellar; the boy escaped into a vicious snowstorm and managed to make his way to the Segren house before collapsing. Now he fears that his parents may have been murdered.

It becomes clear that there is long-standing resentment and competition between Big Hans and Pa Segren, so it is only reluctantly that they manage to agree to set off with Jorge for the Pedersen farm. Circumventing the obstacles of weather and their own antagonism for each other, they arrive and come on the intruder's frozen horse. Hiding in the barn—they are afraid of traversing the open space to the house—they contrive the unlikely project of tunneling unobserved through the snowdrift on the far side of the house. This fails, so they finally decide to risk moving across the yard. Jorge goes first and succeeds, but when his father tries to follow, he is felled by a gunshot. Jorge breaks through a basement window and, anxious and shivering, he awaits the fatal confrontation. No one, however, ever appears. The story concludes with Jorge alone in the Pedersen house, where he considers the presumed deaths not only of the neighbors but also of his own parents and of Big Hans as well. A surprising warmth slowly suffuses him: It is a burning joy, a satisfaction that comes from the brave completion of his duty and, apparently, from having been liberated from the vicious domination of the adults in his life.

*Themes and Meanings*

Each of the characters in "The Pedersen Kid" seeks to create a feeling of inner springtime to battle against the bleak physical environment and the empty prospects of living in a loveless household: Big Hans with his pornographic pictures, Pa with his whiskey, Jorge's mother with her diligent maintenance of domestic organization and routine, and Jorge with vague dreams of prowess and freedom. Their secret lives are also the sole source of self-worth in the story, for intimacy and compassion are utterly absent. (One profoundly revealing memory of Jorge's is of his father's destruction of a favorite picture book, which had been a rare secret pleasure in his life.) It is no wonder, then, that Jorge immediately resents the appearance of the frozen child because the ministrations he earns represent a quality of attention that Jorge himself has never enjoyed. (Pa smacks his son for waking him, and Jorge silently blames the Pedersen Kid; he consoles himself with the thought that the naked boy's penis is smaller than his own.)

With the resuscitation of the frozen child comes the bringing to life of his awful tale, and each of the eventual "rescuers" accepts the truth of it—and thus, the responsibility this occasions—for very private reasons. Big Hans, who has saved the boy, probably has a special stake in the version of reality he offers because it vindicates and extends his sudden ascendancy; Pa goes along out of spite for Big Hans, and out of fitful anger over the discovery of his hidden store of whiskey; Jorge is simply bullied into the plot by the men, but his disdain for the Pedersen Kid slowly turns to emulation as he decides to prove himself superior to the neighbor boy under the same critical circumstances. He will outdo him, Jorge thinks, and he imagines himself saving his parents from the killer and thereby proving his own worth once and for all. (That saving his parents would require endangering them first shows that vengeance for years of abuse is a principal motivation, too.)

Each of them sets off in his own story, as it were. However, who is the unseen killer with the yellow gloves who lurks at the end of their difficult journey through the snow? Perhaps he is the Abominable Snowman, winter's own henchman, the environmental harshness personified and personalized. Perhaps he is the instrument of Jorge's heroic growth and of his repudiation of Pa and Big Hans—the test of his mettle and, ultimately, the same eradicator of adult authority for Jorge that he was for the Pedersen Kid. As the events of the story grow increasingly ambiguous, losing themselves within Jorge's dream-riddled mind, other explanations arise, including the possibility that it is Jorge, not the stranger, who has shot and killed his father, fulfilling a wish he had during an idyllic summer when, armed with a broomstick, he roamed the countryside pretending to blast anyone who happened by. Under this interpretation, the yellow-gloved man serves as an imaginary screen protecting Jorge from the unmediated awareness of his guilt.

"The Pedersen Kid" is pervaded by conflicting images of warmth and coldness, exposure and sanctuary. In fact, the snow itself offers opposing qualities—it is both blanket and grave, refuge and death threat, and its coldness burns. Symbolic wombs, tunnels, and shelters all establish the desire for inviolable solitude and rejuvenation, and all prove transitory until, having made his way through the harsh trials of the journey, Jorge burrows into the Pedersen basement, where he is seemingly rewarded with the warmth of an energized consciousness (unless he is suffering the hallucinations that precede freezing to death). While it is irrelevant to speak of the real, totalizing meaning of "The Pedersen Kid," it can be said that Jorge's final ability to author his own destiny transforms a desperate landscape into an imaginative realm of vital possibility. His is a victory of artistic consciousness.

*Style and Technique*

It has been argued that "The Pedersen Kid" is William H. Gass's most traditional story, for not only does it include conventionally established characters, setting, and action, but it also is overtly indebted to Freudian, Christian, and heraldic archetypes and offers easily identifiable themes—the initiation of a young man into experience, the maturation of the artist, and the struggle between man and nature—that place the story comfortably within the province of realistic fiction. What sets it apart from tradition is what makes all of Gass's writing unique: the luxuriant texturing of the prose itself. Gass has remarked that the only events in his texts are sentences; in other words, the manner of the telling is the tale being told. Whether it be the spare, brittle language, which seems to have been petrified by exposure to the forbidding Dakota territory, or the lush, rolling consciousness of Jorge Segren's interior world, the physicality of the words is its own justification. Words are by no means mere scaffolding for the story; instead, they are rigorously, lovingly designed to be lingered on.

Indeed, Gass's style constitutes one of the most distinctive signatures in contemporary American fiction. In a story as relentlessly ambiguous as "The Pedersen Kid," style is the one thing that unquestionably "happens."

*Arthur M. Saltzman*

# A PEDESTRIAN ACCIDENT

*Author:* Robert Coover (1932-    )
*Type of plot:* Absurdist
*Time of plot:* The mid-twentieth century
*Locale:* A large metropolitan area
*First published:* 1969

> *Principal characters:*
> PAUL, a man who has been run over by a truck and should be dead
> TRUCK DRIVER, the man who was driving the truck
> POLICE OFFICER, the individual who tries to control the crowd that gathers to watch the spectacle
> CHARITY GRUNDY, a seventy-year-old woman who invents a story to fit the circumstances and to try to explain them

*The Story*

A postmodern story in the absurdist tradition, "A Pedestrian Accident" recounts a nonsensical story about a man who has been run over by a six-wheel truck. After the accident, the man, Paul, remains conscious and is aware of what is going on around him within his range of vision. Even after the truck backs over him again and then pulls forward so that his body is mangled and torn, Paul remains conscious. Alternative explanations are that he is dead, but still able to observe real events taking place around him; that he is not dead but fantasizing; or that he is dead and removed to another level of reality just as "real" as the experiential world, but different from it. In postmodernist fiction, it is not necessary that choices be made. A reader simply accepts the absurd situation as it is given in a hypothetical world whose dimensions are different from those of the real world. Whatever the dimensions of an author's "made" world, one is dealing with storified experience, in fact not any different from all other "stories" that have been created by storytellers from prehistoric times to the present. Thus, a story written in this mode has the same kind of validity as stories written or told long ago that have passed into history as myths, legends, or reputedly factual accounts. A story is a created experience, whether it is about the girl next door who had a date with the football hero or about Cinderella and her Prince Charming. Consequently, a story about a man who should be dead witnessing an absurd burlesque being acted out before him can have as much meaning as a biblical account of miracles accomplished, for example, by Paul, Jesus's apostle.

The events that take place around the Paul of "A Pedestrian Accident" seem to be parts of a burlesque, a vaudeville show, or a Punch and Judy puppet show. The truck driver, with his rolling body and his little hands flying wildly about, thrusts himself in and out of the cab window as if he is being controlled by the strings of a puppeteer.

The driver's words, which become a refrain repeated throughout the story with only slight variations, begin in such a way as to underline the theatrical aspects of his role: "Listen lays and gentmens I'm a good Christian by Judy a decent hardwork in fambly man." The police officer, with the tiny mustache and the notebook, who is constantly fingering his epaulets and acting in the name of the law, seems a straight man to Charity Grundy's comic act as she struts, postures, and grimaces across the stage of Paul's vision.

The woman and the police officer take part in a comic dialogue whose purpose is to explain who Paul is. Charity, a seventy-year-old woman with a pasty face, thick rouge, and a head covered with ringlets of sparse orange hair, identifies Paul as Amory Westerman, her lover, who came to her door carrying a heavy sea chest and whom she had desired only to mother, though circumstances got out of hand. As she recites her story, Charity dances about and plays to the crowd, and they begin to toss pennies to her in appreciation for the excellence of her act.

When the doctor arrives center stage, Mrs. Grundy retires to the rear, where later Paul will observe her setting up a ticket booth and charging admission to the play being enacted. The appearance of the doctor causes the police officer to breathe a sigh of relief because his authority is being superseded by that of the doctor, but Paul becomes even more terrified and believes that with the appearance of the doctor he is in real trouble. The doctor makes a routine examination of a man who is lying half-buried under a truck. Because the doctor will not allow Paul to be moved because he may have a broken neck, the police officer and truck driver can think of nothing to do but to pull the truck off Paul, which means running over him again. The truck driver misunderstands the officer and begins to go backward over the body before he is told to move forward. This moving of the truck at the direction of the doctor results in Paul's being run over again and again.

When the doctor determines that he cannot help Paul, he lectures Paul on the meaning of life and death and orders the police officer to send for a priest. Paul's eyes close, and when he awakes the streets are empty except for an old man who looks like the priest he had expected. Before long, however, Paul realizes that the man is not a priest but a beggar, and he is waiting for Paul to die so that he can appropriate Paul's torn clothes.

At the end of the story, a small dog has arrived and apparently recognized that Paul's body can provide food. Rain begins to fall and Paul hears the sound of other approaching dogs.

*Themes and Meanings*

It has become a commonplace of criticism to note that Robert Coover considers the world to be a collage of fictions created by human beings. After a while, human beings forget that they have themselves created the fictions, and they act as though the fictions are shaping them and dictating their behavioral patterns. At this point, when the fictions lose their validity and efficacy, the fictions need to be destroyed so that other fictions can be created. Because the world is composed only of fictions, however, a fiction-maker's only choice is to repeat the past, using the old fictions, but at the same time re-creating them by rearranging them to make them more pertinent to the present time. Thus, the role of the artist is to create new fictional forms out of the old residues. Artists must always be aware, however, that what they are creating is fiction and not an objective view of reality.

In "A Pedestrian Accident," several fictions are in operation. There is the symbolic substructure of Christian belief. Paul, as apostle, preaching the gospel of Jesus in the hope of everlasting life, whose conversion on the road to Damascus is accomplished in a blinding flash of light, is likened to Paul, the pedestrian, carrying the book, whose conversion is accomplished by a sudden flash of light and a blaze roaring out of the back of his head. (The apostle Paul was beheaded.) In his "Everyman" role, Paul is Adam to Charity's Eve, as well as Amory Westerman, symbol of Western man who is loved "amore" not in a brotherly way similar to the Greek "agape," but in a "coupling unequaled in the history of Western concupiscence!"

Paul is also Solomon Grundy, who was

> Born on Monday
> Christened on Tuesday
> Married on Wednesday
> Took ill on Thursday
> Worse on Friday
> Died on Saturday
> Was buried on Sunday
> And that was the end of Solomon Grundy.

In the Western world, when "miracle" cures gave way to doctors with "scientific" cures, doctors assumed the importance of older gods, and people placed them in godlike roles. However, doctors are not miracle workers when it comes to life and death. In "A Pedestrian Accident," the doctor lectures Paul:

> New life burgeons out of rot, new mouths consume old organisms, father dies at orgasm, mother dies at birth, only old Dame Mass with her twin dugs of Stuff and Tickle persists, suffering her long slow split into pure light and pure carbon!

Unable to accomplish the cure, the doctor fades into shadow and appears again as that prosoppoeia of patience, the priest, but priest fades into beggar, who simply waits for Paul to die.

*Style and Technique*

"A Pedestrian Accident" is from Coover's collection of short stories called *Pricksongs and Descants* (1969). The title of the collection refers not only to the recurring theme of sex and death, including the violent and the grotesque, but also to the musical terms that define a form of music in which variations play against a basic line.

"Pricksong" is synonymous with "descant." Events in "A Pedestrian Accident" are counterpointed against the familiar literary themes of Paul the Apostle, theatrical farces, and the surrealist montage of doctor, priest, and beggar. This kind of counterpointing results in multiple perspectives and points toward an understanding of the broad fictional base on which comprehension of the universe rests. With Coover, as with many other postmodernist writers, a reader is asked to consider the primacy of self, not for purposes of solipsism, but to emphasize the creative power of human beings.

Nineteenth century culture stresses empiricism—the primacy of objective reality. Twentieth century "new physics," however, insists that there is no objective reality different from what individuals perceive. Individuals, however, cannot have complete knowledge simultaneously of all the facts because the very act of observing the system changes the system. Ordinary language, which is based on the old concepts of space and time, is no longer appropriate to describe the findings of modern physics. Thus, in contemporary science, the ordinary has given way to the fabulous; fact and fiction, as they were once perceived, have become blurred; and an artist such as Coover takes delight in fantastic inventions, hoping to change the world by reinventing it.

*Mary Rohrberger*

# PEOPLE LIKE THAT ARE THE ONLY PEOPLE HERE
## Canonical Babbling in Peed Onk

*Author:* Lorrie Moore (1957-    )
*Type of plot:* Psychological, autobiographical
*Time of plot:* The 1990's
*Locale:* An unnamed midwestern town
*First published:* 1997

> *Principal characters:*
> THE MOTHER, a writer
> THE HUSBAND, the father of the baby
> THE BABY, a boy about one year old

*The Story*

"People Like That Are the Only People Here" is told in the third person through the perspective of a mother who discovers that her baby has cancer. The principal characters and the doctors are not named. The mother is a writer who must use her utmost intellectual and emotional resources to get through her baby's radical nephrectomy in a pediatric oncology unit at a children's hospital.

With little warning other than the baby's appearing to be slightly ill, the mother discovers a blood clot in her baby's diaper. She phones a nearby pediatric clinic and is urged to bring the child in right away. After a quick examination, the baby is whisked away to the radiology unit. The surgeon soon appears to announce that the baby has a cancerous tumor, requiring a radical nephrectomy and possibly chemotherapy.

The husband's response, although alarmed, is practical. The first thing that he tells his wife is to take notes, and then he begins to worry about money. He soon attempts to devise a step-by-step plan for them to get through the ordeal. The husband is not cold; he simply talks and acts in a way that might be expected of a man.

The mother, however, is not one to take such a practical, mechanical approach. Her next impulse is to turn to God, in whom she does not firmly believe. Her god ends up looking a lot like the manager of Marshall Field's, and as such, she initially attempts to bargain with him. The manager of Marshall Field's (now God) offers the mother only the reassurances she might easily glean from fiction-writing techniques: One cannot know the narrative of his or her life in advance; there must be surprises or otherwise it is not life; the idea that anyone really has a clue about how the world works is laughable.

The husband continues to urge his wife to take notes, even to write a piece of nonfiction or journalism for money. The mother initially balks at the idea, but she does begin to note things (the reader never sees her actually writing). She notes that nearly all cancer victims in the pediatric oncology unit are males. They come from deceptively sweet-sounding towns like Janesville or Appleton, places undoubtedly poisoned by agricultural and industrial pollutants. The mother notes the dress and demeanor of the other cancer patients' mothers; she initially feels alienated from the large, cheerful women. The mother hears the usual platitudes such as "one day at the time" but finds little comfort in them.

Before the operation, the surgeon tells the parents that this tumor is not particularly aggressive but that it does tend to metastasize on the lungs. This cancer, the surgeon assures them, is the best kind of cancer that the baby could have. The mother and the husband are left to get through the last day before surgery. In a hospital lounge, they hear many war stories from the other parents who are battling the cancers of their children. These parents have pulled through the first shocking diagnoses, multiple hospitalizations, and even comas brought on by chemotherapy. The mother has momentary thoughts of hopping a bus and running away, but she is grounded by these parents who have suffered for a long time without allowing themselves to fall apart.

The baby's tumor turns out to be relatively minor (for cancer, that is), and the parents are allowed the option of careful monitoring rather than chemotherapy. On the way out of the hospital, one mother offers the consolation that there is a great deal of collateral beauty in their experiences. The mother is too distracted to consider collateral beauty at this time; she just wants to get herself and the baby out of the hospital as quickly as possible. However, in the last lines of the story, she suggests that the story itself is her notes on this experience.

*Themes and Meanings*

"People Like That Are the Only People Here" is one of Lorrie Moore's most autobiographical stories. She suffered through a similar ordeal with her son, Benjamin. This story is more than a story about how a mother would cope with learning that her baby has cancer; it is a story specifically about how a writer who is a mother would cope with this discovery. A writer's ordeal is not radically different from any other parent's ordeal in a similar situation, but her means of coping with the ordeal will inevitably bear the marks of her occupation as a writer. It is the writer's business to make sense out of and to bring order to the messy, sometimes tragic components of human life. This writer and mother is faced with a situation that does not make sense; she is faced with the task of articulating something unthinkable: Her baby has cancer.

The mother's first response is similar to the response of any mother: disbelief, denial, self-blame, and anger. The husband's suggestion that she take notes initially strikes her as insane, but taking notes, or putting her experience into words, is the writer's only defense. Even the god that she quickly makes up (the one that looks like a manager at Marshall Field's) can only console her with advice about the elements of good narration. The writer often does not know the full narrative in advance. Not knowing is a gift in life as well as in narrative. If one takes away surprises, one takes away life and the fun of living.

The writer and mother feels inadequate to the task assigned to her. After all, writing fiction is her specialty, not nonfiction or journalism, which is often written more for monetary gain. She knows that her suffering cannot be fully communicated, no matter how skillful a writer she is, and she feels alone. Words—whether those found in conventional platitudes or those that arise from her own quirky, ironic voice—do little to console her.

For a time, the mother and writer must give up on trying to make sense of the whole ordeal. Instead, she focuses on simply getting through her baby's surgery. She now listens attentively to the other parents of cancer victims. They offer the only wisdom available: It is something that she has to pull through, not through courage, exactly, but through an unquestioned sense of obligation. Pulling through becomes the focus of the rest of the story. The writer in the mother realizes that the narrator who eventually tells the story will already be someone other than who she is right now. She also realizes that the act of writing creates a tidiness that belies the incoherence of the experience itself.

In many ways, "People Like That Are the Only People Here" is both a celebration and denunciation of the power of writing. If the writer and mother is unable to make sense of a baby getting cancer, she is at least able to convey enough of what the experience must be like. She finds the collateral beauty of the experience even if she resents the implication that there is anything to be gained by such a horrific ordeal. In the last lines of the story, she disparagingly refers to the entire story as notes and sardonically demands money. One gets the impression that any words used to convey the near loss of a child must necessarily cheapen the real suffering of real mothers.

*Style and Technique*

The plot of "People Like That Are the Only People Here" is predictably linear; the only surprise may be that the tumor is not as bad as feared and that the baby goes home, without having to undergo chemotherapy. The focus of the story is on the mother and writer's coping techniques, which, as mentioned earlier, have a lot to do with writing itself.

Moore's story reads very much like a series of notes on the ongoing experience. Breaks in the notes are indicated by extra line spacing. These notes are more than diary entries and less than a coherent, unified story. This lack of cohesion is probably deliberate on Moore's part, a true case of form reflecting content. Her narrative technique illustrates her rejection of the notion that such a horrific experience can be understood, ordered, or unified into one coherent whole.

Moore's trademark humor is subdued in this story, naturally, but it is not absent. There are traces of humor even in the first paragraph when the mother imagines any number of unlikely reasons there would be a blood clot in her baby's diaper. The subtitle itself is humorous, and her depiction of God is humorous. Throughout the story, the mother is allowed her moments of ironic reflection or occasional sarcastic gibes. There is never any danger, however, of Moore's humor undermining the magnitude of the experience attributed to the mother. This humor seems absolutely necessary to maintain some distance between the storyteller and the story. Otherwise, the story itself might have never been told.

*Nancy E. Sherrod*

# PEOPLE OF THE DOG

*Author:* Alma Villanueva (1944-        )
*Type of plot:* Social realism
*Time of plot:* The late twentieth century
*Locale:* Mexico City
*First published:* 1990

> *Principal characters:*
> THE BOY, a street urchin
> A YOUNG MAN, Quetzalcoatl, an Aztec god
> THE BABY WIND GOD
> A SOCIAL WORKER

*The Story*

An unnamed boy comes to Mexico City to escape an abusive home, where the new man takes his food, hits him with his fists until he bleeds, and threatens to kill him. His mother tells him tearfully to go to the city, where she hopes he will survive. Almost ten years old, the boy sleeps with four other boys, two of them younger, all of them tormented, and one of them raped by older boys.

In his fantasy, the little boy sees a young man, "his entire body . . . tattooed with snakes, birds and circles . . . with the wind god clinging to his back." The young man gets into a boat, and the boy feels the water at his feet, remembering that he has not bathed since he left his mother's house. He jumps in the boat after the young man, attracted by the happy expression of the baby wind god. He paddles rapidly; the young man's tattoos begin to move faster and faster; the baby wind god laughs. The boy is no longer tired, no longer hungry; he is no longer in pain, no longer afraid. He cannot remember any suffering. In his vision, he swallows a small piece of lightning that comes from the mouth of the baby wind god. He sees a city and many brave Indians, and the scene reminds him of Mexico City when he first saw it, before it devoured him. An eagle flies from the mouth of the baby wind god and lands on a cactus. He sees the young man again, whose face is divided into gentle and fierce aspects. The baby wind god changes into a thin white cloud, which the boy inhales. The boy thinks he will not remember if he is dead, but he will remember Quetzalcoatl.

A Mexican woman with noticeable Indian features bends over the boy's dead body. He is covered with a filthy blanket and wears shoes stuffed with rags to keep out the cold. A tube of glue lies next to him. His face shows no pain, only peace. Another boy has called her because his friend would not wake up. He went with a man who gave him money and some pills. Another little boy is missing, he says, and he thinks the older boys may have killed him. The woman wonders if perhaps the dead boy is better off than the living ones. She will call the police, who will dispose of the poor boy's body as if he were a dog. She does not realize that "the ancient one, Quetzalcoatl, came from a clan called the Chichimecs. People of the Dog." She covers the dead boy's face with the dirty blanket, and the baby in her womb jumps suddenly, causing her to sigh deeply.

## Themes and Meanings

This is clearly a story of social protest. Dedicated to the children of Mexico City, this story of an unnamed boy's short life is modeled after the life of many hundreds of children in the large cities of Latin America. The boy's Indian descent is suggested by his thick, black hair and the poverty of his village home. There are other indications as well: his vision of the Aztec god, Quetzalcoatl; his vision of the Mexico City of long ago, when there were Indians everywhere; the image of the eagle landing on a cactus.

According to their history, when the Aztecs found an eagle with a snake in its mouth sitting on a cactus, they were to build a new city there and they would have great prosperity. They found just such a divine sign near a lake and, obeying their gods, they constructed the famous city of Tenochtitlán. Twentieth century Mexico honors its Aztec heritage by displaying these symbols on its national flag and currency. The present-day Mexico City was built over Tenochtitlán; the Spanish conquerors built on the foundations and bodies of the conquered Indians. The boy's vision of a former Mexico bustling with Indians seems quite apt, as does his view of the eagle-cactus story: Instead of having a snake in its mouth, the boy's eagle lands on the cactus, looks from side to side, and defecates, representing the new Mexico of conquered peoples—a Mexico of poverty rather than prosperity.

Quetzalcoatl was one of the most important of the Aztec gods. Portrayed as a young man or an enormous feathered serpent (the name means "plumed serpent"), he was Lord of the Winds. Those born under his sign were considered unlucky. They could expect to be paupers and homeless beggars, thus imitating the snake that goes about homeless and naked, exposed to the forces of nature, or akin to the wind that roams restlessly from one place to another. The Aztec legend that Quetzalcoatl would return contributed to their defeat by Hernán Cortés, in whom they believed they saw the manifestation of their long-awaited god. After they welcomed Cortés with great honors, he used their confusion to bring about their ruin.

As an Indian Mexican, the boy in the story is a helpless member of a large underclass, victim of an empty present and a hopeless future. As the story implies, there are many such children living in the streets of the city, where, because of their youth and innocence, they are easy prey to older, more experienced outcasts. They suffer from homelessness, hunger and starvation, and physical and sexual abuse, and often resort to exchanging sex for anything that might alleviate some of their suffering. Their use of drugs—especially the common practice of sniffing glue—is less an indication of their lack of morality or proper values than it is an act of desperation. Glue-sniffing is known to suppress pain and hunger. Hence the boy's vision, which makes apparent his welcome loss of memory and sensation. Alma Villanueva's interpretation of his glue-induced high emphasizes the beauty of his flight of fancy, his spirit traveling freely where his body cannot go. Glue-sniffing is known to cause serious brain damage; it can lead to a quick and sudden death. Villanueva's description of the boy's dreams does not romanticize the boy's drug use and death, however: The dream symbolizes the boy's return to his own people, the "people of the dog," of the Aztec deity Quetzalcoatl. If only in death, the boy escapes the new Mexico City, the one that ate him up, and flies with the wind god to the old city, which is filled with strong and fearless Indians. The story ends with the woman's sigh, implying the presence of the wind god—Quetzalcoatl—at the boy's passing.

*Style and Technique*

The most immediately observable technique in this brief tale is the use of italics in the first section. Italics are often used to represent a character's thoughts; here they indicate the little boy's unconscious. The two sections of text differ not only in typography, but also are physically divided by three symbols signaling a change. Leaving the boy's unconscious, the narration moves from first-person to third-person omniscient narration from the woman's point of view.

The mythology of ancient Mexico provides both the frame and the content of "People of the Dog." Villanueva's use of Quetzalcoatl, the symbol of the eagle and the cactus, and the wind god, makes possible the coexistence of a present and a long-ago past. The present is modern-day Mexico, while the past is the Tenochtitlán before the Spanish conquest in the early 1500's. Villanueva suggests that this past is shared by twentieth century Indians like a Jungian collective unconscious. When the boy dies, his unconscious does not remember death, but rather comments that he will remember birth. Much like the Christian belief that death is a passing on to a new life, the boy is born into his native heritage and delivered from the tragedy of his earthly existence. Although the story takes place in Mexico, the attention to Aztec legends reflects the Chicano interest in regaining the historical homeland known as Aztlán. Villanueva, a Chicana whose grandmother was a Yaqui Indian from Sonora, Mexico, sends her tragic young character home.

*Linda Ledford-Miller*

# A PERFECT DAY FOR BANANAFISH

*Author:* J. D. Salinger (1919-    )
*Type of plot:* Psychological
*Time of plot:* 1948
*Locale:* South Florida
*First published:* 1948

>*Principal characters:*
>SEYMOUR GLASS, a psychologically disturbed army veteran
>MURIEL GLASS, his wife
>MURIEL'S MOTHER, unnamed
>DR. RIESER, a psychiatrist
>SYBIL CARPENTER, a child four or five years old
>MRS. CARPENTER, her mother

*The Story*

"A Perfect Day for Bananafish" is composed of three interconnected story lines, the first and third of them realistic, the second a kind of fantasy. As the story opens, Muriel Glass is alone in her hotel room, presumably in Miami Beach, waiting for her call to her mother to be put through. She is polishing her fingernails when the telephone rings, but she does not drop everything to answer it. She replaces the cap of her nail polish, gets an ash tray, sits down on one of the twin beds, and answers the telephone on the fifth or sixth ring.

Muriel's mother, talking from a northern city, is worried at not having heard from Muriel sooner. As the conversation progresses, it becomes increasingly evident that something is seriously wrong with Seymour, Muriel's husband, who had been mustered out of the army after World War II and who has been hospitalized up until now. Muriel has waited for him through the war and during the time he was hospitalized.

Muriel's mother is particularly distressed to learn that Muriel allowed Seymour to drive the car on their trip to Florida. He has already damaged Muriel's father's car by driving it into a tree, which he seems to have a compulsion to do. The mother urges her daughter to come home at once. She tells Muriel that her father will pay for her to take a trip away by herself to think things out. Muriel mentions that she met the hotel's psychiatrist, Dr. Rieser, who asked her if her husband, who looks wan and pale, is ill.

Muriel also asks if her mother knows where a book of German poetry is that Seymour sent her from Germany. Seymour considers the poems to be by the only great poet of the century, presumably Rainer Maria Rilke, and wants Muriel to learn German so that she can read them. Muriel tells her mother that Seymour is now by himself on the beach, where he refuses to take off his terry cloth robe because he does not want people to stare at his tattoo. Her mother says, "He doesn't have any tattoo! Did he get one in the army?" Muriel assures her that he did not.

The scene shifts to a beach, where little Sybil Carpenter is talking with her mother, who is about to go off to have a martini with a friend. She tells Sybil to go and play, and she promises to save her the olive from her drink. Sybil walks a quarter of a mile down the beach, where she finds her friend Seymour Glass. She is petulant because she has heard that he let another little girl sit on his bench when he was playing the piano in one of the hotel's public rooms. As the two go to the water, Seymour suggests that perhaps they can catch a bananafish. He tells Sybil that it is a perfect day for bananafish. Seymour pushes her out almost too far on a rubber raft, and she makes him take her back to shore. On the way, he tells her that bananafish swim into holes where there are bananas and stuff themselves on them, sometimes eating as many as seventy-eight at a time. This makes them so fat, naturally, that they cannot get out of the hole, and they die there. Sybil tells Seymour that she has just seen a bananafish.

The final scene of the story has two parts. In the first, Seymour gets into the hotel elevator, and when it starts to move, he accuses a woman with zinc salve on her nose, someone whom he does not know, of staring at his feet. She says that she is merely looking at the floor, but Seymour continues making his accusation volubly to the point that she becomes flustered and asks the elevator operator to let her out at the next floor.

Seymour leaves the elevator when it gets to his floor and goes to his and Muriel's room. Muriel is asleep in her bed. He goes to his suitcase, takes an Ortiges calibre 7.65 automatic revolver from it, sits down on his bed, looks at Muriel, then puts a bullet through his right temple.

*Themes and Meanings*

The meanings of "A Perfect Day for Bananafish" have been much discussed. On one hand, a number of reputable critics think that the story simply relates some events in a day that culminated in the suicide of a disturbed person. Other critics think of the story as a metaphorical representation of what happens to sensitive people in a materialistic society filled with people who are as greedy as the bananafish about which Seymour tells Sybil. J. D. Salinger is fond of writing about the phoniness of modern society, as he did so effectively in his best-known novel, *The Catcher in the Rye* (1951). "A Perfect Day for Bananafish," especially on its metaphoric level, explores the same theme.

Seymour, whose name perhaps indicates that he sees more clearly than other people, has dubbed his wife "Miss Spiritual Tramp of 1948," and this designation, about which Muriel tells her mother, refers probably to Muriel's tendency always to do what is best at any give time or in any situation. She is a capable person, but she has no staunch set of values. She is malleable, and Seymour does not appreciate her malleability. Although Muriel waited for Seymour through the war and through his hospitalization, Seymour sees her as someone with whom he cannot communicate.

Seymour constantly does things to unnerve people and to make them notice him. He complains that people stare at his tattoo, even though he does not have a tattoo; he accuses an innocuous stranger of staring at his feet, even though she is not doing so; he asks Muriel's grandmother about her plans for dying; he puts a bullet through his head, in what is seemingly an unpremeditated act, to unnerve his wife and to make her notice him. The irony is that Muriel is sufficiently in control of her emotions that she will probably cope with Seymour's death just as she has coped with other problems in her life. Perhaps, then, Salinger's ultimate message is that futility pervades anything that sensitive people do to give themselves identities.

Seymour is comfortable in the presence of children. This is because he is essentially a child himself. He has not grown up; he cannot face the realities of life as Muriel can. Her strength and adaptability contribute to his weakness and inflexibility.

"A Perfect Day for Bananafish" is important in a number of ways. It is the initial story in the Glass family epic, which Salinger was to write about frequently in his stories and in both *Franny and Zooey* (1961) and *Raise High the Roofbeam, Carpenters and Seymour: An Introduction* (1963). It also was one of three Salinger stories that were accepted for publication in *The New Yorker* in 1948, an event that marked the beginning of a long, exclusive association that the author had with *The New Yorker.*

### Style and Technique

Salinger has a strong sense of the dramatic, and he often constructs his stories as though they were plays. In "A Perfect Day for Bananafish," one finds the elements of a three-act play, the third act of which has two scenes. Salinger appears to have an inherent understanding of dramatic technique, and he is able to integrate this into his writing of short stories.

"A Perfect Day for Bananafish" demonstrates how well Salinger uses specific detail in his work. The first section of the story is particularly strong in its use of such detail. Salinger turns Muriel's polishing of her fingernails into a carefully detailed and telling act that reveals her personality extremely well. The reader immediately sees in Muriel a woman in control. When the telephone rings, she does not have the immediate response that is common to most people in twentieth century society. She lets it ring until she has done what she has to do; then, with complete mastery of the situation, she answers the phone.

Muriel also controls quite convincingly the telephone conversation with her mother, who certainly is a woman of strong convictions and definite personality. Salinger is particularly deft in not allowing readers to see Muriel and Seymour in any sort of interaction. The only time they are together in the story, Muriel is asleep. By handling his materials in this way, Salinger leaves it to the reader to suppose what their times together must have been like.

Salinger's wit helps to build his readers' impressions of Muriel. He tells them that she does not drop everything to answer a telephone, that "she looked as if her phone had been ringing continually ever since she had reached puberty." Perhaps Salinger's greatest triumph in terms of technique is that he always evinces a respect for the intellectual capacity of his readers.

*R. Baird Shuman*

# PET FLY

*Author:* Walter Mosley (1952-    )
*Type of plot:* Character study
*Time of plot:* The 1990's
*Locale:* New York City
*First published:* 1999

> *Principal characters:*
> RUFUS COOMBS, an African American mail clerk
> MONA DONELLI, a white secretary
> LANA DONELLI, her twin
> ERNIE, his boss and mentor
> MR. DREW, who receives the harassment complaint
> MR. AVERILL, a vice president

*The Story*

"Pet Fly" is a first-person story told by African American Rufus Coombs, a recent college graduate who was relegated to the mailroom of Carter's Home Insurance despite applying for a professional-trainee position. It opens with his appreciation of the vivacious Mona Donelli, a flashy dresser with a gregarious attitude. Although he notices her on his first day on his new job, he works his mail route for three weeks before he decides to get to know her better.

Rufus has had generally friendly but not intimate relationships with his coworkers, and he mistakes Mona Donelli's friendliness as an invitation. After meeting a rather chilling reception when he tries to strike up a conversation with her, he asks Ernie, his immediate supervisor and sometime confidant, for answers. Ernie reveals that Mona's identical twin Lana works for the same company, which explains the mixed messages Rufus has received.

Vaguely stirred by his recollections of the two sisters, Rufus soon finds excuses to drop by Lana's third-floor mortgage department as often as possible. Trouble ensues when he good-naturedly comments on her attire and quickly buys her a succession of increasingly expensive presents, which he leaves on her desk. Too late, he discovers that his advances are unwanted. Without warning, he is summoned to Mr. Drew's office, where he is shown the pink sexual harassment slip that Lana had filed.

Rufus is a man who would not hurt a fly; in fact, he feeds and even talks to the fly he finds in his apartment. His sensitivity is also shown in less bizarre ways. He chose an eighth-floor apartment because it has a view of the river even though he could have had a cheaper room on a lower floor. He has good relationships with his mother and a former girlfriend, although the latter only infrequently returns his calls.

When Rufus is first called on the carpet by Mr. Drew, he is so stunned by the accusations that he cannot bring himself to refute the charges. Instead, he can only think of applying for another job, especially when Mr. Averill, the vice president in charge of nonprofessional employees, summons Rufus to his office. The scene that unfolds is either a shocking instance of the misogynistic ways in which men conspire to keep their corporate power or a test to determine if Rufus is the miscreant that the sexual harassment slip indicates.

In a climactic moment, Mr. Averill tries to balance the magna cum laude success Rufus enjoyed in college with the insensitivity evident on the pink harassment slip. Seeking a common bond, the vice president brags that he could have five or six of the women in the office. He argues that the women would not think of it as harassment because, unlike Rufus, he would be direct in his manner. Rufus does not dispute this claim and is rewarded for his silence with a promotion to professional trainee.

Returning to his apartment, Rufus finds the fly has died. Placing it in one of the unused crack vials he found on his way home from work, he buries it under the expensive bonsai tree he had purchased but not had time to deliver to Lana. When he next gets in touch with his mother, she thinks the miniature tree is something he bought for himself and that a real bed might be his next purchase.

*Themes and Meanings*

Ernie provides Rufus with his closest human relationship at work. They talk for hours at a stretch, and it is Ernie's influence in the company that finally saves the young man's career. From the older African American man, Rufus learns such valuable lessons as the importance of maintaining good relationships with one's coworkers and, especially, one's immediate superior. From the near calamity with Lana, he has, it is hoped, learned the importance of maintaining decorum at the office and being sensitive to the discomfort his actions may cause coworkers.

The narrator is so isolated in the city full of strangers that his fixation on the flies he sees at work and at home is a rather pathetic stopgap effort. His willingness to form bonds with a fly may indicate his suitability for a satisfying relationship with his own species; he is, after all, a man who likes animals.

On another level, the story demonstrates how the latent racism of late twentieth century American society can foster misunderstandings in the workplace. The representatives of both races depicted in the story tend to misinterpret each other according to culturally determined paradigms. The greatest irony of the story is that Rufus suspects that his problems with Lana stem from racial discrimination; it turns out that she cannot guess his race and is even dating an African American. Similarly, Ernie, as a member of the older generation, does not really trust his white employers, but ultimately it is their trust in Ernie's judgment that saves Rufus.

*Style and Technique*

In keeping with its narrator's moral simplicity, "Pet Fly" is a conventionally plotted, straightforward narrative. Things happen in cause-and-effect pattern, and the chronology of the piece is realistically presented and preserved. Like John Updike, Walter Mosley has chosen an environment and situation with which most modern urban readers can identify. The method is so subtle that "Pet Fly" may seem like a sexual harassment prevention scenario such as those developed for job training purposes. There is more to the story than that, however, and focusing on the ways in which Mosley has made Rufus a sympathetic character should help the reader realize the dramatic potential of several recent developments in American culture.

Because of his choice of first-person point of view, Mosley cannot realistically render the thoughts of any character except his narrator. This lends some delightful ambiguity to the story, as is evident in the scene in which Rufus is promoted. Either Rufus's silence suggests that he shares Mr. Averill's opinion of women or it implies that he is not an insensitive lout who is guilty of harassment. Somehow, Mr. Averill finds it to be the proper response and dismisses the accusations. He could be acting out of sympathetic misogyny or because he understands that Rufus is essentially incapable of the brutish behavior the harassment charge suggests, but his motivation is lost behind the impenetrable barriers of age and race that separate the boss from the narrator.

Another advantage of the author's choice of first-person point of view is that the reader is more likely to accept some of the narrator's rather strange traits, like his willingness to treat flies as though they are suitable companions. The apparent honesty of this admission underscores his protestations of complete innocence in regard to the harassment charge. The reader tends to side with his interpretation of the events because he is so seemingly open in his revelations about his houseguest, the fly.

The author takes great pains to portray the relative paucity of objects in Rufus's apartment, yet his narrator is acutely aware of the social significance of Mr. Averill's having more office space than Mr. Drew as an indication of the former's greater corporate power. The reader is more likely to side with Rufus as an obvious underdog because of his lack of possessions; they are so few that he can easily inventory them. The meticulous care with which he similarly itemizes a succession of fast-food dinners further establishes his lower- or middle-class background. His evident pleasure when recalling brand names and specific food orders such as a Beef Burrito Supreme from Taco Bell suggests the unsophisticated tastes of someone who is from a relatively disadvantaged background.

The fly is an important symbol in the story; perhaps it represents a persistent nuisance like that experienced in some forms of sexual harassment. Its interment beneath the miniature crab apple tree might suggest that Rufus will similarly bury his feelings for Lana, which have been innocuous but are now completely behind him in any case.

The story also challenges the preconceptions of white America about the urban problems of drugs and crime. When Rufus thinks of crime, it is only as a potential victim; he fears he would have been robbed if he had chosen an apartment on a lower floor. His motives for picking up unused crack vials off the street are less clear, but his use of a crack vial as a coffin for the fly suggests that they were benign. At the end of the story, his mother's suggestion that he buy a bed indicates that his lack of furniture is caused by his poverty and not drug abuse or general neglect.

*Randall Huff*

# PET MILK

*Author:* Stuart Dybek (1942-    )
*Type of plot:* Psychological
*Time of plot:* The mid-twentieth century
*Locale:* Chicago
*First published:* 1981

> *Principal characters:*
> THE NARRATOR, a young man living in Chicago
> KATE, his girlfriend

## The Story

"Pet Milk" is told from the perspective of a young man as he recalls his youth in an ethnic neighborhood in Chicago and the course of his relationship with his girlfriend in the year after they graduated from college. The story begins with the narrator musing in midwinter about the patterns made by the addition of Pet evaporated milk to a cup of coffee. The swirls of the mixture lead through a series of associations to the thought that evaporated milk is an emblem of an earlier time in his life when a first-generation family had to find an adequate substitute—Pet milk for fresh cream—to compensate for the limits imposed by their economic condition.

Images from his grandmother's home establish something of the ethos of an urban community in which "all the incompatible states of Europe were pressed together" and then lead toward a more recent time when the swirl in a liqueur glass in a Czech restaurant connects the past to the recent present when the narrator and his girlfriend, Kate, have begun to spend time together for drinks after work. The restaurant has been designed to give the residents of the neighborhood a touch of their origins in Europe, and an older waiter's continental charm encourages the romantic aura that is gradually enveloping the young couple.

The story shifts at this point to the immediate present on the narrator's twenty-second birthday, a warm spring day in May. To celebrate, he orders champagne and oysters, a conspicuously upscale and flamboyant choice in contrast to the standard fare—sausage and potatoes—on the menu at the Pilsen. The spirit of the occasion arouses the emotions of the couple, and instead of ordering dinner, they leave the premises to find a suitable location for a more intensely intimate evening. Because the narrator shares an apartment and Kate lives in a suburb north of the city, they head toward a local park, but when they discover that the gate is locked, they board the last express train to Evanston. There are no seats available, and the couple, finding the conductor's compartment empty, enter the small enclosure and shut the door.

As the train rushes through the city, the couple embrace, their bodies moving in a rhythm that is accentuated by the motion of the train. An aura of eros envelops them, and the powerful emotional reaction of the narrator is conveyed through a series of familiar landmarks that he recognizes from many previous rides along this track. Past experience and a vision of a possible future blend in a moment of heightened awareness.

   In the aftermath of the passionate encounter, the narrator begins to notice the faces of passengers on the platform as the express train slows down while passing through local stations. His senses sharpened by his involvement with Kate, he has a moment of brief and temporary insight about the character of the people he sees. In particular, his attention is caught by a sixteen-year-old high school boy, who grins when he sees the couple and starts to wave at them. The narrator falls into a comfortable reverie in which all the images of the ride blend and blur into a mood of lassitude, but the image of "that arrested wave" stays with him. It induces a reflective recapitulation of his life through the past half-dozen years, and as the story concludes, the narrator remembers how he stood on the station in similar fashion, his life and future open but uncertain, eager for some sign of life's bounty. His last thought is that he would "have loved seeing someone like us streaming by."

*Themes and Meanings*

   Stuart Dybek's story joins the theme of assimilation into a cultural mainstream with the traditional narrative of a young man passing through adolescence toward the maturity of adulthood. The protagonist is a third-generation member of a family that immigrated to the United States from Europe, quite possibly the Czech Republic, since his favorite restaurant is called the Pilsen after the famous Czechoslovakian source of lager. In the first section of the story, Dybek establishes the ambience of an ethnic neighborhood within the vast city of Chicago, mentioning that his grandmother would search for the language of the Old World on the radio and that she would elegantly ask his young friends, "Do you take cream and sugar?," an echo of a European custom. Although his recollections are pleasant, there is also an implication that the entire family shared the same dwelling when he was growing up, an indication of the difficulties of finding private, personal space.

   From a social foundation in a community that has re-created aspects of its European heritage in the United States, the narrator moves toward young manhood as a part of a process that blends Old World customs with the opportunities afforded by an open, less-structured society. His developing relationship with Kate is energized by the options that they have. After working to pay for college tuition in mundane labor, they are both astonished and delighted to "find real jobs." Her background is not defined, but her thoughts about graduate school in Europe and his about joining the Peace Corps suggest their idealism as well as their international orientation. It is apparent that this is the first serious relationship either of them has experienced, and the sense of mutual awakening enhances their obvious attraction for each other. Although the roots of their relationship reach back toward their families' origins, the course it follows is toward an America in the 1960's that permitted new patterns of behavior and styles of self-definition previously unavailable.

   This path is metaphorically paralleled by the train they take in an attempt to reach the suburb beyond the inner city, a place in which obvious ethnicity is blurred by the mixture of people whose increasing mobility is an indication of choice beyond a prescribed cultural identity. The fact that they are compelled to create an intimate personal space within a cramped compartment, surrounded by an anonymous public, underscores the difficulty of marking out their own territory, as well as its necessity. The narrator's recital of familiar landmarks along the route from "a lifetime of rides"—Wrigley Field, billboards, an old cemetery—combined with the vivid sensations he feels, describes the flux that is forming the psyche of the evolving adult. Dybek's intention is to produce a portrait of a thoughtful, perceptive person, keenly attuned to his environment and able to find language that demonstrates his sensitivity and intelligence. The title of the collection in which "Pet Milk" appeared, *The Coast of Chicago* (1990), suggests the contours of a new continent in which Dybek's protagonist can explore both psychic and geographical terrain. The direction of his journey is toward a place in which what has taken place in his life can be assimilated and perhaps transcended. Writing after the disappointments of the previous two decades were manifest, Dybek is recalling an era when the world seemed fresh and alive with promise and possibility.

*Style and Technique*

Dybek uses "Pet Milk"—canned, evaporated milk, often used in place of fresh cream—as a defining and controlling symbol in the story. What captures his attention is the way in which "Pet milk swirls in the coffee," creating a visual symbol that connects the separate sections of the narrator's life. "Today I've been drinking instant coffee," the story begins, as Dybek constructs a frame that surrounds the narrative action, containing the immediate present as well as an earlier time when his grandmother used Pet milk as a means of maintaining gentility despite economic limitations.

The symbolic swirl—a figure for the flux of the narrator's life and an emblem of an aesthetic sensibility that finds patterns of meaning in action—appears next in a liqueur glass when the narrator is on a date. Here, it is described as "smoke in repeated explosions," operating as a visual equivalent for the stirring of emotion. As his friendship with Kate develops, the narrator playfully interferes with the waiter preparing the liqueur, suggesting that he is no longer entirely a spectator, but the waiter is still concerned that the narrator is too contemplative concerning the swirl and that he might enter more fully into an active role.

This leads toward the extended metaphor that operates in the second part of the story. The subway track to the outer suburbs is used as a version of the road of life, a traditional literary device that has allegorical overtones, and in this case, the ride itself is used as a vehicle for presenting the acceleration of sensation that the narrator undergoes. The penultimate paragraph of the story is written as a lyric evocation of physical arousal, and the relaxation of tension that follows coincides with the train "braking a little from express speed." Then, in the last lines of the story, the narrator returns to the past, seeing in the boy on the platform a replica of his own youth, the smoke from his cigarette a lingering, brief reference to the swirl that initiated the narrative.

*Leon Lewis*

# PETER RUGG, THE MISSING MAN

*Author:* William Austin (1778-1841)
*Type of plot:* Fantasy
*Time of plot:* The 1820's
*Locale:* The northeastern United States
*First published:* 1824, 1827

>   *Principal characters:*
>     JONATHAN DUNWELL, a New Yorker who travels a great deal on
>       business
>     PETER RUGG, a man cursed to wander the roads around Boston
>     JENNY RUGG, Peter's daughter and hapless traveling companion

*The Story*

The first part of the story takes the form of a letter in which Jonathan Dunwell explains how, in 1820, he first encountered a man and a child mounted on a "chair" (the chassis of a carriage without the protective shell it was built to carry) pulled by a black horse. The mysterious stranger, who seemed to be pursued by a relentless storm cloud, impatiently asked the way to Boston and was sorely distressed to find that he was heading he wrong way. Dunwell then relates how the driver of the coach on which he was traveling told him that the stranger had been wandering the roads for longer than he could remember, always in a desperate hurry, always asking the same question, and always confused by the answers he received.

Dunwell goes on to explain that on making further inquiries in Boston he was told that one Peter Rugg of Middle Street was on his way home from Concord one night in 1770, on a chair pulled by a bay horse, when he was overtaken by a violent storm. Although a friend living in Menotomy pleaded with him to stay the night, Rugg insisted on continuing his return journey, swearing a terrible (but unspecified) oath that he would reach home that night or never.

In the second part of the story, which was added three years later, Dunwell tells of another meeting with Peter Rugg in Richmond, Virginia, in 1825, when Rugg's fearsome horse—which some observers take for an ox, and whose hoofprints are cloven-footed—outgalloped two noted racehorses. He relays accounts of several other reported meetings, which have informed him that Rugg's wanderings are now ranging far and wide through Maryland, Virginia, New York, and Delaware as well as Connecticut. Soon afterward, Dunwell relates, he had a chance to accompany the exceedingly confused wanderer on a ride through New York City—a city in which Rugg could hardly believe, any more than he could believe in the "United States."

Eventually, Dunwell explains, he found himself in attendance at an auction of Rugg's long-derelict property in Middle Street. During this auction, Rugg finally reached his destination, after an absence of some fifty-five years—but he had not come home, because his home no longer existed; the storm had ceased to bother him and his transfigured mount had ceased to draw him astray, but—as a mysterious voice from the crowd took the trouble to spell out—he had lost everything he once possessed and the New World had no place for him.

*Themes and Meanings*

Like Washington Irving's famous tales of "Rip van Winkle" and "The Legend of Sleepy Hollow," both of which were issued in *The Sketch Book of Geoffrey Crayon, Gent.* (1819-1820) not long before the first appearance of William Austin's work, the tale of Peter Rugg is an Americanization of a European legend. Its model is the tale of the Flying Dutchman, the spectral ship whose ill-tempered captain swore an oath that he would round the Cape of Good Hope in spite of a raging storm and was cursed to keep trying—without ever succeeding—forever.

Rugg, like the main characters in Irving's two classic stories, is a Dutchman by extraction, but he is not such a comical figure as Rip van Winkle or Ichabod Crane, and the sinister aspects of his fate are not so lightly treated. The period of his exile is a crucial epoch in American history, and his alienation from the course of events is all the greater for his ignorance of the War of Independence and the rapid development of the United States. Initially confined to the immediate environs of Boston, his mistaken roads gradually take him farther and farther afield, into a nation that is growing and flourishing while he remains becalmed in his personal pre-Revolutionary backwater. Whereas the Flying Dutchman of old represented merely the folly of swearing reckless oaths, Peter Rugg represents something much more complex and profound: the folly of making haste to remain the same and the hopelessness of an impatient failure to go with the historical flow. His poor wife hardly figures in the story at all; Rugg is a "missing man" because of what he misses rather than because he is missed.

The seemingly neglected figure in Peter Rugg's story is that of his daughter Jenny, who never uttered any kind of oath but has had to endure her father's miserable, bedeviled, and storm-tossed fate regardless, wretchedly stuck at ten years of age for more than half a century. This may seem unjust, especially as Jenny's plight remains conspicuously unconsidered within the story—but the mysterious voice from the crowd that delivers the final verdict on Peter Rugg when the wanderer bemoans the loss of his home speaks only to him when it says that he can never have another. Jenny, now that she has rejoined the stream of time, still has a future; precisely because she is a child, she is not bound to the legacy of her forefathers. She still has time enough, and certainly has motive enough, to become an American.

*Style and Technique*

Austin's story uses a documentary format, distancing the reader from the events by presenting them in a summary form, carefully rearranged by an intermediary. This method of literary presentation was very common in the early nineteenth century, when tellers of tales—especially tall tales—found it a useful means of advertising the "authenticity" of their narrations and bidding for an extra measure of plausibility. Because modern readers have become much more accustomed to the impostures of fiction and much more sympathetic to literary invention, the documentary method has fallen into disuse, but it has several virtues that modern storytelling methods sometimes strive in vain to reproduce. Austin's tale has a wonderful economy, covering an enormous reach of narrative ground at a very rapid pace, with admirable efficiency.

The cost of this kind of economy is a lack of involvement with the characters, but Peter Rugg's plight is the kind of phenomenon that is best observed at a contemplative distance, with calculated objectivity. He is a mystery and a symbol as well as a pitiable creature; it is perhaps as well that the reader cannot get very close to him. Although the narrative technique used in the tale has fallen out of fashion, it is certainly arguable that individuals such as Peter Rugg are most usefully observed by a viewpoint character whose attitude is calmly detached, scrupulously clinical, and determinedly analytical.

The final speech by the anonymous voice in the crowd equips the story with a explicit moral, of a sort that has fallen even further out of fashion than the documentary method of representation, but it is offered with polite discretion. The dispassionate way in which the "facts" have been previously set out will not let this moral stand as a summary, let alone a dismissal of the complex issues raised by the narrative. The elements of the story have been laid before the reader, in a succinct and orderly manner, and the reader's own judgment of what has happened is bound to take the whole pattern into account, far outreaching the narrow and formal moral.

The vocabulary of a story written nearly two hundred years ago is bound to seem archaic to a modern reader, especially when its subject matter spans fifty years of its own history, but Dunwell's reportage makes every attempt to be frank and straightforward—as surely befits an item of authentic Americana. Austin's tale is an obvious adaptation of a European legend, but that serves to make it more authentic as an item of Americana, not less, because that kind of adaptation is the heart of America's historical project. The seeding, germination, and flowering of the United States of America has, in essence, been a gradual adaptation of the descendants first of displaced Europeans (and later of others) to a new way of life and sense of purpose, which embodies a new frankness, a new straightforwardness, and a new determination to make history at a faster pace than it was ever made before. The devil-led Peter Rugg, the missing man, emphasizes by his plaintive absence everything wonderful that happened in the progressive city of Boston while he was gone.

*Brian Stableford*

# PETRIFIED MAN

*Author:* Eudora Welty (1909-2001)
*Type of plot:* Realism
*Time of plot:* The late 1930's
*Locale:* A small southern town
*First published:* 1939

> *Principal characters:*
> LEOTA, a hairdresser
> FRED, her husband
> MRS. FLETCHER, her customer
> MR. AND MRS. PIKE, a couple who rent a room from Leota and
> Fred
> MR. PETRIE, the petrified man at the local freak show
> BILLY BOY, the Pikes' son

*The Story*

The story opens abruptly in a beauty parlor with the animated conversation be-tween Leota and her shampoo-and-set customer, Mrs. Fletcher. Amid a number of un-related subjects, Leota mentions a Mrs. Pike in passing, piquing Mrs. Fletcher's curi-osity. The Pikes, Leota explains, are a couple renting a room from her and her husband, Fred. The conversation wanders from topic to topic, until Leota blurts out that someone has seen Mrs. Fletcher on the street and discerned that she is pregnant. This galls Mrs. Fletcher, and she demands to know who reported this so she can plot her social revenge. Their conversation is then interrupted by a child's voice, who asks, "Why? What're you gonna do to her?"

The voice belongs to Billy Boy, Mrs. Pike's precocious son, who stays with Leota in the beauty parlor because he has been asked to leave the millinery store where his mother works. Leota finally reveals that it was the mysterious Mrs. Pike who identi-fied Mrs. Fletcher's condition and launches into a series of non sequiturs about Mrs. Pike's good qualities. In the midst of her monologue, Leota mentions that she and Mrs. Pike attended the traveling freak show that came to town.

Among the freaks they encountered were a set of Siamese twins in a bottle, a tribe of Pygmies, and the petrified man, who digests his food and "before you can say 'Jack Robinson,' it's stone—pure stone." As the conversation reaches its end, Leota reports their visit to a fortune-teller, Lady Evangeline, who proclaimed that Mr. Pike was faithful to Mrs. Pike and predicted that he would soon come into money. The scene ends with Mrs. Fletcher's disparaging remark about Mrs. Pike's looks.

A week later, Mrs. Fletcher returns for her appointment and Leota begins another gossipy conversation that winds its way through such topics as Mrs. Fletcher's shape, a Mrs. Montjoy's prematurely gray husband, and, finally, back to Mrs. Pike. "Well!

How's Mrs. Pike . . . who spreads it around town that perfect strangers are pregnant?" Mrs. Fletcher demands. Leota is clearly perturbed by the topic and gradually reveals the happenings of the previous week.

Mr. and Mrs. Pike, it seems, had read one of Leota's police magazines and recognized an old acquaintance, a Mr. Petrie, as a man wanted for the rape of four women in California. Mr. Petrie turned out to be the petrified man at the freak show, worth a five-hundred-dollar reward. Leota reports that Mr. Pike at first wanted to let Mr. Petrie go, because he had once lent Mr. Pike money, but Mrs. Pike put her foot down and insisted that they turn him in to the police. Leota is distraught that she herself was not lucky enough to identify the wanted man, claiming that "that ole petrified man sure did leave me with a funny feelin'."

The story ends with Leota taking out her frustrations on the Pikes' Billy Boy, spanking him for his impolite manner. Billy Boy has the last word, stomping through the group of "wild-haired ladies," shouting, "If you're so smart, why ain't you rich?"

*Themes and Meanings*

Critics often describe this story as a study of the vulgarity or grotesquerie of modern life, and certainly Eudora Welty uses the beauty parlor and the freak show here as microcosms of small-town America. Leota, a stereotypical gossiping beautician, goads her clientele into revealing their vanities and their pettiness. In the case of Mrs. Fletcher, it embarrasses her that a stranger could detect that she is pregnant. Leota emerges as a self-aggrandizing, basically cynical person whose care for her customers extends only so far as it benefits her.

Mr. Petrie, the convicted rapist who has been masquerading at the freak show, is not the only "petrified man" in Welty's story. Each male character, except for Billy Boy, is in his own way a hardened or stale version of manhood, dominated in an unhealthy way by the woman in his life. In the story's final scene, Welty leaves it to the bratty Billy Boy to have the final word, a stinging rhetorical question about human motive. He is the only character in the story capable of speaking without pretension or posture, and he clarifies the story's theme. Basic human dignity easily gives way to ugly character assassination when the self is placed at the center of relationships. Welty seems to be making the point that no one in the story, females included, can rise above his or her shortsighted and selfish ambitions.

The real freak show is located not in a traveling sideshow but in the very beauty parlor where Leota holds forth, creating disguises and false identities for the women who seek her magic. Thus, Welty strips away the veneer of respectability that distinguishes Leota and Mrs. Fletcher from Mr. Petrie.

*Style and Technique*

"Petrified Man" basically consists of two sets of conversations between Leota and Mrs. Fletcher; the story's "action" takes place wholly in these conversations. In small-town America, much of what constitutes "real life" consists of the images created by conversationalists such as Leota and Mrs. Fletcher, and the dialogue between these two characters is thus a perfect device for capturing the banality and pretentiousness of much human encounter.

Welty was a master at depicting in fine detail the life of the small southern town, and "Petrified Man" bears the verisimilitude that has earned for her this reputation. She effectively employs the visual, tactile, and olfactory images that place the reader in the beauty parlor with Leota and company. Though the reader never directly confronts the Pikes, Leota's husband Fred, or Mr. Petrie, Leota's vivid descriptions serve well enough as surrogates. Despite her own posturing, Leota's dialogue cannot help but reveal the truth about herself and others, and this is a tribute to Welty's skillful use of the style and substance of the small-town southern experience in the story's extended conversations.

*Bruce L. Edwards, Jr.*

# A PIECE OF NEWS

*Author:* Eudora Welty (1909-2001)
*Type of plot:* Psychological
*Time of plot:* The 1930's
*Locale:* Southern United States
*First published:* 1937

> *Principal characters:*
> RUBY FISHER, a barely literate country woman
> CLYDE FISHER, her husband, a still operator

*The Story*

Ruby, a southern woman, has come in from the rain and is drying herself off and talking to herself. The scene is a primitive and remote cabin, perhaps in the author's native Mississippi. That she talks to herself so easily indicates that she is used to being alone. She cries out in astonishment that the sample of coffee on the table is wrapped in newspaper, and the narrator relates that "She must have been lonesome and slow all her life, the way things would take her by surprise."

Ruby suffers from cabin fever, a depression resulting from a nearly total isolation from the world, a condition often afflicting the rural poor in a time when modern transportation and communication did not extend to them. Ruby seldom sees anyone other than her husband, and she has no radio or telephone to fill the void. With little stimulation from the outside, the newspaper becomes a delightful diversion. She spreads it out before the fire and is astonished by so many words, and at best she can only trace out a few of them. Suddenly her own name leaps out from the page: Ruby Fisher! With difficulty she reads the short and utterly ambiguous announcement: "Mrs. Ruby Fisher had the misfortune to be shot in the leg by her husband this week."

Ruby does not realize that this is merely a coincidence of names. In her ignorance and superstition, she is trapped in a primitive confusion between a symbol and what that symbol represents, just as primitive people sometimes believe that the spirit of a person is contained in the name. Her name on the page has a powerful magic far greater than her own feeble authority. Her first reaction is fear and anger. How could her husband Clyde do such a thing to her? She calls to him, but Clyde is at the whiskey still in the woods, waiting out the thunderstorm.

Slowly she starts to understand what has happened. In talking to herself, she concludes that Clyde, however he may have mistreated her, has never shot her in the leg. She reflects on the times she has gone out to the road to stop cars and to lure the drivers to the cotton gin shed. Even when Clyde had found out about it, he did no more than slap her.

Ruby's mind runs imaginatively to wild melodrama. What if Clyde did shoot her, not just in the leg, but in the heart? She projects her own death scene, in which she lies beautiful, desirable, and dead. At her death, Clyde will feel a terrible repentance. He will have to buy her a dress to bury her in, and he will appreciate her as he looks on her grave.

As Ruby ruminates, Clyde suddenly appears in the room, dripping from the heavy rain. Crude and insensitive, he gruffly asks what is for supper and pokes her with the butt of his gun. Ruby goes about preparing his meal, but this time she has the secret of the newspaper within her as she moves about the room. She is aware of his watching her and feels seductive, making many unnecessary movements back and forth. Clyde evidently catches something of her mood, because he promptly accuses her of going hitchhiking again. She nervously spills coffee on his hand, and he threatens to beat her.

After Clyde finishes eating, Ruby expectantly shows him the newspaper. At first, he is flushed with anger and denial; it is a lie that he ever did such a thing. The truth of the circumstances comes to him more quickly than it did to his wife. They look at each other, and "some possibility stood timidly like a stranger between them and made them hang their heads." He throws the newspaper into the fire and points out to her that it was a Tennessee newspaper and referred to another Ruby Fisher. He spanks her good-humoredly across the backside. "My name is Ruby Fisher!" she protests. A spark of recognition passes between them. As she looks out the window, the storm rolls away like a wagon crossing a bridge.

## Themes and Meanings

At first reading, it may seem that nothing happens in this story, that it is plotless, perhaps even pointless. A closer reading reveals it to be a warm, rich, and subtle portrayal of character. As improbable as it may seem at first, this is a story about seduction—about a wife, no longer young, who accidentally receives a means of feeling her own importance and of attracting the attention of her husband. Ruby lives a brutalized life, isolated and outside the law. She is no more than an object to Clyde in his own deprived life. In her desperate bid for attention, she picks up men on the highway, a behavior that compels Clyde at least to notice her existence. Although no authorial attention is focused on it, it seems significant that Ruby has no children, no role to play except to provide meals for her husband. She longs for his acceptance, or at least acceptance by someone.

The coincidental use of Ruby's name in the newspaper serves to make Ruby more interesting to herself and, consequently, more interesting to Clyde. Something has happened to her in the world (although it is merely accidental) that gives her something different to talk about. The little news article has a significance to Clyde as well. It appears to accuse him of an act that he did not do, but that he might well be capable of doing. Clyde savors the sadistic possibility of catching her misbehaving ("Some day I'm goin' to smack the livin' devil outa you"), but the episode compels him to acknowledge his mistreatment of her. They face each other with a new recognition on both sides. In crying out, "It was Ruby Fisher! . . . My name is Ruby Fisher!" she demands his recognition. Clyde playfully slaps her on the backside, acknowledging her demand. It has become a game between them. To these emotionally impoverished people, this apparently trivial awareness represents an important change in their lives.

To some extent, the author plays off against stereotypes of the gun-toting, moonshining southern hillbilly of the movies and popular fiction. This social group already had been given a broadly comic send-up by the American writer and dramatist Erskine Caldwell and had been granted a profound ironic dignity by William Faulkner. Eudora Welty also gives these people a considerable sympathy and dignity. No matter how ignorant and foolish Ruby and Clyde may appear, their struggle to understand themselves is universal and thoroughly human.

*Style and Technique*

The story's point of view is entirely Ruby's, centering on her partial discovery of what is wrong in her life. Although sensitive, Ruby is inarticulate, forcing the narrator to step in with a number of direct statements to let the reader know what is going on. Clearly, the narrator has a power of generalization denied to Ruby: "She stood in front of the cabin fireplace, her legs wide apart, bending over, shaking her wet yellow hair crossly, like a cat reproaching itself for not knowing better." The story, however, provides images that have a strong relationship to Ruby's psychological stages. One image used throughout is the thunderstorm, an often overused device that signifies emotional stress, although it is unobtrusive here. It serves in the story to isolate Ruby even more from her husband, and as an appropriate background for the magic moment of discovering her name in the newspaper.

Also significant is the connection between this discovery and her desire for pregnancy. Having spread out the newspaper, "she watched it, as if it were unpredictable, like a young girl watching a baby." While she is preparing Clyde's dinner, "There was some way she began to move her arms that was mysteriously sweet and yet abrupt and tentative, a delicate and vulnerable manner, as though her breasts gave her pain." The episode creates a sensual arousal in Ruby, which is now directed toward her husband.

*Bruce Olsen*

# A PIECE OF STEAK

*Author:* Jack London (1876-1916)
*Type of plot:* Social realism
*Time of plot:* The early 1900's
*Locale:* Sydney, Australia
*First published:* 1911

*Principal characters:*

TOM KING, an aging prizefighter who desperately needs a win in order to feed his wife and two children

HIS WIFE, a working-class woman who does not know what the family will do if Tom loses

SANDEL, a young New Zealand fighter whose future in Australia depends on his fight against Tom King

*The Story*

Tom King is a big brute of a man who looks every inch the champion prizefighter he was twenty years ago. Times are harder now. He seldom gets a good match and even has trouble finding work on the docks. As the story opens, Tom is finishing a meager meal of flour gravy and bread. He had been craving a piece of steak since the morning, and his poor wife had tried to get meat from the local butchers, but they refused her credit. She purchased the bread with their last few shillings and borrowed the flour from a neighbor. There is no food in the house. She eats nothing herself and has sent their two children to bed without supper. She knows that Tom needs all the nourishment he can get. In less than two hours, he will be fighting a younger man from New Zealand for a thirty-pound purse. She tells Tom that he must win, and Tom reassures her, determined "to get meat for his mate and cubs," or else his family will go hungry.

Without money for a cab, Tom walks the two miles to the arena and wonders how many more fights he has in him. Boxing is really all he knows how to do, and he knows that the young fighters sooner or later beat down the older ones. How much longer does he have? Tom remembers his first fight against an "old un." Stowsher Bill was his name, and after Tom had beaten him, the older boxer sat weeping in the dressing room. He had laughed at the misfortune of the old fighter then, but youth is now his nemesis. It is his turn to face the superior speed and stamina of someone almost twenty years younger. Had he known years ago that this would be happening to him, would he have stayed in boxing? No one explained that to him, but had he been told, he doubts that he would have listened. Boxing was too much fun, and it was easy then.

Tom knows that youth must be served. He is doubly concerned because he has not been able to train properly or maintain a decent diet. Drawing on considerable experience and skill, he hopes to conserve his own strength and wear down his muscular young opponent, Sandel. As expected, Sandel, whose career depends on beating Tom, immediately attacks with a flurry of blows. Seldom throwing a punch, Tom fights defensively, moving slowly but ducking expertly and allowing few of the blows to hit home. In the third round, Sandel momentarily drops his guard, and Tom lands home a staggering right hook that drops the younger man to his knees, but he is able to recover. By round seven, Tom is utilizing every trick he knows to conserve his strength. He clinches frequently and breaks slowly, forcing Sandel to support his weight. He seldom leaves his side of the ring and makes sure to be near his corner when the round is over so he can simply step back into his chair. However, on and on comes Sandel.

In the tenth round, Tom lands two bone-crushing right uppercuts, knocking Sandel off his feet and to the floor. Tom moves in with other smashing blows, and a knockout by the veteran fighter appears likely. The bell sounds, however, and between rounds, Sandel regains his strength and composure. The fight becomes grueling in the eleventh round. Still hungry and inspired by thoughts of a piece of steak, Tom musters all of his strength and delivers yet another punishing series of punches to Sandel. The young boxer falls back, and Tom staggers after him, his legs giving way and his stamina already gone. Sandel suddenly shoots back, pushing aside the weak and futile blows of his spent opponent. Another punch, then another, and finally the one that sends Tom through the black veil of unconsciousness.

Tom bears Sandel no ill will for knocking him out. He had done so to older fighters; his turn simply has come. The knot in his stomach reminds him of his abiding hunger, and Tom is certain that a piece of steak would have given him the strength to put Sandel away. After dressing, he walks toward home alone, thinking about what has just transpired. He decides against having a drink at the neighborhood saloon, and moves on, thinking more deeply about the present and what the future holds. His wife will be waiting, but how can he tell her that he has lost? He is hungry and broke, and it will be a week before his aching hands can do even dock work. Sitting on a street bench, he begins to sob, and now understands why Stowsher Bill had broken down and cried so long ago.

*Themes and Meanings*

Dominating this story are two influences that shaped much of Jack London's writing: Social Darwinism and sympathy for the working classes. Tom King personifies the concept of survival of the fittest. His profession, prizefighting, is based on the demonstration of one man's strength, stamina, and cunning over another's. In his younger days, the system of which he is so much a part worked well for Tom. He was a champion and had little sympathy for those left crying in the dressing room. However, despite his still fearsome physique, Tom is growing old, and his turn for crying is at hand. It is the law of the jungle.

His profession might be violent, but Tom himself is a very sympathetic character. Fighting is a way of life he has come to love. He is also a father and husband who grieves for his family. His devotion to his family is clear. Tom knows his limitations, and one must wonder if he would have risked the fight against the younger Sandel were it not for the dire straits of the family. Skilled at nothing except fighting, Tom is a man trapped by circumstances, though he entered prizefighting voluntarily and knows he must live with that choice. He does not indulge in self-pity, but the realization that he has failed his family is heartbreaking, and so he cries.

There is a grim determinism in this story that London would apply to the poor generally. London himself grew up in a working-class neighborhood and knew the odds against escaping the poverty of his childhood. However, he did it, and one can see in the will and determination of the aging Tom King the latent power of the proletariat. It is too late for Tom; the system of prizefighting that nurtured him has brought him low and threatens ruin to his family. The political purpose of the story is relatively unobtrusive, carefully subordinated to the character of Tom King and his struggle to survive.

### Style and Technique

London was a literary craftsperson who mastered the short-story form. "A Piece of Steak" demonstrates several elements of his mature style. London understood the advantages of the flexible third-person narrator and utilized it with consummate skill and grace. "Let the reader learn," he once advised a young writer, "through the minds of the men themselves, let the reader look at the question through their eyes." Hence, the reader is immediately and intimately drawn into Tom King's thoughts and feelings. Although unattractive in so many ways, Tom King becomes a tragically sympathetic character.

This is a wonderfully controlled story that does not waste a single word. It moves forward on two fascinating levels: One is the objective reality of the fight itself, its importance to the two fighters, and its graphic brutality. The other is psychological, for Tom gradually realizes that he is finished as a boxer and has nowhere else to go. His ruminations also set the stage for and complement the detailed descriptions of the fight sequence. The story itself is epitomized by its title. That piece of steak is an integrating symbol that brings together several themes and adds to the remarkable internal consistency of the story. London thus captures the essence of Tom King, both as an individual and as an archetypal figure.

*Ronald W. Howard*

# THE PIECE OF STRING

*Author:* Guy de Maupassant (1850-1893)
*Type of plot:* Social realism
*Time of plot:* The 1880's
*Locale:* Goderville in Normandy, France
*First published:* "La Ficelle," 1883 (English translation, 1903)

*Principal characters:*
MAITRE HAUCHECORNE, the protagonist, an old Norman peasant
M. MALANDAIN, the harness maker and an enemy of
Hauchecorne
THE MAYOR OF GODERVILLE, a pompous man

*The Story*

Set in a little Norman village, "The Piece of String" concerns several months in the life of Maitre Hauchecorne, an old peasant. On an autumn market-day in Goderville, Hauchecorne is about to enter the square when he sees a piece of string on the ground and, being of the saving kind, retrieves it. As he does so, he becomes aware that an enemy of his, M. Malandain, the local harness maker, is watching. Ashamed to be seen picking up a remnant of string, the protagonist furtively hides it in his clothing and then pretends to be looking for something of value on the ground. With his head bent over in his intent search, he moves on toward the market.

A few hours later, Hauchecorne is having his noon meal at the local tavern, Jordain's, which is filled with local peasants, their gossipy chatter, and the powerful odor of food cooking. Twice the meal and the chatter are interrupted: first, by the voice of the town crier, who gravely announces the loss by M. Houlbreque of a pocketbook containing five hundred francs; second, by the appearance of the chief of gendarmes, who summons Hauchecorne to see the mayor on village business.

Leaving his meal, the protagonist hurries to the mayor's office, where he is unofficially confronted with the charge of having found Houlbreque's pocketbook and of keeping it. The sole witness to the incident is Malandain, says the mayor. Hauchecorne sputters in rage at the accusation coming from his enemy. His defense—one that he shouts over and over—is that no one could seriously mistake a pocketbook for a piece of string. Those present do not believe him, and they say so, which enrages Hauchecorne even more. Malandain appears, and his reiterating of the charge against the protagonist leads to a lengthy and bitter exchange between them. To prove his innocence, Hauchecorne insists on being searched. He is, but no pocketbook or large sum of money is found on him. The mayor dismisses him with the warning that as mayor he will consult a higher authority in the matter.

Out in the village again, old Hauchecorne finds that many of the peasants have already heard of the event, and to set the record straight Hauchecorne begins to restate what he told the mayor and the others: He found a piece of string and saw no pocketbook; to dramatize those points he turns his pockets inside out. Both his friends and strangers boldly tell him that they place no faith in his story, that he is indeed an old rascal and a rogue.

On the way home that night, and after his evening meal, he again stops neighbors and strangers and again goes over his litany of facts relative to the string and the pocketbook and the mayor's false accusation. Once more, no single peasant will step forward to support his claim of innocence.

The day's events have made him ill. The next day, however, the pocketbook and its contents have been found on the road and returned to their rightful owner. In his hour of triumph, Hauchecorne goes into the village and endlessly recounts the charge made against him the previous day and then the good news that fully exonerates him. Indeed, he spends the rest of the day on the road, returning often to the square to spread the news. At first he is convinced that his big adventure has ended most favorably for him, but as the day wears on, he senses that something is wrong: "He was easy now, and yet something worried him without his knowing exactly what it was. People had a joking manner while they listened. They did not seem convinced. He seemed to feel their remarks behind his back."

One week later, having brooded over the collective reaction to his supposed vindication, the protagonist returns once more to the Goderville market and once more confronts his peers with the details of the found string and the lost and returned pocketbook. On the streets and in Jordain's, the response to Hauchecorne is the same: He is guilty and both he and they know it. From time to time that day, he is even told that he had an accomplice who gave back the pocketbook, once Hauchecorne's name had become implicated in the theft.

Angry, dejected, and confused, he is unable to finish his meal at Jordain's and is forced to return home amid the sound of mocking laughter. Going over and over in his mind the events that began one week before, Hauchecorne tries to come to terms with what has happened to him. He is positive of one thing: He is unable to prove his innocence because his reputation in Goderville for being crafty is well-known: "He was, perhaps, capable of having done what they accused him of and even of boasting of it as a good trick." In other words, his reputation has preceded him—and it does not stand him in good stead now.

Once he had prided himself on his tricky business practices, but now he understands that those practices have predisposed his peasant neighbors and friends to doubt his innocence. The Norman peasant, suspicious by nature, is ready to think the worst of old Hauchecorne, and he does.

The injustice of it all weighs heavily on the protagonist's mind. He sees himself as being alone in the community (in fact, Guy de Maupassant does not mention Hauchecorne's family, if he does have one). He knows, too, that he has no defenders and many accusers. His brooding continues. His mind begins to be affected by his need to convince them that he is no dissembler. Hauchecorne goes forth every day in the village, redoubling his efforts to persuade any and all that he spied a piece of string in the road and put it in his pocket; about the pocketbook, he knows nothing. The cruelty of the peasants is such that Hauchecorne becomes in short order a butt of public jokes. The more they ask him to recite his tale of woe, the more elaborate and the more subtle his argument for his innocence becomes; as always, he is never believed.

The protagonist falls ill in late December and is bedridden. Early in January, he dies; in his deathbed delirium, his denials of wrongdoing are focused in a single phrase uttered repeatedly: "A little bit of string—a little bit of string."

## Themes and Meanings

In "The Piece of String," Maupassant is dramatizing at least two of his more familiar themes: his intense dislike of the peasantry and the peasants' abiding distrust of one another. Although Maupassant came from a well-to-do Norman background, his disillusioning experiences as a private in the Franco-Prussian War served to harden his soul against the lower class. In addition, his years of sharp scrutiny of their Norman ways and mores—their everyday habits—strengthened his cynical attitude toward them. It is generally agreed that he was misanthropic, but never more so than when he set his sights on those Norman men and women. Their hardiness and endurance notwithstanding, Maupassant's composite portrait of them is almost without qualification unflattering, and often sardonic. So he often enumerates their failings: They are greedy and deceitful, and they can be very treacherous.

Early in "The Piece of String," he sets the tone for their behavior that will follow. Gathered in the Goderville marketplace, they are ever trying to discover "the tricks of the man and the defect in the beast." Those two phrases, "the tricks of the man" and "the defect in the beast," say it all. Indeed, the trick in Hauchecorne is that he surely had a hand in the loss of the pocketbook; the defect in him is that he foolishly and vainly persists in voicing his innocence long after anyone has even thought him to be innocent, if ever anyone did.

Maupassant was no sociologist, and he did not expand on the fact that hundreds of years of debasement caused the peasants to see themselves as individuals who, by their intrinsic nature, were both unworthy and untrustworthy. Ironically, when Hauchecorne goes home after being mocked out of town, he arrives at the same conclusion that Maupassant had held for years. That is, Hauchecorne's Norman simplicity readily understands that there is considerable justice in the peasants' disbelief of his story. The peasants' ingrained suspiciousness has singled out this old man as a thief, even disregarding the fact that the pocketbook had been recovered a day later; this, too, is how Maupassant treats his peasant: as a man not to be trusted.

## Style and Technique

In Maupassant's most famous story, "The Necklace," he makes a summary statement that in a sense stands for what much of his fiction is about: "How small a thing is needed to make or ruin us!" Apropos of that, it seems safe to say that rarely, if ever, does one find his works reaching the high tragic intensity of the ancient Greek dramatists or of William Shakespeare; Maupassant's emotional compass is so often much more modest and confined. Many of his more than three hundred short stories treat his favorite subject: the Norman countryside and its inhabitants, meaning—almost always—the peasants. It surely does not take much to undo them, or to ruin them, insists Maupassant.

His technique in "The Piece of String" is to prove that fact to the reader. At no point in the tale is the Hauchecorne-Houlbreque incident worth much more than a quick retelling or a passing remark. It is anecdotal at best. After all, no cataclysmic tragedy has taken place: A purse is lost, and is found—and an old man has been accused of finding and keeping it. To be sure, it is a trivial incident among modest lives, lives that do not count for very much in the more significant scheme of things, a cynic might say. To reinforce aesthetically the smallness of the incident's dimension, Maupassant uses several devices. One is to employ relatively short paragraphs (relative to the generally longer ones he had been using) once the corporal of gendarmes calls Hauchecorne away from the tavern dining room to confront the mayor. This device is Maupassant's way of reflecting the smallness of the string (and its lack of real value) and the trivial nature of the incident overall. By the end of the story, the reader will surmise that quite ironically the string is significant (it is the protagonist's only piece of evidence) and that the incident is genuinely tragic (it serves to bring about the pitiful Hauchecorne's death in a most direct way).

A second device, one similar to the first, is the use of a kind of fragmented dialogue. There is no dialogue, in fact, until the protagonist is sent for by the mayor. From that point until the end of the story, the dialogue is brief; no single speech overwhelms the action, and the dialogue is strung out as Hauchecorne, in a whole series of brief encounters, tries heroically to establish his credibility. The dialogue mirrors his desire to tell, again and again, the truth. In a sense, Maupassant's style seems to be a true artistic medium: The form and the meaning become one.

*Gerald R. Griffin*

# PIERRE MENARD, AUTHOR OF THE *QUIXOTE*

*Author:* Jorge Luis Borges (1899-1986)
*Type of plot:* Metafiction
*Time of plot:* 1918-1934
*Locale:* Nimes and Bayonne, France
*First published:* "Pierre Menard, autor del *Quijote*," 1942 (English translation, 1962)

> *Principal characters:*
> PIERRE MENARD, an obscure author
> THE NARRATOR, who examines the work of Menard

## *The Story*

The title of this story indicates that Jorge Luis Borges is engaging in his customary mischief of rearranging the universe, for almost any reader of the fiction of this master storyteller would know that the author of *El ingenioso hidalgo don Quixote de la Mancha* (1605, 1615; *The History of the Valorous and Wittie Knight-Errant, Don Quixote of the Mancha*, 1612-1620; better known as *Don Quixote de la Mancha*) is not Pierre Menard but Miguel de Cervantes (1547-1616). The narrator begins by relating the details of his encounter with Menard through a series of mutual friends, in particular the baroness de Bacourt and the countess de Bagnoregio, formerly of Monaco but now married to an international philanthropist in Pittsburgh, Pennsylvania.

The narrator lists what he calls the "visible" work of Menard, comparing his enumeration of works to the catalog prepared by Madame Henri Bachelier and published by a newspaper suspect for its Protestant tendencies. The list includes translations of classical authors, treatises on philosophical and metaphysical problems, monographs on poetic language, and various works of poetry. The narrator then turns to the other, more important work—the subterranean, heroic, peerless, and unfinished. This extraordinary composition consists of two chapters and a fragment of a third chapter of *Don Quixote de la Mancha*. Menard's work is not another *Quixote*; rather, it is the *Quixote* itself.

Menard's inspiration came from two sources: a fragment by Novalis (1772-1801), which deals with the theme of a total identification with a given author, and an unnamed parasitic book that places a classic fictional character in a modern setting. Menard attempted to create a few fragments that would coincide word for word with the *Quixote*, not by copying the text but by assimilating it completely and then inventing it anew.

Menard first tried to accomplish his task in 1918 by becoming Cervantes—knowing Spanish well, fighting the Turks and the Moors, and forgetting the history of the world from 1602 to 1918. He then discarded that plan and adopted another, which led to the final invention analyzed by the narrator. He wrote the *Quixote* from the experience and perspective of the twentieth century author Pierre Menard.

The result of Menard's endeavor is three passages that coincide in every textual detail with the corresponding chapters of Cervantes's *Don Quixote de la Mancha*. As the narrator observes, however, there is a vivid contrast in style. Cervantes's style is contemporary and natural; Menard's is archaic and affected. Cervantes's view of history as "the mother of truth" is merely rhetorical; Menard's history as engenderer of truth is an astounding and original concept.

The narrator reasons that Menard's greatest contribution is his enrichment of the art of reading through the techniques of deliberate anachronism and erroneous attribution. Menard's illuminating labor has made possible the reading of great classics as contemporary works. To read the original text of the *Iliad* (c. 750 B.C.E.; English translation, 1611) as a twentieth century romance or William Shakespeare's *Hamlet, Prince of Denmark* (1600) as a story of modern intrigue is to fill these classic works with an extraordinary sense of adventure.

*Themes and Meanings*

In many ways, the story of Pierre Menard is representative of the work of Borges, for it is a manifestation of the processes of fictional invention that have made him one of the most influential twentieth century writers. In fact, this story deals with the process itself of literary artistic creation. It is, then, a commentary on what happens as Borges invents his fiction, just as it is an analysis of the creation of the work of art by Menard, or by Cervantes, or by any other artist.

Borges treats this theoretical question with respect to the *Quixote* in several of his other short fictions and essays included in the first collection of Borges's work widely available in English, *Labyrinths: Selected Stories and Other Writings* (1962, 1964). The essay "Partial Magic in the *Quixote*" analyzes the doubling of the fictional text through the invention of a manuscript on which the *Quixote* is based, a technique that confuses the distinction of fiction and history and has been the origin of the concept of metafiction developed by the literary critics of the 1970's and 1980's. "A Problem," which is a parable, pursues further the question of the historicity or fictiveness of the manuscript and its supposed author, Cide Hamete Benengeli. The "Parable of Cervantes and the *Quixote*" explores the relationship of Cervantes to his character, Don Quixote, a question that Borges also confronts in the narrative about Menard.

The story of Pierre Menard poses a theme that Borges examines in many of his works: the relationship of the fictional world portrayed in the text and the world of real, historical experience. The passages are identical—those of Menard and those of Cervantes—but the difference of three centuries in the experience of the perceivers of the text (the readers and the authors) alters the essence of the fictional reality that arises from the text. The clearest example of the influence of the reader's perception is seen in Borges's comments on the language of the two apparently identical passages. Because of the reader's own linguistic experience, Cervantes's use of language is rhetorical but contemporary, while Menard's is archaic and affected.

It is evident that for Borges the experience of reading is a process of transforming the fictional world into an interiorized experience analogous to historical experience. That process is a phenomenon inextricably bound to the circumstance of the reader.

*Style and Technique*

Borges's concept of the relationship between the text and the perception of the reader is a manifestation of his concept of existence as a function of the perception of things. This idealist view of human experience is evident in all the writings of Borges. He develops his fiction not through realistic descriptions or character portrayals but through emphasis on the ideas and linguistic processes of his characters. The story about the author of the *Quixote* is, above all, an analysis of Menard's obsessive concern with the possibility of creating the literary work as an intellectual exercise. The task represents an intellectual challenge, and the accomplishment of the task has significance for the essential meaning of the universe.

Because of the emphasis on the private intellectual experience of the character, the typical language of storytelling is replaced in Borges's fiction with the linguistic techniques more commonly found in the essay. Even in the stories of Borges that have a well-defined plot, such as "El jardín de senderos que se bifurcan" ("The Garden of Forking Paths") or "El milagro secreto" ("The Secret Miracle"), the interest lies not so much in what happens, but in the character's intense rationalizing and intellectualizing about his predicament. In "Pierre Menard, Author of the *Quixote*," Borges emphasizes the intellectual activity of Pierre Menard and develops only marginally anything that could be called a plot.

The list of Menard's publications and the references to the testimonies of the friends of Menard concerning his work do not further the development of the "story"; rather, they reinforce the importance of the intellect and the rational in Menard's experience. They also disarm to some extent the intensely serious rational nature of the narrative through subtle, sophisticated humor. The incongruity of the countess from Monaco who ends up in Pittsburgh and the doubtfulness of Madame Bachelier's testimony because of its appearance in a Protestant newspaper are examples of Borges's wry cynicism about his own analytical approach to human experience.

This ratiocinative emphasis results in a narrative language that is clear and concise. At some points, "Pierre Menard, Author of the *Quixote*" is difficult, as are all of Borges's stories. The difficulty, however, never results from an imprecision of language, but rather from the complexity of Borges's ideas and the obsessive intensity of his concerns.

*Gilbert Smith*

# PIGEON FEATHERS

*Author:* John Updike (1932-    )
*Type of plot:* Coming of age
*Time of plot:* About 1930-1950
*Locale:* A farm outside Firetown
*First published:* 1961

> *Principal characters:*
> DAVID KERN, the protagonist, an adolescent boy
> ELSIE, his mother, a romantic
> GEORGE, his father, a cynic
> GRANMOM, who suffers from Parkinson's disease
> THE REVEREND MR. DOBSON, the Lutheran minister

*The Story*

During the year of his life that this story covers, David Kern must come to grips with many things that are changing and chaotic. The external action of the story is concerned with his family's move from Olinger to a farm, his mother's birthplace but an unfamiliar world for David and his father. Besides the usual adjustments—to a new school, a new youth group at church—David must also deal with dissension between his parents about the move. His mother loves the farm and feels a deep kinship with the soil. His father, on the other hand, is uncomfortable there. Bitter and sarcastic, he tries to reduce every argument to chemistry, his college major and, presumably, the subject he teaches. Further complicating the family's life is the presence of Granmom, who used to work this farm with her husband but is now crippled and bewildered by Parkinson's disease. She irritates her daughter and seems always to be in the way.

These external conflicts closely parallel the internal action of the story. David is moving away from the safe, easily understood attitudes of childhood toward a confrontation with frightening and confusing adult realities. At first, this movement is only a formless dread of change. As the story progresses, however, it becomes a specific fear that death is absolute and final, thereby negating any meaning in life.

The story opens on Saturday of the second week after the move to the farm. David tries to work off some of his disorientation by arranging the family's books, mostly old college texts and novels that belonged to his mother. He opens H. G. Wells's *The Outline of History* (1920)—he had once read Wells's *The Time Machine* (1895)—and reads Wells's account of Jesus: an obscure political agitator who by some accident survived his own crucifixion and became, thereby, the central figure in a myth that grew into a church. That God had allowed such blasphemy to exist and to be recorded in a book seems, to David's shocked mind, to give it credibility and to cast other long-held but unproven ideas into doubt. He has never been visited by Christ. Even answered prayers could have been coincidences.

Later that same evening, while his mother and father are conducting an endless argument about organic farming, David, still distracted by the formless dread that is growing within his shocked, disillusioned mind, takes a flashlight and visits the outhouse. The image of an insect that alights on the lens and is projected by the flashlight with an X ray's magnification onto the wall seems, to David, an exact vision of death: a long hole in the ground down which one's body passes until it mixes with deep underground stone and dirt. This revelation of extinction is so frightening that all of his earlier dread coalesces into absolute terror. He races back to the house, where his mother and father are still arguing, and goes immediately to Webster's Dictionary, where he looks up "soul." He finds some comfort in its careful stipulation that the soul is "usually held to be separate in existence" from the body, and from death.

This assurance does not stay, however, and David's search for some proof that will justify the hope that something about human existence outlasts death dominates the remaining episodes of the story. His disillusionment deepens as he confronts the traditional sources of knowledge: his minister, the Bible, his parents. He disturbs the adolescent politeness of his catechism class by asking the Reverend Mr. Dobson about the status of the soul's awareness during the interval between death and the Day of Judgment. The minister's pat answer, accompanied by his assurance that such things do not really matter in the eyes of God, angers David. He believes that Christianity has betrayed him. Later, he can find no answers in his grandfather's Bible. His mother, who urges him to talk about his experience with the Reverend Mr. Dobson, suggests that he will feel differently about such things when he is older and more experienced.

David's father's sardonic advice is to look forward to death because life itself is only a curse to be endured. Nowhere—not in crowds of adults, in religious services and writings, in school, not even in pinball or the vigorously destructive chores with which he assists his father that winter—can he find any clues or hints that help him defend against his fear of death.

Ironically, Granmom's request that he use the Remington .22 rifle that he got for his fifteenth birthday to rid the barn of pigeons who are nesting there precipitates the climax of David's preoccupation with death. Although initially hesitant to shoot anything living, he finds the killing of the pigeons strangely exciting. He kills the first as it is outlined against a hole in the barn's roof. When the others, disturbed by the report, head for the escape hole, he fires again and again. He kills six pigeons in what seems a frenzy of firing, pumping a full clip of eight bullets into the lifeless body of one of the pigeons that blocks the hole. Afterward, as he buries the dead pigeons, he examines the complex geometric patterns of blue, gray, lilac, white, and salmon feathers. He finds in the intricate design of the birds' wings the natural order he has been seeking. Suddenly, this is the proof he has needed to justify his hope that death is not final. Surely "the God who had lavished such craft on these worthless birds would not destroy His whole Creation by refusing to let David live forever."

*Themes and Meanings*

The central issue of "Pigeon Feathers" is David Kern's search for a belief to compensate for his loss of confidence in the ideals and institutions of childhood. In re-creating this universal conflict, John Updike presents David's confrontation with an unsettling idea, Wells's summation of the life and significance of Jesus Christ. Once he accepts the historian's skepticism, David's doubts about long-held religious beliefs multiply. When the adults he questions answer him with only vague platitudes, he feels betrayed—not only by Christianity but also by the adult world that he used to re-gard as omniscient. Every experience intensifies his fear of the ultimate betrayal: that death is the end of everything. He keeps alive the possibility of hope but is tormented by fear that such hope is yet another delusion. Finally, he finds the answer in his own experience. His examination of the slaughtered pigeons leads him to a conclusion of his own: If order exists in such mundane aspects of nature, then God's plan for hu-mankind, his most complex creation, must surely extend beyond the temporary ex-tinction of death. This realization, with its affirmation of the immortality of the soul as well as its validation of life itself, fills David with joy. The reader, who may or may not agree with David's revelation, nevertheless recognizes that experience, however am-biguous or complex, is an adult's source of truth.

*Style and Technique*

Updike underscores the movement of the plot and the motivational processes of David Kern's mind with a series of parallel incidents and images. For example, the image, early in the story, of an insect caught in the flashlight's beam becomes a vision of death: man trapped at the bottom of a deep hole. At the story's climax, this image recurs when the pigeons, seen in silhouette as they seek to escape the dark barn through a sunlit hole, are methodically destroyed by David's rifle shots. This image connects David's early terrors with the older, harder David, who enjoys the power he has over the pigeons' life and death.

Similarly, David has observed an intricate pattern of natural order in the physical configuration of his dog Copper's nostrils and whorling hair. This image foreshadows the geometrical precision and order of the pigeons' wings and anticipates the recogni-tion that accompanies the climax of the story. Such careful attention to minute sensual details makes the reader aware of Updike's careful attention to symmetry and struc-ture. The resonances created by parallel images and repeated scenes establish a dis-tinct harmony between the story's content and its form.

*Patricia A. Finch*

# PIPA'S STORY

*Author:* Lan Samantha Chang (1965-    )
*Type of plot:* Magical Realism, family
*Time of plot:* 1949
*Locale:* A rural Chinese village and Shanghai
*First published:* 1993

> *Principal characters:*
> PIPA, a young Chinese girl
> HER MOTHER, a village woman who works in charms
> LAO FU, a friend of Pipa's mother
> WEN, a rich Chinese merchant
> MEISI, one of Wen's servants

*The Story*

A young woman named Pipa leaves her Chinese village to work for a wealthy family in Shanghai. Because Pipa's mother works in charms and makes potions, she is a powerful figure in her village. When Pipa prepares to leave, her mother mixes potions to protect her against bodily harm as well as herbs that will fix her past in her memory and never allow her to forget her mother, no matter how far away she goes. The mother also asks Pipa to promise her to take a small stone with her and to find the heart of the house in which Wen, the man for whom she is going to work, lives and to hide the stone there. She tells Pipa not to tell anyone what village she is from and not to tell anyone her mother's name.

Pipa gets a ride to Shanghai with her mother's family friend Lao Fu. When she arrives, she is terrified by the size of the city. Reaching the house where she is to work and watching her mother's friend drive his cart away, she thinks she has said her last good-bye to her village and her mother. After years of avoiding her mother's sight, Pipa feels she is now in a place where her mother cannot see her; she is so filled with conflicting emotions about this that she vomits on the side of the road.

Pipa makes friends with another young woman named Meisi who works in the Wen house. She allows the stone, which her mother sewed up in her smock, to be thrown away. When Wen learns that Pipa can read, she is given a more important role in the household than simply being a maid. Later, when Lao Fu comes back to Shanghai to see how Pipa is doing, he tells her a story about when Wen was a young man and was a friend of her father. He tells her how her mother had an astounding talent for finding anything that was lost. Lao Fu also tells her that he, her parents, and Wen went into business together gathering ginseng roots to sell. However, Wen was a ruthless, ambitious young man who wanted Pipa's mother for himself. One foggy day, Pipa's father disappeared, and Pipa's mother, pregnant with Pipa, mourned for him and would not have anything to do with Wen until her husband's body was found. In the spring, the body was found at the bottom of a ravine, lying on a bed of pinkish quartz. Pipa's mother knew that the death was not an accident and accused Wen of killing her husband. Wen left the village and disappeared for years. Pipa tells Lao Fu that the story has nothing to do with her and that she will not keep her promise to her mother. However, when Wen sexually assaults Pipa's friend Meisi, she finds the stone, a piece of pinkish quartz, and hides it in his bed.

When the communists enter the city, they behead Wen. Pipa never sees her mother again; the communists execute her as a witch. Pipa goes to Taiwan and gets a job in a library. She gets married and has two children, but the smell of smoke always reminds her of her mother.

*Themes and Meanings*

In its delicate treatment of the past's impingement on the present and in its complex combination of the political, the personal, and the supernatural, "Pipa's Story" reflects, the narrator says, how people's buried pasts are like ginseng roots, all with different shapes. Selected for *The Best American Short Stories, 1994*, "Pipa's Story" is the only tale in Lan Samantha Chang's debut collection, *Hunger: A Novella and Stories* (1998) that is not based on Chinese immigrants in the United States. Although the plot of the story focuses on a young woman who leaves her Chinese village to work for a wealthy man in Shanghai, the thematic heart of the story is the relationship between the girl and the mother. The mother, reputed to have supernatural power, is such a powerful figure in her village that Pipa thinks she will disappear if she does not escape the shadow of her mother. When the mother gives Pipa a small stone from the area where her husband's body was found to hide in the heart of Wen's house, it is clear that even though she is leaving, her obligation to her mother accompanies her.

When Pipa learns how Wen, her powerful employer, once desired her mother and murdered her father just before she was born, she is torn between her wish to break free of her mother, insisting that none of the story has anything to do with her, and her sense that even her flight from her mother fits into some incomprehensible design. "Pipa's Story" mixes history with folklore, for when the communists execute Wen, it is not clear whether this is a result of Pipa's mother's curse on him or his political beliefs.

"Pipa's Story" is a carefully constructed fiction about how the past cannot be ignored and how family ties exceed any conscious effort to escape them. Although the execution of Wen is political, for he has become rich by working with foreign capitalists, at the same time, it is personal, punishment for an old crime that Pipa's mother will not forget and that she does not let her daughter forget. The story ends with Pipa, a grown woman with a family, thinking it is not wise to look back too long and deep on what has taken place in the past. However, even as she thinks this, she remembers in great detail the fire that the communists started when they reached Wen's section of the city. She remembers how soldiers led Wen out of the house and made him kneel before them. When Wen held his head high, one of the soldiers twirled a machete so that the blunt side came down on Wen's neck to make him fall forward. Pipa recalls that everything was momentarily silent until the soldier raised his arm again and "the sharp blade sliced all our lives in two." In this vividly remembered image, Pipa unites the powerful political implication of the communist takeover with the equally powerful personal implication of her mother's vengeance.

## Style and Technique

When Chang's first book, *Hunger*, appeared, it received almost universally positive reviews. Several reviewers compared her to other Asian American women writers such as Amy Tan and Maxine Hong Kingston. However, although it is true that Chang explores some of the same themes and cultural issues as those established novelists of the Chinese immigrant experience—especially the familiar Asian American conflict between parents and children and the Old World and the New—other reviewers compared Chang to such expert stylists of the short-story genre as James Joyce and Bernard Malamud. The latter may be a more apt comparison, for Chang's stories are not focused so much on the timely social issues faced by Chinese immigrants as they are concerned with more universal issues such as the delicate fabric of family relationships, loneliness, memory, desire, ambition, and loss. Chang herself has said that she is more interested in things that happen over and over again than in time-bound contemporary events. "Pipa's Story" is more concerned with the stylistic union between the past and the present, the cultural and the personal, than it is with political issues.

The fact that "Pipa's Story" and other Chang stories have been enthusiastically received for their universality, lyricism, and formal control rather than for their cultural specificity and postcolonial political stance perhaps signals that in the late 1990's the focus of contemporary fiction was more on what unites people as humans rather than what separates people as members of different cultures. However, Chang's emphasis on the human universal rather than on the politically particular and her insistence on tight formal and stylistic control in her fiction have been the sources of the only negative reviews she has received. An M.F.A. graduate from the famous University of Iowa writing program and a Wallace Stegner Fellow at the equally famous Stanford University writing program, Chang has been accused by some critics as exhibiting basic, writing school predictability and formal control. This criticism may, however, be a result of a general preference among academic critics in the late 1990's for the political realism of the postcolonial novel over the lyrical formalism of the post-Chekhovian short story.

*Charles E. May*

# THE PIT AND THE PENDULUM

*Author:* Edgar Allan Poe (1809-1849)
*Type of plot:* Gothic
*Time of plot:* May, 1808
*Locale:* Toledo, Spain
*First published:* 1842

### Principal characters:

THE NARRATOR, a victim of the Spanish Inquisition, sentenced to
death by torture
THE NARRATOR'S UNSEEN TORMENTORS, Inquisition monks
GENERAL LASALLE, the leader of the French forces that end the
Inquisition

## The Story

The first-person narrator informs the reader that he is trying to recall and write down everything that happened to him earlier. He describes the Spanish Inquisition's sentencing him to death, a sentence that he could not understand because of his extremely nervous state. When he regained consciousness temporarily, he felt himself being carried down and down into an apparent abyss. Later, when he was fully conscious, he knew that he was lying on his back in an oppressive, damp environment. Finally daring to open his eyes and finding himself in absolute darkness, he imagined that he was buried alive. Food and drink were provided to him only when he swooned or slept. Later, while investigating his surroundings, he narrowly escaped falling into a deep pit to a certain death. Shaken, but relieved, he fell asleep. When he awoke, some light entering the dungeon made it possible for him to compare the room to his calculations made in the dark.

Soon he discovered that one form of torture and execution had only been replaced with another, for he was strapped to a table so that only his head and left arm could be moved slightly. A large razor-sharp pendulum suspended overhead drew nearer with each pass. The ponderous rate at which it descended increased his agony, for he had to await death for what seemed to be many days. At last he developed a plan: He smeared some scraps of meat on his ropes so that the rats in the cell came to gnaw on them. Just as the pendulum brushed his skin, the ropes were loosened enough to allow him to escape. His relief was again short-lived, for the walls of his cell became hotter and hotter, forcing him toward the pit in the center of the room. When he resisted, his invisible tormentors moved the walls so that he was squeezed toward death by heat or by falling into the pit. At the moment when he was losing his foothold, the machines were suddenly turned off, and the walls receded. Just before he fell into the pit, he was rescued by General Lasalle, the leader of the French army, which had just invaded Toledo.

## Themes and Meanings

One obvious theme is the inexorable passage of time, ending in death as the final outcome of all life. The pendulum, usually associated with clocks and time, here combines the two elements, for it is one of two possible means of execution, and it is also compared to the scythe wielded by Father Time. The other obvious symbol of death is the pit, a synonym with death or Sheol since biblical times.

The horrors of the Spanish Inquisition are also treated specifically. This is not, however, a diatribe against Spain or a laudatory statement about France. Instead, on a more universal level, it shows the cruelty that humans exercise on their fellow human beings. Edgar Allan Poe uses the historical background solely to render the story more believable and, thus, more frightening. His purpose is to create a nightmare in which the reader becomes a coparticipant with the protagonist, sharing in the terror and the suspense.

## Style and Technique

The first-person narration, in which the "I" remains unnamed, causes the reader to identify with the protagonist. The obvious disadvantage of the use of the first person—the knowledge from the outset that he manages to escape because he has lived to tell his story—is overcome by Poe's ability to create such tension and illogical fear that one forgets this fact.

The protagonist's dread is shared by the audience, for both are ignorant of the character's environment and his ultimate fate. Therefore, suspense is maintained, for the reader and the narrator discover each detail simultaneously. As each new fact is revealed, there is a temporary feeling of relief, which is destroyed as new, more awful terrors become known. This alternation of relief and renewed terror ultimately causes the reader to doubt that any escape is possible, despite the fact that, logically, the narrator must survive in order to write his account.

Another technique that contributes to the nightmarish atmosphere of this tale of horror is the distortion of time, space, and reality. The narrator says that the pendulum's descent was "only appreciable at intervals that seemed ages. . . . Days passed— it might have been that many days passed." Perception of space is also altered and unreliable. A room thought to have a perimeter of one hundred paces is, in reality, much smaller. In addition, the room's shape and characteristics are changed by unseen forces: The walls can be heated and moved, light can be provided or withheld, the pendulum can be stopped and started. The character's swoons and exhausted sleep exacerbate the confusion, for they cause gaps in the reader's knowledge about reality. After each period of unconsciousness, something in the environment has been changed, so that one fears these so-called respites.

Poe's psychological portraiture is masterful as he evokes, for example, the sensations of losing and regaining consciousness. Especially realistic is his description of the mental state of the narrator as he is being sentenced: The condemned man focuses on unimportant images—the curtains; the candles, which become phantasmagoric; the thin, white lips of the judges, which move but emit no comprehensible sound:

"And then, all at once, there came a most deadly nausea over my spirit, and I felt every fibre in my frame thrill as if I had touched the wire of a galvanic battery." This attention to detailed accounts of sensations, smells, sounds, thirst, and hunger makes the narration credible and even real for the reader. In addition, the writer of the account stresses that this is unlike fiction: "Such a supposition [that I was dead], notwithstanding what we read in fiction, is altogether inconsistent with real existence."

After all the foiled, character-generated escapes, the final rescue is anticlimactic but welcome nevertheless. This use of *deus ex machina*, the resolution of the problem by a force exterior to the action of the story, is rather surprising because it is used infrequently in Poe's stories. Its use is justifiable, however, for the story is historically based.

*Eunice Myers*

# PKHENTZ

*Author:* Abram Tertz (Andrei Sinyavsky, 1925-1997)
*Type of plot:* Fantasy
*Time of plot:* The 1950's
*Locale:* Moscow
*First published:* 1967 (English translation, 1968)

*Principal characters:*
ANDREI KAZIMIROVICH SUSHINSKY, the alias of an alien from another planet posing as a hunchback, the narrator and protagonist
LEOPOLD SERGEYEVICH, a hunchback
VERONICA GRIGORIEVNA, a girl in love with Andrei
KOSTRITSKAYA, a landlady who bears the name also given to Leopold's wife
A SMALL CHILD, Leopold's son

*The Story*

"Pkhentz" is a fantastic tale of science fiction, describing the emotional experiences and survival techniques of an alien from another planet whose spaceship goes off course and crash-lands somewhere in Siberia. The alien is the sole survivor of the crash. In order to survive in a hostile environment, he disguises himself as a human being, assumes the alias Andrei Kazimirovich Sushinsky, and eventually obtains work as a bookkeeper in Moscow. Although the creature is vegetablelike, with numerous appendages, he manages to pass as human by strapping his extra appendages to his body, hiding them under human clothing. He also wears a wig and rubberlike ears. Thus disguised, he resembles a human hunchback. Gradually, the alien, Andrei, who is both the story's narrator and its protagonist, reveals the emotional strain he has endured by being forced to pose as a human being for the past thirty-two years. He must be ever vigilant not to reveal his true identity and thus rejects the sexual advances of Veronica Grigorievna, a young girl who lives in the same communal apartment house as he and who is attracted to him.

As an alien creature, he finds the human body repulsive. He longs for contact and association with creatures like himself, and hastens to make the acquaintance of Leopold Sergeyevich, a hunchback whom he encounters in the laundry—he has mistaken Leopold for a fellow creature from his native planet in disguise like himself and goes to Leopold's apartment to reveal himself as a fellow alien. Andrei addresses Leopold by using the code word "Pkhentz," a "sacred name" which Andrei remembers from his distant homeland. Leopold fails to recognize the word, maintains that he has nothing in common with Andrei, and rejects him as a hunchback more loathsome and hideous than himself. In desperation, Andrei grabs Leopold, shakes him, and attempts to force him to acknowledge their kinship. As Andrei touches Leopold, however, he feels body heat and immediately realizes that Leopold is indeed a human being and not an alien like himself. He excuses himself and quickly departs.

Andrei then falls ill from dehydration. Realizing that he will die soon, he determines to return to Siberia to the scene of the crash of his spaceship and live out his remaining days without a disguise. He determines to wait until the first frost and then ignite himself with a match. In the meantime, he will gaze at the heavens, attempt to distinguish the star from which he came, and long for his native land. The story concludes with Andrei apostrophizing his native land using the term "Pkhentz" and other words that he still remembers from his lost, native language.

*Themes and Meanings*

Although ostensibly a work of science fiction, "Pkhentz" may be read as a satiric allegory on the tragic consequences of the Russian Revolution, as well as a commentary on the plight of the creative artist in the Soviet Union. The alien lands in the Soviet Union in the first part of the twentieth century, at the time of the Russian Revolution in 1917. Abram Tertz (the pen name Andrei Sinyavsky used for political reasons) suggests that the Bolshevik seizure of power was a mistake similar to the mistaken crash-landing of the alien spaceship that went off course and took seven and a half months to land, approximately the same amount of time between the Russian Revolution in February, 1917, and the Bolshevik seizure of power in October, 1917.

The Russian Revolution, like the crash-landing, was an unintended, chance happening. The alien states: "In fact we had no intention of flying into space . . . we were going to a holiday resort. . . . Then . . . something occurred, . . . we lost buoyancy . . . and down we fell, into the unknown, for seven and a half months we went on falling . . . and by pure chance we landed up here." The alien, like Robinson in Daniel Defoe's *Robinson Crusoe* (1719), is the sole survivor and must face the problem of adapting himself to a hostile environment. "The air was wrong, the light was wrong, and all the gravities and pressures were strange."

Tertz draws an analogy between the alien's hostile environment and the hostile political atmosphere confronting writers after the revolution. He personally identifies himself with the alien by giving him his own first name, Andrei. The alien's assumed identity as half-Russian, half-Polish, recalls Tertz's personal biography. Most significant, the alien loses sight of one eye in 1934, the year of the first Congress of Soviet Writers, which followed the 1932 edict of the Communist Party, in which all writers were organized into a single union with a single board of censorship. At the 1934 convention, the delegates approved a Party resolution establishing the doctrine of socialist realism as the sole standard for writing. Henceforth, all literature would be realistic in form and socialist in content. This doctrine stifled literary creativity and resulted in a uniform, conformist art to which Tertz objected.

In an original and provocative book-length essay, *Chto takoe sotsialisticheskii realizm* (1959; *On Socialist Realism*, 1960), Tertz attacked socialist realism. He called for a new "phantasmagoric art . . . in which the grotesque will replace realistic descriptions of ordinary life" and which will "be truthful with the aid of the absurd and the fantastic."

Through his fantastic tale of the plight of Andrei, the alien, Tertz associates the position of the alien as an outsider and nonconformist with that of the writer in the Soviet Union. At the end of the story, Tertz suggests the need to overcome the cultural isolation that Russian writers have experienced by being separated from their Western European counterparts. When the alien apostrophizes his lost homeland in his native language, which he only dimly remembers, he uses two Western European words, *bonjour* and *gutenabend*. The concluding apostrophe is Tertz's plea to reestablish the link between Soviet literature and a lost linguistic and cultural tradition represented by both prerevolutionary Russian literature and the literature of Western Europe.

> Oh native land! PKHENTZ! GOGRY TUZHEROSKIP! I am coming back to you. GOGRY! GOGRY! GOGRY! TUZHEROSKIP! TUZHEROSKIP! BONJOUR! GUTENABEND! TUZHEROSKIP!
> BU-BU-BU!
> MIAOW-MIAWO!
> PKHENTZ!

*Style and Technique*

Tertz achieves his "phantasmagoric" view of reality by using an alien creature from another planet as his narrator. He thus compels the reader to view the world through the eyes of the alien and presents the reader with an unconventional perspective on human habits and customs. Even the most common elements of daily human life are made to seem strange. Sausage and scrambled eggs are perceived as "a gut that's swallowed itself garnished with stillborn chickens." The normal human body is viewed as grotesque, and the alien is puzzled by society's puritanical attitudes toward sex, which is shrouded in secrecy. He finds human clothing distasteful and longs to shed his disguise and reveal the full splendor of his appearance. When he disrobes, his body opens up like a palm, extending his four limbs or hands like branches and revealing eyes in his hands and feet, the crown of his head, and the nape of his neck. He regards himself as "the only example of that lost harmony and beauty" that characterized his homeland.

The only human beings with which the alien can identify are hunchbacks; and the plants he most admires, collects, and cares for are cacti, which he refers to as his "little hump-backed children." When the alien attempts to make contact with the hunchback Leopold, he expresses his delight in "this skillful caricature of humanity, this art which was all the more like the real thing because it was so absurd." For Tertz, only absurd, fantastic images can reveal the fundamental absurdity of life.

Although physically unattractive by conventional human standards, the alien is spiritually beautiful. He is sensitive, sincere, caring, and has a strong sense of his own moral worth and dignity. He values his uniqueness and wishes to hide from humans in order to protect himself from their scorn. Tertz's satiric method is brilliantly employed when the alien contemplates his fate, were his true identity to be revealed. Academics would rush to examine, question, and interrogate him in disregard of his feelings and wishes. He would be commercially exploited through theses, films, and poems. The novelty of his appearance would result in new fashion trends. "Ladies would start wearing green lipstick and having their hats made to look like cactus." Children, streets, and dogs would be named after him. He would become "as famous as Lev Tolstoy, or Gulliver, or Hercules. Or Galileo Galilei."

By associating the alien with the heretics Tolstoy and Galileo, Tertz underscores the role of the alien as nonconformist. His identification of the alien with Hercules, a mythical hero, reinforces the role of the alien as hero of the story. Most important, however, Tertz associates his art with a satiric literary tradition represented by Gulliver, the hero of Jonathan Swift's *Gulliver's Travels* (1726). The alien, like Gulliver, has made a fantastic voyage and has viewed his surroundings from the perspective of an outsider. Tertz thus reaffirms the value of satire and fantasy as a healthy corrective to the shortcomings of human beings, their foibles, and their societal conventions.

*Jerome J. Rinkus*

# THE PLEASURE OF HER COMPANY

*Author:* Jane Smiley (1949-     )
*Type of plot:* Social realism
*Time of plot:* Probably the 1970's
*Locale:* An American university town
*First published:* 1981

*Principal characters:*
FLORENCE, an unmarried nurse
FRANNIE HOWARD, her next-door neighbor
PHILIP HOWARD, Frannie's husband
BRYAN, Florence's boyfriend

*The Story*

When Philip and Frannie Howard move into the old Victorian house next door, Florence is immediately taken with her neighbors, especially Frannie. The two women become friends, and Florence spends more and more of her time at the Howards' house. Florence's time with the Howards is a series of seemingly tranquil domestic moments: drinking coffee at the maple kitchen table, easy conversations while preparing dinner. The women talk of everything, it seems, except marriage, which is a mystery to Florence. Frannie never shares confidences about Philip or their life together, which makes Florence curious. Frannie tells Florence that she had several women friends before she married, but that changed immediately. She says it is as if there is no room for an intimate woman friend when there is a husband, as if Philip would have to give way if Frannie were to have a truly close woman friend.

The relationship of the three neighbors evolves beyond talk to one of easy silence. Florence often sleeps at the Howards' and wakes up to tea and buttered toast in the morning. After Christmas, Frannie tells Florence that she and Philip are separating. Frannie moves to a small apartment, and Florence avoids Philip when she sees him in the neighborhood. When Florence visits Frannie, Frannie never talks about her marriage. Florence waits expectantly for Frannie to say something, anything that will help her to understand marriage and what happened between Frannie and Philip. When Florence and her new boyfriend, Bryan, visit Frannie, she admires his ability to ask Frannie directly whether she will go back to Philip.

Florence keeps up her regular visits to Frannie, sometimes spending the night. They have long talks about all the things they will do together. When Florence talks about her relationship with Bryan, she leaves space between her words so that Frannie can speak if she wants to, but Frannie never does. One of the few things she tells Florence is that she and Philip lost a baby. Frannie was prediabetic without knowing it; the baby died during labor. She says no more on the subject.

Looking out her window at Philip's house, Florence wonders about him and his marriage. As curious as she is about the Howards' marriage, she does not want to hear anything about Bryan's former wife—in fact, her mind wanders whenever he talks about his former wife or marriage. One day, Bryan mentions that Frannie's name came up at lunch. Florence defensively demands to know what was said. Her name was simply mentioned, Bryan replies. This seemingly trivial detail suggests to Florence that Frannie's life extends far beyond Florence's grasp and ability to contain her. She is jealous.

Frannie invites Florence to join her for an early-morning picnic at a friend's house. They take champagne and French bread, and they pick strawberries out of the garden. For both women, this is a sensual, luxurious experience. Frannie's gaze strays to the house beyond the garden; Florence's thoughts turn to Bryan, and she wonders what time it is. They soon depart.

Florence and Bryan have fallen in love. One evening they are having an especially playful time together, joking and laughing with each other. Just as Florence imagines that they will begin to make love, Bryan announces that he has seen Frannie with a woman who, he believes, is her new lover. This breaks the spell they have enjoyed during the evening and preempts their lovemaking. While Bryan falls asleep, Florence jealously imagines Frannie with this woman.

The next morning, Florence stops by Frannie's apartment. Frannie's things are in the street. As Florence stands looking at them, Frannie and her lover, Helen, drive up. Frannie is moving into Helen's house. The introductions are awkward. Florence and Helen survey each other. When Florence offers to help, Helen tells her they are nearly finished. There is little more to say. Florence turns and runs down the street to her car.

Back at her own home, Florence is waiting for Bryan to come and take her swimming. Outside, Philip is cutting the grass and trimming his hedges. She tries to sneak into the house before Philip notices her, but he calls to her. After some small talk, Philip invites Florence to see the work he has done since her last visit.

The house feels spacious and there have been many changes. Florence tells Philip that she misses the things that are now gone, that she loved the days and evenings when the three of them sat around, sipping brandy and talking. It was more than just friendship, she says; it was like being a member of their family. Philip responds teasingly that those were lovely times, with him in love with Frannie and Frannie in love with Helen. He confesses that they used Florence to take the focus off the issue of their marriage and Frannie's attraction to Helen. This gives her painful insight into Philip and Frannie's marriage and, in some measure, into all marriages.

As Bryan drives up to her house and gets out of his car, Florence learns from Philip some of the secrets of marriage: that she was the only one of the threesome who was happy, that all the secrets of marriage are not necessarily disclosed, and that it is worth finding out for oneself. Just as Bryan reaches to press the doorbell at Florence's, she calls out to him, letting him know where she is.

*Themes and Meanings*

"The Pleasure of Her Company" is a study of marriage, intimate friendships between women, and how marriage and friendship fit—or do not fit—together. Florence's curiosity about the Howards' marriage comes close to voyeurism. The story states several times that Florence finds marriage a mystery, and Florence constantly tries to manipulate conversations so that Frannie will talk about Philip and their life together. Frannie is reticent, more of a listener than a talker, especially on this subject. Florence attempts to piece things together in her naïve way.

One of the most telling of Frannie's few confidences is that she lost all of her women friends when she married Philip. She says she has not had a close woman friend since marrying Philip, although she had had three or four before. There is not room for both a close woman friend and Philip in her life.

When Frannie and Philip separate, Florence's curiosity about their marriage intensifies. Again she tries to elicit confidences from Frannie, but Frannie says little. It is not until late in the story that Florence begins to realize that Frannie is slipping from her grasp, that she cannot contain her friend's life within her own. Even as she sees Frannie's life exclude her, she believes that at least they had a special friendship before the separation, before Helen. Philip disabuses Florence of this notion, telling her that their friendship was not what she thought it was. The intimacy she felt was a farce designed to smooth over a difficult period in the Howards' marriage. Philip tells Florence that she cannot begin to understand marriage by studying someone else's. She must solve the mystery and find intimacy in her own marriage.

*Style and Technique*

Jane Smiley explores the complexities of friendship and marriage by looking at ordinary people and the minutiae of their lives, deriving meaning metaphorically from everyday details. One of the most telling metaphors of the story is a dress that has fallen from its hanger. The day the Howards move into their new house, Florence walks past the boxes and piles of clothing left on the sidewalk. Among these things is a white dress that may be a wedding dress; Florence is not sure. Tissue paper fills out the bodice; a sleeve has slipped from the hanger. Florence straightens the dress on the hanger, and then, embarrassed that she might be seen, hurries on.

This scene, trivial on a first reading, is rich with foreshadowing and metaphorical meaning. It is revealing that Florence cannot tell whether this is a wedding dress, just as it is significant that the dress—as the marriage—is shaped into fullness artificially. Something is not quite right with this dress: It has slipped free of its support, and Florence reaches out to fix it. Florence escapes quickly after straightening the dress, fearful of being seen, as later she wants to understand the Howards' marriage but is too embarrassed to question Frannie directly. The next morning the pile of belongings is gone, except for the dress, which lies on the grass "like a snow angel." Despite Florence's attempt to care for the dress, it falls anyway, abandoned.

*Julie Thompson*

# THE POET

*Author:* Hermann Hesse (1877-1962)
*Type of plot:* Fantasy
*Time of plot:* Unspecified
*Locale:* China
*First published:* "Der Dichter," 1913 (English translation, 1961)

> *Principal characters:*
> HAN FOOK, a young Chinese poet
> MASTER OF THE PERFECT WORD, an old man
> HAN FOOK'S FATHER

*The Story*

A young Chinese, Han Fook, is possessed by the desire to perfect himself in the art of poetry. Despite his youth, he has already written poems and is respected by the learned men of his province. He is a handsome youth whose loving parents have recently arranged a marriage for him with a beautiful and virtuous girl. Nevertheless, Han Fook is not satisfied; his heart is still filled with the longing to become an accomplished poet.

One evening a lantern festival is being celebrated beside the river. From the opposite shore, Han Fook watches the guests arriving and sees a thousand lights shimmering on the water, reflections from the lanterns. The sounds of zithers and flutes drift toward him, and the night sky appears to hover over the festival like a temple. As much as he wants to join the festivities with his bride-to-be, so much more does he want to remain here, to observe, to take in the scene until he is able to express what he sees in a perfect poem. He realizes that he will always be a lonely spectator of life, and his only true happiness will come if he is able to capture all of life in poetry; only in this way can he possess life.

As he stands entranced, he hears a rustling noise and turns to see an elderly man in purple robes leaning against a tree. Han Fook greets him with the respect that is due an elder. The old man smiles and recites several verses that express in beautiful lyric forms the very thoughts that have been in Han Fook's mind. "Who are you?" Han Fook asks in amazement, and the old man answers, "If you want to become a poet, come to my hut where the great river begins in the north-western mountains. My name is Master of the Perfect Word," and then he is gone. Han Fook can find no trace of him and thinks that he must have imagined the whole experience. He hurries to the festival, but amid all the gaiety he continues to hear the mysterious voice of the old man, and his own soul seems to have departed with him.

Several days later, Han Fook's father is about to call relatives and friends together to announce the date of his son's wedding, but Han Fook begs him to delay. He wants more time to be alone with his thoughts and his poetry. The father is surprised but grants him the wish. He may spend a year pursuing his dream, for perhaps it was sent by a god. "Perhaps it will take even two years, who can know," answers Han Fook.

After writing his bride a letter of farewell, Han Fook follows the great river to its source, where he finds the bamboo hut and the old man seated before it playing the lute. The master does not greet his guest, but only smiles and lets his fingers run over the strings. The sounds enchant Han Fook, who now becomes his servant and his pupil. He soon learns to despise the poems he has already written and forgets all those that he has studied. The old man scarcely speaks to him but teaches him instead to play the lute, until his entire being is flooded with music.

After two years, his goal seems as distant as ever, and he is homesick. The master, as if reading his thoughts, tells him, "You are free to go wherever pleases you." Han Fook goes home, arriving early in the morning. Listening at the window of his own home, he hears his father's heavy breathing as he sleeps. At his bride's home he climbs a pear tree, and through the open window he can see her combing her hair. As he compares this picture with the one he has painted in his thoughts of home, however, he realizes that he must be faithful to his inner voice, which is still calling to him. In the dreams of poets there is a beauty and dignity that he would seek in vain in the reality of life. Without announcing his visit, Han Fook returns to the elder.

Now that Han Fook has mastered the lute, the old man teaches him to play the zither, and months fly away like snowflakes in the wind. Once Han Fook dreams that he is at home, planting a tree in his own garden. His wife is standing beside him, and his children are consecrating the tree with wine and milk. Then, however, he awakens to find himself in the hut with the master, who is slumbering nearby. Suddenly he feels a bitter hatred toward this man who seems to have destroyed his life and cheated him of a future. He wants to kill him. At this moment the old man opens his eyes, smiles, and says, "Remember, Han Fook . . . you are free to do whatever pleases you. You may go home and plant trees, you may hate me and kill me, it is of little consequence."

"How can I hate you," Han Fook realizes aloud. "It would be as if I hated heaven itself." Thus he stays and learns to play the zither and to compose poetry. What outwardly appears to be an art expressing only the simple and unpretentious things, he finds, can move the listener's soul as the wind moves the surface of the water.

Han Fook no longer knows how long he has lived with the master, but one morning the master is gone. Han Fook takes the lute and begins his homeward journey, and along the way he is greeted in the manner reserved for old and respected men. When he arrives in his village, he finds that his father, his bride, and his relatives are dead. That evening, the village is celebrating the lantern festival, and he stands across the river, leans against a tree, and plays his lute. The women sigh and look with rapture into the night, and the young men call out to the lute player, whom they cannot find, saying they have never heard such music. Han Fook can only smile and watch the reflection of the lanterns in the water. He cannot distinguish them from the real lanterns, and there seems to be no difference between this festival and the one of his youth, when he first heard the words of his master.

*Themes and Meanings*

"The Poet" was written in 1913, shortly after Hermann Hesse had finished his novel *Rosshalde* (1914; English translation, 1970), a thinly veiled portrait of his own life, in which he painfully analyzed the plight of an artist who is burdened by ties to his family, while his nature demands that he devote himself solely to his art. The shorter work is a more imaginative variation on the same theme. It is also the first work to reveal Hesse's growing preoccupation with the East and a prelude to his most lyric novel, *Siddhartha* (1922, English translation, 1951), in which Hesse expresses his religious beliefs against the background of Buddhistic India. Here, too, a younger apprentice discovers the harmony of the universe as he lives with a simple, smiling ferryman in a hut near a river. Whereas *Siddhartha* deals with the search for the meaning of life in religious terms, "The Poet" expresses Hesse's earlier and misdirected dream that he could find and express this meaning in art alone.

The repeated emphasis on music reveals it as a voice of universal harmony, a role foreshadowing the music theme in Hesse's final novel, *Das Glasperlenspiel: Versuch einer Lebensbeschreibung des Magister Ludi Josef Knecht samt Knechts hinterlassenen Schriften* (1943; *Magister Ludi*, 1949; also known as *The Glass Bead Game*, 1969), in which the Music Master becomes a transfigured saint who bears a likeness to the Master of the Perfect Word and to the elder Han Fook.

*Style and Technique*

"The Poet" is a fantasy, or *Marchen* (fairy tale). As such, one expects it to be imaginative and timeless, which it is. The language is lyrical, rhythmical, and simple, and, despite the exotic setting, the symbolism is not difficult. The lantern lights reflected in the water portray the artist's extrasensory perception of the link between the world of reality and the world of the spirit. Hesse's glowing praise of poetry and the revered, purple-robed poet reveal the author's conviction that the real meaning of life can be found and expressed in art. Finally, the resemblance of Han Fook to his master in the last scene emphasizes Hesse's vision of the recurring voice of the artist and the timeless essence of his message.

*Lewis W. Tusken*

# A POETICS FOR BULLIES

*Author:* Stanley Elkin (1930-1995)
*Type of plot:* Parody
*Time of plot:* The twentieth century
*Locale:* Unspecified
*First published:* 1965

> *Principal characters:*
> PUSH, the narrator, a bully
> EUGENE KRAFT, one of his victims, a boy with a glandular
> disorder
> JOHN WILLIAMS, a new boy in the neighborhood
> MIMMER,
> SLUD,
> CLOB, and
> FRANK, several of Push's victims

## The Story

The narrator, a brash schoolboy who calls himself "Push the bully," reveals whom he hates ("new kids and sissies, dumb kids and smart, rich kids, poor kids, kids who wear glasses, talk funny, show off") and what he likes, such as the specific ways he torments his victims. One day the obsequious Eugene Kraft, who suffers from a glandular disorder that makes him drool, comes to tell Push about a new boy in the neighborhood. Push has bullied Kraft into continually drinking water, and now forces him to swallow directly from the kitchen faucet. When Kraft meekly complains that the water is hot, Push assures him, with specious logic, that hot water evaporates better. After he makes Kraft gulp and stammer through his report, Push goes to confront the new boy, John Williams, whom Kraft characterizes as a kid-and-a-half.

In contrast to Push and the other local boys—Kraft, Mimmer, Slud, Clob, and Frank—John Williams does not suffer any physical, intellectual, or moral disability. Worldly, educated, self-confident, charitable, handsome, and athletic, he possesses no visible defects, seeming, in name as well as nature, to belong to a higher social order. Unlike the others, he is immune to Push's bullying.

Capable only of understanding the world as a place of imperfections, in which defect confers identity, Push is helpless to grasp the possibility of a flawless person. At Williams's home, Push's agitated efforts at bullying are easily negated by Williams's litany of care and concern for a man who is in pain, an old woman, a worried husband, and a wife in despair. Empathy and concern are foreign to Push; he winces and accuses Williams of being a lover and a bully.

During the days that follow, Push watches helplessly as Williams takes root at school, earning the admiration of his new classmates as well as the teachers and administrators. To the boys Push has bullied, Williams becomes a hero. He patiently reviews lessons with Mimmer, the "dummy"; he visits the gym with Slud, the "cripple"; he has Frank push aside the rich desserts that make him obese; and he teaches the physically repulsive Clob that true beauty comes from within. Even Kraft, whose glandular disorder seems beyond help, seems happier in Williams's company. In their love for the hero, their fear of Push is forgotten, and he, marginalized and baffled, remarks that he can understand people's hatred and grievance, but not their love or contentment.

The pivotal indignity occurs when Williams approaches Push at home, inviting him to talk. When he tells Push that he thinks he can make him happier, the bully becomes enraged at being treated like a victim. Although certain that he will lose, Push reasons that drawing Williams into a fistfight will demonstrate to the others that Williams does not have perfect knowledge or perfect charity: He will lose his aura of infallibility.

When Push strikes him, Williams quickly strikes back with unexpected zeal, and then strikes once again. Dazed, Push loses touch with the reason for his attack. On the ground, he cringes before Williams's next righteous blow, knowing only that he does not wish to be hurt. Instead of punishing the subdued Push, Williams charitably offers him his hand in friendship. Lonely and physically hurt, Push feels the need for such friendship. He is encouraged to shake Williams's hand by the other boys, Push's former victims, whose afflictions Williams has tended and whose self-esteem he has worked hard to elevate.

On the verge of joining the crowd, Push jerks back. Suppressing his own need for companionship, he vows that John Williams will never have him and realizes suddenly that it is this, his own crude independence, that constitutes Williams's lone defect. In a world once again free of perfection, Push is again Push the bully. He turns and excoriates the newfound happiness of the others. He contemptuously informs them that they will never be free of their infirmities; they are what they are: "Slud may dance and Clob may kiss but they'll never be good at it. . . . Will Mimmer do sums in his head? How do you like your lousy hunger, thin boy?" Kraft, crumbling under Push's derision, cries for someone to silence him and finally rushes at Push himself.

Despite his firm belief in the "bully's poetics," which are predicated on the nonexistence of magic, Push summons up what he calls "real magic at last: the cabala of my hate, of my irreconcilableness." He not only repels Kraft with a word but also curses him, paradoxically curing him. He causes Kraft's saliva to dry up, amazing everyone, even John Williams. They gather around the dry-mouthed and choking Kraft. Having momentarily longed for their acceptance, Push now declares, "I can't stand them near me. I move against them. I shove them away. I force them off. I press them, thrust them aside. I push through."

*Themes and Meanings*

"A Poetics for Bullies" subverts the generic boy's story, exemplified by the works of Thomas Hughes and Horatio Alger, in order to depict the destructive, antisocial forces underlying the growth and affirmation of the self. Although the protagonist, Push, characterizes himself as "the incarnation of envy and jealousy and need," he nevertheless fulfills the classic role of hero by confronting a superior adversary and prevailing through determination, grit, and ingenuity. Ironically, Push gains a deeper and more mature sense of self—the goal espoused by conventional pedagogical literature as a crucial step in the socialization process—but does so only by rejecting society and holding fast to his own antisocial characteristics.

Insecurity plagues the protagonist of a typical boy's story, and Push's initial covetousness betrays a longing to be other than he is. Stanley Elkin ironically has Push mask his adolescent uneasiness in a declaration of a love for the American ideal. "Do you know what makes me cry?" he asks, innocently; "'The Declaration of Independence.' 'All men are created equal.' That's beautiful." In Push's immature view, the democratic society is a safe haven from the isolating effects of his own differences.

In the midst of the final, climactic confrontation with John Williams, Push no longer yearns to escape from himself. He says, as if emerging with a new acceptance of his own characteristics, "I vie, strive, emulate, compete, a contender in every event there is." He recognizes and courageously accepts that it is hate at the core of his identity. He proclaims, "I will not be reconciled, or halve my hate. It's what I have." The others, who have allowed John Williams to aid them, have submerged their identities, entering into what Elkin vividly portrays as a homogeneous, insipid society. When Push dries up Kraft's defective glands—an act of magic unavailable to him earlier—he obliterates Kraft's identity. That such an act would be viewed as a cure, not only by the caricature of society within the story, but by the reader as well, constitutes the story's final, inescapable irony.

Overturning the standard conclusion of the boy's story, in which the protagonist reaches maturity and thereby gains admission into society, Elkin suggests that individual maturity is diametrically at odds with society; that society provides its citizens with warm feelings of security and belonging, but exacts the high price of their independence or mature individuality. This is the transaction that Push heroically rejects.

*Style and Technique*

As the story's title suggests, by joining two oppositional ideas—poets, or painstaking precision, with bullies or bulls, heedless or clumsy force—"A Poetics for Bullies" playfully subverts the normal usage of language. Push's boasting is rife with puns. He says that there is "only casuistical trick. Sleight-of-mouth, the bully's poetics." By drawing "sleight-of-mouth" from the idiom sleight-of-hand, Elkin not only aptly and originally names the kind of verbal tricks played by his protagonist but also demonstrates the kind of violence that he, the author, will do to, or the kind of liberties that he will take with, the language. The notion of doing violence, which is a kind of bullying, and taking liberties, which is a license associated with poetry, is, of course, directly relevant to the meaning of the story. The synthesis of violence and poetry is repeated

Masterplots II

when Push chortles, "Physical puns, conundrums. Push the punisher, the conundrummer." Puns are related to punish; and, perhaps, conundrums are related to drumming, as in beating or hitting.

Elkin gives several of his minor characters—Kraft, Mimmer, Slud, and Clob—names that invoke the gross and farcical failings of base menials in Shakespearean comedies, such as *A Midsummer Night's Dream* (1595). Perhaps the most central subversion of language occurs with another title, the Declaration of Independence. It is by relinquishing his attachment to this document and the notion that "all men are created equal" that Push is able to assert his own, personal independence. Thus, Elkin ironically offers the Declaration of Independence as a barrier to independence, a symbol of social pressure to conform.

*Michael Scott Joseph*

# THE PORTABLE PHONOGRAPH

*Author:* Walter Van Tilburg Clark (1909-1971)
*Type of plot:* Fantasy
*Time of plot:* Unspecified
*Locale:* Western United States
*First published:* 1941

> *Principal characters:*
> DOCTOR JENKINS, an old intellectual
> AN UNNAMED MUSICIAN, who is ill
> A MIDDLE-AGED WRITER
> AN UNNAMED MIDDLE-AGED MAN

*The Story*

The story opens at the end of a desolate, late autumn day in the aftermath of a great war. The landscape is a vast, empty prairie, with nothing but the fading traces of battle to be seen. Civilization is dead, and few survivors have been reduced to a primitive state. In an earthen cave, four men huddle by a small peat fire; what wood there is must be saved for the coming, deadly winter. Doctor Jenkins is wrapping up four books from which he has been reading: the Bible, the works of William Shakespeare, Herman Melville's *Moby Dick: Or, The Whale* (1851), and Dante's *La divina commedia* (c. 1320; *The Divine Comedy,* 1802), the only books he has saved from the catastrophe. These books, he remarks, contain what was good in the old civilization, even though they could not save that civilization. He adds that he hopes that they will help the people of the next civilization to be strong enough that they will not fall behind when they become clever.

One of the other men is a writer, but he has nothing on which, or with which, to write. He says enviously that because Jenkins has the books, Jenkins will have a little soul left until he dies. That is, the books embody and give soul, although the meaning of the word is ambiguous. Jenkins grudgingly offers to let the others hear his phonograph, a windup machine. Because one of the guests is a musician, Jenkins says he will use one of his few steel needles, instead of the thorns he normally uses. Jenkins pulls out his records, a mere dozen, reads the titles, and then allows the youngest guest, the sick, coughing musician, to select the one that he wants to hear, a Claude Debussy nocturne. They listen raptly; for the others, the music calls up memories, but the musician hears only the music, the pure sound, pure beauty.

When it is over, the young musician departs into the darkness and cold outside abruptly, without saying anything; the others thank Jenkins. He promises them that next week he will play another record. After they have gone, Jenkins stands in the entrance of his cave, peering, listening; he hears what he had expected, a coughing, and thinks he sees a moving shadow. He goes back into his cave and, listening often, hides his records, phonograph, and books in a hole behind his makeshift bed. At the very last, he shifts his ragged bed to face the piece of canvas that is his door, lies down, and then feels, with his hand, a piece of lead pipe.

*Themes and Meanings*

For a very short story, "The Portable Phonograph" develops unusual complex thematic matters. When it was published, there was already war in Europe and a well-founded fear that the United States would soon be involved. The story, both in the manner of its telling as well as in what it tells, develops themes that are not time-bound. Walter Van Tilburg Clark is posing questions about human nature, not just discussing particular historical circumstances.

There is a deliberate indeterminacy as to what human nature may be and how it relates to its own achievements. For example, technology, which has been created by humans, has destroyed itself and so destroyed humans; or, perhaps, human beings, having made technology, have misused it and destroyed themselves. Only in a civilized world is there technology, and technology is control over, sometimes destruction of, nature. Because civilization can be antinature and antilife, it can be an evil. Outside the cave, there is only nature, uncaring about humankind, held off only somewhat by books and music. Elsewhere in his work, Clark has affirmed the natural and primitive man, but here primitiveness is not a simple good.

Jenkins's wish for the future, that the ones to follow will learn the best of the old civilization from its books, suggests that he still believes that humankind can learn, can truly progress. He believes that human beings may be capable of achieving technological progress and yet use it for good and beautiful purposes, of living in harmony with the natural. There is also a hint that nature itself may offer some hope, although humankind has little to do with this. After the description of tank tracks and bomb craters, the first paragraph ends with the picture of a few young trees "trying again."

All of this is only a wish. The actualities of the events say that people have killed and very probably will continue to kill one another; the end of the story disturbingly suggests that the young musician, no doubt dying from his disease, may nevertheless be capable of killing Jenkins in order to acquire the phonograph and the records. He may kill, not for power, but for the temporary possession of a certain kind of beauty. Perhaps Clark's use of music is intended to emphasize the terrible nature of this breakdown of civilization. Music is the nearest art to purity, especially the art of someone like Debussy. The books that Jenkins has preserved are contaminated by social, political, religious, and moral content, and so could stir one to act, but Debussy's music should not. Paradoxically, if the writer so envies Jenkins the books that he seems to be a threat, he is much less a threat than the musician is. If the ill musician, apparently the least dangerous of men, is capable of murdering, that would imply that no amount of civilization will save humankind from its impulse to evil.

There is a further irony about art here. What Jenkins had been reading is from William Shakespeare's *The Tempest* (1611); the envious writer is a creator; one can say that he is an image, or perhaps a counterimage, of Prospero in the play. Human creativity has always been associated with an affirmation of life. Prospero, however, has a book, a book by which he brings about good, but the writer in "The Portable Phonograph" not only has no book but also cannot make one, cannot create. The thematic statement is that creativity itself is also problematic.

One must note that there are no women in the story. They may exist somewhere in this world, but absence itself is a statement. Their absence emphasizes violence, death, and the improbability of continued life. By implication, it is males who have brought about the catastrophe; it is males who will continue on, but without women they cannot continue long.

*Style and Technique*

Clark's language is relatively simple, for he is emphasizing what happens, not language in itself. It is a language of concrete images, especially of winter; the points are made largely through the use of imagery, not assertion. Clark develops his themes, however, through the use of a varying point of view as well as of the overall structure, and these two techniques are intimately allied.

Structurally, the story moves from a general view of humankind to the particular. As the story begins, the world is presented from the outside, almost as though through the lens of a camera. These images are of a cruel and unforgiving natural world, and so become comments. For only a sentence or two, an authorial voice tells us what those images mean. This is the one place that this judging, moralizing voice enters. Most of the story does not force the reader to accept a particular meaning, but the authorial voice is momentarily necessary in order to establish the generalizations.

It is the telling of most of the story from the outside, however, that suggests the difficulties of saying what humankind is. Clark does not explain what people are; the interpretation is up to the reader.

When the point of view first shifts to a personal view, the thoughts of the individuals, it is momentarily to the mind of the musician, not to Doctor Jenkins. This is significant, for the musician thinks only that he does not have much future. The reader is never in his mind again and so cannot know whether he may be willing to kill for that short future. The reader enters Jenkins's mind only indirectly: The reader knows that he is listening for the cough but is not told why. Nor is it explained why the lead pipe is comforting. This indirection is one more element in the terrible and threatening ambiguity of the story.

*L. L. Lee*

# THE PORTOBELLO ROAD

*Author:* Muriel Spark (1918-    )
*Type of plot:* Ghost story
*Time of plot:* 1930-1950
*Locale:* London, rural Great Britain, and the British colonies in Africa
*First published:* 1958

> *Principal characters:*
> NEEDLE, the narrator, one of a group of friends
> KATHLEEN, Needle's best childhood friend
> JOHN (SKINNY), another childhood friend
> GEORGE, the fourth of the group of friends

*The Story*

This episodic story begins with an account of how Needle got her unusual nickname: by reaching into a haystack on which she and her friends, George, Kathleen, and John, were playing and accidentally impaling the fleshy part of her thumb with a needle that lay hidden in the hay. After some minor first aid, George marks the occasion by taking a photograph, which serves throughout the story as a memento of the youthful friendship that these people shared—a friendship that survives, although in modified form, through a lengthy period of change as they mature.

As the first episode marks the earliest event in the chronology of the story, the second marks virtually the latest. Needle describes an accidental meeting with George and Kathleen that occurs many years after the haystack episode, when Kathleen is nearing thirty-five years of age. Needle is passing through the Saturday crowds in the Portobello Road, an open-air market area of London, when she comes across her two old friends, who are now married to each other. Acting under an inner prompting, Needle speaks to George, who is horrified to see her. When he tells Kathleen that Needle is nearby, she insists that he is mistaken because, as she remarks at the end of the episode, Needle has been dead for five years.

The remainder of the story recounts the progressive decline of the unusual relationship between these four childhood friends. Although Needle does not use the term, she clearly suggests in the succeeding narrative, an interlude between the second and third episodes, that she is spending the time after her death clearing up the "unfinished business" of this relationship. The nature of that business is, in large part, both the source of the story's interest and the basis of its surprising conclusion.

In the third episode, Needle picks up the chronological account that begins with the haystack episode at the beginning of the story. No longer mere children, the four friends are preparing to take up adult lives in London and the south of England, far from their native territory on the Scottish border: John, nicknamed "Skinny," goes to study archaeology; George and Kathleen, to take up connections with wealthy family members; and Needle, to undertake a career as a writer. George soon decides to go to Africa and work on his uncle's tobacco farm, and his approaching departure from familiar surroundings and friends makes him both anxious and eager to remind them that they must maintain their friendship. In the way of persons whose early friendships survive changing adult interests, the four keep track of one another despite the changes.

John arranges a job for Needle as secretary to an archaeological dig in Africa, where the two have the opportunity to see George again and to discover his dissatisfaction and sense of isolation, as well as the fact that he is living with Matilda, a woman of mixed race, who is pregnant by him. Needle soon quits her job with the party of archaeologists and scrapes together a living as a columnist for a local paper. She meets George once again, just before World War II breaks out, and he gives evidence of jealousy over her apparent attachment to John and her coolness toward him. In a fit of honesty, George tells Needle that he has secretly married Matilda because she refused to live with him any longer unless he did so. He has since arranged, through the wealth of his uncle, to get Matilda to live separately from him, although he cannot persuade her to divorce him because she is Catholic. Perhaps regretting his candor, George insists that Needle promise never to tell the secret he has shared, and she does so, leaving Africa shortly thereafter, just as the war breaks out.

After the war, which George spends away from England, the other three friends keep up a casual but earnest friendship. Needle and John are almost ready to marry when John contracts tuberculosis, and during the period of his convalescence abroad, Needle lives in England, contriving to piece together a living from a variety of odd jobs as a writer, publicist, and companion. Kathleen suddenly calls her with news: George is back in England and apparently eager to reestablish old ties, even though the other three have not heard from him for almost ten years. Kathleen seems quite eager to welcome him back on the old terms, or perhaps even closer ones, but Needle is less sanguine.

Needle leaves the south of England for a brief holiday, during which she learns by letter that Kathleen and George are seeing much of each other. When she returns to London, Kathleen arranges for her to spend a weekend at a country house belonging to Kathleen's aunt; George is living nearby and is expected as a guest at dinner. When Kathleen is delayed, Needle goes down to the country house alone, with the object of buying groceries and other supplies.

At a nearby farm, where she has gone to buy milk, she meets George, bound on the same errand. George asks to accompany her to the house, and when they stop to rest on a haystack along the path through the farm, she soon discovers that he has an important matter to discuss with her: He plans to marry Kathleen, and he wants further assurance that Needle will not tell the secret about Matilda, to whom he is still legally married. Needle refuses, telling him unequivocally that she will tell Kathleen about Matilda if he attempts to marry her. At this response, Needle reports that "he looked as if he would murder me and he did," by stuffing hay into her mouth until she suffocated.

Her body is later discovered, and George is questioned by the police, but no charge can be brought against him. Although the police check George's African history and discover the fact of his living with Matilda, the marriage itself remains undiscovered. Kathleen and George are married, and the interval passes until Needle speaks to George once more, in the Portobello Road on a Saturday morning.

In the concluding section, Needle explains how she and George begin to look for each other on Saturdays in the Portobello Road; George is both attracted and repelled by the ghost of the woman he murdered. In the end, he is driven almost mad, and Kathleen has all that she can do to keep him away from the road on Saturday mornings. John finally persuades them to emigrate to Canada—where George will be free of the compulsion to visit the road—and the long-standing, unusual relationship among the four friends finally dissolves.

*Themes and Meanings*

Several motifs that recur in much of Muriel Spark's fiction appear in this story as well: the indirect reflection of Catholic doctrine, the concern about religion generally and about the afterlife in particular, the representation of love relationships between persons of different races, and the discovery and analysis of confused values.

In this story, however, the focal point of thematic development seems to be that of expectation: the kinds of expectation that persons may reasonably have of their friends and lovers, and the kinds that are unreasonable or otherwise illegitimate and inappropriate. Kathleen is a good-hearted person who cannot see the bad points of anyone she has chosen to befriend, and whose expectations are constantly out of concord with the reality that she is nevertheless quite able to ignore.

George is the epitome of unreasonableness, a childish and immature creature who expects everyone else to conform to his own plans and goals, who finds it necessary and possible to deal harshly with anyone who stands in his way, but who is nevertheless incapable of accepting the responsibilities that such expectations entail. John, although the least developed of the main characters, seems clearly to be a character with very limited expectations of others: His reticence and diffidence, especially in regard to his supposed love for Needle, apparently mask a profound mistrust of those whose relationships and understandings he should value.

Finally, Needle—although she tells the story—reveals herself as a person fundamentally incapable of commitment to a relationship. Unlike Kathleen or George, who can accept the intimacy of closeness, Needle shows that she resists such intimacy by her refusal to make any commitment to John. On the positive side, however, Needle shows that the expectation of principled action is the grounds of her own behavior, and she maintains her standards of action, even though the cost is higher than she might have expected.

*Style and Technique*

The principal structural device of the story is the episodic arrangement that allows the narrator to move from one event to another without following a rigorously chronological order. Information is presented appropriately, but the surprising announcement of Needle's condition, as well as the long delay in the narration of her death, are effective only because Spark has prepared the reader to accept such unlikelihoods by the neat diversions from a strict chronological account.

Spark's typically wry and understated manner contributes much to the success of the story. The matter-of-fact tone of the narrator's voice, even when narrating unlikely events, is in itself highly persuasive, so that the reader is almost taken in by the remarkable occurrences that Needle describes. Throughout, the relatively narrow emotional range that Spark allows her narrator to use also contributes to the control of the story's effect and to the seeming realism of the account: One might easily imagine a ghost speaking thus, without rancor but also without enthusiasm.

*Dale B. Billingsley*

# THE POST OFFICE

*Author:* Liam O'Flaherty (1896-1984)
*Type of plot:* Parody
*First published:* 1954
*Locale:* Western Ireland
*Time of plot:* The 1950's

> *Principal characters:*
> MARTIN CONLON, the postmaster of Praiseach
> THE YOUNG MAN, a visitor to the post office
> THE YOUNG AMERICAN WOMAN, a friend of the young man
> THE YOUNG SPANISH WOMAN, another friend of the young man

*The Story*

The setting for this quick-paced story is the Irish village of Praiseach, which means "confusion." It is an appropriate title, because from the very moment the three strangers (two women and one man, all dressed in the height of fashion) arrive in this isolated village, confusion reigns. The action takes place in the post office of Praiseach, a dingy little stone building ruled over by the local postmaster, Martin Conlon. Described by Liam O'Flaherty as "a middle-aged man of great size, a good part of which lay in the region of his stomach," Martin has a fear of being dismissed from his job that is exceeded only by his fear of sending telegrams.

It is pension day in Praiseach, so there are dozens of old people waiting for Martin to cash their government pension checks. One of the three strangers, the young man who is dressed like a "foreigner" but who speaks Irish like a native, adds even greater turmoil to this already confused situation by requesting to send a telegram to the United States. On hearing the word "telegram," "Martin started violently and gripped the edge of the counter with both hands. His face looked horrified."

Thus begins a long series of comic exchanges, with the young man trying to get hold of a telegraph form, on one hand, and Martin doing his best to dissuade him, on the other. Martin tries everything to get the young man to send his message from Galway, even pointing to the American woman's shiny red Cadillac (which is quite a contrast to this shabby village) and saying, "With a car like that one outside, she wouldn't be half an hour going into the town."

The young man, however, does not wish to be put off. He insists, to the great amusement of the locals who know of Martin's fear, that the telegram must be sent from Praiseach. He explains that the Spanish woman, the darker of the two women, has a friend in Los Angeles whose ancestors hailed from Praiseach. The woman has promised, at all costs, to send a telegram to her friend from his ancestral village. What makes it worse, however, from Martin's point of view, is that the message is a poem in Spanish.

Father Tom, the parish priest, briefly enters the scene. He is out looking for his dog, and, in his search, stumbles into the post office. He finds Martin's predicament as amusing as do the local villagers. After a few words of false sympathy, the priest leaves the post office, laughing loudly.

Eventually, under continued pressure from the young man, Martin agrees to send the telegram. He then has a series of confrontations with the telephone, both brief and amusing, in which he speaks to seemingly everyone but the one person he is trying to reach. Three times he rings for the Galway operator, and three times he is connected to conversations that are already in progress. There is one in which "the angry voice of a single man made itself violently manifest to the drum of Martin's ear." In no uncertain terms, the voice accuses Martin of trying to cheat him out of some fish. When Martin tells him that he has no fish for sale, the man calls him a liar. They are then disconnected.

The Galway operator finally rings him, with the message that a local man is dead. This is duly passed on to the locals surrounding Martin, but then the operator hangs up. Martin goes through the same process again, ringing for the operator but getting the wrong connections. Eventually, he reaches a man who is also trying to reach another place. Martin tells him that he is in Praiseach (confusion), and the man laughs and says, "We are all in it, as far as I can see."

This confusion continues long into the story, with Martin becoming progressively more befuddled and frustrated. In the end, he can only hold his head in his hands and allow the American woman to make the phone call. This she does promptly, reading each letter of the poem (which is by Federico García Lorca) into the phone.

The story ends as it began, with utter chaos. While the American woman is on the phone, the locals begin to crowd around Martin and demand their pensions. He, in turn, shouts at them to behave. The soldier, an old man who entered with a letter he wanted someone to read to him, advises the young man for the fifth time to "have a go" at the American woman. In the meantime, the Spanish woman is marching around the room, "with her arms stretched out and head thrown back," reciting passionately:

> Era madrugada. Nadie
> pudo asomarse a sus ojos
> abiertos al duro aire.
>
> (It was dawn. Nobody
> could fathom her eyes
> open to the hard air.)

*Themes and Meanings*

At first glance, there is little in this story to suggest that there are any deep themes or meanings. Indeed, for all practical purposes, the story looks like little more than a satirical sketch on life in the west of Ireland. By using the name Praiseach, O'Flaherty seemingly wishes to create a portrait of chaos, confusion, and formlessness. In this he is successful, but there is far more to the story than simply unbridled confusion.

This story is about a clash between two cultures, the traditional and the modern, and how the former is helpless when faced with the latter. As postmaster of Praiseach, an "obscure and miserable village," Martin Conlon represents the old tradition. The young women, on the other hand, represent all that is modern in the world, with their sleek cars, clothes, and manners. The young man, with his fancy clothes yet fluent Irish, stands as a bridge between the two cultures.

The clash between the two cultures comes over the sending of the telegram, itself a representation of the modern culture. When presented with this challenge, the traditional culture—represented by Martin—simply cannot respond. Indeed, Martin's sole reaction is precisely in tune with the name of his village: confusion. It is the American woman, the symbol of modern culture, who finally completes the telegram.

O'Flaherty also seems to believe that this modern culture will eventually take over the traditional, for the young man, standing as a bridge between the two cultures, certainly favors the modern side. He is humbled by it, telling the soldier that he is not good enough for the American woman. However, at the same time, he takes great pleasure in mocking the traditional culture of Praiseach.

*Style and Technique*

O'Flaherty's style in this story, like the majority of his fiction, is simple and straightforward. To create a comic sort of narrative, he relies on both exaggeration and repetition. When the villagers in the post office find out that Martin must send a telegram, they do not simply smile knowingly at one another, but they "burst out into full-bellied and joyous laughter. The rollicking sound could be heard away out on the road. People stamped on the floor and thumped one another in the sides with merriment." Again and again this exaggeration occurs in the story.

There is also heavy use of repetition. Four times in the space of the story, Martin screams at the local villagers to keep quiet. Three times he gets a bad connection on the phone, and three times he looks at the strangers with hatred for having asked him to send the telegram.

At times, these techniques are a bit heavy-handed and almost seem to beg for a laugh. At others, though, the reader cannot help but smile. There is one digression in which an old woman looks at the toes of the two foreign women and, seeing that they are painted red, asks the young man: "What class of disease is that?" He responds that they caught a disease in the Amazon that is causing their toes to rot slowly, inch by inch. The old woman screams and flees the post office, leaving her pension money behind.

In the end, however, the humor is of secondary importance, for O'Flaherty has created a story and characters that personify the name of the village—confusion. This he does admirably.

*Michael Verdon*

# POWERHOUSE

*Author:* Eudora Welty (1909-2001)
*Type of plot:* Psychological
*Time of plot:* The late 1930's
*Locale:* Alligator, Mississippi
*First published:* 1941

> *Principal characters:*
> POWERHOUSE, the leader of a jazz band, a famous black musician
> who plays piano and sings
> VALENTINE, a member of the band who plays the bass
> LITTLE BROTHER, a member of the band who plays the clarinet
> SCOOT, a member of the band who plays the drums
> THE NARRATOR, an unnamed white man

*The Story*

Eudora Welty is known for her compelling characters, and the protagonist in this story, Powerhouse, is certainly one of her most striking creations. A famous black musician, Powerhouse is appropriately named, for his outstanding characteristic is the creative power of his imagination. This creative power is portrayed over the course of one evening in a small town in Mississippi, during the late 1930's, when the Jim Crow laws of segregation were in effect, as the band plays for a "white dance"—a dance that only white people may attend.

At the opening of the story, the narrator, an unnamed white member of the community, begins with a lyrical celebration of Powerhouse on the night of the performance. The narrator sees the musician as someone who is "marvelous, frightening," someone who is capable of casting everyone in the audience "into oblivion" with his performance. Powerhouse is like a magician with his band. From his first note—which "marks the end of any known discipline"—onward, Powerhouse brings the audience under the spell of his creative power, which is constantly improvising and also constantly seeking expression.

After the opening sections of the story, the narration shifts beyond the white narrator to a more objective reporting of the events. Late at night, the band begins to play the one waltz of the evening, a request, and during this sad song, Powerhouse suddenly declares to the other members of the band that he has received a telegram that reads that his wife, Gypsy, has died. This declaration is the beginning of an intermittent jive that carries through the rest of the story. While playing, the other band members ask Powerhouse about her death, and Powerhouse begins to weave a story of receiving the telegram with such convincing detail, relating such pain and despair, that the reader becomes caught up in the imaginative reality of it and begins to wonder if, in fact, Powerhouse's wife has died.

After the song ends, it is midnight, and Powerhouse calls for an intermission. Because Alligator, Mississippi, is segregated, black people cannot be served in white establishments, so the band leaves the dance hall to walk to a café in "Negrotown." Outside, it is a bad night, rain is falling, but a large crowd of about one hundred black people, "ragged, silent, delighted," greet the band; under the eaves of the hall outside—because they could not attend the segregated dance—these people have been listening to the music.

At the café, which is a "silent, limp room" with a "burned-out-looking nickelodeon," the band orders beer, and Powerhouse requests a record by Bessie Smith, the great blues singer. As the jukebox plays and the band drinks beer, Powerhouse once again begins the jive about his wife, creating the circumstances of her suicide. He tells of how she was in so much anguish that she jumped out the window of a hotel, and he goes on to speak of how her brains were all over the sidewalk. One of the band members protests that these details are too graphic, too awful.

The jive continues, now developing around a "crooning creeper" who has been taking Powerhouse's place with his wife, a man whom Powerhouse names as Uranus Knockwood. Uranus Knockwood is described in such detail, with such compellingly realistic flourishes, that the audience in the café "moans with pleasure," and the waitress declares that the story has to be "the real truth." Powerhouse then tells her that the story is not true, that "Truth is something worse, I ain't said what, yet. It's something hasn't come to me, but I ain't saying it won't." He asks if he should tell that truth when it does come to him, and the band begs him not to.

On the walk back to the dance hall, Powerhouse again begins the jive about Uranus Knockwood, and he is so persistent that Scoot, the drummer, asks if perhaps Powerhouse should not phone his wife. An ominous tension animates this moment, for the imaginative reality that Powerhouse has created is an expression of his fears that his wife is unfaithful to him and that she is prone to the kind of despair that ends in suicide. However, when Powerhouse declares that he will not call her, with the implication that he will not give in to his fears, the moment of crisis has passed.

The story ends with the band playing "Somebody Loves Me." The white narrator's voice, as at the beginning of the story, once again relates the action. Powerhouse sings the lyrics, "Somebody loves me! Somebody loves me, I wonder who!" and as he sings the next line, "Maybe . . . ," he glances around "the place where he is"—the white dance hall, a world of segregation and prejudice—and "a vast, impersonal, and yet furious grimace transfigures his wet face." He suddenly ends the song, "Maybe it's you!" The meaning of this last action carries the connotation that as an artist, Powerhouse has a vision of a love that perhaps can go beyond the circumstances of this life—in his case, a life of segregation and prejudice, a world of fear and pain and despair.

*Themes and Meanings*

The power of the artistic imagination is the basic theme that Welty explores in this story. That imagination is what gives Powerhouse his ability to cast a spell over his audience, to draw them into a reality that he creates with his voice and his piano, and with the members of his band. The small-town narrator articulates the fascination of this man, declaring, "He's a person of joy, a fanatic. He listens as much as he performs, a look of hideous, powerful rapture on his face." The creative energy that flows from Powerhouse is something beyond the limits of ordinary existence, as the power of the artist transforms ordinary lives, enabling others to experience the world in a different way.

That same imagination enables Powerhouse to give expression to his fears: In the jive story about the death of his wife, and then about the singer, Uranus Knockwood, who had taken Powerhouse's place with his wife, Powerhouse creates an imaginative reality that he may confront and dispel, so that he may continue to function as a man of the world. Powerhouse recognizes the nature of his fiction, so that when the waitress questions him about the "real truth" of his wife, he tells her that the incident did not happen; however, he goes on to say that "Truth is something worse"—the real facts of humankind's existence are terrible. However, he, Powerhouse, believes that he has the ability eventually to grasp that truth and then to relate it to others. The implication is that he will relate it as an artist through the medium of his music, through the jazz blues that he plays.

The setting contributes to the strength of the theme, for the fact that Powerhouse is a black musician playing in the segregated South, a place where black people cannot even come into the hall and dance to his music, gives added pain and despair to the already bleak circumstances of the human condition.

*Style and Technique*

Welty has stated that when an author is writing a story, "I think it may be wrong to try for beauty; we should try for other things, then hope." In this story, one of the things Welty tries to achieve is a sensitive rendering of the setting, her native Mississippi. In order to portray the setting properly, Welty uses the technique of presenting Powerhouse first through the voice of the small-town white narrator, who vividly embodies the provincial sensibilities of this segregated community when he declares that "Powerhouse is not a show-off like the Harlem boys." The narrator, however, is not comfortable with Powerhouse, and in the statement, "You know people on a stage— and people of a darker race—so likely to be marvelous, frightening," the narrator's fascination with, and fears of, Powerhouse emerge. Powerhouse is, after all, a black man performing before an all-white audience, but beyond that, he is the kind of person who will take one beyond the limits of his known existence, and such people seem dangerous.

The imaginative, creative power of Powerhouse is suggested by the story's language, with its great, vibrant energy. The word patterns are intense and lyrical, particularly in the opening section, where a stream of phrases and incomplete sentences serves to generate the excitement of the subject and to take the reader beyond the limits of an ordinary story. Welty believes that "stories make words new," and with her dynamic style in this story, readers feel as if they had never read these words before. In addition to her vivid, descriptive passages, Welty shows herself to be a master of dialogue, as the jive among the band members achieves its own kind of lyricism. The overall use of language is itself a tribute to the creative power of the imagination—this is one story wherein subject and technique are one, and, as in the highest art, are essentially indivisible. In telling the story of Powerhouse and his imagination, Welty achieves that beauty of artistic form that she believes to be the "reward" of the sensitive writer.

*Ronald L. Johnson*

# PRELUDE

*Author:* Katherine Mansfield (Katherine Mansfield Beauchamp, 1888-1923)
*Type of plot:* Psychological
*Time of plot:* The early twentieth century
*Locale:* New Zealand
*First published:* 1917

> *Principal characters:*
> LINDA BURNELL, the protagonist, whose life is threatened every
>     time she gives birth
> STANLEY BURNELL, her husband, whose greatest wish is to have
>     a son and heir
> ISABEL, their oldest daughter
> KEZIA, the middle daughter, much like her mother in
>     temperament
> LOTTIE, the youngest daughter, still nearly a baby
> MRS. FAIRCHILD, Linda's beloved mother, the stabilizing female
>     force in the household
> BERYL FAIRCHILD, Linda's unmarried younger sister

*The Story*

"Prelude" describes a move that the Burnell family makes from one house to another. With most of their possessions already in transit, the Burnell women are in a buggy that is packed so tightly that there is no room for Lottie and Kezia. Mrs. Fairchild decides to leave the children with a neighbor until they can be brought later by the grocery man in his wagon. For Kezia and Lottie, the journey to the new house begins at night when everything familiar is left behind, and the carriage rattles into unknown country and along new roads and steep hills, down into bushy valleys and through wide shallow rivers. As they reach the great new house, it appears to Kezia as a soft white bulk stretched on a green garden.

When they enter the house, Kezia's lamp reveals wallpaper covered with flying parrots. The dining room has a fireplace, and this center is occupied by the family. The windows are bare but, by the next morning, Beryl will have hung red serge curtains. From this point on, there is a careful room-by-room description of the house. There are four bedrooms upstairs. The servants sleep downstairs in rooms just behind the kitchen. From the windows of the kitchen it is possible to see the washhouse and scullery. The nursery has a fireplace and a table where the children have their meals. The drawing room is described after it has been put in order. As Beryl and Mrs. Fairchild establish daily routines, there emerges a complete floor plan of the house and yards. The windows and the views from them orient the house to the garden and to the light of the sun and the moon. Packing cases disappear, beds are made, pictures are hung, the kitchen is made neat, and everything is put in pairs and on shelves. Daily life is organized into patterns.

Plans, also, are made: Mrs. Fairchild will make jam in the autumn; Stanley speaks of bringing men home from the office for Saturday lunch and tennis. The children are sent to play in the garden, their play becoming an imitation of life in the house, but that play is only a prelude to their experience when they leave the garden and go down to the creek, for the garden, which is detailed with as much care as the house, is the prelude to the dark bush that lies beyond it.

Kezia explores the well-laid-out, neatly arranged flowers and orchards, always aware of what lies beyond, of what is on the other side of the drive, the dark trees and strange bushes, the frightening side. Driving through the bush at sunset, Stanley is overcome with panic that does not subside until he has been reassured by the sound of Linda's voice that everything is in order. It is in Linda that the two realities find accommodation, life seen as a necessary prelude to death.

Although it is not stated in the story that Linda is pregnant, there is a suggestion that she either is or soon will be. Stanley's gift of oysters, which Linda puts aside, is recalled when the servant girl reads in her dream book that a party in a family way should avoid eating a present of shellfish. Removed, unconcerned in the caring for the children and the household, Linda's one function seems to be a creative one. While her mother and sister busily put the household into order and tend to the children, Linda is most often apart, alone in her room, alone in the garden, away from the dinner table when the family is eating, at the end of the drawing room when Beryl and Stanley play cribbage. Mrs. Fairchild and Beryl dress conventionally, but Linda does not dress as the other women do. Instead, she is draped in a shawl or a blanket. The romantic aura thrown about Linda suggests another aspect of the feminine mystique bound up in birth-giving, from which arises the shadowy figure of the mother-goddess who is intimately connected with the moon and the earth.

Stanley, on the other hand, is identified with the sun. On the first morning in the new house, he stands in the exact center of a square of sunlight. This initial identification takes on greater proportions as the household comes to life and everything revolves around him and the urgency of his departure. The horse and buggy must be readied; he must make his daily journey, timed with the appearance and disappearance of the sun in the sky. All day, the activities of the house will prepare for his return, and when he comes home, everything is bathed in bright, metallic light.

*Themes and Meanings*

Essentially, "Prelude" is about time and place as they affect a single family. There is the time that is measured by the clock and to which the characters respond with daily routines; there is the time of a larger order, that of generations in history; there is time in an even larger, grander sense, the time of nature, of the movement of the planets through the heavens, rotating about the sun. A corresponding sense of place is achieved as the family moves through prescribed paths and areas. The family moves from one house to another, from city to country; the characters move from house to garden and back again into the house; they move from family rooms to private rooms, and finally they move from reality to dream to fantasy in the innermost circle of all.

Time and place are parallel. The personal time that governs daily activities is ordered by clock time, which, in turn, corresponds with the movement of the earth around the sun. The planetary motions suggest that larger order of historical time made parallel with the generations of the family delineated in all its tenses, past, present, and future. An absolute time transcends planetary motions, extending beyond the finalities of life and death, and accounts for the individual's attempts to impose structure, order, and meaning on life, to escape the narrow boundaries imposed by life to freer realms of death, to overcome the restrictions imposed by society. Such is the closely woven complex of relationships in "Prelude" that at any specific moment in time, a larger construct of meaning can be derived.

Readers of this story find themselves caught up in these various aspects of time. They see a family for the calendar space of seven days; they become familiar with daily routines that measure time like a clock. They see the years of the past merge in the present moment so that the future is always on the point of becoming one with the present, and sometimes does. The child becomes mother and the mother becomes child. Generation is followed by generation in one unbroken sequence. The century plant is coming into bloom again; in another century it will bloom again as it has bloomed in the past. The universe spins on its axis; the planets move about the sun, eternally, through endless space at incredible rates as the sun rises and sets. However, all the different times are simultaneous and exist as one in the human mind.

Within the interior regions of the mind, themes are developed. Human concerns are presented: problems of human existences, meanings of life and death. People respond in different ways. Some accept life without question and seek only to achieve order and control over the chaos of living; the questions of these people concern operational means, the design of routine. Stanley is an example. Life, for him, is a matter of regulating daily routines. His is a conventional notion of the well-ordered life. However, Stanley is both man and child, the "master" of the house and the object of the care and responsibility of the members of the household. That there is something wrong with his simplified notion of living is suggested by the panic he experiences when he approaches the house at night and the anxiety he feels in the morning before work.

In contrast, Linda accepts nothing, neither the principles of life nor her role nor Stanley, as the answer to larger problems. Her concept of life is broad. It extends to include all things, even the minute, inanimate objects that she invests with her own mobility and awareness in much the same way that the mother gives life to the children that she bears unwillingly. Her life revolves around the more fundamental question of the conflict between the will to survive that is part of the human makeup and the equally strong drive and need for death.

*Style and Technique*

To the inexperienced reader of Katherine Mansfield's stories, it must seem that nothing of any significance ever happens. Plot, as one used to know it and still finds it in occasional fiction, has disappeared. The old plot line that could be charted—rising action, climax, falling action—has given way to a line that does not rise very much and then stops somewhere and remains hovering. In contrast to the traditional emphasis on what happens, Mansfield's stories emphasize why it happens, which is an altogether different thing. In a story such as "Prelude," details do more than set the scene; objects, characters, and incidents and their positions make a tangential point; nothing is apparent, everything is implied.

With an *in medias res* beginning, there is no formal introduction, no exposition, no particular setting of scene. Plunged immediately into a story, without time to accommodate to a new situation, readers are thrown into an imbalance that they must immediately work to set straight, and they have no bearings except those that the story provides.

Once in a Mansfield story, readers are moved through a series of incidents that are no more than incidents until relationships are discovered. Ordinarily, relationships are revealed through details that are charged with symbolic significance, image patterns that move to metaphoric levels, and symbolic actions. Details, properly chosen, provide the texture of an experience; sense data ground readers in the concrete, convincing them of the reality of a scene. In her stories, Mansfield causes readers to become immersed in the sensory, invoking all five senses to provide immediacy and intensity.

Mansfield's symbols emerge from the story itself; they are formed from the natural materials that create the texture of the experience. Thus, the juxtaposition of Kezia with both Linda and Mrs. Fairchild forms a strong symbolic relationship. So close are the affinities between Kezia and Linda that at times it is possible to see Kezia as an apparition of the past, Linda as child. Their fantasies and dreams are interchangeable. Their common fears and love of Mrs. Fairchild unite them. It is around Kezia and her confrontation with death that a major part of the story revolves. After Pat, the manservant, kills the duck that will be used for dinner, Kezia is first thrilled by the sight of blood, and then she is appalled. She rushes at Pat, putting her arms around his legs and screaming to him to put the duck's head back on his body. That Kezia comes to a similar intuitive knowledge of life and death as Linda is made clear at the end of the story when Kezia tiptoes away from the mirror in the same way that Linda had earlier turned her head as she passed the mirror.

*Mary Rohrberger*

# PRETTY ICE

*Author:* Mary Robison (1949-    )
*Type of plot:* Domestic realism
*Time of plot:* The 1970's
*Locale:* Ohio
*First published:* 1977

> *Principal characters:*
> BELLE, a woman in her mid-thirties
> HER MOTHER
> WILL, her fiancé

## The Story

Belle is expecting the first visit from Will, her fiancé, to her small hometown in Ohio. He is coming from Cambridge, Massachusetts, where he has been conducting research in botany. They met there when he was attending Boston University and teaching undergraduates and she was working toward a doctorate in musicology. Their courtship took place during those years of study.

Belle stays up the whole night before Will arrives, working on figures in her checkbook, drinking coffee, pacing back and forth, and returning to her calculator. She takes pleasure in adding up numbers. At 6:15 in the morning, she is called away from her addition by her mother, who is waiting in the car to take Belle to the train station. Belle has never learned to drive a car.

There has been a lot of snow recently, and now an ice storm has coated the trees. Driving is somewhat hazardous, and Belle's mother drives carefully. On the way to the station, Belle mentions that Will, who is a plant taxonomist, recently was turned down for an important and lucrative grant because the committee decided that the research he had been conducting for the past seven years was irrelevant. Belle mentions that she thinks it might be a good idea to postpone the wedding until Will is financially more stable. Her mother advises her not to wait too long.

Along the route, they pass a fading billboard that advertises the dance studio that Belle's father and mother once ran. This reminds Belle of the flashy sports car that her father and mother once had, and of the pleasure she took when her father would take her for rides in it.

When they arrive at the train station, Belle notices that Will has put on weight and seems puffy. She lets him kiss her, and then Belle's mother kisses him. Will sits in the back seat, and Belle sits up front with her mother. The mother suggests that Will stay at her house in Belle's old room, but Belle quickly suggests they find a motel for him. She notes that there is really not room for him at her place, either, because she has her tax materials strewn all over. When Will suggests that the two of them go out for breakfast after he gets settled, Belle puts him off, again mentioning that she needs to clean up her tax materials.

As they leave the station, Belle's mother mentions that her husband's name also had been William, and that he had been quite handsome. Belle reveals that it had been in the dance studio, when she was twenty-one years old, that her father pointed a service revolver down his throat and took his life.

Even though she has taken this route many times, Belle's mother gets lost on the way home. Rather than becoming discouraged by this, she notes that the ice storm was beautiful. They are in no hurry to get Will to his motel, after all, so why not just wait a while and enjoy the beauty around them. Belle surprises herself by agreeing with her mother. She smiles at Will but thinks that it will be the last time that she does so.

*Themes and Meanings*

On the surface, "Pretty Ice" appears to be a story about a woman's cooling relationship with her fiancé, but it is more than that. By the end of the story, Belle appears to have come to a decision to end her engagement, not only because Will has lost his source of income but also because she no longer finds him attractive. She says nothing good about him in the course of her narration, and she takes the side of those who have declared his seven years of research to be superficial. She does not kiss him, although her mother does. She does not invite him to stay with her and does not want him to stay with her mother. She does not even want to have breakfast with him.

Most readers will recognize that the calculations Belle has been making all night long before Will's arrival have more to do with the relationship than with her tax returns. It is ominous for Will that Belle finds herself taking pleasure in the sums she is getting.

This is only one of the relationships with which Belle is having problems. She seems to be unusually dependent on her mother for someone of her age; it is not until her mother starts honking that she allows herself to be driven to meet her fiancé. She disparages her mother throughout the story, even resenting the little car her mother bought after her father's suicide. She expresses a resentful sense of inadequacy in comparison to her mother's great popularity with men, noting that her mother probably dated more men in a single year than Belle has dated in her entire life. By story's end, she seems to have bonded more completely with her mother, almost in defiance of Will and her father. If the new car suggests her mother is willing to get on with her life after the suicide, Belle's ultimate choice of her mother suggests that she herself is not.

The third relationship is the most important, because it explains the others. Although her father died just when Belle reached full adulthood, she apparently has never forgiven him for abandoning her. When she recognizes that her fiancé has the same name, she returns the rejection she felt from the suicide. Significantly, it is soon before this decision that she observes a skater skating backward, perhaps symbolizing Belle's desire to return to an earlier, more graceful time in her life.

*Style and Technique*

Mary Robison is noted for her clean prose that neatly embodies a great deal in a few words, giving the reader insight into an entire life by looking closely at small moments of that life. One technique by which she compresses much into a small space is her suggestive use of images that take on allegorical importance. In "Pretty Ice," the narrator is obsessed with calculations and numbers, with parting her hair down the middle to make sure that everything falls evenly into two equal halves. Even her study of music seems to have resulted not in a free-flowing approach to life, but in looking at high-tension towers and seeing in their cables memories of the staff lines on a sheet of music.

Most important, there is Robison's play on the word "superficial." Will's research project has been rejected because it was seen to be superficial, criticism that Belle ultimately shares not only of the work but also, it seems, of Will himself. One might also say that Belle's mother has a superficial way of relating to others, clear especially in her decision not to mention the research problem to Will and in demanding that her husband's death not be discussed. She prefers to remember him as a beautiful dancer—someone who, in effect, skims gracefully across surfaces. Most pointedly, though, Belle unconsciously identifies with just this aspect of her departed parent: his preoccupation with cartography, atlases, and the distances between points.

Robison has chosen an unreliable narrator, therefore, because she provides the reader with enough information to force an ironic distance between what Belle observes and what a more objective reader might conclude. By having Belle conclude that Will is superficial in the very paragraph that she happily identifies with her father's obsession with maps, Robison calls into question her narrator's apparently freeing decision to end her engagement. The reader is left wondering whether Belle has condemned herself to a slow suicide at home, because beneath the surface beauty of the ice storm lie damaged trees that will have a difficult spring. This is the wisdom that Will brings the narrator, but it is an insight to which she pays no attention. Her father's graceful dancing, however, did not save him from whatever deep-seated problems remained far beneath the surface.

The story's play on types of superficiality provides the story with a certain ambiguity: Is Belle's rejection of Will a healthy assertion of her own independence apart from a father who could not handle life, or is it her more complete identification with that father, at the expense of a deeper relationship with a living human being?

*John C. Hawley*

# PRINCE OF DARKNESS

*Author:* J. F. Powers (1917-1999)
*Type of plot:* Satire
*Time of plot:* The early 1940's during World War II
*Locale:* A town in the American Midwest
*First published:* 1946

*Principal characters:*

> FATHER ERNEST BURNER, age forty-three, a priest long overdue for a routine promotion
>
> THOMAS NASH TRACY, a high-powered insurance salesperson and "Big Catholic Layman"
>
> FATHER QUINLAN, a newly ordained priest who crosses himself sloppily enough to be a monsignor
>
> FATHER KEEFE, Quinlan's friend, also newly ordained
>
> THE DEAN, Burner's cold superior at St. Patrick's church
>
> FATHER ED DESMOND, Burner's friend, currently being treated in a hospital for alcoholism
>
> THE ARCHBISHOP, an ascetic intellectual who tests and judges Burner

*The Story*

The story's title, "Prince of Darkness," alludes to the devil. Father Ernest Burner is an ambitious but unsuccessful priest who lacks a spiritual vocation. He goes through the empty motions of his clerical duties during the morning, noon, and night of one day, but still craves a parish of his own. Fat, sweaty, and impatient, he stares with malignant eyes, seethes with resentment, and is crudely blasphemous. He uses his Roman collar as a putting ring in golf and deposits a burnt match in a holy-water font.

Dwelling in his private hell, Burner is surrounded by infernal associations. He finds red-hot believers a devilish nuisance, demolishes the perfect rose window of a grapefruit, operates on the principle of discord, constantly smokes, shuns the light, rigs up a darkroom, gropes blindly in the shadows, applies a cloven foot to the gas pedal, and garrotes his image of St. Christopher. The dean, his superior, referred to Burner (because of this darkroom) as the "Prince of Darkness," and the name caught on in the diocese.

Burner's conversation with Tracy, who is trying to sell him an insurance policy, reveals that he has little spiritual reserve on which to draw in old age. He seeks mundane security in the immediate future rather than eternal salvation in the next world. Burner's talk with the young priests, Quinlan and Keefe, exposes his gluttony and obesity, his lack of literary taste, his cynical skepticism, and his indifference to a mother in the parish who wants to add a star for her son, who is away at war, in the "servicemen's flag" in the church.

In the afternoon, Burner hopes to take a flying lesson (his idea of heaven) but is earthbound by the rain. He fantasizes about becoming a flying Junker and quotes Hermann Göring's philistine dictum: "When I hear the word culture, I reach for my gun." Scheming for ways to acquire a parish, even a rural one, he orders a smoking hamburger at a drive-in restaurant. He then recalls his examination of a child who was about to be confirmed. He asked her to name the seven deadly sins, unaware that he embodies all of them. He feels pride toward his parishioners and the archbishop; covetousness for insurance money; lust when he hears the clicking of high heels; anger when quarreling with his fellow priests; envy toward the rapidly promoted young vicar general; sloth in preparing sermons and hearing confessions; and (though the child is reluctant to mention this manifest sin for fear of offending Burner) gluttony during his greedy meals.

Burner toys with the idea of dying for the faith but wisely rejects the notion of becoming an army chaplain in order to advance his career. He remembers his humiliation when a Catholic magazine printed "circular" for "secular" in one of his awkwardly written articles and earned for his fat self the degrading nickname of "circular priest." His visit to the alcoholic Father Desmond, who is recuperating in a hospital, provides a warning of what happens to worldly priests with no true calling.

At night, while inattentively hearing confessions in the cathedral, Burner summarily dismisses a young woman who has married outside the faith and practiced birth control. His harsh, bullying manner fails to satisfy the spiritual famine of the sinners who come to him for comfort. His interview with the archbishop, which Burner hopes will satisfy his long-nourished ambitions, provides an ironic parallel to his dialogue in the confessional as well as a subtle instruction in the pitfalls of piety.

The archbishop gives him a series of minor tests and Burner clumsily fails all of them. He chooses the hard rather than the soft chair, denies his friendship with Father Desmond (as Peter denied Christ), is ignorant of the writings of Saint Bernard, lacks musical appreciation, refuses a glass of wine and a cigarette, acknowledges that there has never been a Saint Ernest (though he previously ironically imagined prayers to Saint Ernest Burner, Help of Golfers), and foolishly believes it important to kiss the archbishop's ring.

As Burner leaves the cathedral, he can scarcely see the cross on the dome. He disobeys the archbishop's explicit orders, prematurely opens the letter concerning his new appointment, and is shocked to discover that he will be an assistant at yet another parish.

*Themes and Meanings*

"Prince of Darkness" concerns the conflict between spiritual and material values in a priest who has followed a false vocation, become morally impoverished, and failed in his duty to both humanity and God. The key question, raised by the archbishop, is this: Where is the devil today? He answers that the devil is within us. Like Satan in

Christopher Marlowe's play *The Tragedy of Doctor Faustus* (1592) and in John Milton's epic poem *Paradise Lost* (1667, 1674), Burner is damned and lives in his own earthly hell.

Author J. F. Powers subtly suggests, however, that Burner is not all evil and even has some redeeming features. He is slightly repelled by Tracy's insurance pitch and thinks of him as a buzzard. He feels sorry for the mother whose son's star is missing from the church servicemen's flag. He buys hamburgers for the eighth-grade boys, is touched by a lad's desire to be a priest ("like you, Father"), and wants to spare him the terrible fate of a false vocation. He is embarrassed by the child's reluctance to name the seventh sin of Gluttony. He is saddened to have to disappoint (once again) his aged mother, who hoped to be the housekeeper in his own parish. He is thankful for the example—if not the advice and judgment—of the exemplary archbishop. The archbishop (who quotes Matthew 10:34, "I come not to send peace, but a sword"), has disturbed his complacency and forced him to look within himself. If he heeds the archbishop's warnings, he may still be saved.

*Style and Technique*

The most significant literary influence on Powers's chaste, chiseled, and ironic style is James Joyce. Like Joyce in *Dubliners* (1914), Powers satirizes weak priests and describes in a style of scrupulous meanness the paralysis of a significant segment of society. Like Joyce in *A Portrait of the Artist as a Young Man* (1916), he defines his character in terms of the seven deadly sins.

Also like Joyce, Powers is a densely allusive author who conveys his meaning through biblical and literary references. Burner does not reject the olive branch (Genesis 8:11) from Tracy, who has the voice of the good and faithful servant (an allusion to the parable of the talents—Burner has surely buried his talent—in Matthew 25:21). Greedy for material security, he ignores Quinlan's advice to "Take nothing for your journey, neither staff, nor scrip" (Luke 9:3). Quinlan is unable to see God in a few church buildings as Moses saw the Lord in the midst of a burning bush (Exodus 3:2). Burner is a priest of the highest order, of Melchizedek (Genesis 14:18), but he is tempted by money and, as the archbishop observes (conflating allusions to Matthew 19:24 and Luke 13:24), he gives the rich consolation and makes the eye of the needle a gate.

Powers also alludes to the sweetness and light passage in Jonathan Swift's work of nonfiction *The Battle of the Books* (1704) and to Karl Marx's statement that religion is the opiate of the masses. He considers golf to be a great secular symbol and quotes three lines from T. S. Eliot's *The Rock: A Pageant Play* (1934) about a thousand lost golf balls. These effective allusions suggest an ideal standard of religious belief and behavior that is neither achieved nor approached by the priests or the laity in an age of secular materialism.

*Jeffrey Meyers*

# THE PRISON

*Author:* Bernard Malamud (1914-1986)
*Type of plot:* Naturalistic
*Time of plot:* The 1940's
*Locale:* New York City's Greenwich Village
*First published:* 1950

*Principal characters:*
TOMMY CASTELLI, a twenty-nine-year-old candy store owner
ROSA AGNELLI, his wife
UNCLE DOM, his uncle
AN UNNAMED TEN-YEAR-OLD GIRL
HER MOTHER

*The Story*

Tommy Castelli's prison is the candy store in which he has worked for a decade. Renamed by his wife, Rosa, who disliked his original name of Tony, Tommy was born and raised near this store. He dreamed of escaping from the tenement in which he was brought up, but by the time he was sixteen he had dropped out of a vocational school, where he trained to be a shoemaker, and was running out of options. Adrift and seeing little promise for his future, Tommy began running with a gang that had the money to buy silver café espresso urns and television sets and host the pizza parties that impressed the girls they admired. Their wherewithal was derived from shady dealings, among which was a liquor store holdup.

Meanwhile, Tommy's father arranged for him to marry Rosa Agnelli, whose father agreed to bankroll a small candy store in Greenwich Village for the newlyweds. Not attracted to Rosa and reluctant to spend his life running a candy store, Tommy fled to Texas, where he bummed around for a while. Finally, however, he returned to New York. His friends and relatives were convinced that he had returned home to marry Rosa and set up the store Mr. Agnelli had proffered. His father's marriage plans materialized, however, largely because Tommy failed to object. Now, ten years later, Tommy is twenty-nine and he finds his life a crushing bore. He regards the candy store, above which he and Rosa live, as his personal prison. Day after day, he works from eight in the morning until almost midnight, taking only one break, an hour in the afternoon when he goes upstairs to nap.

Tommy has tried to enhance his profits by putting a punchboard and a slot machine in his store. When the slot machine appeared, however, Rosa's father stormed into the shop screaming that Tommy was a criminal. He broke the offending machine to pieces with a hammer. Ironically, the police raided candy stores in the area the very next day, arresting the proprietors who had slot machines, and Tommy narrowly escaped arrest.

Every Monday morning, a ten-year-old girl who lives nearby comes in to buy two rolls of colored tissue paper for her mother, who gives it to the children whom she tends for them to make cutouts. Tommy keeps the paper in the back of the store and thinks it peculiar that the girl never accompanies him there, because that is where he also keeps the comic books to which most of his juvenile customers gravitate. He speculates that the girl may be afraid of the dark.

One day, however, after Rosa has installed a mirror in the store's shadowy area, Tommy notices that when he goes for the girl's colored tissue paper, she reaches into the candy case and takes out several candy bars. When he returns, the girl—a picture of innocence—pays for the paper with two dimes and leaves.

This petty theft arouses in Tommy memories of his favorite uncle, Dom, who skirted the law and ended up in prison. Tommy knows that he must do something to turn the girl away from her shoplifting, which is apparently becoming habitual. After much thought, he decides to write her a note telling her not to steal any more, reminding her that continuing to steal will make her suffer for her whole life. He puts the note inside the wrapper of a candy bar that he knows she will take.

On the following Monday, Tommy awaits the light-fingered girl all morning. As luck has it, she is later than usual. Rosa comes downstairs to relieve Tommy, who has no choice but to go upstairs for his daily nap. Rosa lets him nap unusually long; when he comes back downstairs, he hears screeching. Rosa has caught the thieving girl stealing and is shaking her. Tommy intervenes, striking his hysterically enraged wife hard on her mouth. At this moment, the girl's mother arrives, inquiring about the fracas. Rosa shrieks that the girl has stolen candy, but Tommy intervenes saying that he has let her take it. The terrified child tries to mollify her mother by telling her she has stolen one of the candy bars for her. The mother rails, calling her daughter a little thief and promising punishment. As the mother drags her daughter from the store, the girl turns to Tommy and sticks her tongue out at him.

*Themes and Meanings*

Despite his checkered early years, Tommy Castelli is basically a decent person trapped in a boring job, sharing his life with a woman whom he has never loved. His incarceration, like that of many working people, does not involve sprawling gray buildings with watchtowers and barbed wire. Rather he is trapped in a way of life that he cannot abide. As the monotony of his routine weighs on him, he is forced to acknowledge that this is his life and that it is unlikely ever to change significantly. Catching the ten-year-old in her petty theft adds a bit of interest to Tommy's otherwise banal Monday and adds a moral dimension to his life. Bernard Malamud's choice of the day is calculated: Monday marks the beginning of the week. For Tommy, beginnings are not happy events because what stretches out beyond them is incredible sameness. The word that best describes Tommy's life at this point is drab.

When Tommy spots the young girl stealing candy, he fleetingly sees a mirror image of his younger self. The mistakes of his early life have resulted in his being in his depressing, dead-end situation. Sensing in the girl an opportunity to save someone from a similar fate, he sets up his act of salvation secretly and with calculation. He writes the note, puts it inside the wrapper of the strategically placed candy bar, and awaits the new beginning that he envisions.

However, in life as Tommy generally perceives it, any plan to do good is scuttled inevitably by chance happenings, quite in keeping with the conventions of literary naturalism. Rosa shatters Tommy's plan, but her intrusion is a mere shadow of what Rosa has done to Tommy's life. She obviously dominates him; he accepts her domination passively, as indicated by his accepting a new name at Rosa's behest.

When Tommy intervenes between Rosa and the girl, he is neither on his wife's side nor on the side of right as society normally defines it. His slapping Rosa hard on her mouth represents his venting of a lifetime of frustration; the girl has provided Tommy with the excuse that he needs to retaliate against Rosa's years of control over him. However faint, that slap is Tommy's primal scream. Malamud does not suggest, however, that the event he describes marks a turning point for Tommy. Quite the opposite. The girl whom Tommy seeks to rescue is so oblivious to his intended kindness that she defiantly sticks out her tongue at him as her mother drags her away. Humans, Malamud seems to suggest, fail to understand or appreciate kindness. He also makes one wonder to what kindness might lead. Tommy's prisonlike candy store is, after all, a manifestation of Mr. Agnelli's intended kindness to him and his daughter.

### Style and Technique

"The Prison" is straightforward and matter of fact. Malamud tells it directly without moralizing or editorializing. Save for its final page, the story is told in the third-person singular, with an omniscient narrator, and it contains no dialogue.

Malamud successfully builds a foreboding quality into the story by referring obliquely to Tommy's early illegal activities and to his Uncle Dom's imprisonment. He gives few details about either but makes it apparent that the specter of imprisonment looms constantly. The irony of the story, however, is that Tommy, as his fate has decreed, is imprisoned as much as any convicted felon serving a sentence in the state penitentiary—and his is a life sentence with little hope of parole.

Readers get to know Tommy quite well. Malamud's other characters in this story are not fully developed, although Rosa is revealed in some detail through Tommy's interaction with her. The girl, who is central to the story, is described physically and through her covert actions. Her psychological motivation is unclear, nor does it need to be clarified. What is important to the story is Tommy's psychological motivation in trying to save the girl from her thieving ways.

"The Prison" is one of four short stories that Malamud, who generally focuses on Jewish Americans, wrote about Italian Americans. It is also one of several he wrote about shopkeepers, who were also the focus of his later novel, *The Assistant* (1957). Clearly, Malamud understands the city and the little people who keep it running in their often frustrating daily occupations.

*R. Baird Shuman*

# PRIVATE DOMAIN

*Author:* James Alan McPherson (1943-    )
*Type of plot:* Satire
*Time of plot:* The 1970's
*Locale:* New York City
*First published:* 1969

> *Principal characters:*
> RODNEY, a young black university student
> LYNN, his live-in lover
> WILLIE, a down-and-out black man
> CHARLIE PRATT, a white man who admires black music

*The Story*

This is an ironic story, with a somewhat bitter bite, about a young black man named Rodney who, because of his middle-class background and education, has so thoroughly accepted the white man's values that he must make a self-conscious effort to learn the ways of the streetwise black in order to be "in" with his "hip" and self-consciously liberal white friends.

The story begins with Rodney buying drinks for a down-and-out black man named Willie in return for being "educated" in the slang and musical knowledge of the urban "cat." Willie instructs Rodney that one's "bag" is where one keeps things one does best and that whatever is in one's bag is one's "thing" or "stick." Willie also tells him about a large rock-and-roll memorial in Cleveland in which a famous singer, "Fatso Checkers" (a fictional name for Chubby Checkers), did not appear but was replaced by another singer, "Dirty Rivers" (a fictional name for Muddy Waters), who improvised a song onstage that made the "cats" go wild because they "dug" it so.

When Rodney leaves the bar, he worries about being in this particular area of the city; is suspicious that the neighborhood blacks, with their shifty eyes and broad black noses, are after his money; and is relieved to find that no one has broken into his car. When he hears some young boys singing an obscene but childish rhyme, he is repulsed at first but then thinks that it is clever and memorizes it. When the boys follow a black prostitute down the street, making obscene references to her genitals, he is only sorry that he did not bring his notebook. During all this activity, Rodney's attitude is like that of a sociology student who is studying an exotic, foreign culture. He even tries to quiz a young man selling a Muslim newspaper about why he became a Muslim so that he can make such an experience intellectually his own.

Rodney's middle-class "white" prudishness is revealed when he returns home to his black girlfriend and scolds her for sitting cross-legged on the floor so that her panties show. When, using the new slang he has picked up, he tells her that if sitting like that is her "thing," she should put it in a separate "bag" and bury it someplace, she chides him by calling him "bay-bee," a term that he hates in private, although he obviously desires such affectation of black slang in public. When his white friend Charlie Pratt calls, inviting him to listen to some music with some other "cats," he says "cool," although Pratt makes him feel uncomfortable by being proud to use the vocabulary that Rodney had been trying to forget all his life.

At the party, Pratt, a devotee of black music who owns more than two thousand records of blues, gospel, folk, and jazz, shows off a new "find"—a rare album by Roscoe and Shirley from 1964. Rodney thinks about how, in 1964, he was trying to make up for a lifetime of not knowing anything about Baroque; now that he knows about Baroque, he has never heard of Roscoe and Shirley, but he tries to hide his unease by relating Willie's story about the rock-and-roll memorial. Pratt, however, in a bit of one-upmanship, not only knows about the concert but also has tapes of Dirty Rivers's impromptu vocal. As they listen to the tape, Pratt's white guests arrive and obviously look to Rodney as the resident expert on all things black. Rodney improperly beats time to the music, but he knows that as he is the only black male in the room, the others will assume that he alone knows the proper beat and will follow his lead. Rodney knows that he has to feel more from the music than the others and thus exclaims, "[M]ercy! mercy! mercy! This cat is together." Only Rodney's girlfriend Lynn knows how phony his act is.

The climax of the story comes when Pratt and Rodney get into an argument about whether Dirty Rivers or Ashy Williamson is the best singer with the most soul. Although Rodney affects his secondhand "black" knowledge, Pratt proves to be more "black" than he is, gaining the agreement not only of his white friends but also of Rodney's girlfriend. Bested and backed up against a wall, Rodney waits a few moments and then, to no one in particular, repeats the obscene rhyme he heard earlier from the street children, and thus ironically wins back his temporarily lost regard as the resident streetwise and hip black. The story ends on the way home as Lynn chides him, in typical middle-class fashion, for being the life of the party and letting his color come through. All that Rodney can think about is going back to talk to Willie some more, building up his collection of Ashy Williamson records, and definitely not making love to Lynn.

*Themes and Meanings*

The point of James Alan McPherson's story is quite clear. Rodney is a seriocomic version of the black man who has so assimilated himself to the white man's values that he feels cut off from his racial culture. However, rather than wanting to return to that culture, he condescends to it even as he believes that he must gain some of its external manifestations as a way of becoming accepted in the white man's world. Thus, the story is an irony-within-an-irony. Rodney is a bigot both to whites and to blacks, at times hating everyone, bouncing back and forth between two value systems. The metaphor he uses is that of a coin spinning inside his brain. Sometimes it lands heads up, signifying an affinity toward someone, sometimes heads down, signifying distaste. He refuses to dislike anyone absolutely because he believes that such would be uncomfortably close to bigotry.

Rodney has this double attitude toward Willie, toward Lynn, toward Charlie Pratt—indeed, toward everyone in the story. When he loses the argument with Charlie, the coin spins in his mind faster and faster until it stops on that side where he keeps his bigotry almost locked away. Rodney does not try to learn black slang and acquire street knowledge simply to impress his friends; McPherson's irony and satire of the middle-class black situation cuts deeper than that. Rodney both wants and does not want to be black. He scorns blacks such as Willie even as he admires them. He envies Pratt for being comfortably "black" in his musical knowledge, even as he despises him for ironically being more "black" than he is.

Rodney is a sexual prude, which the story suggests is typical of the middle-class white, but he is fascinated by a stereotype of black sexuality that is denied him. For example, he is somewhat repulsed by Lynn's open sexuality, even as he enjoys it. He enjoys making love to her, but only in the dark. He does not like to make sounds during lovemaking but feels uneasy when Lynn does not. In short, he is presented as a man with all the sexual inhibitions of the middle-class white who finds "black sexuality" (whatever that is) both obscene and irresistible. Rodney is a satiric, comic version of the archetypal black "outsider" or "underground man," made famous by Richard Wright and Ralph Ellison. However, McPherson's twist on this theme is to place Rodney in a "private domain," caught between the inhibited white culture and the hip world of the urban black.

*Style and Technique*

The story is told in a straightforward manner by an omniscient narrator who refuses to judge Rodney or his hip white friends. Rodney's own behavior and pathetic-comic efforts to be culturally black, in spite of the fact that he is racially black, are sufficient for the reader to make his or her own judgment. The story is a combination of sly comic satire and serious social criticism. Although no background exposition is provided to explain how Rodney is the way he is, it seems clear that McPherson is trying to draw the reader's attention to the dilemma of the young black male caught in between two worlds.

Although Rodney is presented as a ridiculous figure, there is also something very sad about his dilemma. The story reverses the usual black "outsider" theme with a satiric style that makes it possible to laugh at Rodney, but it does not negate the seriousness of the fact that Rodney is forever caught in a no-win situation of trying to be both white and black at the same time. It is perhaps an indication of growing social awareness that McPherson can write such a story that is less angry than it is characterized by a complex mixture of comedy and pathos. At least the so-called black social problem has been so internalized that black writers such as McPherson can feel comfortable playing with it in a comic and satiric manner.

*Charles E. May*

# PRIZE STOCK

*Author:* Kenzaburō Ōe (1935-    )
*Type of plot:* War
*Time of plot:* Summer, 1945
*Locale:* A mountain village in Japan
*First published:* "Shiiku," 1958 (English translations, "The Catch," 1966, and "Prize Stock," 1977)

>          *Principal characters:*
>          "FROG," the narrator, a teenage Japanese boy
>          "HARELIP," his teenage companion
>          HIS YOUNGER BROTHER
>          HIS FATHER, a hunter and trapper
>          THE BLACK AMERICAN SOLDIER, a prisoner of war of the villagers
>          "CLERK," a one-legged town official

*The Story*

"Prize Stock," for which Kenzaburō Ōe received Japan's prestigious Akutagawa Prize in 1958 while he was still in college, tells the tragic tale of a downed black American soldier in the last summer months before Japan's unconditional surrender ending World War II in September, 1945. The black soldier at first terrifies, then mystifies, and ultimately befriends the Japanese villagers who are told to hold him captive. When orders arrive that he is to be transferred, a tragic misunderstanding leads to his death.

The story begins at dusk when the narrator Frog and his younger brother finish sifting through the ashes by the village crematorium, looking for uniquely shaped bones to use as play medals. Joined by their friend Harelip, nicknamed for his untreated birth defect, the two boys observe the low overflight of a huge American plane before returning home to the second floor of the village storehouse. Their taciturn father prepares the evening meal, after which the boys and their father go to bed.

Before morning, the village is awakened by the sound of a huge crash farther up in the mountains. The adult men go to investigate, forbidding the children to trail along. Harelip amuses himself by letting the village girls play with his penis at the communal spring. In the evening, the men return with their "catch," the black American soldier who survived the plane crash. None of the villagers has ever seen an African American, and they consider him less an enemy than a strange big beast.

Because they cannot talk with their prisoner, they lock him in the basement of the storeroom and chain his ankles with a boar trap. The next day, Frog and his father walk to the nearby town to report their "catch" and ask for instructions. Clerk, a one-legged minor official, jokes with Frog about the captive. Returning to their village, Frog helps his father carry food to the prisoner. Suspicious at first, the black soldier finally takes a drink and hungrily eats the local food.

As the black soldier does not display any threatening behavior, his care is soon left to the village boys, foremost the narrator, his younger brother, and Harelip, who guard their prisoner fiercely. They delegate the emptying of the prisoner's dump bucket to other children and grow increasingly familiar with their "catch." Noticing that the chain of the boar trap cuts into the man's infected ankles, Harelip frees him. Encouraged by the prisoner's cooperative behavior, the children let him out to catch fresh air, and none of the adults object.

Every day, Frog and his friends become more attached to the soldier. They bring him a toolbox to repair the boar trap, and when Clerk damages his artificial leg on a visit to the village, they let the prisoner repair it. Finally, they take their "catch" to the spring, letting him bathe in the nude. Impressed by the size of the black soldier's penis, Harelip fetches a female goat, but the prisoner fails to copulate with the animal.

Finally, Clerk tells the villagers that the soldier is to be transferred. Frog grows alarmed. He talks to the prisoner and touches his body in an agitated and panicked manner. Suddenly, the black man takes the narrator hostage and barricades himself in the storeroom cellar, clearly afraid for his life. As the villagers debate a course of action, Frog is confronted by a man who has suddenly become the enemy again.

The next morning, the villagers break into the storeroom. Using Frog as a human shield, the captive fails to stop the hatchet blow delivered by the boy's father, which smashes Frog's left hand and the skull of the black man. Waking from his trauma-induced delirium, Frog watches the storage of the prisoner's corpse in an abandoned mine, for his cremation is forbidden. Clerk joins the children sledding down the slope on the tail of the downed American plane and is thrown off and killed when his head hits a rock. Frog realizes that war has brought an end to his childhood.

*Themes and Meanings*

"Prize Stock" is a powerful story, from the Japanese point of view, of encountering an amazing and fascinating stranger. The attitude of the isolated villagers to their prisoner is central to Ōe's tale. Initially, they look for the expected enemy, white Americans, to emerge from the downed plane. The African American is a big surprise. He is first considered to be a beast and likened to a farm animal by his captors. He becomes humanized only in close contact with his captors.

The importance of language for the establishment of common human bonds is a second major theme. The villagers' view of the black soldier as a big beast is reinforced because he cannot speak to them to demonstrate his intelligence and they cannot talk to him. Only when he repairs the boar trap and Clerk's artificial leg does he establish part of his humanity as a tool-using, sentient being.

Cultural sexual stereotypes are also a theme of the story. The teenagers are clearly impressed by the unfamiliar size of the captive's genitalia, which, in their minds, reestablishes the stranger's animalistic nature. Earlier, Frog confided how he viewed the exposed vaginas of the bathing nude village girls as unimpressive and threw small stones at them to show his disdain. He considers the black man's penis to be beautiful and out of this world.

The effect of war on human behavior and its attendant human cost is the final theme unifying all aspects of Ōe's masterful story. Ordinarily, the villagers would not imprison a stranger, who is first regarded as the enemy then relegated to the level of beast before he becomes a friend to their children and helpful in the village. When the war-related order for his transfer arrives, the soldier justifiably worries he may be executed. His defense destroys his friendship with Frog and turns him into the enemy in the eyes of everybody. The adult world, with its wars and cruelties, does not allow for a continuation of the playful coexistence of the prisoner and the village children. For Ōe, to become adult also means to lose childhood dreams of a benevolent world.

*Style and Technique*

John Nathan's 1977 translation of Ōe's story captures well the stylistic nuances of the original version. Frog's narration is characterized by its mix of juvenile inconsideration, naïve wonder, and a bit of callousness. His language shows that he and the other village children are a fiercely competitive lot, fighting with each other for the best access to any novelty in their lives. Frog is an astute observer. His narration includes commentaries on the variations in the sunlight that illuminates his native landscape, as well as his descriptive evaluation of human emotions, and the processes transforming his self.

The villagers constantly refer to their prisoner of war as a "catch," like an especially valuable animal that has been finally trapped. This idea is stylistically reinforced by Ōe's choice for the occupation of the father as a hunter and trapper. Just as he regularly brings home trapped and shot animals, one day, he is among the first of the villagers returning with the black man. The idea that war has dehumanized people and reduced them to the status of wild animals is well conveyed by Ōe's particular term for the prisoner. When the captive watches Frog's father kill and skin a trapped weasel for its pelt, there is an ominous sense of foreshadowing for the fate of the black soldier.

The story opens and closes near the village crematorium, symbolizing the pervasiveness of death even in an apparently idyllic rural landscape. Frog digs for human bones to use as toy medals, a poignant antiwar commentary. Foreshadowing is used skillfully in this short story, which moves from children's play to the effects of war back to children playing with their "catch" until the adult world intervenes. The problematic transition from childhood to adolescence is stylized through the relationship between Clerk and Frog. Like two people struggling for the right to name the other, they each have nicknamed the other, indicating that Frog is on the verge of achieving power even as a teenager.

After the black soldier is killed, Frog becomes an outsider. With his smashed left hand, he receives a symbolic wound, similar to a rite of passage into adulthood and similar to Clerk's missing leg. Invited by Clerk to join the sledding children, Frog declines this symbolic act of rejoining childhood. While the children use both their legs to steer clear of dangerous rocks, the one-legged Clerk fails in this maneuver and dies. Frog, clearly wiser than the older man, survives to pass into full adulthood.

*R. C. Lutz*

# THE PROBLEM OF CELL THIRTEEN

*Author:* Jacques Futrelle (1875-1912)
*Type of plot:* Suspense
*Time of plot:* 1905
*Locale:* Boston
*First published:* 1905

> *Principal characters:*
> AUGUSTUS S. F. X. VAN DUSEN, a scientist and the protagonist,
> known as "The Thinking Machine"
> HUTCHINSON HATCH, a newspaper reporter who assists Van
> Dusen
> DR. CHARLES RANSOME, a scientist who challenges Van Dusen to
> escape from death row prison cell 13
> ALFRED FIELDING, an ally of Ransome
> THE WARDEN OF CHISHOLM PRISON, who is charged with keeping
> Van Dusen prisoner for one week

*The Story*

Augustus S. F. X. Van Dusen, Ph.D., L.L.D., F.R.S., M.D., M.D.S., is a scientist and logician. The popular press made him known as "The Thinking Machine" when, a novice at the game of chess, he challenged and beat a chess master, bringing to bear logic rather than familiarity with the game. He spends much time in his own small laboratory, from which emanate ideas that deeply influence the scientific world. He claims that logic can solve all problems, and his self-confidence is equal to his achievements.

Visiting him one evening, fellow scientists Charles Ransome and Alfred Fielding are irritated by that confidence. Trying to imagine a situation that logic alone cannot master, Ransome mentions prisons, saying that even The Thinking Machine cannot reason his way out from a prison cell. Van Dusen claims that, indeed, he can do so. That same night, Ransome and Fielding arrange for Van Dusen to be imprisoned in death row cell 13 of Chisholm Prison. They deliver him to the warden of that prison. Before being taken to his cell, Van Dusen makes several eccentric, but apparently harmless, requests. He asks that his shoes be polished; he also asks for tooth powder and twenty-five dollars in the form of one five-dollar and two ten-dollar bills. The warden honors the requests, and The Thinking Machine, after being thoroughly searched, is taken to his cell, still promising to rejoin his friends for dinner at the end of one week.

In the days that follow, several events shake the warden's faith in his escape-proof prison. While Van Dusen talks with jailers and examines his cell in order to plan his escape, he also begins to leave a series of notes, giving them to his jailers or dropping them from his barred windows. He uses part of his white shirt as paper, and he continues to write on white linen even after the warden takes this shirt away. Moreover, The Thinking Machine has found substances to serve as pen and ink, although he took no such materials to the cell. In the notes, Van Dusen includes two five-dollar bills; he entered the cell with only one. The warden arranges a 3:00 A.M. search but finds little more than a dead rat stuck into an old pipe. After the search, The Thinking Machine produces still more small bills and even coins. At the same time, another prisoner, housed in the cell directly above Van Dusen's, screams in the night, terrorized by a mysterious voice that seems to know all about his crime. He has been accused of killing a woman by throwing acid in her face, and now this voice speaks to him of acid in the dead of night until he hysterically confesses the killing.

The events continue until the seventh day, which is much quieter except that an arc lamp illuminating the prison yard fails. This causes the warden to call the electric company. As the electricians are due to arrive, the warden goes downstairs where he finds Ransome and Fielding waiting at the gate; this is the day on which The Thinking Machine has promised to accomplish his escape. As they stand together by the gate, the warden receives a special delivery letter from The Thinking Machine, confirming their dinner engagement for that evening. The warden sends a guard to check on The Thinking Machine. The guard reports that he is lying quietly in his cell.

The electricians arrive, as do two newspaper reporters. One reporter is Hutchinson Hatch; the other is The Thinking Machine himself, who takes the group back to his cell. There, he shows the men a yellow wig atop a blanket. When he rolls back the blanket, he reveals, carefully arranged on the bed, a dagger, three files, ten feet of wire, some thirty feet of strong rope, a pair of steel pliers, a tack hammer, and a pistol. He also points out that all the window bars and the lower bars in the cell door have been cut through.

At dinner that night, he explains what he has done. When he entered the cell, he says, he noted the rats. Observing that they were field, not house, animals, he watched until he found that they were entering and leaving the cell through abandoned pipes. Using thread from his stockings, he attached a note and a ten-dollar bill to a rat and frightened it back through the pipe to the other end, where it emerged in a field outside the prison walls. The boy who found the bill and note took them, as instructed, to Hatch, who cooperated for the sake of the sensational news story. Hatch returned to the ground outside the prison, found the pipe, and attached a wire, which The Thinking Machine drew back into his cell. From then on, the wire provided a means for sending items of all kinds back and forth. It was in the process of testing the pipe as a speaking tube that Van Dusen inadvertently terrified the convict in the cell above. To inhibit the warden's zeal, The Thinking Machine stuffed a dead rat in the pipe's mouth, and, through the lining of his shirt, which he retained, and ink made of shoe polish, he produced the notes that distracted the warden from the actual escape method. At the last, Van Dusen cut the feed wire to the arc lamp with an acid-tipped wire. The final deception, disguising Hatch and Van Dusen among the electricians, was arranged by Hatch, whose father manages the electric company.

*Themes and Meanings*

"The Problem of Cell Thirteen" presents a simple locked-room puzzle; it does not offer the reader symbolic or thematic complexity. If there is a theme, it is that shared by the Sherlock Holmes stories of Arthur Conan Doyle and the C. Auguste Dupin tales of Edgar Allan Poe: the victory of the man of intellect over the man of action. Like Holmes and Dupin, The Thinking Machine is a mastermind, but he is a considerable weaker figure than they: His grotesque and weak appearance is stressed even in the story's opening paragraphs, while he makes a pathetic figure when he undergoes the prison search, and his appearance in the cells elicits the warden's pity.

*Style and Technique*

According to E. F. Bleiler, editor of *Best "Thinking Machine" Detective Stories* (1973), which includes "The Problem of Cell Thirteen" and eleven other Thinking Machine tales, the Jacques Futrelle hero occupies a significant place in the development of detective fiction. While The Thinking Machine shares his intellectuality with Holmes and Dupin and shares some of their eccentricities, Futrelle moves the world of the detective toward the greater realism that characterizes detective fiction in the later twentieth century. He drew such fiction away from the exotic murder weapons and haunted manors of Doyle and the Parisian drawing rooms of Poe toward the everyday life and the realistic dialogue of working police officers and journalists and actual ladies and gentlemen.

Sentences and language, too, are simple and direct. Futrelle was primarily a journalistic writer. "The Problem of Cell Thirteen," in fact, was published as a six-part serial in the *Boston American* between October 30 and November 5, 1905; prize money was offered to readers who could devise methods for Van Dusen's escape. The ease of writing and naturalness of diction and, especially, of dialogue cause the Thinking Machine stories to seem considerably less dated than are many American and British works written in that last glittering decade before the 1912 *Titanic* disaster in which Futrelle died and the outbreak of World War I in 1914.

*Betty Richardson*

# THE PROCURATOR OF JUDEA

*Author:* Anatole France (Jacques-Anatole-François Thibault, 1844-1924)
*Type of plot:* Social realism
*Time of plot:* 57 C.E.
*Locale:* A hill above Baiae, near Cape Misenum in Italy
*First published:* "Le Procurateur de Judée," 1892 (English translation, 1896)

Principal characters:
AELIUS LAMIA, a Roman citizen and scholar
PONTIUS PILATE, the former procurator of Judea

*The Story*

Aelius Lamia, who is sixty-two years of age and afflicted by a discomforting illness, has left Rome to take the waters at Baiae, a seaside resort. One day, having tired of his fellows, he climbs the hill above the town to read *De rerum natura* (c. 60 B.C.E.; *On the Nature of Things*, 1682), Lucretius's celebrated treatise on the philosophy of Epicurus. While making way for the passage of a litter bearing a gloomy aristocrat he is astonished and delighted to recognize a man whom he has not seen for twenty years—a man whom he met during an eighteen-year period when he was exiled from Rome by the emperor Tiberius. Although the man in question, Pontius Pilate, does not immediately recognize his old friend, he is quick to embrace him on hearing his name.

Both men have fond memories of the time they spent together while Pilate was procurator of the Syrian province of Judea. In those days, Pilate entertained the exile generously and introduced him to Herod Antipas. On his eventual return to Rome—sanctioned by Tiberius's successor Caius—Lamia had repaid Pilate's generosity with a gift of money but completely lost track of his friend thereafter. Pilate, who is now in his seventies, explains that he retired long ago to his estate in Sicily, from which he has now emerged in search of palliative treatment for his gout.

Lamia asks Pilate why he took early retirement from public service and became a virtual recluse. Pilate explains that he was driven from his former position by an unfortunate chain of circumstances. After putting down a Samaritan insurrection he sent the rebel leaders for punishment to the proconsul Vitellius. After the rebels complained that Pilate had provoked their actions, Pilate had to go to Rome to justify his actions. Tiberius died while Pilate was traveling, and the new emperor—swayed by the opinions of his childhood friend Agrippa, a relative and avid rival of Herod Antipas—refused to hear his case, thus forcing his early retirement.

Lamia wonders whether Pilate might not have proceeded more gently against the Samaritans, but the older man rejects the argument. Pilate reminds his friend of shared occasions when they could observe the unreasonableness and obduracy of the rebelliously inclined Judeans. After Pilate laments the terrible injustice of his fate, the men agree to meet for supper on the following day.

The old men continue their discussion by lamenting the fact that Roman society is no longer what it was, having been spoiled by an influx of foreigners and a general decline in standards of dress and behavior. Pilate proudly reflects on various great engineering feats initiated by the emperor Augustus—his great inspiration. He then tells the sad tale of his own attempt to build an aqueduct that would have supplied Jerusalem with fresh water, and how the ungrateful inhabitants of the town forced him to abandon the project. This leads Pilate to rail against the local customs that he had been forced to support, including the prolific and endless demands made on him by the Jews to license the execution of any of their own people who violated their taboos.

Intent on diverting the conversation toward more pleasant topics, Lamia attempts to sing the praises of the women of Judea, extolling their beauty. This calls forth another diatribe from Pilate on the sacredness of marriage and the looseness of the young Lamia's morals, but Lamia is by now lost in fond reminiscence of a particular courtesan of Jerusalem. Recalling how she eventually forsook her profession in order to follow a young Galilean magician, he asks his friend if he remembers the man, whose name was Jesus of Nazareth. Pilate declares he has no memory of any such person.

*Themes and Meanings*

The fame of this story rests on its last line of dialogue. Anatole France always enjoyed startling and undermining the assumptions of his contemporaries, especially in matters of religion. In "The Human Tragedy" (1895), for example, a virtuous monk imprisoned by corrupt churchmen is delivered from that evil by Satan. In *The Revolt of the Angels* (1914), Satan politely declines to lead a second revolution against God on the grounds that the cause of moral progress should not be advanced by violence. Works such as these carried forward a rich French tradition of criticism of the Church and its clergymen, rather than the actual tenets of Christian faith, that had already extended from François Rabelais to Charles Baudelaire. "The Procurator of Judea" was similarly designed to shock and annoy, but it also makes a serious point about the artificiality of history and seeing the past through the lens of hindsight.

France was to expand further on the theme of "The Procurator of Judea" in his philosophical novel *The White Stone* (1905). This book includes an exemplary tale, set a few years later, in which a group of Roman exiles encounters a ragged wandering preacher. They are as unanimous in declaring that the faith he is preaching cannot possibly endure as they are in hoping that the newly proclaimed emperor will preside over a dramatic resurgence of the fortunes of Rome. The irony is sharpened by the fact that the reader not only knows what became of the preacher (Saint Paul) but also the failure that was actually wrought by the emperor (Nero). Similar playfulness is foreshadowed in "The Procurator of Judea," in which France is careful to use the name Caius to disguise the emperor known to history as Caligula; he also is scrupulous in saying nothing about the matters that were eventually to make the latter name notorious.

"The Procurator of Judea" also foreshadows *The Revolt of the Angels*. The book that Lamia carries up the hill to his meeting with Pilate in the story is *De rerum natura*, the same book that reveals to a skeptical guardian angel in the novel that the claims made by the God of the scriptures are not to be taken at face value.

The philosophy outlined in *De rerum natura* is founded in the claim that if there actually ever were any gods, they are quite irrelevant to the explanation of the way the world is now—which must proceed from the assumption that the universe consists of matter in motion and that morality is something that must be made by men and for men. (Anatole France was well aware of the irony implicit in the fact that all of Epicurus's own writings—unlike those of Plato and Aristotle—were lost, partly by virtue of their deliberate suppression by men who walked in fear of all manner of gods.) "The Procurator of Judea" is a straightforward extrapolation of this Epicurean axiom. It suggests that Jesus, if he actually existed, is of no particular relevance to the modern world as a person, and that the worthiness of his teachings—which France did not doubt—arises from their intrinsic merit as moral arguments, not by virtue of their source.

The story itself does not pass judgment on Pontius Pilate's sense of grievance, nor on his sense of values. If the reader comes away with the impression that the people of Jerusalem really were unreasonable in demanding so many death sentences for blasphemy that no one could be expected to remember any one of them, or that the city would have benefited far more from an aqueduct than from a surfeit of priests, that is not because the author embarks on any spirited advocacy of these cases. All France does, in his scrupulous fashion, is to declare that this is the way these two characters would have seen their situation and assessed their fortunes; it is precisely because France attempts to do no more than this that the reader is inclined to believe him.

The past, as L. P. Hartley has observed, is a foreign country whose inhabitants see and do things differently; we cannot expect them to share our perceptions of the significance of their actions and achievements. "The Procurator of Judea" provides a useful service in reminding us that if Pontius Pilate died a bitter man, he had his own reasons.

*Style and Technique*

Anatole France is well known for his style, a sense of language touched with irony at all the foibles of humankind. In "The Procurator of Judea" he achieves his purpose of undermining the religious assumptions of his contemporaries through a subtle form of misdirection that enables him to present a surprise ironic ending. Readers will quickly recognize the name of his principal character, Pontius Pilate—the biblical figure notorious for overseeing the trial and execution of Jesus Christ. They cannot, however, know what later became of Pilate. France adds to this difficulty by obscuring the narrative's historical framework when he hides the identity of the reigning Roman emperor, Caligula, behind his less well-known name, Caius. This device helps to give readers pause about Pilate's identity, ensuring that the story's ending catches them by surprise. The surprise ending, in turn, reinforces the supreme irony that the person responsible for perhaps the most significant event in history is not even aware that he is associated with it.

*Brian Stableford*

# PROFESSION: HOUSEWIFE

*Author:* Sally Benson (1900-1972)
*Locale:* Suburban United States
*Type of plot:* Social realism
*Time of plot:* The 1930's
*First published:* 1938

> *Principal characters:*
> DOROTHY GRANNIS, a newly married woman
> JOE GRANNIS, her husband
> A MAGAZINE SALESPERSON

*The Story*

This story begins with a description of the house in which Dorothy and Joe Grannis live—the breakfast nook, the gingham curtains, and the painted tabletop where Joe sits reading his morning paper. Dorothy opens a letter from a couple she has invited to visit. The woman has written to say that she and her husband cannot accept the invitation. Dorothy is angry, but Joe—who has expected this response—feigns surprise. He tries to encourage his wife by suggesting that the couple may be able to come another time, but Dorothy sees through the woman's excuse. She knows that the couple do not want to socialize with them.

As the dialogue proceeds, it becomes clear that this is Joe's second marriage. The friends of his marriage have not carried over to his new marriage. He and Dorothy have few friends of their own. Dorothy quit her office job when she married and now has little contact with people. She has not kept in touch with the women with whom she formerly worked. There appears to be only one couple with whom the Grannises socialize, and Dorothy, humiliated that this couple have begun to suspect that she and her husband have no other friends, rejects Joe's suggestion that she invite them over in place of the couple who have just rejected their invitation.

All of this makes for a lonely and uninspiring life for Dorothy. After Joe leaves the house, slamming the front door behind him, Dorothy washes the breakfast dishes, then walks into the dining room, where she admires the silver lined up neatly in the drawers of the sideboard. Upstairs she straightens the bedroom; just as she finishes, the doorbell rings. Looking out the window, Dorothy sees a young sales representative with a briefcase.

The sales representative makes his pitch, offering Dorothy a free book with "five hundred tested recipes, how to set your table for any occasion, and other helpful household hints." Dorothy is shrewd enough to tell him that she knows the book is free only if she subscribes to something, and she wants to know what. Caught slightly off guard, the sales representative acknowledges that the gift is conditional; to get it Dorothy must sign up for a three-year subscription to *Good Homes Magazine*. Saying that he will return later in the afternoon, he offers to leave the book with Dorothy so she can look it over and decide.

Dorothy naps until the early afternoon, then makes herself lunch and leaves for the village to get her hair washed and waved. After returning home, she goes upstairs to her room, where she changes into her housecoat, lies on the bed, and lights a cigarette. The doorbell rings; it is the young sales representative returning for his book. Dorothy lies down again and smokes her cigarette, listening to the bell ringing ever more urgently. Finally, she retrieves the book from downstairs and returns to her room, where she rips the pages from its spine and tears them in half. After bending the cover, she gathers the ripped pages and walks to her bedroom window. The sales representative is relieved to see her, but to his amazement, Dorothy opens the screen and drops pieces of the destroyed book to the lawn below. After beginning to pick the pieces up, he soon realizes the futility of the task. He and Dorothy stare at each other before he walks away. Dorothy returns to her bed, lights another cigarette, and lies staring at the ceiling.

*Themes and Meanings*

Sally Benson's short story is a portrayal of the American suburban housewife of the 1930's. Because Dorothy Grannis is a potentially interesting character, she is too undeveloped and one-dimensional to function as the story's main subject. "Profession: Housewife" is not intended to be a character study; Dorothy merely represents a wider phenomenon experienced by many women of her time period. The title also works to inform the reader that Benson's concern here is with the role of the housewife at that moment in history. She particularly emphasizes the housewife's loneliness, frustration, and rage as Dorothy lives out one tedious, narrowly circumscribed day of her married existence.

The story opens with the detailed description of the Grannises' middle-class kitchen, and the first emotion that Dorothy expresses is anger at having her invitation turned down. In fact, she is so angry at this snub that she slams her hand down on the table, spilling her coffee. The ensuing dialogue between her and her husband reveals that Dorothy believes she is doing everything right, that she is following the rules that accompany her job as housewife. She keeps a clean house; however, a spotless house cannot begin to compensate for her loneliness. Further, Joe's parting shot—that he cannot help it if she cannot make friends for herself—stings her. Wounded, Dorothy withdraws, giving Joe no more than a formal, indignant reply.

Dorothy then goes through the minutiae of her daily tasks of washing breakfast dishes, hanging pajamas, and making beds. She takes a nap before noon. She makes herself a simple lunch. All these little tasks are devised to get her through a day. At one point, when she looks at the clock and realizes that the morning is still early, she tries to slow her movements in order to fill the time. This is a woman who has little to do, and the boredom of her life frustrates and enrages her.

It is ironic that the ringing of Dorothy's doorbell does not announce a release from her boredom and rut of domesticity; it is not an unexpected visit from a friend with whom Dorothy may spend a pleasant morning. Rather, it is a sales representative whose wares—*Good Homes Magazine* and the complimentary book of recipes and household hints—is designed further to entrap Dorothy and capitalize on her frustrating lifestyle. Dorothy's manner with the sales representative is so hostile and confrontational that he grows uncomfortable; he unwittingly becomes the focal point of Dorothy's frustration and anger.

There are also subtle references to the social forces that contribute to Dorothy's isolation. This was a time when working women frequently gave up their jobs when they married; their disconnection from their jobs often also meant a loss of friendships with their workmates. The brief paragraph that describes the office at Dorothy's former workplace suggests a camaraderie and a liveliness that are absent from her present life.

Other forces that exert pressure on Dorothy and help to ensure her loneliness are the unwritten social laws that dissolve friendships in the event of divorce and that drive Dorothy to keep up appearances so that their one friendly couple will not fully realize the extent of her dependence on them for social interaction. Dorothy is thus isolated not only physically but also socially.

*Style and Technique*

Unlike the more austere and cleaner styles of some of her contemporaries, Benson's makes liberal use of descriptive words and phrases to explain the scenes, tones, and emotions contained in her story. For example, when Dorothy and her husband argue about the rejected invitation, Dorothy pushes up the sleeves of her housecoat "with a hard, deliberate gesture." Dorothy's hostile, unwelcoming manner with the sales representative causes him to shift "his feet in embarrassment."

Much of this description is applied to the house as the setting and source of Dorothy's drama and pain. Illustrating that the cleanliness and decoration of the house may have no direct relationship to the lives of those living in it, Benson points out, in her account of the Grannises' argument, that the kitchen is "bright, shiny." Possessions intended as valuable for their beauty and worth are devoid of meaning, as Dorothy walks through her dining room looking at a silver bowl, candlesticks, and silverplated ware. Although everything is fastidiously neat and clean, it gives Dorothy no pleasure.

*Julie Thompson*

# THE PROPHET FROM JUPITER

*Author:* Tony Earley (1961-      )
*Type of plot:* Satire
*Time of plot:* 1927-1990's
*Locale:* The mountain country of western North Carolina
*First published:* 1993

*Principal characters:*

THE DAM KEEPER OF LAKE GLEN, the protagonist and narrator
ELISABETH, his wife
RANDY, the assistant dam keeper, an orderly at a local hospital
ARCHIE SIMPSON, aka The Prophet from Jupiter, a developer from
    Florida
JUNIE WILSON, an unemployed African American

*The Story*

"The Prophet from Jupiter" is a first-person narration in which the dam keeper of a lake created when a small town was flooded intermingles incidents from his own life with a selective historical recounting of the lake's effect on the region. It begins with a topographical description of the lake, establishing the location of the dam keeper's house just above the lake shore, a perimeter encircled by homes on small lots that are occupied primarily by tourists and visitors.

As the dam keeper explains that his primary concern is to maintain the lake at a constant level, he introduces some of the people whose presence defines the character of the community, including Archie Simpson, a real estate developer from Jupiter, Florida, whose "message" from God has transformed him into a "prophet," and Junie Wilson, an African American who wanders through the neighborhood with no apparent purpose or direction, but according to Archie Simpson, has "the gift of true sight."

The dam keeper's account is directed toward an explanation of why he plans to leave the area, centered on the deterioration of his marriage and his sense that the entire region is permeated with a kind of curse stemming from the decision in 1927 to destroy Uree, the town that was flooded to form the lake. His separation from his wife, Elisabeth, now pregnant with the child of the new police chief, parallels the disconnection of many people in the area from their surroundings. He enjoys fishing with his only friend, Randy, the assistant dam keeper, but recognizes their fundamental differences. Randy is sensible and practical in a way that constrasts with the dam keeper's moods and uncertainties, a man able to comfortably adapt to the environment in contrary to the dam keeper's sense of anomie and alienation.

The dam keeper intersperses observations about his life and his job with recollections of the reactions of the people who lived in Uree when the decision was made to build the dam, showing how their lives were disrupted and how they have tried to cling to some vestige of their previous existence. The four sons of "Old Man" Burdette drag their father's Reo truck out of the lake and restore it; "Aunt" Plutina Williams had to be carried into the truck when she refused to leave her house. The night before the water rose, Jim Skipper set his house on fire. The week before, the Lake Glen Development Company moved all the remains from the Uree Baptist Church graveyard. The current mayor of Lake Glen came to the town in 1931 on his summer vacation from Chapel Hill, and the dam keeper's presentation of the events of the mayor's life are marking points on a path through the half-century of the town's past.

As the narrative progresses, the dam keeper turns his attention to the transition from the summer tourist season toward changes that occur in the climate and in the communal mood during the fall. Bizarre behavior in the present seems to echo accounts of strikingly odd incidents in the town's history, while the dam keeper tries to balance the requirements of his job with his inclination toward the same kind of idiosyncrasies that he has been describing. Just before Christmas, a duck trapped on the frozen lake's surface is pursued by a dog, which falls through the ice.

The Prophet from Jupiter succeeds in rescuing the dog, but with the whole town watching, he disappears beneath the ice, joining the ghost houses under the water. Stunned by what he has seen, the dam keeper concludes his narrative with an overarching summary of the town's entire history so that "all the ghosts of Lake Glen buzzed in my ears like electricity." His final vision compresses time into an eternal moment, which increases the mysterious nature of the place while implying that the seemingly random circumstances that he has been relating might coalesce into some cosmic conception of ultimate clarity.

### Themes and Meanings

The dam keeper of Lake Glen is a man fascinated by a world from which he is estranged. In an attempt to understand who he is, how he has reached this condition of existence, and what kind of sense he might make of his life, he is obsessed with the history of the flooded town, Uree, which he has learned through the stories of his neighbors. For him, the decision by various powerful outside commercial interests to destroy a living community was the precipitating action that has resulted in a psychic blight that adversely affects nearly everyone living in or visiting Lake Glen. The dam keeper's own troubles, significantly centered on his failure to communicate with his wife and their fruitless attempt for seven years to conceive a child, are presented by Tony Earley as an analogue for the pervasive dysfunction that defines the social nexus of the town.

The dam keeper observes that his job is to "maintain a constant pond level," and this responsibility is a figure for the elusive psychic equilibrium that he seeks, and which the town lacks. When he confesses that he has always wanted to "drop the lake down far enough to see what is down there," he is encapsulating both his geophysical and psychological yearning. He has stated that he thinks that the dam is "an unnatural thing," which he tellingly compares to a diaphragm.

Even in a place in which somewhat unconventional behavior is not uncommon, the dam keeper is separated from the community by individual peculiarities. He is a true descendant of the old town of Uree, troubled by a religious consciousness that makes him the *real* prophet of the region, haunted by the lives of previous generations, alienated from the profiteers, marketeers, and gawking visitors who have come to the lake searching for hedonistic gratifications. He has a curious kinship with Junie Wilson, the town's ultraeccentric, who eventually loses all semblance of sanity. As a way of diverting his attention from his difficulties, he has set himself the goal of landing a fabled huge catfish rumored to be cruising the lake's bottom. He sees this quest as a way of placing himself in the town's historical record, a way to be remembered after he has left the area and a way to do something tangible that will solidify his spiritual inclinations.

Earley has chosen the particular vocation for the narrator so that he can develop a pattern of meanings through the use of water as a central symbol. In addition to the traditional associations that water carries, Earley sees it as both natural force and essential substance, threatening destruction in the flood of 1928, offering opportunity for exploitation, and providing the ingredients for fertility and regeneration. The barren disappointment of the dam keeper's marriage is marked by numerous references to liquidity and flow, and his cryptic pronouncement, "I am the man who didn't miss his water," is rife with implications for his life.

*Style and Technique*

"The Prophet from Jupiter" is developed as an intricate narrative scheme based on the flow of structured consciousness in the dam keeper's mind. Rather than a stream of random thoughts delivered as they occur, the narration is presented as the consequence of constant reflection on the town, the lake, its history, and its inhabitants. Earley has carefully arranged details so that the mix of historical recollection and an evolving present-tense narrative displays the patterns of thought that define the dam keeper's character. The realistic aspect of the details tends to ground the more fantastic aspects of the eccentricities displayed by both the narrator and most of the people he recalls and renders. His world is constructed out of a fusion of the mundane and the marvelous, revealing a place that is recognizable as a feature of American life and as an artistic creation teeming with symbols and emblems that operate as comments on the lives and fates of the characters.

Although the dam keeper is often opinionated and sometimes judgmental, particularly in terms of his values, his voice takes on a distinctive signature primarily through his tone of awe and even bewilderment. Cryptic comments seeded with implications like his observation that "in North Carolina, even in the mountains, it takes more than a month of your life to live through August" are typical. He is somewhat stunned by the human capacity for emotional intensity, including his own, and his generally matter-of-fact recitation of unconventional behavior does not disguise his fascination with the wild variety of responses to circumstance.

When a storm threatened to destroy the dam, Big Julie Cooper, according to accounts, shot twenty-four development company mules to reinforce the structure. Rotting mules then force workers putting a roof on the hotel to wear camphor-covered masks over their mouths until bears from the nearby mountains devour the remains, which are eventually covered with a thick growth of kudzu, the ubiquitous imported vine that has overrun considerable parts of the region. The dam keeper's pervasive curiosity about what it all could mean, what lies beneath the surface of everything, and how he might make some sense of his life amid all the assorted phenomena provides the energy that sustains the narrative throughout the story.

*Leon Lewis*

# PROWLER

*Author:* Elizabeth Tallent (1954-    )
*Type of plot:* Domestic realism
*Time of plot:* The late 1980's
*Locale:* Santa Fe, New Mexico
*First published:* 1989

> *Principal characters:*
> DENNIS, a divorced man
> FRANCESCA, his wife, mother of their twins
> CHRISTIE, his former wife
> ANDY, their thirteen-year-old son

## The Story

"Prowler" focuses on a divorced man named Dennis as he struggles with his emotional reactions to the unexpected return of his former wife to New Mexico and his growing separation from his thirteen-year-old son, Andy. The story opens with Dennis in a frustrating conversation with Christie, his former wife and mother of Andy. She has stopped by on a spur-of-the-moment visit and has asked to have Andy spend the summer with her and her new baby. Christie has spent the last year in Paris, France, but has suddenly returned to the United States, leaving the father of her young daughter behind.

Dennis does not want to let his son go with the boy's mother. While in Europe, she has called Andy rarely, even letting a month go between calls. He does not trust Christie; he sees her as flighty, as inconsistent. Dennis also worries about Andy. He is unsure of Andy's smooth friend, Leo; Dennis imagines Leo getting Andy into trouble, perhaps drugs.

After Christie leaves, Dennis goes upstairs and talks with his current wife, Francesca. She is at the edge of sleep, having been sick, along with their twin infants. Dennis grouses about Christie's irresponsibility, but Francesca tries to point out how unfair Dennis is toward his son Andy's relationship with the boy's mother. She does not defend Christie, but she does believe Andy needs to see his mother.

The next day, Dennis tells Andy that his mother has returned. Andy had noticed that something was wrong with his father and wonders if his mother's sudden reappearance is what is troubling his father, but Dennis explains that he has been unable to sleep. Andy changes his shirt, and his father explodes when he sees Andy has gotten a tattoo. Dennis demands to know if Andy's troublesome friend Leo had put Andy up to this decision, but Andy insists that it is his body and he can do with it as he chooses. Dennis recalls a variety of times Andy has hurt himself, thinking back, for instance, to a bloodied lip back when Andy was five. He realizes that Andy is managing to separate himself a little from his father. Dennis realizes there is now something about

Andy that Dennis hates. He does not believe he could ever hate anything about his boy and realizes that his former wife is the only other person who might share this feeling with him. He grounds his son and, for the next two days, does not return phone calls from Christie.

Dennis has been unable to sleep and decides to stop by Christie's apartment unannounced. She is not home, but Dennis correctly guesses where she hides a key. He enters the apartment and studies its disarray. After peering into the different rooms, he finally reaches the one planned for Andy. He cannot help but like the room, a place he was not intended to see. He lies down on Andy's bed and dozes off for his first real sleep in days. He dreams a dream that he believes should have been Andy's. It is of Andy, as a young child, playing with his mother. Mother and son laugh together, as cutout animals come to life. Dennis finally awakes and sneaks back out of the apartment, leaving no sign of his presence.

The story ends with Dennis and Andy in the car, outside Christie's apartment. Andy worries for a moment that they have not called ahead, but then he jumps out of the car, bag of clothes in hand, to spend the weekend. Christie looks back at Dennis, with a puzzled look, but he just waves at her.

*Themes and Meanings*

Dennis is a planner and an organizer. Professionally he is an architect, a person who controls and designs space. He is frustrated that the rest of his world is not as neat and orderly as he is. However, the rest of the world does not share this ideal. Christie lets him know she will not apologize for being unpredictable. Dennis loves the old trees that surround his house, but beavers come up from the river to gnaw on them. As he tries to construct an argument his current wife will accept, she dozes off. Though he can still ground his son, Dennis has to realize the boy is growing up. Andy now has a life that contains secrets, aspects that are unknown and uncontrolled by his father.

Dennis has worked hard to reconstruct his life after his frustrating first marriage and his difficult divorce, but he has to learn that he cannot control life. Children get sick. They make decisions, such as to get a tattoo, which will show their parents that their children have lives of their own. As much as Dennis would like to control the events in his life, in this story, he learns to let things happen spontaneously. By the end of the story, he can bring his son to the boy's mother without planning and without negotiating the precise parameters of their visit.

Dennis has changed, a little. At the start of the story, he is frustrated at his former wife Christie's affectations, with her secretiveness and her inconsistency. He wants to refuse to let their son go with her and tries to paint a picture of her behavior that is dangerous. His role is to be the steady responsible parent, which means seeing his former wife as unreliable. However, when he steps outside his role and sneaks into her apartment, he sees that she loves their son, too. Her love for their son is strong and tender. He is the secretive prowler of the story's title, but his decision to essentially break into her apartment and her life enables him to see her relationship with Andy in a different light. Dennis can see things through his former wife's eyes rather than strictly through his own.

*Style and Technique*

"Prowler" does not build through plot but through layers of careful description. Attention to descriptive detail is a critical aspect of this story. Elizabeth Tallent describes Dennis's house and later Christie's apartment with an eye for details that say something about the personalities of the characters.

Dennis's house is sheltered and private, hidden by trees. Though he lives in New Mexico, in a place full of bright sunlight, not a lot of light comes in through the windows. His family is secreted upstairs, which is lit by a single candle, and Christie does not feel allowed to see her son Andy's room. It is Dennis's house, his private life. Andy's room is a reflection of his personality. Tallent describes the realistic paintings Andy does of fast motorcycles, juxtaposed with a small photo of the European author Franz Kafka.

When Dennis prowls in Christie's apartment, he sees a side she might not reveal to him. As a reflection of Christie's personality, the apartment is disorderly, and Dennis originally wants to begin arranging things, putting them in their place. However, as he looks about, he is struck by the warmth of the home she has created. When Dennis looks into what will be Andy's room, he finds she has created an interesting and imaginative room for Andy, a place in which to dream. The room enables Dennis to finally relax.

This story contains an underlying motif of fairy tales. It is structured around three visits, each unannounced. Also, Francesca illustrates children's books. Her drawings are intricately detailed, and she is drawing a wolf that looks so real Dennis fears that it has eaten someone. Dennis tries to recall a fairy tale in which someone returns for a cherished child. He views his world as filled with scary threats, as is any fairy tale. He worries that his son is in the thrall of his friend Leo, who, though thirteen like Andy, somehow has a girlfriend old enough to drive. Dennis's worries leave him unable to sleep, opposite of the typical magic spell. He watches his second wife and their twin babies slide easily into the sleep he cannot achieve. It is only after he surrenders to impetuousness himself that he is able to dream.

By the end of the story, he is able to let his son Andy go. Dennis does not know what the future may hold and he does not understand how he has come to accept the changing relationship he has directly with Andy and indirectly with his former wife, but he is now able to stand back and let life happen to the people he loves.

*Brian L. Olson*

# THE PRUSSIAN OFFICER

*Author:* D. H. Lawrence (1885-1930)
*Type of plot:* Psychological
*Time of plot:* 1914, before World War I
*Locale:* Germany
*First published:* 1914

> *Principal characters:*
> THE CAPTAIN, about forty years old
> SCHONER, his orderly, about twenty-two years old

*The Story*

In this classic story of sexual repression and tension that, when released, explodes into maddened violence, D. H. Lawrence examines the psychology of two men, both German soldiers. The captain, a Junker aristocrat, tall, muscular, and an expert horseman, is accustomed to domineering his soldiers just as he subjugates horses. He is, however, isolated from the vital life of other soldiers; fortyish and unmarried, he has had occasional mistresses but has always returned from their arms with greater tension and irritability after he resumes his military duties. Cold, impersonal, and harsh, he is subconsciously tormented by repressed homoerotic desire for his young orderly, Schoner, whose name means "more beautiful" in German, and whose vigorous physical presence is "like a warm flame on the older man's tense, rigid body."

In the most extensive section of the story, part 1, Lawrence develops the theme of conflict between these men, who are locked in a fatal struggle for domination of both body and spirit. With mounting fury, the captain attempts to break down his orderly's will. At one point, he demands to know why Schoner has a piece of pencil stuck behind his ear. When he learns that the young man has been writing a letter to his sweetheart, the officer humiliates the youth. By the end of this section, the two men are driven by hatred and self-loathing.

In part 2, the psychological conflict reaches a climax through physical release in a scene of terrible intensity. Watching with hypnotic fascination while the captain drinks a mug of beer, Schoner is maddened by the sight of the older man's throat; he lunges toward the captain, strangles him against a sharp-edged tree base, and stares in shocked horror—but also satisfaction—as the older man expires.

In part 3, Schoner stumbles through forest brakes to a high mountain range; his vision clouded by delirium, he perceives a landscape transmogrified into sinister colors and vague shapes. Sick from fever, probably "brain fever," he twists in a paroxysm on the grass until his eyes go black, so that he cannot see the distant, gleaming mountains.

In the briefest section, part 4, Schoner is discovered, barely alive, by soldiers who drop his body in horror when they gaze on the youth's open, black mouth. Later, the remains of the two men are placed at the mortuary, side by side: one rigid and the other young and unused, almost as though he might be roused from a slumber. In death they are not divided.

## Themes and Meanings

This story of elemental attraction and repulsion between two men of different temperaments can be understood on at least three levels of meaning. On the simplest level, the captain and his orderly are locked in a struggle for domination on one hand, for submission on the other. At the beginning of the story, the captain persecutes Schoner; his brutal will focused on breaking the spirit of the young man, he achieves his goal of mastery in the letter scene, but his victory leaves him depressed rather than elated. In the second section, Schoner, the former victim of persecution, turns about to strangle his adversary, but his brief triumph brings no joy, for in a vertigo of dizzying emotions, he falls prey to delirium and madness.

On a more complex level, the struggle between antagonists is a classic exposition of sadism and masochism, the two forces seemingly opposed but actually correlative. At first, the captain is the sadist; later, Schoner reverses his role to take the captain's. Even so, can either man be understood as a masochist—one who takes psychological pleasure in abuse? Schoner's suffering under the blows of his superior officer cannot be avoided; as a soldier, his power to disobey his leader is limited. Nevertheless, Lawrence allows the reader clues to perceive that, even in his misery, Schoner is mysteriously attracted to the captain. The older man's domination touches in him the quick of his erotic energy. Similarly, Lawrence allows the reader scope to observe how the captain, in his death throes from strangulation, is curiously submissive, as though his body were pressed beneath the weight of his lover.

On the highest level of abstraction, the struggle can be seen as one involving the repressed homoerotic (not explicitly physical homosexual) urges of two men, each transforming desire into hatred, hatred into desire. The captain's erotic attachment to the youth is more nearly evident, although Lawrence's exposition of that compulsion is subtle and indirect. Unable to express openly his suppressed passion for the youth, the captain is filled with self-disgust. Schoner's reciprocation of this passion—which he similarly represses—is less evident, even from a close reading of the text. Nevertheless, by murdering the captain in a way that grotesquely parodies an act of love, he releases himself briefly from the tension of his erotic constraints and is "satisfied"; then, in madness, he destroys himself through repressed grief over the loss of his hated-beloved. In death the two men are laid body to body, their passion never achieved, their vitality wasted.

## Style and Technique

In this story of compulsion, Lawrence creates a mood of nearly intolerable tension, broken at last, suddenly and elegiacally, at the conclusion. He sustains this mood, at least in part, by symbolic use of three repeated words: neck (or throat), dryness (or thirst), and the color red (contrasted at times with black or green). The three symbols are presented together in the first section, when the orderly drinks a bottle of red wine, some of which spills on the tablecloth. Gazing with hatred at this innocent act, the captain subconsciously identifies the wine with blood, the neck and throat of the young man with erotic tenderness. Later, in part 2, the captain's repressed sexuality is symbolized by the dryness of his own throat, which Lawrence describes as "parched." While Schoner watches the captain drink, in a reversal of the earlier scene, his mind snaps, his repressions explode into furious action, and he springs for the older man's throat.

Finally, in part 3, the horror of the soldier's panic is represented by his own parched throat, "thirst burning in his brain." The glistening, green corn that he views (contrasted against the image of a woman with a black cloth on her head) represents his decline into madness. Lawrence's symbolism for green in this context is not, as is common in other writers (or, for Lawrence, in other contexts), luxuriant growth or vitality, but irrationality and terror (as in Vincent van Gogh's green billiard table in *The Night Café*, 1888). In the final scene, the three dominant symbols come together. Schoner is discovered desiccated, "his black hair giving off heat under the sun." His mouth is open, but not red with the promise of life; instead it is open (dry) and black. Through these persistent symbols, operating powerfully below the level of awareness, Lawrence unifies the conflicting emotions of the story and concentrates them with great force.

*Leslie B. Mittleman*

# THE PSYCHIATRIST

*Author:* Joaquim Maria Machado de Assis (1839-1908)
*Type of plot:* Satire
*Time of plot:* The early nineteenth century
*Locale:* Itaguai, a town near Rio de Janeiro
*First published:* "O alienista," 1881-1882 (English translation, 1963)

> *Principal characters:*
> Dr. SIMAO BACAMARTE, the psychiatrist
> DONA EVARISTA DA COSTA E MASCARENHAS, his wife
> CRISPIM SOARES, a druggist, one of Bacamarte's closest friends
> FATHER LOPES, the vicar
> PORFIRIO CAETANO DAS NEVES (STEWED CORN), a local barber

*The Story*

According to the town chronicles, Simao Bacamarte, one of the greatest doctors in Europe, turned down two extremely prestigious crown appointments to return to his native Itaguai and devote his life to science. He settled there and married Dona Evarista, the story goes, not for love, but because she seemed to him a biologically promising specimen to mother his children.

When the children fail to come, Bacamarte dedicates himself to an exhaustive study of sterility. Realizing the therapeutic value of study itself, he hits on psychopathology, a then-unknown specialty in the realm, as a way not only to contribute to science but also to alleviate his disappointment in not having an heir.

He appeals to the town council for aid, and, to support him, it enacts a tax on the plumes on the horses that pull funeral carriages. With this money, Bacamarte erects the Green House, which will be both asylum and laboratory for his studies of mental illness. Within months, the Green House is home for madmen and madwomen of all varieties. Bacamarte becomes so involved in his studies of these pathetic cases that he ignores all else in life, and he finally has to send Evarista on her longed-for journey to Rio de Janeiro to keep her happy. Now free to labor without interruption, he develops a new theory that the slightest sign of lack of equilibrium is proof of madness, and by the time Evarista returns from Rio de Janeiro, the Green House is full to the rafters with people who have loaned away an inheritance, demonstrated excessive interest in a house ("petrophilia"), or are unfailingly polite.

Almost everyone in town by now has a relative or loved one behind bars, and a minor revolt led by the barber Porfirio (called "Stewed Corn") thus swells to a mob and storms Bacamarte's house. A troop of dragoons arrives to quell the disorder, but many of its number defect to the "Stewed Corners," and in a matter of minutes the barber has taken over the town and deposed the council. Porfirio goes to see Bacamarte and offers a compromise, which prompts another barber, Joao Pina, to depose Porfirio. Government troops finally arrive to restore order, whereupon Bacamarte commits Porfirio and fifty of his followers to the asylum. Within months, the psychiatrist discovers some flaw in most of the population, including his wife (who, he finds, exhibits "vestimania," or excessive preoccupation with clothing), his friend Crispim Soares, and the president of the town council. With four-fifths of the population interned, he comes to the realization that his theory is flawed, and he now decides that complete equilibrium, not its lack, is proof of madness. He releases the patients and starts his search for persons of irreproachable virtue, starting with Father Lopes and the only honest councilman, and ending with Porfirio, who has refused to lead a new revolt.

Such chronic virtue, the psychiatrist soon discovers, is easily cured, and in the end he has effected a cure on every one of the perfectly balanced persons in town—until he realizes that he himself is above reproach. He interns himself in the Green House and dies before finding a cure for his indefectibility.

*Themes and Meanings*

The arbitrary line that society draws to separate those mad from those sane is clearly the essence of this story, but the story is also an ironic study of credulity, vanity, and humankind's chronic weakness for simple solutions. The general theme of madness versus sanity has a long literary history, and it is one that Joaquim Maria Machado de Assis explored in other short stories and at least two of his major novels. Because the theme is simply one of the declensions of the larger theme of appearance versus reality, it is probably fair to say, in fact, that it appears in some form in most of his fiction.

In the context of time and place, the irony is especially acute, because Brazil was a country in which faith in the ability of science to solve any problem had great currency in the late nineteenth century. Indeed, positivism became a sort of second national religion, and it contributed the national motto "Order and Progress," which still appears on the Brazilian flag and which still seems to hold great appeal for Brazilians. Critics have noted the particular relevance of Machado de Assis's treatment of the psychiatrist here because of Brazilians' fondness for, and obeisance to, any high-sounding credential.

Bacamarte initially appears to be not much more than a charlatan, but because he is not even aware of the misery that results from his unremitting egotism, he is oddly naïve as a villain. What he turns out to be is a sort of embodiment of the eccentric but dedicated scientific spirit, ready to make any sacrifice in the name of the advancement of knowledge. Because, like all the other characters, his actions are at the same time guided by his colossal vanity, the story stands not only as an ironic inquiry into the mind of a megalomaniac but also as a commentary on the chronic human problem of self-delusion.

*Style and Technique*

Machado de Assis is considered the most "English" of Brazilian writers because of his subtle and often biting sense of humor and because of his laconic and understated diction. In part for the same reasons, he is a writer almost impossible to insert neatly into general observations of Brazilian literary history; his novels and short stories have none of the quality of datedness that is so evident in the works of most of his contemporaries. Though uncommonly long for a Brazilian short story, "The Psychiatrist" is an example of Machado de Assis's skill as an illusionist.

The story is ostensibly drawn from a documentary source, the town's chronicles, which makes of the entire tale a single preterit narrative block, a piece of history. Though there are numerous characters, only one, Bacamarte, is of real importance. Time is repeatedly compressed by summaries in which months of time are reduced to a single line. These manipulations all contribute to a very tight narrative scheme that in fact obeys the classic reductionist form of the genre.

Machado de Assis is also a master stylist. His narrator is privy to the contents of the chronicles on which he bases the story, but he never betrays any of the credulity the characters all show as a fundamental trait. The narrator consistently employs euphemisms, multiple adjectivation, and pseudophilosophical asides to create the illusion of an elegant and cultured style, but what these devices really create is a narrative style just a shade too grand for the implausible sequence of events. The result is that Bacamarte (the name means "blunderbuss") is constantly seen in the light of a not altogether gentle irony, so that at the end, the cause of his death, like the cause of everything else, seems to be a simple case of incurable vanity.

*Jon S. Vincent*

# PSYCHOPOLIS

*Author:* Ian McEwan (1948-       )
*Type of plot:* Psychological
*Time of plot:* The 1970's
*Locale:* Los Angeles, California
*First published:* 1978

> *Principal characters:*
> THE NARRATOR, an English traveler who is staying in Los
> Angeles
> MARY, the co-owner of a feminist bookstore
> TERENCE LATTERLY, an American scholar who earlier met the
> narrator in England
> GEORGE MALONE, the proprietor of a rental shop beneath the
> narrator's apartment

*The Story*

The narrator begins his account of a sojourn in Los Angeles by describing the first weekend he spent with Mary, whom he met in a feminist bookstore on his second day in the city. She asks him to chain her to the bed and makes him promise that he will not unchain her for twenty-four hours no matter how fervently she pleads for release. He keeps his promise, although she does indeed demand to be freed. When they go out later to eat, however, their main topic of conversation is the social and economic collapse of England.

The narrator's apartment in Santa Monica is above a shop that offers rental equipment for parties and—in a seemingly bizarre juxtaposition—for the care of invalids. The shop's proprietor, George Malone, develops an interest in the narrator after hearing him practice playing his flute. George takes the narrator out to a bar, gives him directions to the beach, and begins driving him around so that he can get a better grasp of the city's size and disposition. The narrator is also contacted by a old acquaintance, Terence Latterly, a delicate young scholar spectacularly unlucky in love, who recounts a tale of his most recent humiliation by the unkind object of his current romantic obsession, a woman named Sylvie.

The bored narrator's desultory flute playing encourages George to make further attempts to cultivate his friendship, culminating in an invitation to visit his house in Simi Valley. On the weekend before his departure for New York, the narrator accepts this invitation, taking Mary and Terence with him. George's two sons from his failed marriage are also at the house, on one of their regular visits, but they are determinedly unobtrusive. The four adults are moved to discuss the propriety of corporal punishment and the politics of educating children in religious faith, but they eventually move on to more controversial ground and begin playing with George's gun. To bring the occasion to a conclusion, the narrator attempts to play a Bach sonata on his flute; he cannot finish it, but his audience applauds his efforts anyway.

## Themes and Meanings

The story maps out the narrator's halfhearted attempts to get an imaginative grip on the city of Los Angeles. This process extends through a series of absurd encounters, whose matter-of-fact perversity seems to the narrator to embody the contradictions inherent in the city and the ultramodernity of which it is the perfect symbol.

Mary is an articulate and outspoken feminist who nevertheless wants to be tied up and then to have her demands for release ignored; she also does not want to analyze or discuss her impulses. Her hastily contrived relationship with the narrator, though casually sexual, contains no evident trace of affection or intimacy. George and Terence find it hard to relate to the narrator's ironic observations, thus making them seem rather alien to him. George needs to think twice before realizing that his suggestion that the best English wheelchairs must be made by Rolls-Royce is a joke, and Terence cannot see any absurdity in a restaurant named the Doggie Diner even when the narrator carefully explains the meaning of the English colloquialism "dog's dinner."

Terence's relationship with Sylvie and George's relationship with his sons seem, in the cursory glimpses offered to the narrator and the reader, to be as devoid of any rewarding attachment as the narrator's relationship with Mary.

When all four characters eventually come together, the culture clashes between George and Mary, George and Terence, and Mary and Terence are as obvious as those between the three Americans and the English traveler, but their conflict is listless and taken for granted all round, with not the slightest expectation of resolution. The narrator, by contrast, is much more acutely aware of the social distances continually brought to his attention by his confrontations with the landscape and citizens of Los Angeles, and he experiences their hollow futility as a kind of mental infection. The changes that he undergoes as he is overwhelmed by the vastness and impersonality of the city are not entirely unwelcome, though; there is something to be treasured in the passive attitude forced on him by the overcomplicated environment, and he is already anticipating the nostalgia with which he will look back on it before he actually departs.

There is a definite pathos in the way in which the narrator is driven by boredom to resume his long-postponed quest to master the Bach sonata and in his utter failure to bring that project to a satisfactory conclusion, but the utter inhospitability of the ultramodern city to such exquisite adventures is no simple tragedy in this story, although it might well have been represented as such in the work of an older and more Eurocentric writer. Instead, the narrator's failure to produce a music appropriate to the time and place in which he finds himself becomes a revelation of the inanity of the ambitions and expectations that led him to set off on his escapist journey into the American cultural wilderness. The ungraspable vastness of the "city of the mind" is an opportunity as well as an oppression, which transcends and defies ironic interpretation.

*Style and Technique*

The story is told in a steadfastly laconic manner, the narrator remaining bogged down in a kind of emotional torpor until the final moment of private revelation that he experiences when he fails to complete his rendition of the Bach sonata. The opening incident, which describes the phases of the narrator's understated experiment in bondage, sets this tone very neatly. The subsequent descriptions of the narrator's impressions of the beach scene and Terence's account of Sylvie's cruel exploitation of his excessively romantic offer maintain the same underlying note while carefully elaborating the theme.

The eventual summation of this whole enterprise is the deliberately anticlimactic episode in which Terence aims the gun at George and pulls the trigger. Even though George is the only one who had noticed that Terence had removed the bullets from the gun, neither Mary nor the narrator is aroused to violent anxiety by this apparent assassination attempt. Indeed, the conversation thereafter flows more easily and more politely than before, unpunctuated by any tangible melodramatic alarm. The story does not end with this incident, because the whole point of undermining its climactic status so drastically is to stress that there is no possibility of ending an account of this sort with a bang or even a perceptible whimper.

As the title of the story indicates, the real "central character" of the story is its setting, not its nameless narrator. Everything the narrator does, says, thinks, and feels—especially the tone and manner of the voice in which he relates his experience to the reader—is a reaction to the all-encompassing presence of a city like none he has ever encountered before: a city that stretches from horizon to horizon and beyond, which contains multitudes and yet contrives to separate them from one another, in body and mind alike, more widely than any Londoner could ever have imagined possible while contemplating Los Angeles at a distance through the media of cinema and television.

When the narrator agrees so readily with Mary's suggestion that England is in a state of collapse, he is talking about his own estate of mind rather than the actual society or economy of his homeland; the England that has collapsed is the model contained in his consciousness, which cannot survive confrontation with the sheer enormity of the American psychopolis. When Mary, Terence, and George begin an animated discussion of religion—no less animated for the fact that none of them is really a committed believer—the narrator finds himself suddenly possessed of urgent and unironic views of a kind to which he could never have fallen prey in his native environment. He is beginning, in spite of himself, to become acclimatized—and that is why his feelings, slightly awakened from their former torpor, are so perversely mixed when he contemplates his departure, while reveling in the wholly undeserved but not entirely insincere applause of his makeshift audience.

*Brian Stableford*

# THE PUGILIST AT REST

*Author:* Thom Jones (1945-     )
*Type of plot:* Philosophical realism, war
*Time of plot:* The 1960's and 1980's
*Locale:* San Diego, other parts of the United States, and Vietnam
*First published:* 1991

> *Principal characters:*
> THE NARRATOR, a Marine who served in the Vietnam War
> JORGESON, his friend in the Marines
> HEY BABY, a Marine who harasses Jorgeson

## The Story

The story opens at boot camp for the United States Marines in San Diego, California. One man is nicknamed "Hey Baby" because he has been caught writing a letter to his girlfriend when he should have been studying his rifle specifications. The narrator, another Marine in training, takes a dislike to Hey Baby because he continually harasses Jorgeson, the narrator's friend. Jorgeson is the only one at boot camp who has not dedicated himself to becoming a Marine; he dreams of becoming a beatnik or an artist. Although the narrator is serious about his training and becoming an elite paratrooper, he is fascinated by Jorgeson's dreams.

Hey Baby's dislike for Jorgeson leads him to knock the other man down. The narrator comes up behind Hey Baby and clubs him in the head with the butt of his rifle. Hey Baby is unconscious for three days and permanently injured. Although the narrator worries that he could be in trouble for his rash act, no one reports him.

After boot camp, the narrator intentionally flunks out of com school, so he can be sent to the infantry. He meets up with Jorgeson, who is now dedicated to the Marines, and the two work to join a reconnaissance patrol. They soon go into enemy territory.

The first trip starts badly. A corporal with less than two weeks to go in Vietnam is sent across an open field. The narrator is sent off from his group to investigate a pile of dirt that might indicate the presence of a tunnel. No sooner does the narrator separate from his group than mortar fire comes in. The narrator is thrown to the ground by the force of the blast. From a distance, the narrator watches as North Vietnamese soldiers attack. Most of the Marines are already dead, and the narrator's friend Jorgeson and another lieutenant are the only ones shooting back. The narrator tries to fire, but his weapon is jammed from dirt thrown up in the earlier mortar explosion.

As the narrator feverishly tries to clean his weapon, he watches a rocket tear off the lieutenant's shoulder. Jorgeson shoots several attackers and then picks up a larger machine gun that had been carried by one of the experienced Marines. The gun's owner had yet to speak to the narrator because the narrator was a newcomer and therefore bad luck. Jorgeson begins to turn back the attackers but is hit by a rocket.

From a distance, the narrator watches as the enemy troops check to see if all the narrator's group is dead. He realizes that no one has noticed him and radios for an air strike. Finally, one soldier begins to head in the narrator's direction, but Jorgeson screams and distracts him, allowing the narrator to escape. Jets roar in and drop napalm. The narrator is the only survivor and takes credit for the dead enemy troops.

Although he had not actively participated in his first fight, the narrator becomes a violent man. He kills enemy soldiers in later battles and goes on three tours of duty in Vietnam. His violence continues when he returns to the United States. He becomes a Marine boxer. He boxes a more powerful fighter and wins the match, but that evening, he passes out from a strong headache, and a year later, he begins to have seizures.

The narrator begins to reflect on his life. He wonders why he has become such a violent man, someone who intentionally hurts people. The narrator tells the story of Theogenes, a Greek pugilist who supposedly won more than fourteen hundred fights, hundreds of years before the birth of Christ. He wonders if people are any better now than in those savage days. He explains that he has become a pessimist and suffers from dark depression. His seizures have grown more frequent, and he faces serious, risky brain surgery. He laments the person he has become and wonders if anything can save the people of the world from their terrible fates.\

*Themes and Meanings*

The meaning of life and fate, against a person's responsibility for his or her actions, is the central focus of the story. The narrator reflects on the sort of person he has become, someone willing to permanently injure Hey Baby and someone more than willing to kill people in Vietnam. A central image is that of the pugilist Theogenes, a Greek fighter described as the "greatest of gladiators." In ancient times, competitors were strapped to huge rocks and fought to the death. The narrator describes a statue he guesses might be Theogenes. After carefully describing the musculature and the physical damages from boxing, he turns to the man's expression, one of "weariness and philosophical resignation." The narrator wonders if the fighter would be happy as a nobody, a farmer, and if the fighter is proud of who he is.

The story illustrates the many twists and turns life can have. The narrator chooses to participate in the Vietnam War as part of the infantry, but he runs and hides and spends his first battle trying to clean his rifle and attempting to rinse his eyes. He tells lies, claiming to have been the hero his friend Jorgeson actually was. He has to acknowledge to himself that he has talked Jorgeson into following the narrator's path rather than pursuing his dream of being an artist. The narrator has to acknowledge that he took a terrible beating in a boxing match just to impress his friends.

The narrator also reflects on how his injury has made him a kinder person. He argues that the world is a terrible place, full of evil. He suggests that the philosopher Arthur Schopenhauer was correct in his pessimistic view of life. To understand evil, though, the narrator says people should not look at big examples happening in faraway places, such as ethnic cleansing, but at little, nearby ones. Though the United States is a place with many material advantages, the narrator tells people to "take a walk through an American prison, a nursing home, the slums . . ."

However, though the narrator's view is dark and pessimistic, he also argues for the existence of God. He has been afflicted with seizures that leave him unable to leave his house, but his epilepsy also gives him moments in which he knows God is real.

In the end, the story offers a series of events in which fate catches a character by surprise and changes that character's life for the worse. The first character affected is Hey Baby, who goes from tormenting someone weaker to suffering from an injury for the rest of his life. The narrator witnesses the violent deaths of his friends and colleagues. He is saved by blind luck and bumbles while the others die. The narrator's fascination with violence brings him to serious injury as well, yet it teaches him about kindness and the mysteries of existence.

*Style and Technique*

"The Pugilist at Rest" uses startling juxtapositions to create a memorable effect on the reader. The story opens humorously, with the stories of how tough boot camp is, as a drill sergeant crudely mocks Hey Baby's love letter to a girlfriend who will soon dump him. Jorgeson's artistic yearnings and his wry comments on the Marines are soon contrasted with the narrator's brutal assault on Hey Baby.

Next the narrator carefully describes how beautiful the Marine dress uniform is, but that calm moment matches a brutal moment of war. During his first battle, the narrator feverishly fumbles with cleaning his rifle, dropping the same pieces over and over, in a bumbling dark comedy, as he describes the terrifying deaths of the other soldiers.

As the story progresses, each section contrasts with earlier ones to build an ever-deepening, reflective piece. The story moves from early humorous moments, through violent, frightening ones, to the calm, final reflective moments. The early moments are blind to the dangers that are to come, and the philosophical thoughtfulness of the close has been earned by the terrors in the middle of the story. The first half of "The Pugilist at Rest" is a retelling of a series of events, but the second half is an essay. The story shifts from dreams of girls and artist's garrets and being a hero to an exploration of the connections between the epileptic seizures of Russian novelist Fyodor Dostoevski. In a few pages, the story shifts from a Marine writing a letter that opens "Hey Baby" to a discussion of epilepsy and how it may have enabled different mystics throughout history to understand God.

"The Pugilist at Rest" demonstrates the author's characteristic voice: a first-person narrator with a wildly ranging voice. A typical Thom Jones narrator is intense, practically ranting. The narrator here moves between angrily cursing his fate and his own stupidity to thoughtfully reflecting on his philosophy of life. The language ranges wildly as well. At times it is full of slang and crude insults, then the narrator's next sentence is elevated and precise. The major battle scene uses the specific jargon and rough language of men at war, but juxtaposed against this are clinical descriptions of injuries, as a careful doctor might offer.

*Brian L. Olson*

# THE PUPIL

*Author:* Henry James (1843-1916)
*Type of plot:* Domestic realism
*Time of plot:* The 1850's
*Locale:* Nice, Venice, and Paris
*First published:* 1891

> *Principal characters:*
> PEMBERTON, the tutor
> MORGAN MOREEN, his adolescent pupil
> MR. MOREEN, Morgan's father
> MRS. MOREEN, Morgan's mother

*The Story*

Needing money, Pemberton agrees to become the resident tutor of the eleven-year-old Morgan Moreen, whose heart condition prevents him from attending school. Pemberton's initial impression of Morgan is not favorable; though the child seems intelligent, he is not physically attractive and looks as if "he might be unpleasant."

Soon, though, Morgan is the only member of the family whom Pemberton does like. He must threaten to leave before the Moreens pay him even a portion of the salary they owe him, and eventually he tutors for free simply because he has grown fond of his pupil. They become so close that Pemberton suggests that they "ought to go off and live somewhere together."

Morgan is as eager as Pemberton to leave his family, whom both recognize as adventurers, gypsies who repeatedly move from city to city and hotel to hotel because they cannot or will not pay their bills. The family finances eventually become so desperate that, in Venice, Mrs. Moreen asks Pemberton to lend her sixty francs. Pemberton can only laugh. "Where in the world do you suppose I should get sixty francs?" he asks.

Immediately afterward, Pemberton is invited to return to England to tutor a rich but dull youth whose parents want to prepare him for Balliol College, Oxford. Pemberton accepts the appointment, at Morgan's urging, because he hopes to earn enough money to allow him to support Morgan.

The new post does indeed pay well, but Pemberton abandons it when Mrs. Moreen writes to him that Morgan is desperately ill. Arriving in Paris, Pemberton realizes that he has been tricked; Morgan has indeed been ill, but not so "desperately" as his mother pretended.

Despite the deception, Pemberton resumes his nonpaying post as tutor, though without enthusiasm. One afternoon in the winter, Pemberton and Morgan go for a walk. When they return, they find the Moreen family in turmoil, for they are being evicted for failing to pay their hotel bills. Mr. and Mrs. Moreen offer Morgan to Pemberton, for they no longer want the expense of rearing the child.

For Morgan, this rejection by his parents is the fulfillment of his dreams. He has never liked their ways and has yearned to go off with his tutor. His joy, however, is short-lived; the excitement kills him. True to their characters to the last, Mrs. Moreen blames Pemberton for having taken the child on too long a walk, and her husband claims that Morgan's heart was broken over the prospect of leaving his parents.

## Themes and Meanings

Morgan's death sadly vindicates Pemberton's observation that his pupil is "too clever to live." Morgan is the most perceptive of the story's characters, and that clearsightedness produces both his charm and his undoing. His parents and siblings see and feel nothing and never show embarrassment. Even when their world crumbles about them at the end of the story, they feel no shame; they bear the death of Morgan like "men of the world." In contrast, as soon as Morgan realizes that his parents are being evicted, he blushes "to the roots of his hair" at their "public exposure."

For Morgan's parents, life is surface and appearance. They are always "looking out," which means that they are never introspective. Their only concern is to make a good show. Hence, they spend no money on Morgan's clothes: He never appears in public. Their very name suggests this focus on the outside, for moreen is a coarse fabric with a smooth exterior.

Even Pemberton, supposedly Morgan's tutor, proves himself less perceptive than his charge. When he is first hired, he fails to draw any conclusions from the fact that Mrs. Moreen says nothing about paying him, nor does he realize that her soiled gloves suggest the state of the Moreen family finances. When Morgan interrupts this first interview to say, "We don't mind what anything costs—we live awfully well," Pemberton does not understand that the Moreens care nothing for cost because they never pay their bills.

Pemberton is more sympathetic than the elder Moreens. He willingly divides his limited funds with his pupil, even buying clothes for him because Morgan's parents will not. However, he does not measure up to his pupil in 3wisdom or generosity. Morgan is prepared to give Pemberton his very life, but Pemberton does not want it.

Pemberton realizes that the Moreens cannot continue to live like gypsies indefinitely, and he expects that when the end comes, each family member will try to save himself or herself without regard to the needs of the others. He is correct in this assessment; in the final scene, the older son, Ulick, has already vanished, the daughters are nowhere in sight, and the parents try to dispose of Morgan without consulting him. However, Pemberton, too, behaves like "a man of the world." He is not pleased when Morgan finally is offered to him because he worries about practical matters: "Where shall I take you, and how?" He does not relish the role of "a floating spar in case of a wreck." Though his generosity is not put to the test, one is not certain that Pemberton would have accepted the child.

Early in their relationship, when Pemberton claims to find Morgan's parents charming, the child, recognizing that his tutor is merely trying to be polite, tells him, "You're a jolly old humbug!" In the end, Pemberton does prove to be a humbug; after raising Morgan's hopes of escape, he shrinks from the opportunity and responsibility.

## Style and Technique

Henry James tells the story objectively from Pemberton's perspective, never intruding his own opinions. However, irony abounds to highlight the discrepancies between appearance and reality. Thus, Pemberton accepts the position of tutor because he needs money to pay his hotel bill, yet in the course of his employment he will, together with his employers, avoid many another such charge. Though Pemberton is nominally the tutor and Morgan the pupil, the child proves to be the more clever of the two.

He also seems older and more experienced. Indeed, while he is the youngest member of the household, he notes that his older brother imitates him, and he refers to himself as if he were the patriarch of the family: "I'll take their affairs in hand; I'll marry my sisters," he reassures Pemberton. Such a self-image is not wholly fanciful because his parents do behave like irresponsible children and only he shows concern for their reputation.

However, another irony is Morgan's weak heart. Of all the characters, he is the most generous. He repeatedly urges Pemberton to leave his family because he knows that he never will earn any money from them, and he is willing to give away his very life. All the others are more or less self-centered; even Pemberton's heart is not as great as Morgan's.

The numerous ironies not only emphasize the deceptiveness of appearances but also add an element of humor that diminishes the sense of tragedy. Pemberton laughs when he is asked to give money to the people who should be paying him. Pemberton agrees to work for free if he can tell Morgan that the Moreens are not paying him; immediately afterward, Pemberton discovers that Morgan already knows this "secret." These repeated reversals distance readers by giving them a sense of superior knowledge or insight. They are thus able to judge the characters dispassionately.

Perhaps James has in this way introduced a final irony. The reader responds to Morgan's death, as the Moreens do, like "a man of the world." Has James tricked his audience into becoming like these unsavory characters? Pemberton succumbs to their spell; he really does find them charming and finally behaves like them. Because Morgan's death does not seem tragic, is the reader, too, composed of moreen?

*Joseph Rosenblum*

# THE PURLOINED LETTER

*Author:* Edgar Allan Poe (1809-1849)
*Type of plot:* Mystery and detective
*Time of plot:* The nineteenth century
*Locale:* Paris, France
*First published:* Unauthorized, 1844; enlarged and authorized, 1845

     *Principal characters:*
        C. AUGUSTE DUPIN, an amateur detective and friend to the
          narrator
        THE NARRATOR, a friend to Dupin who serves as the auditor for
          most of the details of the narrative
        MONSIEUR G——, the prefect of the Parisian police
        MINISTER D——, who steals the letter

*The Story*

The unnamed narrator and his friend, C. Auguste Dupin, are interrupted by the intrusion of the prefect of the Parisian police, who bursts in to tell the tale of the theft of a compromising letter from the bedroom of the queen by the unscrupulous Minister D——. The contents of the letter are never made known, but the prefect avers that he has been charged with retrieving it, and he further reveals that so long as the letter remains in the minister's possession, he will hold the queen in his power. The prefect details to the narrator and Dupin the extent of his searches of the minister's apartments, and he confesses that even though he and his assistants have searched in every possible place, leaving no place unexamined, all of their efforts have been in vain. The letter remains concealed in a place undiscoverable by anyone.

Dupin questions the prefect closely about the methods and the places of his search, suggesting that it would appear that the letter is no longer in the minister's apartments. He nevertheless advises the prefect to search them once more, inquiring as he does about the exact physical appearance of the letter, as well as its contents. The prefect departs in despair, and the story shifts immediately to his return to Dupin's apartment a month later, at which time the letter remains, as far as the prefect can discern, in the possession of the minister. Dupin inquires as to the amount that the prefect would be willing to give to possess the letter, and when the latter names the sum of fifty thousand francs, Dupin offers to produce the letter for the sum named. He does so, much to the astonishment of both prefect and narrator (who is present at this second meeting as well), and after the departure of the prefect, tells the narrator how he came to recover the letter from the minister.

The secret of Dupin's success, he asserts, lay in his capacity to read the intentions of the minister more accurately than the Parisian police. Briefly, Dupin realizes that rather than hiding the letter in some ingenious contraption or out-of-the-way place, the minister would realize that all such efforts would be fruitless in concealing the item from the searches that were bound to ensue on his having stolen it. Consequently, Dupin surmises that the minister would hide the letter in plain sight.

In a visit to the latter's apartments, and under the cover of wearing dark glasses, Dupin surveys the sitting room and notices the letter dangling from a ribbon in the center of the mantelpiece, even though its outward appearance is such as to deny this possibility. Leaving a gold snuffbox in the minister's quarters, Dupin thus provides himself with an occasion to return on the following day, at which time he arranges for a diversion that allows him deftly to substitute a facsimile of the letter for the authentic article and thus to possess himself of the letter and earn the reward. The tale ends with Dupin's account of his previous relations with the minister, as well as the revelation of the message that Dupin had inscribed on the inside of the facsimile. The words are a citation from an eighteenth century play about the legend of the house of Atreus: "So funereal a design, if it is not worthy of Atreus, is worthy of Thyestes."

*Themes and Meanings*

"The Purloined Letter" has been the subject of considerable commentary, most interestingly as the bone of contention between two of the more prominent contemporary French thinkers, the philosopher Jacques Derrida and the psychoanalyst Jacques Lacan, who have argued about the story's pertinence to the themes and significance of psychoanalysis. It would require considerable space to lay out the complicated arguments that each of these thinkers mounts in reading Edgar Allan Poe's tale, but one could characterize this debate briefly as signifying the difference between a reading of the story as presenting readers with a definite and finitely circumscribed set of meanings (roughly Lacan's position) and one that denies categorically, on behalf of Poe's story, the possibility that any definitive interpretation of the elements in this or any narrative can ever be produced. One could say, perhaps too schematically, that Derrida's claim rests primarily on the fact that the precise contents of the letter are never revealed, and that therefore the letter itself becomes an emblem of the indeterminacy in meaning that the tale enacts. Certainly the central tension in the story between the calculating and rationally motivated Dupin and the more shadowy narrator—whose relation to Dupin is established in prior stories, "The Mystery of Marie Roget" and "The Murders in the Rue Morgue"—as well as the difficulty of knowing precisely how to apply the closing citation to the case of the minister and his actions, suggests that Lacan's more or less straightforward symbolic interpretation of the tale as an allegory of sexuality misses many of the subtlest discriminations that the narrative establishes.

Once one has opened up the possibility that all is not as it seems—and this is the very possibility on which the plot turns because it is the appearance of the letter itself that is crucial to its concealment by the minister—it is not simple to begin to pin down the meaning of individual elements. Nor is it absolutely certain at the end that Dupin has in fact delivered the original letter to the prefect because he might, with the knowledge of the original's contents, have prepared a facsimile and retained the original for purposes that he does not here reveal. In truth, readers know little more about the facts of the matter at the end than they did at the beginning, although they have been initiated into an astonishingly intricate web of stratagems.

### Style and Technique

Like many of Poe's tales, this one is written in a complex idiom that smacks of archaism—and did so even at the moment of his writing. The language tends to be somewhat stilted, and the insertion here of foreign phrases (mostly, although not exclusively, French) puts the situation and the characters at some distance from the average reader. Poe is careful to set the tale in a distant and alien locale, the ambience of which is minutely evoked, with precise references to quarters of Paris, to articles of clothing and furniture, and to the whole unfamiliar business of court intrigue. The net results of these distancing effects are to render the tale more exotic and to make the preternatural powers of observation and ratiocination exhibited by Dupin appear plausible in the context. To the extent that the world of the story is clearly not one familiar to any of Poe's readers, contemporary with the tale or subsequent, it can be argued that the extraordinary events of the plot seem less fantastic. In such a world, such characters may be said to make sense.

The narrative itself is so constructed as to reinforce the sense of mystery that pervades this world, as the position of the narrator remains entirely obscure from beginning to end. He never reveals anything substantive about himself, and one might surmise that he is merely a formal device for getting the story told, a means for introducing the real protagonist, Dupin, and for giving the latter an occasion to speak because it would be unlikely, given the discretion of Dupin's character, that he would readily tell his own story. However, one is led always to speculate on the motivations of this character, on his precise relationship to Dupin, and on the degree of knowledge to which he himself can with justice lay a certain claim. It would be mistaken simply to slot him into the position of the Sherlock Holmes foil, the ingenuous Dr. Watson.

By framing his tale in the discourse of this elusive narrator, Poe inaugurated what would become an important tradition in European and American short fiction, visible, for example, in the works of Henry James, where the relationship between narrator and what is narrated is often problematic and somewhat mysterious. While it is generally thought that the genre of detective or mystery fiction, which Poe with considerable warrant has often been said to have initiated, issues in definite solutions to the crimes or other enigmas that form the basis of the plot, one is left wondering in the case of Poe just what it is that has been revealed. Certainly one would want to know the contents of the purloined letter of the title, but this is precisely what is never revealed. It may be a mark of Poe's genius that he recognized as an intrinsic property of narratives what Diane Arbus once remarked of photographs: that they are secrets about secrets; the more they tell you, the less you know. Such might be the very motto of Dupin, or even of the narrator, for it is in the relation between their two tellings that the structure of this story resides.

*Michael Sprinker*

# PUTOIS

*Author:* Anatole France (Jacques-Anatole-François Thibault, 1844-1924)
*Type of plot:* Fantasy
*Time of plot:* About 1900
*Locale:* Paris and Saint-Omer, France
*First published:* 1904 (English translation, 1915)

> *Principal characters:*
> PUTOIS, an imaginary gardener invented by Madame Eloi
> Bergeret
> MONSIEUR LUCIEN BERGERET, professor of philosophy at the
> Sorbonne
> MADEMOISELLE ZOÉ BERGERET, Lucien's older sister
> PAULINE BERGERET, Lucien's daughter
> MONSIEUR and MADAME ELOI BERGERET, the parents of Zoé and
> Lucien
> MADAME CORNOUILLER, a distant relative of Madame Eloi
> Bergeret
> MONSIEUR MARTEAU and
> MONSIEUR GOUBIN, disciples of Lucien Bergeret

*The Story*

As Zoé and Lucien Bergeret reminisce about their childhood in Saint-Omer, Zoé asks her brother if he remembers Putois. His enthusiastically affirmative reply leads to a recital, by sister and brother speaking alternately, of a complete physical description of Putois. Lucien's teenage daughter, Pauline, listens to this recital in amazement and asks why they have memorized this curious piece of prose and why they recite it with such pious solemnity. Amused by Pauline's question, Lucien and Zoé explain that the description of Putois is a revered text in the Bergeret family because Putois was the most familiar figure of their childhood, even though he did not exist—or rather, had a special kind of existence. Putois was "born" at a mature age, invented by their mother when Lucien and Zoé were young children and the family was living quietly in the northern French town of Saint-Omer. Their peaceful life was interrupted when they were "discovered" by a great-aunt of Madame Bergeret, named Madame Cornouiller, who insisted that the Bergerets must dine with her every Sunday, as is done in the best families. This social obligation quickly proved to be so boring that the Bergerets began to look for polite pretexts to decline the imperious Madame Cornouiller's standing invitation.

After exhausting such obvious excuses as illness, the desperate Madame Bergeret one day blurted out that they could not come the next Sunday because they were expecting their gardener. Asked who their gardener was, Madame Bergeret invented the name Putois. Certain that she knew this person, Madame Cornouiller cautioned Madame Bergeret to beware of Putois, because he was considered a lazy good-for-nothing and a vagabond. That was how Putois came to exist, and how he acquired a distinctive character.

Zoé and Lucien are interrupted by the arrival of two disciples of Professor Bergeret, Monsieur Goubin and Monsieur Marteau, who are given a rapid summary of the origin of Putois so they can join the family discussion. Told that Putois came into existence when Professor Bergeret's mother named him, and that he at once became an active influence in the town, Monsieur Goubin objects, arguing that because Putois's existence is only imaginary, he could hardly have had any influence on others. To this, Professor Bergeret replies that mythical figures, though imaginary, have always had a profound influence on people, and that Putois was obviously a mythical figure, though a very minor and local one.

That point settled, the disciples ask Bergeret to tell them more about Putois and his reputation in Saint-Omer as an evil spirit. Monsieur Bergeret recounts for them the role of Madame Cornouiller in developing still further the bad reputation she had initially assigned to Putois. Reflecting that the gardening services of Putois would cost her less than those of her own gardener, Madame Cornouiller insisted that her grandniece send Putois to her. Madame Bergeret promised to do so, but when, as expected, Madame Cornouiller complained that he had not appeared, Madame Bergeret explained that Putois was a strange and elusive person, and that he was probably hiding. Feeling challenged, Madame Cornouiller asserted that she would find Putois, and she went about asking relatives, friends, neighbors, servants, and merchants if they knew him. Only two or three admitted having never heard of him; the rest claimed to know him, but not where he could be found. One day, Madame Cornouiller arrived breathlessly at the Bergerets', saying she had just seen Putois and had called out his name. Putois had turned around briefly, but then had hurried away. She added, triumphantly, that now she knew what he looked like. He had an evil countenance, just as she expected.

Soon thereafter Madame Cornouiller accused Putois of stealing three melons from her garden and gave a detailed description of him to the police. Her description appeared in the Saint-Omer newspaper and was promptly adopted as a sacred text by the delighted Bergeret family. Next, Putois was accused of having seduced Madame Cornouiller's cook. Before long, all of Saint-Omer suspected Putois of every evil deed reported. Putois thus became the talk of the town. His nefarious exploits were legion. Public belief in Putois's existence had become so strong that even Madame Bergeret wondered whether her "white lie" might have been divinely inspired truth.

*Themes and Meanings*

The central theme of "Putois" is certainly the propensity of human beings to invent myths as a way of explaining the evils of the world they inhabit. Anatole France handles this theme in a distinctly humorous vein, naming his mythical figure "Putois," which means a skunk. The name thus comically suggests both the inescapable pervasiveness of his presence and the disagreeable and unsavory nature of his social activity. The humor is unmistakably tinged with mockery, so that the theme of myth-making becomes a critical analysis of the way society, in a small town, will distort the reality of its political, economic, and social relationships, and even of its history, in the interests of adjusting the world to the society's beliefs and prejudices. As a mythical figure, Putois has the essential virtues—or vices—needed for the role: He is elusive but seemingly ubiquitous, his persistent presence is undesirable because of his questionable character; yet, paradoxically, his questionable character makes him the ideal person to blame for whatever evils befall the community. The community's subconscious need for a scapegoat gives Putois such existence as a mythical figure may possess.

Some readers interpret the process by which Putois gradually becomes a reality as a symbolic representation of how rumors spread in a community. Such readers see the story's central theme as rumor-mongering, and Putois as a symbol for scandalous gossip or ugly rumor. Still other readers, noting that the story was first published while France was obsessed with the Alfred Dreyfus affair, have suggested that Putois symbolizes any forged or counterfeit reality, like the forged documents fabricated by the military to "prove" Dreyfus guilty, or the falsified history invented by the government to justify its claim that the spy in their midst had to be a Jewish officer of Alsatian origin. Such readers thus see "Putois" as a satirical parody of the Dreyfus affair, exposing it as a gross miscarriage of justice. However readers choose to characterize the central theme of "Putois,"—myth-making, rumor-mongering, or counterfeiting reality—they are clearly all seeing the same meaning in "Putois": a humorous portrayal of the human need to find a scapegoat to explain away the experience of evil.

*Style and Technique*

As a writer, France is perhaps best known for his witty portrayal of life's ironies and for the purity and clarity of his classical style. "Putois" offers an excellent illustration of both qualities. For example, the grotesque and self-contradictory description of Putois, recited so solemnly at the beginning of the story, is rendered even more comical by Bergeret's comment to his daughter that the text should be treated piously as sacred family liturgy, to be passed on from generation to generation. This "devout" sentiment, from an acknowledged skeptic in matters of religion, sounds an ironic counterpoint that brings a knowing smile to the lips of the alert reader.

As a master ironist, France can surprise his reader into frank laughter as well as inspire the silent knowing smile. Speaking of Madame Cornouiller's cook, whose unexpected pregnancy was attributed to Putois, the author remarks that the cook was thought by everyone to be safe from the dangers of love because of her luxuriant beard. A deft ironic touch, encapsulating the sense of the whole story, is put into the mouth of Eloi Bergeret, who notes that he would not be a good citizen if he informed the people of Saint-Omer that Putois does not exist because one must think twice before depriving a community of an important article of faith. Such wry observations, expressed in elegant, well-turned sentences, illustrate why France is so successful in this small comic masterpiece in communicating both theme and meaning so clearly and concisely.

*Murray Sachs*

# PUTTERMESSER PAIRED

*Author:* Cynthia Ozick (1928-      )
*Type of plot:* Psychological
*Time of plot:* The late twentieth century
*Locale:* New York City
*First published:* 1990

> *Principal characters:*
> RUTH PUTTERMESSER, an unemployed attorney in her fifties,
>     seeking an ideal mate for a marriage of minds
> RUPERT RABEENO, a painter in his mid-thirties who copies
>     famous paintings for postcards

## The Story

Ruth Puttermesser, a New York attorney, has set aside gainful employment to live on her savings and think through her fate. In her fifties, she has a strong self-image of being brainy, cherishes a devotion to the nineteenth century novelist George Eliot, and finds herself very much alone. Dismayed to recognize her signs of aging, she decides she should marry. Ruth idolizes Eliot—another homely female intellectual, but one who found a happy fate—and lives in her subjective reality of "selected phantom literary flashbacks." She has immersed herself in biographies of Eliot and in Eliot's letters, nurturing a dream that she will meet a latter-day copy of George Lewes, Eliot's intellectual companion and lover, and share with him the same transcendent intimacy of souls ascribed to Eliot and Lewes by her biographers and portrayed in Eliot's letters. New York, however, seems to be filled only with the self-regarding egos of shallow and isolated failures at marriage, with the leftovers and mistakes who flirt superficially, mask their vulnerabilities behind flippancy, and neglect their children.

At a gathering at which she has chanced on such types, Ruth feels aloof and yearns to find virtue, knowledge, mutuality, and intellectual distinction embodied in a contemporary Victorian gentleman—another Lewes. Then she sees a man some twenty years younger than she is and connects him with her vision of Lewes. She is hurt that he does not even notice her.

Soon afterward, Ruth sits in the Metropolitan Museum, reading Eliot's letters; gradually she becomes aware that a painter is copying one of the masterpieces to be used as a postcard. Striking up a dialogue about whether his work is mimicry or reproduction, she discovers that he is the same young man whom she recently noticed. His name is Rupert Rabeeno. Fascinated by his insistence that he does not duplicate but, rather, reenacts a process, she is convinced by his lively talk that she has found her Lewes and invites him home for tea. They begin reading Eliot's novels together, which Ruth sees as reenacting the nightly reading by Eliot and Lewes and, therefore, as building the same mental and emotional intimacy that the nineteenth century couple had shared. Rupert often interrupts the reading to recount details of his past. When Ruth feels the time is right, she shares her dream of ideal friendship, directing Rupert's attention to Lewes and believing that Rupert understands her as Lewes understood and sympathized with Eliot. He signals his apparent rapport by moving in with her.

When they begin reading Eliot's biographies, Ruth is disturbed to discover that Rupert previously had known little of Eliot and nothing at all of Lewes or John Cross, the man twenty years her junior whom Eliot married after Lewes's death. As they take turns reading aloud, reenacting Eliot's life, Rupert shows far more energy and enthusiasm for reenacting the role of Cross, creating a Cross quite different from Ruth's understanding of him, than he has shown for complying with Ruth's wish that he try to make himself into Lewes. Although Ruth insists that Eliot and Cross were true lovers, Rupert maintains that Cross never consummated his marriage. Rupert believes that Cross's attempt to make himself into an intellectual copy of Lewes to keep Eliot from feeling the loss of her longtime companion caused Cross's nervous collapse and leap into the Grand Canal of Venice during their honeymoon. Rupert's re-creation of Cross trying to be Lewes for Eliot is so convincing, so alive, that it leaves Ruth feeling that he has taken Lewes, the great mind and generous soul of her dream, from her and given her instead the athletically and practically focused Cross, man of the outdoors. When Rupert next proposes marriage, however, Ruth feels reassured that he really does understand ideal friendship and will be her Lewes. On their wedding night, Rupert repeats his reenactment, charging toward the window Cross-style, but leaving by the door, as Ruth calls after him, forced to acknowledge that he is only a copyist.

*Themes and Meanings*

Ruth Puttermesser is Cynthia Ozick's protagonist in two earlier stories: "Puttermesser: Her Work History, Her Ancestry, Her Afterlife" and "Puttermesser and Xanthippe." In these stories, at the ages of thirty-four and forty-six, Ruth attempts, through fantasy, to create a significant role for herself in a world of values that she has created from literary sources. For example, she envisions William Blake's mercy, pity, peace, and love reigning in New York, and she sees the Brooklyn Bridge as the harp that Hart Crane called it. In both stories, Ruth is returned to the limited and unpromising world of actuality. Ozick, through these and other stories and essays, has established herself as a writer whose themes depend in part on a sense of intertextuality with literature and history. Also related is her earlier story "Levitation," in which a married couple, both writers, think of themselves as being like Eliot and Lewes, but their mental limitations and self-focus make the comparison ironic.

Similarly, Rupert the reductionist, who recognizes that his talent is only postcard-size, is an ironic impersonator, re-creating fully neither the art he copies nor the historical Lewes or Cross. As Ruth recognizes briefly, he shrinks mastery, dwindling it to a size he can call his own. Insisting that he cares not for the dead and past, that he is the one who is alive, he is driven to diminish the power of great artworks into the four-by-six-inch cards that he makes. Unable to reenact the masterful mind that was Lewes, he reconstructs the less daunting Cross as a figure whom he can mimic. Ruth's retreat from the life around her, the thirst she feels for a time machine to take her to her image of life with Lewes, a life of courtliness and distinction, leaves her vulnerable. She is unable to recognize herself as one of many lonely singles, such as those in the personals advertisements. Although she protests consciousness of her stunted experience and secluded loneliness, she deludes herself into believing that Rupert will and can be Lewes to her, that their marriage will be a wedding of soulmates. Overwhelmed by her sense of diminution as an aging woman, she snatches at Rupert's energetic immediacy as a stimulus for her own revitalizing, as evidence that she is not the crone she sees in her mirror.

Ruth is among the "lonesome atoms" that make up the nonrelational world as her neighbor, Raya Lieberman, describes it, a motif in the story. Absorbed by her idealizing, she lacks perception about the world around her; for example, she wears patent leather high heels out into the snow, instead of the galoshes worn by the others. From Rupert's perspective, individual perception and interpretation create mastery, so that his imitation is not fraudulent, as Ruth sees it. His impersonation of Cross, which leaves Ruth feeling routed, undermines Ruth's ideal of virtue and knowledge. He has, at least, invented himself.

*Style and Technique*

Ruth's perspective as a limited omniscient center of consciousness guides the reader through the story. Her reading and her memories of passages from biographies of Eliot present a backdrop for the exchanges between Ruth and Rupert and for Ruth's inward musings, sometimes perceptive, but more often delusory. The chasm between the authentic personal sympathies of Eliot and Lewes, and the ersatz, almost trivial developments between Ruth and Rupert that she grasps at as ideal friendship, creates sustained irony, intensified by section titles with ambiguous applications to both Eliot's and Ruth's lives.

Adding to the irony is the suggestiveness of the titles of paintings that Rupert copies. The first, Jacques-Louis David's *The Death of Socrates* (1787), implies an end to the rationalism by which Ruth has formerly described herself and its replacement by the subjective reality she and Rupert pursue each night. This recalls the reflections of the bridges in the River Seine that Rupert claims compete with the bridges over the river to be perceived as the true world. Other subjects suggest Rupert's mastery, through assertion of his perception, over mythology, the natural world, a domestic scene, and a painting of Venice's Grand Canal, presaging his reconstruction of Cross's mentally disturbed leap into that water. Only at the end is that mastery dramatized, as Ruth must drop her sentimentalizing.

*Carolyn F. Dickinson*

# THE PUZZLEHEADED GIRL

*Author:* Christina Stead (1902-1983)
*Type of plot:* Social realism
*Time of plot:* The 1950's
*Locale:* New York and London
*First published:* 1965

*Principal characters:*
    AUGUSTUS DEBRETT, a good-natured businessperson
    BEATRICE DEBRETT, his wife
    HONOR LAWRENCE, a young woman of uncertain background
    TOM ZERO, a partner in the firm where Debrett works
    MYRA ZERO, Tom's wife
    JAY HEWETT, Honor's first husband

*The Story*

Augustus Debrett hires Honor Lawrence as a file clerk for his company, although she has no discernible qualifications. He is taken with her youth and her sweet, wistful quality. As time passes, he learns that she lives with her father in appalling poverty and that her brother is a successful artist. When Debrett's burgeoning business acquires a new bookkeeping machine, Honor quickly learns to operate it, but she refuses to accept the job of bookkeeper even though it would mean a raise in salary. She will not deal with the moneymaking aspect of the business, calling it unworthy. Tom Zero, a handsome young lawyer in the firm, suggests they fire her, but Debrett is impressed by the fact that Honor has given up a raise on principle, so she stays.

Honor shows up unexpectedly at Zero's apartment one day during working hours and breaks through Mrs. Zero's reserve with stories of her life dominated by a mean and miserly father. Honor's mother, who was also ill-treated by her father, is dead, and she wants nothing as much as a room of her own in someone's house. Sympathetic Mrs. Zero promises to think about the problem and finds Honor touching, even when she shows up at the Zero's apartment unexpectedly for dinner the following evening.

Debrett, whose wife is away visiting her mother with their infant son, comes home from work one night to find Honor in his apartment. He sends her home, ignoring her innocent suggestion that she stay there with him. When his wife and son return, Honor makes an unexpected call on Beatrice Debrett. Beatrice invites Honor for dinner, during which the girl's extreme poverty and lack of normal experience are highlighted.

Honor's eccentricity is further emphasized when Palmer, a visiting engineer from the Midwest, invites her out for lunch and tells her of his wife and children on their farm in Ohio. Honor does not show up for work the following week, although her father and brother both come looking for her. Her father is an Italian immigrant who barely speaks English; her family name is Tommaseo, which she and her brother have changed to Lawrence. Debrett is shocked to learn that the girl is only sixteen. A short time later, Debrett's firm breaks up and he finds a new job on Wall Street. Palmer, the engineer who had invited Honor to lunch, receives a letter from his wife in Ohio. A young girl arrived at the farm claiming that she knows Mr. Palmer and has decided to stay. Mrs. Palmer is taken with the girl although she does no work in the house or on the farm, even when asked. When Mr. Palmer returns, the girl slips away without a word.

Two-and-a-half years later, Honor shows up at Debrett's Wall Street office to borrow money to live on until she leaves for Europe with a wealthy woman who has taken an interest in her. Two days later she is back; the woman has made sexual advances toward Honor and then thrown her out when she resisted. She next takes up with the matron of a mental home, an alliance that also ends badly when the matron treats her like a madwoman. Tom Zero runs into Honor on the street looking frayed and exhausted, but she refuses his offer of help and disappears, weeping.

Debrett settles his wife and son in Nice while he looks for work in Europe. Honor again surfaces unexpectedly. In Berlin, he receives a late-night call from an associate in London about a Mrs. Hewett who has turned up at their office claiming a close friendship with Debrett. She needs ten pounds to keep from starving. When it is determined that the woman is Honor Lawrence, Debrett approves the loan. On his return to London, he finds a letter from her explaining that she married Jay Hewett, a childhood friend, but found him dreadful and mad and left him. Debrett eventually leaves his wife for another woman, but as he and his new wife meander about Europe, he imagines that he keeps seeing Honor.

In New York on a business trip about three years later, Debrett again encounters Honor Lawrence. She tells him she married a South African she met in a gallery in Europe, but when she went to South Africa, his family had her deported and put their child in an orphanage. She now has no money, but plans a trip back to South Africa. She also has a venereal disease that she believes the South African gave her. When questioned, she is vague about her relationship with Hewett. While visiting an exhibition of the artwork of Honor's brother, Debrett is approached by Hewett, who claims to have known all about Debrett for years. Hewett has been in love with Honor since childhood, but his stories about her and Debrett's stories about her are quite different, although they both believe the girl never lies.

Some time later, Debrett hears that Hewett ran into Honor and found her sick and dishevelled. Although poor himself, Hewett offered to take care of her in the name of love, but she rejected both his offer and the idea of love. Finally Hewett learns of her solitary death, and disappears himself. Debrett continues to believe that he sees Honor from time to time in her younger incarnation.

*Themes and Meanings*

Perhaps the most important character type in Christina Stead's work is the tyrannical father of a daughter who longs to escape. Such characters appear in her novels *Seven Poor Men of Sydney* (1934), *For Love Alone* (1944), and *The Man Who Loved*

*Children* (1940). Stead's work is highly autobiographical, and it is assumed that the character is based on her own domineering father, from whom she herself struggled to escape.

Honor Lawrence, the puzzleheaded girl of the title, is another heroine whose life is shaped by her overbearing father, Tommaseo. Tommaseo is an immigrant who, by the meanest penny-pinching, managed to set himself up as a fruit and vegetable dealer. He watched every bite his children ate, denied them clothes and pleasures, and took the key whenever he left the tenement, forcing his wife and children to huddle on the stairs. Worst of all were the violent scenes that he made at home and in public. Now that the children are older, he expects them to give him all their pay. Honor is still living with her father and longing for freedom when the story opens. Much of her motivation may be seen as attempts to acquire this freedom: her odd intrusions into other people's lives, her refusal to work when she lives on the Ohio farm, and her two unsuccessful marriages.

Another factor that influences Honor is the position of women, biologically and socially. Both Beatrice Debrett and Honor are women who dislike sexual relations and marry only because they have few other options. Beatrice becomes a lonely, embittered woman by the end of the story, and Honor grows poorer and sicker until she dies. Honor Lawrence plays out a major theme in Stead's work: the struggle to maintain one's integrity in the face of society's rules. Some of Stead's characters manage to survive intact, but others, like Honor, are defeated. They remain true to their vision at any cost, and go under because they cannot compromise their individuality.

*Style and Technique*

In creating the enigmatic Honor Lawrence, Stead provides numerous details about the urban poverty in which the girl grew up and still lives. Repetition and accumulation of detail are among Stead's typical stylistic devices.

The generally loose structure of Stead's plots consists of scenes in which character is slowly revealed. In this way, "The Puzzleheaded Girl" moves around in time, unified by a series of encounters with Honor Lawrence as she pursues her haphazard life. In many scenes, the girl speaks for herself in dialogue, oration, argument, or justification. There is no authorial interpretation; when not speaking for herself, Honor is seen through the eyes of the other characters as they meet her or talk to each other about her, usually with very different views. The irony created by the different characters' expectations of Honor is the central device providing tension in the story.

A master of dialogue, Stead has her characters speak in an ordinary way, but Honor's speech is simple and stylized, almost childlike. This adds to the irony, for in some ways the girl is very clever, which is only slowly revealed. Stead's story ultimately assumes an almost mythic quality as Debrett muses on Honor's puzzling character, pondering what he calls her "sacred character, those the gods love, or hate: it's the same."

*Sheila Golburgh Johnson*

# QUEEN OF DIAMONDS

*Author:* Michael Anthony Dorris (1945-1997)
*Type of plot:* Domestic realism
*Time of plot:* 1987
*Locale:* The Pacific Northwest
*First published:* 1987

> *Principal characters:*
> RAY, the narrator, a fifteen-year-old girl
> CHRISTINE, her Native American mother
> ELGIN, her African American father

## The Story

Ray, a tall, thin, fifteen-year-old, is visiting her Native American mother in the hospital. As the two play cards, Ray realizes that Christine, her mother, cheats in order to win. Ray also notices that her mother seems suddenly smaller, as though she had shrunk. The daughter thinks to herself that this hospital visit might be different, that Christine really might have a disease. Christine's changed image, however, is a result of her husband's having entered the room. Elgin, Ray's father, is an African American who has not spoken to Ray in six months.

Although both Ray and Christine exhibit signs of hope that Elgin will stay, he says he has come to return his wife's car. Christine begs him to keep the car in order to pick her up when she is released from the hospital, but Elgin declines. Christine grows furious in the face of Elgin's indifference. Ray, who relates the story, understands that Christine expects Elgin to reconsider. Elgin backs out of the room and Ray flees too, to avoid her mother's furor. Later, as she crosses the hospital parking lot, Ray sees someone trying to break into her mother's car. Only after she karate-chops the would-be thief does Ray realize it is her mother in disguise.

Christine tells Ray that the only thing she has that is worth anything is her car insurance, and because she has been reduced by Elgin to nothing, she plans to commit suicide so Ray can collect the benefits. Ray responds by calling Christine's bluff. She tells her mother she is sure Christine is headed for Tacoma, where she always threatens to go when she is depressed, although she never actually goes.

Christine drives to Tacoma, accompanied by Ray, who refuses to remain behind. When they reach the park in Tacoma, Christine tries to get Ray out of the car, but Ray won't move. She tells Christine, "You win. . . . Go for it. I just hope the policy is paid." Christine hesitates, but turns her key in the ignition. Out of gas, the car will not start.

After a few awkward moments, Ray and her mother laugh at the irony and the futility of their situation, and walk together to a gas station.

## Themes and Meanings

In the second paragraph of "Queen of Diamonds," Ray comments that nothing her mother wants is out of her reach. The literal reference is to such hospital paraphernalia as a pillow and a desk, but the metaphorical meaning illuminates a prominent theme. Christine is the "Queen of Diamonds" because her expert manipulations have allowed her to survive. Her trump in life is fate, the magical entity with which she repeatedly deceives, and occasionally defeats, reality. However, Christine knows what she will not admit; her wins involve cheats. "I quit when I'm ahead," she says, later adding, "The object of the game is to reduce everything to one stack."

Just as she plays her cards, Christine reduces her passion in life to one object, the love of a husband incapable of achieving stability. The stakes increase as her manipulations escalate; Christine's hospital stays have yet to be caused by disease, and most of her ailments surface in the middle of the night. Christine's frenetic denial in the form of excessive consumption of alcohol finds its obsessive/compulsive and passive/aggressive mirror image in her constant manipulations. In the hospital, the carefree party girl becomes the penultimate victim, demanding the last rites.

Wandering the hospital corridors, Ray feels invisible. Her reference extends beyond the people in green uniforms whom she passes; she knows it is her parents who ignore her. Ray's statement, "The lobby is deserted, but I know my way around," alludes to the fact that Ray has learned to negotiate life on her own.

Ray fantasizes about encountering her father as he conducts his mail route, but because he is not a full-time employee, his track is unpredictable. Just as Elgin is a temporary postal carrier, he is a part-time husband and father with an unpredictable track. Hence Ray, the child who gets lost between Elgin's shuffle to fulfill his whims and Christine's shuffling of the cards with which she bets her future, copes on her own. The wisdom she has gained through hard-won experience causes her to reverse roles with her mother. Christine, who early in the story tells Ray she folds too easily, eventually succumbs to Ray's bluff. When Christine threatens suicide, Ray insists on going along for the ride.

Christine heads for her destination, but reality is not her strong suit. The very mechanism that allows Christine to fantasize and maintain the illusion of strength also dooms her to a life of denial. Christine controls so successfully because she is the author of her escapades; she thrives only in the realm of possibility. Ray emphasizes this by stating, "Most of the time Mom is off to the races, excited at every chance," and "The future never discouraged her before, since she doesn't think about it from a distance."

When Ray and Christine reach the park where Christine threatens to drive off a cliff, it is Ray who challenges her mother to go through with her threat. Ray does so because she bets Christine lacks the courage to kill herself, that Christine's energy stems from her theatrics. For the first time, Ray acts like her mother's daughter, throwing caution to the wind and wagering all. After a moment's hesitation, Christine presses the accelerator to meet Ray's challenge. The car, however, is out of gas, and Christine is miraculously saved. Fate alone intervenes.

The hospital card game parallels the game mother and daughter play in Christine's car, with Ray and her mother both winners, of sorts, as they translate their losses into gains. Christine, cursed with living a fantasy, converts her imagination into her salvation. She would seem to be no match for Ray, who sees her parents and understands their motives more clearly than they ever could. Ray's knowledge of human behavior allows her to survive and permits her to challenge her mother with the truth.

As Ray and Christine trek to the gas station following Christine's failure to kill herself, they share a laugh. Mother and daughter verge on surrendering to each other those feelings that have led them to deal with each other as opponents, and they silently declare a draw.

When they arrive at the gas station, Christine once again assumes a role to persuade the attendant to grant them a lift. The climax in Ray and Christine's relationship—Ray's calling Christine's bluff, and Christine's thwarted attempt to go through with it—has not permanently altered their behavior, but has only made each more certain of the other's capabilities.

Themes in "Queen of Diamonds" include reality versus fantasy, the irony of a child's maturity exceeding that of her parents, the irony of survival mechanisms serving as the tools of defeat, the irony of someone good and wise and healthy being born of broken and defeated parents, and the notion that misplaced love can poison—just as true love can heal—weak and wounded relationships.

*Style and Technique*

Michael Anthony Dorris punctuates the informal conversational style in "Queen of Diamonds" with dry, wry humor that heightens every irony while ensuring that the story's characters remain individuals rather than stereotypes. When Ray tries to figure out why her mother is so upset by her father's indifference, she reflects, "Being married never stops either one of them from doing what they want. It doesn't interfere." The humor of that last sentence simultaneously adds poignancy and subtracts sentimentality from the text. Dorris's dependence on declarative sentence structures strong on nouns and verbs and sparse in adjectives forces the reader to see exact word pictures that reflect the strengths of his characters.

Rich in metaphor, "Queen of Diamonds" compares fantasy to reality, using a card game and its players' comments to reveal character and motive. Dorris's choice of narrator is also worth noting. Ray tells the story from her point of view, the only perspective from which the reader can discern Ray's maturity and wit as a result of being privy to her thoughts. Because Ray's parents spend most of their time and energies caught up in their own dilemmas, Ray's role as narrator cleverly combines the distanced, objective stance of the disassociated with the inside knowledge and keen sense of observation that only an intimate could possess.

Realistic dialogue that includes sentence fragments and profanities, as well as short paragraphs that mimic the staccato leaps of unreasoned, if not unreasonable, thought, add to Dorris's simple, elegant style.

*L. Elisabeth Beattie*

# THE QUEEN OF SPADES

*Author:* Alexander Pushkin (1799-1837)
*Type of plot:* Psychological
*Time of plot:* The 1830's
*Locale:* St. Petersburg
*First published:* "Pikovaya dama," 1834 (English translation, 1896)

> *Principal characters:*
> HERMANN, the protagonist, a Russian officer of German descent
> THE COUNTESS, an aged noblewoman
> ELIZAVETA IVANOVNA, the poor ward of the countess
> PRINCE PAVEL TOMSKY, the grandson of the countess
> CHEKALINSKY, the proprietor of a gambling parlor

*The Story*

As the story opens, a group of young military officers are playing cards into the early morning. One officer remarks that Hermann, an officer in the Engineer Corps, likes to watch the others play, but he himself does not play. The prudent and industrious Hermann replies that he is attempting to build a fortune and does not want to risk the essential in order to gain the superfluous. Prince Pavel Tomsky changes the conversation by telling the story of his grandmother, a strong-willed socialite when she was younger. While on a trip to France, the young beauty lost a large sum at cards, a sum that her long-suffering husband refused to give her in order to honor her debt. The countess ran to a friend, the count St. Germain, who gave her the secret of victory at cards. The countess returned to the tables the next evening, regained the money that she had lost, and settled her debts.

The officers who have listened to the story react to it in different ways. One believes that the story is fantasy, another that the cards were marked, and a third that the victory was a result of pure chance. Although Tomsky cannot explain what happened, he believes that a secret exists and that his grandmother has been derelict in not passing it on to her family. On this note, the officers break up their card game as the sun begins to rise.

The narrative changes to the countess, who is now an elderly lady unable to do much but terrorize her domestic staff. Elizaveta Ivanovna is a ward of the countess and completely dependent on the old lady for her sustenance. Elizaveta's life is difficult, as she endures the conflicting orders and irrational opinions of the countess and can find no way out of her predicament.

One afternoon, Elizaveta looks out the window as she is sewing and spies a young officer standing on the corner and staring at her window. It is Hermann, who was strongly impressed by Tomsky's story about his grandmother and wishes to learn the secret of the cards before the countess dies. He stands on the corner and dreams of ways to enter the house and confront the countess. When he notices Elizaveta Ivanovna at the window, an idea comes to him. He sends letters to her, some taken word-for-word from German novels, in which he professes his love and importunes her for a meeting. After an initial reluctance, Elizaveta Ivanovna, viewing the young officer as a potential deliverer from her dreary existence with the countess, concocts an elaborate plan to let the young officer into the house and into her room for a private meeting.

All goes according to plan; Hermann sneaks into the house while the countess and Elizaveta are at a ball. Instead of going to Elizaveta's room, however, he enters the room of the countess, hiding until her return. Hermann surprises the old lady and pleads for the secret. The countess refuses to divulge the secret, and Hermann, losing patience, threatens her with a pistol. Seeing the gun, the countess gives a start and dies, presumably of fright. Hermann sneaks off to Elizaveta's room, informing her of events and explaining why he had gone to the countess's room. Elizaveta is broken-hearted, as she realizes that Hermann was cultivating her friendship in order to gain money, not because of love.

Although Hermann's conscience is dulled by his obsession and his main regret is the loss of the secret, he still feels obligated to attend the old lady's funeral. As Hermann looks into the casket to pay his last respects, the countess seems to open her eyes and wink at him. Taken by surprise, he falls backward to the floor and has to be helped up. Unnerved by this experience, he decides to eat a good meal and drive away his fright with wine.

After coming home and falling into a deep sleep induced by the wine, Hermann awakens at three in the morning. He looks at the window and sees a face looking at him. The face disappears; then Hermann hears the door to his anteroom being opened. A ghostly apparition slides into his room, and Hermann realizes that the countess is paying him a visit. The old lady tells a frightened Hermann that she has been commanded to reveal to him the secret that he desired: He is to play a three, seven, and ace three nights in a row, and then never play again. The apparition disappears; Hermann, now fully awake, finds his valet asleep and the outer door locked. Was it a vision or a dream?

Hermann's life now takes a new turn. Thoughts of the countess are displaced by an obsession with three, seven, ace; even women and inanimate objects begin to look like one of the three numbers. Hermann debates whether to resign from the army and go to the great gambling halls of Paris; meanwhile, a renowned Moscow gambler, Chekalinsky, opens a gambling parlor in St. Petersburg. His decision thus made for him, Hermann is introduced to Chekalinsky by a friend and is allowed to play. He bets his patrimony, forty-seven thousand rubles, and plays a three. Hermann wins, and Chekalinsky, ever affable, pays the young officer. The large bet of the first evening attracts a small crowd when Hermann returns on the second evening, places ninety-four thousand rubles on the table, and wins with a seven. A bit distressed, Chekalinsky pays Hermann.

On the third evening, Hermann returns to the gambling hall. He places all of his winnings on the table and prepares to play. The other gamblers cease their play and surround the table of Hermann and Chekalinsky, who is visibly nervous. The suspense builds as the play commences. Hermann, desiring to play the ace, inadvertently and possibly through excitement pulls out the queen of spades by mistake and loses everything. As he stares at the queen, it seems to wink at Hermann, who remembers the wink of the countess in the casket. He leaves the hall as play resumes, and Chekalinsky begins smiling again. In an afterword, Alexander Pushkin informs the reader that Hermann is now insane, confined to a hospital. Elizaveta has married and is supporting a poor ward.

## Themes and Meanings

Pushkin's "The Queen of Spades" is considered one of the seminal short stories of Russian literature, the beginning of a rich tradition. The main theme, however, is a moral borrowed from the ancient heritage of Latin and Greek literature: the golden mean. Hermann is a Russified German, a device in Russian literature used to depict the virtues of prudence, moderation, and hard work—the opposite of another stock device, the Russian who goes to extremes and lives life to the fullest. Obsession with winning money deflects Hermann from the correct path and disaster ensues; he goes broke and mad at the same time. The obsession also kills his humanity as he callously misuses Elizaveta, is responsible for the death of the countess, and then represses any feeling of remorse that he felt for this act.

Another view sees the story as the depiction of the power of the supernatural. If man tempts fate, then he is liable to punishment. The game is a symbol of life governed by fate; Hermann tries to short-circuit the process by using the secret and is destroyed.

A third view sees the queen of spades as the countess's revenge on Hermann for being frightened to death. Perhaps all three views are valid interpretations of the tale.

## Style and Technique

Pushkin lived in a time of transition for Russian literature, from Romanticism to realism. This story is a Romantic tale of fantasy told in a realistic manner. The author employs the techniques of classicism that would become the staple of the realistic short story: economy of words, elimination of superfluous detail, and emphasis on a single theme. As a result, the story moves quickly and keeps the reader's attention directed to the main point.

The interest of the reader is also kept alive by the inclusion of elements of fantasy, especially the vision of the countess after her death. It is unclear whether the countess really appears or whether the drunken Hermann is merely imagining the entire episode. If the vision is a figment of his imagination, how is he able to win the first two times? Is it mere chance? Pushkin leaves clues, such as repeating, "It seems as . . . " The puzzle is not conclusively answered, however, and each reader is able to draw whatever conclusion he or she wishes. By means of this technique, Pushkin not only retains one's interest during the story but also keeps one thinking about the story long after the original reading.

*Philip Maloney*

# A QUEER HEART

*Author:* Elizabeth Bowen (1899-1973)
*Type of plot:* Domestic realism
*Time of plot:* Unspecified; perhaps the 1930's
*Locale:* A small town in the Midlands of England
*First published:* 1941

> *Principal characters:*
> HILDA CADMAN, a widow in her sixties
> ROSA, her elder, unmarried sister
> LUCILLE, her daughter, also single

*The Story*

Hilda Cadman is cautiously and clumsily disembarking, backward, from the bus that has brought her home from town. A heavy-set, jolly, friendly woman, she enjoys her frequent trips to the nearby town, where she knows and is known by everyone. As the bus continues to travel up the hill, she realizes that the only happy part of her day has ended. Her solid, somber, stucco house, named "Granville," has been her home for many years, nevertheless she is reluctant to go inside.

Since the death twelve years ago of Mr. Cadman, Hilda and her daughter Lucille, unmarried and no longer young, have lived together with occasional visits from Hilda's sister Rosa, also a widow. Since Mr. Cadman's death, Rosa's visits have become longer and longer, and Hilda has gradually realized that her sister and her daughter are in league against her, always carping and criticizing her, darkening the gloomy house with their cheerless meekness. Now Rosa has collapsed and is dying in the upstairs spare room. Lucille chides her mother for her frivolousness, doing her best to make Hilda feel inconsiderate and thoughtless for being away so long and for buying herself a small, pretty scarf.

While Hilda drinks tea alone in the kitchen, reflecting on her happy past life with her husband, who had acted as a defense against her older sister, Lucille comes downstairs to tell Hilda that Rosa wants to see her. Brought back to the present after having recalled the good times that she and her husband had enjoyed as members of the jolly set, Hilda is again forced to act with reluctance.

Rosa accuses her sister of having a shallow heart and says smugly that she could have had a vain, wicked heart. Then Rosa recalls the Christmas, when she and her sister were little girls, that Hilda got the fairy doll on the top of the Christmas tree because she sang for it. Rosa claims that God then taught her to pity Hilda for having a vain heart.

Hilda feels sorry for Rosa's implacable resentment of her and says silently, "You poor queer heart, eating yourself out, thanking God for pain." Aloud, Hilda says that she and Rosa are alike in setting their heart on things, and wishes that Rosa had had that fairy doll that Hilda does not even remember.

*Themes and Meanings*

In this short, simple story, Elizabeth Bowen presents two contrasting characters, elderly sisters who have followed their natures and lived very different lives.

The focus of the story is on the differences between the two main characters. Hilda, the younger of the two, exemplifies a warm, sociable person who enjoys a good time—who derives pleasure from looking at the big cafés, the buses, the movie theaters, and the shops. She is saddened by Lucille's alienation from her, but does not allow the constant condemnation of her daughter and her sister to affect her own outlook on life.

Rosa, on the other hand, has a cold nature and has imposed it on her niece, wrapping "her virginity round her like someone sharing a mackintosh." In striking contrast to her younger sister, Rosa harbors resentment, even for a disappointment that occurred so long ago that Hilda has forgotten all about it.

The title of the story suggests the basic theme: After Rosa accuses her of being shallow, vain, and silly, Hilda pities her and wishes she could do something to make up for that disappointment that has stayed in Rosa's heart all these years. It is too late to make up for it, Hilda realizes as she thinks about Rosa's "queer heart." Because of her outgoing, generous nature, Hilda understands why Rosa has wanted to dominate Lucille, in effect stealing her from her mother. Hilda sees the mean-spirited capture of Lucille's heart as Rosa's revenge over the Christmas tree doll, and forgives her.

Bowen thus delineates two opposite natures, or hearts. She shows the simplicity of the one who lives in the moment, taking pleasure from small things, quite unaware that her cheerful nature has provoked envy in her sister's heart, just as did her long, blond hair and pretty ways as a child. Rosa's cold nature, by contrast, has brought her to her deathbed in rancor and resentment and poisoned Lucille's life.

*Style and Technique*

Bowen tells this story in a straightforward, simple style, proceeding chronologically except for Hilda's occasional ruminations on the past. The most meaningful parts of the story are presented in dialogue, brief conversations between Hilda and Lucille and between Hilda and Rosa. The talk is natural, credible, and revealing of the speakers' natures. The author does not state her theme, but merely suggests it through what the characters say to each other.

Bowen's use of exceptionally clear and strong images helps to convey the meaning of the story also. For example, Hilda's face is "as ingenuous as a little girl's" and "her smiles were frequent, hopeful and quick." Twice Bowen uses the word "irrepressible," underscoring the quality of Hilda's personality. After Hilda's widowhood, Rosa "started flapping round Granville like a doomful bird."

Life has not been all good for Hilda, but on the whole she has had a good time. She thinks, "A real good time always lasts; you have it with all your nature and your nature stays living with it." When confronted by Rosa's deeply unforgiving nature, Hilda merely pities her with gentle sympathy.

*Natalie Harper*

# THE RAGMAN'S DAUGHTER

*Author:* Alan Sillitoe (1928-    )
*Type of plot:* Social realism
*Time of plot:* The 1950's and 1960's
*Locale:* Nottingham, England
*First published:* 1963

> *Principal characters:*
> Tony, the narrator, a loader in a warehouse, formerly a petty thief
> Doris, the schoolgirl daughter of a scrap merchant

## The Story

As Tony, the narrator of the story, is leaving the warehouse where he works as a cheese loader, the police question him about a suitcase that he is carrying out. It is empty, as it happens—returned by a friend who had borrowed it and had been hoping to keep it for himself.

This short opening episode, embellished with some pithy references to the police, economically establishes that Tony and his workmates are no respecters of private property and that the police are their common enemy. Tony elaborates his attitude toward the law in a comic account of cheese stealing and of the relish with which he and his family savor the stolen food, thus revealing himself as a married man with a poorly paid job and with a history of lawbreaking.

He then looks back to his childhood and explains his development as a habitual thief, starting with his experience in the infants' school when, sensing something morally wrong with the idea of a "buying and selling" lesson, he pocketed the token coins without detection or punishment. Subsequent childish experiments taught him that, although "money was trouble," it was safer to steal money than things, and that it was best to keep silent. Petty thieving soon became a way of life.

Tony's account of the delight with which he used to plunge the goods he had stolen into the river demonstrates his contempt for possessions and consumerism and, by implication, for an unjust and hypocritical society. He expresses his notions of an ideal society, in which everyone is equally provided for and equally treated, in the only terms with which he is familiar: like a prison, but with everyone free.

The evolution of his antiauthoritarian philosophy is essential to an understanding of his relationship with Doris, whom, in the recollected part of the narrative, he meets at a fish-and-chip shop, and who agrees to accompany him on his thieving "expeditions" (her word). Doris, who is still at school, has no need to steal; her father is a prosperous scrap merchant. She does it "for kicks."

From their first joint expedition, Tony recognizes Doris as the ideal partner-in-crime. Unlike the lads who have occasionally joined him, she is deft, quiet, and efficient. The excitement of the theft is transformed into sexual excitement: Tony is in love.

The quality of his love is highlighted in a dramatic description of Doris's arrival on horseback at the backyard of his run-down street, to the astonishment of the neighbors. Doris, "all clean and golden-haired on that shining horse," as he recalls in a later part of the story, symbolizes Tony's aspirations for a freer lifestyle—something of the reverse, perhaps, of the knight in shining armor whisking the lady away in traditional legend.

Tony and Doris get into the habit of depositing the goods they steal in back gardens or through mailboxes, to give the finders happy surprises. With his accumulation of stolen money, Tony buys a motorcycle and whisks Doris off for rides in the industry-scarred countryside—a token of his dream of a shared country life with her.

The sequence of successful expeditions, in which their love is consummated with mounting passion, leads to a heady climax, which takes place in the storeroom of a shoe shop they have broken into. Inching his way around in the dark, Tony finds the till and fills his pockets with bank notes.

Suddenly Doris switches on the lights. She tries on shoe after shoe, tossing them across the room as she rejects them, while Tony acts as her wild and willing shop assistant. It is a gesture of defiance, a consummation of "living for kicks." When Tony, sensing danger, switches the lights off, the darkness brings them back to reality. With the inevitable arrival of a police officer, Tony's ability to ensure that Doris escapes and that the bank notes are "posted" in the mailbox of a nearby house before he is arrested shows that his code of morality can be sustained even at the moment of crisis.

During three years at Borstal (a reform institution for young offenders), he hears nothing from Doris and is tortured by doubt about whether she—and the liberating future she represents—will still be there when he is released. The news, on his release, that she has been married, has given birth to his son, and has been killed with her husband in a motorcycle crash is a mortal blow to his aspirations. It sends him on a senseless thieving trip that lands him back in jail. In the last incident of the recollected narrative, he glimpses his son, playing in the woods with Doris's father—a poignant reminder of what might have been.

This brings Tony back to the present and explains why, despite his challenging attitude toward life, he has become a conventional family man and has "gone straight"—except that, like his workmates, he keeps himself, his wife, and his two children eating well by stealing food from the warehouse.

*Themes and Meanings*

Like many of the antiheroes of Alan Sillitoe's early stories and novels, Tony is a young, working-class man who is alienated by the harsh conditions of his neighborhood and the false values of the world outside.

Social class is a key element in the story, as its title emphasizes. Had Doris been, for example, a banker's daughter, she would have been beyond Tony's reach and would not, in any case, have visited the fish-and-chip shop, a central feature of the British working-class lifestyle. Her father's trade is also a working-class symbol; Tony can identify with and even envy a person who started out as a humble rag-and-bone man and grew prosperous on other people's throwaways.

Although Tony has developed his own moral code in direct conflict with orthodox morality, he is not an outsider. References to a shared class attitude to private property run throughout the narrative, from the man at the beginning who had hoped to keep the borrowed suitcase, to the woman toward the end who, finding the stolen bank notes pushed through her mailbox, spends the money on pleasure (as Tony rejoices to discover later) and tells everyone that it came from a loving relative. Tony carries this attitude to its extended conclusion by destroying or giving away the consumer goods he steals.

At the time of his narrative, he has learned enough to be sharply critical of contemporary society—the inequalities, dishonesties, and obsession with possessions that he has observed. Unlike Sillitoe, however, he does not think in political terms. When he describes his vision of an ideal society and adds that he does not know what it would be called, Sillitoe is in effect inviting the reader to make a political judgment by recognizing a naïve version of socialism.

The story is both a criticism of contemporary society and a moving personal tragedy. The feeling that life could and should be different runs all through Tony's account of himself and shapes his private dream of a wandering country life with Doris, with her crisp, cool looks, her yellow hair, and her liberated spirit. After her death, he recalls the moment when he switched out the lights in the shoe shop. "We both went into the dark," he says, "and never came out." The ultimate tragedy, in Sillitoe's terms, is not that Doris died, but that Tony's aspirations died with her.

*Style and Technique*

Sillitoe's use of the first-person narrative form establishes the story's tone of gritty realism, which was a strong characteristic of the upsurge of regional literature in the 1950's and 1960's—a movement in which Sillitoe played a leading role.

Born and brought up in the industrial, mid-England city of Nottingham, Sillitoe is one of the few contemporary British writers with a solidly working-class upbringing and work experience. His reproduction of the local patterns of speech is therefore very authentic.

He uses two styles of vernacular in this story: The pithy, working-class slang and idiom of Tony's direct narrative is a little more self-conscious than the broad Nottingham dialect in which Tony recounts his bantering conversations with neighbors and friends.

The idiomatic narrative style that Sillitoe has given to Tony is very economical. Ideas are encapsulated in a few choice words, and each sentence is taut with meaning. Tony is able to share his assumptions about life with the reader by using crisp, vivid similes that are culled from his own experiences but have universal nuances.

The use of Tony as narrator also enables Sillitoe to present him from two points of view—as Tony sees himself in the very specific context of his own experiences and comprehensions, and as he appears in the broader and more generalized context that Sillitoe, through occasional small nudges, invites the reader to provide.

*Nina Hibbin*

# THE RAGS OF TIME

*Author:* Barry Targan (1932-    )
*Type of plot:* Domestic realism
*Time of plot:* Probably the 1970's
*Locale:* A college town north of New York City
*First published:* 1979

> *Principal characters:*
> THOMAS WILKINS, a forty-four-year-old English professor
> MILDRED WILKINS, his wife
> FAY LESTER, one of his students
> NEIL, his sixteen-year-old son

*The Story*

During one semester, Thomas Wilkins, a middle-aged professor of English literature, for the first time finds his neatly ordered existence threatened by his overwhelming passion for a student, Fay Lester. From the time that he was offered his first teaching job—which he accepted immediately, although it meant giving up his long-planned first trip to Europe—his life has been on a steady course, which he has no desire to derail. Thomas and his wife, Mildred, live a contented, temperate life, with their two sons, Neil and Peter. The only disturbance in their lives comes from the stormy adolescent moods of Neil, their older son. Now, however, Thomas is enthralled by the sensual Fay, who arrived at his college preceded by stories of having ruined the academic career of a young professor at the last college she attended. Although disinterested in her studies, Fay is intelligent, or at least clever. During a meeting in Thomas's office to discuss her spotty academic performance, she manages to hold her own in the discussion, arguing that contrary to Thomas's assertion that all the seventeenth century poets he teaches wrote from a religious perspective, John Donne's poetry celebrated earthly love, not spiritual love.

Thomas is bewildered and distressed by his growing obsession with Fay. He has been attracted to students before occasionally, but not to the point of obsessing over the girl and rearranging his schedule so as to see her as often as possible. The only remotely similar experience in his life was worshiping an extravagantly beautiful and unobtainable cheerleader at his high school.

When Thomas's brother and his family visit for Thanksgiving, the holiday traditions and family activities soothe Thomas's passions, and he believes he has exorcised Fay from his fantasies. He is thrown off balance, however, by his intense reaction when she does not show up at class after the long weekend, and he is disconcerted when she wanders into his office later that same day. After making excuses for her absence from class, Fay tries to persuade Thomas to assign her a topic for her term paper, but he refuses to do so, saying that a student's choice of a topic gives him an idea of what she has learned. Fay then suggests that perhaps she could avoid writing the term paper. After a long silence stretches between them, he acknowledges that might be possible. She immediately takes charge of arranging their assignation, then leaves.

Having finally decided to act on his fantasies, Thomas is no longer consumed by passion any more than Fay is. What he wants is simply to do what he is going to do, "to do this outrageous and nearly irrational thing." On the day of their encounter, Thomas arrives calmly and promptly at the arranged apartment, and Fay quickly leads him into the bedroom. Just before allowing Thomas to enter her, Fay suggests that she should not have to take the final exam either, and he assents. Afterward, Thomas walks back to his office to catch up on correspondence.

Returning home at his usual time, Thomas finds his usually stolid wife, Mildred, nearly hysterical because state troopers have charged Neil with rape. Accompanying Neil to the police station, he learns that Neil and two friends had sex that afternoon with a teenage girl who had a reputation for promiscuity. The girl's father soon agrees to drop the charges, and the boys are released.

On the day of the final exam, Fay comes to class but submits a blank test booklet. Thomas gives her a C grade for the semester and feels that the chapter is closed. A few days later, he is working in his office, thinking about the week that he and Mildred will soon be spending with friends in New York City, when Fay bursts in, screaming at him for giving her a C. Thomas is genuinely confused, believing that Fay never cared about the grade, and tries to explain to her that it would look strange if someone who had earned an A found out that she had gotten one also. She is furious, raging that she worked for her grade too, and accusing him of trying to extort more sexual favors for a higher grade. When she realizes that he has no further interest in her, and no intention of changing her grade, she leaves. Thomas returns to contemplating the New York restaurant at which he has reservations for the next night, and anticipating the meal he will order. "Vichyssoise, artichoke vinaigrette, escargots, coq au vin, a 1969 St. Julien. A supper you could count on."

*Themes and Meanings*

Barry Targan's "The Rags of Time" illuminates the conflicts of a settled, middle-aged man confronted with a strong impulse to risk sexual infidelity, tied to his memories of his high school attraction to an unobtainable cheerleader and his son's dramatic sexual initiation. Neither Thomas nor his wife has a great sexual appetite; his life has been devoid of passion with the exception of his worshiping the cheerleader from afar. His life also has been relatively safe and risk-free, except for a long-ago incident in which he was buried for several minutes under a snowbank. Secure in an academic career that has progressed on schedule since his first teaching job, Thomas has no interest in writing anything other than articles on arcane topics for scholarly journals. He prefers interpreting the thoughts and feelings of the risk-takers to taking the risks himself. Content in his tender but placid marriage, he is unsettled to find himself bewitched by a bright but indifferent student. When Fay makes herself available, however, his focus switches from her as a person to the idea of the adventure itself.

Neil's experience of losing his virginity sharply contrasts with his father's adolescent fantasizing about the cheerleader; in Thomas's high school fantasies, the girl he desired was important, but unobtainable, whereas Cecily is easily obtainable, but unimportant. Neil's adolescent experience emotionally mirrors his father's adult experience with Fay, however; both males are more interested in the experience itself than in the person. Neither male seems likely to suffer any harmful consequences from his action, but each of the females is punished—Fay by getting a lower grade than she expects; Cecily by the double standard that brands her conduct as shameful while that of Neil is a source of amusement to his parents' friends, and, his father expects, will be admired by his friends at school.

*Style and Technique*

Thomas is the most sharply and clearly drawn of all the characters. Reinforcing the fact that he and Mildred live a life dominated by the intellect, not by the senses, none of the family members is described physically. The only character for whom Targan provides any physical description is Fay, and then only a few words when Thomas goes to meet her at her friend's apartment. Further distancing Thomas from the physical and sexual dimension, Targan does not indicate whether Thomas enjoys having sex with Fay, or whether it was more exciting than his sex life with Mildred, who is apparently his only previous sexual partner. The reader only learns that he leaves Fay soon after the act, feeling neither guilt nor exuberance. He reflects that taking this risk gives him a sense of accomplishment similar to what he feels when he has an article accepted for publication in *Seventeenth Century Studies*: "Then and now his life seemed stronger, better balanced . . . running on evenly, well tuned, which was all that life was supposed to do."

Lines from the poetry of the seventeenth century authors in whom Thomas specializes are integrated throughout the story. The title is from John Donne's poem, "The Sunne Rising": "Love, all alike, no season knowes, nor clyme,/ Nor houres, dayes, moneths, which are the rags of time." These lines appear in the story in one of the quotes that Fay uses to rebut Thomas during their first argument in his office.

*Irene Struthers Rush*

# THE RAID
## A Volunteer's Story

*Author:* Leo Tolstoy (1828-1910)
*Type of plot:* Realism
*Time of plot:* The 1850's
*Locale:* The Russian Caucasus
*First published:* "Nabeg: Razskaz volontera," 1853 (English translation, 1909)

Principal characters:
THE NARRATOR, unnamed
CAPTAIN PAVEL HLOPOV, a Russian army officer stationed in the
Caucasus
MARYA IVANOVNA HLOPOV, the captain's aged mother
ENSIGN ANATOLE IVANOVICH ALANIN, a soldier in the captain's
regiment
IVAN MIHAILOVICH HASANOV, a Russian cavalry officer
LIEUTENANT ROSENKRANZ, a Russian officer

*The Story*

The anonymous narrator begins by describing how a certain Captain Pavel Hlopov visits him in his hut in the Russian Caucasus to inform him of an impending Russian military action against the native Tatar tribesmen. As a consequence of their conversation, the two men begin to discuss the concept of bravery. Captain Hlopov offers a definition of bravery that reminds the narrator of Plato's definition; the captain says quite concisely: "He's a brave man who behaves as he ought." The narrator adds that the man who risks his life out of vanity, or curiosity, or greed cannot be called brave, while a man who refuses to face danger out of duty to his family or on conscientious grounds cannot be called a coward.

The narrator is a former neighbor of Captain Hlopov's mother, whom he visited before coming to the Caucasus. The old lady, Marya Ivanovna Hlopov, worships her son and has prayed for him since he went into the service eighteen years ago. The captain was wounded severely four times but has kept this information from his mother, who thinks that he has been safe all the while. Although the captain rarely writes and never visits his mother, he does send her money every year. Before the narrator departed for the Caucasus, he had agreed to deliver a black religious amulet from the mother to her son. When he arrives in the Caucasus, the narrator delivers the gift, which deeply touches the captain.

The next day, at four in the morning, the captain arouses the narrator and invites him to join the military operation. As they ride, the narrator is impressed by the splendid scenery and fauna and flora of the mountain setting. A young ensign in the captain's regiment, Alanin by name, overtakes them and rides by, delighted at his first chance to be in a real battle. The young soldier's romantic attitude toward battle mildly annoys Captain Hlopov.

The narrator gives a detailed profile of a Lieutenant Rosenkranz, a romantic type who often assumes a kind of Byronic pose—distant, contradictory, and misunderstood by those around him. The narrator notes with interest the pre-battle activities of the soldiers—playing cards, telling jokes and stories, and singing. "It was as though no one could conceive that some of them were destined not to come back along that road."

The narrator describes in detail the life at the Russian fort and is struck again by the casual attitude of everybody toward the upcoming battle against the Tatars. Nature in the mountains is so picturesque and splendidly romantic that it is hard to imagine the possibility of danger and death so close at hand. He sums up the paradox: "Everything evil in the heart of man ought, one would think, to vanish in contact with Nature, in which beauty and goodness find their most direct expression."

Soon Tatar torchlights are seen in the distance, signaling other tribesmen that the Russians are approaching. The Russians ford a river and are soon exchanging gunfire with the Tatars. The Tatars fall back, and the Russians advance, shelling a Tatar village with artillery.

The Tatar village is sacked by the Russians, and one old Tatar is taken prisoner. As the Russians advance beyond the village, the enemy's resistance becomes stronger. The real confrontation begins. Lieutenant Rosenkranz and the young Ensign Alanin are in the thick of battle and are enjoying it. Only Captain Hlopov calls a Russian retreat and offers no excuses or explanations for his seemingly cowardly actions. "This, to my thinking, is the peculiar and noble characteristic of Russian courage," observes the narrator.

As if fulfilling the captain's prophecy that the ensign's fear of nothing is immature and foolish, Alanin is wounded and carried off for treatment. The doctor is not able to stabilize the young man, and Ensign Alanin dies. The detachment marches back to the fortress singing in the moonlit Caucasus night, their mission accomplished.

*Themes and Meanings*

In "The Raid" (subtitled "A Volunteer's Story"), Leo Tolstoy offers a fictional elaboration of Plato's theory of courage. For Tolstoy, real bravery is in the knowledge of what one should and what one should not fear. Contrary to more typically romantic notions of bravery, in which the hero is the one who goes against exaggerated odds with no rational thought of the consequences (as does, for example, Ensign Alanin), Tolstoy defines bravery as the ability to size up a situation and act logically (as does Captain Hlopov). More elaborate, but similar, examples of Tolstoy's theory of courage are found frequently in his later fiction, especially in *Voyna i mir* (1865-1869; *War and Peace*, 1886).

In a broader sense, "The Raid" is a compelling account of people's fear, anxiety, and cowardice in the face of death. Tolstoy is particularly interested in describing different people's reactions to war and combat, especially how they deal with the ever-present possibility of being killed. Although Tolstoy himself later became a pacifist and an active opponent of war and the use of force that war represents, there is in "The Raid" praise (sometimes subtle, more often overt) for such values as patriotism, loyalty to country and comrades in arms, and duty. Tolstoy moralizes very little about the horrors of war. Instead he approaches war as a kind of necessary category of history. As such, it is philosophically neutral, beyond good and evil. Although the lives of some are winnowed away in war, those who survive have added another dimension of valuable experience to their personal lives, which have been enhanced by the exposure to danger and uncertainty, ultimately resulting in an increased love of life.

*Style and Technique*

The Caucasus frequently served as a backdrop for Russian Romantic writers in the early decades of the nineteenth century. Tolstoy, well aware of this tradition, infused his lyrical passages describing nature with a touch of irony, trying to bring out the paradox of war and killing in a perfectly peaceful and majestic setting. The narrator describes the local color in vivid detail but is somehow unable to reconcile completely the gratuitous killing and carnage of war within such a unique and beautiful setting. The narrator has very keen senses, and he describes the sounds, smells, and sights of harmonious nature around him. At the same time there is no sentimentality about the narrator's feeling toward nature; he simply is impressed and enjoys the new experience in his life. Finally, the contrast between the tranquillity of nature and the violence of war becomes so strong that Tolstoy as narrator is able to "estrange" the reader's perception of the paradox.

*R. E. Richardson*

# RAIN

*Author:* W. Somerset Maugham (1874-1965)
*Type of plot:* Realism
*Time of plot:* During or immediately after World War I
*Locale:* Pago-Pago, American Samoa
*First published:* 1921

> *Principal characters:*
> SADIE THOMPSON, a prostitute
> THE REVEREND MR. DAVIDSON, a missionary
> MRS. DAVIDSON, his wife, also a missionary
> DR. MACPHAIL, a physician
> MRS. MACPHAIL, his wife

*The Story*

When a measles epidemic temporarily prevents the Davidsons and the Macphails from continuing their journey to Apia, Western Samoa, they find themselves stranded in Pago-Pago. Though the two couples have socialized on shipboard, they are very different: The Davidsons, who have been absent from their medical and religious mission north of Samoa for a year, are religious zealots whose single aim in life is to convert Samoans to Christianity. They are a drab and humorless pair who associate with the Macphails only because the rest of the ship's passengers seem "fast" by comparison. Though the women find much to talk about, the men share only an association with medicine, for Dr. Macphail is a shy, contemplative man to whom religion means little.

When it is announced that they will be unable to leave the island for at least ten days, the energetic Davidsons take action. Through his influence with the governor, Davidson is able to find them rooms in the establishment of Mr. Horn, a local trader. Mrs. Davidson, with characteristic efficiency, helps the rather ineffectual Macphails settle into the boardinghouse, determined to make the best of things in spite of the bleak environment.

Soon Macphail learns that another of their shipmates will be lodging at Horn's, a second-class passenger named Sadie Thompson. Sadie, en route to Apia where a job supposedly awaits her, has been judged "fast" by Mrs. Davidson and Mrs. Macphail for dancing with the ship's quartermaster at the shipboard party the night before the landing at Pago-Pago. Vulgar in appearance and speech, Sadie is a friendly and vivacious sort who seeks, in the ensuing days, to enliven the depressing boardinghouse by giving frequent parties, loud and raucous affairs attended solely by the island's sailors. One evening the couples' dinner conversation is interrupted by especially loud noises coming from Sadie's room on the floor below. As they try to talk over the din, Davidson has a sudden revelation: Sadie, who boarded the ship at Honolulu, must be a denizen of Iwelei, that city's notorious red-light district, which has only recently been shut down through the efforts of Hawaiian missionaries. Further, she must be plying her trade here in Pago-Pago—just below them in her room at Horn's.

Over the objections of Macphail, who considers Sadie's actions none of their business, Davidson insists on storming into her room and trying to break up the party. As his wife and the Macphails listen, Davidson is thrown out of the room by the sailors. After the Davidsons go to their room, the party starts up again, even louder than before.

The arrival of the ship in Pago-Pago has coincided with the beginning of the tropical rainy season, and rain falls almost ceaselessly during the time period covered by the story—torrential, oppressive rain, which depresses the Macphails and greatly adds to the sense of claustrophobia that permeates the story. During a rare dry spell on the day after Sadie's party, Mrs. Macphail and Mrs. Davidson twice encounter Sadie, who treats them rudely. Mrs. Davidson is certain that Sadie will regret having made an enemy of Davidson, who is tireless and vengeful in his battle against sin, but when he announces later that day that he intends to try to save the prostitute's soul, even his wife is shocked: Surely the woman has sunk too low to be reformed. Davidson's reply that no sinner is beyond God's mercy leaves little doubt of his confidence that Sadie can be converted, and he has his first session with her that very day. It seems to be a standoff. Sadie is coarse, brazen, unrepentant; the Reverend Mr. Davidson is determined.

Time passes on the island and the rain seems as though it will never stop. The weather, the climate, and the islanders are grating on Macphail's nerves. One day Sadie calls him to her room, where she discloses that Davidson has convinced the governor to force her to leave on the next boat. Unfortunately for her, its destination is San Francisco, to which she does not want to return. She asks Macphail to speak to the governor for her: Why cannot she be allowed to leave on the next boat for Sydney instead? Sympathetic to her plight and irritated by Davidson's lack of compassion, Macphail agrees. The governor stands by his decision, however, obviously intimidated by the missionaries' influence in the region. Macphail is disgruntled and more disgusted than ever with Davidson's intractability.

That evening, a distraught and disheveled Sadie comes to plead with Davidson for mercy. She admits that she is wanted by the police in San Francisco, and begs Davidson not to make her return. The missionary remains unmoved, however, despite Macphail's pleas on her behalf. When Sadie becomes hysterical, Macphail helps her to her room. Later that evening, after Davidson has led the group in praying for her soul, the calmed and ostensibly contrite Sadie sends for Davidson, saying that she is ready to repent. Davidson stays with her until two o'clock the next morning and declares the next day that he has brought her to the Lord.

Sadie's sessions with Davidson continue for several days, during which time the rain, the heat, and the mosquitoes make life on the island nearly intolerable. Macphail looks forward to the day when Sadie's departure will break the tension that her religious conversion has brought to the boardinghouse. Davidson, exhausted from spending much of each night with Sadie, is nevertheless in a state of spiritual rapture. Sadie seems to have accepted the fact that she must return to the United States to face her punishment. This uncomfortable state of affairs continues until the morning that Sadie's ship is to sail for San Francisco. Just after dawn, Macphail is awakened by Horn, who tells him that his services are needed. Horn leads him to the beach, where a group of Samoans stand huddled around a body. Macphail is shocked to find that the dead man is Davidson, who still holds the razor with which he has slit his throat. After making arrangements with the police, Macphail returns to Horn's boardinghouse and asks his wife to break the news to Mrs. Davidson. Abnormally calm, Mrs. Davidson asks to see the body.

On the way back from the mortuary, the Macphails and Mrs. Davidson are startled by the sound of Sadie's gramophone, which had been silent since her supposed conversion. Sadie herself has reverted to her former ways: Dressed in her old flashy costume and heavily made-up, she is entertaining a sailor. When she sees Mrs. Davidson, she spits at her. Mrs. Davidson hurries to her room, and Macphail chastises Sadie. What does she think she is doing? Fixing him with a look of intense hatred, Sadie gives Macphail the key to Davidson's suicide: "You men! You filthy, dirty pigs! You're all the same, all of you. Pigs! Pigs!" Macphail realizes in a flash the reason for the guilt that has driven Davidson to kill himself.

*Themes and Meanings*

Setting is central to the effectiveness of "Rain." Probably the most famous of W. Somerset Maugham's numerous tales set in the tropics, "Rain," like others of its kind, is an exploration of what happens when East meets West in a tropical setting. The clash between Pacific and European cultures informs every aspect of "Rain," and for each Anglo-Saxon character, the tropics represent some different and alien reality. The Davidsons see the South Seas as a vast pagan chaos waiting to be colonized and Christianized. For Sadie Thompson, the islands represent an escape, a place to begin life anew, far away from the repression exercised by Davidson and his kind. Even the even-tempered Macphail is affected by the strange world of the tropics: Appalled by the squalor and disease of Pago-Pago, he is driven to distraction by the unremitting rain. Much like "The Letter" and "The Outstation," two of Maugham's other South Seas tales, "Rain" is a study of the bizarre behavior that results when a European temperament must face prolonged exposure to tropical climates and customs.

"Rain" is also a bitter indictment of intolerance, both political and religious. The Davidsons are self-righteous and authoritarian, accomplished destroyers of Samoan culture. Mrs. Davidson is a cold and prudish woman to whom even European-style dancing is immoral, and it is little wonder that Davidson seeks sexual satisfaction from a prostitute. Davidson himself is merciless in his cruel insistence that Sadie return to the United States; he is a single-minded bigot whose suicide is the product of an unbearable but self-imposed religious guilt. In that it criticizes and exposes the colonizers who would transform the tropics into a morally upright and repressive extension of the West, who seek to impose white culture and religion on the world at large, "Rain" is a powerful critique of American and Western European imperialism.

*Style and Technique*

"Rain" is told primarily from the point of view of Macphail, an intelligent and modest man to whom the world of the Samoan Islands is entirely unfamiliar. Thus, the reader shares with Macphail the sense of newness, of exoticism of setting and climate so central to the story's effectiveness. Macphail's viewpoint controls the reader's perceptions in other ways as well, particularly as concerns the relationship between Sadie and Davidson: Because Macphail is basically an agnostic, willing to live and let live, he serves as an obvious foil to Davidson, and the reader comes to share with Macphail an impatience with the missionary's religious authoritarianism. Like Macphail, the reader ignores hints of what is going on between Davidson and Sadie until the end of the story when, with Macphail, the reader must reinterpret past events in the light of Davidson's suicide. This masterful use of a limited point of view ensures that the surprise ending delivers a strong perceptual shock.

Maugham's prose is famous for its directness, its urbanity, and its polish. Like much of his fiction, "Rain" is written with a minimum of ornamentation, concentrating almost unflinchingly on the narrative line. Maugham thought of himself primarily as a storyteller rather than as a literary artist, but "Rain" belies such modesty. Not only is it a highly entertaining morality play about temptation, sin, and salvation, but also, at its best, it is an incisive and even allegorical critique of the white man's colonial impulse.

*J. D. Daubs*

# THE RAINY MOON

*Author:* Colette (Sidonie-Gabrielle Colette, 1873-1954)
*Type of plot:* Horror
*Time of plot:* The mid-twentieth century
*Locale:* Paris
*First published:* "La Lune de pluie," 1940 (English translation, 1959)

*Principal characters:*
THE NARRATOR, an author
ROSITA BARBERET, her typist
DELIA ESSENDIER, Rosita's married sister

*The Story*

The narrator of the story, an author, comes for the first time to the apartment of her new typist, Mlle Rosita Barberet. The typist's apartment is situated on Montmartre, where the narrator herself once lived. However, there have been many changes since the narrator resided on the Butte: Some of the street names have been changed, and buildings have been repainted or torn down altogether. During the course of their conversation, the author goes to the window to inspect the view; unconsciously, her hand rests on the window catch. The unusual catch—a cast-iron mermaid—jars her memory, and suddenly the author realizes that she used to live in this very apartment.

She does not reveal this discovery to the efficient, birdlike Rosita, but instead asks her to retype a page, stalling for time to inspect the room. The author is especially curious to see again her old bedroom and, as she leaves, pretends to mistake the bedroom door for the door to the corridor. Before she can twist the knob, however, Rosita bars the way.

On her next visit, the author learns (through unsubtle questioning of the typist) that Rosita's sister lives in the bedroom. Apparently, the sister has been "ill" and confined to the room. The author's romantic imagination paints a picture of a young woman forsaken by her lover, pining away in the same bed where the author herself once pined for a departed man.

Her guess is actually close to the truth. When the author next comes to the apartment, Rosita is distraught and weepy. The typist confesses that her sister's character has changed for the worse since her husband, "the faithless Essendier," deserted her. The author decides not to pursue the matter; yet, as she is leaving, a small rainbow appears on the wall, a reflection caused by the sun hitting an imperfection in the window pane. The author is again reminded of her past—she had called the reflection her "rainy moon," greeting it as an optimistic sign. Rosita confides, however, that her sister considers the little fan of colors a bad omen. Her curiosity again aroused, the author bluffs her way into the bedroom and meets the beautiful, cold Delia Essendier, who has taken to bed not to pine, as the writer had fancied, but to sulk. Annoyed yet intrigued by this saturnine young woman, the author asks her why she does not work like her sister does.

> "I work too," she said stiffly. "Only nobody sees what I do. I wear myself out; oh, I wear myself out. In there. . . . In there. . . . "
> She was touching her forehead and pressing her temples.

Nevertheless, the challenge affects Delia, for one day shortly thereafter the author arrives to find her engaged in needlework. Delia remarks that it is good for her to handle pointed things. The author makes a joke of this seemingly inane comment and goes out to make a purchase from a street vendor. As she rushes back inside, she bumps into a fatigued-looking man who is staring fixedly at the Barberet window.

Rosita—seeming suddenly aged herself—explains what has been "wearing out" her sister: Delia has been convoking, or summoning through intense concentration, her husband. Supposedly, the result of convocation is, for her husband, death. When Colette expresses disbelief in convocation, Rosita assures her that it is quite common, citing several examples even in the same neighborhood.

Although not convinced, the author is disgusted by this evil endeavor and vows never to return to the Barberet apartment. However, weeks later, she begins haphazardly running into Delia, whose confinement has apparently ended. The young woman "looked pale and diminished, like a convalescent who is out too soon, pearly under the eyes, and extremely pretty." Finally, the author catches sight of Delia at a fried-potato stand. Ravenously eating potato chips, Delia is now dressed all in black, wearing the widow's crepe.

*Themes and Meanings*

With its voodoo overtones and macabre O. Henry ending, "The Rainy Moon" is a tale told primarily for impact. Delia's convocations, her "need" to handle pointed things (suggesting that she is either mentally or actually gouging her husband's likeness), and the transfixed man in the street escalate the reader's suspense. Although in the story the symbolic nature of the rainy moon is uncertain (the author sees it as a good sign; Delia labels it bad), Colette explains elsewhere that she meant the ephemeral image to suggest the iridescent halo around the moon foretelling foul weather. Despite all these ill tidings, the conclusion is still surprising. Perhaps the reader, like the narrator, makes the mistake of deciding too quickly what is possible and what is not.

However, the bizarre finale should not overshadow the original weird coincidence. Not only does the author return unknowingly to her old apartment, but there she finds a seeming time twin: a young woman deserted by her man, taking refuge in her bed, and even wearing the same type of tasseled slippers that the author used to wear. Is this not a coincidence as disturbing as the "coincidence" that Delia convokes her husband and her husband dies? Colette's point is not that voodoo works or that there are supernatural forces in play because an author once lived in her typist's apartment, but rather that no one really knows what exists beneath the veneer of a "coincidence." There may be other powers at work, or there may not be. It might be unwise to discount any possibility.

## Style and Technique

In "The Rainy Moon," the writer's style and the character of the narrator-author are practically indistinguishable. Both are reticent, seemingly disinterested, and intuitive.

Colette's style is reticent because, although she offers many details about her personal life, the reader nevertheless completes the story feeling as though he or she really knows very little about her. With scant preamble, she makes a baldly honest and self-astute comment such as " . . . a solitude that bore no resemblance to peace had wiped all the life and charm out of my face." Then she withdraws from her statement as precipitously as she introduced it, leaving the reader to speculate on why she was solitary and discontent. Just as Colette the character does not bother to share with Rosita the astonishing discovery that she used to inhabit this very apartment, neither does the narrator Colette share explanations with the reader. Her reticence implies that some things are inexplicable, while other things are explicable yet better left unexplained.

Feigning disinterest, the author barges into Delia's bedroom on the pretext of aiding the young woman. However, her true purpose is to satisfy her own curiosity about this virtual specter of her former self. Similarly, Colette's style is superficially disinterested. She renders a seemingly dispassionate and cool record of events; yet there is an undercurrent of deep sensitivity, if not deep emotionality, constantly held in check, running through her work. Her disinterest is but a facade; no one in the story has greater emotional investment in the events in the Barberet apartment than does the author.

Finally, Colette is an intuitive writer rather than an empirical one. Some of her intuitive flights could be termed "digressions." In the middle of recounting the Barberet tale, she suddenly talks of the pleasantness of picnics in the Bois, her mother's perspective-restoring visit, or an eventless dinner in a neighborhood café. Although ostensibly discursions, these snapshots serve several important purposes. Scenes of normalcy provide contrast for the culminating evil in the Barberet apartment and, at the same time, add to the tale a journal-like realism, intimating that, no, this is not a contrived story but simply a diary of events. Ideally, these "digressions" beguile the reader into identifying with the author's "normal" life, then whisper to him or her, See what eerie and unexplainable things lurk close to you.

*Susan Davis*

# RALPH THE DUCK

*Author:* Frederick Busch (1941-    )
*Type of plot:* Domestic realism
*Time of plot:* The mid-1980's
*Locale:* A northeastern U.S. college campus
*First published:* 1989

> *Principal characters:*
> THE NARRATOR, a forty-two-year-old security guard and part-time
>   student
> FANNY, his wife
> HIS ENGLISH PROFESSOR
> A RED-HAIRED FEMALE STUDENT

*The Story*

The unnamed narrator, awakened at 5:25 A.M. by his vomiting dog, reveals that he has misbehaved the previous night, making his wife cry. He intimates that his behavior was part of a pattern and that his marriage has problems. They once had a daughter, but she evidently died in early childhood; he is less than forthcoming about details in this, as in most areas of his private life. He calls himself the oldest college student in the United States, although he knows it is not technically true. At forty-two years old, however, he is nearly twice the age of the average undergraduate on his campus, old enough, significantly, to be most students' father. He is a military veteran, although just too old to have served in Vietnam. As an employee of the college, he is allowed to enroll for one class per semester and figures that he can finish his undergraduate degree in another sixteen years. Distanced from his classmates by both age and class—it is an elite private school—he has disdain for their smugness, their self-indulgence, and their privilege. He is also suspicious of his English professor, who is younger than he, handsome, and rather too slick. The professor seems to hope that the narrator is a Vietnam veteran, particularly a Special Forces operative.

The story moves by a series of encounters with a red-haired coed and the professor, while scenes with Fanny serve as punctuation or commentary. In the first, he finds the young woman standing outside her dormitory in her bathrobe and rubber-bottomed boots, crying that her father does not love her. When she says no one loves her, he gives her a hug and gets her to safety. His thanks is a mild reprimand from the head of nonacademic services for the physical contact. Shifting to his role as student, he finds himself corrected by the professor for using a four-letter word in a theme on Faulkner. The professor corrects him while using the same word himself, trying to prove that he is no prude in these matters. The narrator sees the professor as slumming, with his working-class-chic style of dress—denoted by his ironed dungarees—and his studied, regular-guy mannerisms.

After attending, and sleeping through, Akira Kurosawa's *The Seven Samurai* (1954) with Fanny, he has two telling encounters with the professor. In the first, he lies by saying that he did kill people in Vietnam, fulfilling the professor's fantasy image of him. Then the narrator submits a brief anecdote about a character called Ralph the Duck, in which the tiny, helpless Ralph is sheltered by his mother, for an assignment called "Rhetoric and Persuasion." The professor gives him a grade of D. While they discuss the paper, the red-haired student arrives at the professor's office for what is clearly a romantic assignation. These two moments cement both the narrator's opinion of the professor and the student's credentials as a confused and misused young woman.

These matters come to a head during a winter storm, when the narrator must traverse a dangerous road to reach a quarry above campus, where the young woman has gone after taking an overdose of pills. He finds her and, with a combination of physical effort and talk, gets her to the hospital. His chief rhetorical ploy is to elaborate on his Vietnam lie in an attempt to convince her not to die. The irony is not lost on him. He also reveals that he and Fanny once had a child, thereby connecting this girl, who is someone's child, with the girl they lost. When he returns home, he and Fanny discuss what will become of the young woman when she recovers, and what her family will do for her. Fanny, who loves and even admires him despite his shortcomings, asks how he got the girl down to safety. He says he used rhetoric and persuasion, and she tells him to go in before class to get the professor to raise his grade.

*Themes and Meanings*

Despite the odd title, this story shares with many stories of the 1980's certain basic elements: the disaffected protagonist whose life is at a standstill, his shaky marriage and unhappy personal history, a significant encounter that takes him outside himself, and the movement toward knowledge of self.

The story explores a number of issues, perhaps chief among them the question of what it means to be a man in the late twentieth century and all that such a question entails: self-knowledge, communication, relationships, gender roles, heroism, parental responsibility. At the beginning of the story, the narrator seems to feel useless in his life. His marriage is rocky and his daughter is gone. He is a student on a very slow track. His military service, at the freight yards in Baltimore handling war equipment and supplies, was less than heroic. His attempts at communication, both with Fanny and in his English class, are exercises in frustration, and his hugging of the student is misinterpreted as sexual harassment. His status as a perpetual college student suggests that he has not quite arrived at full adult status, which is reinforced by his sense of failure as a parent.

Saving the young woman, then, addresses many of the narrator's needs simultaneously. Alone in her nightgown in a snowstorm, she is the orphaned waif for whom he becomes the father figure, seemingly the only adult who truly cares about her. Her predicament puts him in the role of hero, and driving up to the quarry and back constitutes heroic action, despite his matter-of-fact tone. His steed, as befits a somewhat

ironic hero, is not a white horse but a battered Ford Bronco. He must use his persuasive powers to save someone who does not wish to be saved. He also confronts the one
fact he would most like to avoid, that he and Fanny had a daughter once. The importance of that fact to him becomes clear when the local police officer tells him he has
been saying "Don't let her die" over and over like a mantra and "She better not die this
time." His daughter has already died, and he will not let this second, surrogate daughter die.

However, the narrator is a hero with limited powers. His best efforts can only accomplish so much; the miracle of restoring the girl to health falls to someone else.
Even that may be enough. In a world where the other adults—parents, administration,
the professor—have failed to care for the young woman, the love he gives her is the
only thing that can save her life. That he has reached a new stage of manhood is indicated by his improved relations with Fanny at the story's end. She is crying again, but
with understanding and love this time.

*Style and Technique*

Frederick Busch employs the contemporary realistic mode sometimes called mini-
malism: comparatively flat narrative style, first-person point of view, limited scope of
action, relatively small emotional shifts in the resolution. It is sometimes claimed that
nothing happens in these stories. At their best, however, as with this story, they demonstrate how much can be accomplished with limited material. The style of this story
is largely an outgrowth of the character of the narrator. His voice, world-weary, ironic,
and flat in the post-Hemingway manner, controls the action and the rate of revelation.
By turns funny and bitter, he recounts the events from the inside, ruling out any larger
perspective, any pretense of objectivity. He does not see what he has revealed about
himself until he has already revealed it, if then.

This method of presentation puts the emphasis squarely on the narrator and his personal development. The reader becomes aware not only of the encounters but also of
the main character's responses to them as the central issue: What does the narrator
learn? How does he change? To what extent does he grow? His restricted vocabulary
and limited verbal range stress that this story is truly his, while at the same time they
suggest other limitations that he is striving to overcome. He is not capable of taking
an Olympian view, indeed seems incapable of getting outside himself to look at
events, until he finds himself caring for someone else toward the story's end. These
minimalistic narrative elements, which can tend toward cliché in the contemporary
short story, work admirably in "Ralph the Duck" precisely because they are in the service of a character and a story that demand such a treatment.

*Thomas C. Foster*

# THE RAM IN THE THICKET

*Author:* Wright Morris (1910-1998)
*Type of plot:* Domestic realism
*Time of plot:* June 23, in a year near the end of World War II
*Locale:* A town in Pennsylvania
*First published:* 1948

> *Principal characters:*
> ROGER ORMSBY, the protagonist, a storekeeper
> VIOLET ORMSBY, his wife, whom he calls "Mother," and an
>     activist
> VIRGIL ORMSBY, their son, killed in the war, a hero

*The Story*

"The Ram in the Thicket" falls into three sections, each distinguished by the point of view assumed by the third-person narrator: In the relatively long first section, told from the point of view of Roger Ormsby, Roger awakens in the morning, prepares breakfast, and calls Violet, his wife, of whom he habitually thinks as "Mother"; in the second section, told from Mother's point of view, she arises and dresses; in the third section, which returns to Mr. Ormsby's point of view, the two of them eat breakfast and prepare to leave for the ceremony at which Mother will sponsor the USS *Ormsby*, named in honor of Virgil Ormsby, their dead son. Although the external action is slight, psychological action is dense with conflict, implication, and irony.

As the story opens, Mr. Ormsby is dreaming. He has been staring at a figure on a rise with the head of a bird; the figure is casually holding a gun, and above his extended right arm hovers an endless procession of birds. Mr. Ormsby, though his wrists are bound, reaches out to the friendly birds and with that gesture becomes free. The first thing he sees when he awakens is a photograph of his son Virgil, referred to throughout as "the boy," standing on a rise and casually holding a gun, thus identifying the boy with the figure in the dream. The gun, which he holds as though it were a part of his body, is clearly phallic.

In his waking ruminations, Mr. Ormsby recalls having, years before, given the boy a gun "because he had never had a gun himself. . . ." The boy's relationship to his gun was remarkably natural, but Mother disapproved. A founder of the League for Wild Life Conservation, she ironically stands against things natural. Though she is skilled in identifying birds, it is the boy who is, implicitly, identified with them as free, natural creatures. In sharp contrast to the boy's naturalness, Mr. Ormsby recalls that "Mother had slept the first few months of their marriage in her corset—as a precaution and as an aid to self-control." As he dresses and shaves, Mr. Ormsby thinks of Mother's obsessive neatness, which has made the house barely habitable. When the boy was young, the house was redecorated and Mother covered everything with newspaper, at which time Mr. Ormsby began having his pipe in the basement, and the boy took to the outdoors.

After tiptoeing downstairs, Mr. Ormsby begins preparing breakfast, but, when he feels a stirring in the bowels, he retires to his basement toilet, a quiet dark place that gives him the privacy he wants. Once, when the boy accidentally discovered him on the stool and said "et tu, Brutus," they laughed until their sides ached, and he felt closer to the boy than at any other time in his life. Upstairs, continuing to prepare breakfast, Mr. Ormsby is diverted again, this time by a stench from the jars of left-overs in the refrigerator that Mother will not allow him to throw away. When the boy was quite young, he went into the living room filled with Mother's guests and displayed something in a jar. Mother, suspecting a frog or something of the sort, was horrified, but after the boy announced that it had come from the icebox, she never forgave him. The moldy food is one of many images of ugliness beneath a pleasing surface, suggesting the falsity of the Ormsbys' lives and the repressions that fill their subconscious minds. Breakfast almost prepared, Mr. Ormsby calls, like an invocation, "Ohhh Mother!"

The second and much briefer section of the story shifts to Mother's point of view. She rises like a goddess, but comic incongruities undercut her grandiose pretensions: After having groped about for her corset and wriggled into it in the dark, she intones *"Fiat lux"* as she turns on the light. In the locked bathroom, she turns on the water before she sits on the stool and, when she is finished, simulates a shower, including a dampened shower cap, to cover up the flush of the toilet. Since Mr. Ormsby, as the reader has already learned, is acutely aware of her subterfuges, she ironically dramatizes what she intends to cover up.

The concluding section returns to Mr. Ormsby's point of view. In the course of breakfast, he timidly ventures an opinion. Mother at first ignores him, but, when he dares to repeat it, her mustache begins to show, and he knows that she is angry. Saying that he can go to the ceremony without her, Mother leaves him in helpless torment, but she relents. Despite her personal feelings, she explains, she has responsibilities and cannot, like some people, simply act as she pleases, which, of course, is exactly what she is doing.

### Themes and Meanings

The story explores male-female relationships in contemporary society. Mother and the boy embody antithetical attitudes and values, with Mr. Ormsby caught between his feelings of kinship with the boy and his subservience to Mother. Mother is clearly the ascendant figure in the household; moreover, she enjoys comparable social status as a community leader, indicating that her values reflect the prevailing values of society.

Mother stands for, among other things, decorum, control, and purity. Her values may have merit, but she pursues them in defiance of nature. Her unnaturalness is evident in the corset she wears to enforce sexual restraint, in elaborate subterfuges to cover up bodily functions, and in self-identification with the Diety. The boy, in contrast to Mother's prudish, sterile femininity, stands for masculinity and is associated with the out-of-doors, nature, freedom, heroism, and mortality. Just as Mother denies the flesh, the boy accepts it.

Mr. Ormsby, caught between the values embodied by Mother and by the boy, yields to Mother's power and thereby betrays his own masculinity. When the boy is killed, so is a part of Mr. Ormsby, and though it is the boy who is dead, Mr. Ormsby is not quite alive. The title, "The Ram in the Thicket," alludes to the story of Abraham and Isaac. Abraham, about to sacrifice his son Isaac in obedience to God's commandment, is spared at the last moment by an angel sent from God and offers up instead "a ram caught in a thicket" (Genesis 22:13). Mr. Ormsby worships the goddess Mother, a mortal creature who ludicrously presumes to unnatural perfection. Despite the affection he feels, he allows his son to be driven from his home and he sacrifices his own masculinity in subservience to Mother. Unlike Abraham, he will not be the father of many nations.

*Style and Technique*

To compensate for the paucity of dramatic action, Wright Morris uses a variety of stylistic devices and techniques to enrich and enliven his story. Vivid images and provocative symbols abound—guns, birds, Mother's corset, and moldy leftovers are examples—and language is dense with implication, such as Mr. Ormsby's effort "to keep the springs quiet" when he rises so as not to disturb Mother. Reversals and surprises keep the reader's attention, as when Mr. Ormsby lights a match in his basement cell to read the telegram about the boy's death and discovers Mother's hoard of illegal canned goods. Interruptions and delays create suspense, as when Mr. Ormsby is about to venture an opinion but must help with the dishes and defer to Mother's observation of a thrush before he finishes his thought. Even within sentences Morris creates suspense through interrupted constructions: "The way the boy took to the out-of-doors— he stopped looking for his cuff links, began to look for pins—was partially because he couldn't find a place in the house to sit down." The substitution of the comma for a conjunction after "links" keeps the sentence moving and is another typical stylistic device.

Much of the impact of the story is shaped by various ironic contrasts. Some, not placed in direct opposition to one another, are relatively subtle, such as Mother's creation of light in the attic in contrast to Mr. Ormsby's striking matches in his basement cell. Others are immediately apparent, as when Mother grandly writes on a notepad "*Ars longa, vita brevis*" while sitting on the toilet stool. The story repeatedly juxtaposes things natural to things unnatural, contrasts underscored by a cliché to which Mr. Ormsby has frequent recourse: "It was only natural."

*Jerome Cartwright*

# THE RANSOM OF RED CHIEF

*Author:* O. Henry (William Sydney Porter, 1862-1910)
*Type of plot:* Wit and humor
*Time of plot:* The early twentieth century
*Locale:* Summit, Alabama
*First published:* 1907

> *Principal characters:*
> SAM, the narrator
> BILL DRISCOLL, his confederate
> JOHNNY DORSET "RED CHIEF," the kidnapped boy
> EBENEZER DORSET, Johnny's father

*The Story*

The pattern of "The Ransom of Red Chief" is suggested by the first sentence of the story: "It looked like a good thing: but wait till I tell you." The story is essentially ironic; in a series of comic reversals, the expected event is replaced by its opposite. From the name of the town where the story takes place, Summit, which is perfectly flat, to the end of the story, where a fat man outruns the thin narrator, that which the narrator anticipates never does occur.

The "good thing" that Sam and Bill have planned is a kidnapping. Early in the story, they select a quiet, sleepy town, a wealthy man with an only son, and a cave where they can keep their victim. They rent a buggy and approach the small boy with the promise of candy and a buggy ride. At this point, the first reversal occurs. Instead of sweetly climbing into the buggy, Johnny Dorset hits Bill Driscoll with a brick and fights violently when the two men drag him into the buggy. Although Sam and Bill get the boy to their cave hideout, another reversal occurs while Sam is returning the buggy and walking back. During Sam's absence, the captor and the captive change roles, seemingly only in play but actually in real control of the situation. When Sam returns to the cave, he finds Bill, badly battered, playing the captured trapper to Johnny's heroic Indian, who calls himself "Red Chief." Appropriating Sam for his game, Johnny announces that Bill is to be scalped and Sam burned at the stake.

From this time on, Johnny is in power, annoying his captors with chatter and questions, keeping them from sleeping, terrifying Bill with an attempted scalping at daybreak—followed by an attack with a hot potato and later with a rock—and generally enjoying himself so much that he seems disinclined to return home. Finally, Sam mails the ransom note, but the reply makes it clear that Ebenezer Dorset recognizes his son's power. The father demands a ransom of $250 from the kidnappers, in return for which he will take Johnny back. Bill, who has already tried to send Johnny home, begs his confederate to agree, and Sam himself is now willing to pay to get rid of the child whom the con men had abducted. Johnny, however, does not wish to leave his captors. They must scheme to get him back to his father as once they had schemed to get him away from home, and finally, they must run at top speed to escape the boy who does not wish to lose his new playmates, the would-be kidnappers who have become his victims.

*Themes and Meanings*

"The Ransom of Red Chief" is not simply a story in the O. Henry tradition of surprise endings; it is also a story in the pattern of classical comedy, which assures the reader that sometimes in this world the underdog can win. Generally, however, slaves or servants, wives or lovers, have prevailed by outwitting their masters. In "The Ransom of Red Chief," the kidnappers are defeated not by any scheme devised by Johnny but simply by his nature. Johnny is, himself, the ultimate ten-year-old terror, certainly worse than most small boys his age but not so unlike them as to be a monster. Part of the humor of the story comes from Johnny's relationship to the generic ten-year-old boy. Like the generic boy, he asks questions, rambles, fantasizes, and enlists playmates. While Sam and Bill could have coped with the average ten-year-old, they are helpless in Johnny's hands because Johnny is not average. He is tougher, meaner, and wilder than the ten-year-old whom these street-smart criminals thought they were victimizing.

A second element in the underdog theme involves the city and the country. The sophisticated con men, Sam and Bill, select Summit, Alabama, for the scene of their crime because they think that the country bumpkins will be easy to fool: their law officers inept, their bloodhounds lazy, and their weekly rural newspapers ineffectual. Sam's visit to the bewhiskered, tobacco-chewing citizens of Poplar Grove is related with unconcealed contempt. However, a small rural boy and his practical father defeat the crooks without even resorting to the law or the newspapers. The implication is that just as some children are tougher than adults, some rural people are tougher than city people. Sam and Bill have erred in selecting underdogs.

They have certainly erred in casting Ebenezer Dorset as an underdog. Their original information should have warned them. The man is stingy and mean, a "mortgage-fancier," a "forecloser." However, Sam and Bill think of him only as a father, who customarily is indeed the underdog when his only child has been kidnapped. The father, however, knows his son, knows him well enough to insist that he be returned when the neighbors could not object. A tough man himself, he does not underestimate the toughness or the nastiness of his only son, a boy whom even he can control for no more than ten minutes. Furthermore, Ebenezer Dorset knows what things are worth, and he can estimate the value to the kidnappers of being relieved of Johnny.

The rural father and the rural son, then, do not need to outwit the kidnappers. They simply outwait them. To the reader's delight, the story suggests that a kidnap victim and his father can be the instruments of poetic justice, leaving the criminals both physically and financially defeated by their seeming inferiors.

*Style and Technique*

"The Ransom of Red Chief" derives from the tall tale so familiar in American humor. Ordinarily, the tall tale answers a question: "How big was the ox?" "How slow was the horse?" In this story, the question is, "How bad was the ten-year-old boy?" Thus, the tall tale simply exaggerates reality; in this case, the reality is the average ten-year-old boy, and the exaggeration is Johnny Dorset.

The narrative technique of the story is also reminiscent of the tall-tale tradition. Sam, the leading con man, speaks in the first person, as if relating his story to an audience: "Wait till I tell you," "Yes, sir, that boy seemed to be having the time of his life." He is given to malapropisms, such as "philoprogenitoveness," and to literary words, such as "sylvan" and "dastardly," which suggest that he is overreaching his real capacities, as he does in the story. However, both Sam and Bill can use the language of frontier America, too, comparing Johnny to a "welter-weight cinnamon bear" or a "two-legged skyrocket" when they choose to exaggerate, saying that Johnny has "somewhat got on my nerves," in a comic understatement.

Nor is the story without its scenes of comic pathos, all related by Sam, as when Bill apologizes for releasing Johnny, then turns to find the boy behind him and seems for a time to be losing his sanity. It is Sam who describes Bill's pleas, which finally result in a "getaway" from the kidnapped boy and in paying the "ransom" to his father.

Because the story is written in the comic tradition, it lacks the sentimentality that has dated some of O. Henry's other stories. Fusing as it does the elements of classical comedy and those of the American tall tale, "The Ransom of Red Chief" is one of the writer's most successful productions.

*Rosemary M. Canfield Reisman*

# RAPE FANTASIES

*Author:* Margaret Atwood (1939-      )
*Type of plot:* Social realism
*Time of plot:* The late twentieth century
*Locale:* Toronto, Canada
*First published:* 1975

> *Principal character:*
> ESTELLE, the naïve narrator

*The Story*

Developed through the literary device of dramatic monologue, this story presents virtually no exposition and little recognizable plot. The reader must wait patiently for tidbits of information while wading through the inane rambling utterances of a protagonist who is obviously speaking to a male not directly involved in the story.

Estelle, the narrator, undertakes her quixotic wanderings by relating an incident that took place earlier in the week. During her lunch breaks at work, she customarily spends time with her office mates—Sondra, Chrissy, and Greta—playing bridge, delving into office gossip, and commenting on the world as they see it. On this particular day their game is interrupted by a more serious matter when Chrissy alludes to a magazine article she is reading about the rape fantasies of women.

As the co-workers take turns sharing their ideas on the topic, Estelle grows more critical not only of their perceptions of rape and rapists but also of each of the other women. She appears to be unaware, however, that through her derogatory descriptions of them, she is disclosing her own underlying insecurity, envy, and frustration.

After recapping her version of the remembered conversation, Estelle launches into the particulars of her own fantasies and it is at this point that the character becomes more fully rounded. She seems convinced—or is attempting to convince her current implied listener—that she is capable of thwarting any potential attacker and that, ultimately, through reason and care, she can touch the core of the rapist and permanently convert him. In viewing herself as a defender of the downtrodden and redeemer of the disillusioned, Estelle unveils her need for control over her own life.

In one imagined encounter, she is approached on a darkened street by a strange, physically repulsive man. Rather than experiencing fear or feeling traumatized in this fantasy, Estelle empathizes with the attacker and expresses genuine pity for his unattractiveness. She takes control by recommending that he visit her dermatologist.

In another such imaginary tryst, Estelle is lying in bed with a cold as her potential rapist climbs through a window. Ironically, he also has a cold and they blissfully share a box of tissue. In her third and most farfetched daydream, Estelle attempts to discourage an attack by telling the rapist she has leukemia. Naturally, in her limited scope, the attacker has been similarly diagnosed, and they move in together and fantasize about funeral arrangements.

Even in her most frightening fantasy—a devil-possessed man who enters her mother's house through a basement coal chute—Estelle is triumphant in outwitting the rapist and in saving herself. This is the most intriguing scenario of her presentation, for not only is she moderately frightened for once, the scene possibly symbolizes her psychic makeup. (The psychoanalytic school of literary criticism might interpret her fear as springing from her seeing the villain penetrating an opening not intended for his use; while the feminist perspective could ascribe the feeling to the violation of the perceived safety of her mother's house.)

*Themes and Meanings*

In most of Margaret Atwood's fiction, a female protagonist is presented as a victim, typically of a male-dominated lifestyle or of a sociopolitical patriarchal order. "Rape Fantasies" is no exception in drawing this portrait of the female as victim; however, in this story, Atwood deviates from her standard mode of repressed heroine. Estelle is a victim of her own naïveté, convinced that she is capable of trusting or managing those persons who dwell within her limited frame of reference and that she is equipped to handle whatever situations might arise from such associations.

The author paints Estelle's character into a vaguely defined landscape that the reader can only surmise is a singles' bar or comparable locale, and peoples it with a solitary, unidentified male listener. Due to the first-person narration and the monologue style of delivery, the reader is exposed to a limited, likely unreliable, reality— that of Estelle and her delusions of competence and control.

Perhaps the most interesting aspect of the story is what is left unwritten—that of Estelle's enigmatic listener and his reaction to her mindless diatribe. From subtle hints, one can assume he is a person Estelle wishes to impress, but the story offers no closure and the reader can only guess at his perceptions and the ultimate outcome.

The central character drifts through her own fictions, firmly believing that rape is something that could happen only to someone else and that if she is incorrect in that assumption, she could reason with a potential attacker and avert the actual act. She takes this warped logic one step further to place her fantasized self in the role of savior, noting that once the imagined rapist is within her logical powers, she can then convert him to a goodly person, convince him to repent, and possibly manage to make him fall in love with her.

The need for control is a major theme in this story. Through her fantasies, Estelle seeks to manipulate her environment and to exert control over her mundane life, her vapid acquaintances, and her apparent alienation. Underlying this will to control lurks a secondary theme, which graphically illustrates how little humans, and women in particular, are aware of their own vulnerability and to what lengths many are willing to go to avoid a lonely, isolated existence.

Although the references are not always blatant, Atwood habitually touches on feminist issues in her work. It would seem, on first reading, that "Rape Fantasies" is an exception; however, on digging deeper, one can identify the locus of emptiness, isolation, and desperation that defines many of Atwood's other female protagonists. Thus, a victim is still a victim regardless of the cause of her victimization. Although much of the barrenness and despair in the life of this character originates from within Estelle herself, it is heightened by her perceived hostile environment and her friend-less plunge into the group-dominated universe of the city.

Estelle is an antiheroine, a character who proselytizes through negative example. Even though her monologue is replete with flashes of anecdotal wit, the reader soon discovers this to be a feeble attempt by the protagonist at being a clever conversationalist and that she is, at heart, deadly serious and likely devoid of humor. The story is open-ended; however, it is an easy task to envision the character being sucked into the blackened lungs of the city, desperately seeking companionship and compassion, procuring love in places where it is least likely to exist, and of arriving, still alone but no longer naïve, at a negative, embittered end. Regardless of her assertion of her own humanity in the concluding paragraph, Estelle is never fully developed as an individual imbued with the strength and conviction to carry on. In spite of her own innocent and misdirected beliefs, she is no survivor.

## Style and Technique

The predominant literary technique employed in "Rape Fantasies" is borrowed from the realm of poets and playwrights. Atwood employs a dramatic monologue, wherein one speaker relates information to an implied listener who does not participate in the action. Used successfully by such classic poets as Robert Browning and T. S. Eliot, the dramatic monologue tends to reveal facets of the speaker that she or he may assume are hidden. By describing others in a negative vein or by unconscious slips of the tongue, the protagonist lifts her mask and permits a view of her truest self.

Stylistically, "Rape Fantasies" illustrates the literary tenet that the reader cannot and should not completely trust the reliability of a first-person narrator in her depiction of events or interpretations of behavior. Although Estelle is not mad, as many first-person narrators tend to be, she is certainly self-absorbed, and her narration is filtered through her own pathetic perceptual screen. She is never less credible than when she proclaims, "I'm being totally honest."

Another mark of Atwood's fiction is her creation of landscapes, such as the horrendous futuristic milieu of Offred in *The Handmaid's Tale* (1985) or the constricted, myopic anorexia of Marian in *The Edible Woman* (1969). The landscapes, although consciously penned, tend to register in the unconscious and, consequently, to haunt the reader long after her work is finished. The landscape in this story is not as vividly drawn as that in some others, but one gets an uneasy sense of the drab office, the dreary bar, and the hungry city eager to consume yet another witless victim.

Regardless of one's final assessment of Estelle and the apparent fact that her current and consequent problems spring from her own beliefs and actions, one is left asking "What if ?" That, according to Flannery O'Connor, is the mark of good fiction.

*Joyce Duncan*

# RAPPACCINI'S DAUGHTER

*Author:* Nathaniel Hawthorne (1804-1864)
*Type of plot:* Gothic
*Time of plot:* The late eighteenth century
*Locale:* Padua, Italy
*First published:* 1844

*Principal characters:*
GIOVANNI GUASCONTI, the protagonist, a student at the University of Padua
DAME LISABETTA, his landlady
DR. GIACOMO RAPPACCINI, a scientist and physician
BEATRICE RAPPACCINI, his daughter
DR. PIETRO BAGLIONI, a professor of medicine at the University of Padua

*The Story*

A young man named Giovanni rents a room in an old edifice belonging to a family whose ancestor was listed among the sufferers in Dante's *Inferno*. It looks down on a luxuriant inner garden belonging to a neighbor, Dr. Rappaccini. The garden is brilliant with exotic blooms, the most spectacular, a shrub growing by a ruined fountain. It is covered with rich purple blossoms. Dr. Rappaccini often tends the garden, but he is always protected by heavy gloves and sometimes a face mask. His lovely daughter, Beatrice, takes no such precautions, however, and she is the only one who touches the handsome plant with the purple blooms. She tends it as though it were a beloved sister.

Giovanni has a letter of introduction to a Dr. Pietro Baglioni, a professor of medicine at the university, who once knew his father. Dr. Baglioni warns him to keep away from Rappaccini, a brilliant scientist but one inclined to sacrifice anything and anyone to his scientific experiments. He is an expert in poisons and is known to have developed new varieties of herbs more poisonous than those in nature.

Such information lends substance to Giovanni's lurid imaginings about the garden and the girl. He had once thrown her a bouquet that had seemed to wilt the moment she picked it up. He also fancied that a butterfly that hovered close to her face had died suddenly in midflight.

These forebodings do not prevent him from entering the garden when his landlady, Lisabetta, offers to show him a secret door into the inner courtyard. Beatrice comes out to meet him, and they are drawn to each other immediately. When he asks for a blossom from the shrub at the ruined fountain and reaches out to pluck it, Beatrice cries out in alarm, seizes his hand, and warns him never to touch it. The next morning, the place where she grasped his hand is painful and inflamed.

Giovanni continues to visit Beatrice, until he notices with horror that flowers will no longer remain fresh in his own hands. As an experiment, he exhales a long breath on a spider that is industriously weaving a web in his room: The spider curls up and dies immediately. Tortured now by fear and resentment, Giovanni paces the streets of Padua, where Dr. Baglioni sees him and divines the reason for his distraction. Dr. Baglioni brings him a silver vial containing an antidote that was originally created to counteract the poisons of the Borgias. He instructs Giovanni to give the antidote to Beatrice to counteract the deadly fumes in which she has lived.

When Beatrice again calls from the garden, he goes down to her with hatred and resentment in his heart, instead of love. He curses her for contaminating him with her poison. Beatrice is crushed by his cruel words, having always assumed that he was safe so long as he did not touch her or the flowers. He accuses her of deliberately trapping him to share in her isolation from the world. This she passionately denies, "I dreamed only to love thee and be with thee a little time, and so let thee pass away . . . ; for Giovanni, believe it, though my body be nourished with poison, my spirit is God's creature and craves love as its daily food."

Giovanni is somewhat mollified and tells her of the antidote that Dr. Baglioni provided. Perhaps they can both escape the garden. Beatrice agrees, but adds emphatically, "I will drink; but do thou wait the result." She does so and dies at the feet of Giovanni and her father.

*Themes and Meanings*

This parable of the Fall from innocence in a poisonous garden of Eden has several levels of meaning, not all of them explicitly stated. The Eden analogy is certainly clear, and one may assume that the garden, with its ruined fountain, is in some sense a microcosm of the fallen world cursed by sin and death. Perhaps it is the world that might ensue if scientists value knowledge and power more than human love.

Nathaniel Hawthorne suggested in other stories as well, such as "The Birthmark" and "The Great Carbuncle," that the scientist in his intellectual pride might destroy the natural blessings that God has provided. This sentiment was a fairly common one at the time. The technique of grafting plants was recently discovered and widely distrusted as an impious if not dangerous interference with God's intentions. While such processes seem innocent enough today, readers may certainly recognize the "mad scientist" motif still popular in science fiction.

The imagery of the story, however, is primarily religious and moral. Granted Rappaccini's malevolent impact, Giovanni falls from grace not entirely through the machinations of a satanic scientist. To be sure, the young man seems to have been lured deliberately into the garden by the doctor, not by Beatrice herself, to serve as a companion for the isolated girl. He falls not because of Beatrice's evil nature, but because of his own shallow capacity for love. Giovanni's shortcomings in the face of an admittedly tainted world are repeatedly suggested: "His love grew thin and faint as the morning mist," "that cunning semblance of love which flourishes in the imagination, but strikes no depth of root into the heart." Before he descends to the garden on the last occasion, he mutters venomously, "She is the only being whom my breath may not slay! Would that it might!" Given this preliminary evidence of Giovanni's malice, the dying words of Beatrice ring true: "Farewell, Giovanni! Thy words of hatred are like lead within my heart; but they, too, will fall away as I ascend. Oh, was there not, from the first, more poison in thy nature than in mine?"

If Beatrice, unlike Giovanni, is innocent of malice, that sin most damned in Dante's *Inferno*, the moral status of Dr. Baglioni, giver of the antidote that kills, is most ambiguous. Dr. Baglioni stands in a godlike position above the garden in the closing scene calling down his judgment from the balcony: "Rappaccini! Rappaccini! and is this the upshot of your experiment!" That would seem to reflect God's moral indignation, except that Dr. Baglioni is also suspect as harboring considerable malice for Rappaccini as a professional rival. Moreover, there is a distinct implication that Dr. Baglioni knew that his antidote would kill, not cure, Rappaccini's daughter. This ambiguity may suggest simply that the real world of Dr. Baglioni and the untested Giovanni is already contaminated, or it may suggest that God himself, who created a garden with the foreknowledge of humankind's fall, is somehow implicated in the sin and death that inevitably follow.

*Style and Technique*

This story is obviously replete with literary symbols, some of them pointing in seemingly opposite directions. Although the function of Beatrice suggests Eve, often blamed for Adam's fall, her name recalls that other Beatrice who rescued Dante from sin and escorted him into Heaven.

If one looks at the story from the viewpoint of Freudian psychology, one might suspect that the "original sin" of this virginal Eve is simply her inborn sexuality and the "original sin" (though not the final sin) of Giovanni is plain lust. One might even imagine that the lethal, purple plant so close to the fountain of life might signify, in dream language, the female sexual parts that he must not touch. Nowhere is that inelegant word "lust" used, yet the description of his obsession seems to convey it:

> She had at least instilled a fierce and subtle poison into his system. It was not love, although her rich beauty was a madness to him; nor horror, even while he fancied her spirit to be imbued with the same baleful essence that seemed to pervade her physical frame; but a wild offspring of both love and horror that had each parent in it and burned like one and shivered like the other.

Seldom has the forbidden term "lust" been evoked in such rich and gothic prose.

The deliberate mention of Dante at the beginning, the viewpoint of Giovanni from his balcony looking down as into a pit, the poisonous vapors presumably arising from it, all suggest the ledge overlooking deepest Hell where Dante and Vergil discussed the different degrees of sin, beginning with lust and ending with malice and betrayal.

However, at the bottom of this pit, at the center, is not Lucifer, or even Rappaccini, presumably his agent, but a fountain. There is no evidence that the water itself is polluted. Beatrice's innocent spirit is several times likened to a fountain:

> Many a holy and passionate outgush of her heart, when the pure fountain has been unsealed from its depths and made visible in its transparency to his mental eye; recollections that, had Giovanni known how to estimate them, would have assured him that all this ugly mystery was but an earthly illusion.

Thus, the traditional association between evil and physical nature, magnified in the story, may seem real or illusory, depending on the purity of the human heart.

*Katherine Snipes*

# RASHŌMON

*Author:* Ryūnosuke Akutagawa (Ryūnosuke Niihara, 1892-1927)
*Type of plot:* Fable
*Time of plot:* The late twelfth century
*Locale:* Kyoto, Japan
*First published:* 1915 (English translation, 1930)

*Principal characters:*
AN UNEMPLOYED SERVANT
AN OLD WOMAN

*The Story*

In "Rashōmon," Ryūnosuke Akutagawa depicts the plight of an out-of-work servant who ponders his fate at Rashōmon, the gate of a dilapidated building in twelfth century Kyoto. The servant knows, or believes, that in order to survive he must resort to theft, but he is at first reluctant to steal. In the course of the story, however, his encounter with an old woman, herself a thief, causes him to change his mind, or it enables him to rationalize resorting to theft as a way of life. His decision to steal is undoubtedly influenced not only by the unsettled times, but also by the deathly atmosphere of Rashōmon. It was precisely that setting that appealed to Akira Kurosawa, the film director who used Rashōmon to convey a sense of corruption and decay in his film *Rashōmon* (1950), which has as its sources not only Akutagawa's "Rashōmon," but also his "In a Grove."

Rashōmon, with its peeling paint and weather-beaten pillars, serves as a symbol for the ruins of Kyoto, which has been plagued by a series of disasters such as earthquakes, fires, tornadoes, and famines. The gate has become a refuge for wild animals and thieves, a depository for unclaimed bodies, and a haunt for crows, which feed off the bodies. In this gloomy setting—it is dusk, and a steady rain is falling—a dismissed servant thinks about his future and reluctantly concludes that if he is to survive he must steal. In an effort to find better shelter from the rain and the cold he climbs a ladder into the loft, where he sees a light. As he approaches the light, he sees that it is held by an old woman, who is pulling the hair out of the head of one of the decaying corpses.

As he watches the woman, the servant grows increasingly angry and self-righteous until he finally gains the courage to confront her. Sword in hand, he springs into the loft, blocks the woman's escape, asks her what she is doing, and throws her to the floor of the loft. When he realizes that she is at his mercy, he assures her that he is not a police officer and again demands to know what she is doing in the corpse-filled loft. This time she gasps out the answer that she uses the hair to make wigs. The woman, who fears for her life, desperately tries to justify her action by stating that she is sure that the dead would not mind her taking their hair, and then she adds that the woman before her had committed the crime of selling snakes as dried fish. Comparing her crime with the dead woman's, the old woman explains that no "wrong" was involved since both would have starved otherwise and that both consequently had no choice. She ends by reiterating her belief that the dead woman would forgive her.

The old woman's justification of her actions ironically serves in turn to justify the servant's decision to steal from her because he, too, would otherwise starve. He rips off her kimono, flings her among the corpses, and flees into the night and into obscurity. After he leaves, the old woman recovers, crawls to the loft ladder, and stares into the darkness.

### Themes and Meanings

In "Rashōmon," Akutagawa probes the subtle relationship between setting and character. Twelfth century Kyoto becomes an emblem for desolation, decay, and death: The entire city has been plagued by natural disasters (earthquakes, tornadoes, and fires) and by famine, but the spiritual "famine" is no less important. In order to survive (and the story concerns the conflict between morality and survival), people have smashed the Buddhist icons and sold the pieces for firewood. In effect, then, Akutagawa indicates that in desperate situations people not only abandon morality but also use and exploit it as they would any other material at hand. Given his need to survive, the servant who steals the kimono is merely acting as the townspeople have acted.

Set against this general picture of physical and spiritual desolation is Rashōmon, which represents the entire city. With its peeling paint and weather-beaten pillars, the dilapidated structure serves as a haven for wild animals and thieves and as a repository for unclaimed corpses. The only other visitors are the crows, which feed on the dead bodies. Thus, in his description of the gate, Akutagawa has provided images of decay, immorality, and predatory behavior. The crows prey on the dead bodies; the old woman preys on dead bodies; the dead woman had preyed on her customer; the servant preys on the old woman—all in the name of survival. (In fact, the servant's dismissal may have been caused by his master's need to survive financially.)

Other negative images pervade Akutagawa's description of Rashōmon: the overgrown tall weeds, the crumbling stone steps, and the white bird droppings—all attest Kyoto's decline, so widespread that the servant's dismissal seems trivial by comparison. In fact, the individual seems insignificant against the backdrop of physical, cultural, and moral bankruptcy. Adding to the general gloom are the dusk, with its associations of death and ambiguity, and the steady rain, which has forced the servant to seek shelter. In one sentence, Akutagawa combines the dusk and rain with a sense of the ominous: "As evening descended, a low cloud, dark and foreboding, loomed heavily above the corner rooftiles."

Because the setting is so negatively described, the servant is understandably pessimistic about his fate. Cold, wet, and hungry, he has no prospects of gaining employment and can see only his impending death, unless he resorts to theft. Stealing is, he believes, the "only way out," but he cannot "bring himself to do it," primarily because of his weakness: He is a coward who quickly resolves to steal but lacks the will or courage to do it. Because he fears the dead, he clutches the sword at his side; it is only when he sees the old woman, not a strong young man, that he decides to "summon his strength" and attack her. Before he can act, however, he must abhor the old woman's action so that he can rationalize his action as being motivated by principle. The author thereby establishes the servant as a weak person who seeks both a suitable victim and a justification for his crime. In effect, while the setting does provide a backdrop against which his action seems consistent, the servant does have a choice and cannot evade responsibility for his actions by comparing his crime to the old woman's or her victim's.

*Style and Technique*

In the course of the story, Akutagawa uses imagery not only to establish the setting, but also to portray his characters. The servant is first compared to the lone cricket, which "clings" to the pillar but later abandons his "perch"—much like the fleeing servant. When he climbs up the loft ladder, the servant is "quiet as a lizard" and stealthy "as a cat." He fears that his corpse will be thrown into the loft as would a "stray dog's." The old woman's arm is like a chicken's, and she is twice compared to a monkey. Through his imagery, Akutagawa suggests that these two characters have forsaken their humanity and have become caught up in a struggle for survival. When he describes the old woman's eyes as being those of a "bird of prey," he also ties the characters to the crows that prey on the dead.

Even though such imagery does not present the characters favorably, Akutagawa treats the old woman and the servant with light irony: The author is rather condescending, but he is not harsh or contemptuous of the thieves. For the most part, Akutagawa uses the third-person point of view but filters much of the story through the mind of the servant. On the other hand, the narrator occasionally editorializes about the servant so that his audience will not have any doubts about the servant's motives or his self-deception. The narrator uses the phrases "in fact" and "the truth is that" when he first discusses the servant's desperate plight. When the servant grows increasingly angry with the old woman's theft from the dead, he is being a hypocrite, for he has already decided to steal to survive. The narrator points out the hypocrisy: "He had, of course, already forgotten that only a few minutes earlier he himself had made up his mind to become a thief." From this point on the narrator suggests that the servant, knowing he controls the situation, manipulates his emotions in order to justify his actions: "His hatred returned, only this time he controlled it." When he uses the old woman's rationalization, the servant joins her in the predatory behavior symbolized by the crows and encouraged by the setting of death and decay. The servant's moral decay is his inner corruption, which is mirrored by his physical corruption and affliction: On his cheek there is a festering pimple that oozes "red pus." Until he finds the rationalization he seeks, the servant picks at his cheek; he uses that same hand to steal from the old woman when he is finally free of nagging moral scruples.

*Thomas L. Erskine*

# RAYMOND'S RUN

*Author:* Toni Cade Bambara (Miltona Mirkin Cade, 1939-1995)
*Type of plot:* Social realism
*Time of plot:* The 1960's
*Locale:* Harlem, New York City
*First published:* 1971

> *Principal characters:*
> HAZEL ELIZABETH DEBORAH PARKER, a young girl better known
> as Squeaky
> RAYMOND, her mildly retarded brother
> GRETCHEN, her rival on the track
> CYNTHIA, a classmate

*The Story*

The first-person narrator, Hazel Elizabeth Deborah Parker, known as Squeaky, is a young girl growing up in the Harlem section of New York City. Squeaky prides herself on her performance on the track and her ability to care for her mildly retarded brother Raymond.

A little girl with skinny arms and a high-pitched voice, Squeaky is a self-confident, cocky youngster who boasts that everyone knows she is the fastest thing on two feet. Squeaky takes her running seriously; she is not afraid to practice high stepping out on the street where anyone can see her. She is also a responsible and caring child. Although Raymond is actually older, Squeaky thinks of him as her little brother because he is less bright than she is. She is proud of her ability to care for him, protecting him from the taunts and threats of other children.

The May Day celebration in the park includes a race, but the most important event is the maypole dancing. Squeaky has refused to participate because she is uncomfortable getting all dressed up in a white dress and shoes to dance. She is a practical girl who describes herself as "a poor Black girl who really can't afford to buy shoes and a new dress you only wear once." She is there to compete in the track meet. Secure in her identity as a runner, she explains that she uses her feet for running, not dancing.

Squeaky's main competition is a new girl, Gretchen Lewis, whom Squeaky has tried to size up on the basis of a few brief contacts. When Gretchen smiles at Squeaky during one of their encounters, Squeaky does not think it is a real smile, because, in her opinion, girls never really smile at each other. As Squeaky checks out her rival on the day of the race, she notices that Gretchen kicks her legs out like a pro, and she begins to look at Gretchen with respect.

As she crouches down waiting for the crack of the pistol to start the race, she notices that Raymond is on the other side of the fence "bending down with his fingers on the ground just like he knew what he was doing." As she runs, Squeaky glances over to watch her brother running on the sidelines. He runs in a unique style, with his palms tucked up behind him, but Squeaky sees that he has the potential to be a good runner. She remembers that he always keeps up with her when she trots around the neighborhood.

When the race ends, Squeaky is thinking of how she could give up her own career as a runner to concentrate on coaching Raymond, rather than listening for the announcement of the winner. Because she already has a room full of trophies and ribbons, and Raymond has nothing, she thinks that she could help him get some recognition as a runner. Squeaky changes as she shifts her attention from herself to her brother. As she hears her name announced as the winner, she is already focusing on Raymond's future. Although Raymond was not actually in the race, this was really his run.

When Squeaky realizes that winning is not everything, she sees Gretchen in a new light, as a person who also works hard to achieve her goals. She looks at her former rival with new respect, thinking that perhaps Gretchen is the type of person who would help coach Raymond. The story ends with Squeaky and Gretchen exchanging a big smile of respect that is "about as real a smile as girls can do for each other, considering we don't practice real smiling every day."

## Themes and Meanings

"Raymond's Run" first appeared in 1971 in *Tales and Stories for Black Folks*, and was published in *Redbook* in June, 1971. In her works, Toni Cade Bambara seeks to portray the positive side of African American family life and the strengths of the African American community. In discussing her work, Bambara has said, "I work to tell the truth about people's lives; I work to celebrate struggle, to applaud the tradition of struggle in our community, to bring to center stage all those characters, just ordinary folks on the block . . . characters we thought we had to ignore because they weren't pimp-flashy or hustler-slick or because they didn't fit easily into previously acceptable modes or stock types."

In "Raymond's Run," Bambara portrays a child's world with sensitivity and understanding. Squeaky engages the reader's interest because she allows the reader to see this world through her eyes. She is spunky and outspoken, tough, sassy, and bright, with a big reputation, but she is also a responsible and caring person. Other children in the story serve to further define Squeaky's character. She is a hard worker and not ashamed of it. In contrast, her classmate Cynthia does not want anyone to know how hard she works. Cynthia practices the piano at home, but at school acts surprised that she is able to play Chopin waltzes. On the other hand, Gretchen, like Squeaky, is an honest competitor, who takes running seriously.

The story is set in the streets and parks of Harlem, the area in which Bambara herself grew up. Bambara places the action on specific streets as her characters race down Amsterdam Avenue, stroll down Broadway, and prance down 34th Street. Squeaky knows that she must be on guard, and survives in the neighborhood because she is always ready to protect herself and Raymond. This is a place where people may take

Raymond's allowance or ask where he got "that great big pumpkin head." Squeaky does not go in for chitchat; she says she would rather "just knock you down right from the jump and save everybody a lot of precious time."

Another characteristic of Bambara's fiction is her portrayal of different generations interacting within a neighborhood. Squeaky's neighborhood is peopled with characters of all ages. Old people sit in the sun "getting upset with the pigeons fluttering around them, scattering their newspapers and upsetting the wax-paper lunches in their laps." Parents come to the park wearing corsages and breast-pocket handkerchiefs. Young men with baseball caps on backwards lean against the fence twirling basketballs on their fingertips.

Bambara's characters typically are decent people who care about each other and respect other people for their unique contributions. Squeaky accepts Raymond for what he is, cares for him, and enjoys his company. For example, when she studies for her spelling test, she asks Raymond to quiz her even though it slows her down. She realizes that this builds his confidence, and believes that helping each other is important. Later in the story, she looks beyond his mental limitations to see his potential as a runner and vows to help him succeed.

*Style and Technique*

Bambara uses a first-person narrator to show the neighborhood through the eyes of a child. Use of the present tense creates a sense of immediacy. Bambara's choice of words, sentence structure, and manner of expression are all simple. Of the thirteen sentences that make up the first two paragraphs, six begin with "and" and three begin with "but." The result is a colloquial style appropriate for the young narrator. The young characters speak in the language of the playground with all its vitality and humor. The children banter and exchange insults, referring to other children as "Fatso," "her freckle-face self," or "Mary Louise Williams of Raggedy Town, Baltimore," and call Mr. Pearson "Jack and the Beanstalk."

Bambara paints her characters with a few deft strokes. Squeaky's father is described as a "thirty-five-year-old man stuffing himself into a PAL pair of shorts" to race his daughter down Amsterdam Avenue. He gives her a "two-hydrant head start" and runs "with his hands in his pockets and whistling." Cynthia clutches "the lace on her blouse like it was a narrow escape." Mr. Pearson, with his clipboard, cards, and whistles, is both a symbol of authority and an object of ridicule. Bambara speaks of the "high standards our community has regarding verbal performance." Surely, the language of "Raymond's Run" meets those standards.

*Judith Barton Williamson*

# THE REAL THING

*Author:* Henry James (1843-1916)
*Type of plot:* Social realism
*Time of plot:* The 1890's
*Locale:* London
*First published:* 1892

> *Principal characters:*
> THE NARRATOR, an artist
> MAJOR and MRS. MONARCH, a middle-aged couple who want to
> be models
> ORONTE and
> MISS CHURM, professional models

*The Story*

An artist is visited one day in his studio by a middle-aged couple, Major and Mrs. Monarch. At first the artist assumes that they have come to commission a portrait, but he soon learns that they want, instead, to pose as paid models. He observes that the Monarchs, though on the edge of poverty, are an eminently respectable pair, well-mannered, immaculately poised—in effect, as their name suggests, the very embodiment of taste, refinement, and class.

Hoping that they might prove ideal subjects for a series of illustrations he is engaged in creating for a publisher, the artist agrees to hire them, though their very authenticity causes him to have vague misgivings. They are the "real thing," but they are still amateurs, and the artist is more confident of his ability to work with his professional models, Oronte and Miss Churm.

Miss Churm is an ill-mannered cockney who "couldn't spell and loved beer" but who can represent anything from an aristocrat to a beggar. The artist regards her as an excellent model. As for Oronte, he is an Italian vagrant who found his way to the artist's studio and who has become as good a model, in the artist's eyes, as Miss Churm. He is, the narrator relates, as good at posing as an Englishman as Miss Churm is as an Italian.

Against these two, the Monarchs must compete for the artist's favor, though at first they assume that their own credentials as aristocrats will be warrant enough for their success. Try as he might, however, the artist cannot do anything with them. He draws Mrs. Monarch many times, in many ways, always failing to capture what he wants. With Major Monarch the situation is worse, his representation being always gigantic and out of scale. Eventually the artist manages several drawings with both husband and wife and sends them to the publisher for approval.

Meanwhile, a fellow artist and friend of the narrator has returned from Paris, where he has studied some of the great works and where he has, as the narrator says, "gotten a fresh eye." Viewing some of the artist's illustrations with the Monarchs as models, the friend expresses his disapproval. The artist insists that the illustrations are good, but his friend counsels him to get rid of the models or risk his career.

Despite his friend's remonstrances, the artist continues to keep the Monarchs as models, not so much out of respect for their gentility as out of compassion for their impoverishment. Ultimately the artist rejects them by working exclusively with Oronte and Miss Churm. "I can't be ruined for you," he tells the major, petulantly.

In a final humiliation, the Monarchs plead for a position, even offering to act as servants. For almost a week the artist keeps them on, but in the end, saddened by their failure, he pays them off and never sees them again.

## Themes and Meanings

"The Real Thing" is an extraordinarily subtle work demanding, like much of the work of Henry James, sensitivity and perceptiveness from the reader. The theme, one of James's recurring preoccupations, is the artist's honest struggle with his material, a struggle to render a subject in all of its multifaceted meaning. The Monarchs are the real thing, but their very authenticity, their very perfection is somehow not enough for the artist to capture. As the ideal, they are easily recognizable yet just as elusive. The artist's struggle to paint them ends in failure because, though it is the nature of art to be always striving for perfection, on the human level of the artist, it must always miss— perfection being beyond human attainment.

In this sense, "The Real Thing" is suggestive of a short story by Nathaniel Hawthorne, a writer whom James admired and about whom he published one of the first critical studies (1879). In that Hawthorne story, "The Artist of the Beautiful," Owen Warfield—whose name signifies the artist's dilemma, the warfare between ideality and reality—strives for the perfection of his art, but in the struggle destroys his creation. So too, in "The Real Thing," the artist is unable to capture fully what the Monarchs are and must turn them away, although, as he says, he was happy "to have paid the price—for the memory."

In this sense, too, the characters of Oronte and Miss Churm amplify the meaning. Unlike the Monarchs, they are not the aesthetic ideal, but the mundanely real, the concrete, the actual; these qualities the artist is most successful in dealing with. The question becomes, then, whether the artist's achievement is in the ability to capture the ideal on its own terms, or, rather, is in the ability to shape phenomena into a form that merely suggests or approaches the ideal. Significantly, the artist in James's story is engaged in a series of illustrations for a magazine called *Cheapside*, a wonderfully apt appellation, connotative of quality as well as locale: The artist is a commercial success; he is becoming popular and is fearful for his reputation. Pursuit of the Monarchs (as Owen Warfield's invention was a mechanical butterfly) means failure. Working comfortably, risk-free, with his professional models ensures success in the marketplace. He is, in this light, a second-rate artist, having, in his own words, "an innate preference for the represented subject over the real one."

Finally, a second theme runs simultaneously along with that of the artist's struggle with his material: the demise of the aristocratic class in a society more and more fluid, increasingly amenable to the rising lower orders who make things work. The Monarchs can be seen as anachronisms, unable in their effete gentility to compete with the aggressive versatility of the worldly middle class. So ill-equipped are they for survival in the society of shifting values that they fail even at being domestics, unable even to serve where once they were so obviously served.

Oscar Wilde perceived the decay of the aristocracy in his brilliant comedy of the same period, *The Importance of Being Earnest: A Trivial Comedy for Serious People* (1895), in which aristocratic drawing-room manners and life-styles are parodied into absurdity. In one scene, for example, Lady Bracknell sums up her nephew's attributes thus: "He looks everything but has nothing." If the same could be said of the Monarchs, it is a declaration less humorous and more pitiful.

## Style and Technique

Published a few years before the great novels of James's so-called late style, characterized by rhetorical complexity, "The Real Thing" is interesting as an example of its author's successful use of the "popular" style to convey the more serious meanings already discussed.

The story moves quickly, gracefully, with an elegant, precise prose recalling the sparkle of James's earlier works such as *Daisy Miller* (1879) and *The Portrait of a Lady* (1881). The first-person narration is successful in establishing a central point of view—James's trademark—while maintaining the lively, spontaneous tone. Additionally, by allowing the artist to speak for himself, James brings his dilemma into sharper focus, making it a personal drama rather than a dry monologue or a mere critique of aesthetic theory disguised as a story. The artist's personality is keenly felt—his wit, his compassion, even his delusion of someday capturing the real thing.

Finally, and characteristically, the story is marked by an intriguing use of names, an almost Dickensian exuberance and unabashed simplicity. The name "Monarch" is obviously suggestive. So, too, is the grossly discordant "Churm" and the shallow flashiness of "Oronte." The name of the artist's friend, Claude Rivet, suggests the iron-bound commercialism by which the Monarchs are judged. Even the title of the novel for which the artist is providing illustrations, *Rutland Ramsey*, suggests a mild parody of James's own first novel of artists in Rome, *Roderick Hudson* (1876).

*Edward Fiorelli*

# A REASONABLE FACSIMILE

*Author:* Jean Stafford (1915-1979)
*Type of plot:* Sketch
*Time of plot:* The mid-twentieth century
*Locale:* Adams, Colorado, a fictional composite of the towns of Boulder and Colorado Springs
*First published:* 1957

> *Principal characters:*
> DR. WOLFGANG BOHRMANN, a graciously aging philosopher, a retired academic, a prodigious correspondent, and an uncommonly generous man
> MRS. PRITCHARD, Dr. Bohrmann's loyal housekeeper
> HENRY MEDLEY, the insufferable interloper, the uninvited and protracted houseguest of his intellectual mentor Dr. Bohrmann
> GRIMALKIN, the ginger cat, lord of the manor
> HEDDA BOHRMANN, Dr. Bohrmann's deceased but fondly remembered wife

*The Story*

"Change is the only stimulus," insists Dr. Wolfgang Bohrmann on retiring from a career of teaching at Nevilles College in Adams, Colorado. Instead of resigning himself to spending the remainder of his allotted years in quiet retirement, Dr. Bohrmann embarks on a variety of engrossing pursuits, not the least of which is having a new house built for himself, a "house of tomorrow—cantilevered, half-glass—six miles out on the prairies." From his position on one of the house's many decks, the enthusiastic professor emeritus can command an expansive view of the Rocky Mountains and the ever-changing panorama of cloud and sky: "there dark rain, here blinding sunshine, yonder a sulphurous dust storm, haze on the summit of one peak, a pillow of cloud concealing a second, hyaline light on the glacier of a third."

From his aerielike perch, Dr. Bohrmann inhales the invigorating air of freedom; loosed from his career bonds, he is free to explore the numerous hobbies that intrigue his curious mind. A man of wide-ranging interests, he occupies his time studying Japanese, learning the art of engraving, exploring the mysteries of mycology, and growing Persian melons. Having carved his own private space within a landscape that he loves, Dr. Bohrmann is not prepared for the sudden arrival of a young easterner, Henry Medley, who informs the old gentleman of his intention to pay him a prolonged visit so that the two may get to know each other personally after having corresponded for some years. Dr. Bohrmann, astonished at the prospect of having a houseguest ("not through any want of hospitality but because it was a matter that had never arisen"), nevertheless rallies to the occasion and has his housekeeper, Mrs. Pritchard, prepare the spare room for his visitor.

The ubiquitous Mrs. Pritchard, "shaped like a pear" and having "a blue mustache under a fleshy and ferocious bill," harbors a deep suspicion that the arrival of the professor's disciple may not be a very pleasant event. Indeed, when Henry Medley, true to his name, unloads his gear from the taxi (a pup tent, a portable grill, a sleeping bag, "two bulging Gladstones, a typewriter, a tennis racket, a pair of skis, a rifle, a fishing rod and tackle box, a recorder . . . and two large boxes of cuttings of field flowers from the Hudson Valley . . . "), Mrs. Pritchard senses that his will be no abbreviated visit, for skis cannot be used, even in the mountains near Adams, until late fall or early winter at best. Dr. Bohrmann, whose magnanimous hospitality becomes taxed by Medley's invasion of his home, tries to maintain his habitual friendly demeanor, but as days pass, it becomes clear that the overbearing English teacher plans to stay.

The drama of the story builds as Dr. Bohrmann, urged on by Mrs. Pritchard's concerned prodding, attempts to free himself from Medley's grasp. He longs for his highly prized solitude, which Medley has broken by his noisy, persistent presence. Perhaps the most overwhelmingly unbearable aspect of Medley's omnipresence is his infatuation with his mentor, which leads him to agree, wholeheartedly and constantly, with whatever Dr. Bohrmann says. Although Bohrmann scolds Medley for his sin of "impassioned, uncritical agreement," he soon discovers that the young man simply has no ideas of his own. While overtly brilliant, for Medley "had apparently read everything and forgotten nothing," Bohrmann's protege "was so unself-centered that Dr. Bohrmann began to wonder if he had a self at all." In short, Henry Medley is an intellectual robot, a "reasonable facsimile" of the true intellectual and spiritual offspring that Dr. Bohrmann once desired more than anything else in the world.

Once Dr. Bohrmann realizes that Medley must go—must be evicted, albeit gently, if need be—the focus of the story turns to a most essential yet rather unusual character, Bohrmann's cat, Grimalkin. As fate (or fortune) would have it, Henry Medley suffers an excruciating allergy to cats, and even though the professor has agreed to restrict Grimalkin to the outdoors during Medley's stay, Mrs. Pritchard intervenes, allowing the animal to slip into the house just long enough to keep the dander level painfully high. Finally, in a voice punctuated with explosive sneezes and with an expression dampened by tears of allergic agony, Medley announces his intention to depart. No character is more pleased than Grimalkin, who, having been unceremoniously ousted by Medley's arrival, equally unceremoniously deposits a farewell gift on the mat outside Medley's door as he prepares to leave—a dead gopher. With a sense of unspeakable relief, Dr. Bohrmann returns to the life he most enjoys, free from the "sapping tedium of Medley's monologues and interrogations" that had seemed to rob him of his own personality.

*Themes and Meanings*

Jean Stafford is fond of exploring the parallel between the landscape of the Rocky Mountain West and characters indigenous to that region. She believes that the Colorado spirit is reinforced by a strength of character, an inimitable independent personality, which makes people straightforward, resilient, and above all intrigued by life's potential. As Dr. Bohrmann himself observes, there is a special ingredient found in the Rocky Mountains that gives characters a certain Western charm. "Once they were out in the world, they seldom came back to Adams, and when they did, they were not the same, for they had outgrown their lucubrations; they were no longer so fervent as they had been, and often their eyes strayed to their wristwatches in the midst of a conversation." Just as Stafford herself never returned to the Rocky Mountain West to live after leaving the area when she finished her university education, other characters who move away in her fiction seldom come back to live. However, those who remain, like Dr. Wolfgang Bohrmann, epitomize a certain quality not to be found elsewhere.

Another theme frequently found in Stafford's short stories and novels is the importance of a character's past experiences on his present life. Often her characters seem anachronisms in the society in which they live. Dr. Bohrmann, for example, relishes his retirement in his new house, but he also fills the new space with artifacts of his past, symbols of a former life that he would never forsake simply because it was out of date. Stafford recognizes the universality of human experience and urges readers to become aware of the value of the past.

Stafford echoes the theories of Virginia Woolf and D. H. Lawrence with regard to the centrality of character in fiction, insisting that her characters be, above all, dynamic, believable, and real for the reader. In a letter to the Pulitzer committee in 1969, Stafford wrote: "I want, in a novel, a tarnished, perhaps, but nonetheless sterling hero or heroine; I don't want everybody to be a simon-pure alloy of base metals." Thus, in her collection of short stories entitled *Bad Characters* (1964), she portrays individuals whose lives are far from perfect but who nevertheless live determinedly. Stafford's devotion to physical and psychological realism gives her fiction the solid, earthy quality so integral to the American literary tradition.

*Style and Technique*

Critics have long credited Stafford with having a vivid, descriptive style that shows her deep reverence for the power of the English language. When "A Reasonable Facsimile" appeared in print, Stafford's acquaintance Eudora Welty commended her story, writing, "Oh, Jean, I love all the detail and the splendor." Saul Bellow, another admirer of Stafford's writing, sent her a congratulatory note, remarking: "I liked all the stories, but the one about the old professor and the young know-it-all best." Through her elaborate descriptions of characters and settings, Stafford is able to create an atmosphere as realistic as, for example, many found in Charles Dickens's novels. In "A Reasonable Facsimile," Stafford presents the professor so thoroughly that the reader really feels as though he has met the old gentleman.

The narrator pulls the reader into the actual theater of the story: "Imagine, then, this character, with his silver beard, wearing a hazel coat-sweater from J. C. Penney. . . . Or look at him pottering in his pretty Oriental garden. . . . See him in his sleek, slender blond dining room eating a mutton chop or blood pudding with red cabbage."

Stafford's style also develops a firm sense of place, for she uses actual and specific locations to give her fiction that local-color flavor most often found in realistic fiction. As a result, her fiction presents an atmosphere that becomes more crucial than plot itself; her characters emerge as sculptured identities rather than mere outlines of personalities. Reading Stafford's short stories gives one the ability to journey deep inside the souls of her characters and to cheer with glee when Dr. Bohrmann finally boots that upstart Medley right out the door.

Another stylistic element characteristic to Stafford's fiction is her use of an exhaustive and intricate vocabulary that makes heavy demands on the contemporary reader. Her style challenges the reader to accompany her narrators on journeys of language exploration. Few modern readers would be able to grasp Stafford's vocabulary at first glance; for example, when one learns that Dr. Bohrmann's retirement activities include the study of "mycology, and mycophagy as well," one knows that this is a man who is not content with studying the mundane disciplines of scholarship. The professor's "monograph on Maimonides for the *Hibbert Journal*" tempts even the most hasty reader to reach for the nearest dictionary.

In addition to her use of elaborate descriptions, Stafford also reveals a marvelous ear for the varieties of speech that enrich the English language. Who is able to resist a smile at Dr. Bohrmann's reaction to Medley's annoying, exhaustive commentary: "I think you have made a Jungfrau out of the hill of a pygmy mole." Medley himself is described as "brilliant, though undisciplined and incorrigibly high-falutin' . . . ," and even minor characters speak with genuineness as they describe the main character: "You should have seen mein Herr Doktor Professor this morning, with his cat and his fiddle, ready to hop right over the moon." One can certainly see the truth in Stafford's comment to one of her editors: "My mother tongue has been, from the beginning of my life, my dearest friend."

Stafford strove throughout her life to defend the language against the destructive influences of cant and imprecision. Readers soon discover that Stafford's language is as elaborate as her subjects are diverse, and that her ability to expand the language rather than to reduce it (as did many modernist writers) makes her fiction a study in the limitless power of the human imagination.

*Mary Davidson McConahay*

# A RECLUSE

*Author:* Walter de la Mare (1873-1956)
*Type of plot:* Ghost story
*Time of plot:* The 1920's
*Locale:* Rural England
*First published:* 1926

> *Principal characters:*
> CHARLES DASH, a young man, the narrator
> A HORSEMAN, unnamed
> MR. BLOOM, owner of Montresor
> S. S. CHAMPNEYS, Mr. Bloom's late secretary

*The Story*

In spite of Mr. Charles Dash's promise to make his record "as full, concise and definite as possible," this story, like the estate Montresor, wears "a look of reticence." The plot is straightforwardly, even naïvely, developed, but as the events of the story unfold with increasing complexity, the reader is sent back to earlier parts of the story or out of the story altogether by allusions—to symbolic forms, to folkloric associations, to literary and extraliterary sources. Though on a first reading the story seems all too clearly banal, further perusals fascinate—trap—the reader by revealing ever more frustrating (thus interesting) patterns of inconclusiveness, loose ends not explained by any authorial intervention and beyond the explanatory powers of the narrator, Mr. Dash.

The story proceeds simply enough, Mr. Dash making only the most superficial connections between its parts. His initial musings on life's "edges"—Walter de la Mare included this story in his collection *On the Edge* (1930)—give haphazard rise to memories of Mr. Bloom of Montresor, whose estate is for sale, and to the question, "But was it discreet of them to describe the house itself as an imposing mansion?" This question tells the reader much about Mr. Dash, especially in readerly retrospect, for his quibble and his off-hand reason for it—"A pair of slippers in my possession prompts this query"—reveal a fastidious but superficial intellect, quite ready to cry "*Distinguo!*" but rarely if ever prepared to follow up. In a more serious way, this tendency is revealed in his excessive relief to be gone from the "dismal reminders" of death afforded by his convalescing friend; Mr. Dash notices all the right things but knows the significance of none, as shown further by his comment on the gray-faced horseman: "So far as I can see he has nothing whatever to do with what comes after—no more, at most, than my poor thin-nosed, gasping friend." These are to Mr. Dash all oddities, remarkable, and so remarked on, but no more.

At first, the reader sees no further than Mr. Dash does, but as this superficial narrator's observations accumulate, the reader's role becomes more and more active. As

Mr. Bloom remarks in contempt of Mrs. Altogood, vaunting his own occult attainments, "There are deeps, and vasty deeps." It is an ambiguous comment, yet ambiguity befits a story whose depths remain largely undefined, but whose very lack of definition asks readers to try to plumb those depths, to create them, as it were, in the very act of reading.

Mr. Dash's actual encounter with Mr. Bloom is compounded of numerous tiny suspenses, each contributing to the almost overwhelming suspense of the story itself, which is then anticlimactically dissipated by the indefiniteness of the apparition seen and by the final paragraph about Mrs. Altogood and her "gallipot of 'tiddlers.'" The initial empty appearance of the house is answered by the emptiness of Mr. Dash himself, though the narrator is typically quick to pull back from what his observation might imply: "His house had suggested vacancy, so did he—not of human inmate, that is, but of pleasing interest!" He returns to this idea later, when he is less inclined to soften its significance: "What was wrong with the man? What made him so extortionately substantial, and yet in effect, so elusive and unreal? What indeed constitutes the reality of a fellow creature in himself? The something, the someone within, surely, not the mere physical frame."

Unlike the story's author, who was willing to admit the impossibility of answering most questions yet pursued them all of his life, Mr. Dash believes that answers are available but allows his odd blend of skepticism and civility to prevent their active pursuit. Pushed by his exigent situation to admit the questions, Mr. Dash's tendency is to comment on the absurdity of the situation, and his admission that his sensations of distaste "lie outside the tests even of mighty Science" is for Mr. Dash a dismissal, not an opportunity for a broader or deeper mind.

The reader, meanwhile, accumulates the ingredients of horror: the silence surrounding Montresor, the missing key, the "dead-white" lake, Mr. Bloom's odd hesitations at doors, the flatness of his voice and the immobility of his face, his obvious expectation and fear of only he knows what, hints at deaths and hauntings, the yellow dog that skulks from the corner just when the reader expects something else, finally the voices and footsteps, the "hallucination" in Mr. Bloom's bed, and the narrator's dash to safety. These and the other richly contiguous particulars of "A Recluse" pull the reader through the story and set him on a hunt for patterns and connections. Mr. Dash's final misgivings, however, even his notion that he ought to have made "amends" for his running away from Montresor, are formulated conventionally (Mr. Bloom "has gone home," he has "taken his wages") and though Mr. Dash takes more seriously than heretofore the reality of a less physically tangible world than the one he sees, his mind remains superficial: "I know of no harm he did."

### Themes and Meanings

Doris Ross McCrosson has written of de la Mare: "Should anyone be looking for answers, he has none. . . . He questioned everything, never arrogantly, however, because he believed—in fact, it was the only thing he seemed certain of—that all of life is shot with strangeness and mystery." The story "A Recluse" bears out this assertion, but it makes certain distinctions: The narrator, Mr. Dash, recognizes the predominance of questions in the story he tells, yet the story does not ask the reader therefore to consider him a mouthpiece for the author, one appropriately aware of the difficulty of what de la Mare called "the whole question of the relation between the living and the dead." Mr. Dash, as his name suggests, retreats from the truth of what confronts him—an ironic retreat, since he has accused Mr. Bloom of "showing himself incapable of facing facts." De la Mare's use of such a narrator forces the reader also to choose between running away and facing facts. The story offers this choice in the form of loose ends, a series of inconclusive elements simply presented by Mr. Dash, but forming patterns of significance—though no firm answers—for the reader.

The gray-faced horseman is one of the first inconclusive elements in the story. Here Mr. Dash, as usual, notices all the right things, even makes some appropriate connections, but adds, "Why I have mentioned him I scarcely know, except that there he was, for an instant, at those gates." Later he suspects that Montresor's effect on him has something to do with "the queer gesture and the queerer looks of my cardboard-boxed gentleman on horseback," but he finds little further reason in the odd encounter. The reader finds himself at first in much the same situation, but hindsight provides a context of significance for the "pseudo-miller" of Montresor.

Horsemen are often messengers or otherwise portentous, and this one mutely fulfills the expected function with his dismissive gesture of "unnecessary violence." Then Mr. Dash's quotation of the old song introduces into the picture the traditional association between millers and the Devil, and though it is merely the "indiscriminately hairy face" that brings this ditty to the narrator's mind, the association raised suggests some connection with the theme of death running through the later parts of the story: On the one hand, one thinks of the vision of Saint John: "I saw . . . a pale horse, and its rider's name was Death, and Hades followed him." (Revelation 6:8); on the other hand, the mysterious cardboard box this horseman carries suggests secrets and the possibility of their revelation—Pandora's Box, perhaps, and its association with the mysteries of the human unconscious. These allusions give the horseman a more exact function as messenger (though neither a strictly theological nor a rigorously psychological one), for they portend the hauntedness of Montresor, its aura of present death, and the challenge these present to Mr. Dash's persistently flippant externality.

More significant and comprehensive as an inconclusiveness is the matter of the dead secretary, S. S. Champneys, particularly since Mr. Dash believes that he has himself been invited somehow to take Mr. Champneys' place in the household at Montresor. Mr. Bloom's apparently ingenuous remarks about his former companion's death do not seem to arouse Mr. Dash's suspicion that anything out of the way has happened here. Indeed, he considers that though "lung trouble" appears to have killed Mr. Champneys, "exasperation and boredom alone would have accounted for it." Neither do Mr. Bloom's references to his personal wishes—"to go quickly"—even accompanied as they are by Mr. Bloom's startling gestures of head and eyes. Nor, finally, do Mr. Bloom's rather threatening references to Mr. Dash's own death.

These unrecognized or unacknowledged threats, coupled with Mr. Bloom's apparent desire to keep Mr. Dash at Montresor, suggest that Mr. Dash is similarly incorrect in his failure to connect Mr. Bloom more than casually with Mr. Champneys' death or with any irregular disposal of his remains. That Mr. Champneys' death has something to do with Mr. Bloom's occult experiments is suggested by Mr. Dash's remark that "this house was not haunted, it was infested. Catspaw, poor young Mr. Champneys may have been, but he had indeed helped with the chestnuts." The more immediately horrible inference is not even hinted at by the narrator, yet the surprise entrance of Chunk, the dog, and "the crunching of teeth on bones" are accompanied by this odd exchange:

> "You greedy! You glutton!" Mr. Bloom was cajoling him. "Aye, but where's Steve? An animal's intelligence, Mr. Dash"—his voice floated up to me from under the other side of the table—"is concentrated in his belly. And even when one climbs up to human prejudices one usually finds the foundation as material."

A moment later: "'That animal could tell a tale.' The crunching continued. 'Couldn't yer, you old rascal? Where's Steve; where's Steve?'" The reader naturally wonders who Steve is and later learns that Mr. Champneys' initials are "S. S." His mother addressed him as "Sidney"; did Mr. Bloom call him "Steve"?

*Style and Technique*

De la Mare's employment of loose ends extends to the witty diction of "A Recluse," where wordplay sets up patterns of verbal echo in the text. The word "imposing" in the story's second paragraph is a good limited example. Here Mr. Dash is quibbling with the auctioneers' use of the term, suggesting that it is an indiscretion. In its usual sense, though, the word cannot be called indiscreet: Montresor is plainly an impressive sight. Mr. Dash, however, suggests the word's less pleasant senses with his equivocation, and his entire story ostensibly springs from a desire to explain that the word is indiscreet because Montresor is not what it seems, is in fact a mansion "practising imposture" (as the *Oxford English Dictionary* defines a no longer current meaning of "imposing").

Again, in his final comments on Mrs. Altogood as "a Thomasina Tiddler"—a trifler, that is, not up to the seriousness of Mr. Bloom's occult researches—Mr. Dash employs his terms equivocally. He also considers Mrs. Altogood to be dabbling in "those obscure waters" and leaning "over a gallipot of 'tiddlers'"—a small container, that is, of small fish. Mr. Dash's pun is an obvious one, but it establishes an inescapable contrast with Mr. Bloom's "vasty deeps," suggesting that Mr. Bloom has so far accustomed himself to the "Serpentine" (in contrast to Mrs. Altogood's "gallipot") that he has become master of the big fish—perhaps one of the big fish himself (in contrast to Mrs. Altogood's "tiddlers"). Here Mr. Dash provides as well the watery imagery of the human unconscious, which he has chosen to ignore.

The word "edge," finally, creates a more extensive verbal ambiguity. It opens the story, of course, but Mr. Dash dismisses it as too vague and prefers "the central." However, the concept appears repeatedly in the story, both in its primary sense—besides "edge," the terms "borderline" and "Jordan" refer in this story to the boundary between life and death—and in two others. During the evening, Mr. Dash says, his host "would . . . edge off toward the door," move furtively to listen for noises. More important, Mr. Bloom is "on edge" and even acknowledges his "edginess." He is upset, but the word also suggests the ambiguity of Mr. Bloom's relationship to life (in Mr. Dash's sense) and the "other side."

Such cases of verbal indeterminateness are the particular exemplars of de la Mare's style of inconclusiveness in the story, by which he invites the reader to participate with him in the act of establishing significance and at the same time challenges the concreteness of the categories cherished by every Mr. Dash.

*Jonathan A. Glenn*

# THE RED CONVERTIBLE

*Author:* Louise Erdrich (1954-    )
*Type of plot:* Realism, coming of age
*Time of plot:* The early 1970's
*Locale:* American Indian reservation in North Dakota
*First published:* 1981

> *Principal characters:*
> HENRY LAMARTINE, a Vietnam War veteran who suffers from
>   post-traumatic stress disorder
> LYMAN LAMARTINE, his younger brother

*The Story*

"The Red Convertible," which also forms a chapter in Louise Erdrich's novel *Love Medicine* (1984, 1993), is the story of two Native American brothers, Lyman Lamartine and his older sibling, Henry, Jr. Narrated by Lyman, the story explores the relationship between the brothers before and after Henry's combat experience in Vietnam, where he was held as a prisoner of war.

The story begins on an American Indian reservation in North Dakota. Lyman has received a large insurance check after a tornado destroyed his restaurant. He and Henry, a laid-off factory worker, buy a red convertible. Free of daily responsibilities, they take to the open road in their flashy automobile. Along the way, they pick up Susy, a Native American woman who is hitchhiking. After giving her a ride to her home in Chicken, Alaska, they spend the summer with her family. Their idyllic journey comes to an end when they return to their reservation and discover that Henry, who had volunteered for military service, has been called to report for duty.

After nine months of combat duty in Vietnam, Henry is captured by the North Vietnamese and imprisoned for six months. During Henry's absence, Lyman restores the travel-worn car. Working on the convertible provides Lyman with a tangible link to his brother. When Henry finally returns home, he is profoundly changed. Gone is the fun-loving child, and in his place is a jumpy, mean, and withdrawn man who rarely speaks. He spends his days sitting quietly but restlessly in front of the color television set. Because there are no Native American doctors on the reservation, Lyman and his mother consider sending Henry to a psychiatric hospital but ultimately reject the notion. Instead, Lyman believes that the red convertible might somehow bring the old Henry back.

Taking a hammer to the car, Lyman beats the body and undercarriage out of shape. It takes a month for Henry to notice the damage, but when he does, he berates Lyman for allowing the car to deteriorate. He sets about fixing it himself, without Lyman's help. Lyman is disappointed because he had hoped that he and Henry would repair the convertible together, thereby reestablishing the close bond they had once shared. As

Henry works on the car, he seems to revert to his prewar self, but the change proves to be superficial. After the car is restored, Bonita, Henry and Lyman's younger sister, takes a picture of them standing in front of the now-pristine automobile.

Henry suggests that they take the car for a spin, and the men head for the Red River. It is early spring, and the river is swollen with water from melting snow. As they sit on the bank, Lyman becomes aware of a squeezing sensation in his chest and realizes that he is feeling the same anguish that Henry is experiencing at that moment. Frightened, he shakes Henry's shoulders and yells, "Wake up, wake up, wake up, wake up!" Henry, resigned, tells Lyman, "It's no use," and insists that Lyman take the car as his own. Lyman protests that he does not want the car, and the brothers engage in a fist-fight. Suddenly they stop fighting and start laughing uncontrollably. The tension is broken, and Henry begins to dance wildly. Telling Lyman that he needs to cool off, Henry runs to the river, jumps in, and is taken by the current. Lyman realizes that his brother is in trouble and calls out to him. Henry replies in a detached way, "My boots are filling," and then drowns. Lyman dives in to try to save him but is unsuccessful. After climbing out of the water, he drives the car to the bank, releases the clutch, and lets the car slide into the river after his brother.

*Themes and Meanings*

Louise Erdrich's story can be viewed through the lenses of both modern history and American Indian cultural mores. From the mid-1960's to the mid-1970's, the United States drafted thousands of men to fight in the Vietnam War. Because the warrior tradition is a key concept in Native American culture, the number of American Indian men serving in the military is among the highest of any ethnic group. As warriors, Native American men uphold the honor of their tribe and prove themselves as men. A warrior puts his life on the line as the ultimate sacrifice to ensure his people's survival. Facing death in battle is a spiritual rite of passage and an important step in gaining respect and status in the Native American community.

When Henry volunteers for active duty, he is maintaining these distinctive cultural values. However, serving in the white man's war leaves Henry psychologically fragile and emotionally lost. One of the more grotesque images Erdrich uses to illustrate the extreme damage to Henry's psyche is the blood dripping down his chin after he has bitten through his lip while watching television. He does not notice that he is bleeding when he sits down at the dinner table and begins to eat. Lyman notes that Henry is swallowing his own blood as it mixes with the bread in his mouth. Vietnam veterans from many different backgrounds suffered from post-traumatic stress disorder after they returned home from the war, but Henry's case is made worse by the fact that his cultural expectations as a Native American warrior have not been fulfilled. For him, there is no glory or honor, only anger, despair, and hopelessness.

"The Red Convertible" is also a bitter coming-of-age story. At the beginning of the narrative, the brothers enjoy a carefree camaraderie as they take off in their new car and travel from state to state, visiting other reservations. Their visit to Alaska takes on an otherworldly quality in that their stay with Susy's family harkens back to the distant past when Native American traditions remained intact and unsullied by European influence. During the summer they spend in Chicken, they live in mythic time in a place in which the sun never sets and each day flows seamlessly into the next. Just before they leave for home, Henry dances with Susy perched on his shoulders, her long hair swinging around him. He comments that he always wondered what it would be like to have long hair. Ironically, his "borrowing" of a woman's tresses is the closest he comes to resembling his warrior ancestors. As a contemporary United States Marine, his hair is shorn, and he is sent to fight in a controversial war against a nation that is no direct threat to his own country. His disillusionment coupled with the humiliation of his imprisonment as a prisoner of war cause him to lose his innocent idealism as well as his cultural bearings. Henry's mental state has a direct impact on his family, especially his brother. Henry's postwar illness and subsequent suicide initiate Lyman into the adult world.

*Style and Technique*

A member of the Turtle Mountain Band of Chippewa, Erdrich considers herself a storyteller first and a writer second. Love of storytelling, which grew out of tribal oral tradition, is a primary means of keeping Native American cultural values alive within the community. The first-person narrative technique Erdrich employs in "The Red Convertible" reflects her affinity for storytelling. She has often said that she "hears" her characters talking before writing dialogue. Lyman speaks in his own voice, which lends an immediacy and poignancy to the narrative. The first-person narration also allows Erdrich to convey the speech patterns of modern Native Americans and to portray the hardships of reservation life realistically.

In addition to Lyman's first-person account, the fact that the story is told from his point of view is also a significant element of the narrative structure. Throughout most of the work, Lyman uses past tense when he recounts events and when he quotes himself, Susy, his mother, and Bonita. However when he quotes Henry, he always uses present tense, even if the action takes place in the past. Present tense is also used exclusively from the time the brothers arrive at the Red River to the end of the story. For Lyman, Henry does not exist in the past. Instead, Lyman's loss of his brother is always fresh, like a wound that will not heal.

Finally, the red convertible itself serves as a narrative device to illustrate Henry's changing mental state throughout the work. When Lyman and Henry first purchase the automobile, Lyman describes the car as "reposed" and "calm," which reflects Henry's personality at the beginning of the story. Later, after Lyman damages the car, Henry seems to recognize that the dented convertible is a physical reflection of his wounded psyche. In repairing the automobile, Henry is attempting to heal himself. When he fails to achieve the same state of wholeness as the car, he realizes that it is "no use," and tries to give the convertible to Lyman. Lyman, who realizes that the car mirror Henry's struggles, transfers complete ownership to Henry by sending it into the river after his brother drowns.

*Pegge Bochynski*

# THE RED-HEADED LEAGUE

*Author:* Arthur Conan Doyle (1859-1930)
*Type of plot:* Mystery and detective
*Time of plot:* 1890
*Locale:* London, England
*First published:* 1891

> *Principal characters:*
> SHERLOCK HOLMES, the world's greatest detective
> DR. JOHN H. WATSON, his friend and biographer
> MR. JABEZ WILSON, the owner of a small pawnshop
> JOHN CLAY, alias
> VINCENT SPAULDING, his assistant

*The Story*

When Dr. Watson visits the apartment of his friend Sherlock Holmes, he finds the world's first consulting detective in conference with a client with bright red hair, Mr. Jabez Wilson. Holmes invites Watson to remain and to hear the client's unusual story. Wilson, a man of about sixty, is a not very successful small businessperson; the most noteworthy thing about him is the flaming color of his hair. After introductions all around, Wilson explains how upset he has been by a recent incident, so upset that he has come to Holmes for his help.

Wilson says that he is a man of very settled habits, a bachelor who almost never deviates from the daily routine of running his pawnshop. At least, he never deviated until he heard of the Red-Headed League. One day in his shop, his assistant, Vincent Spaulding, called his attention to an advertisement in the newspaper that announced an opening in the Red-Headed League. The announcement promised a salary of four pounds a week (about twenty dollars at the time of the story) for "purely nominal services" to the candidate who was accepted. The amount was a considerable sum at the time, especially if the duties were slight, and Spaulding urged Wilson to apply. The timid pawnbroker did so, but only after Spaulding practically took him to the office mentioned in the ad.

There Wilson heard the story of an eccentric American millionaire who had left a fortune to provide an income for Londoners with red hair as bright as the millionaire's had been. Wilson was accepted into the League. He learned that the nominal duties consisted only of his coming to the office from 10:00 A.M. until 2:00 P.M. each day and copying out the *Encyclopaedia Britannica* in longhand. Since most of Wilson's business was done in the evening, he was delighted at the chance to supplement his income. This he did for eight weeks, getting well into the "A" volume, until one day he arrived at the office to find it closed, with a notice on the door that the Red-Headed League had been dissolved. He was so disturbed by the thought that someone had been playing a practical joke on him that he came to Holmes for a solution.

Holmes points out that Wilson has lost nothing—indeed, has made thirty pounds—but says that the case is remarkable. Holmes soon discovers that Spaulding, who encouraged Wilson to apply, is not all that he seems. The assistant came to Wilson recently for half-wages, claiming to want to learn the business. Although perfectly satisfactory as an assistant, Spaulding has an interest in photography, has set up Wilson's cellar as a darkroom, and is down in the basement every minute that Wilson does not need him in the shop above. Holmes promises to look into the case, and Wilson leaves.

Holmes and Watson first visit the district in which Wilson's shop is located, where Holmes does some mysterious things: He asks directions from a clerk at the pawnshop; he taps the street outside with his walking stick and remarks that the case is complicated by the fact that it is Saturday. Later, he asks Watson to meet him at Baker Street that evening at ten, and to come armed. When Watson arrives, he finds two other men there: Peter Jones, an inspector from Scotland Yard, and a Mr. Merryweather, a bank director. Holmes takes them to a branch of the City and Suburban Bank, a branch located in the same district as Wilson's pawnshop. There they enter the vaults of the bank, where Merryweather shows them a shipment of thirty thousand gold coins they have recently received from the Bank of France. Holmes says that they may have some time to wait, and they sit quietly in the dim vault.

After about an hour, they see a glint of light from the floor: A paving stone moves, and a man's face appears from the hole. He climbs out, and Holmes and the inspector seize him.

Holmes later explains his reasoning: He became suspicious when first he heard that Vincent Spaulding had taken Wilson's job offer at less than the normal wages. His time in the cellar suggested that there would be found the real interest of Spaulding. The business of the Red-Headed League seemed to be a trick to get the sedentary Wilson out of the shop for some hours each day so that Spaulding and his confederates could do whatever they were up to, unobserved. When, on his visit to the area, Holmes tapped the pavement and heard a hollow sound, he concluded that they were tunneling beneath the street to the branch bank in question. When he asked the pawnbroker's clerk, Spaulding himself, for directions, Holmes recognized him as John Clay, a notoriously cunning criminal. The rest was the simple matter of gaining entrance to the bank vault—Holmes reasoned that the robbers would strike on Sunday, when the bank was closed—and waiting for them to appear.

*Themes and Meanings*

Arthur Conan Doyle wrote so many Sherlock Holmes stories, all of which can be found in collected editions, that it is hard to imagine a time when the character of the famous detective was new and fresh in the public imagination. Two novels featuring Holmes, *A Study in Scarlet* (1887) and *The Sign of Four* (1890), were published with only mild success. It was not until the publication of the first Holmes short story, "A Scandal in Bohemia," in 1891, that the detective became immensely popular. It was to capitalize on this public demand that Doyle wrote "The Red-Headed League."

The story is above all a vehicle to display the remarkable reasoning ability of Sherlock Holmes, a man who is able to impose order on a seemingly meaningless jumble of experience. Experience in the Holmes stories only seems, however, to be meaningless: For someone who, like the detective, observes closely and interprets correctly, the world is a book to be read.

In "The Red-Headed League," the character of Holmes is the theme, and in the story Doyle continues to supply information about the background, tastes, and habits of his greatest creation. It is in this story that the reader learns that Holmes has a "poetic and contemplative" side to his nature, one that is illustrated when Holmes interrupts his detective work to attend a violin concert. One finds out as well that Holmes himself is a musician and a composer "of no ordinary merit." Through the almost casual introduction of details such as these, Doyle created a character who escapes the bounds of fiction, becoming almost lifelike in his solidity.

A subsidiary theme may be present, too, represented in the adage "You can't cheat an honest man." Throughout the story, Doyle delicately hints at Wilson's greed, the most telling example of which is his hiring of Vincent Spaulding because Spaulding agrees to work for half-pay. From that decision, all of Wilson's troubles spring.

*Style and Technique*

The style of the story is one that was to become customary in the Holmes adventures: Watson narrates the tale from his viewpoint as an on-the-spot observer. He provides Holmes (and Doyle) with the means to build suspense because, although Watson is present to see all of Holmes's actions, he does not understand their significance. Thus, the unlocking of the mystery is postponed until the end.

The technique of building suspense by holding off the explanation is usually employed several times in a typical Sherlock Holmes story, and this one is no exception: First, there is the small demonstration of Holmes's ability when Wilson first enters the Baker Street flat and Holmes deduces many facts about him from his appearance. The postponement is only momentary in this prelude, so to call it, because Holmes explains the inferences he draws from watch chains and calluses and the like. Nevertheless, the technique has been used to show Holmes's powers, and his revelation at the end of the story of a greater chain of inferences has been prepared for by the less important scene at the beginning.

"The Red-Headed League" was a story of which Doyle himself was proud: At the conclusion of a contest held by *Strand* magazine, asking readers to pick their favorite Sherlock Holmes stories, Doyle contributed a list of his own, on which "The Red-Headed League" ranked second only to "The Adventure of the Speckled Band"; Doyle rated it so high, he said, because of the originality of the plot. It is hard to argue with that view. The trick to remove Wilson from the scene of the crime and Holmes's equal cleverness in preventing the crime continue to make the story memorable.

*Walter E. Meyers*

# RED LEAVES

*Author:* William Faulkner (1897-1962)
*Type of plot:* Satire
*Time of plot:* The nineteenth century, before the American Civil War
*Locale:* Yoknapatawpha County, Mississippi
*First published:* 1930

*Principal characters:*
HERMAN BASKET and
LOUIS BERRY, Chickasaw Indians
THE BLACK MAN, a body servant to the dead chief
MOKETUBBE, the new Chickasaw chief
ISSETIBBEHA, the recently deceased chief
DOOM, the chief before Issetibbeha
OLE GRANDFATHER, a snake

*The Story*

The situation at the beginning of "Red Leaves" is presented in a dialogue between sixty-year-old Herman Basket and his companion Louis Berry. The two are carrying out an assignment demanded by the age-old custom of some Mississippi Indians of burying slaves with the body of a chief. The two Indians are looking for the body servant of Chief Issetibbeha, who has just died under questionable circumstances. The servant is a black slave from Guinea. In mock-heroic tone and diction, the seekers discuss the fact that the man does not want to die. Bits of information regarding the past history of three successive chiefs and the Chickasaw's keeping of black slaves are shared.

Part 2 gives more detailed information on the chiefs, from Doom, the father of the dead chief, to his son Issetibbeha, and finally to Moketubbe, the son of Issetibbeha and the newest chief. More information is given on the relationship between the Chickasaw and their slaves. For example, Doom hunted his slaves as if they were animals; Issetibbeha mated with a slave and sired Moketubbe. The conversation in this section is an earlier version of the one between Basket and Berry in Part 1: The slaves are a burden, but they are too valuable to get rid of; they could be eaten, but they probably do not have a good taste.

Of special interest is the story of the origins of the palace, a river steamboat brought on rollers by slave labor from the river some miles away. Again, there is reference to the slippers with the red heels, brought from Paris some years before by Issetibbeha: They serve the same purpose for the chiefs as a crown for a king. The picture of 250-pound, five-foot Moketubbe forcing the slippers on his too large feet is ludicrous, and his wearing the slippers while his father is still alive bodes ill for Issetibbeha. The digression continues with the fact that Issetibbeha lived for five more years and then he died. It ends with a return to the story's present with the words "That was yesterday."

Part 3 of "Red Leaves" resumes the dialogue between Basket and Berry. They are concerned that the chase will be too long, that the chief's body will begin to smell, and that the food for the many celebrants of the occasion will give out too soon. Their mock-heroic style continues as they blame the white man for all of their troubles—blame him, that is, for foisting the blacks on them. The two report to the indolent Moketubbe, who will lead the hunt.

Part 4 shifts attention to the black body servant. He is described as forty years old and having served the chief for twenty-three years. A slight time shift relates his observations on the day the chief lay sick. From a hiding place in the loft, he has followed closely the reports of the illness and the death of Issetibbeha, listening after dark to the sound of the drums. He also hears the sound of "two voices, himself and himself," discussing the fact that he, too, is dead. He begins his flight, stopping at the plantation to receive assistance from the other blacks there, then plunging into the wilderness. On two occasions he is nearly apprehended by Indians. At sunset he is slashed by a cottonmouth moccasin, which he treats as a totem animal: He addresses it as "Ole Grandfather" and touches its head, letting it strike him again and again. He contemplates once more the fact that he does not wish to die.

Part 5 continues the chase but shifts to a less serious tone. The huge Moketubbe is being carried on a litter by alternating crews of Indians as he leads the pursuers. Again, he is a ludicrous figure as he tries to wear the royal slippers; the similarity to the plight of Cinderella's big-footed stepsisters is too obvious to miss. The hunt goes on into the sixth day, with the predicted shortage of food for the guests and the odor of the dead chief both coming to pass. Another odor is also of concern: that of the body servant with snake's venom in his veins. Will he be of any use to Issetibbeha in the Happy Hunting Grounds? The slave is told that he has nothing to be ashamed of, that he has run well. His shouting, talking, and singing have ceased as he quietly watches his captors.

Part 6 concludes the story in three pages covering the return to the plantation. The man stalls for time, asking for food, which he unsuccessfully tries to eat, and water, which he goes through the futile motions of drinking. His cry of "ah-ah-ah" is answered by the last word of the story when Basket says "come."

*Themes and Meanings*

Treated from various viewpoints is the primitive ritual of human sacrifice as practiced by these Indians. Reference is made to a now discarded ritual of cannibalism, but the ritual of burying the chief's servant with him is at the time of the story still practiced, although some of the superstitious feeling for it has disappeared. Where the viewpoint is that of the Indians, the attitude is one of complaining about the inconvenience of such ritual, as if to say, "let's get on with it before the body becomes too rank." The chief is much too fat and lazy to lead the hunt as tradition demands he must; the sixty-year-old Herman Basket would much prefer not to be in the position of organizing the expedition; there is even a statement or two blaming blacks for the inconvenience. The Indians never question directly their belief in Happy Hunting Grounds or in the idea that chiefs need a horse, a dog, and a servant to hunt there, yet the implication of their attitude is that of doubt, perhaps disbelief; the ritual is continued because it is a tradition honored by time—thus the many references to past observances.

When the viewpoint is that of the body servant, there is a realistic facing of the inevitable while regretting and trying to postpone if not prevent it. No longer is there speculation on customs or inconveniences: The vital matter of life and death dominates every concern, a matter that has been treated by Basket and Berry somewhat flippantly at times, casually or realistically at others. The tone, when the focus is on the slave is always deadly serious.

*Style and Technique*

William Faulkner has woven into "Red Leaves" two stories carefully unified into one. The first is a humorous narrative of Indians honoring an outdated ritual. The treating of such serious matters as the poisoning of chiefs and the burying of men who, at least for the moment, are still alive, would suggest a lofty, solemn tone. Faulkner indeed assumes such a tone in the lofty diction of the Indians, a style suggestive of the King James Bible, and in the dutiful manner in which Basket and Berry carry out their responsibilities. However, the underlying tone is ironic: What the Indians say is not in harmony with the way they say it. Frequent references to the incongruities in the lives and persons of the three chiefs contribute to this undertone. The fact that none of them is a full-blooded Chickasaw, that the newest chief is half black but no more than one-eighth Chickasaw, raises doubts as to the legitimacy of the succession. The strong suggestions of royal poisonings confirm such suspicions. The use of a deteriorated steamboat for a palace and ill-fitting slippers for a crown reinforce the opinion that these are not legitimate chiefs; yet their credentials are impressive enough to qualify them for a dog, a horse, and a servant in the Happy Hunting Grounds. The ambiguous attitude toward the keeping of black slaves also suggests humor and irony.

The other story, the wilderness tale of a runaway slave being pursued by his Indian masters so that he can become a human sacrifice to their timeworn superstition, lacks the glibness of humorous speech. The slave is often silent; when he speaks, the words are agonizingly forced; at times they are incoherent. His plight is real; his fear is genuine; his emotions are intense. The wilderness through which he flees is also realistic, even naturalistic, for in spite of his valiant effort, he knows his doom is inevitable. The fear, the darkness, the exhaustion, the beat of the drums—all reflect an attitude in complete contrast to that of the Indians.

Faulkner frequently found opportunity to use his stories more than once. "Red Leaves" was published originally in 1930 in *The Saturday Evening Post*. The next year it was included in his first collection of stories, *These 13*. In 1950 he included it in his most complete collection, *Collected Short Stories of William Faulkner*, edited by Joseph Blotner and published by Random House (this is the edition followed herein). Five years later he revised the story of the servant's flight through the wilderness for his collection of hunting stories entitled *Big Woods*.

*George W. Van Devender*

# REDEMPTION

*Author:* John Gardner (1933-1982)
*Type of plot:* Domestic realism
*Time of plot:* The 1940's
*Locale:* New York State
*First published:* 1977

> *Principal characters:*
> JACK HAWTHORNE, a twelve-year-old boy
> DALE, his father, a farmer
> HIS MOTHER
> PHOEBE, his sister

*The Story*

Twelve-year-old Jack Hawthorne is driving the cultipacker on his father's farm when his seven-year-old brother, David, riding on the back, falls off and is run over and killed. Believing that he could have saved his brother if he had thought clearly, Jack blames himself. His father, Dale, is nearly destroyed by the accident and periodically rides off on his motorcycle, cursing God and himself, contemplating suicide, and seducing women with his tears. Although Dale does not blame Jack consciously, his behavior intensifies Jack's guilt. Dale's actions also increase his wife's sorrow, but she only cries at night behind closed doors. Barely able to move, she still takes care of her children and does her work. Religious faith and support from friends enable her to go on. She keeps her children busy with chores and activities, including piano lessons for Phoebe and French horn for Jack.

Jack's behavior initially parallels his father's. Driving the tractor, he condemns himself for not saving his brother and thinks of suicide. Jack always tells himself stories as he works. Before the accident, they were fantasies about sexual conquest and heroic battles. Now they are pitiful stories in which he redeems himself by sacrificing his life for others. Jack keeps aloof from people, becoming silent like his father and uncles, who never talk about their problems or feelings. Jack feels closer to the cows than he does to human beings. Finding momentary solace in nature, feeling at one with it all, he can forget about David temporarily, but he cannot sustain this escape.

One day when Phoebe brings lunch to Jack in the field, and he begins drinking his tea, she asks if he wants to say grace. Trying not to upset her, Jack says that he already said it, but not out loud. He realizes that if he did not say grace, Phoebe might think that there is no heaven, that their father would never get well, and that David was dead. Dale, thinking of his family, like Jack empathizing with Phoebe, realizes that he is hurting them and returns home to stay. Coming in the house one evening after doing his chores, Jack sees his father kneeling in front of his mother with his head on her lap, crying. Phoebe is hugging both parents. Dale calls to Jack, who joins them, but he says to his father so softly that no one can hear: "I hate you." Jack keeps himself even more secluded now that his father is home. He uses all of his spare time practicing his French horn and fantasizing about leaving them all. One day when he asks his teacher, the arrogant Yegudkin, if he thinks that he, Jack, will ever play like him, Yegudkin laughs dismissively. Humbled, Jack nevertheless agrees to return the next Saturday for his lesson. Outside, with his horn under one arm, his music under the other, Jack plunges into a space made for him by the crowd of shoppers, starting home. Like his father before him, he will be welcomed warmly back into the family.

## Themes and Meanings

"Redemption" is about ways of coping with loss, grief, and guilt. Because these are universal experiences, the story is ultimately about coping with the human condition. Unable to accept his own fallibility, cursing God's injustice, Jack's father, Dale, abandons reason and responsibility and indulges his emotions. Jack's mother and sister find solace in work, religion, and friends. Jack tries to lose himself in nature, but finds only temporary relief. Ultimately, he turns to art, exemplified by his earlier fantasies of heroic battle and sexual conquest, as well as by his later stories of self-pity and self-abasement. These fantasies try to evade reality, paralleling Dale's behavior.

John Gardner's story mirrors Jack's experience. Only by confronting reality directly and clearly, Gardner implies, can Jack achieve redemption. The process results in humility, which leads to self-forgiveness, and to empathy, which leads to the forgiveness of others—including Jack's father. This permits Jack to rejoin the family, to accept the human condition. Unlike the fantasies, which are emotional and self-indulgent, this kind of art is rational and consoles the reader. "Redemption" can help relieve the pain of life and create a sense of union with the human community.

"Redemption" contrasts two types of behavior. One is self-centered, arrogant, cruel, irresponsible, and lawless. The other is self-sacrificing, humble, empathetic, responsible, and moral. Dale and Jack at first exemplify the negative way, while Jack's mother exemplifies the positive. Dale is more responsible for David's death than Jack, for allowing such young children to ride on dangerous farm equipment. Dale cannot change the fact that David is dead, but he runs away, instead of being concerned with the living—his wife, Jack, and Phoebe. It is cruel for him to let Jack feel responsible not only for David's death but also for Dale's pain.

Jack's mother is never named in the story, signifying her humility and self-sacrifice, in contrast to her husband's egotism and self-indulgence. She stays home and cares for Jack and Phoebe, doing the best that she can to endure and teaching her children to do the same. She turns to religion and friends to provide emotional and spiritual support. At the end of the story, Jack accepts his mother's way as best. He has noticed that cows sometimes go through holes that they themselves make and then cannot get back. Jack is like these cows: After Yegudkin's laugh humbles him, he finds his way back to "Christ's flock," when the crowd opens, and he plunges in, starting home. These dazed-looking people are "herding along irritably, meekly, through painfully bright light." This is the light of reality: Children sometimes die in accidents.

*Style and Technique*

Gardner uses the third-person, limited omniscient point of view, presenting the story through Jack's consciousness, because it is Jack who must come to terms with his recurring memories of David's death. In line with this, the story circles back to the death scene three times. Initially, Jack recalls his sister's scream, sees the wheels of the cultipacker reach his brother's pelvis, and watches blood pour from David's mouth. The second return is vaguer, without specific details, indicating Jack's attempt to repress the memory. His whole body flinches from the image. The third memory includes details omitted from the first and second: "And now, from nowhere, the black memory of his brother's death rushed over him again, mindless and inexorable as a wind or wave, the huge cultipacker lifting—only an inch or so—as it climbed toward the shoulders, then sank on the skull—and he heard . . . his sister's scream."

This sentence is a good example of Gardner's style. He recreates the accident in language. Beginning the sentence abruptly with "and" mirrors the shock of the memory coming without warning. By interrupting the main clause with phrases, Gardner slows and lengthens the sentence, creating a slow-motion effect, the way Jack sees it in his mind. The phrase "only an inch or so," enclosed in dashes, is an impediment in the sentence, as David's shoulders are to the cultipacker. The phrases "climbed toward the shoulders," "then sank on the cheek," and "flattening the skull," contain the same number of syllables, giving equal time to each aspect of the action. A rising effect is achieved in the first, containing three stressed and two unstressed syllables, as the cultipacker lifts. A falling effect is achieved in the second and third, each containing three unstressed and two stressed syllables, as the cultipacker comes down on David's cheek and skull. The realism of this style reinforces Gardner's theme that reality must be faced to achieve redemption.

Gardner also uses words the way a composer uses notes. This technique is especially appropriate to express the idea that art has redemptive power. Key words are repeated, sometimes in variations, for example, "dark," "darkly"; "cave," "cavernous"; "warm," "warmth"; "herd," "herding." In another kind of variation, Gardner uses words with similar meanings, such as "aloof," "alone," "apart"; "herd," "flock," "community." Another set of words refers to emotions: "anguish," "anger," "rage"; "smiled," "cheerful," "happiness." Gardner also combines such words in phrases, creating motifs as in music: "sheep among sheep," "herding warmth," "Christ's flock."

Such words and phrases combine and recombine throughout the story, making associations in the reader's mind. The effect is largely subliminal on a first reading, but subsequent readings bring the associations into consciousness. The negative words collect into one group, associated with Jack and his father, the positive ones into another, associated with Jack's mother and Phoebe. These two groups create a counterpoint of discord and harmony, which is resolved at the end of the story in the episode with Yegudkin, a sort of coda to Gardner's symphony.

*James Green*

# REMBRANDT'S HAT

*Author:* Bernard Malamud (1914-1986)
*Type of plot:* Psychological
*Time of plot:* The 1960's
*Locale:* New York City
*First published:* 1973

> *Principal characters:*
> ARKIN, an art historian at a New York art school, age thirty-four
> RUBIN, a sculptor and teacher at the same art school, age forty-six

*The Story*

After his wife left him, Rubin, the sculptor, took to wearing various odd hats. Now, at age forty-six, he favors a visorless, soft, round white cap. Arkin, the art historian at the New York City art school where Rubin also teaches, thinks that the hat "illumines a lonely inexpressiveness arrived at after years of experience." He tells Rubin that the hat resembles Rembrandt's hat—the one that Rembrandt wears in the profound self-portraits of his middle age. The day after Arkin makes this remark, Rubin stops wearing the hat and begins to avoid him.

Arkin—"a hypertensive bachelor of thirty-four"—has considered himself friendly with Rubin, although they are not really friends. Arkin has been at the school for seven years, having left an art curator's job in St. Louis to come to New York. Arkin could never get Rubin to say anything at all about his artwork. Arkin remembers that when he first arrived, Rubin was working in wood, altering driftwood objects with a hatchet. At that time Rubin was persuaded by the director of the art school to present an exhibition—his only one. The exhibit was not a success, and Rubin spent the time sulking in a storage room at the rear of the gallery. Recently, Arkin suggested that it might be a good idea for Rubin to show his new work, which is constructed from welded triangular pieces of scrap iron. The suggestion obviously irritated Rubin.

After the hat remark, months pass during which Rubin avoids Arkin. After a while Arkin, too, becomes irritated, reasoning that "he didn't like people who didn't like him." He usually worries, however, that it might be his fault. He decides that he has probably done three things to alienate Rubin: not mentioning Rubin's driftwood show; suggesting the possibility of a new show that Rubin obviously does not want; and commenting on Rubin's white cap. He makes up his mind to apologize to Rubin and to put their acquaintanceship back on its normal track.

Before he is able to apologize, Arkin receives a present for his thirty-fifth birthday from one of his students: a white ten-gallon Stetson hat. Immediately after Rubin sees the Stetson, it is stolen. Arkin realizes that Rubin is the thief. Even though they try to avoid each other, they begin to encounter each other everywhere they go. At this point, "The art historian hated Rubin for hating him and beheld repugnance in Rubin's eyes." After a yelling scene between the two in front of the art school, Arkin again realizes that he should apologize, "if only because if the other couldn't he could."

Half a year after the yelling scene, on his thirty-sixth birthday, Arkin decides to visit Rubin's studio to look around for his Stetson. He inspects Rubin's work in welded triangular iron pieces, set amid broken stone statuary he has been collecting for years. Rubin has come from abstract driftwood sculptures to figurative objects such as flowers and busts of men and women colleagues. He discovers only one lovely piece: a sculpture of a dwarf tree. Arkin begins to understand why Rubin does not like to talk about a new exhibition of his work—for there is only the one fine piece.

Several days later, Arkin is preparing a lecture about Rembrandt's self-portraits. In doing so, Arkin realizes that it is not Rembrandt's hat that resembles Rubin's white cap; rather, it is the expression in the artist's eyes that is similar: "the unillusioned honesty of his gaze." Rembrandt's expression is "magisterially sad," as Arkin notes. Realizing this, Arkin decides to put himself in Rubin's position. He realizes that his previous remark about the hat was too much for Rubin to bear, because it forced him to ask himself once too often: "Why am I going on if this is the kind of sculptor I am going to be for the rest of my life?"

Finally realizing this, Arkin goes directly to Rubin's studio. Shortly afterward, Rubin enters, and the first thing Arkin says concerns the dwarf tree: "It's a beautiful sculpture, the best in the room I'd say." At this, Rubin stares at him in anger. Arkin then apologizes for his earlier remarks, and Rubin beings to cry. Arkin immediately leaves.

After this, the two men stop avoiding each other. They speak pleasantly when they meet, which is not often. One day Rubin reappears in his white cap—the one that seemed to resemble Rembrandt's hat. The narrator's concluding remark is "He wore it like a crown of failure and hope."

*Themes and Meanings*

Bernard Malamud presents the idea that art and beauty are difficult taskmasters. When Rubin measures himself as an artist, what scale is he to use—perfection in beauty and form? Indeed, is he to compare himself with one of the world-acclaimed master painters, Rembrandt? If these are to be his standards, then how is Rubin to measure up? In case he should try to stop thinking about the quality of his art, the comic Arkin is sent to keep him on his toes. Here Arkin serves much the same purposes as the troublesome Susskind in Malamud's "The Last Mohican."

Arkin reminds Rubin about Rembrandt, hence of Rembrandt's beautiful achievements in art as well as the recognition the world has accorded Rembrandt. Rubin, on the other hand, has had only one exhibition of his work—seven years ago—and has produced little or nothing of merit since then. Rubin is painfully aware of this himself. At forty-eight years of age toward the story's end, Rubin has few years left to produce beautiful work, and somehow his welded iron triangles do not produce much hope in the reader's mind. This is the reason for the sadness Arkin notices in Rubin's eyes. Since Rubin shares his pursuit of beauty with some of the greatest artists of the past, however, perhaps one may hold out hope for him. At the least, perhaps the pursuit of the beautiful is its own reward.

A second theme that Malamud pursues is the difficulty of human relationships. Arkin, a well-meaning fellow if ever there was one, despite his best intentions frequently wounds Rubin. When he finally realizes, however, that he is responsible for alienating Rubin, Arkin apologizes and asks forgiveness. Thus, Malamud demonstrates effectively that despite their difficulty, human relationships are possible so long as one is willing to make the effort and take the responsibility.

*Style and Technique*

Although "Rembrandt's Hat" uses a third-person narrator to present the characters, much of the story is built around Arkin's interior monologues. These monologues, delivered by the super-sensitive art historian, add a special comic touch to the story. The monologues, as well as the dialogue, are presented in the Jewish idiom of New York City.

Malamud's title secures the reader's attention at the outset, and he focuses the opening two pages of the story on this white cloth hat. The third-person narrator says that "Rubin wore it like a crown"; the last line in the story, describing the hat as a "crown of failure and hope," returns to this image, investing it with a deeper understanding of the artist's quest.

Malamud keeps a sharp thematic focus on the two men; indeed, they are the only characters who appear in the story at all except for the two-sentence appearance of an art student who gives Arkin the cowboy hat. The only aspect of the men that is mentioned is their mutual interest in art and in each other. Arkin's thoughts—through which the reader sees Rubin for the most part—are kept focused on Rubin and on their strained relationship. In this way, Malamud keeps the reader focused on his main interest: the difficulties of a life devoted to art.

*A. Bruce Dean*

# REMEMBERING ORCHARDS

*Author:* Barry Lopez (1945-     )
*Type of plot:* Antistory
*Time of plot:* The late twentieth century
*Locale:* Oregon and California
*First published:* 1991

*Principal characters:*
THE NARRATOR, a typesetter
HIS STEPFATHER, an orchardist
RAMON CASTILLO, his stepfather's assistant, a young and talented
orchardist

## The Story

Written more in essay than story form, this first-person narrative reveals how the narrator has only belatedly resolved some important differences in his life. These differences appear in two primary forms: those that he willfully maintained between himself and his stepfather from the age of twelve until well into his adulthood and those between the outwardly ordered, apparently immobile orchard groves and their living residents, growing "in a time and on a plane inaccessible" to the casual observer.

The narrator's stepfather was an orchardist "of the first rank" who was nurturing and confidently rooted in the world, while the narrator was full of desire to travel from the time his stepfather entered his life until he left home for college. As a youth, the narrator regarded the differences between his stepfather and his hired helper, Ramon Castillo, as reflecting more favorably on Ramon. He regarded Ramon as more sophisticated at the time because of his obvious expertise in gardening, his completely composed attitude, and his many girlfriends.

Not only did the narrator fail to understand his stepfather's basic humility, he also misinterpreted his stepfather's true love for his work—which the narrator saw as merely a form of pride or gratification. As a teenager, he acknowledged only his stepfather's slavish attention to details, the outward results of the orchardist's craft, and the prisonlike orderliness of his orchard rows. Both his stepfather's orchards and his stepfather himself offered much more than a casual, or perhaps indifferent, view of their surfaces might have revealed.

Now living far from his rural childhood California home, the narrator has found serenity among the filbert orchards near his riverside home in western Oregon. Even the not-too-distant apple and pear orchards of central Oregon contribute to his peace of mind. He recognizes that his peace is linked, through the orchards, to his stepfather, who is now dead. The only lingering discontent that he feels is his shame at not recognizing earlier the depth and purpose of his stepfather's life. Nevertheless, he has now found such serenity that he accepts everything peacefully, even his previous losses and sorrows. Only now, after years of observation, does he see the "exquisite tension" of life straining forth from beneath the external immobility of each growing fruit tree.

## Themes and Meanings

Because Barry Lopez's story assumes the outward appearance of an essay, it is difficult to ascribe to it any specific setting, plot, or action. Its setting—if such must be defined—is within the writer's mind, for the reader hears only the voice of the narrator, explaining how he ultimately understood that his stepfather's world and his own are in fact the same. In building toward that understanding—which comes not at the end but in the middle of the story (after which it is reinforced by the rest of the story), the author uses "two very mundane observations" of surprisingly strong revelatory impact.

Those observations, beginning with a mere speeding "glance" at a "single broken branch hanging down" in a snow-covered filbert orchard, remind the narrator, as if in photographic negative detail, of an earlier memory of Ramon Castillo standing in the moonlight, "gazing at the stars." It is at that precise moment of visionary recall that the orchards, which the narrator once viewed as "penal colonies" with "the trees as prisoners," become for him individual trees, alive, "like sparrows frozen in flight," and "like all life—incandescent, pervasive." The narrator asserts that in that moment he feels "like an animal suddenly given its head." Suddenly, he is freed of all questions and indecision.

Oddly enough, throughout the entire story the only character mentioned by name is Ramon Castillo, whom the narrator once admired greatly when Ramon was his stepfather's assistant. Although Ramon, an unmarried man in his twenties, was skilled in the arts of the orchardist, as well as the arts of the lover, he apparently lacked something essential—possibly constancy of affection or a genuine feeling for his craft. In any case, he remained aloof from the complete living world. In contrast, the stepfather was not only strong and passionate but also gentle and compassionate, bringing peaceful serenity to his marriage, to his work, and, eventually, to his stepson. Much more than an earthbound and lifelong farmer, the stepfather had also been a World War II pilot in the Pacific; after the war, he had helped to establish Claire Chennault's famous Flying Tigers in China. It was while he was in China that he developed some knowledge of and appreciation for Chinese culture.

The narrator claims to have forfeited more than just the time and the rich heritage he might have shared with his stepfather, but also a type of serene knowledge or attitude that enriches everything, including married life. He has no regrets, however, for he has serenity now, because of his stepfather. All his conflicts have been resolved. In fact, the title, "Remembering Orchards," might equally well have been "Remembering Stepfather," for it is in many ways a supremely sophisticated version of the classic college composition assignment, wherein students are asked to describe a person of some personal importance to them.

Ultimately, the narrator draws a metaphorical parallel between the life and practice of his orchardist stepfather and the life and practice of the typesetter stepson. Both are inextricably linked by orchards. The narrator now walks in orchards both real and metaphorical, and, just as his stepfather once used his hands to prune and shape the growing fruit trees, the narrator now uses his hands to craft metaphorical orchards that also bear fruit, in the form of the words that arise through the process of typesetting, and, by logical extension, through the process of writing that the author of "Remembering Orchards" uses.

*Style and Technique*

As its title suggests, "Remembering Orchards" is reflective, recalling many glimpses from earlier times in the narrator's life, especially from the ages of twelve to seventeen, when he lived with his mother and stepfather. The incomplete understanding the narrator had then contrasts with the clarity of vision that he now enjoys, a clarity that illuminates those remembered glimpses with remarkable insight and powerfully figurative language of haunting precision.

As the reader progresses through the story, many similes lead toward the overall metaphor, that of typesetting as the narrator's equivalent of his stepfather's orchard gardening. Among these similes is the narrator's recollection that his stepfather moved gently and fluidly, but with such confident strength that his movements are best described by the Chinese simile, "like silk that hits like iron." The narrator clearly sees his late stepfather's carriage as "a spring-steel movement that arrived like a rose and braced like iron." Even in the stepfather's tragically premature end by chemical poisoning, his image is fixed in a botanical simile that reveals a powerful but dying man, "contorted in his bed like a root mass."

The stepfather's epitaph, consisting of lines from a Robinson Jeffers poem that were placed on his headstone in a filbert orchard by his loving spouse (the narrator's mother), also describes the stepfather metaphorically: He was "the spirit/ Of the beauty of humanity, the petal of a lost flower/ blown seaward by the night wind, float[ing] to its quietness" and eternal rest. These well-chosen words and images bring peace, not simply to the narrator/author, but to the reader as well. Lopez may have written a story that looks like an essay; however, it reads like poetry.

*William Matta*

# "REPENT, HARLEQUIN!" SAID THE TICKTOCKMAN

*Author:* Harlan Ellison (1934-    )
*Type of plot:* Science fiction
*Time of plot:* The near future
*Locale:* An unspecified city on Earth
*First published:* 1965

> *Principal characters:*
> EVERETT C. MARM, the Harlequin, a man who ignores time
> ALICE, his wife
> THE MASTER TIMEKEEPER, the prosecutor and enforcer, also known as the Ticktockman
> MARSHALL DELAHANTY, a man whose time is up

*The Story*

The story opens with a passage from Henry David Thoreau's essay "Civil Disobedience" (1849), which concludes, "A very few . . . serve the state with their consciences also . . . and they are commonly treated as enemies by it." The story then jumps to the future, when a man has come to the attention of the Ones Who Keep The Machine Functioning Smoothly, because he has become a personality. Known as the Harlequin, because of the clownish costume that he wears and the pranks that he plays, he is dismissed by the masses, but is loved by the people who need heroes and villains, and is considered a dangerous rebel by the powerful elite. His file, timecard, and cardioplate are turned over to the Master Timekeeper, who is known behind his back as the Ticktockman. The Ticktockman informs his staff that they know what the Harlequin is, but they must find out who he is.

The Harlequin is sitting aboard his air-boat overlooking the Time-Motion Study Building. He grins and dives, swooping over the ladies of fashion riding on the slidewalk. Having created a diversion, he swoops over the factory workers, releasing $150,000 worth of jelly beans, which work their way into the mechanism of the slidewalk, causing a disruptive seven-minute delay. The Harlequin is electronically summoned to appear before the Ticktockman, but he causes an even greater disturbance by appearing three-and-one-half hours late, only to sing a silly song and vanish.

The Situation Analysts, called in to count the jelly beans and tabulate their findings, are thrown a full day behind in their schedules. They are left asking how they got "into this position, where a laughing, irresponsible japer of jabberwocky and jive could disrupt our entire economic and cultural life with a hundred and fifty thousand dollars worth of jelly beans." In this futuristic society, time has become so important, it is not merely a minor inconvenience to be late, it has become a sin, and, ultimately, a crime. The Ticktockman has the authority to subtract late time from a person's life and, when time runs out, to turn off that life. Schedules must be met because it is patriotic.

The Harlequin is revealed as Everett C. Marm, who is arguing with his wife, Alice, about his time-disrupting activities. She complains that his running around annoying people is ridiculous. He promises to be home at ten-thirty, then runs off to be late again. He has notified the officials that he will attend the International Medical Association Invocation at 8:00 P.M. They are preparing a trap to catch him, but are snared in it themselves when he laughingly appears early. In a parenthetic explanation of what could happen to the Harlequin when he is caught, an anecdote is inserted describing how Marshall Delahanty's cardioplate is blanked and his life terminated when his time runs out.

The Harlequin's final escapades throw the shopping schedule off by hours when he taunts construction workers and shoppers at the Efficiency Shopping Center, "Don't be slaves of time . . . down with the Ticktockman!" He has now gone too far. Every known technique is applied, and they catch the Harlequin, the man with no sense of time. When the Ticktockman commands the Harlequin to repent, he sneers in reply. The authorities do not want to create a martyr by terminating Everett C. Marm; they want to make of him an example. The Harlequin is sent to Coventry where he is brainwashed, and he emerges confessing to the public that he was wrong. The Harlequin has succeeded in bringing about change, however: When the Ticktockman is accused of throwing off the schedule by coming to work three minutes late, he vehemently denies the charge, but then goes gleefully into his office.

*Themes and Meanings*

Harlan Ellison is not subtle in developing "'Repent, Harlequin!' Said the Ticktockman" as an example of the value of civil disobedience, even when only the slightest progress is made at great personal expense, including the destruction of the individual. He begins by informing the reader of his intent, and ends by explaining the moral to the reader. Ellison couched this overriding theme within a satiric attack on the time-and-motion studies prevalent during the mid-1960's as a method to improve workers' productivity. Ellison was morally outraged at the institutionalization of human stupidity, and the general public's complacency in allowing themselves to be led into various modern forms of slavery.

"'Repent, Harlequin!' Said the Ticktockman" shatters the theory that increasing attention to timetables and efficient human motion not only would improve productivity but also would improve the quality of life. Instead, the resulting society reduces people to mindless robots marking time to an oppressive government's regimented schedules. These time-and-motion theories are lampooned by the violent responses to the trivial delays caused by the Harlequin. Society's increasing regard of punctuality is carefully developed, while other usual trappings of fiction are kept to a minimum. Once the point of the Harlequin's protests is made, he is captured by the Ticktockman, who demands that he repent. When he smugly refuses, he is brainwashed with no regard to plot or character development. The satire of time-and-motion studies is complete, and the broader theme of the value of individual sacrifice is shown, when the Ticktockman himself playfully throws off the schedule by three minutes. The world will be different because of the Harlequin.

*Style and Technique*

Ellison patterned the character of the Harlequin more on himself than any other character he has created. He is an outspoken social critic with a remarkable, almost savage wit. His outrage at the ludicrousness of sociopolitical fads and the stupidity of the people who support them are both at play in this story. While the Harlequin is wreaking havoc on business and government schedules by diving at shoppers, dumping jelly beans onto slidewalks, and shouting insults from the top of the Efficiency Shopping Center, a playful tone is maintained by the ridiculousness of his antics. The ludicrousness of time-and-motion proponents is further satirized by chronicling the events that transform tardiness into criminal behavior punishable by death. The story's reader is likely to have a grin pasted on his or her face much like the one pasted on the face of Everett C. Marm. The same grin must be on the face of the Ticktockman at the end of the story when he denies being late and enters his office going "mrmee, mrmee, mrmee."

Ellison has been a leading proponent in the move to expand science fiction beyond its early taboos regarding sex and violence, as well as to expand its literary parameters. This story is an example of his refusal to follow a straight narrative line and his willingness to break into the story with comments directed to the reader. Ellison was also aware that much of his audience was composed of young science fiction fans who were not schooled in other literary genres or their traditions, so he carefully guides his reader through the story's episodes and rather blatantly explains its theme. Ellison did not want the reader to skip the extensive epigraph, or to miss the relationship between it and the story; therefore, he begins his tale by presenting Thoreau's view on civil disobedience as though it is part of the story, and explains what it is about "for those who need to ask."

Ellison next informs the reader that he will first tell the middle of the story, then the beginning, and let the end take care of itself. When he interjects the experience of Marshall Delahanty, he openly labels it a footnote, the point of which is to show what could happen to the Harlequin if his identity is discovered. Finally, at the end of the story, he refers the reader back to Thoreau and makes the point that sacrifice is worthwhile if even a tiny amount of progress is made. By openly drawing attention to the mechanics of the storytelling process, Ellison tells an engaging story in a nontraditional manner and instructs the novice reader in how to negotiate its form and meaning.

*Gerald S. Argetsinger*

# A REPORT TO AN ACADEMY

*Author:* Franz Kafka (1883-1924)
*Type of plot:* Animal tale
*Time of plot:* The early twentieth century
*Locale:* Perhaps Hamburg
*First published:* "Ein Bericht für eine Akademie," 1917 (English translation, 1946)

> *Principal character:*
> ROTPETER, the narrator and protagonist, an ape that is becoming
> human

*The Story*

Asked by a scientific academy to report on his former life as an ape, Rotpeter responds by saying that his development into a human being during the last five years has erased virtually all memories of his youth in the Gold Coast. In his address to the distinguished gentlemen of the academy, he concentrates instead on his penetration into the human world, where he now feels well established as an accomplished artist in variety shows.

According to his captors, he was shot twice by members of an expedition of the Hagenbeck circus, on the cheek and below the hip. The first wound gave him his name, Rotpeter ("Red Peter"), which he finds distasteful but which differentiates him from a trained ape named Peter that has recently died. He is not at all bashful about showing his second wound to journalists, especially those who claim that he has not completely suppressed his ape nature. In the interest of truth, he believes that he may take down his pants whenever he wishes to reveal his well-groomed fur and the maliciously inflicted wound.

His first memories stem from the time of his captivity in a small cage in the Hagenbeck steamship. Overwhelmed by distress at not having a "way out" for the first time in his life, he was unusually quiet, which was taken as a sign that he either would die soon or could be easily trained. Realizing that he could not live without some kind of way out, he decided to cease being an ape. This solution meant, however, neither escape nor desire for freedom "in all directions," a quality he perhaps knew as an ape and for which some humans long. Freedom is among the noblest of human self-deceptions, comparable in his mind to the precarious movements of trapeze artists in the variety theaters.

The quiet that the ship's sailors afforded Rotpeter allowed him to observe them carefully. They moved slowly, often sitting in front of his cage, smoking and watching him in turn. He began to imitate them, first spitting in their faces, then smoking a pipe. It took him weeks to bring himself to drink schnapps. One sailor in particular persisted in giving him drinking lessons. Rotpeter watched attentively as the man uncorked a bottle and repeatedly set it to his lips. Eager to imitate him, Rotpeter soiled his cage, to the sailor's great satisfaction. Then, with an exaggerated didactic gesture, the sailor emptied the bottle in one gulp and ended the "theoretical" part of the instruction by rubbing his stomach and grinning. It was now the ape's turn, but despite all of his efforts, he could not overcome his aversion to the smell of the empty bottle when he brought it to his lips.

One evening, the ape grabbed a schnapps bottle that had been left in front of his cage. It was perhaps during a party—a gramophone played—and a number of spectators gathered around as he uncorked the bottle, raised it to his mouth, and emptied it without hesitation. He then threw away the bottle, not in despair but as an artist. His senses intoxicated, he called out suddenly "Hallo," and with this cry "leaped into the human community." Although his voice failed him for months afterward and his disgust at the schnapps bottle increased, he had found his way out: He would imitate humans.

After his arrival in Hamburg for training, he did not hesitate to choose between the two paths open to him: zoo or variety stage. The zoo was only a different sort of cage. Wearing out many instructors in the process, he learned rapidly how to abandon his ape nature. When he became more confident of his abilities and the public began to follow his progress, he hired his own teachers, placed them in five neighboring rooms, and learned from them simultaneously by jumping from one room to another without interruption.

Looking back on his development, Rotpeter is relatively happy with the gains he has made, yet he is also aware that his enormous exertion has given him only the "average culture of a European." Nevertheless, it has provided him with his way out, his human way out. He has "taken cover"; this was his only path, for he could not choose freedom.

During the day, he lounges in his rocking chair and looks out the window. His impresario sits in the anteroom and waits for his ring. In the evening there is the performance, followed by social or scientific gatherings. Afterward, he comes home to a small, half-trained chimpanzee, with whom he takes his pleasure according to the manner of apes, yet whose sight he cannot stand in the daytime.

On the whole, he has achieved what he had set out to achieve. He does not want any human judgment of his efforts, but rather wishes only to spread knowledge and to report. To the distinguished gentlemen of the academy as well, he has only reported.

## Themes and Meanings

In the fall of 1916, six months before the composition of "A Report to an Academy," Franz Kafka wrote Felice Bauer, the woman to whom he was engaged twice and who played such a major and traumatic role in his life from 1912 to 1917, that he had an "infinite desire for autonomy, independence, freedom in all directions." Torn between the demands of artistic freedom on one hand and ties to his family, work, and possible marriage on the other, Kafka insisted on the former in order to pursue his writing. While Rotpeter, in his report, adamantly denies himself such a desire for limitless freedom, he also vividly demonstrates the weaknesses of his artistry and the extent to which he has compromised his life. However, given his capture and the loss of his original freedom, Rotpeter's ruthless pursuit of his way out of captivity has succeeded in gaining for him freedom of movement, respect, and fame.

Rotpeter remains peculiarly suspended outside both the ape and the human communities, and his case eludes human judgment, which he does not want anyway. As he well knows, he is not a human, but only mimics human behavior as a means of remaining on the path that he has chosen for himself. In human terms, his art is not true art (but rather imitative and neither original nor creative), and his measure of freedom is not true freedom (he has sacrificed his real self for the sake of his career). In his own terms, however, especially compared to his first days of captivity in the steamship, he has achieved an astounding degree of success: He can read and write and think rationally and has become a moderately cultivated and sophisticated being. Although commentators have often understood the story as a satire of conformity and accommodation to a superficial culture, the ape in fact remains a critical outsider; whatever laughter his report engenders comes less at his expense than at that of the civilization that has forced him into such narrow choices.

*Style and Technique*

The virtues and shortcomings of Rotpeter's talent as a mimic are readily apparent in the language and style of his address, which is an unconscious yet masterful parody of academic oratory. Its comic incongruities arise from the fact that he is so unaware of how empty and hollow his high-flown phrases sound. In proper deference to his learned audience, Rotpeter uses a considerable amount of metaphor, philosophical reflection, complex sentence structure, exclamation, and wit to tell his life story. Thus, he speaks of the five years that divide him from his apehood as "a time that is perhaps short when measured on the calendar, but infinitely long when galloped through as I did, accompanied in stretches by admirable men, advice, applause, and orchestral music, but basically alone, for all accompaniment kept itself—to keep to the image—far in front of the gate."

Elsewhere, Rotpeter speaks of the drunken sailor wanting to "resolve the riddle of my soul," of how his "ape nature raced rolling over itself out of me and away, so that my first instructor almost became apish as a result," of his intellectual progress as a "penetration of the rays of knowledge from all sides into the awakening brain." These rhetorical flourishes underscore both his shrewd verbal dexterity and the superficial and trivial speech of those whom he mimics so well.

*Peter West Nutting*

# THE RESEMBLANCE BETWEEN A VIOLIN CASE
# AND A COFFIN

*Author:* Tennessee Williams (Thomas Lanier Williams, 1911-1983)
*Type of plot:* Domestic realism
*Time of plot:* About 1923
*Locale:* Clarksdale, Mississippi
*First published:* 1950

> *Principal characters:*
> TOM, the narrator, a boy about twelve years old
> HIS SISTER, unnamed in the story, who is two years older than he
> HIS MOTHER, also unnamed
> GRAND, Tom's grandmother
> RICHARD MILES, a handsome seventeen-year-old boy who plays
> the violin
> MISS AEHLE, a music teacher from whom Tom's sister and
> Richard Miles take lessons

## The Story

Tom, the twelve-year-old narrator, is bewildered because suddenly his sister is receiving all the attention from his mother and grandmother. The girl is said not to be feeling well, a euphemism for the fact that the physical manifestations of her passage from childhood to womanhood have just begun to show themselves. When Tom becomes frustrated with the situation and yells at his sister, his grandmother, who usually treats him with great gentleness, twists his ear. Tom wants his sister to go out and play but is told that she must practice her piano, which she starts to do. When Tom asks Grand why his sister cannot practice later, the girl flees from the piano in tears and goes to her bedroom. Tom does not know what to make of any of this.

The girl's rites of passage are symbolized by her being taken downtown by her mother on an expedition from which Tom is excluded. When his sister and mother return, the girl's long hair has been cut: "The long copperish curls which had swung below her shoulders, bobbing almost constantly with excitement, were removed one day." Tom's relationship with his sister has changed in ways that he cannot quite fathom.

Tom's sister takes piano lessons from Miss Aehle, a spinster who is extremely encouraging of all of her students' abilities, regardless of whether they are gifted. She need not exaggerate, however, to praise the musical virtues of Tom's sister, who is a quite gifted pianist for her age. Soon, Miss Aehle's students are to give a concert in the parish hall of Tom's grandfather's church. Tom's sister and Richard Miles are to play a duet: she at the piano, Richard at the violin. The two practice constantly, both alone and together, in preparation for the event. These are troubling days for Tom's sister, because her musical talent seems to be declining. She has great trouble remembering the music, and her fingers are not working well.

Richard, who is handsome, talented, and sensitive, has obviously stolen the heart of Tom's sister, and Tom also feels a sexual attraction to Richard. He is disturbed at the awakening of his own sexuality: "How on earth did I explain to myself, at that time, the fascination of his [Richard's] physical being without, at the same time, confessing to myself that I was a little monster of sensuality?" Not only has Tom lost his sister as a playmate, but he also finds himself in an unmentionable and, at the time in which the story is set, unthinkable competition with her for the affections of the same boy.

The concert takes place, and Tom's sister, almost pathologically shy and sensitive, nearly goes to pieces before it. She complains that her hands are stiff. She fills her room with steam from the bath and opens the windows, which Grand closes, saying that the girl will catch her death of cold, whereupon the girl uncharacteristically snaps at the grandmother. Finally, she gets to the parish hall and tries to play her duet with Richard. She is so nervous that she cannot remember the piece beyond the first few pages, so she keeps returning to the beginning. Richard follows skillfully and does what he can to be understanding and encouraging. He plays loudly when she is making mistakes, and the pair receives an ovation, largely because of Richard's skillful handling of a tense situation.

On the drive home from the parish hall, Tom's family remains silent. Soon the family moves from the South. They learn that Richard, who had always seemed too good to be real, has died of pneumonia. The narrator muses on how Richard's violin case had looked like a little black coffin made for a child or a doll.

*Themes and Meanings*

Tennessee Williams is said to have used his short stories as sketch pads for his plays. Certainly, in the case of "The Resemblance Between a Violin Case and a Coffin," the situation is reversed; it is the story in the Williams canon most closely related to *The Glass Menagerie* (1944). The story is autobiographical in all of its details, although the time sequence and locales are slightly distorted.

Williams's own sister Rose was the very essence of Tom's sister in this story, a beautiful but wretchedly insecure adolescent who grew into a neurotic and, finally, psychotic woman. Rose eventually had to be institutionalized and was lobotomized, after which she required custodial care lasting all of Williams's lifetime. In actuality, Rose played the violin, not the piano, as the sister in the story did; in *The Glass Menagerie*, Rose fantasized about her collection of glass animals, the only things with which she felt safe and somewhat secure.

Williams constantly explored the question of what inroads the real world makes on the psyches of sensitive people. The Blanche DuBois-Stanley Kowalski relationship in *A Streetcar Named Desire* (1947) centers on this same consideration. Blanche is the typical idealized southern woman who, like the women in Williams's own family, has retained the gentility of the South's vanished glory but has fallen on hard times. Stanley Kowalski represents the modern industrial age that will bring the gentle southerners to their knees, but in *A Streetcar Named Desire*, at least, not without the connivance and enticement of these southerners. In "The Resemblance Between a Violin Case and a Coffin," the unfeeling world is more vague than it is in some of Williams's other work, but it is still devastating to the sensitive.

Williams is concerned with sexual pressures as a root cause of human tensions, and "The Resemblance Between a Violin Case and a Coffin" clearly illustrates the effect of these pressures on the central characters in the story. However, Williams also drops hints about the effects that such pressures have on the parents in the story. Williams writes of the mother, "Upstairs my mother began to sing to herself which was something she only did when my father had just left on a long trip with his samples and would not be likely to return for quite a while."

Obviously, the parents in the story do not have a close or loving relationship. As the story unfolds, Tom is systematically excluded from the family, a boy among three women—a grandmother, a mother, and a sister—who whisper among themselves about confidences to which the boy is not privy. The healthiest person in the story, Richard Miles, is ironically the one who does not live to maturity. One senses some kind of perverse divine retribution in the fact that the sister lives on with her great emotional pain, that Tom lives on with his unresolved guilt and his feeling of detachment from those he loves, while Richard, who seems well adapted to his world, is taken from it.

The theme of personal isolation pervades the story, for despite the fact that members of families cling to one another, the individual members of the family are very much isolated in their own discrete worlds. Tom's sister, as she is seen here, is in the process of constructing around herself the wall behind which she will spend her life. In *The Glass Menagerie*, the wall becomes so strong as to be virtually impenetrable, and so did it come to be in the case of Williams's own sister.

*Style and Technique*

Williams's style in this story is one of surface gentleness that masks the great cruelties of life that lurk just below the surface. In this story, having assumed the persona of a pubescent boy, the author never deviates from that point of view. Readers see the world that Williams is revealing to them just as a twelve- or thirteen-year-old child would see it. No omniscient insights destroy the illusion Williams initially creates.

Williams's women cannot accept realities. They have enough of the southern lady about them to be exceedingly vulnerable to the hurts that are a part of daily life for most people. They agonize over what to most people would seem to be routine events. In dealing with her daughter's first menstruation, Tom's mother (and the grandmother as well) makes of it something almost mystical rather than something quite natural. The message the young girl derives from this is that women are supposed to be sickly during their menstrual periods. She learns quickly that her expected behavior must demonstrate her delicacy, and in meeting her parental (and grandparental) expectations, she sows the seeds for a life of emotional delicacy and physical weakness.

In this story, one sees the interplay of love and death that literary critic Leslie Fiedler finds at the heart of much American fiction. The title bears the suggestion, and the story carries it through. One might ask, "Who is dead?" Is Tom's sister really not more dead than Richard Miles? She has experienced a death of the soul, while Richard has lived his life vitally, self-assuredly. He remains a vivid memory in the minds of those whose lives he touched.

*R. Baird Shuman*

# RESERVATIONS
## A Love Story

*Author:* Peter Taylor (1917-1994)
*Type of plot:* Domestic realism
*Time of plot:* The early 1950's
*Locale:* Cincinnati, Ohio
*First published:* 1961

*Principal characters:*
FRANNY CROWELL MILLER, a young bride
MILES MILLER, her twenty-six-year-old husband
BERNICE, a maid at the country club
BILL CARLISLE, an assistant manager of the hotel
A PROSTITUTE

*The Story*

Because of poor weather, Miles Miller and his bride, Franny Crowell Miller, must abandon their hotel reservations in Bardstown, Kentucky, and spend the first night of their honeymoon in the same local hotel in which Miles stayed immediately before his marriage.

The story begins in a locker room of the country club where the bride, Franny, and the country club maid, Bernice, are meeting the groom, Miles, so that the couple may leave for their honeymoon undetected by their guests upstairs in the ballroom. Franny is naïve, untraveled, and possessed of only a finishing school education, but she has a certain self-confidence in the narrow, affluent, country club milieu in which she has been reared. She betrays her skittishness when she mistakenly fears that Miles is not in the locker room to meet her, but the pair are reunited and leave on their wedding trip after Franny hugs the maid Bernice, for whom she has never previously cared.

The locker room scene sets the tone of the story and begins to suggest the reservations that both partners feel going into their marriage. The backgrounds of the bride and groom—she a local girl, he an attractive stranger from California—are woven into the plot, as are the concerns and reservations of the two people as they enter matrimony.

When they arrive at the hotel, the bride imagines that the doorman and bellboys are leering at her in a knowing way, thus underscoring her nervous virginal state. Further embarrassment is avoided when a woman who is obviously a prostitute joins the couple in the elevator but deliberately debarks on a different floor so as not to embarrass the bride.

As the bride and groom sip champagne in their room, all seems well until Franny accidentally locks herself in the bathroom and cannot get out. As Miles tries unsuccessfully to take the door off its hinges, tension mounts and the couple start to hurl accusations of minor duplicity at each other. Franny charges that she had her mother write to friends in California to check up on Miles's family and that she put her father up to testing Miles to be sure he was not after her money; further, Miles carried on a flirtation with one of Franny's friends and slapped Franny once when he was jealous of her kissing another man at a party. The situation is deteriorating badly when Franny discovers that the bathroom also has a door connecting to the next room. The couple in the next room, the assistant manager of the hotel, Bill Carlisle, and the prostitute, have heard the crying and shouting and discover the connecting door as well.

Franny does not know who is in the next room, but she both desires their help and fears having them see her in her negligee and nightgown. The assistant manager uses his pass key to unlock the bathroom door from his side, then cowers in the bed with a sheet over his head so he cannot be recognized. The prostitute, who is fully clothed, sees Franny dash into the waiting arms of Miles, who is standing in the hall in his pajamas. Franny recognizes her rescuers in the next room, as does Miles, but he tries unsuccessfully to convince her she is mistaken. She is not deceived, but they drop the subject in favor of discussing their newfound knowledge about each other. Relieved to have gotten their guilty admissions off their chests, they sincerely believe that they will never deceive each other again or be troubled by differences in their upbringing or by their mixed motives in marrying each other.

## Themes and Meanings

The primary meaning of "Reservations: A Love Story" is conveyed by its antithetical title. The story is a love story, even if its title contains a trace of irony, even if its two protagonists go into their marriage with reservations. The reader may think initially that Franny and Miles have entirely too many reservations and areas of duplicity, but on further reflection one realizes that they are typical of any young couple. Peter Taylor helps the reader to see their genuine love for one another as well as gaping areas of difference and suggests implicitly that all marriages are made of such materials.

Both Franny and Miles want marriage on their own terms. Franny is delighted to find a charming, promising husband with no parents or brothers and sisters, and friends so far away that they will rarely visit; she plans to stay in her hometown and transform Miles into a Crowell, instead of making herself a Miller. Miles, on the other hand, wishes to marry an unspoiled innocent girl, unlike the girls with whom he attended college, and is delighted to find Franny in Cincinnati, a midwestern city that is largely southern in its orientation. Franny is sexually innocent, but is not artless and has distinct plans for absorbing Miles into her vision of upper-middle-class life. The reader senses enough steel in Miles to surmise that he will play that role only up to a point.

Franny's sojourn in the locked bathroom and her rescue by the prostitute and her customer, hotel assistant manager Bill Carlisle, are the catalysts that make evident the differing temperaments and aims of Franny and Miles. The comic nature of the situation undercuts the gravity of their differences and leads the reader to have hope for this marriage of opposites.

*Style and Technique*

Taylor's writing style is straightforward and unembellished. His great strength is his perfect ear for southern dialogue and narration and his acute knowledge of the mores of affluent twentieth century southerners. The voice of his narrator might be that of one of Franny and Miles's wedding guests. The narrator is a careful observer and shows considerable insight into the meaning of the tale at its end, but he is of Miles's set and knows their folkways firsthand.

As a writer of manners, Taylor depicts social differences well. Franny is a well-reared southern lady who treats the country club maid Bernice with a proper combination of artless condescension and easy affection. She is gracious to the prostitute at the end of the story. Men of lower social station than hers, however, make her nervous: The bellboys and elevator operator convey a disquieting sexuality in their joking, undeferential manner, while the possibility of meeting the assistant hotel manager Carlisle makes her anxious before she sees him with a sheet over his head. Clearly the coarseness and sexuality of men below her station challenge the perfectly arranged world in which Franny has been reared and expects to live.

Miles loves Franny for her naïveté and instinctive good manners and overlooks her unkind mimicry of the bellboys; he fails to see a steel will in his pretty young bride. In many ways, Miles acts as a foil for Franny and her world. He knows and accepts the rougher world of business and of the hotel manager, but he seeks to shield Franny from such knowledge. When she correctly identifies the prostitute and Carlisle at the end of the story, Miles goes to absurd lengths to convince her otherwise. He wishes to keep her as unaware of the wiles of the world as he believes her to be, and she is willing to foster his illusions up to a point. She will agree with him, but she knows what she knows.

Taylor is a master of the short story whose forte is depicting modern affluent southerners, just as John Updike and John Cheever excel at depicting a similar class of New Yorkers and New Englanders. His stories often capture a moment in time in the period between 1920 and 1960, an era in which the South was changing quickly but vestiges of the old life remained. "Reservations: A Love Story" takes place in the 1950's milieu from the escape of the bride and groom through the little boy's locker room of the country club to the embarrassment of being rescued by a prostitute and her customer. Taylor's faithful pen uses the gossamer threads of social convention to depict the reservations and duplicity of a young couple as they begin married life and suggests that all love stories are woven of such materials.

*Isabel B. Stanley*

# RESIDENTS AND TRANSIENTS

*Author:* Bobbie Ann Mason (1940-    )
*Type of plot:* Social realism
*Time of plot:* The mid-twentieth century
*Locale:* A small town in Kentucky
*First published:* 1982

> *Principal characters:*
> MARY, the thirty-year-old narrator
> STEPHEN, her husband
> LARRY, her lover, a dentist

*The Story*

Mary, the thirty-year-old narrator, has moved back to her hometown in Kentucky after being away at college for several years. She has returned to Kentucky to care for her parents; after they retire to Florida, she and her husband, Stephen, move into their old farmhouse. Mary loves the land and the stately old farmhouse that "rises up from the fields like a patch of mutant jimsonweeds." Because her mother cannot bear to think of moving her things out of the house herself, she has left Mary in charge of selling the house and their belongings.

When Stephen moves to Louisville to take another job, Mary stays in the farmhouse to prepare for the sale of the property, agreeing to join him after the house is sold. Now Mary realizes that she does not want to leave; also, she has taken a lover. After a routine visit to the dentist's office, she has started seeing the dentist, Larry, a man with whom she went to school. Larry had been wild in high school, but he married, settled down in his hometown, and continued to live there after his divorce. Like Mary, he loves this part of Kentucky and has no desire to move.

One afternoon, Stephen calls to inform Mary that he has found a house in Louisville and wants her to join him there. Although he is eager to buy the house, Mary hesitates to make the commitment. She reminds Stephen that her father, who always warned her to avoid debt, is paying cash for his condominium in Florida. Stephen tells her that attitude is ridiculous. He is also reluctant to have Mary's eight cats move into the house with them.

Unlike Stephen, Larry does not mind having the cats around. He visits Mary almost every day and does not even object when her cats walk on top of the bed. Mary tells Larry that she read that scientists once thought that wild cats who established territories were the strongest, while the transients were the losers. Now, she says, scientists wonder if the transients are the most curious and intelligent, and therefore the superior ones.

One evening when Mary and Larry are driving to her house, they see a wounded rabbit on the road. Mary becomes upset when she notices that the rabbit's back legs have been crushed. It hops up and down in place, unable to move off the road. By the time they reach her house, Mary is nearly hysterical. As Larry tries to comfort her, the phone rings and Larry answers it. Stephen is on the phone; Mary tries to explain why Larry is there. In the course of the conversation, Stephen admonishes Mary to be more flexible and open to change. As she listens to him, Mary thinks that he is processing words, and envisions him as floppy like a Raggedy Andy doll.

When she hangs up the phone, Mary runs out to see Larry standing on the porch. Unable to make the choice between staying with Larry or moving to Louisville with Stephen, she looks for a sign to guide her. Just then Brenda, the cat with one blue eye and one yellow eye, comes up the lane toward the house. As she looks at the cat, she sees that the blue eye looks red and the yellow eye looks green, like the lights on a traffic sign. Mary realizes that she is "waiting for the light to change."

*Themes and Meanings*

One major theme in Bobbie Ann Mason's work is the effects of rapid social change on ordinary people. "Residents and Transients" concerns the conflicts that arise when the main character must make the decision to move on or stay, to be a transient or a resident. In her twenties, Mary had been a transient, living in a commune in Aspen and backpacking through the Rockies. Now she and Larry are residents, content to live in the same town where they grew up. They appreciate the land and the comfort of familiar territory in a slower-paced world. Stephen is a transient, eager to move on to new challenges. He is not originally from Kentucky and has no particular ties to the area. Mary's parents, former residents, are now transients, having given up their home and belongings to move to Florida in retirement.

In describing characters, Mason focuses on their attitudes toward money and security. Larry is a conservative person, born in the area, settled and comfortable. He plays Monopoly seriously, carefully pushing a little iron token around the game board. He moves cautiously, whether he is eating french fries or working on the teeth of a hemophiliac. He is conservative in other ways, saving water in his office by installing a switch to cut off the water so that it does not run constantly.

Mary's family has been conservative. Her grandmother buried money in the backyard and saved ten thousand dollars from her Social Security checks during the last ten years of her life. Mary's mother could not bear to have her belongings taken from the house, so she left everything in place, just as it had always been. Not wanting to part with anything, her mother has left useless old things around the house. Mary is like her mother in many ways. She collects cats and has an attachment to the place that is nearly impossible to break.

In contrast, Stephen is a Yankee with no ties to the past. He lives in the present, eager to move on and up. He is willing to take a gamble with money. He wants to build a life in the big city of Louisville. He works with computers and word processors, and talks about investments, flexibility, and fluid assets.

Mary appears aimless and bewildered when confronted with change. She talks about her college years, but she does not mention a career or any type of job. She drifts along with no real purpose, living in her parents' house, playing with the cats, and spending time with Larry. Unable to choose between her husband and her lover, reluctant to move out of the old farmhouse, Mary waits for some external sign to guide her. Unfortunately, the sign, the cat's eyes, show both red and green, and the story ends with Mary still unsure of her decision.

*Style and Technique*

Mason uses a first-person narrator to reveal the main character's attitudes through a series of interior monologues. As Mary struggles to make decisions about her life, she focuses on ordinary, everyday activities, such as playing Monopoly and watching cats. Mary's life is portrayed in surface details, in descriptions of the house and the cats. She describes other characters in the way they react toward money and possessions. At times, the possessions reflect another aspect of a personality. For example, Larry's truck "has a chrome streak that makes it look like a rocket," and the doors are painted with flames. Perhaps the truck represents the conservative dentist's wild past.

Mason describes scenes in brief, vivid passages. While they are eating in a restaurant, Mary studies "the saw handles, scythes, pulleys . . . mounted on wood like fish trophies." This arrangement of farm tools represents an important part of the community's past. When Mary and Larry circle West Kentucky in Larry's small plane, they get an aerial view of "eighty acres of corn and pasture, neat green squares." Mary loves this part of Kentucky, whether viewed from a distance or up as close as her parents' farmhouse with the "old white wood siding, the sagging outbuildings."

Mason uses symbols to illuminate the story. The rabbit, for example, is caught in the middle of the road, trying to move with its front legs, grounded by its crushed back legs. Mary is like the rabbit—grounded, unable to move. The word processor, an impersonal, fast-moving machine that spews out words, is a metaphor for the rapid changes going on in the world.

Mary exists suspended between nostalgia for the past and apprehension about her future. The thought of selling her parents' house and moving to Louisville leaves her feeling rootless. Her relationships are unraveling. She is separated from her husband; her parents are more concerned with their lives in Florida than in what is going on at their old home. Mary will be forced to leave the house, because her parents need the proceeds from the sale to buy their condo in Florida. Because Mary has made no decision by the story's end, the story is left unresolved. The story closes with the image of the cat's eyes showing both red and green.

*Judith Barton Williamson*

# THE RETURN OF A PRIVATE

*Author:* Hamlin Garland (1860-1940)
*Type of plot:* Domestic realism
*Time of plot:* 1865
*Locale:* Near LaCrosse, Wisconsin Territory
*First published:* 1891

> *Principal characters:*
> PRIVATE EDWARD SMITH, the hero, a sickly Civil War veteran
> returning home after four years
> EMMA SMITH, his young wife, who has cared for their three
> children and the farm in his absence
> WIDOW GRAY, also called "Mother Gray," a kindly neighbor
> JIM CRANBY and
> SAUNDERS, two veterans who served with Private Smith and who
> are also returning home

*The Story*

"The Return of a Private" begins on a train from New Orleans carrying Northern veterans back to the Midwest. They are among the last to leave the South; sickness and wounds delayed their departure until August. Only four or five are left to get off the train at LaCrosse. One of them, Private Edward Smith, still suffers from fever and ague. It is two o'clock in the morning, and rather than spend their money for a hotel room, Smith and two compatriots decide to bed down in the train station. The two other veterans arrange their blankets so that their sickly friend might be more comfortable, but Private Smith has trouble sleeping. The war has left him worn out and infirm and in no shape to care for his heavily mortgaged farm or to provide for his young wife and their three children.

As Sunday morning dawns, the three veterans look across the Mississippi River and to the hills beyond, invigorated by a familiar landscape that they have not seen for several years. They buy some coffee, eat their army hardtack, and then begin walking along the road toward the hills and home, stopping now and again to let Private Smith rest. Jim Cranby, the oldest of the three, expects that he will get home just in time to surprise his boys at evening milking. Private Smith muses aloud that Old Rover will no doubt be the first of his household to run out to meet him, but when he mentions Emma, his voice breaks and is silenced by emotion. Saunders, the youngest of the three, seldom says a word. His wife will not be waiting for him; she died the first year of the war, having caught pneumonia laboring in the autumn rains to bring in the harvest. The veterans know one another well; it is a friendship born in the hardships of war.

Coming to a fork in the road, Private Smith says farewell to his friends; they promise to keep in touch, and he reassures them that he will be all right walking alone. They stop and wave at a distance, and Private Smith thinks of the good times they have had in the midst of the terrible war. He also thinks about Billy Tripp, his best friend from home, and how Billy was laughing one minute and dead from a "minie" ball the next. Billy's mother and sweetheart will want him to tell them all about the untimely death of handsome young Billy. Private Smith walks on slowly.

The scene now shifts several miles up the road to the little valley, or coulee as it is called, where Emma Smith is beginning another Sunday morning worrying about her husband and their uncertain future. Six weeks before, Edward wrote that he would shortly be discharged but has sent no other word since. She thinks about the farm he had labored so diligently to keep up. It is a shambles. Before leaving for war, Edward had contracted with a man to take care of the farm, but the man ran away in the night, stealing some farm equipment in the process. The neighbor who is now renting the land is naturally harvesting his own crops first. Thinking about her three children, Emma looks around her and weeps. Rather than be overcome by despair, she hastily dresses nine-year-old Mary, six-year-old Tommy, and four-year-old Ted, and they go down the road to Mother Gray's.

Widow Gray has a house full of children and a heart full of love. Worn down by constant labor, she is happiest when she is sharing what little she has. It is Sunday, and her girls are expecting their beaux; son Bill and his family arrive for dinner, and Widow Gray is beside herself with joy to see Emma and her little brood coming down the road. The Gray household is filled with a contagious conviviality that makes Emma momentarily forget her sadness. The dinner itself is a farmer's feast, with platters of corn and potatoes and pies of various kinds. After the meal, the women linger at the table, and Widow Gray reads the tea leaves, producing shrieks and gales of laughter from her daughters as she predicts the coming of handsome callers. Turning to Emma, she says that a soldier is on his way to her. Just then, Widow Gray looks out the window and sees what appears to be a soldier walking up the road just beyond the house. Emma tries to get his attention, but he seems not to hear.

Running up the road toward her farm, Emma is not sure that the soldier standing by the rail fence is really her husband Edward. He is so thin and pale. They suddenly recognize each other, kiss, and reunion of husband and wife, father and children, begins. The reader is told that it is a sight that Tommy, the six-year-old, will always remember with affection. As Emma takes Edward inside and prepares some biscuits, he is overcome with joy and relief at being home with his beloved wife and children. Here is his life, his happiness, in this run-down little cabin.

The homecoming is presented in bittersweet terms to the reader. The familial affection is almost overpowering, and yet the trials and tribulations that await both Private Smith and Emma are everywhere lurking in the background. Private Smith knows the hardships that are before him, but "his heroic soul did not quail." In prose that reaches poetic eloquence, the narrator relates that Private Smith fights a hopeless battle against injustice and the harshness of nature. Nevertheless, there is dignity in his struggle.

## Themes and Meanings

Hamlin Garland was at the forefront of the realist movement. He called it "veritism," and it led him to reject virtually all the romance and sentimentality that had traditionally clothed stories about the farm family. Garland knew the poverty, injustice, and dullness of rural life at first hand and conveyed that understanding with exceptional clarity in his early writings. "The Return of a Private" is a case in point. Although the focus here is on the homecoming itself, the hardships of working the land are always present. The land is not kind, and nature takes her toll, in terms of worn-out bodies and shattered dreams; as Widow Gray makes clear, though, the generosity of the human spirit is able to prevail under even harsh conditions.

Garland was a critic of land speculation and banks. A follower of economist Henry George, he saw the ubiquitous mortgage as the primary reason for the poverty of farm life. At one point in this story, the narrator even contrasts the sacrificing patriotism of Private Smith, who left his farm, wife, and babies to fight for the North, with the selfish millionaires who sent their money to England for safekeeping. Private Smith is constantly aware of the insatiable mortgage, ever threatening to devour all that he has worked for, including the security of his family. The injustice of it all is palpable, and it is relieved only slightly by the strength of character of the victims themselves. There are glimpses of a depressing determinism that presages the naturalism of later writers such as Stephen Crane and Theodore Dreiser.

Despite the cultural and material poverty he describes, Garland affirmed the dignity and nobility of the human spirit. Conditions might be harsh, but tenderness and family affections still survive, as does the struggle of the father and the mother to make a better life for their offspring. Still, there is no retreat to sentimental optimism. One finishes the story convinced that the protagonist and his family are good, loving, and deserving. However, it is clear that they cannot overcome the drabness and harshness of their environment. Their joys, whether visiting Widow Gray or simply resting together outside by the well, are all the more poignant because they are so few.

## Style and Technique

Clear, concise descriptions of people and places are hallmarks of Garland's style. The story indicates that the narrator is the son Tommy, now grown up and looking back on the return of his father and the futile struggles that the entire family waged against poverty that stifled both body and soul. This revelation adds to the basic credibility and realism of the story. Saying just so much but never too much is a technique that Garland mastered early, especially in presenting his characters or describing the landscape. The characters are ordinary, rather drab, and yet so sympathetic that their plight reaches out to the reader.

Garland was a precise recorder of life on the prairie, and he wrote as one who loved it and yet deplored it. Dramatic contrasts are everywhere to be found demonstrating the poverty of the environment and the goodness of the people. Intimate details are also added at the right time in the story—it might be Edward saying goodbye to

Cranby and Saunders, or coaxing his shy children to him with three red apples, or Emma fixing biscuits and blushing at her husband's compliments. The author also captured the dialect of the Middle Borders with remarkable felicity.

In "The Return of a Private," Garland wove together theme, character, and landscape into a powerful statement about the ordinary and sometimes forgotten people of the prairie. Indeed, not the least of his contributions to literature is his wholehearted devotion to American themes. He took the trials and tribulations of the common people and rendered them in starkly realistic prose. In this and other stories, Garland followed his own injunction to portray life as it is.

*Ronald W. Howard*

# THE RETURN OF CHORB

*Author:* Vladimir Nabokov (1899-1977)
*Type of plot:* Psychological
*Time of plot:* 1920
*Locale:* A German city
*First published:* "Vozvrashchenie Chorba," 1925 (English translation, 1976)

> *Principal characters:*
> CHORB, a destitute Russian émigré and litterateur
> MR. KELLER and
> MRS. KELLER, his Russo-German in-laws

*The Story*

The Kellers, smug, prosperous philistines, return home after an evening at the opera and a nightclub. The maid tells them that their son-in-law, Chorb, supposedly on his honeymoon in the south of France, has paid a call, saying that his wife is ill. He is staying in the same disreputable hotel where he and his bride spent their wedding night, after fleeing the elaborate reception arranged by her dismayed parents. Although Chorb has promised to call in the morning, the alarmed couple immediately sets out for the hotel.

The wife is in fact not ill, but dead. Nearly a month earlier, the laughing girl had accidentally touched a fallen roadside power line. Chorb's world has ceased to exist:

> Her death appeared to him as a most rare, almost unheard-of occurrence; nothing . . .
> could be purer than such a death, caused by the impact of an electric stream, the same
> stream which, when poured into glass receptacles, yields the purest and brightest light.

The young husband wishes to possess his grief alone, "without tainting it by any foreign substance and without sharing it with any other soul." For this reason, Chorb has not informed the parents but rather has undertaken a ritualistic return journey.

The bereaved bridegroom decides to re-create, to immortalize, the image of his dead wife by retracing step-by-step their long, autumn-to-spring honeymoon journey. The re-created image will, he hopes, replace his bride. Starting from the place of her death, Chorb attempts to relive each of their memories, the small shared perceptions with which they delighted each other: the oddly marked pebble found on a Riviera beach, the winter in Switzerland, the autumn walks in the Black Forest where they saw an iridescent, dewdrop-covered spiderweb radially spanning two telegraph wires, perhaps, Chorb now thinks, prefiguring his bride's fate. Completing his reverse journey, Chorb has arrived back at their starting point.

The young writer checks into the same disreputable hotel and by chance gets the same shabby room that he recognizes by the picture over the bed. He also recognizes the green couch on which he spent their chaste first night while she slept in the bed. He recalls his bride's amusement at the seedy establishment and their glee at having escaped her stuffy parents and their reception. The room seems haunted: A mouse rustles behind the wallpaper, and the light bulb hanging from the ceiling sways gently. Though exhausted by his sleepless, three-week journey, Chorb is too distraught to rest and sets out for a nocturnal walk. As he wanders, he recalls a wedding-eve stroll with his laughing, skipping bride. Finding himself at the house of his in-laws, he learns from the maid that they are at the opera and leaves word that their daughter is ill.

Chorb realizes that he is now back at the source of his recollections. He needs only to spend one night in their former hotel room, and the ordeal will be over. Her image will be complete. He senses, however, that he cannot spend the night alone in the haunted room. He must have a companion. At length, he finds a prostitute, who accompanies him to the room where she has spent other nights. Chorb, to the surprise of the untouched girl, immediately falls asleep. The prostitute prowls about the room, fingers the dead wife's clothes in a trunk, and finally goes to sleep. The air is rent by a visceral scream. Chorb has awakened to find his "wife" beside him in the bed. The terrified girl leaps up and turns on the lamp to find Chorb huddled in the bedclothes with his hands over his face, through which one eye can be seen burning "with a mad flame." Chorb gradually recognizes the prostitute and gives a sigh of relief. His ordeal is now over. He moves to the green couch and gazes at the girl with "a meaningless smile." Still terror-stricken, she scrambles to dress.

Voices and steps are heard in the corridor, and there is a knock on the door. The girl flings it open to meet the stupified gazes of Keller and his wife. Responding to a signal from the hotel employee, she bolts out as the in-laws enter. The door closes. The girl and the bellboy wait at the door, listening. Silence reigns.

*Themes and Meanings*

Vladimir Nabokov's title, "The Return of Chorb," points to his major theme. Chorb's return takes place on two levels: the geographical and the psychological. The former merely frames and provides a set of cues for the latter's world of memory. Nabokov's central theme, one common to much of his work, is the relationship of the memory of things past to present reality. If Chorb succeeds in re-creating his bride in memory, he thinks, he will have exorcised the tragedy and possess her forever; he will be able to live again. This is the goal of his reverse journey through space and time. However, reality proves him wrong. Although momentarily relieved of his tragic burden when he awakes, he immediately faces the tragicomic denouement with his in-laws. One cannot successfully live in a world of idyllic memories, no matter how richly reconstituted.

The story also has a subtle undercurrent of the supernatural. The bride dies the purest of deaths, killed by that same stream of electricity that pours into glass bulbs and gives the brightest light. It is not by chance that Chorb is unaccountably distressed by the gently swaying light bulb in his hotel room. As Nabokov once remarked in a discussion of the occult: "Electricity. Time. Space. We know nothing about these things."

The always laughing wife may have returned to play a joke on the husband (the comic fiasco of the ending) or to try to jolt him into the loving realization that he must live in the present, not in shared memories of their brief past.

Chorb is perhaps not fated to be a great writer, for he lacks the toughness of mind to live in the present. There is a hint that his mind has snapped as he sits peeping out with his mad, flame-filled eye and then gazes at the prostitute with "a meaningless smile."

## Style and Technique

Nabokov was one of the great twentieth century masters of structure and style, in both his Russian and his English works. "The Return of Chorb" is a good example. Nabokov employs an omniscient narrator who focuses on the Kellers in the opening and closing sections (both set in the present) and on Chorb in the longer middle section, which alternates between the present of Chorb's return and the past of his memories. Events in the present trigger memories of related scenes from the past. The mention of the wife's "illness" evokes Chorb's reminiscence of her death and his slow return journey, the picture in the grubby hotel room, the lovers' wedding and flight to the hotel, and Chorb's walk, his wedding-eve stroll with his fiancé. The striking thing about Nabokov's narrative technique is that it proceeds in two directions at once. The present-tense narration, beginning with Chorb's return, moves in the normal forward direction; the past-tense narration stages Chorb's tragedy in reverse order: the death and return trip, the wedding night, the wedding-eve stroll. The two time-lines proceed in opposite directions and are linked by the web of memories just as in the image of the two telegraph lines spanned by the iridescent spiderweb.

Nabokov's development of the characters is also noteworthy. The narrator's contempt for the unimaginative, bourgeois Kellers is evident. Both are stout, and Herr Keller's face is "simian." Their level of taste is satirically reflected in the slippers (hers red, with cute little pom-poms) placed by the newlyweds' intended bedside on the throw rug, with its incongruous but prophetic motto, "We are together unto the tomb." They stand in grotesque contrast to the sensitive Chorb, an artist caught up in his subtle perception of the wonder of reality. This sense of wonder is shared by his laughing, nameless bride, who is mysteriously and fatally linked with images of electricity and falling leaves.

Nabokov is justly famed as a master of the precise verbal detail ("The same black poodle with apathetic eyes was in the act of raising a thin hindleg near a Morris pillar, straight at the scarlet lettering of a playbill announcing *Parsifal*"). Detail is also sometimes used for narrative purposes. A good example is the "lovely blond hair" found in the hotel room's washbasin by Chorb's bride. The hair belongs to the blond prostitute, a frequent "guest" at the hotel, who later spends the night with Chorb. There is even a faint suspicion that Keller may have been her client at the time the hair was left. Also to be noted is the humorous irony in which the narrative's elegiac tone is deliberately shattered by the abrupt if understated comic fiasco of the ending.

*D. Barton Johnson*

# RETURN TO RETURN

*Author:* Barry Hannah (1942-　　)
*Type of plot:* Antistory
*Time of plot:* The 1950's to 1970's
*Locale:* New York City and cities in Louisiana
*First published:* 1975

*Principal characters:*
　　FRENCH EDWARD, a tennis professional of exceptional beauty
　　BABY LEVASTER, his sidekick and admirer
　　DR. JAMES WORD, his other major admirer and the focus of his
　　　　excessive hatred

*The Story*

A brain-damaged tennis professional, French Edward, and his sidekick and unoffi-
cial manager, Baby Levaster, are a most unlikely pair. Edward is presumably the happiest man on the court and may also be the prettiest. Levaster, a self-hating, hard-
drinking, part-time physician, is quite unattractive. In a segmented dream memory,
Levaster revisits the often picaresque adventures of their collective past. He and Edward
first became acquainted as high school athletes in Vicksburg, Mississippi. Levaster
was a better tennis player initially, but after the local college tennis coach, Dr. James
Word, begins working with Edward, it is his life that is changed by the sport.

French Edward is not grateful to his mentor. He discovers that his mother, Olive, is
having an affair with the bald but virile Dr. Word, and he senses that he himself is also
the object of his coach's sexual interest. Edward is so filled with hatred that he wants
to blot out what offends him. He challenges Word to a tennis match that he intentionally prolongs in the hope of driving his sixty-year-old opponent to heart failure. Instead, Dr. Word has a stroke, which costs him almost all of his sight and the part of the
brain that monitors the amplitude of his speech. These handicaps do not stop him from
zealously following the career of the man he calls his son. Word, accompanied by his
brother, Wilbur, pursues French Edward from tournament to tournament.

At first, Edward is only marginally conscious of this continued attention; he has his
own priorities. While studying at Louisiana State University, he meets and marries a
Franco-Italian woman. Her father has grown rich from pinball and wrestling conces-
sions and sees in Edward's mastery of an upper-class sport the family's only claim to
glory. Baby Levaster responds to Edward as the embodiment of qualities that he is
painfully aware that he personally lacks: youthful beauty and physical elegance.
Levaster periodically abandons his medical practice to follow Edward on the professional tennis circuit.

Word follows Edward also, but mostly at a distance, and only rarely does he confront Edward after a match and give him a "hard, affectionate little nip of the fingers,"
an act that drives the tennis pro to the boiling point.

On a bridge over the Mississippi River, Edward finally confronts the family secret that has tormented him for so long. In the presence of his parents, Word, and Levaster, he informs his father of Olive's continuing infidelity. In response, Word runs from the group as if to cast himself over the railings of the bridge, Edward runs as if to stop him, and both men plummet into the river. Apparently, only French Edward survives.

Levaster awakens from his combination of memory and dream just in time to drive Edward to another tournament. His mental powers impaired by his near-drowning, but his athletic body functioning superbly on automatic pilot, Edward is about to serve match point when Levaster whispers as if his whole existence depended on that single act, "Hit it, hit. My life, hit it."

*Themes and Meanings*

One of twenty stories in Barry Hannah's first published collection, *Airships* (1978), "Return to Return" was salvaged from an aborted novel. Five years later, "Return to Return" appeared as the initial section of *The Tennis Handsome* (1983), a novel that reintroduces the three principal characters of the original story and further develops their collective narrative.

The novel's title signals one of the writer's major themes in "Return to Return." French Edward, in his role as "The Tennis Handsome," assumes legendary stature as the incarnation of comeliness and strength, much like "the Handsome Sailor" in the posthumously published novella *Billy Budd* (1924) by the nineteenth century U.S. novelist Herman Melville. Like Billy Budd, French Edward serves as a standard by which all the other characters are measured.

Although Baby Levaster, a physician, is clearly the intellectual superior of college dropout French Edward, the unprepossessing Levaster nevertheless covets Edward's physical beauty and yearns for his mindless athleticism. Levaster himself recognizes the "perfect mental desert" of Edward's brain, a condition that makes it possible for him to respond so instinctively to the game without the distraction of thought.

Levaster longs to merge his mind with Edward's body, an opportunity that presents itself after the tennis pro nearly drowns. This role as companion and surrogate memory is the closest Levaster can come to the state of being he sees represented in French Edward.

Dr. Word also seeks to possess Edward, and through his sexual relationship with Edward's mother, Word feels that the tennis pro is his own progeny. Word eschews reason in favor of instinctive behavior. This accounts for part of his attraction to Edward, the natural athlete, and part of his inability to abandon his attachment to Olive.

The title "Return to Return" also reinforces meaning. To "return serve" is a tennis term denoting the act of hitting the ball back to one's opponent; the continuity of any tennis match depends on the ability of both players to keep the ball in play so that return follows return. Thus tennis is a metaphor for life, wherein each action impels a reaction.

In this regard, part of the attraction that Edward holds for Baby Levaster is the tennis pro's ability to react instinctively on the court as well as in life. His actions combine the nature of a priest with that of a brute. Edward is a priest in the sense that he does not want the game or his life to be fouled by personal ugliness. Thus, he punishes himself for ill will on the court by soft-serving to players that he personally dislikes. He is a brute in the sense that his animal strength and speed have made it possible for him to perfect a new, dangerous brand of tennis.

For Levaster, who hated to see pain and blood, who shot at would-be muggers in Central Park with popcorn-filled bullets, and who "dragged himself from one peak of cowardice to the next," thus learning the many humiliations that life hands the average person, Edward offers vicarious victory in the face of defeat.

When Edward is about to hit the ball at story's end, to Levaster's eye, he hits for everyone, and there is "something peaceful in the violent sweep of his racket."

*Style and Technique*

At the heart of Hannah's style is a love for language: One of his principal characters is named Dr. Word. At times, this affection impels his prose to aspire to the condition of poetry. Even at these moments, the beauty wears a smile, and the occasional purple passage is touched by humor. When Levaster asks Wilbur Word how Vicksburg has changed, for example, the reply is "nothing explosive, kudzu and the usual erosion." Hannah is a master of the lush, rhythmic southern idiom.

In addition to heightened language, Hannah's narrative strategy is marked by surreal incidents and eccentric characters. "Return to Return" is episodic, and each section advances the plot line like the return of a serve prolongs a tennis match. In one section, Dr. Word is struck in his one good eye by a tennis ball intentionally and vindictively aimed by a tennis player outraged by Word's loud support for French Edward; in the next section, Olive confesses in a letter to her son that his sports-mad father once tackled a player during a high-school football game he was hired to referee. In rapid succession, Hannah serves the reader one wacky incident after another.

Each section is also peopled by characters whose eccentricity is similar to the comically grotesque denizens of the fiction of Flannery O'Connor, the modern American writer to whom Hannah is most often compared.

Even the minor characters are memorable. These include the phlegm-hacking, fish-colored South African tennis star Whitney Humble, who plays against Edward twice in the tale; the promiscuous, teenage runaway Carina, who shares Levaster's New York apartment and thinks that Edward "looks like love"; and Edward's large-nosed, big-breasted wife Cecilia Emile, who paints watercolors "so demure they resisted making an image against the retina." Like doctors Levaster and Word, these minor characters also serve to define the protagonist French Edward through their confrontation with and reaction to his presence.

In the final analysis, Hannah celebrates survivors, no matter how unlikely. In a world that the narrator at times describes as "vicious" and "soilsome," the act of making it from one day to the next is a cause for celebration.

*S. Thomas Mack*

# THE REUNION

*Author:* Maya Angelou (Marguerite Johnson, 1928-    )
*Type of plot:* Social realism
*Time of plot:* Probably the 1930's or 1940's
*Locale:* Chicago's South Side
*First published:* 1983

> *Principal characters:*
> PHILOMENA JENKINS, an African American jazz pianist
> BETH ANN BAKER, a rich white woman

*The Story*

The story's title produces an expectation that characters soon to be introduced will share nostalgia of bygone days and long for happier hours that can never be fully recaptured. A few opening words laced with irony, however, dispel this anticipation. The appearance of a particular white woman in a jazz club, the Palm Cafe, jolts the narrator, whose surprise is intensified by the fact that the lady in question appears to be dating a black man. Faced with a seeming impossibility the narrator consults her long-term memory, checking for accuracy, and concedes that this nemesis of her past, and not a double, is indeed sitting there, waiting to hear the Sunday afternoon matinee of the Cal Callen band.

As the band leader introduces the instrumentalists, the narrator, Philomena Jenkins, hears his usual hip patter with half a mind; the other half is captured by the spectacle of Miss Beth Ann Baker, former Georgia Peach and Miss Cotton Queen, the richest girl in the town of Baker, Georgia, sitting beside a good-looking black man. When Cal Callen introduces the lady piano player by name, Philomena sees Beth squint at her in mutual recognition. This brief acknowledgment causes Philomena to miss her cue in the opening interlude. While a few bars of the music escape her, Philomena detects in Beth's expression a look that is familiar, but too vague to name. Philomena uses the feelings that look evokes to dig down into the next jazz number, "Round Bout Midnight." Beth's presence now seems to facilitate Philomena's finding "the places between the keys where the blues and the truth lay hiding." As Philomena identifies with the inconvenience, lack of privilege, and heartache the song calls forth, the notes blend with her understanding of how these realities have shaped both her life and her music. The tangible symbol of all the pain and hurt the knowledge engenders is now embodied by Beth, the little rich girl who had everything.

Philomena bitterly recalls how her parents, servants for the Baker family, had received so little compensation for their sweat that they could not afford to buy new clothes for their daughter, yet they were called treasures and gems by their employers. Philomena remembers having to work so hard as a youngster that stolen, midnight hours were all she could get to practice the piano. As she thinks back to all the times at school when she was called the "Baker Nigger," feelings of resentment swell and she fantasizes about the disrespect she can finally show Beth to her face.

Philomena's solo contribution of thirty-two bars to the song wins the audience's applause—a sign of great approval from the tough, predominantly black audience, which is characteristically stingy with its praise. When the number ends, Philomena is set to flaunt her success before Beth, but when she looks at the table where the young woman and her date were sitting, they are gone.

Philomena completes the set. During intermission, she retires to the dark end of the bar. The emotional edge caused by the near reunion returns, and she slips back into a bitter reverie. Suddenly Beth, alone, appears beside Philomena. In an awkward beginning, Beth brushes off the past and launches into an explanation for her being in the club with a black man. She tells Philomena that she is engaged to the man, Willard; that they are happy; and that her parents will no longer speak to her. As Beth proudly explains that she acquired Willard by her own initiative, and that he is the first thing she has ever owned that no one has handed to her, Philomena is reminded of Beth's spoiled mother, who often showed the effects of too much whiskey. Philomena sees plainly that Willard is a toy for Beth, who can afford to play with him for a while, but when his presence becomes too inconvenient, she will discard him and quickly return to her life of privilege.

When Beth offers to make Philomena a part of her weekend plans and even extends an invitation to the wedding, Philomena looks beyond Beth's affair with Willard and remembers how Beth's father had played the same skin game, leaving as proof three children by different African American women whom he ignored once he lost interest in them sexually. Refusing the opportunity to hurl accusations and delve into the past, Philomena simply replies, "Good-by Beth. Tell your parents I said to go to hell and take you with them, just for company."

With the reunion behind her, Philomena feels unburdened. Through tears of relief, she realizes more clearly that her music is power—refined by hard work, dedication, and love—and that it has greater lasting value spiritually than Beth's money, which buys only hollow privilege and fleeting pleasure.

*Themes and Meanings*

Maya Angelou once said, "I speak to the black experience but I am always talking about the human condition—about what we can endure, dream, fail at and still survive." Her protagonist in "The Reunion" epitomizes a survivor in the mold of her description. She is the archetypal black female artist who has struggled to overcome formidable social obstacles and has risen to achieve greater self-understanding and greater appreciation for her talent, honed to perfection by adversity.

In this story, one hears echoes of Angelou's famous autobiography, *I Know Why the Caged Bird Sings* (1970), for Angelou, like the character in the story, suffered through a troubled childhood in which racial discrimination was an everyday reality; like Philomena, she endured hardships to develop her art. Angelou reveals her acute understanding of human nature when she paints Philomena as neither saint nor victim, despite the fact that Philomena's aspirations are spiritual and she has been victimized. She realistically portrays her protagonist as tough, worldly-wise, and unforgiving. Accepting Philomena as a true-to-life human being, the reader understands why she is unbending in the way she resents the wrongs she has suffered and why she feels she owes nothing to her oppressor. At the same time, the reader respects and cheers for the female character who has fashioned a place for herself as a piano player in an otherwise all-male band, gets the billing of "a looker and a cooker," and lives up to it. As "a cooker" is a slang term for one who can perform any task as an expert, its use in this story is an ironic pun, because women usually prepare meals.

*Style and Technique*

The story's first sentence establishes the rhythm that plays throughout like a piece of jazz music. Angelou adeptly paces the story like a musical score by means of repetition and variations on ideas. For example, when Philomena begins with the incredible information that Miss Cotton Queen Beth is dating a black man, she drives the point home by stating first that the young woman is out with the man, then she repeats the word, and finally comes back to expand, "like going out," magnifying more than she explains. This kind of repeat and variation is used effectively throughout the story, calling to mind the parallel jazz structure of a riff.

Analogous to jazz, which is streetwise and hip, the language of "The Reunion" projects the same ambiance through ideas expressed in prose rich in metaphor and earthy expressions. Such language not only makes the story colorfully cool, but enhances Angelou's ironic intentions. For example, instead of saying that Philomena was shocked when Beth said she was engaged to marry a black man, Angelou has Philomena reflect on the moment this way: "I'm proud of my face. It didn't jump up and walk the bar."

*Sarah Smith Ducksworth*

# REVELATION

*Author:* Flannery O'Connor (1925-1964)
*Type of plot:* Psychological
*Time of plot:* The 1950's
*Locale:* Georgia
*First published:* 1964

> *Principal characters:*
> MRS. RUBY TURPIN, a self-righteous woman
> CLAUD TURPIN, her husband
> MARY GRACE, a Wellesley student

*The Story*

While Mrs. Turpin and her husband Claud are waiting in the doctor's office for treatment of Claud's bruised leg, Mrs. Turpin strikes up a conversation with some of the other patients but becomes annoyed with a Wellesley student, whom she thinks is fat and ugly and who scowls at her. Mrs. Turpin notices that the girl, Mary Grace, seems to be staring at her malevolently, and when she tries to engage the girl in conversation, she is snubbed. As she sizes up the people in the doctor's office, Mrs. Turpin classifies them, as is her wont. She thinks that Mary Grace's mother is stylishly dressed and pleasant, in contrast to the woman with the small child sitting nearby, whom she regards as white trash.

While talking to Mary Grace's mother, Mrs. Turpin concentrates her attention on herself. As the reader soon learns, she is normally preoccupied with herself. She thinks about how fortunate she is to be who she is, rather than being black or merely white trash. Just as she comments to the others on how grateful she is for all she is and has, she is suddenly assaulted by Mary Grace—struck by the book that she has been reading. As she struggles to escape, Mrs. Turpin feels as if she is watching the event from far away. When Mary Grace is sedated, Mrs. Turpin asks her what she has to say for herself and waits as if for a revelation. Mary Grace calls her a warthog and tells her to go back to Hell.

Because she believes that Mary Grace had something to say to her rather than any of the others in the doctor's office, who were more deserving of such reprobation, Mrs. Turpin sees herself as being singled out to be given a special message. As she thinks over the revelation later, she becomes angry, and it continues to prey on her mind.

Later, while talking to the black women who work for her husband, Mrs. Turpin relates the incident, and the women commiserate with her, telling her how sweet and nice she is. Still, she realizes how empty their sympathy is, recognizing the accustomed role blacks play in their dealings with whites. As she goes out to water down the pig parlor, she continues to mull over the incident in her mind. She speaks to God, asking why he sent such a message to her when there are so many others more deserving, ending with asking God just who he thinks he is.

Finally she has a vision of a bridge that extends from the earth through a fire, and on the bridge are troops of souls whom she recognizes as blacks and white trash being washed clean for the first time in their lives. At the end of the procession, she sees staunch, respectable middle-class people such as Claud and herself, and she sees by the shock on their faces that these people have had their virtues burned away. As she turns off the water and slowly walks back to the house, she hears only the voices of the souls in her vision singing hallelujah.

## Themes and Meanings

Though the message of "Revelation" is clear, its impact is underplayed; the reader is left unsure about what Mrs. Turpin has learned from the revelation she has received. It is through the title and the name of the girl, Mary Grace, and chiefly Mrs. Turpin's reactions that the revelation that comes to her is emphasized.

The revelation is prepared for by the author's exposition of the character of Mrs. Turpin at the start of the story. The story is narrated from the third-person limited-omniscient point of view: Events are narrated in the third person for all the characters in the story, except for Mrs. Turpin. Others are described as Mrs. Turpin perceives them. Interspersed with the narrative are the thoughts of Mrs. Turpin about how superior Claud and she are to others and how she likes to classify people.

The narrator speaks of how Mrs. Turpin is accustomed to lying in bed at night, contemplating the virtues of different people. In her classification, she puts blacks on the bottom (she usually refers to them as "niggers" not with malice, but through custom), white trash next, then homeowners, followed by "home-and-land owners, to which she and Claud belonged," ending with people with a large amount of money, who should be beneath Claud and her. At this she thinks of a black dentist who unaccountably has more material possessions than she and Claud do. When she contemplates these values while lying in bed she usually falls into utter confusion trying to figure out why Claud and she are not at the top: "All the classes of people were moiling and roiling around in her head, and she would dream they were all crammed in together in a box car, being ridden off to be put in a gas oven."

The author's language gives several clues about Mrs. Turpin. First, her phrase "she and Claud" shows her self-centeredness because she places herself before Claud, contrary to proper usage. Later, she compounds this error with the phrase, "Above she and Claud," an error made by those who think they are more educated than they are.

More telling is the final metaphor of confusion used by the author. The obvious association with the Holocaust in Nazi Germany passes an unequivocal judgment on the kind of morality that is represented by Mrs. Turpin. Although Mrs. Turpin is sometimes troubled by the contemplation of her role on earth, she has a closed mind about her sense of superiority. However, she is forced to confront her self-concept, and with the final revelation it is uncertain how she will react to this knowledge—whether she has acquired a new awareness of herself and a new humility. Judging from Flannery

O'Connor's penchant for stories of "redemption through catastrophe," it is probable that such is the intended theme.

*Style and Technique*

As noted above, Mrs. Turpin's thoughts are conveyed by an omniscient narrator who otherwise narrates the events of the story from the third-person point of view, picking up Mrs. Turpin's judgments of most of the events. The reader cannot be certain whether Mary Grace, as Mrs. Turpin believes, is really fixing her eyes on Mrs. Turpin in hatred. What is important is that Mrs. Turpin thinks so, and this belief leads her to expect some sort of revelation from the girl. The girl's name is also important (as is the title, which gives the reader the main clue to the theme of the story), combining the word "grace" with the holy name Mary, an indication of the grace that Mrs. Turpin receives in gaining a revelation that can lead to her redemption.

At the same time, the point of the story is not overly emphasized by the author. Rather, the theme arises naturally, as O'Connor presents objective details through the consciousness of Mrs. Turpin, letting the reader decipher what impact the events finally have on her.

*Roger Geimer*

# A REVENANT

*Author:* Walter de la Mare (1873-1956)
*Type of plot:* Ghost story
*Time of plot:* 1932
*Locale:* Wigston, England
*First published:* 1936

> *Principal characters:*
> PROFESSOR MONK, a man of letters, lecturing to a small literary society
> THE GHOST OF EDGAR ALLAN POE, a member of the audience
> THE REVEREND MR. MORTIMER, the chairman of the lecture
> A YOUNG GIRL, unnamed, a member of the audience

*The Story*

Though the title "A Revenant" proclaims that this is a ghost story—and it is—it reads more like an essay, a discourse more on ideas than on events or characters. In this aspect, the story's structure is twofold: It is a duel of intellects between Professor Monk and the ghost of Edgar Allan Poe, the professor's assertions about Poe followed by Poe's rebuttal. The story is also a study of Professor Monk—limited as his character is by academic habits of mind and waffling prudery—and as such its structure, like the professor's lecture, is fourfold: a lengthy introductory section establishing time, place, and characters; a synopsis of the professor's lecture up to 8:46 P.M., when the present action of the story begins; the continuation of the lecture to its end; and two responses, the chairman's public response followed by Poe's private one.

The introductory section establishes two sides to Professor Monk's character: his habitual complacency and his present profound disquietude. The former is revealed in the professor's preference for "a sober and academic delivery," in his rejection of gestures and any sort of staginess, in his determination to appeal to the intellect alone, in his "modest satisfaction" with this lecture and its systematic organization. His disquietude is expressed by his sudden sharp awareness of where he is, his acute sense that he is alone, and the "amazing rapidity" of the speculations that agitate his thoughts. Mediating between these two aspects of Professor Monk's state of mind is the "challenge" offered by the darkly cloaked stranger at the back of the hall, of whose presence, apparently, only Professor Monk is aware.

The professor's lecture seems an odd tissue of qualifications, full of "but" and "though," "on the other hand," and "nonetheless." In the portion of the lecture preceding 8:46 P.M., summarized here by the narrator, Professor Monk focuses largely on Poe's character ("arrogant, fitful, quarrelsome, unstable") and on his failure to find material success. What little the professor does say about Poe's work itself is done briefly and apparently contradictorily, announcing that "craftsmanship, artistry . . .

[are] vital alike in prose and verse" and proceeding directly to fault Poe's poems for their "flawless mastery of method." Like an anatomist with the human body, the professor fails to deal creatively with the whole of the phenomenon his lecture purports to treat, yet he does not realize why he finds Rembrandt's *Anatomy Lesson of Dr. Nicolaes Tulp* (1632) flickering through his mind; his statements, like Rembrandt's painting, remain "curiously detached"—that is, curiously disconnected—and his intellect falls somehow between the two sides of his own advice: "Life, like a lecture, is a succession of moments. Don't pay too extreme an attention to any one or two; wait for the end of the hour." He takes his lecture, for its own sake, too seriously, failing to take its subject seriously enough; his lecture, consequently, fails to make sense of the writings he purports to be expounding or of the man he actually treats. Professor Monk's lecture continues after 8:46 P.M. as a series of discrete comments— contiguous but barely linked—and turns ever and again from Poe's writings to Poe the man.

If the professor has erred on the side of "academic mouthings and nothings," as Poe's ghost later claims, the lecture's chairman, the Reverend Mr. Mortimer, misses any point a literary lecture may have, his ignorance illustrating one argument against what the professor has offered his audience: The chairman seizes on all the least relevant points in the lecture and fluently constructs from them an "urgent lesson." Probably the only person who has had an actual literary experience at this lecture is the schoolgirl who asks for Professor Monk's autograph, and she has attained her experience by ignoring most of what the lecturer says, concentrating instead on the loveliness of the poems she has learned in class.

The encounter that follows with the ghost of Edgar Allan Poe is the crisis of Professor Monk's life, for Poe's rebuttal is at once so incisive and so acid that it completely changes Professor Monk's "view of himself and even of his future." He may continue to insist on existing "within strict limits," and he understands what has happened to him as "a piece of mere legerdemain," yet his final "Ah, yes" seems at least to acknowledge the truth of what Poe's ghost has said:

> Opinions, views, passing tastes, passing prejudices—they are like funguses, a growth of the night. But the moon of the imagination, however fickle in her phases, is still constant in her borrowed light, and sheds her beams on them one and all, the just and the unjust.

## Themes and Meanings

As an essay, "A Revenant" opposes two viewpoints, Professor Monk's and Edgar Allan Poe's. The professor's position is equivocal, however, for his theory and his practice are at odds. "He preferred," the narrator explains, "facts to atmosphere, statements to hints, assumptions, 'I venture's', and dubious implications." However, his lecture is compounded largely of atmosphere, hints, assumptions, and all the rest. His sober academic manner has been, even by the professor himself, mistaken for scholarly method, the dryness of his delivery for depth of understanding, and the constant qualification of his statements for critical acumen. His unfitness—and, by extension, the unfitness of many academics—to venture into the world of literary criticism is evidenced by his discontent with the nature of its subject: "Poetry may, and perhaps unfortunately, must appeal to the emotions and the heart."

Ironically, Poe's ghost seems to agree with the remainder of the professor's statement, that "the expounding of [poetry] is the business of the head." Quoting Poe's own essay on "The Poetic Principle," the ghost asserts that "we must be cool, calm, unimpassioned." In a sentence deleted from the ghostly quotation, Poe wrote, "We need severity rather than efflorescence of language." At the same time, however, the specter insists on the aspect of the poetic impulse that Professor Monk finds so unfortunate; he argues, indeed, that "imagination" is no "mere faculty," but is a "sovereign power," a "divine energy." Poe's ghost further demands of the professor a definition of poetry, or at least some reference to Poe's own definition. The ghost thus calls into question the professor's ability even to speak of poetry, since he seems unable to appreciate it, and the acuity of his intellectual method, since he has failed even to define his terms.

The method followed by the ghost in his rebuttal is simpler yet more comprehensive than the professor's own lecture. He begins by summarizing Professor Monk's attitude toward his subject by adducing "the tone, the flavour, the accent" of the lecture and noting how poor a basis for the critical endeavor such an attitude is. He proceeds to critique the lecturer's treatment of Poe the man, noting that he has turned tragedy into melodrama and that his words have revealed his feelings, hinting at opinions such as "mountebank, ingrate, wastrel, fortune-hunter, seducer, debauchee, dipsomaniac." The specter prepares for his next point by finding an area of common ground and then attacking the professor from that vantage:

Oh yes, I agree that a man's writings indelibly reflect him and all of him that matters most. And since your poet's are all that is left of him in the world, and they alone are of lasting value, should we not look for him there? Did you attempt to depict, to describe, to illuminate that reflection? No: for that would have needed insight, the power to divine, to re-create. You are a stern and ardent moralist, Professor. But since when has the platform become the pulpit? It needs, too, little courage to attack and stigmatize the dead.

Again the ghost calls into question the professor's intellectual acumen by reminding him of the title of his paper—"The Writings of Edgar Allan Poe"—and by using such terms as "groping" and "fatuous" to describe the professor's treatment of poetic technique; his "remarks on the art of writing," the specter adds, "were nothing short of treason to the mind. They were based on inadequate knowledge, and all but innocent of common sense."

Walter de la Mare's discursive intention may, perhaps, be found in the specter's suggestion that "man's feeblest taper [is] . . . a dual splendour—of heat and light." Professor Monk professes but half that formula—light—and he fails even there because of the confusions he entertains, the distinctions he does not make, and the knowledge he simply does not have.

*Style and Technique*

De la Mare's discursive intentions have been tempered in "A Revenant" by the machinery he employs to lend both mystery and importance to the presence of a ghost at Professor Monk's lecture. His gradual introduction of the stranger, for example, piques the reader's interest primarily by what is not told. Initially, no reason is offered for the professor's disquiet, but a series of incomplete ideas leads to the latecomer's introduction; "one single exception," "he knew why," "Then what was wrong?" are offered, paragraphs apart, without completion, raising questions in the reader's mind: Who is the exception? What is the reason the professor knows? Why does he not answer the question?

Again, Professor Monk's "punctual interruption" is presented in terms appropriate to the occasion. The story's first notice of the "sudden, peculiar, brief, strident roar" describes it thus: "On his way to the Hall he had noticed—incarnadining the louring heavens—what appeared to be the reflected light from the furnaces of a foundry. Possibly it was discharging its draff, its slag, its cinders." The next explicit notice of this infernal interruption occurs when it takes the position of a place-name in the specter's statement, "I am from . . . " It is noticed again as Professor Monk hesitates before leaving the anteroom of the lecture hall. This foundry's presence, then, provides a structurally significant objective correlative for the revenant's larger meaning when he asks, "Is there not a shade of the Satanic in these streets?"

Finally, the "piercing cold" of the specter's hand acts on Professor Monk as spiritual shock therapy: "A sigh shook him from head to foot. A slight vertigo overcame him. He raised his hand to his eyes. For an instant it seemed to him as though even his sense of reality had cheated him—had foundered." De la Mare has, then, used the ambivalent reality of life and death, waking and sleeping, to call into question the limitedness of Professor Monk's sense of the reality of art and the imagination; the ghost of Edgar Allan Poe is sent to remind Professor Monk—and the reader—that logic is only half the tale and that the transcendent invites "cachinnation" only from "fools."

*Jonathan A. Glenn*

# THE REVERENT WOOING OF ARCHIBALD

*Author:* P. G. Wodehouse (1881-1975)
*Type of plot:* Satire, wit and humor, frame story
*Time of plot:* 1928
*Locale:* London and Sussex, England
*First published:* 1928

> *Principal characters:*
> MR. WILFRED MULLINER, an English gentleman and narrator
> ARCHIBALD MULLINER, his nephew
> AURELIA CAMMARLEIGH, the woman Archibald pursues

*The Story*

Mr. Wilfred Mulliner, in the bar parlor of the Angler's Roost, relates how one of his nephews, Archibald, wooed Aurelia Cammarleigh.

From a window of London's Drones Club, Archibald espies a beautiful girl waiting for a taxi. He gets her name from Algy Wymondham-Wymondham, who suggests that Archibald introduce himself to her at Ascot. She lives with her dotty aunt, who believes that Sir Francis Bacon wrote William Shakespeare's plays. What, Archibald wonders, could he offer to impress someone like Aurelia? He is renowned for his imitation of a hen laying an egg, but that is all. Such coarse buffoonery must be far beneath her.

When Archibald meets her at Ascot, she asks about his egg-laying imitation, but he sternly denies it. She allows him to call on her. Realizing that he will have to get past the aunt before seeing Aurelia, he gets a few books so he can look into these Shakespeare and Bacon fellows. Pretending to be a nonsmoker, teetotaler, and Bacon admirer, he is invited for a long visit to the aunt's country house in Sussex. This fails to cheer him, though, because Aurelia's presence makes him tongue-tied and he dumbly pines for her.

After dressing for dinner in the country house, he finds that the younger guests have gone out, leaving him alone with the aunt, who inflates her lungs and launches into the remarkable Baconian discovery made by applying the plain cipher to Milton's well-known epitaph on Shakespeare. Archibald gamely and deftly parries the conversation, but not before midnight does he manage to escape to his room. Climbing wearily into his bed, he finds it short-sheeted, an "apple-pie bed." Although normally quite the trickster himself, in this depressed mood, he is not appreciative; he just rips out the sheets and sleeps between the blankets.

A few hours later, a thunderous snoring awakens him. Armed with a cake of soap for the blighter's mouth, he heads out his French windows. Through the other room's curtains, he hears Aurelia and another girl discussing first her snoring bulldog, then Archibald. Ignobly, he keeps listening. Aurelia says the odds are against she and he becoming a couple, and his heart sinks. She says that she did like him at Ascot and was intrigued by Algy's tales of the egg-laying imitation, but Archibald denied that ability. Then, observing him with her aunt, she found him to be anything but the bonhomous old bean of his reputation. She adds that she is sick of being looked at reverently, as he is so wont to do. What she really wants is a sprightly trickster who enjoys life. The other girl says she made the apple-pie bed, and Aurelia replies that she wishes she had thought of it herself, adding that she now plans to drop the snoring dog in Archibald's window. The eavesdropping Archibald quickly returns to his room, and when he hears footsteps outside his room, he begins his celebrated hen imitation.

As the imagined egg is laid, he sees the lovely face of his dreams, peering through the curtains with a look of worship. He pleases her further by performing four hopping and clucking encores, then goes on to dispel the rest of the aunt-inspired false persona, after which the couple head off hand in hand to put the snoring dog in the butler's pantry.

*Themes and Meanings*

P. G. Wodehouse (pronounced "Wood-house") wrote several series of stories around characters including Mr. Mulliner, Ukridge, Lord Emsworth, Psmith, and the best known of them all, Bertie Wooster and Jeeves. All are set in the same general milieu of well-off English families with comfortable lives, country houses, and gentlemen's personal gentlemen. The lead characters often drink enough alcohol to float a boat, yet suffer none of the ravages of alcoholism, other than the occasional hangover. Undisturbed by any woes of poverty, murder, or similar real-world concerns, these characters need concern themselves with nothing other than the situation at hand.

In the Mulliner series, the vast and varied multitude of Mr. Mulliner's relatives allows Wodehouse to spin completely different tales in different settings, with different characters. At the same time, the narrating gentleman and his Angler's Roost public house give the reader a comforting constancy. Whether it is nephew Augustine the curate, cousin Montrose the film director, or nephew Archibald, one can feel that the forthcoming story has already proven itself interesting.

"The Reverent Wooing of Archibald" is typical of Wodehouse stories. The author, who continued to produce stories and novels until his death at age ninety-four, spent that entire career honing his stereotypical parodies of the overly rich elite. Two of his most common themes are a gentleman's escape from matrimony and his pursuit thereof. This story demonstrates the latter.

From the very beginning of the story, Archibald marks his romantic objective with great fervor, and he then devotes all of his efforts to no other goal. He does not have to go far to identify her, and even his introduction to her at Ascot is skimmed over. The unwavering pursuit actually begins with Archibald's preparation for meeting the aunt. He perceives that the path to Aurelia must lie through her aunt, so he must set out to convince the aunt of his worthiness. To accomplish this, he must demonstrate an ability to converse in her favored topics and must also avoid any of the traits that might offend her. Therefore he denies the use of alcohol and tobacco and especially the unsophisticated ability to imitate a hen. Realizing that he knows nothing at all about Shakespeare or Bacon, he prepares for the conversation by having his manservant fetch appropriate books, which he spends a fortnight studying. With this hurried background, he submits himself to the aunt's stultifying discourse, all for the purpose of getting her approval for him to court her niece.

*Style and Technique*

Although Wodehouse liked to set many of his tales in oddly named villages, such as Little-Wigmarsh-in-the-Dell or Lower Briskett-in-the-Midden, this story staidly begins in London and moves to the plainly named Brawstead Manor in Sussex. The dialog also is somewhat restrained, as compared with much of Wodehouse's work.

Wodehouse employs his usual degree of exaggeration in "The Reverent Wooing of Archibald," which, like most of Wodehouse's works, has the exaggeration of slapstick but none of the associated tedium. When Archibald first lays eyes on the beautiful Aurelia, his thought is not merely that she is attractive and that he might like to meet her; as his narrating uncle puts it, he worshiped her with a passion that might make him lose his reason. When he embarks on his imitation of a hen laying an egg, he does not just cluck and wave his elbows; he leaps and flaps and crows himself purple in the face, finally alighting atop the chest of drawers.

Another aspect of Wodehouse's penchant for exaggeration is the extreme ignorance of the lead character. Just like his more famous character Bertie Wooster, Archibald is portrayed as being ignorant and lacking even the most basic education, yet able to hold his own in his stratum of society. His uncle says Archibald is not just an ordinary pinhead but an exceptional one. If his brain were made of silk, he would have had a hard time finding enough material to make pants for a canary. The very start of his plan to win the fair Aurelia involves his having no knowledge whatsoever of William Shakespeare or Francis Bacon. It is part of Wodehouse's talent that he can make the reader believe that such a character can carry on a normal life among the elite.

*J. Edmund Rush*

# THE REVOLT OF "MOTHER"

*Author:* Mary E. Wilkins Freeman (1852-1930)
*Type of plot:* Social realism
*Time of plot:* The late nineteenth century
*Locale:* A New England village
*First published:* 1891

> *Principal characters:*
> SARAH PENN, a New England farmwife
> ADONIRAM PENN, her husband
> SAMMY and
> NANNY, their children

*The Story*

Sarah Penn feels compelled to challenge the status quo and assert her own moral imperatives against the more prosaic desires of her husband, Adoniram. Sarah is not by nature a hellion or a woman intent on challenging male dominion; she is a long-suffering wife who has waited forty years for her husband to honor his promise to build a new house to accommodate their domestic needs. Through all these years, she has been the consummate helpmate who devotes the bulk of her energies to ensuring that none of her husband's wants go unmet.

As the story opens, it is early spring and the land is full of new growth and unseen blossoms. Sarah and Adoniram are engaged in a dialogue that is both sparse and familiar. The conversation, sparked by Sarah's inquiry regarding the digging going on in the adjacent field, ends when Adoniram refuses to discuss his decision to build yet another new barn in the exact location where he had once promised to build a new home to replace the old homestead.

Despite her obvious displeasure, Sarah returns to her household chores. She even defends her husband's actions when their daughter, Nanny, complains that his decision to build a new barn disregards their need for a better house. In Sarah's view, Adoniram has been a good provider and has always attended to their needs without delay. They have, in her estimation, a house that is commodious despite its physical limitations. She trusts in her husband's judgment, much as she might in the forces of Providence, and remains convinced that there is a master plan.

Sarah's resignation to her husband's will is part of a persona she has crafted over the years. Just as she has grown used to his taciturn nature, she also has come to anticipate his obstinacy. Confronted with her daughter's distress, however, she tries once again to impress on him the need for a new house to replace the one that is "scarcely as commodious for people as the little boxes under the barn eaves were for the doves." When her masterful appeals fall on deaf ears and Adoniram refuses to change his plans, she resumes her customary duties without a word of complaint.

Shortly thereafter, Nanny mentions holding her wedding in the new barn, and Sarah experiences something of an epiphany. Her response suggests that she has just detected the higher purpose implicit in Adoniram's actions. Although she says nothing to Nanny, when her husband returns a short time later, she greets him at the door and then lingers, as if trying to flesh out a vision.

As the barn nears completion and Adoniram prepares to move in his stock, a letter from Sarah's brother fortuitously arrives, inviting Adoniram to come to Vermont to buy the kind of horse he has been wanting. Just what part Sarah has played in this invitation is not clear, but her reaction suggests that she has done something and hopes that her husband will accept, thereby giving her the time she needs to take advantage of his providential absence.

The hours following his departure are active hours, filled with the previously "unseen blossoms" mentioned earlier. After she instructs the delivery boy to place the new hay in the old barn, Sarah begins packing. Within hours, she has moved all of their worldly possessions into the barn. When the new cows arrive, she places one of them in the old homestead so that when her husband returns, he will realize how serious she was when she accused him of housing his cattle in better accommodations than those in which he has raised his family.

The town's reaction to Sarah's willfulness is predictable. So, too, is Adoniram's initial shock, and his eventual capitulation to Sarah's mandate that he complete her dream by adding such finishing touches as doors, windows, and partitions. As Sarah has known all along, Adoniram—unlike the minister who ineffectually attempts to convince her of the error of her ways—has a fundamental respect for Sarah and will do right by her.

## Themes and Meanings

Throughout the narrative, it is clear that Adoniram and the majority of the townsfolk adhere to a strict division of labor. From Adoniram's perspective, what goes on in the barns, fields, and sheds is none of Sarah's concern. From the town's perspective, any woman who willfully upstages her husband by commandeering one of his barns must be either insane or fundamentally lawless. By alluding to the town's reaction, Mary E. Wilkins Freeman offers objective evidence of the debilitating impact that preconceived notions can have on both the individual and the community at large. She underscores her point by dryly noting that any deviation from the town's routine is enough to stop all progress.

Freeman is both sympathetic and opposed to the norms that strictly define spheres of action. She casts Sarah as a woman who indulges her husband's every whim, while painting Adoniram as a man who is simply incapable of understanding his wife's reactions or comprehending how important a new house has become to her. His confusion is suggested midway through the story, when Freeman notes that despite the admiration that the neighbors have for the fast-growing barn, Adoniram often returns from his inspections with an air of injured dignity. He very much wants Sarah to rejoice in his success and to share his pleasure. Hence, his final comment: "I hadn't no idee you was so set on't as all this comes to."

His shock and lack of understanding are used not as an indictment, but as a statement about the normative way of life in small New England villages. Adoniram is portrayed not as an evil man, but as one who is oblivious to anything beyond his own sphere of influence. So long as his needs are tended to, his only concerns are increasing his holdings and bettering his ability to provide for his family in the ways in which he has been taught. So long as his family is not objectively suffering, he feels he is fulfilling his marital contract.

Sarah is less interested in the quantitative gains and more interested in the qualitative aspects of her family's life. While she appreciates all Adoniram has done to give them a sense of security, she is concerned with her daughter's future and feels that a new house is a prerequisite for Nanny's future well-being. It is for this reason that she must strike out in her own direction and demonstrate to him that there is a world beyond the barns and sheds that he holds so dear.

Freeman's depiction of the son, Sammy, leaves the reader with a sense of hope. While he is depicted initially as a coconspirator with his father, he ultimately emerges as a man who is willing to adapt to new circumstances and put himself on the line in defense of change. Although his voice quavers, his defense of his mother's decision bravely announces the advent of a new era.

### Style and Technique

Freeman employs a terse style that relies on significant, and often comic, gestures rather than on extended narrative or description. She complements this style with both biblical and historic allusions, likening Sarah's "meek vigor" to that of New Testament saints, and comparing Sarah's transformation of the new barn to General James Wolfe's decision during the French and Indian War to gain the element of surprise by launching a surprise attack from the plateau above Quebec.

In her portrayal of Sarah, Freeman makes it clear from the beginning that she is describing a capable and devoted woman whose meekness was the result of her own will, not someone else's. Her ability to make their "little box of a house" into a home worthy of the finest suitors and to make shirts from scanty patterns testify both to her Yankee ingenuity and to her self-reliant spirit. It comes as no surprise, therefore, when she seizes the opportunity and moves the family into the new barn.

Throughout the story, Freeman relies on understatement. There are no great confrontations and no pivotal moments. Instead, there is a building of nuance that leads the reader to anticipate that a change is about to take place. When the change does come, the actions are depicted in a matter-of-fact way that reinforces Sarah's contention that if one is sufficiently patient, one will find a way to reap the rewards earned during a lifetime of service.

*C. Lynn Munro*

# A REVOLUTIONARY TALE

*Author:* Nikki Giovanni (1943-    )
*Type of plot:* Social realism
*Time of plot:* The 1960's
*Locale:* A city in the United States
*First published:* 1968

*Principal characters:*
KIM, a young African American woman
HER MOTHER, a supervisor in the welfare department
HER FATHER, a social worker
BERTHA, her roommate, a black activist

*The Story*

Kim, an African American woman in her early twenties, is explaining to someone that it is her roommate Bertha's fault that she is late. Kim was politically conservative until she became friends with Bertha, a black activist. Under Bertha's influence, Kim has grown her hair out into an Afro and has stopped getting involved with white men. This ideological decision, however, has cost her money, for she had been receiving some financial support from white men. Now that she has no income, Bertha suggests that she get a job; however, Kim decides to go on welfare instead.

When the caseworker discovers that Kim's parents both work at the welfare office, she angers Kim by huffily announcing that she is not eligible. As Kim chases the caseworker down the hall, her mother comes down the hall crying. Kim tries to convince her mother that it is important to the black revolution that she get welfare, but her mother orders her to either go to graduate school or get a job. Kim is shocked because her mother usually goes along with whatever she wants to do. Her mother, however, says that she has read all of the black revolutionary literature Kim has given her and listened to her many speeches, and now it is time for Kim to listen to her.

Kim calls her father to take her to lunch. When she complains about her mother's orders, he agrees that it is not fair and says her mother never should have said such a thing—Kim should simply get a nice job and not even worry about going back to school. Her father patiently explains that if she wants to improve black people's lives, she must set a good example. He criticizes the black leaders whom she admires because they have never held real jobs requiring them to punch a time clock. Her lunch ruined, Kim goes home to type her résumé.

After making several typing errors, she stretches out on the floor and dozes off. She dreams of a university chasing her down the street; as she runs away, she is swallowed up by a social agency. She wakes up screaming, sure that whatever fate befalls her, she will be destroyed. Then she thinks about all the students whom she could convert if she were back in school and realizes that if she applies to a graduate program in social work, both her parents will be pleased.

When Kim is accepted to a program that is to start in nine months, Bertha is excited but Kim cries. She finally decides she has survived worse things—such as missing out on having sex with an attractive white man while on a civil rights march in Mississippi—so she surely can survive this unpleasantness. She dresses and goes to a bar, where she runs into a black man whom she knows, and goes back to his apartment and spends the night. Kim becomes convinced that if she tells the college placement office that she has been having sex and enjoying it, they will rescind their acceptance. To her surprise, they send her a letter applauding her willingness to try new things and congratulating her on her honesty.

When Bertha does not sympathize with Kim for not being rejected from graduate school, Kim puts drain cleaner in her coffee. When it has no effect other than loosening Bertha's bowels, Kim decides that she is a failure. She sends a second telegram to the school:

PLEASE BE ADVISED STOP HAVE PUT DRANO IN ROOMMATE'S COFFEE STOP SHE LIVES STOP I AM A FAILURE YOU MUST REJECT ME STOP

They reply with a long letter apologizing for not having completed her placement, explaining that they are a bit behind, and admiring her ingenious way of expressing her needs. Kim is becoming terrified that if she does not come up with a scheme to get out of this, she will end up with a degree, working for an agency, and becoming decent and responsible—the very things that she hates.

Kim next decides that she can escape this fate by telling the school that she has no money, and will need a grant and a stipend. Convinced that she has finally gotten out of returning to school, she goes back to devoting her time to the revolution. First she works on a black arts festival; then she helps start an underground paper, *Love Black*, aimed at black people who seldom read. Her deeper involvement with the Black Power movement refines her ideas on the social system in which the movement is operating, and gives her the impetus to attend graduate school. She decides, however, to walk there, not realizing how long it will take. That, she says, is why she is late.

*Themes and Meanings*

Nikki Giovanni's story is in the form of a lengthy monologue to an unnamed listener, apparently someone at the college in which Kim has enrolled. Through the monologue, Giovanni portrays the evolution of a young, privileged, previously conservative, middle-class black woman from slogan-spouting radicalism to responsibility. She also uses the story to introduce her audience to some of the leaders of the Black Power movement, and, in the last part of the story, provides a grounding in some of the ideas regarding class, economics, and politics that informed the movement.

Kim's father and mother, seen only briefly at the beginning of the story, are remarkably tolerant of her flirtation with the black revolution. It is not made clear whether they simply have been indulging their high-spirited daughter as she flirts with a radical new philosophy, or if they are really in tune with her but feel unable to express such radical views in the light of their middle-class achievements and lifestyle. When Kim's mother tearfully confronts her in the welfare office, it is clear that she is not merely embarrassed by Kim's applying for welfare, but feels threatened by Kim's bringing her radicalism into her workplace. After recounting how she and Kim's father tolerated Kim's being expelled from school for drinking, getting involved with men they did not like, and even being featured in the newspaper for protesting the Vietnam War by dancing on a table during President Lyndon Johnson's speech at the Democratic Convention, she wails, "But this is my job! Your father and I have worked very hard to give you everything we could."

*Style and Technique*

"A Revolutionary Tale" relies on the self-centered, first-person narration of an educated but unfocused young woman. Although its time frame is the length of a single conversation, the narrator matures greatly over the course of the story. When the story begins, Kim is self-centered and refuses to take responsibility for her actions. First she whines that her troubles are all the fault of her roommate, then she proceeds to implicate the system and her parents as well. After she finally decides to apply for graduate school, she sits back "while others stronger and wiser than I would determine my fate." Once she is accepted into graduate school, she attempts to get them to reject her rather than withdrawing her application, although in an amusingly creative way.

Giovanni's use of language in "A Revolutionary Tale" helps to make the narrator credible. There is a believable balance between standard English, which befits the educated young woman who was "Ayn Rand-Barry Goldwater all the way" before coming under Bertha's influence, and the slang appropriate to a street-smart young black woman in the 1960's.

In line with the narrator's maturation, the tone of the writing changes fairly abruptly in the middle of the story. The story begins in a farcical vein, as Kim and others describe her attention-getting antics in a deadpan fashion. When Kim begins making a real contribution to the black revolution through her work on the magazine *Love Black*, however, she changes from a spoiled girl focused on partying to a concerned citizen of the society that she hopes to help create. The narrative then abandons its comic tone to address more serious issues. It is unlikely that the ideas she is spouting are original to her, but she has moved far beyond the girl who was distressed because she could not contribute to the revolution just by sleeping with financially generous white men and sharing the wealth.

At the end, she informs her listener that one of the reasons she is late is because she decided to walk to school rather than fly or hitch a ride. Wherever Kim has gone in reality, or how she has gotten there, metaphorically, she has traveled a life-altering distance from the spoiled party girl to someone who will be a contributor to the revolution that was previously only a game to her.

*Irene Struthers Rush*

# THE RICH BOY

*Author:* F. Scott Fitzgerald (1896-1940)
*Type of plot:* Psychological
*Time of plot:* The 1920's
*Locale:* New York and Florida
*First published:* 1926

*Principal characters:*
> ANSON HUNTER, an attractive, charming, but arrogant young man from a wealthy and prestigious family
> PAULA LEGENDRE, a beautiful, wealthy young woman who falls in love with Anson but later marries another man
> DOLLY KARGER, an attractive young woman from new money who is attracted to men who are not attracted to her
> AUNT EDNA, Anson's aunt by marriage
> CARY, the young lover of Edna
> THE NARRATOR, an unidentified friend of Anson

*The Story*

Anson Hunter, the rich boy for whom the story is named, aptly portrays F. Scott Fitzgerald's fascination with an analysis of the rich as

> different from you and me. They possess and enjoy early, . . . [which] makes them soft where we are hard, and cynical where we are trustful. They think, deep in their hearts, that they are better than we are because we had to discover the compensations and refuges of life for ourselves.

As a child, Anson is cared for by a governess and is secluded from contact with his social peers. His fraternizing with the local town children helps instill his feeling of superiority. His education is completed at Yale, where he makes connections in the business and social worlds. He establishes himself in a New York brokerage firm, joins the appropriate clubs, and commences to maintain an extravagant lifestyle, arrogantly frowning on excessive behavior in others that he finds acceptable for himself.

Anson serves in the Navy but is not changed by the experience. While in Florida at a training base, he meets Paula Legendre, a woman of his class and social standing. As he himself admits, their relationship is superficial, based on common upbringing and expectations. Paula and her mother accompany him north, and while there he arrives at their hotel one evening, inebriated. Paula and her mother react negatively to this improper behavior, but Anson never apologizes. Later, when he becomes drunk and fails to keep a date with Paula, she breaks the engagement. Anson, however, continues to believe that he has control over Paula, that she will, in fact, wait for him forever. When he and Paula meet again, his arrogance prevents him from recognizing Paula's weakening attraction and patience toward him: "He need say no more, commit their destinies to no practical enigma. Why should he, when he might hold her so, biding his own time, for another year—forever?" Because of this attitude, Anson loses her. He receives word that she will marry someone else.

His loss of Paula shocks him, but he continues his wild life and becomes involved with Dolly Karger. His relationship with Dolly is gamelike; when she tries to make him jealous, he purposely wins her back, only to show her who is in control, and then promptly rejects her. When she accompanies him to the country for the weekend, he goes to her in her bedroom, but at the last minute, the image of Paula intervening between them, he, close to tears and projecting his anger on Dolly, breaks away from her: "I don't love you a bit, can't you understand?"

Anson prides himself on his ability to control the lives of other people, and when he learns that his Aunt Edna is having an affair, he informs her and her lover that it must end. He states that failure to do so will cause him to inform his uncle and the young man's father. This threat gains the result he desires. He gives his motivations as the prevention of a scandal, which would reflect on him as well as on the rest of the family, and the protection of his uncle. Primarily, however, it is simply a way for him to assert his superiority. The lover dies, either by accident or by suicide, but Anson feels no remorse. He is banned from his uncle's house, an act that Anson believes is unjustified.

As Anson approaches thirty, he becomes more conscious of his position in society; he teaches Sunday school, sponsors young men for various clubs, and, with the deaths of his mother and father, becomes head of the family, assuming responsibility for his brothers and sisters, particularly financially and socially. He continues to give advice to his friends, especially to those recently married. Despite his continued drinking and partying, the older generation considers him reliable and safe because of the air of self-assurance that he exhibits. Finally though, his friends establish their own lives and interests and find him less necessary.

His loneliness becomes evident to him one evening at the beginning of summer when he tries to find someone in New York with whom to spend the evening, and everyone he knows, including people he has not seen since college, is either busy or out of town. The thought of being alone frightens him, and he glimpses the emptiness of his life. On this evening he accidentally meets Paula, recently remarried and pregnant. They travel up to the country for the weekend, and, after a pleasant meal, the husband leaves them alone to catch up on old times. When Anson learns from Paula that she never loved him, that she is now happy with her husband, Anson is devastated. He returns to the city but breaks into tears easily and seems unable to go on with his life. Although Anson is certainly upset about Paula, it is typical of him that he is not upset that Paula is married or pregnant or happy; his pride is wounded because she had not loved him as he assumed she had.

His work suffers, and his colleagues become worried about him. They urge him to take a voyage and, accompanied by a male friend, the narrator, he plans to depart. Several days prior to their departure, Anson learns that Paula has died during childbirth;

nevertheless, he departs for Europe as planned. On the voyage, Anson takes up with another young woman, reverting to his old ways, without benefiting from his experiences. The narrator-friend concludes, "I don't think he was ever happy unless someone was in love with him, responding to him like filings to a magnet, helping him to explain himself, promising him something. . . . Perhaps they promised that there would always be women in the world who would spend their brightest, freshest, rarest hours to nurse and protect that superiority he cherished in his heart."

*Themes and Meanings*

Fitzgerald depicted the lifestyle of the Lost Generation of the 1920's, those rich young people who blamed the evils of the world on the previous generation and rejected their parents' value system of duty to society and family but also failed to establish a new system. Instead they adopted an irresponsible, cynical, extravagant way of life, which Fitzgerald recognized as essentially devoid of meaning or fulfillment. Certainly Anson is depicted as a superficial character who has no concern for anyone other than himself and who consistently fails to learn from his experiences. Fitzgerald's belief that the rich pay a price for their self-imposed isolation is demonstrated in "The Rich Boy." Anson is rich and different, and the penalty that he pays for his sense of superiority is that he never achieves a meaningful relationship with anyone. Fitzgerald explored the basic psychological drives and how they are satisfied by the very rich. He learned that the possession of wealth was bought at the price of individualism and of increased responsibility to others. His character Anson never learns this lesson. He refuses to take responsibility for his own actions, never considering his effect on the lives of others. Anson is a user of people; he views them as merely objects on which to exert his influence, thus reinforcing his sense of superiority, as exemplified particularly by his treatment of women: Paula, Dolly, and Aunt Edna.

As a child, Anson recognizes the unchallenged superiority of the rich, and "he accepted this as the natural state of things, and a sort of impatience with all groups of which he was not the center—in money, in position, in authority—remained with him for the rest of his life." However, this superiority has its price; closeness to other people becomes unavailable to him. His relationship with Paula illustrates this. Anson admits "that on his side much was insincere, and on hers much was merely simple," thus indicating his lack of true involvement as well as his feeling of superiority toward her. However, Paula is drawn to Anson:

> [He] . . . dominated and attracted her, and at the same time filled her with anxiety. Confused by his mixture of solidity and self-indulgence, of sentiment and cynicism—incongruities that her gentle mind was unable to resolve—Paula grew to think of him as two alternating personalities. When she saw him alone, or at a formal party, or with his casual inferiors, she felt a tremendous pride in his strong, attractive presence, the paternal, understanding stature of his mind. In other company she became uneasy when what had been a fine imperviousness to mere gentility showed its other face. The other face was gross, humorous, reckless of everything but pleasure.

Anson believes that Paula will wait for him forever, but he is mistaken. He claims that it is Paula's action in ending their relationship, rather than his own that necessitated it, which has made him a cynic, thus refusing to take responsibility for the demise of their relationship.

This arrogance surfaces again in his affair with Dolly and his cruel treatment of her: "He was not jealous—she meant nothing to him—but at her pathetic ruse everything stubborn and self-indulgent in him came to the surface. It was a presumption from a mental inferior and it could not be overlooked. If she wanted to know to whom she belonged she would see."

There is no compassion in Anson. He firmly believes that he knows best for everyone, or that whatever is best for him is what must be, despite the effects on others. He does not merely offer advice to friends and family; he forces it on them. Understandably people begin to resent this and withdraw from the area of his control. After he totally humiliates Aunt Edna and her lover and destroys any hope of happiness for them, he calmly returns home, believing that he has done the right thing, even feeling self-satisfied with his actions.

Despite his experiences, Anson never changes. On a superficial level he adopts the responsibilities of head of his family, of church member, and of civic leader, but morally he remains unconcerned with the welfare of anyone other than himself. This arrogance and selfishness lead him into an empty, cynical, and callous way of life. This is aptly illustrated when, on the trip abroad after Paula's death, he bounces back to his irresponsible, charming, witty self as he makes the acquaintance of yet another beautiful young woman.

*Style and Technique*

The story is told by a first-person observer-narrator, who identifies himself as a friend of Anson. As Anson's confidant, the narrator is privy to Anson's thoughts, yet he is able to relate his perception of events objectively, particularly as one who has not been reared in wealth. Thus, he is the persona of Fitzgerald and is able to interpret the effects of Anson's actions objectively, though with more compassion toward Anson than Anson exhibits toward others; thus, the narrator also serves as a foil to Anson.

The psychological realism evidenced in "The Rich Boy" is accomplished through Fitzgerald's close attention to detail and through a consistent, believable portrayal of the characters' thoughts, actions, and personalities. He divulges to the reader the inner workings of the mind of a wealthy, arrogant young man and the social influences that have formed him.

*Jane B. Weedman*

# THE RICH BROTHER

*Author:* Tobias Wolff (1945-        )
*Type of plot:* Domestic realism
*Time of plot:* The 1980's
*Locale:* Northern and Central California
*First published:* 1985

> Principal characters:
> PETE, a man in his early forties
> DONALD, his younger brother
> WEBSTER, a hitchhiker

*The Story*

Pete and Donald are brothers who have little in common. Stable and successful Pete is a real estate agent in Santa Cruz. He has two daughters, a sailboat, and a great deal of money. Donald is something of a drifter, never keeping a job for long, often migrating from one religious commune to another. While Pete is at home in the world and looks healthy and comfortable, Donald is gaunt and obsessed with the fate of his soul.

Pete seems to have taken after their parents, who are both dead. Like them, Pete wants simply to be a decent person and not make a fool of himself. Donald insists on taking himself very seriously, though, and is often taken for a fool. For all of his success, Pete feels implicitly judged by Donald, who wonders why Pete insists on purchasing new goods when old ones are still perfectly usable. Donald, however, has a history of financial insolvency and of depending on Pete to get him out of jams.

Donald has joined a commune outside Paso Robles, California. After a few months his letters end and Pete becomes concerned. He finally calls Donald and convinces him to leave. Since Donald's car has been repossessed, Pete has to drive downstate and pick him up. The day before Pete leaves on the journey, he receives a letter from the head of the commune indicating that Donald has not left voluntarily: He has been expelled. When Pete meets up with Donald, he asks about the circumstances of his expulsion. Donald explains that he was too impractical for the group. For example, when they sent him to go shopping, he ended up giving away all the groceries to the first poor family he saw. When trying to cook for the group, he started a fire.

Pete gives Donald one hundred dollars. As they travel up the coast, they stop at a gas station and Donald invites a hitchhiker to join them. The man, who tells them his name is Webster, begins an elaborate story about having to reach his daughter, who has suddenly taken ill. Webster says this is all part of a long string of troubles that began when he took his wife to open a gold mine in Peru, where she developed a mysterious disease and died. Now Webster is trying his best to raise shares in the gold mine so that the poor Peruvians can benefit from their natural wealth.

Pete is skeptical about Webster's story, but he makes the mistake of falling asleep. When he awakens, Webster is gone—along with the hundred dollars that he gave Donald. Donald has bought a share in Webster's gold mine. An argument ensues, in which the brothers bring up old grievances. The most surprising is Donald's claim that Pete often tried to kill him. When as a child Donald had a serious intestinal operation, both boys got the idea that his stitches could easily rupture and poison his system. Pete, however, frequently snuck into Donald's room at night and punched him in his wounds.

That Donald would use Pete's hard-earned one hundred dollars to buy a share in a phony gold mine is the last straw for Pete; he puts Donald out of the car in the middle of nowhere. Before he goes far, however, he decides that his wife will never understand how he could leave his brother behind. He turns the car around to find his brother.

*Themes and Meanings*

Pete seems to have his life well organized; he is a responsible, highly successful citizen. He has done everything right and is justly proud of the rewards of his hard work. Donald, on the other hand, seems to be a mess. He is something of a hippie, moving from ashrams to other forms of communitarian living. He seems to have little sense of the value of money, often borrowing from others, never paying them back. When he does have a bit of money, regardless of the source, he tends to give it away to the first person who asks for a handout.

Even among his hippie friends, he stands out as childish; they eject him because he cannot function in a way that they are used to. He spills soda on his brother's beautiful new leather upholstery and seems amazed that Pete is upset over such a meaningless possession. He even wears his clothes inside out, totally unconcerned over his appearance.

However, Pete is showing signs of having something of a midlife crisis, centered principally around the question of what all his work and accomplishments really mean. Tobias Wolff gradually reveals symptoms of the problems Pete is facing. The reader may be surprised to learn that Pete does, indeed, dream about Donald, just as Donald had suspected, which Pete at first denies. The content of the dream is rather startling, as well: Pete mentions that, in the dream, there was something wrong with him, not telling Donald that the problem was that Pete was blind, and that Donald was somehow helping him—leading him, one assumes. Even more surprising is Pete's grudging admission that he frequently beat up his younger brother. Thus, when Donald claims that Pete has real problems, and that they center on his not having a real purpose in his life, the reader gradually suspects that Wolff is on Donald's side in this matter.

Donald's very presence serves as a question for Pete, who wonders how anyone can exist in such a haphazard and dependent way. Donald inadvertently wears his T-shirt inside out, so that the words "Try God" are facing inward. Wolff seems to suggest that Donald constantly reminds himself of these words and only secondarily addresses them to his brother. His focus is interior, spiritual, aimed at another world—and, therefore, bizarre in the eyes of a materialist such as Pete.

As the story ends, Pete finds himself pondering the possibility that there may be more to life than his limited view has allowed him to see. What if Donald's naïveté is the beginning of wisdom? He finally recognizes and accepts his own dependence on Donald. Although the two brothers have little in common, the story demonstrates that they are inseparably paired and need each other. This inescapable relationship is their shared wealth.

*Style and Technique*

This story has strong biblical overtones, beginning with its ironic title. The reader assumes that Pete is the rich brother but learns by story's end that this may not be so. Donald has a certain freedom that comes from his independence from material goods, and this brings him a richness that Pete can never experience. Wolff makes indirect allusions to several similar stories from the Testaments.

Anyone familiar with the biblical story of Cain and Abel will hear implicit echoes of Yahweh's question, "Where is thy brother?" and Cain's sarcastic reply: "Am I my brother's keeper?" This is Pete's question throughout the story, and he finally comes to the conclusion that yes, he is his brother's keeper. Leaving him out on the road would, in his view, be equivalent to sentencing him to death—a guilt that he cannot bear.

The story of the prodigal son echoes in Wolff's story as well. Here is Donald returning to the fold of Pete's home after losing everything out in the world. Pete is the resentful older brother who has labored all day in the field; Donald implicitly teaches Pete the need for generosity.

The story of the rich man and the publican seems an appropriate parallel as well. Pete is much like that rich man, proud of his accomplishments, especially proud of his generosity toward his worthless brother. Donald, on the other hand, if not especially humble, is nevertheless on a fumbling quest that preoccupies his whole life. Early on, he admits that he has made a mess of things and asks for a kind of mercy from Pete.

Some of Wolff's language also recalls the Bible, especially the simplicity of his story's opening. Thus, Wolff uses a kind of intertextuality to pack a great deal into a simple story of internecine struggle.

*John C. Hawley*

# A RIDDLE

*Author:* Antonio Tabucchi (1943-     )
*Type of plot:* Domestic realism
*Time of plot:* The 1980's
*Locale:* Paris, Limoges, and the road from Biarritz to San Sebastián, Spain
*First published:* "Rebus," 1985 (English translation, 1987)

> *Principal characters:*
> THE NARRATOR, a mechanic who calls himself the marquis of
>     Carabas
> MIRIAM, the countess of Terrail, who hires the narrator to drive
>     her to Biarritz
> THE COUNT, Miriam's husband
> ALBERT, a race car driver
> MONSIEUR, The man to whom the narrator tells his story

*The Story*

   The narrator sits in a bar telling a story to a man identified only as Monsieur, and he begins with a dream of Miriam, the countess of Terrail, he had the night before, seeing her walking on the beach at Biarritz. The dream prompts him to recount the whole riddle of his journey with her, but first he reminisces about his experiences with Albert, a race car driver whom he met in Saint-Denis, and the car that Albert claimed had belonged to Agostinelli, Marcel Proust's driver. Albert and the narrator, a mechanic, soon team up in running an auto repair shop, with Albert finding the vintage cars to restore and the narrator handling sales. The narrator then tells of having met Miriam at Chez Albert, a bistro near the Porte Saint-Denis in Paris.

   After Miriam introduces herself, the narrator jokingly says that he is the marquis of Carabas. Miriam tells him not to joke about being the marquis, announces that someone wants to kill her, and walks out after leaving her name and phone number on a matchbox. The narrator does not call her, but a few days later, her husband, the count of Terrail, arrives at the narrator's office, explaining that his wife wants to take their 1927 Bugatti Royale to Biarritz and proceed to a car rally in San Sebastián, Spain. The count thinks that his wife has asked the narrator to drive her to Biarritz, and he presents him with a large check and a request that he refuse the countess's proposal. The narrator refuses the check and truthfully denies any knowledge of such an offer, and the count leaves. This arouses the curiosity of the narrator, who has admitted to being "stuck in a morass of boredom," and he immediately calls the Hôtel de Paris and leaves a message for the countess.

   The narrator picks up the Bugatti and has it repaired to perfection, even having an elephant hood ornament carved from wood and chrome-plated. He calls for the countess at the Hôtel de Paris. The count says he will meet her in Biarritz in a week, and the narrator and the countess depart in the Bugatti but, at the countess's insistence, follow a long route that takes them to Limoges, where they spend a night in a hotel as a married couple, under the narrator's name. The next day means another irregular route and a night in Pau. In Biarritz on the third day, Miriam promises the riddle of their journey will be explained after the race.

The course follows a winding route around curves that overhang the water, and the narrator and Miriam play tag with a young couple in a 1922 Lambda. When the Lambda deliberately swerves toward them, the narrator brakes, accelerates, and knocks the Lambda off the road but with no harm to the occupants. After minor car repairs in San Sebastián, they drive back to France, where the narrator notices that the wooden elephant has been replaced by a metal one, but when he moves to open it, Miriam turns "ashen grey" and dissuades him.

They spend the night in Biarritz, making love. In the morning, the narrator confiscates a revolver he finds in Miriam's handbag and then leaves in a taxi with Miriam's promise to meet him at the beach. When the narrator looks for the count at the train station, he learns that he did not arrive as he had promised and has not checked in at the Hôtel des Palais. Finally, a phone call to the Hôtel d'Angleterre reveals that Miriam has already checked out and driven away. Musing on his odd adventure, the narrator confesses to having once put an ad in *Le Figaro*: "Lost elephant looking for 1927 Bugatti." Thus ends the riddle.

*Themes and Meanings*

The theme that introduces the bizarre events of "A Riddle" is the narrator's ennui. He states: "I had come to a standstill; I was stuck in a morass of boredom, in the lethargic mood of a man who is no longer very young, but completely an adult, who is simply waiting for life." This boredom explains why he changes his mind about the countess. He ignores her plea until the count offers to pay him off; then the challenge stirs him to action. That he later yearns for the romance and excitement of his trip in the Bugatti becomes clear in his ad about the lost elephant, but he is left with only his memories.

It is his dream of Miriam that prompts him to tell his story to Monsieur at the bar. He dreams of Miriam walking along an imaginary beach at Biarritz, and he realizes, "with the unsurprised amazement of a dream," that Miriam is dead. Dreams provide us "a plausible solution," he remarks, something that reason with its complexity cannot offer. Tomorrow, he hopes, he may dream that Miriam is alive and that they have kept their appointment. The narrator opens his boozy reminiscence with a brief monologue on dreams, and he ends it with another on the same subject: "Sometimes, when you've drunk a bit, reality is simplified; the gaps between one thing and another are closed, everything hangs together and you say to yourself: I've got it. Just like a dream." The narrator winds down by asking the man at the bar why he wants to hear other people's stories: "Can't you be satisfied with your own dreams?"

The narrator dwells on the "banal" metaphor of life as a journey toward an appointment, a journey marked by "insignificant trips over the crust of this planet." This definition of life leads him to a digression on Marcel Proust's auto tour of the Gothic cathedrals of Normandy with his driver, Agostinelli. He rambles on to Monsieur about his days at the Sorbonne studying literature, and the paper that he wrote on "What Proust Saw from a Car," a piece eventually published in "a third-class magazine." The journey that he makes with the countess is irregular in many ways—in its route, in its adultery, and in its danger and mystery. Moreover, the narrator identifies the journey with real love: "Behind me the road retreated, before me it opened up, and I thought of my life and the boredom of it . . . and I felt ashamed that I'd never known love." Therefore, the self-dubbed marquis of Carabas haunts the bars like a maudlin Ancient Mariner, telling his story of lost love to anyone who will listen.

*Style and Technique*

The riddle, the dream, the journey—these archetypal themes are the soul of storytelling. Creating a first-person narrator allows Antonio Tabucchi to use the long-winded and self-pitying style of the barroom epic. Incorporating Proust into the story thickens up the diction, along with allusions to *Harper's Bazaar* and *Le Figaro*, and the French phrases add a touch of class. Geographical references play a part, too. The narrator meets Miriam at Chez Albert, "near the Porte Saint-Denis [in Paris], not exactly a stamping ground for countesses," and his vintage car shop is on the "fashionable Avenue Foch." The evocative place-names along the way from Biarritz to San Sebastián enrich the narrative texture, ground the dream on solid earth, and carry exotic associations for many readers, as do such proper names as Quai d'Anjou, Pau, and Hôtel d'Angleterre.

A pleasing feature of the narrator's tale is his familiarity with classic cars, and their names trip fondly off his tongue. Besides the star of the show, Miriam's 1927 Bugatti Royale coupé de ville and the sinister bright red 1922 Lambda, there are Delages, Aston Martins, a Hispano-Suiza, an Isotta Fraschini, and a 1922 Fiat Mefistofele. Cars are sexy: Albert says of the Bugatti that "it has something of a woman's body about it, a woman lying on her back with her legs out in front of her." The narrator's paean is positively erotic: "A Bugatti Royale on its haunches, climbing a slight incline, with fenders flared, ready to gather speed and intoxication, with power throbbing behind a fabulous radiator grille and, atop it, an elephant with upraised trunk." Genuine romantic love, not just sexual desire, is "the kind that blazes up inside and breaks out and spins like a motor while the wheels speed over the ground." By combining sex and fast cars in a mysterious story of illicit love and violence on the highways of the glamorous French-Spanish coast, Tabucchi strikes a note that rings loud in modern culture.

*Frank Day*

# RIP VAN WINKLE

*Author:* Washington Irving (1783-1859)
*Type of plot:* Folktale
*Time of plot:* The late eighteenth century
*Locale:* The Catskill Mountains of New York
*First published:* 1819

#### Principal characters:

RIP VAN WINKLE, the protagonist, a village ne'er-do-well
DAME VAN WINKLE, his shrewish wife
JUDITH VAN WINKLE GARDENIER, his daughter

### The Story

Rip Van Winkle is a good-natured but unassertive descendant of the Dutch settlers who assisted Peter Stuyvesant in his military exploits. Every small community has someone like Rip: the entertainer of local children, the willing helper of his neighbor, the desultory fisherman—but a man constitutionally unable to work on his own behalf. Rip's farm falls into ruin, his children run ragged, and his wife's bad temper mounts. He takes refuge from Dame Van Winkle in protracted discussions at the village inn, all-day fishing expeditions, and rambles in the mountains with his dog Wolf. It is on one of these occasions that he encounters a company of antique Dutchmen who are playing at ninepins in a natural amphitheater high in the Catskills.

Offered liquid refreshment, Rip drinks himself to sleep, from which he awakens the next morning, as he supposes, to find everything inexplicably changed: his dog gone, a worm-eaten gun in place of the one he had brought, no trace of the bowlers or of their bowling alley. Descending to the town, he finds his old dog strangely hostile, his house abandoned, and even the village inn replaced by a large new hotel.

The first person Rip actually recognizes is his daughter, now a young wife and mother; she kindly takes the perplexed old man home to live with her family. He learns of the death of many of his old friends and of his wife, for whose demise he feels nothing but relief. When he sees his son Rip slouching against a tree, looking much as he himself did "yesterday"—actually twenty years ago—he briefly doubts his own identity.

The larger changes in society are yet more profound. Rip went to sleep a subject of George III and has awakened a citizen of the United States of America under the leadership of George Washington. Although Rip soon falls into his old loitering ways, justified now by his white beard and the absence of matrimonial demands, it takes him some time to absorb the Revolution that has run its full course while he slept. The town has learned to accommodate the new republic, and all the changes lend charm to Rip's fresh recollections of the old order. Rip tells and retells his story, which is accepted most readily by the older Dutch villagers, who have kept alive a legend that Hendrick Hudson's men keep a vigil in the nearby mountains and play at ninepins there regularly in the afternoon. Rip prefers the company of the young, however, not so much to be in touch with the new as to preserve the old in a relentlessly changing world.

## Themes and Meanings

Washington Irving was a nostalgic man in whom a touch of Rip Van Winkle persisted. Like Rip, he was away from home for many years. He was in the earlier years of a seventeen-year sojourn in England when he wrote *The Sketch Book of Geoffrey Crayon, Gent.* (1819-1920) with its two narrative masterpieces, this story and "The Legend of Sleepy Hollow." A conservative who enjoyed the old ways, Irving wrote best when he juxtaposed old and new, tradition and change. His friend Sir Walter Scott encouraged him to rummage in European folklore. Both of the famous stories in *The Sketch Book* are based on German tales; by adapting them, Irving helped to create a distinctively American fiction. Whereas earlier American imitators of European romances and gothic horror stories had suffered from the lack of convincing settings in a land without ancient abbeys and castles, Irving realized the possibilities inherent in the Hudson River Valley, only a day's journey from New York but teeming with romantic possibilities and local traditions that, although they did not date from medieval times, nevertheless went back a respectable two centuries.

In "Rip Van Winkle," Irving seized on the venerable theme of the henpecked husband who turns the tables on his tyrannical wife, a feat Rip achieves by simply outlasting her—with a bit of preternatural help from the crew of Hudson's *Half Moon*. Rip merely desires a leisurely, casual, convivial life, but his wife calls him home from the congenial atmosphere of the inn and lectures him in bed at night. Irving never, however, permits Dame Van Winkle's point of view to obtrude; she does not speak in the story, and Irving elicits no sympathy for her. She is the enemy partly because she embodies a whole culture that is at odds with Rip's values: that of the tidy, thrifty, ambitious Dutch.

Despite the story's German source and its setting in a Dutch-American community, Irving domesticates his material very successfully. First, he deftly captures the beauty of a recognizably American region. The rather brief scene in which the mountains become the setting for fantasy is sandwiched between two thicker slices of late eighteenth century American village reality. By the very act of passing over a signal event in American history, the story draws attention to it. Rip returns to find people talking of the heroes of the late war (some of his friends fought and one died in it), the new form of government (the village schoolmaster is now in something called "Congress"), and national political parties (almost immediately he is asked whether he is a Federalist or a Democrat).

Rip has paid heavily for his secure leisure, for he has lost what should have been the years of his mature vigor and all opportunity to participate in the great events of his lifetime. While loving freedom, Rip placidly endured the tyranny of Dame Van Winkle and King George and has escaped playing any role in the forging of American liberty. He has avoided the tribulations of family life by losing all title as husband and becoming dependent on his daughter, while he has sloughed off his responsibilities as patriot by choosing "overnight" status as a senior citizen.

His easygoing philosophy is completely at odds with that of the great architects of American freedom, including Benjamin Franklin, whose almanac *Poor Richard's* (first issued in 1732) stands at a pole opposite to Rip's sluggishness. Irving even uses Franklin's idiom to describe Rip, who "would rather starve on a penny than work for a pound." Rip would also rather starve himself of any satisfaction for accomplishment such as that permeating Franklin's much admired *Autobiography* (1771-1788).

The other Founding Father prominent in the story is George Washington, whose image has replaced that of King George in front of the new hotel. By virtue of exchanging the life of a country gentleman for the dangers and deprivations of military service in wartime, Washington became "the Father of his country," while Rip's children have in effect grown up fatherless. After the war, Washington, presumably about Rip's age, did not recede into the past but accepted eight years of further responsibility as president.

Irving, named for Washington, was, like Rip, a man who spent much of his life telling stories, but the one he labored at most diligently through his late years was his five-volume biography of Washington, the man after whom neither Rip nor his creator could pattern himself. In Rip, Irving created a character whom the reader can envy— but only by ignoring the implicit reminders of a far nobler type of American.

*Style and Technique*

Irving erected an elaborate facade for the book in which this story first appeared. Purporting to be the work of "Geoffrey Crayon, Gentleman," *The Sketch Book* featured primarily literary "sketches" of the type popularized by Joseph Addison a century earlier and influenced writers as late as Charles Dickens. Irving's sketches are chiefly travel essays of an American in England, written in a graceful, well-bred manner calculated to appeal to the English gentleman as well as his American readers. As a result, Irving became the first American literary man widely read abroad.

Irving further distanced himself from his narrative by means of a headnote alleging the story to be a posthumously discovered work of "Diedrich Knickerbocker, an old gentleman of New York" and a postscript to the effect that Knickerbocker himself had it from a "German superstition," though Irving more or less retracts this suggestion by including a note reputed to be Knickerbocker's own in which the old gentleman claims to have talked with the real Rip Van Winkle himself.

This sort of elaborate hocus-pocus was common in American fiction up to about the middle of the nineteenth century, and readers may compare Irving's frame for this story with Nathaniel Hawthorne's lengthy customhouse essay at the head of *The Scarlet Letter* (1850). Common to both works is a desire both for the freedom from any obligation to respect prosaic everyday life and for an air of authenticity these writers seemed to feel readers of the time required.

Unlike Hawthorne, however, Irving does not aspire to profundity, and his style is much more colloquial and familiar. The dialogue is extremely simple and straightforward, and the descriptions, while effective, are rather understated. Irving's simplicity, which has helped make his tales enduringly popular school texts, is somewhat deceptive, for although Irving is not an ambitious artist, he has an artful way of suggesting more than he seems to say. Thus, the allusions to Franklin and Washington establish the standards of duty and accomplishment against which Rip's withdrawal from responsibility is to be measured. Unlike his greatest American contemporary in fiction, James Fenimore Cooper, Irving seldom overwrites. By describing his mountaineers very little and keeping them absolutely silent, he creates the desired atmosphere of enchantment. He understands the value of describing Dame Van Winkle indirectly through her effect on Rip. In a century of writers always poised to spin great webs of words, Irving demonstrates the virtues of an economical and unpretentious style.

For all its derivative nature, simplicity, and modest statement, "Rip Van Winkle" achieves universal significance. It depicts the pastoral contentment yearned for in a society aware of its own increasing complexity but shows this peace to be purchased at the expense of the protagonist's full manhood and maturity. With considerable justification, "Rip Van Winkle" has been called the first successful American short story.

*Robert P. Ellis*

# THE RISE OF MAUD MARTHA

*Author:* Gwendolyn Brooks (1917-2000)
*Type of plot:* Psychological
*Time of plot:* About 1955
*Locale:* Chicago
*First published:* 1955

> *Principal characters:*
> MAUD MARTHA, who is newly widowed
> MRS. PHILLIPS, her mother-in-law
> BELVA BROWN, her mother

*The Story*

"The Rise of Maud Martha," a very brief and deceptively simple story, opens as a pastor observes the departure of a funeral procession and closes only a short time later, the moment Maud Martha begins crying as they lower her husband, Paul, into his grave. With the precision of the poet she is and the insight of the sensitive observer of human behavior she has always been, Gwendolyn Brooks joins the procession through the thoughts and observations of Maud Martha as she rides in the first car with her mother, Belva Brown, and Paul's mother, Mrs. Phillips. Each carefully detailed picture conveys the lifestyle in which Maud Martha finds herself, from the opening details of the "big and little and few" wreaths with "fresh and barely fresh" flowers, through the placement of Maud Martha in "the longest and shiny-blackest of the long black cars," to the image of an "after-funeral white cake" that closes the story.

Equally vivid are the flashback observations of Paul's death as one of "30-odd" passengers burned in the crash of a streetcar with a gas truck. Ironically, the streetcar was a new model, and its sealed windows sealed the fate of its unfortunate passengers as well.

The violent tragedy is not, however, the focus of Brooks's story. Rather, it is "the women in the street"—from the grieving wives to the high school girl in the crowd "enjoying herself. Seeing Life." Brooks may focus on Maud Martha, but she uses a wide-angle lens, taking in the many faces of grief and contrasting the "'dreadful' blackness" of charred bodies with the formerly "known and despised" blackness of race.

Next Brooks narrows her lens to the three women in the head car and turns up the sound, as Mrs. Phillips eulogizes her son and patronizes her daughter-in-law. Criticism disguised as faint praise fails to provoke a rise from either Maud Martha or her mother, Belva, although Belva does have to snap her lips shut at one point. Maud Martha's only response is "I understand," ambiguously acknowledging Mrs. Phillips's request for visits and her own growing understanding of the real meaning of Paul's death for her.

Reminiscent but not derivative of Kate Chopin's "The Story of an Hour," Brooks's story presents a newly widowed wife who is looking for the feelings that she has been taught to expect from herself but who finds instead inescapable and unpredicted realities. Instead of the self-pity of the abandoned love, Maud Martha discovers in herself only pity for Paul's loss of the physical beauty he loved so dearly. As does Chopin's character, Maud Martha feels in herself a release of freedom and power: "She could actually feel herself rising." The tears that come in time to please the relatives are not for Paul.

### Themes and Meanings

Brooks had introduced her readers to Maud Martha two years before the publication of this story with her novella *Maud Martha* (1953). The young black woman who wanted to "found tradition" for herself, for Paul, and for little Paulette now finds herself caught in and measured by the narrow expectations of physical existence. Mrs. Phillips praises her for giving Paul hot meals: "That's what makes for a healthy man." Blind to the spiritual values Maud Martha might hope to instill in her household, the mother-in-law goes on to suggest that letting ten-year-old Paulette leave school to baby-sit for the smaller children and getting a job would have been the right way for Maud Martha to help Paul.

Like his mother, Paul had loved physical existence and had offered little but "vicissitudes" to his wife. If love makes a man "more than a body" to a woman, Maud Martha realizes, then even when he "happens to be dead, he is still what you love." Physical values, though, are easily and surprisingly turned into "a fire-used, repulsive thing": The body cannot be protected from life's vicissitudes. Even the young girl observing the grief of others is not envied by Maud Martha; she, too, will know loss in time.

For Maud Martha, life with Paul had become dominated by the physical limits of childbearing and problem-solving; he "had made her feel like a pumpkin." Now his death offers Maud Martha another opportunity to "found tradition"; she realizes that her children's lives and her own are now "in her individual power." The physical realities do not go away—the tears and the white cake will both come—but Maud Martha is ready to rise to the challenge once more. In a world that still approves of her because of her tears, the physical sign of grief, the story of her rising has yet to reach the surface of her life.

### Style and Technique

With the eye and the language of a poet, Brooks offers a surface of social realism within which the psychological realities of Maud Martha's thoughts are probed. The opening paragraph describing the pastor watching the departure of the funeral procession has already suggested the shallow reality of surfaces. "It was impossible to tell just what he was thinking," Brooks reminds the reader as she re-creates him; her suggestions range from thoughts about death or its accoutrements to the irrelevance of "strawberries."

Even language can be as shallow as visual surfaces if one does not plumb its depths, and Brooks forces one to read every word of her story thoroughly before exhausting it of meaning. Again, the first paragraph introduces this stylistic density as she describes the quiet closing of the casket lid "to avoid jarring the family." Not only does this shift the reader's focus from the dead man to the surviving family, where it belongs, but it also contains the double meanings for "jar" of upsetting or enclosing. Maud Martha has been "jarred" in her marriage and is about to be "jarred" out of it.

In a story thematically concerned with the limits of physical reality, Brooks also conveys the power of that reality as she personifies the fire as an "invader" eating the trapped "flesh" of the streetcar passengers. The emotions of the women are similarly given physical reality as "ripped-open wounds" and "sores." However, already the reader is offered the values that negate physical realities, as what is considered physical beauty or ugliness becomes its opposite through the intense grief of the women. Establishing physical correspondence for the nonphysical realities with which she confronts the reader allows Brooks to reveal a physical world inseparable from the spiritual. On the other hand, the spiritual is so independent of the physical that when a man is loved, "his physical limits expand, his outlines recede, vanish."

Brooks is not, however, writing a poem here, whatever poetic demands she makes on language. She is telling a story, and her setting provides the backdrop for the inner and outer dialogues that convey the story. Mrs. Phillips is revealed culturally through her dialect as she describes her "boy" as "a-laughin'" and "a-jokin'"; she is revealed psychologically as she qualifies her "praise" of Maud Martha in every sentence until it becomes blatant criticism. Belva Brown reveals her character by what she does not say, and by the struggle she has to keep from saying it.

To understand Maud Martha, the psychological center of the story, however, one must go into her thoughts, even before she has had them. Brooks carefully stretches the limits of the third-person limited perspective to anticipate the realization that is rising in Maud Martha and to trace its growth. Even when Maud Martha has had her epiphany, Brooks phrases it ambiguously: "She felt higher and more like a citizen of—what?" Whereas the physical can reach its final expression in death, the spiritual reality comes in hints. If physical limits seal one in a jar where one can be destroyed by fire, spiritual realization offers one choices. It promises Maud Martha neither approval nor success—merely that "a road was again clear before her."

*Thelma J. Shinn*

# RITTER GLUCK

*Author:* E. T. A. Hoffmann (1776-1822)
*Type of plot:* Fantasy
*Time of plot:* 1809
*Locale:* Berlin
*First published:* 1809 (English translation, 1969)

> *Principal characters:*
> A MAN, one who claims to be the great German composer
>     Christoph Willibald Ritter von Gluck (best-known as
>     Christoph Gluck, 1714-1787)
> THE NARRATOR, a connoisseur of music

*The Story*

On a beautiful fall afternoon, the first-person narrator, a passionate lover of music, sits in one of Berlin's well-known cafés, desperately trying to escape from the loud racket of its obligatory music into the world of pleasant reveries. Brought back from his dreams by the offensive tune of a particularly vile waltz, he suddenly notices that an older man of strikingly mysterious countenance and demeanor has joined him at his table. In an ensuing conversation, the stranger disagrees with the narrator's harsh criticism of the musicians and, to prove his point, asks them to play the overture to Christoph Gluck's opera *Iphigenia in Aulis* (1774). The narrator is quickly caught up in his companion's intense delight and is finally able to hear the heavenly beauty of the composition in spite of the pitiful performance it receives at the hands of the little orchestra.

At the end of the music, the stranger admits that he himself is a composer and proceeds to recount with ever-growing exaltation his way from his boyhood music lessons to the frightening but enchanting realms of music to his final, mystical encounter with the truth of all art. This truth revealed itself to him under the symbol of the sun as an ineffable harmony, a musical triad "from which the chords, like stars, shoot out and entwine you with threads of fire." Overcome by the wild enthusiasm of his own story, the stranger abruptly gets up and vanishes.

That same night, the narrator runs into the mysterious composer for the second time. Fascinated by the extraordinary aura of this man, he invites him to his apartment for a further exchange of ideas. Now it is the older of the two who castigates with great bitterness Berlin's theatrical practice of lavishing all care on the ostentatious production of operas while neglecting their musical integrity. The atrocious liberties directors have taken in the staging of Gluck's works are singled out for particularly impassioned censure. Paroxysms of emotion, this time pain and frustration clearly dominant, finally drive the unhappy man back into the night. Again he departs without a good-bye.

A third meeting comes to pass several months later as the narrator finds his eccentric friend in a state of bewildering excitement outside a theater in which a performance of Gluck's opera *Armida* (1777) is taking place. This time the curious stranger insists on inviting the narrator to his own apartment, which the visitor finds filled with old-fashioned furniture belonging to the era of Gluck rather than that of the early nineteenth century. The host now suggests that he will play the music to *Armida* on his piano and that his guest should turn the pages for him. These pages are, however, to the young man's total consternation, completely blank. The agitated stranger proceeds, nevertheless, to play Gluck's music from the empty pages and does so with a fervor and with numerous, brilliant variations that for the mesmerized listener seem to outshine the genius of Gluck's original. When the performance has come to an end, the stunned visitor begs to know to whom he is talking. The host disappears for a while into an adjacent room, only to reappear in the embroidered court dress of an eighteenth century chevalier. The young man stands paralyzed at the sight. The last words belong to the mysterious man, who now politely introduces himself by saying: "I am Ritter Gluck!"

*Themes and Meanings*

"Ritter Gluck" was E. T. A. Hoffmann's first tale and marked his emergence as one of German Romanticism's most important and influential writers. For many years Hoffmann thought his true calling to be that of a composer or conductor. In 1809, when "Ritter Gluck" was published, he served as orchestral director in the small southern town of Bamberg, and it must have seemed only natural to him to submit his short tale to Germany's leading musical journal, the *Allgemeine musikalische Zeitung*. Hoffmann's preoccupation with music is still quite obvious in the story, and literary critics have occasionally tried to dismiss it for that reason as little more than a barely disguised essay in musical criticism. However, in spite of several musical references that the uninitiated reader today will find difficult to understand or appreciate, "Ritter Gluck" is now widely recognized as one of the finest examples of Hoffmann's literary genius, an amazingly concise prefiguration of several of his most obsessive themes.

The outward, historical circumstances of the modest plot are taken from Hoffmann's stay in Berlin between 1807 and 1808 and, more specifically, center on a performance of Gluck's opera *Armida* that Hoffmann attended and whose staging convinced him of the abominable tastes of Berlin's musical circles. On this experience, Hoffmann built a story that proclaims the fundamental incompatibility between artistic creativity and bourgeois receptivity. This insurmountable conflict between an artist and his audience is heightened by the fact that it merely reflects on a social level an even deeper conflict within the artistic process itself. The true tragedy of the artist must arise out of the recognition that what he or she perceives in moments of creative vision belongs to the realm of the inexpressible—no artistic realization can fully recapture such an experience in its original beauty and intensity.

The mysterious stranger of "Ritter Gluck" escapes his insensitive social environment through ever more self-absorbing flights of the imagination until in a moment of untrammeled exaltation he enters a world of harmony in which the division between nature and art has been overcome. The frustration inherent in such mystical immediacy is that its very essence forbids adequate artistic formulation. Despair thus becomes the inevitable result of any experience of the ultimate. The gifted composer of Hoffmann's tale tries to compensate for his own inability to give voice to the ecstatic harmonies of his mind by employing and improving on the work of another artist, by assuming the identity of the successful composer Christoph Gluck.

The paradox of Hoffmann's position seems to be that precisely those artists who experience most deeply will, of necessity, be driven into artistic impotence that, in turn, must lead to madness and self-destruction. Hoffmann explored these frightful consequences in much greater detail in such characters as the painters Traugott, Berklinger, and Berthold in "The Artus Exchange" and "The Jesuit Church in G." as well as in the fate of the musician Kreisler, the hero of his last novel *Lebensansichten des Katers Murr, nebst fragmentarischer Biographie des Kapellmeisters Johannes Kreisler in zufalligen Makulaturblattern* (1820-1822; *The Life and Opinions of Kater Murr, with the Fragmentary Biography of Kapellmeister Johannes Kreisler on Random Sheets of Scrap Paper,* 1907).

*Style and Technique*

Many of Hoffmann's most prominent stylistic devices can be identified in this, his first tale. Central among these is what has been called his style of two worlds: the unmediated juxtaposition of the ordinary and the extraordinary, the everyday and the uncanny. Again and again, Hoffmann lures the unsuspecting reader with descriptions of great precision into chains of perceptions that, in the end, leave him or her helplessly stranded in a world of fantastic unreality. The figure of the curious Ritter Gluck is only the most obvious instance of Hoffmann's grotesque integration of mutually exclusive perspectives. Is this man a figment of the narrator's imagination, is he the ghost of the historical Gluck, or is he simply a deranged artist? Evidence is presented in support of each of these contradictory explanations.

In the same vein, Hoffmann blurs the distinction between the arts. That he uses words to describe a musical world seems unavoidable. However, when he conveys the ultimate mysteries of musical harmony in the highly visual images of sun and flower, he consciously aims at an artistic vision that would transcend the limits of a person's divided sensorium.

The narrative technique with which "Ritter Gluck" is told seems only to intensify the resulting disorientation. Though the story provides few actions, the speed with which dialogues develop and scenes follow one another provides a dramatic tension that leaves the reader breathless in bewilderment. For Hoffmann, in everything there lurks its opposite: sanity in madness, madness in sanity. It is the unhappy fate of the sensitive soul to be torn apart by being attuned to the fiendish transparence of all reality. Clear outline and identity, mainstays of a secure existence, reveal themselves from this vantage point as nothing but the dubious prerogatives of one-dimensional mediocrity.

*Joachim J. Scholz*

# THE RIVER

*Author:* Flannery O'Connor (1925-1964)
*Type of plot:* Domestic realism
*Time of plot:* The mid-twentieth century
*Locale:* Southern United States
*First published:* 1953

> *Principal characters:*
> HARRY ASHFIELD, a boy four or five years old
> MRS. CONNIN, his baby-sitter, a night-shift worker
> MR. and MRS. ASHFIELD, his parents
> THE REVEREND BEVEL SUMMERS, a teenage traveling evangelist
> MR. PARADISE, a gas station owner who has cancer
> J. C.,
> SPIVEY, and
> SINCLAIR, Mrs. Connin's sons

*The Story*

Early one morning, the tired Mr. Ashfield hands over his son, Harry, to a baby-sitter, Mrs. Connin. Although she has been at work all night, she will keep Harry with her until late that evening. Before leaving the Ashfields' apartment, Mrs. Connin criticizes the cigarette butts that she smells and the modern art that she sees on the wall, and she hears that Mrs. Ashfield, Harry's mother, is ill. As she and Harry leave, she tells the boy that she will take him today to see the Reverend Bevel Summers, who will be conducting a healing service by a local river. When she notices Harry has no handkerchief, she lends him one. As they wait for a trolley, Mrs. Connin asks Harry his first name, and he lies, telling her it is Bevel. She is pleased to hear this and says Harry will have to meet the young reverend, who is a good preacher although he cannot heal Mrs. Connin's husband, who is currently in the hospital. Harry says he wants to be healed, even though all that is wrong with him is that he is hungry. When Mrs. Connin falls asleep on the trolley, Harry hides her handkerchief inside his coat.

In Mrs. Connin's small house away from the city, Harry sees photographs on her walls as well as a picture of Jesus. Mrs. Connin's three sons lead Harry to their pigpen, where they trick him into releasing a pig. Harry expects pigs to look clean and cheery, as in children's books, but the pig that chases him is gray and dirty, with a damaged ear. When Mrs. Connin realizes that Harry does not recognize Jesus in her picture, she reads to him from an old book, *The Life of Jesus for Readers Under Twelve*. In the book, Harry sees Jesus driving pigs out of a man. Harry hides the book inside his coat when Mrs. Connin is not looking.

When Harry, Mrs. Connin, and her children arrive at the healing service, they hear the Reverend Bevel Summers warning people that they should be present for Jesus, not just for healing—that the river that matters, the one that heals, is the river of Jesus's blood, which leads to the Kingdom of Christ. A large, old man with cancer over his ear, Mr. Paradise, heckles the preacher. Mrs. Connin introduces Harry to the preacher, points out that both are named Bevel, and asks him to pray for Mrs. Ashfield. Harry is struck by the man's seriousness and agrees to be baptized so he can go to the Kingdom of Christ, which he imagines is under the river, instead of going home. After his baptism, Harry tells the preacher that his mother's illness is a hangover, at which point Mr. Paradise laughs loudly.

When Harry reaches home, his parents are having a party. Mrs. Connin is shocked to learn that Bevel is not the boy's name and that his parents disapprove of his baptism; she leaves without being paid. Mrs. Ashfield discovers the book Harry has taken, and her guests comment on its high monetary value. As Mrs. Ashfield puts Harry to bed, he says that the reverend told him he is changed.

The next morning, Harry wakes up first, scrounges for food, rubs cigarette ashes into the rug, and decides to return to the river. Mrs. Connin's house is empty when Harry passes by, but as Harry passes Mr. Paradise's gas station, Mr. Paradise spies him and follows. When Harry enters the river to go to the Kingdom of Christ, he has trouble going under the water and staying there. When Harry sees Mr. Paradise coming after him, looking to Harry like a pig, Harry goes under the water again and drowns.

*Themes and Meanings*

Flannery O'Connor sees a world full of social, familial, economic, and even medical problems, and one of her themes is how to rear a child in such a troubled world. At first, it may appear that Mr. and Mrs. Ashfield are terrible parents and that Mrs. Connin does an excellent job of attending to Harry's physical and spiritual needs. O'Connor complicates this theme by showing that Harry has turned out to be a clever and courageous boy, either despite his parents' neglect or because they leave him alone, while Mrs. Connin's sons are mean boys. More than once, Mrs. Connin is described as resembling a corpse. Such comparisons may foreshadow a happy death for Harry; alternatively, they may call into question the value of the ideas to which she introduces Harry. The child-rearing theme becomes more complex at the river; although the Reverend Summers may seem to be a good substitute father for Harry and Mr. Paradise may seem like an abusive parent, at the end of the story, when Harry returns to the river, he wants nothing more to do with preachers. It is Mr. Paradise who gives Harry the needed push to take him where he longs to go.

O'Connor is noted for her stories about religion. This story presents fundamentalists, blasphemers, people with no interest in religion, and, in Harry, a character living in perfectly ignorant innocence about religion. In other O'Connor stories, both fundamentalists and blasphemers can earn her respect, but a major concern for O'Connor in this story is religious ignorance and the extent to which an individual needs to understand the complexities of religious dogma to be considered religious. If Harry has a sense of religion, he appears to create his own religion from scratch in the course of this story. Even when he does receive religious training, from Mrs. Connin's book or from the young preacher's sermon, Harry seems to leave these teachings behind. When he reaches the river at the end, Harry means to baptize himself—without a preacher. In Harry Ashfield, O'Connor depicts either a character pathetically destroyed by his ignorance and his misunderstanding of religion, or one saved by the religion that he, as a free, autonomous individual, constructs for himself.

## Style and Technique

The omniscient narrator often presents events and descriptions from Harry's perspective; although the narrator and the reader are much more knowledgeable than Harry, his understanding of the other characters and of what happens to him is taken seriously rather than being treated as a joke.

As a result, the meaning of much of the most important symbolism in this story is revealed by watching Harry observe the new world he discovers. The river is meaningful to Harry because the preacher tells him that he can go there instead of going home—the Kingdom of Christ as a theological concept and traditional river symbolism mean nothing to Harry. He may simply want a place where he matters, instead of living amid parties for his parents' friends.

When Harry is aware of a traditional meaning, he quickly learns to reject it in favor of a new reality. What he expects a pig to be from reading books at home—a pal in a cartoon—is rejected as soon as he sees the ugly pigs found in the Connins' yard, in Mrs. Connin's book about Jesus, and even in the form of Mr. Paradise. The story encourages the reader to think about what sorts of symbolism a child can understand. Harry knows the name Bevel is significant, but does he know a bevel is an angle that is not a right angle? Harry plays with ashes, but does he see the irony in his surname, Ashfield? Does he think Mrs. Connin is a con artist, or that Mr. Paradise longs for paradise? Do adult readers who catch these meanings have any real advantage over a character like Harry who does not understand jokes?

The story expresses skepticism about the value of many tricks of the literary trade. O'Connor seems to suggest that a simple, perhaps crudely drawn picture of Jesus can carry more punch than a watercolor in a modern art style can, and that she wants to write a story with a strength that comes, in part, from its lack of sophisticated artfulness. O'Connor is famous for her humor, but since Harry is tired of an excess of jokes, this story maintains, for O'Connor, a very serious tone.

*Marshall Bruce Gentry*

# THE ROAD FROM COLONUS

*Author:* E. M. Forster (1879-1970)
*Type of plot:* Psychological
*Time of plot:* The early twentieth century
*Locale:* Messenia, Greece, and London, England
*First published:* 1904

> *Principal characters:*
> MR. LUCAS, an aging Englishman who loves Greek culture
> ETHEL, his daughter
> ARTHUR GRAHAM, Ethel's fiancé
> MRS. FORMAN, an English resident of Athens

*The Story*

The elderly Mr. Lucas has been a Grecophile for forty years. Now in declining health, he has decided to see Greece for himself. What he really seeks during his travels is restoration of youth. He is aware of a diminution in his mental power and seems to understand that his independence will soon end. Although he finds Athens overly dusty and Delphi too wet, his disappointment in the trip stirs feelings of discontent that contrast with his usual indifference.

Traveling on muleback through Messenia, a coastal province southeast of Athens, he presses his mount ahead of his companions and arrives early at a small country inn located among a grove of imposing plane trees, where they plan to have lunch. To his surprise, he discovers water flowing across the road; even more surprising, it comes from a huge, hollowed-out plane tree that leans over the small inn.

Regaining some of his lost confidence, Lucas thinks about the tree and its mysterious spring and decides to enter and possess it. When he enters the hollow space seeking the water's source, he discovers that the tree's interior, the origin of the spring, has been transformed into a variously decorated shrine. Deriving a sense of spiritual fulfillment from the tree, the flowing water, the people living in the inn, and the surroundings, Lucas resolves to remain there for a time. He has acquired a sense of unity that extends to everything in his environment and anticipates that some profoundly moving experience will take place. Although he has found Greece's most famous places boring, he is deeply affected by this obscure country setting.

When the others in Lucas's party arrive, they join him in his admiration of the setting. When he suggests to his daughter, Ethel, that they delay their trip and spend an extra day there, she suggests a week. For her, this response represents a moment of uncharacteristic enthusiasm, but Lucas takes her words seriously. Their travel guide, Mrs. Forman, who earlier identified Lucas with Oedipus and Ethel with Antigone, names the spot Colonus, the site where the life of Oedipus ended. She objects to a delay because it would disrupt their previously arranged schedule. When Ethel inspects the inn and finds the accommodations unsatisfactory, she concludes that she must take her father away for his own good. Against his stubborn opposition, Lucas is placed on his mule by Arthur Graham, his daughter's fiancé, and the party continue their journey, despite frantic efforts by the inn's owner and her family to delay them.

A few months later, during breakfast with Ethel in his London apartment, Lucas is busy writing a letter of complaint to his landlord about noises that keep him awake. He is disturbed by music practice from a nearby apartment, assorted street sounds at night, and water gurgling through pipes over his head. Ethel ignores his complaints. She has made plans to marry Mr. Graham within a few weeks, and her Aunt Julia, an unmarried sister of Lucas whom he hates and fears, will come to live in the apartment to care for him.

Unexpectedly, a package containing asphodel bulbs arrives from Greece, a gift from Mrs. Forman. The bulbs are wrapped in an old Greek newspaper, which Ethel proceeds to read. It dates from the time of their trip and contains an article about the deaths of the Rhomaides family—the innkeepers whom they had visited. The plane tree fell onto the inn and killed its inhabitants as they rested on the balcony. From the date given in the newspaper, Ethel determines that the accident occurred the very same night when they considered staying there. She points out to her father how fortunate it was that they left early, but Lucas, busily at work on his letter of complaint, comprehends nothing.

*Themes and Meanings*

A character in E. M. Forster's novel *Howard's End* (1910) advocates connecting the prose (prosaic, rational nature) and the passion (emotional, spiritual nature) in human life in order to make human relationships more satisfactory. Forster was fascinated by the disconnections and disjunctions among human beings and the misunderstandings and conflicts they engender. In an attempt to confront the past of Greek civilization in this story, Mr. Lucas unconsciously seeks to come to terms with his own past life. Because he arrives at the inn earlier than the others, he has more time to be influenced by the setting. He clearly needs to be preparing for death, and he undergoes a profound spiritual experience at the shrine that enables him to see life whole. Instead of leaving images of body parts that were healed or improved at the shrine, as others before him have done, he conceives of leaving an image of a whole man.

Although the others find the lunch stop in this picturesque setting pleasant, they are not so moved, in part because they are not in similarly earnest search of spiritual experiences. Lucas seems detached from the practical demands of the moment, but his companions are concerned with the immediate present. As if to heighten the contrast between the practical and the spiritual, Forster has their guide, an unnamed Greek translator in the travel party, bargain with the innkeeper to purchase a pig. This mundane act takes place while Lucas is working out the meaning of his own transforming event.

Lucas's companions experience conflict, but, as they are acting rationally, are convinced that their acts are for his own good. When Graham forcibly places Lucas astride his mule, he offers an apology and explanation, but he gives up when he realizes that the old man will not understand. When Ethel reads of the accident at the inn, she can only react with relief over their decision to leave, never realizing that Mr. Lucas would have found a happier fate in death at the inn.

Conflicts in the story arise owing to differences in age, timing of the narrative, and values, and Forster makes them appear natural, even inevitable. He suggests that moral choices as well as human relationships are infinitely complex and subtle.

### Style and Technique

The story's title, containing an allusion to a Sophoclean tragedy, suggests the importance of myth to the development of the story's themes. Narrated in the third person, the story incorporates ample dialogue, primarily between Mr. Lucas and his daughter Ethel, to reveal the characters' points of view.

The story is remarkable for its use of symbolism, myth, and irony. The flowing water, the shrine, and the shrine's little ornaments are all symbolic of spiritual experience. Given Lucas's reaction, the country inn symbolizes a final resting place, the end of one's life journey.

The mythic elements derive from the allusions to *Oidipous epi Kolōnōi* (401 B.C.E.; *Oedipus at Colonus*, 1729), by Sophocles. In that tragedy, the blind Oedipus, having suffered in exile for many years, reaches a peaceful rural spot, Colonus, somewhere near Athens. There, accompanied by his daughter Antigone, he experiences a peaceful, happy death. The gods, whose will had imposed on Oedipus a long period of expiation for past misdeeds, once again showed their favor. Like the Greek protagonist, Lucas seeks peace and coherent meaning in life, and these are suggested at the site of the inn.

Lucas's Antigone-like daughter, however, leads him away from his fate for his own good. The story's most telling irony lies in the title. The road to Colonus led Oedipus to peace, atonement, contentment, and meaningful death. The road from his metaphoric Colonus leads Lucas to a querulous, petulant, difficult old age in which he loses his independence and freedom and must endure the autocratic supervision of the unmarried sister whom he hates.

Although the story treats every character briefly except Lucas, the dialogue between Ethel and her father is laced with irony. After Lucas is forced to leave the inn and lapses into an uncaring lethargic state, Ethel comments that her father is once again himself; this is a casual observation to her, but a telling commentary to Forster. Further irony occurs in Ethel's final observation that their departure was providential, a comment that Lucas does not hear because he is working on his letter of complaint.

*Stanley Archer*

# ROAD TO THE ISLES

*Author:* Jessamyn West (1902-1984)
*Type of plot:* Psychological
*Time of plot:* The last Thursday and Friday in January
*Locale:* Tenant City
*First published:* 1948

> *Principal characters:*
> JOHN DELAHANTY, the father
> GERTRUDE DELAHANTY, the mother
> CRESS DELAHANTY, the daughter
> BERNADINE "NEDRA" DEEVERS, Cress's friend

*The Story*

Cress Delahanty, a remedial dance student, is chosen to appear in the Tenant City High School Folk-Dance Festival. The fourteen-year-old girl is thrilled that she has been selected to dance alongside Bernadine Deevers, Tenant City High School's most gifted dancer, in the dance number "Road to the Isles." She has a vision of dancing "not only the outward steps of the 'Road to the Isles' but its inner meaning." Cress feels that she has achieved one of the two great goals in the life of a Tenant High School student, the other being to have Bernadine for a friend. Now that Bernadine is coming to spend the weekend with her, Cress feels as if all of her life's dreams are coming true.

Every winter, since there is little work on the ranch, Mr. Delahanty embarks on a self-improvement program, an idea suggested and nurtured by Mrs. Delahanty. Then every spring he abandons the project as if he had never begun. Last year it was "A Schedule of Exercises to Ensure Absolute Fitness"; this schedule involved running six times around the orchard in short pants, his arms flailing and chest pumping—an embarrassing sight for Cress.

This year Mr. Delahanty's schedule is a reading program from an encyclopedia for the purpose of acquiring all "Human Knowledge in a Year." Mrs. Delahanty is always trying to help Mr. Delahanty to stay on his schedule—before breakfast, before lunch, before supper, and before bedtime. Cress is ashamed of this business of schedules: Her friend Bernadine is far too sophisticated for schedules, and Cress wants to see her parents become what Bernadine would want them to be. Further, Cress is worried that her father might mispronounce the dance numbers and embarrass her in front of Bernadine. Meekly, Mr. Delahanty suggests that he will not open his mouth in the presence of Cress's friends.

Cress reminds her parents that they should address Bernadine as Nedra on Fridays. Naturally, her parents are inquisitive. Cress explains to them about the dubious origin of "Nedra": Bernadine's boyfriend Neddy, who owned two drugstores and to whom

Bernadine said no on a Friday, died the following Friday. The Delahantys are amused and skeptical.

Bernadine comes the next day, Friday, to spend the weekend with Cress. They are getting ready for the folk-dance festival. While getting her costume on, Bernadine confides in Cress: Her parents also used to be like Cress's. They went where Bernadine went and she stayed with them all the time. This year, however, she will not let them go with her to the dance festival because her father made a spectacle of himself, to her shame and chagrin, when he awkwardly danced the Hopak with Miss Ingols, the gym teacher. Bernadine now wants Cress to warn her parents not to make fools of themselves on the dance floor with Miss Ingols in public.

Cress goes to the kitchen to warn her parents. As she is about to open the kitchen door to the porch, she overhears her father and mother talking about her. Unseen by them, she listens. Her parents, especially her father, are very worried about her. Mr. Delahanty is afraid that his daughter, being clumsy in footwork, might make a fool of herself in public by falling on her ear during the dance. He could not bear it if his daughter should experience such a humiliation.

As Cress traces her steps back to her friend, she looks at herself in the bathroom mirror. "I look different," she tells herself. She looks at her image again—it is blurred, wavering, and doubtful; it is no longer the triumphant face she imagined.

Cress tells Bernadine everything about her parents. Indeed, she is proud of them; she is no longer apologetic about her parents; she is not afraid to admit that her father keeps schedules. She proudly announces that her parents are concerned and worried about her because they care. Cress is no longer worried about what Bernadine thinks about her parents. When Bernadine tries to make fun of her father, she tells her to shut up. Cress has grown up.

*Themes and Meanings*

Growing up through the process of change is what this story is about. There are two groups of people involved in this maturation process: two adults and two adolescents.

Of the two adults, one, Mrs. Delahanty, tries futilely and mistakenly to help Mr. Delahanty grow up physically and mentally. Since Mr. Delahanty is a mature adult, Jessamyn West implies, he should not be forced or nudged by his wife to change; his strenuous running and his intellectual schedule-keeping merely make him look ridiculous in the eyes of his adolescent daughter. On the other hand, Mrs. Delahanty does not try to change herself. It is interesting to note that Mr. Delahanty does not try to change his wife at all; he knows that he should not force change on another adult.

The two adolescents, Cress and Bernadine, try to change their parents, who they think are ignorant of the ways of the modern world and naïve in social graces. Bernadine shuts her parents out of her life and refuses to accept their advice. She simply refuses to change her ways and to grow up. Cress, on the contrary, keeps an open mind and remains open to change. In only two or three minutes of conversation heard through a back porch door, Cress gets to know her parents better, and the change in perspective gives her a newfound maturity.

West seems to imply that refusal to grow up and change is a destructive process. Bernadine is described as a "femme fatale": She is capable of performing only Salome's dance of death; she is also somehow involved in the death of her boyfriend Neddy.

*Style and Technique*

The consistent and clever use of the journey motif is the means whereby West achieves unity and coherence in the story. This is best illustrated by the story's title, "Road to the Isles," by the movement involved in the dance routine, by the trip to the festival, and by the transportation to the out-of-town game.

One important characteristic of West's style in this story is that she portrays the world as an adolescent, Cress Delahanty, sees it. The reader is given the realistic impression that he or she is an unobserved spectator of the unfolding drama of Cress's psychological development. In this regard, the reader is like Cress, who, unseen, listens in on her parents' conversation about Bernadine and Cress.

*Zacharias P. Thundy*

# ROCK SPRINGS

*Author:* Richard Ford (1944-    )
*Type of plot:* Social realism
*Time of plot:* 1980
*Locale:* Montana and Wyoming
*First published:* 1982

*Principal characters:*
EARL MIDDLETON, the narrator
EDNA, his girlfriend

*The Story*

Earl Middleton is a man looking to change his luck. He has had his fair share of trouble in his life—troubles with the law, love, and work—and now he is hoping for a fresh start, a new beginning. He decides to hit the road, to get out of Montana, where he has recently gotten into trouble over several bad checks, which can put him into prison in Montana. For Earl, the troubles do not end in Montana. He seems to breed bad luck and trouble, to bring them along with him, even though he claims that he believes in crossing the street to stay out of trouble's way.

For Earl, trouble follows and hounds him like the fumes of exhaust that stream out from the back of his car, a cranberry Mercedes stolen from an ophthalmologist's lot. He gets halfway through Wyoming before the first hint of trouble surfaces: The oil light flashes, which he knows is a bad sign. When the car finally breaks down, thirty miles outside the mining town of Rock Springs, Wyoming, Earl's life unravels faster than he ever could have dreamed. What began as a road trip filled with laughter and love, a new beginning for him, his girlfriend, Edna, and his daughter, Cheryl, turns abruptly into a dead end: a road going nowhere. Even worse, the stolen Mercedes is not the only thing that has broken down: Earl's relationship with Edna turns sour. He is left to deal with the fact that he will always remember Rock Springs as a place where a woman left him, instead of a place where he finally got things going on a straight track.

That night, after Edna goes to sleep, Earl goes outside to the parking lot of the Ramada Inn where, in the morning, he will watch Edna leave on the first bus back to Montana, leaving him alone to care for himself and his daughter. He muses about what separates his life—a life shaped by heartbreak and loss—from the lives of those people who actually own the cars nosed into this lot. He finally realizes that, "Through luck or design they had all faced fewer troubles, and by their own characters, they forget them faster." Earl's story, his epiphany, does not end here. Earl has a few parting words to say before moving on. He poses a series of questions, to both the inhabitants of the motel and the reader: "What would you think a man was doing in the middle of the night looking in the windows of cars in the parking lot of the

Ramada Inn? Would you think he was trying to get his head cleared? . . . Would you think he was anybody like you?" The narrative tension created by being directly addressed at the end of the story, as if pulled in by the shirt collar and then just as suddenly pushed away, leaves readers alone to question their own lives, much as Earl Middleton is left alone, standing on a threshold between the present and the future, waiting and wondering what his next move will be.

*Themes and Meanings*

In typical Richard Ford stories, his mostly male characters live in the vast emptiness of the American West. Raised to stand silent and stone-faced in the presence of trouble and hard times, they must face and ultimately move forward through times of crisis and change. Earl Middleton has lived through, or at least survived, a lifetime of failed relationships. His relationship with Edna, herself no stranger to harsh, heartbreaking encounters with love, began in a bar and was most likely consummated in the backseat of an old Chevy. They are natural-born drifters unburdened by something as bourgeois as an occupation, or a nine-to-five job. If life is not working out in Montana, then it is high time to move on, which is exactly what they do. In the world in which they live every day, there is no such thing as a safety net.

The decision to leave owes nothing to something as structured as a plan. It is purely spontaneous: Find a map, round up a car, and they are ready to go. When Earl walks into the house one afternoon and asks Edna, out of the blue, if she wants to go with him to Florida, her response is a flat, matter-of-fact: "Why not? My datebook's not that full." By nightfall, they are on their way, riding high on the road, hoping against all hope that things will eventually work out.

The American West that was mapped out by novelist Wallace Stegner was once a place where people came to homestead, to lay claim to a piece of the land, but in Ford's stories, a spirit of homelessness seems to have inhabited both the empty space of the land itself as well as those who live on it. Earl Middleton is a living, breathing by-product of this migratory pattern of contemporary living. At the end of "Rock Springs," it does not much matter where he is going. What is clear is that he is gripped by the urge to go, to get anywhere but here. Rock Springs, Wyoming, is a pit stop en route to another town, another woman, all of it viewed through the windows of yet another stolen car.

Earl wants his readers to know that he is one of them. It just so happens that his path in life has hurled him down a road of rundown motels whose neon vacancy signs have stopped flashing, have burned themselves out. All that he asks of the reader is to try to imagine what it would be like to stand with him, for a brief moment, in the middle of the night, in the parking lot of a motel where whatever small-time dreams he harbored earlier that day have all but disappeared. The question still remains, burning like a light: Would one think him a similar kind of human being? Ford forces the reader to consider the possibility that "the difference between a successful life and an unsuccessful one . . . was . . . how many troubles . . . you had faced in a lifetime." In the landscape of Ford's fictional world, trouble always waits around the bend, and he is not about to let the reader forget this. Maybe, if one is lucky, trouble might do one a favor and knock on somebody else's front door.

*Style and Technique*

Of the ten stories in Ford's collection *Rock Springs* (1987), eight—including the title story—are told in the first person, narrated by self-reflective men who seem compelled to tell what happened. The voices behind these stories possess a ragged, rough-hewn lyricism whose loss-tinged, nostalgic narrative tone leans toward the elegiac. Ford earns reader sympathy for men like Earl Middleton—men who might, at first glance, spell nothing but trouble—by exposing the soft sides beneath their typically hard-shelled exteriors. Earl is a thief with a heart, and Ford forces the reader to accept this fact at face value. He achieves this effect in his fiction with a style that is seemingly styleless. He allows his characters not only to feel, but also to respond to the situation at hand.

In "Rock Springs," Ford puts a language of both emotion and rhetoric in the hands of a man not often given the chance to speak, to tell how he views and lives in this world. When Earl directs his closing lament to the reader, it is hard not to align even the coldest heart with his. Ford's storytelling power derives its authenticity and grace from his ability to find the poetry in everyday speech. In a molasses-paced, flat-voweled narrative voice that is boyishly charming and seductive in its apparent simplicity, Ford lures his readers into a landscape of dashed hopes and deflated dreams, breakdowns and breakups, a world where the luckless find the strength to go on living and looking for love, looking right through all the brightly lit signs that keep telling them to stop.

*Peter Markus*

# THE ROCKING-HORSE WINNER

*Author:* D. H. Lawrence (1885-1930)
*Type of plot:* Fantasy
*Time of plot:* 1920
*Locale:* England
*First published:* 1926

*Principal characters:*
PAUL, the protagonist, a preadolescent boy
HESTER, his mother, a beautiful, dissatisfied woman
OSCAR CRESSWELL, his uncle and confidant, Hester's brother
BASSETT, the gardener, an avid horse-racing enthusiast and
gambler

*The Story*

"The Rocking-Horse Winner" relates the desperate and foredoomed efforts of a young boy to win his mother's love by seeking the luck that she bitterly maintains she does not have. By bringing her the luxurious life for which she longs, Paul hopes to win her love, to compensate her for her unhappiness with his father, and to bring peace to their anxious, unhappy household. He determines to find luck after a conversation with his mother, in which she tells him that she is not lucky, having married an un-lucky husband, and that it is better to have luck than money because luck brings money. In response, Paul clearly accepts the unspoken invitation to take his father's place in fulfilling his mother's dreams of happiness. His purpose seems to be fulfilled when, with the help of Bassett, the gardener, he begins to win money betting on horse races. Shortly thereafter, he confides in his uncle Oscar, whom he also considers lucky because Oscar's gift of money started his winning streak.

Paul, Oscar, and Bassett continue to bet and win until Paul has five thousand pounds to give his mother for her birthday, to be distributed to her over the next five years. When she receives the anonymous present, she does not seem at all happy but sets about arranging to get the whole five thousand pounds at once. As a result, Hester becomes even more obsessed with money, increasingly anxious for more. Also, the house, which previously seemed to whisper "There must be more money! There must be more money!" now screeches the same refrain.

Paul, unable to perceive that his mother is insatiable, redoubles his efforts to win more money for her. He hides himself away, alone with his secret source of informa-tion on the outcome of the races. This secret, which he has shared with no one, is his mysterious, nameless rocking horse, which he rides frenziedly until he gets to the point at which he knows the name of the winner in the next big race. Desperate to know the name of the winner in the derby, he urges his parents to take a brief vacation. Summoned back to Paul by a strange sense of foreboding, Hester returns to see Paul fall from his horse after a frenzied ride, stricken by a brain fever from which he never recovers. While Bassett runs to tell Paul that he has successfully guessed the derby winner and is now rich, Paul tells his mother, "I am lucky," and then dies. Thereupon his uncle comments, "he's best gone out of a life where he rides his rocking-horse to find a winner."

## Themes and Meanings

This story is D. H. Lawrence's strongest indictment of materialism and his strongest demonstration of the incompatibility of the love of money and the love of human beings. In Paul's unhappy family, his parents' marriage is unsatisfactory. His mother is sexually frustrated: "She had bonny children, yet she felt they had been thrust upon her." Clearly, she feels not fulfilled, but violated.

However, she does not seek the cause of the failure of her marriage inside herself, but rather outside herself, claiming that she and her husband have no luck. In confiding her disappointment to her son, she seductively invites him to take the father's place in her life by finding luck for her. This task he sets out to accomplish. Thus, the preadolescent boy, who should feel sufficiently secure in his mother's love and in the stability of his family so that he can seek outside relationships and embark on his own sexual course, is arrested in his development. Stuck in an Oedipal bind with his mother, he regresses from adolescent sexuality into sexual infantilism. Instead of riding his own horse, symbol of male sexual power, he rides a rocking horse, an activity that, in its frenzy and isolation, suggests masturbation rather than fulfillment with a partner.

Throughout, Lawrence condemns the modern notion that luck and happiness come from the outside, rather than from within; that happiness must take the form of money and goods rather than of erotic, parental, and filial love. Lawrence also points out, with psychological astuteness, that to supplant love with money is a deception through which everyone can see. In the story, no one is fooled. The mother, whose heart is too hardened to love her children, tries to compensate them with presents and solicitousness, but the children and the mother know the truth: "They read it in each other's eyes."

To give and to receive love, the only true fulfillment in life, is, as Lawrence points out, to relate to but never to control another human being: The loved one always remains mysterious, unknown, unpredictable. Thus, love, freely given and received, is the very opposite of Paul's desperate need to know, to force knowledge, and to predict the future.

Although the reader never discovers how Paul learns the names of the winners, Lawrence hints, at various points in the story, that Paul may be trafficking with false and evil gods. This suggestion is made through his repeated descriptions of Paul's eyes as looking demoniac: "his uncanny blue eyes" that had "an uncanny cold fire in them"; "his eyes were like blue stones." This idea is also suggested by the religious language that surrounds Paul's gambling. Bassett repeatedly refers to Paul's correct prediction by saying, "It's as if he had it from heaven"; "his face terribly serious, as if he were speaking of religious matters"; his manner "serious as a church."

*Style and Technique*

The story begins with the deceptively simple and formulaic language of the fairy tale: "There was a woman who was beautiful, who started with all the advantages, yet she had no luck." This language underscores the inappropriateness of a life lived, as Hester lives it, in the belief that just as in fairy tales, luck and happiness are unpredictable because they come from the outside rather than being matters over which the individual exercises some control.

The supernatural elements in the story, rather than providing an opportunity for escape, augment its sense of reality. The futility of the materialistic quest, and its lack of destination, are well symbolized in Paul's frantic riding of his rocking horse. That the house whispers "There must be more money" seems not so much a supernatural or magical element as a brilliantly sustained metaphor for the unspoken messages that shape and often take over the life of a family. In all, the story is a brilliant study in the sustained use of symbolism to suggest with bold economy the death-dealing consequences of the substitution of money for love.

*Carola M. Kaplan*

# RODMAN THE KEEPER

*Author:* Constance Fenimore Woolson (1840-1894)
*Type of plot:* Regional
*Time of plot:* Not long after the American Civil War
*Locale:* Probably Andersonville, Georgia
*First published:* 1877

### Principal characters:

JOHN RODMAN, a Union Army veteran and keeper of a national
    cemetery
WARD DE ROSSET, a former Confederate soldier
BETTINA WARD, his intended bride
POMP, an old former slave, still loyal to De Rosset

*The Story*

John Rodman, a Union Army veteran who takes care of a large cemetery in which
fourteen thousand Union soldiers are buried, comes to grasp the depth of animosity
felt by southerners against their conquerors, both living and dead. He understands that
although the legacy of hatred may in time diminish, the aftermath of war can be as destructive as war itself.

Having taken a poorly paid job in what was formerly enemy country, Rodman
hopes to recover mentally and physically from the experiences he endured during the
war. The mild southern climate will restore his body, he thinks, while the mechanical
work of groundskeeping, record keeping, and administering in such a quiet place will
restore his tortured mind. Additionally, he hopes to repay his fallen comrades for their
sacrifice to a cause in which his faith has never faltered.

In short order, he learns that those living nearby want no part of him or the cemetery. They regard both as symbols of an unwanted occupation. However, as an open-
minded man, he attempts to acclimate to his surroundings, to find admirable traits in
his poverty-stricken neighbors whom he admires for their soldierly qualities and their
single-minded devotion to a way of life as he tries to adjust to a climate very different
from his native New Hampshire.

One hot day, in search of a cold spring, he finds a great house in total disrepair in
which lives Ward De Rosset, a sick former Confederate soldier now being taken care
of by Pomp, a former slave. Although hungry and wracked with pain, De Rosset is reluctant to accept the slightest favor from a Yankee. However, the extremity of his situation brings him to the tiny cottage that goes with Rodman's position. Although
Rodman has no sympathy for the Confederate cause, he cannot witness a fellow soldier in such distress and attempts to nurse him for about a week until a woman arrives.

Bettina Ward, haughty and unforgiving, but somehow more seductive and intimi-
dating than her northern sisters, rejects Rodman's hospitality, insisting she will pay
for any care given to her fiancé. His patience tried, Rodman replies in kind, demand-

ing thirty dollars, knowing Bettina cannot pay the enormous sum and showing that a hardheaded New Englander is every bit a match for a spirited southerner.

Despite the frost between these two young people, an obvious attraction exists; Bettina at one point goes so far as to comment on Rodman's racially correct "flaxen hair." When De Rosset dies, she determines to leave the area to make an uncertain living teaching in Tennessee. She has come to a grudging respect for the former Yankee officer who nursed her intended. However, when he asks her to be the first to sign the cemetery's guest register, she refuses, though she takes his hand in gratitude before she leaves.

In a final scene, Rodman encounters a Down Easter who intends to tear down the old house in which De Rosset had lived but will sell him its climbing vines for twenty-five cents. Perhaps this commercial spirit and get-up-and-go is as good a remedy as any to help drive out old ghosts.

*Themes and Meanings*

Once widely known, Constance Fenimore Woolson, the grandniece of James Fenimore Cooper, the American novelist famous throughout the world for his Leatherstocking tales of the early frontier, has recently begun to receive notice from feminist scholars who have promoted the work of this intelligent, sensitive, well-read writer. Ironically, "Rodman the Keeper" is difficult to regard as feminist: The women of the story (Bettina Ward and Mary, Rodman's "promised wife") take a distant backseat ethically to the men. To say that, however, is to admit that Woolson is capable of defying conventional expectations unlike so many of her competitors, who were writing sentimental local color stories for publication in magazines and newspapers. A less-talented hand might have made Bettina Ward see the error of her ways and accept the brave Yankee soldier who is as clearly attracted to her as she eventually is to him. That Bettina chooses instead to risk an independent life shows Woolson does not fear straying from popular formulas.

In an awkward digression never satisfactorily developed, Woolson more than once draws the reader's attention to some French lines displayed on Rodman's wall, which are best known in their Italian version, as part of the song "*La donna e mobile*," or "woman is fickle." Rodman even recites the quatrain aloud at Ward De Rosset's request, lingering on one phrase: "*Bien fou qui s'y fie*"—"A fool is he who trusts a woman." This jarring sentiment coming from one who most often reflects Woolson's own thoughts seems to comment not only on Rodman's faithless fiancé, Mary, but also on Bettina.

A more rewarding approach is to regard the story as being about the aftermath of war. Set during the Reconstruction era, less than a decade after the bloodbath that took 600,000 lives, "Rodman the Keeper" concerns itself with what has been learned—or not learned—from that conflict. The story makes clear that lives too must be reconstructed, a lesson Bettina is unable to accept in a fashion that satisfies either Rodman or the reader, though she makes the best effort she is capable of. In addition, the story is about being one's brother's "keeper," to love even those who do not love us.

Again Woolson offers no easy solution. She makes clear that people are a long way from overcoming the bitterness and animosity that causes war and its consequences.

Thus the story is about war and reconciliation like those splendid efforts years later by the German Nobel Prize winner Heinrich Böll. However, whereas Böll often makes his point about the need to love and forgive in heart-piercing language and telling metaphor, Woolson depends on rhetoric and larger-than-life character depictions.

## Style and Technique

This superior local color story is told from the limited omniscient point of view, one in which the narrator enters the mind chiefly of one character, here, John Rodman. However, Woolson not only supplies his thoughts, but she also often encloses them in quotation marks to show that the lonely man has reached a state in which he conducts dialogues with himself and sometimes with the buried dead. For example, he has begun to identify with a dead northern soldier who shared his last name. When he decides somewhat reluctantly to invite the dying Ward De Rosset into his cottage, he mentally consults first the dead Rodman whose approving reply Woolson also records.

By revealing Rodman's attempts to reason out his behavior in a logically articulated fashion, Woolson reveals the very delicate stability of the mind of this as yet unrecovered soldier. Still severely wounded physically and mentally, he has invented a series of therapeutic exercises to help him restore his health. One of the most dramatic of these self-discovered therapies is a method he has found to impose order on his chaotic thoughts. It is, in fact, the same one that American writer Ernest Hemingway would depict his Nick Adams using almost five decades later in "Big Two-Hearted River" (1925), another story about a scarred veteran returned from war who is trying to put together his damaged psyche. Like Hemingway's protagonist, Rodman attempts to impose order by carrying out his affairs and duties in a fashion so systematic that it becomes machinelike. If he makes a single penmanship mistake in copying out the names of the dead soldiers into a new ledger, he rewrites the entire page. He has taken to performing tasks at exactly the same time each day and to inventing little rituals and ceremonies. Woolson conveys Rodman's efforts to do things "by the numbers," as a later generation of American soldiers would say, by repeating such words as "order," "infinite pain," "labor," "exactness," and "precise."

Although the omniscient narrator is capable of labeling Rodman as "cynical" and "misanthropic" at times, it is clear from her quiet and approving voice that she admires his liberal spirit and willingness to become his brother's keeper. Indeed it is difficult for anyone familiar with the biography of Woolson to deny that although Rodman is certainly not Woolson, neither is he completely separate. Like her, he is a northerner temporarily sojourning in the South he both admires and despises. His New England conscience, like hers, rejects the South's carelessness and its pride. He is magnanimous but measured in his charity in that he cannot see it wasted, and like his author, he struggles with an intense depression that he controls only by imposed work habits.

*James E. Devlin*

# ROGER MALVIN'S BURIAL

*Author:* Nathaniel Hawthorne (1804-1864)
*Type of plot:* Psychological
*Time of plot:* 1725 to about 1745
*Locale:* New England
*First published:* 1832

> *Principal characters:*
> REUBEN BOURNE, the protagonist, a young soldier in the French and Indian Wars
> ROGER MALVIN, an elderly soldier
> DORCAS, Malvin's daughter, later Reuben's wife
> CYRUS, Reuben and Dorcas's son

*The Story*

The story opens in 1725, in the aftermath of Lovell's Fight, a battle in the French and Indian Wars. Two soldiers lie wounded in the forest, miles from the nearest settlement, at the foot of a rock that resembles a gigantic gravestone. The significance of this rock is immediately apparent, for the older of the men, Roger Malvin, is mortally wounded. The men have already dragged themselves along for three days, but Malvin knows he will not be able to go farther.

Malvin urges the younger man, Reuben Bourne, to go on without him, to save himself and leave Malvin to die. Reuben is horrified at the thought. Malvin has been his friend and mentor, and Reuben expects to marry his daughter, Dorcas. The two argue at length, Malvin insisting that there is no sense in Reuben staying with him: If Reuben stays behind, he will die, too; if both try to go on together, Malvin will die anyway.

Finally, Malvin tells a story from his own youth, when he fought in another battle against the Indians. His comrade was seriously wounded, unable to travel. Leaving him behind, as comfortable as possible, Malvin was able to go on alone, find help, and return to rescue the other man. Reluctantly persuaded by this story, Reuben at last agrees to go. Malvin's last request is that Reuben return when he can, bury him properly, and say a prayer for him.

Reuben's wounds are also serious, however, and when he is finally found he is too ill to tell his rescuers where Malvin is. Several days pass before he can speak. When Dorcas finally asks about her father, he is too ashamed to admit what he has done; instead, he concocts a story about burying Malvin before departing. (The title of the story is thus ironic, as Roger Malvin never gets a proper burial.)

As the years go by, Reuben and Dorcas marry and have a son, Cyrus. They try to make a living on Malvin's farm, which is one of the largest and richest in the area, but Reuben cannot concentrate on his work and the farm declines rapidly. Consumed by guilt, Reuben becomes more bitter and irritable each year. Finally, he is forced to sell the farm to pay his debts, and the family strikes out into the wilderness to find new land to settle.

Something draws Reuben from the path that he intended to follow. When the family stops on the fifth night, it is at the clearing where he left Malvin's body eighteen years earlier. Reuben and Cyrus set off to hunt something for their dinner. Hearing a sound in the brush, Reuben shoots, only to find he has killed his son on the very spot where Malvin died. Dorcas is as anguished as one would expect, but Reuben is strangely relieved. He believes that he has expiated his sin, and he offers his first prayer since leaving Malvin behind.

*Themes and Meanings*

When Reuben Bourne kills his son Cyrus, he believes that he has atoned for his sin: "His sin was expiated—the curse was gone from him; and in the hour when he had shed blood dearer to him than his own, a prayer, the first for years, went up to Heaven from the lips of Reuben Bourne." The question remains to challenge readers, as it has done for many decades: Of what sin is Reuben guilty?

The narrator takes great pains in the beginning of the story to show the sense in Malvin's proposal. Reuben in fact makes the only rational choice. If he stays behind with Malvin, he will die with him; he cannot save his friend. The narrator presents Malvin's arguments at length and clearly expects the reader to accept them. Some critics have condemned Reuben for abandoning his friend, but most have thought that his leaving was the right decision. Why, then, does Reuben feel so guilty about leaving Malvin behind?

It is a difficult choice to make, of course, and it is to be expected that Reuben will not walk away from his dying friend with a glad heart. His own feelings fluctuate rapidly. He is afraid to stay, afraid to go (not at all unusual for men in combat); at times he feels that he has done nothing wrong, and at other times he almost believes himself a murderer.

True, he does break his promise to return and bury Malvin, but by the time he recovers from his own injuries and is able to fulfill his pledge, it is likely that there would be little left to bury. He lies to Dorcas when she asks him if he has dug a grave for her father; however, is either offense serious enough to sever his relationship with God, or to demand he give up his own dear son in payment?

Probably the reader will not think so, and the narrator strives to create sympathy for Reuben. Certainly he is not a murderer; if he has sinned, it is a sin of omission, not of commission. The important thing, Nathaniel Hawthorne believes, is what Reuben thinks he has done. This is not a story of absolute moral guilt, but of the psychological effects of guilt. Hawthorne is not concerned with whether Reuben has sinned in the eyes of God, or in the eyes of his fellow men. The only thing that matters is that he has sinned in his own eyes.

The theme of the story is what happens to a man who feels guilty, and how he may recover from his guilt. In this story, Hawthorne creates a situation in which the reader can examine these questions without the distractions of moral judgment.

*Style and Technique*

In this story, Hawthorne's main concern is with Reuben's interior development. Interestingly, he provides little physical description of Reuben himself, or of anyone else in the story. Neither are Reuben's farm or the settlement in which he lives presented in much detail. Only two elements of the story are described clearly: Reuben's "interior landscape" and the landscape of the forest where Reuben and Malvin part.

As the story opens, sunbeams filter through the trees to awaken the two men. The narrator describes the setting clearly, both what it looks like and what it feels like. He focuses on the large piece of granite and on a "young and vigorous sapling" near the men. The granite will become Malvin's symbolic gravestone, and the sapling will function symbolically in the story as a parallel to Reuben's development.

The sapling stands over the two men as they argue about what Reuben should do. As he is finally leaving, Reuben stands atop the rock and ties one of his own bloody bandages to the highest branch of the sapling. This flag will not help rescuers find Malvin, for the spot is too well hidden. Reuben intends it only as a token of his pledge and promise.

Eighteen years later, when Reuben returns to the spot, the narrator again describes the setting in detail. The contrast is striking. Where the sunlight was "cheerful" before, the forest is unremittingly "dark and gloomy." Is this the result of years of growth, or has the change occurred in Reuben? The former sapling is now a tall tree, and mostly vigorous and green. However, its tallest branch—the one to which Reuben tied his bloody bandage as a sign of his promise—is withered and dead. Reuben notices this and trembles, for he knows that the branch's death symbolizes his own spiritual decay.

At the end of the story, when Cyrus is dead and his parents find him, the branch suddenly breaks off and falls "in light, soft fragments upon the rock, upon the leaves, upon Reuben, upon his wife and child, and upon Roger Malvin's bones." It does not come crashing down, as one would expect of a dead limb, but falls gently, for this is not a sign of punishment but of atonement. The withered parts are gone now—both Reuben and the tree can flourish again. Roger Malvin has at last had his burial.

*Cynthia A. Bily*

# ROMAN FEVER

*Author:* Edith Wharton (Edith Newbold Jones, 1862-1937)
*Type of plot:* Psychological
*Time of plot:* The 1920's
*Locale:* Rome
*First published:* 1933

> *Principal characters:*
> MR. DELPHIN "ALIDA" SLADE, a middle-aged American tourist
> MRS. HORACE "GRACE" ANSLEY, another middle-aged American
> tourist, a longtime acquaintance of Mrs. Slade

*The Story*

Two old friends, Alida Slade and Grace Ansley, are finishing lunch on the terrace of a Roman restaurant and move to the parapet, where they benignly contemplate the magnificent ruins of the Palatine and the Forum. Remarking that the scene below is the most beautiful view in the world, the two ladies agree to spend the afternoon on the terrace. Alida arranges with the waiter to permit them to stay until evening. They hear their daughters, Barbara Ansley and Jenny Slade, departing to spend the afternoon with two eligible young Italian men, and Grace remarks that the young women will probably return late, flying back by moonlight from Tarquinia. It becomes evident at this point that Grace has a closer relationship with her daughter than Alida has with Jenny because Alida did not know where the girls were going. Also, Barbara remarks a bit ruefully to Jenny as the two of them depart that they are leaving their mothers with nothing much to do.

At that point, Alida broaches the subject of emotions by asking Grace if she thinks that their daughters are as sentimental, especially about moonlight, as they once were. Grace responds that she does not know at all about the girls' sentiments and adds that she doubts that the two mothers know much about each other either. The two women sit silently for a while, thinking about their perceptions of each other.

Alida's perceptions of Grace are recounted as an interior monologue, which continues throughout the story, interspersed with passages of dialogue. As she reflects, she also reveals the circumstances of the years since she first met Grace. Grace had been married to Horace Ansley shortly before Alida had married Delphin Slade. Alida considered the Ansleys nullities, living exemplary but insufferably dull lives in an apartment directly across the street from the Slades in New York City. They had been superficial friends, and Alida had rather closely observed the irreproachable events of the Ansleys' lives for a number of years before her very successful lawyer husband made a big coup in Wall Street and the Slades moved to a more fashionable Park Avenue address. She prided herself on the lively social life that she and Delphin enjoyed, and especially on her own skills as a hostess and a brilliant personality. Both women were widowed only a few months before the time of the story and have renewed their friendship in the common bond of bereavement.

Alida's envy of Grace, despite her disparaging assessment of her, emerges in her thoughts at this time. She wonders how the Ansleys could have produced such a vivid and charming daughter, when her own Jenny seems by comparison so dull. She recalls that Grace was exquisitely lovely in her youth as well as charming in a fragile, quiet way. She reflects that she herself would probably be much more active and concerned if she had Barbara for a daughter.

Grace, for her part, has a mental image of Alida as a brilliant woman, but one who is overimpressed by her own qualities. She remembers Alida as a vivid, dashing girl, much different from her pretty but somewhat mousy daughter. She views Alida's life as sad, full of failures and mistakes, and feels rather sorry for her. Thus, in part 1 of the story, the setting, the situation, and the attitudes of the two women are presented in a manner that suggests a placid, if superficial, friendship of many years' standing, with both of the women secretly feeling some pity for each other's past life.

Part 2 begins with the tolling of the five o'clock bells and the decision of the two women to remain on the terrace rather than going in to play bridge. As Grace Ansley knits, Alida Slade reflects that their own mothers must have had a worrisome task trying to keep them home safe despite the lure of the romantic evenings in Rome. Grace agrees, and Alida continues with speculations about the probability that Barbara will become engaged to the attractive, eligible young Roman pilot with whom she is spending the evening, along with Jenny and the second young man. Jenny, Alida reasons, is only a foil for Barbara's vivacious charm, and Grace may be encouraging the companionship for that very reason. She tells Grace of her envy, stating that she cannot understand how the Ansleys had such a dynamic child while the Slades had such a quiet one. Alida recognizes in her own mind her envy, and also realizes that it began a long time ago.

As the sun sets, Alida recalls that Grace was susceptible to throat infections as a girl and was forced to be very careful about contracting Roman fever or pneumonia. Then she recalls a story of a great-aunt of Grace, who sent her sister on an errand to the Forum at night because the two sisters were in love with the same man, with the result that the unfortunate girl died of Roman fever. Alida then reveals that she used a similar method to eliminate the competition she believed existed between herself and Grace when, as young women in Rome, they both were in love with Delphin Slade. She cruelly reveals that she wrote a note to Grace imploring a rendezvous in the Colosseum by moonlight, and signed it with Delphin's name.

Revealing her hatred further, she gloats about how she laughed that evening thinking about Grace waiting alone in the darkness outside the Colosseum, and how effective the ruse had been, for Grace had become ill and was bedridden for some weeks. Grace is at first crushed to learn that the only letter that she ever received from Delphin was a fake, but she then turns the tables on Alida by assuring her that she had not waited alone that night. Delphin had made all the arrangements and was waiting for her.

Alida's jealousy and hatred are rekindled as she realizes that she has failed to humiliate Grace Ansley, especially when Grace states that she feels sorry for Alida because her cruel trick had so completely failed. Alida protests that she really had everything: She was Delphin's wife for twenty-five years, and Grace has nothing but the one letter that he did not write. In the final ironic epiphany, Grace simply replies that she had Barbara. Then she moves ahead of Alida toward the stairway.

This battle of the two women for the integrity of their own status with respect to the man they both loved ends with the complete victory of the woman who has appeared to be the weak, passive creature. She moves ahead because she is now dominant. The source of Barbara's sparkle is now revealed, and Grace is also now shown to be a woman who defied conventional morality and social restrictions to spend a night with the man she loved. Alida Slade is left only with the dismaying knowledge that she, in her attempt to be hateful and cruel, actually brought about the meeting that produced the lovely daughter she envies her friend having.

*Themes and Meanings*

The title of the story refers to malarial fever, which was prevalent in Rome before the draining of the swamps around the early nineteenth century. This fever was much feared by American tourists, especially those who had young, fragile daughters who might succumb to the ravages of the disease. The chances of contracting the disease were increased greatly after dark, when the mosquitoes that spread the infection were most active. Symbolically, the title also refers to the fever pitch of the passions that were engendered in the two women when they visited Rome as nubile young girls. The surface serenity and static nature of the plot provide ironic contrast to the gradual revelation of the intense emotions that the two women experienced when they were in Rome before.

The story contrasts the abiding hate of Alida Slade with the abiding love of Grace Ansley. Alida's cruelty and hatred, aroused by her fear that Delphin might be attracted to Grace, prompts her finally to reveal her trickery to the other woman. Her intention was clearly to humiliate the other and to bask in her triumphant superiority. Grace reveals, at Alida's goading, that the trickery not only did not work but also was actually the impetus for the birth of Barbara, the child for whom Alida has envied Grace ever since the child was an infant.

Friendship and companionship are superficial social amenities as depicted in this story. Strong emotions are suppressed or at least concealed in favor of outward tranquillity and smooth social relations. However, the deep, hidden emotions have nevertheless driven these women to actions that shaped their lives and characters in profound ways.

*Style and Technique*

The style of the story in its serenity, its quiet setting, and its almost total lack of action well matches the calm control exhibited by Grace Ansley, who turns out to be the victor in the contest initiated by Alida Slade. Although the reader is told that Alida is the dominant, vivid personality, and she clearly takes charge of both the activities (or lack thereof) and the conversation, her attacks on Grace are quietly rebuffed, and she is finally the loser as they mutually reveal information about their past activities.

The story is carefully wrought, so that the shift in sympathy to the timid Grace occurs fairly early, and it comes as a surprise to learn that she was so unconventional in her behavior as to undertake an assignation with another woman's fiancé. Then the final surprise, which is so quietly, and characteristically, announced to the arrogant Alida, serves to end the story with a dramatic flourish that has even more impact because it is so subdued.

*Betty G. Gawthrop*

# ROPE

*Author:* Katherine Anne Porter (1890-1980)
*Type of plot:* Psychological
*Time of plot:* The 1920's
*Locale:* The South, a house in the country
*First published:* 1928

Principal characters:
HE, the husband
SHE, the wife

## The Story

Katherine Anne Porter's simple plot structure belies an insightful rendering of an embittered and ambivalent relationship between a husband and wife who have recently moved to the country from their apartment in town. Despite the generic pronominal references and an ambiguous locale (southern regionalism more in spirit than in fact), the characters are more fully realized than the reader may at first suppose—indeed, each character will flesh out his or her personality by degrees after the inward turning of the first paragraph.

Returning from a four-mile walk through heat and dust, the husband is first greeted by his wife with affection; they exchange playful remarks about their unfamiliar circumstances: She resembles "a born country woman"; he seems like "a rural character in a play." Swiftly, the narrator plunges inside to reveal the essence of what each says to the other. This narrational viewpoint (narrated monologue) involves, at times, not only a rapid switch between characters but also a greater degree of editorializing by the narrator as the tempo of their argument increases.

At first, the wife is mildly disappointed that he has forgotten her coffee; then she spies the broken eggs in the sack—caused by a twenty-four-yard coil of rope; the eggs will have to be used right away, and her plans for dinner are spoiled. Soon, they are arguing with a surprising vehemence, considering the trivial cause. Her passion for order is, in his view, "an insane habit of changing things around"; she, however, "had borne all the clutter she meant to bear in the flat in the town." For the most part, her emotional outbursts are inflected with her own idiom, thinly disguised by the narrator's mediation, but it becomes evident that the pressure of the past is on the point of overwhelming her. Deeper plunges by the narrator inside his character reveal how wide is the discrepancy between what he thinks is wrong with her and what her own near-the-surface reflections reveal.

The rope, which keeps getting underfoot in a figurative sense, lends a bit of grotesque comedy, causing the reader to ponder its obvious symbolic aspects. Although the taunts fly between them, it is clear that they cannot articulate the most deeply rooted sources of their discontent. Aside from the poverty and drudgery of their marriage, she chafes at the housework, even though "getting the devilish house ready for him" pleases her. They are childless, but he cruelly taunts her infertility, wishing she had "something weaker than she was to heckle and tyrannize over." She is also tortured by jealousy and the likelihood that he may have been unfaithful during his stay in town the summer before; he cavalierly dismisses her fear; "It may have looked funny but he had simply got hooked in, and what could he do?"

In contrast to her bitterness, he seems smugly indifferent to probing his own responsibility, exploding in wonderment and fury: "What was the matter, for God's sake?" He knows that it cannot be "only a piece of rope that was causing all the racket," but he deflects her barbs with those of his own by threatening to leave her "with a half-empty house on her hands." Less fragile than she, he assumes a kind of mordant pose about it all: "Things broke so suddenly you didn't know where you were."

He tries to placate her by returning to the village for the coffee, as if that were the source of contention, but she complains that he is deserting her: "Sometimes it seemed to her he had second sight about the precisely perfect moment to leave her ditched." Then she collapses into a fit of hysterical laughter, from which he has to revive her by a violent shaking, and she sends him and his rope down the road with a curse. Alone with his thoughts, he consoles himself with more philosophy: "Things accumulated, things were mountainous, you couldn't move them or sort them or get rid of them."

On his return—again with the rope, which he had hidden and retrieved—he sees his wife waiting; the air is cool and carries the smell of broiling steak; she is attractive, beckoning—and he runs to her. Together, embracing, they return to the house; he playfully coos baby talk to her, and he pats her stomach—a gesture that elicits "wary smiles" from them both. She admires an out-of-season whippoorwill calling its mate (she thinks), and the narrator concludes on an ironically detached note, giving the reader a last glimpse of the husband's mind: Oblivious to the day's strife, he tells himself that he understands her: "Sure, he knew how she was."

*Themes and Meanings*

The rope is the story's central symbol: It binds and oppresses; it lashes and it strangles. Tied together as this couple is, the reader may wonder whether the equilibrium restored to their marriage at the end is merely a temporary respite: Is their need for each other sufficient to overcome the inertia of this kind of anger and bitterness? Like the crab apple fruit itself, the marriage of this pair may well survive on the strength of these intense emotions: Hatred, for them, may be the obverse side of love's coin. In any case, the narrator remains detached from commentary, and the reader must accept the ambiguity of the conclusion. Certainly, their marriage is a hell of their own making.

Porter had married at sixteen and was divorced several years later, so she knew well the forms of dissension that can alienate a couple's affections despite the intimate bond of marriage. The wife of this story, however, is not up to the standards of her later, more fully developed female figures, for example, Miranda of "Pale Horse, Pale Rider" or Laura of "Flowering Judas." For one thing, the wife in "Rope" is not possessed of their powers of self-awareness or their discriminating sensibilities. Strong forces are at work inside her, to be sure, but the narrator will merely report their superficial consequences—for example, she "grew livid about the mouth" and "looked quite dangerous . . . her face turned slightly purple, and she screamed with laughter." Despite her husband's glib confidence that he understands her, the reader cannot so easily reconcile the disproportionate gap between what she says and what she knows to be true in the story world.

*Style and Technique*

The most significant technique is the superb control over point of view, so that characters reveal themselves at the moments of greatest stress. The editorializing function of the narrator is therefore all-important, but it must not seem to be too heavy-handed in manipulating the narrative voice. Porter ensures that the characters' points of view are woven into the narrative in a manner that is consistent and artful. In the first place, she uses narrated monologue rather than other forms of interior monologue, pruning away the unnecessary tags of thinking and saying as well as the signals of quotation. The end result is that the reader "hears" the man and woman in their private voices, when in fact what constitutes the narrative transmission is an aggregate of points of view that mixes the narrator's and characters' voices and which is richly composed of idiom and colloquialism, exclamations, repetitions, and circumlocutions—in short, all the features of a mind instantly verbalizing. In this way, the reader experiences with freshness and immediacy the thoughtless ease with which they wound each other: "Oh, would he please hush and go away, and stay away, if he could, for five minutes? By all means, yes, he would. He'd stay away indefinitely if she wished."

Ultimately, language itself becomes both the theme and the style, causing them to merge into each other with precise diction and economy of choice so that—for all its density and capacity to communicate—the reader experiences this vitriolic exchange of language and realizes that these two cannot say what they most want to say, and that language is itself the source and barrier to a true communication. To this end, Porter makes use of a wide array of the forms of language: from mild profanities (emblematic of their hellish relationship), through a kind of subvocal level (indicated by the narrator's allusions to her feline responses of hissing and clawing), to, finally, that level of self-communion in which the husband will seek to explain his wife's behavior and their crumbling marriage to himself.

Last, there is the narrator's ambiguous silence, looking on dispassionately, allowing things as well as characters to speak for themselves; perhaps this is best exemplified in the lonely bird in the crab apple tree with all its bittersweet allusiveness, suggestive of another Garden and expulsion from it into a hostile and disorderly world.

*Terry White*

# ROSA

*Author:* Cynthia Ozick (1928-    )
*Type of plot:* Psychological
*Time of plot:* 1977
*Locale:* Miami
*First published:* 1983

> *Principal characters:*
> ROSA LUBLIN, the protagonist, a fifty-eight-year-old Polish Jew, a
> survivor of a Nazi concentration camp
> MAGDA, her infant daughter who perished in the camp, to whom
> Rosa nevertheless writes and confides her thoughts
> STELLA, Rosa's niece, who is still living in Brooklyn, also a camp
> survivor
> SIMON PERSKY, a retired button manufacturer who gradually
> becomes Rosa's friend

*The Story*

From the very beginning of the story, Rosa Lublin is described as a madwoman; indeed, the world she inhabits seems composed of as much illusion as reality. After destroying her junk shop in Brooklyn, she has exiled herself to Miami, which she envisions as a sort of Hell of the elderly. She lives in a sordid hotel room with a disconnected phone and keeps as much to herself as possible. Her main form of communication is letter writing; yet her long-dead daughter Magda, to whom she pens lengthy and intimate thoughts in "excellent literary Polish," seems to have more substance for Rosa than the long-suffering niece Stella, who actually supports Rosa and to whom Rosa writes in "crude" English.

When Simon Persky bursts on Rosa's solitude in a coin-operated laundry one morning and attempts to lure her back to the world of the living, she repels his advance, even rejecting their common origins in Warsaw. Rosa insists, "My Warsaw isn't your Warsaw." She pictures his Warsaw as one of alleys strung with cheap clothing and "signs in jargoned Yiddish," while hers was Polish, a place of "cultivation, old civilization, beauty, history." Her parents mocked Yiddish, and the young Rosa was preparing to become another Marie Curie. Persky treats her to a meal in the Kollins Kosher Kameo, which she grudgingly endures, preferring her lonely exclusivity.

When she returns to her hotel, the mail has arrived: Stella's letter announcing that she has finally sent the shawl Rosa requested, and a package that Rosa imagines contains the shawl of her dead infant Magda. Before she can open it, however, she must purify her room and herself; justifying her motives in a long letter to a perfect and adult Magda, she emphasizes the purity of Magda's heritage. Then Rosa ventures out into the dusk in search of a pair of lost underpants that she imagines Persky has "stolen" from her, causing her to feel shamed and degraded. During the search she becomes entrapped on a private hotel beach, behind a barbed-wire fence; she finally gets free but registers her complaint with the hotel's manager, who as a Jew, she reminds him, ought to know better: "In America it's no place for barbed wire on top of fences."

"Cleansed" by the outburst, she returns to her hotel to find Persky waiting in the lobby, and they have tea in her room. Feeling already exposed to Persky, the imagined possessor of her underwear, she opens in front of him, first her thoughts and then the package. To her disappointment it contains, instead of the shawl, only a scientific book. In a fury, Rosa smashes up the tea party, and Persky dashes out.

The next day she has her telephone reconnected, and the real shawl arrives in the mail, though it is now colorless, like an old bandage, and does not immediately evoke Magda's presence for her, as it usually does. Not until Rosa phones Stella "long distance" does Magda come magically to life. Rosa composes another letter to her in which she relates the story of her family's degradation in wartime Warsaw, when Jews were imprisoned in the Ghetto and her family was forced to live among the poor and ignorant in crowded, unbelievably squalid conditions. Through the center of the Ghetto ran the city tram because it could not be economically rerouted around the Ghetto. While people in the Ghetto were prevented from getting on the tram, common Polish working-class citizens, passing from one side of Warsaw to the other, rode through each day, "straight into the place of our misery," to witness her family's shame. One day Rosa noticed an ordinary woman riding the tram with a head of lettuce showing out of the top of her shopping sack. Now, she concludes in the letter to Magda, she has herself become like that ordinary woman with the lettuce in the tram. At that point Magda disappears, because the telephone rings to announce Perksy's arrival in the lobby downstairs, and Rosa invites him to come up.

*Themes and Meanings*

It would be simple enough to read this as a tale of psychic wounds borne by a survivor of the Holocaust, particularly as "Rosa" is a sequel to an earlier story, "The Shawl," which provides an account of a particular experience in the concentration camp involving Rosa, Stella, and Magda and lays groundwork for a probable cause of guilt on Rosa's part.

This would seem further supported by Rosa's explanation of time as a structuring device dividing people's lives into "before," "after," and "during" the Holocaust. Just as the "before" is a dream, she says, the "after" is a joke: "Only the during stays." She condemns those who try to forget the "during," as if she were trapped in that time of horrifying experience, which had the power to transform "before" into "after," or "dream" into "joke."

However, Rosa is trapped not in time but in pride. Although her mind seems often to dwell in the "before," she insists that she does not want to return to that actual time. Her memories serve, rather, to recall the privileged potential that she once enjoyed and to give imaginative shape to the potential perfection that Magda (as Rosa's single accomplishment of any value) might have attained had she only survived, for Magda, too, has the power to transform: Like "the philosophers' stone that prolongs life and transmutes iron to gold," Magda can, through the material agency of the shawl, transform her ordinary mother into "a Madonna." Rosa believes not in God but in "mystery" and attributes such power to the shawl that the object becomes almost a sacred relic in and of itself: "Your idol," mocks Stella, whom Rosa often calls the Angel of Death.

The real means of Rosa's transformation, however, is her pride, her readiness to be recognized as special, if only by Magda. Rosa cannot bear to be thought ordinary; that Persky would take her for "another button"; that Stella would have her "recuperated" or healed of her "craziness," which, if nothing else, sets Rosa apart from the "ordinary."

This same pride is also her cage, her trap, in that it not only holds her apart from her fellowman but also prevents her from recognizing that the distance and misperceptions between herself and others are at least partially of her own making. While she can admit "how far she had fallen . . . nobility turned into a small dun rodent," she does not see that her fallen state comes, ironically, from having set herself so high above her fellowman, past and present. She has discovered the "power to shame" other Jews who did not experience the Holocaust and does not hesitate to hold it over them: "Where were you when we was there?" However, even after having shared a ghastly fate with those other Jews imprisoned with her family back in the Warsaw Ghetto, she can look back now only with contempt and shame at the squalor they imposed on her delicate and sensitive family.

It is, finally, from this same memory—in particular the metaphor of the tram that ran through the center of the walled-off Ghetto with the woman aboard, carrying the lettuce—that Rosa at last draws the key that may release her from her trap of pride. Cynthia Ozick, in "The Moral Necessity of Metaphor," has written, "Metaphor is the reciprocal agent, the universalizing force: it makes possible the power to envision the stranger's heart." When Rosa admits, in her last letter to Magda, "Now I am like the woman who held the lettuce in the tramcar," she has clearly begun to understand, it would seem, what it means to be a stranger, an ordinary stranger, traveling temporarily into a place of "misery," and how she must appear to those less free than she, those others too "deaf" to understand. Rosa, having suffered both humiliation and persistent compassion from Persky, decides finally to reconnect her telephone and invites Persky to "come up" to her room, suggesting both that she is admitting him to her rarefied environment and that she is deliberately reaching out to another human being.

*Style and Technique*

Because Rosa's version of truth is often at odds with other information presented in the story, it is clear that Ozick intends for the reader to question Rosa's reliability. The discrepancies range from something as minor as two different accounts of Rosa's age to the crucial question of whether Magda actually lives, and much ground in between remains open to interpretation. At times the charge of madwoman appears warranted, yet at other times Rosa's faculties seem too accurately to record the cultural and spiritual wasteland around her for her to be anything but painfully sane. Even in acknowledging that some people live only in their thoughts, she seems ironically aware of her own delusions.

The net effect of these conflicting accounts, while demonstrating in an abstract sense the subjectivity of truth, is to establish between the reader and the story's "reality" a tension parallel to that between Rosa and her environment. As he or she participates in Rosa's isolation from an uncertain world with which she is out of step, the reader's sense of reality, as defined by "fact," is undermined.

Rosa's unreliable accounts also cast doubt over the past from which she has "fallen," however, and threaten the very underpinnings of her pride. She seems to protest too much, for example, offering so elaborate an explanation that Magda's father was not a German Nazi that the reader may suspect the opposite to be true. Moreover, Rosa's act of smashing up her antique shop—literally destroying "other people's history"—speaks plainly enough not only of her own subjective view of the past but also of the inadequacy of factual (material) minutiae as a basis for truth. As Rosa fleshes out Magda's "life" with conflicting details, the reader might well question how much of Rosa's own reconstructed past is to be trusted. What, then, of Rosa is true?

This subverting of factual detail finally lessens the reader's dependency on fact as a reliable tool for discovering truth and brings into focus, at the same time, the concept of Rosa's truth as composed of universals—of fatal flaws and qualities of character, of fallen states and states of redemption, of the human need to be accepted, connected, and lovingly interpreted—the truths of myth and metaphor, and of lives taken on faith.

*Sally V. Doud*

# A ROSE FOR EMILY

*Author:* William Faulkner (1897-1962)
*Type of plot:* Gothic
*Time of plot:* About 1865-1924
*Locale:* Jefferson, Yoknapatawpha County, Mississippi
*First published:* 1930

> *Principal characters:*
> MISS EMILY GRIERSON, a southern lady
> THE UNNAMED NARRATOR, a citizen of Jefferson
> HOMER BARRON, Emily's Yankee lover
> TOBE, Emily's black servant
> EMILY'S FATHER, an aristocrat
> COLONEL SARTORIS, the onetime mayor

*The Story*

Although an unnamed citizen of the small town of Jefferson, in Yoknapatawpha County, Mississippi, tells the story of the aristocratic Miss Emily Grierson in a complicated manner, shifting back and forth in time without trying to make clear transitions, the story line itself is quite simple. Miss Emily's father dies when she is a little more than thirty, in about 1882. For three days she prevents his burial, refusing to accept his death. He had driven off all of her suitors; now she is alone, a spinster, in a large house.

In the summer after the death of her father, Miss Emily meets Homer Barron, the Yankee foreman of a crew contracted to pave the sidewalks of Jefferson. They appear on the streets in a fancy buggy, provoking gossip and resentment. Two female cousins come to town from Alabama to attempt to persuade Miss Emily to behave in a more respectable manner. Emily buys an outfit of man's clothes and a silver toilet set. To avoid the cousins, Homer leaves town. Miss Emily buys rat poison from the druggist. The cousins leave. Homer returns; he is never seen again.

A foul odor emanates from Miss Emily's house. After midnight, four citizens, responding to complaints made by neighbors to Judge Stevens, the mayor, stealthily spread lime around the house and in her cellar. In a week or so, the smell goes away.

In 1894, Colonel Sartoris, the mayor, remits Miss Emily's taxes. For about six or seven years, while in her forties, she gives china-painting lessons to the young girls of the town. Then for many years she is seen only at her window. Townspeople watch her black servant Tobe going in and out on errands. A new generation comes to power; they insist that Miss Emily pay taxes on her property. When she fails to respond, a deputation calls on her, but she insists that she owes no taxes, as Colonel Sartoris will tell them (he has been dead ten years).

In about 1925, Miss Emily dies. On the day of her funeral, the townspeople, including some old Civil War veterans, invade the house. Tobe leaves by the back door and is never seen again. One group breaks into a locked room upstairs and discovers the corpse of Homer Barron, which has moldered in the bed for forty years. On a pillow beside him, they find "a long strand of iron-gray hair," evidence that Miss Emily had lain down beside him years after she poisoned him.

## Themes and Meanings

Miss Emily's story is certainly bizarre, suspenseful, and mysterious enough to engage the reader's attention fully. She is a grotesque, southern gothic character whose neurotic or psychotic behavior in her relationships with her father, her lover, and her black servant may elicit many Freudian interpretations. For example, her affair with Homer Barron may be seen as a middle-aged woman's belated rebellion against her repressive father and against the town's burdensome expectations. That William Faulkner intended her story to have a much larger dimension is suggested by his choice of an unnamed citizen of Jefferson to tell it.

The narrator never speaks or writes as an individual, never uses the pronoun "I," always speaks as "we." As representative of the townspeople, the narrator feels a compulsion to tell the story of a woman who represents something important to the community. Black voices are excluded from this collective voice as it speaks out of old and new generations. Colonel Sartoris's antebellum generation is succeeded by one with "modern ideas": "Thus, she passed from generation to generation."

Even though Miss Emily was a child during the Civil War, she represents to generations past and present the old Deep South of the Delta cotton-plantation aristocracy. She is a visible holdover into the modern South of a bygone era of romance, chivalry, and the Lost Cause. Even this new South, striving for a prosperity based on Northern technology, cannot fully accept the decay of antebellum culture and ideals. Early, the narrator invokes such concepts as tradition, duty, hereditary obligation, and custom, suggesting a perpetuation in the community consciousness of those old values. The community's sense of time is predominantly chronological, but it is also like Emily's, the confused, psychological time sense of memory. Like many women of the defeated upper class in the Deep South, Miss Emily withdraws from the chronological time of reality into the timelessness of illusion.

Miss Emily is then symbolic of the religion of southernness that survived military defeat and material destruction. The children of Colonel Sartoris's generation are sent to learn china-painting from Miss Emily in "the same spirit that they were sent to church." It is because "we" see her as resembling "those angels in colored church windows" that her affair with a Yankee makes her "a bad example to the young people."

Given the fact that the Yankee colonel who made the deepest raid into Rebel territory was named Grierson, Faulkner may have intended Emily's family name to be ironic. The insanity of clinging to exposed illusions is suggested by the fact that Miss Emily's great-aunt went "crazy" and that Miss Emily later appears "crazy" to the townspeople. Ironically, even within aristocratic families there is division; her father fell out with Alabama kinsmen over the great-aunt's estate.

Immediately after the narrator refers to Miss Emily as being like an "idol" and to her great-aunt as "crazy," Faulkner presents this image, symbolic of the aristocracy: "We had long thought of them as a tableau, Miss Emily a slender figure in white in the background, her father a spraddled silhouette in the foreground, his back to her and clutching a horsewhip, the two of them framed by the back-flung front door." Her father's rejection of her suitors is like the defeated aristocracy's rejection of new methods of creating a future. Emily's refusal to accept the fact of her father's death suggests the refusal of some aristocrats to accept the death of the South even when faced with the evidence of its corpse. Perversely, "She would have to cling to that which had robbed her, as people will." However, the modern generations insist on burying the decaying corpse of the past.

Miss Emily preserves all the dead, in memory if not literally. "See Colonel Sartoris," she tells the new town fathers, as if he were alive. The townspeople are like Miss Emily in that they persist in preserving her "dignity" as the last representative of the Old South (her death ends the Grierson line); after she is dead, the narrator preserves her in this story. The rose is a symbol of the age of romance in which the aristocracy were obsessed with delusions of grandeur, pure women being a symbol of the ideal in every phase of life. Perhaps the narrator offers this story as a "rose" for Emily. As a lady might press a rose between the pages of a history of the South, she keeps her own personal rose, her lover, preserved in the bridal chamber where a rose color pervades everything. Miss Emily's rose is ironically symbolic because her lover was a modern Yankee, whose laughter drew the townspeople to him and whose corpse has grinned "profoundly" for forty years, as if he, or Miss Emily, had played a joke on all of them.

*Style and Technique*

The extraordinary degree to which the young Faulkner managed to compress into this, his first published story, many of the elements that came to be characteristic of his fiction is the effect of his unusual use of the first-person point of view and his control of the motifs that flow from it.

By confining himself to the pronoun "we," the narrator gives the reader the impression that the whole town is bearing witness to the behavior of a heroine, about whom they have ambivalent attitudes, ambiguously expressed. The ambiguity derives in part from the community's lack of access to facts, stimulating the narrator to draw on his own and the communal imagination to fill out the picture, creating a collage of images. The narration gives the impression of coming out of a communal consciousness, creating the effect of a peculiar omniscience. An entire novel could be developed from the material compressed into this short story.

Is the narrator telling the story in the southern oral tradition or is he or she writing it? To ask basic questions about this unusual collective mode of narration—who, what, where, when, and why—is to stir up many possibilities. The oral mode seems most appropriate, but the style, consisting of such phrases as "diffident deprecation," suggests the written mode.

A pattern of motifs that interact, contrasting with or paralleling one another, sometimes symbolically, sometimes ironically, flows naturally from the reservoir of communal elements in the narrator's saturated consciousness as he tells the story: the funeral, the cemetery, the garages, cars, cotton gins, taxes, the law, the market basket and other elements of black existence, the house, its front and back doors, its cellar and upper rooms, the window where Emily sits, the idol image that becomes a fallen monument, images that evoke the Civil War, images of gold, of decay, the color yellow, dust, shadows, corpses and bodies like corpses, the smells, the breaking down of doors, the poison, and the images of hair.

To lend greater impact to the surprise ending and to achieve greater artistic unity and intensity of effect, Faulkner uses other devices: foreshadowing, reversal, and repetition. Most of the motifs, spaced effectively throughout, are repeated at least three times, enabling the reader to respond at any given point to all the elements simultaneously.

Imitators of the surprise-ending device, made famous in modern times by O. Henry, have given that device a bad name by using it mechanically to provoke a superficial thrill. In raising the surprise-ending device to the level of complex art, Faulkner achieves a double impact: "The man himself lay on the bed" is shock enough, justified by what has gone before, but "the long strand of iron-gray hair," the charged image that ends the story, shocks the reader into a sudden, intuitive reexperiencing and reappraisal of the stream of images, bringing order and meaning to the pattern of motifs.

*David Madden*

# A ROSE IN THE HEART OF NEW YORK

*Author:* Edna O'Brien (1930- )
*Type of plot:* Domestic realism
*Time of plot:* The 1930's to 1970's
*Locale:* Rural Ireland
*First published:* 1978

> *Principal characters:*
> THE DAUGHTER, the unnamed protagonist, a member of a rural
> Irish family
> THE FATHER, a violent drunkard
> THE MOTHER, with whom the daughter is obsessively close

*The Story*

"A Rose in the Heart of New York" chronicles several decades in the lives of a rural Irish family, focusing principally on the daughter, who is born in the story's first scene, and the mother, who is buried in the last. This one turn in the ancient cycle of birth and death constitutes a vivid and moving struggle by both to understand their relationship with each other and with the culture that inevitably shapes them.

If intensity of devotion is a reliable gauge of a happy relationship, then mother and daughter must have been happy indeed. The daughter follows her mother everywhere, watching each of her movements, absorbing her manners and attitudes. The mother dotes on her daughter, sacrificing for her, "spoiling" her as much as their poverty will allow. There is a thin line, however, between healthy devotion and something closer to unnatural obsession, and the reader finds that this line is approached perilously near, if it is not actually crossed.

When the daughter is sent to a convent, she is forced to find some way of living apart from her mother. Her solution to this forced separation is to adopt a nun as a sort of surrogate mother, lavishing her with praise, presents, and devotion and receiving the same in return. That their relationship is unnaturally and unhealthily intense is indicated by the disapproval of the convent superiors. Chastised, the two decide to "break up." Out of the convent, the daughter's life is not so different from many another young woman's; she has affairs, marries "in haste," separates, has more affairs, becomes an independent career woman, and so on. Throughout, her mother never quite leaves her thoughts; in fact, she tends to see her own affairs and life in the light of her mother's life and attitudes. The last scene between mother and daughter occurs when they go on a brief vacation together. They are closer, physically, than at any time since the daughter left home, but closeness brings no revelation. Indeed, they are struck by how little they understand of each other.

In the brief final section, the daughter learns that her mother has died. She rushes home just in time for the funeral. Afterward, she rummages around in her mother's things and finds a letter that her mother had written to an old beau whom she had met while living in New York as a girl. Later, she finds an envelope addressed to her in her mother's handwriting; inside are a few trinkets and a small amount of money. The reader can be forgiven for expecting the letter and the envelope to contain the key to the whole, to provide the revelation or epiphany with which many short stories culminate. Edna O'Brien, however, avoids easy resolutions. The letter is sadly banal; the envelope contains not a word, not a clue to the mystery. The story ends with the daughter farther than ever from understanding her mother or herself.

*Themes and Meanings*

Labeling "A Rose in the Heart of New York" a "feminist" story should not be construed as reducing it to a simplistic set of assumptions about life and literature. Rather, it powerfully and movingly dramatizes exactly what it means to be a woman in modern rural Irish society. The story's feminist theme can best be seen in what the women devote themselves to but what fails or even enslaves them: men, the Church, other women.

Men are less an outright evil than they are facets of a brutal, unyielding landscape. The dominant male figure in the story is the father, a violent drunkard who "takes" the mother in scenes of intercourse more reminiscent of impalement than love or even lust. Two of the daughter's most vivid memories are of the time when the father went after the mother with a hatchet and a later episode when he tried to shoot her. His mellowing with age is less a sign of growing tenderness than of growing senility. If the men in the daughter's life are less violent, neither are they much more satisfying. Her first sexual encounter is banally sordid. She marries a man who dominates every facet of her life, even down to how she should fold her clothes. Rather than a relationship of mutual growth and sharing, her marriage feels "like being in school again." Subsequent affairs bring mostly guilt. In short, not a single man in the story brings to the mother or the daughter the slightest modicum of happiness.

Historically, especially in Ireland, when all else fails, the woman can take solace in the Church. Such is hardly the case in "A Rose in the Heart of New York." Religion is not an overt theme in the story, but a rich pattern of religious imagery shows how subtly important it is in women's lives—and how decidedly it fails them. The first mention of religion is the bottle of holy water that the midwife brings, along with her gauze and other medical supplies. These she administers to the laboring mother who is "roaring and beseeching to God." Does God hear? No one can say, but in her agony the mother drops the crucifix, then dents it by biting down on it in pain. The mother, indeed, is invested with more religious imagery than anything else in the story. Being stitched up after delivery is her "vinegar and gall." She finally rises from bed after the third day. Later, she is attacked by her husband on a hill under three trees—a scene suggesting Christ's crucifixion on Golgotha. Significantly, the nun who replaces the mother in the daughter's affections is seen by her as an "idol," whose gift of a tiny Bible, unreadable, is cherished by the daughter as "a secret scroll in which love was mentioned."

Perhaps mother and nun achieve such godlike status in the daughter's eyes because the traditional religious figures—Father, Son, Holy Ghost, Mary, and so on—offer only false hope. What can be said with certainty is that at no time in the story—at birth, death, or anywhere in between—does religion ease the woman's lot.

Other women offer no more hope than do men or religion. Other than her mother, no woman makes any significant impression on or achieves a lasting relationship with the daughter. Her relationship with her mother, too, comes to seem a kind of death. As a child she wishes to go to Heaven with her mother; after her divorce, her mother writes that her one wish is that they be buried together. However, their last visit concludes with the daughter openly hating her mother and resolving that they will never be buried together.

O'Brien clearly believes that death is less horrible than being buried alive: "buried" by poverty, ignorance, the false hope of religion, sexual dominance, suffocating love. If by the end the daughter has learned that lesson, painful as it is, then perhaps "A Rose in the Heart of New York" should be seen as more affirmative than a catalog of its grim specifics would seem to suggest.

*Style and Technique*

The most interesting technical feature of a story powerful in its simplicity is one that generally is considered a flaw: that is, a lack of foregrounding. A term appropriated from painting, "foregrounding" refers to the added "weight"—length of discussion, intensity of emotion—given to certain scenes that the author considers, and wants the reader to consider, more important than others. Foregrounding may seem especially crucial in a long story such as O'Brien's, one that spans four decades in the lives of its characters, but "A Rose in the Heart of New York" unfolds largely without major scenes on which to hinge the action. The daughter's first sexual encounter, for example, is related in part of a sentence, less space than is devoted to baking a cake. Her marriage transpires and expires in little more than a page, not many more lines than O'Brien devotes to the mother and daughter mending broken water pipes.

One effect of this lack of foregrounding is that the reader infers that, for the woman, such daily minutiae as baking a cake or fixing a leaking pipe are as important—perhaps more important—than often brief and unsatisfying encounters with men. Another effect is the precipitous quality given the action. The mother's and daughter's lives slip by them in a rush, with no heightened scenes to provide revelation, only the understanding that too often women are born and die with precious little joy in between.

*Dennis Vannatta*

# ROSE-JOHNNY

*Author:* Barbara Kingsolver (1955-    )
*Type of plot:* Social realism
*Time of plot:* Probably the early to mid-twentieth century
*Locale:* Rural Kentucky
*First published:* 1988

> *Principal characters:*
> GEORGEANN BOWLES, the eleven-year-old narrator
> MARY ETTA, her teenage sister
> ROSE-JOHNNY, a woman who runs the feed store

## The Story

The fact that Georgeann and her friends are forbidden by all the women in town to speak to Rose-Johnny is enough to pique the inquisitive eleven-year-old's curiosity. That Rose-Johnny has become a legendary horror does not frighten Georgeann; it only makes speaking with her a kind of public dare.

Sent to buy chicken mash after school by her parents, Georgeann meets Rose-Johnny. The woman's very ordinariness almost disappoints Georgeann when she finally meets her: The woman's hair is cut short like a man's and she wears men's Red Wing boots, but the rest of her looks like anybody's mother "in a big flowered dress without a waistline and with two faded spots in front." At the store, Georgeann encounters several local men, who try to warn her away from Rose-Johnny. The things they say sound threatening and seem to frighten Rose-Johnny, but they are incomprehensible to the little girl. Georgeann is all the more confused when Rose-Johnny proves to be a kind, likable soul, who even has a sense of humor. Despite the men's warnings, Georgeann finds herself unafraid of the woman. Trying to make sense of what the men have said, Georgeann asks her Aunt Minnie why girls should not go near Rose-Johnny. Aunt Minnie reluctantly tells her that it is because Rose-Johnny is a "Lebanese," and that she will understand when she is older.

Georgeann concocts a tale, her first important lie, that will allow her to continue going back to Rose-Johnny's feed store. She tells her parents that Rose-Johnny is sick and that Mr. Wall, Rose-Johnny's father and the store's proprietor, has asked her to help out until Rose-Johnny is better. From Rose-Johnny, the little girl learns to care for the pullets and ducklings, weigh packages of seed, and mix the mash. Impressed by Rose-Johnny's skills, she comes to admire the woman more each week. Georgeann also learns to respect different kinds of people. After hours, the customers are poor African Americans, whom Rose-Johnny treats well. For the poorest, she reduces prices by more than half. Rose-Johnny takes pains to teach Georgeann all the names of her African American customers, and she tells her to be sure to say hello whenever she meets them on the street, regardless of who is watching.

At school, Georgeann fights one of the Mattox boys when he calls Rose-Johnny and her perverts. Georgeann declares that she loves Rose-Johnny. To everyone's surprise, though she is younger and smaller, the boy bloodies her nose. The next day, Georgeann asks Rose-Johnny whether the rumors that her father is a "colored man" are true. Rose-Johnny tells her that her father was white, but that every man is some color. Mr. Wall is not her father, but her grandfather; her father is dead. Years ago, her widowed mother loved a "brown" man. After a child was born to the couple, the town lynched the lover and drowned the baby boy in the frozen river, breaking a hole in the ice to do it. To protect her young daughter, Rose-Johnny's mother cut off Rose-Johnny's hair and told her to be Rose and Johnny both from then on. She then drowned herself in the same hole in the ice where her baby died. Rose-Johnny says that the men never bothered her after that.

It is the last time Georgeann and Rose-Johnny meet. Georgeann does not know what happens to Rose-Johnny and Mr. Wall, but they disappear and the store is eventually sold to someone else. There are rumors that Rose-Johnny is dead, but Georgeann prefers to believe that she and her grandfather have moved elsewhere.

On the day that Georgeann and Rose-Johnny have their last conversation, Georgeann's sister, Mary Etta, is attacked by a gang of young men. Although their faces are covered, Mary Etta believes that some of them are from the Mattox family. Georgeann is convinced that this is a case of mistaken identity, and they meant to attack her. She cuts off all of her hair and does the same to a favorite doll, and calls herself George-Etta and her doll Rose-Johnny.

*Themes and Meanings*

In "Rose-Johnny," Barbara Kingsolver attacks racial prejudice and a town's ignorance about and fear of the unknown and the unusual. At the start of the story, the reader believes that the reason for the open hostility the town expresses toward Rose-Johnny is because she is, or appears to be, a lesbian. In fact, Rose-Johnny is "no more lesbian than Lebanese"; the real reason for the hatred is the past love affair between her mother and a "brown" man and the subsequent birth of a baby to the couple. Rather than being the cause of her trouble, Rose-Johnny's sexual ambiguity protects her from the men of the town. Her mother understood that people who feared the unknown and unusual would shun a woman whose sexual orientation was in doubt.

Another theme of the story is the power of motherhood and the power of the bond between mother and child. After the baby Johnny is drowned, Rose-Johnny's mother remakes her daughter, to protect her, into two people, Rose and Johnny both. Then the mother follows her son into the river. Kingsolver has explored how a mother can make two people one, or vice versa, in other stories.

Georgeann looks up to Rose-Johnny in the same way that a daughter looks to her mother for guidance. She describes Rose-Johnny as looking like anybody's mother except for the masculine haircut and the work boots. She thinks Rose-Johnny is the most capable person she has ever met, male or female. When Rose-Johnny disappears, Georgeann repeats what Rose-Johnny did: She remakes herself into two people, herself and her sister Etta, who is a victim of hate in the same way and for the same reasons that the infant Johnny was a victim.

Barbara Kingsolver uses two of her favorite themes, the strong, capable, independent woman and the character who stands out in a crowd, to make a social statement. In a society where nearly all the citizens condone the hatred and fear of the different and unknown, one person can pass on the more positive value of tolerance in a diverse world.

*Style and Technique*

"Rose-Johnny" is a realistic account of prejudice in the South. The setting is rural Kentucky; the people are simple farmers and shopkeepers. Because the narration is not condescending and the reader feels on an intellectual par with the principal characters, the story seems to be universal, not confined to the American South. Kingsolver uses simple, unambiguous language to communicate her message.

The use of an eleven-year-old girl as storyteller enables the reader to look through innocent eyes at the hatred and prejudice of the southern town. Telling the story from a child's perspective puts the reader in the mind of the child. Early in the story, the reader may even feel protective toward the young narrator. The device of making Rose-Johnny sexually ambiguous has its effect. What if Rose-Johnny is a pervert who will harm Georgeann? As Rose-Johnny's character is revealed, however, the reader's fears dissipate. When Rose-Johnny is seen as an ordinary person, and the ugly tale of the real reason for the town's hatred is revealed, the reader may feel a sense of moral superiority.

Georgeann comes of age in the story. It is significant that she is eleven at the story's close, near the age of the traditional child-to-adult rite of passage. The child becomes the mother at the end, renaming her doll Rose-Johnny and taking on the burden Rose-Johnny left behind: fighting prejudice and bigotry.

*Joyce M. Parks*

# ROSES, RHODODENDRON

*Author:* Alice Adams (1926-1999)
*Type of plot:* Domestic realism
*Time of plot:* The 1940's to 1970's
*Locale:* North Carolina
*First published:* 1975

> *Principal characters:*
> JANE, a woman reliving events of the summer when she was ten
>     years old
> MARGOT KILGORE, her mother
> HARRIET FARR, her ten-year-old friend
> EMILY FARR, Harriet's mother

*The Story*

The bright blossoms of the rose and the rhododendron remind Jane of the summer when she was ten years old. During the previous spring Jane's father ran off with a young woman, leaving her and her mother in an antique-filled city apartment in Boston. One evening during a thunderstorm, her mother decides to move to North Carolina and open an antique store. Thus the two find themselves in a small southern town, where Jane first experiences falling in love with a place, a house, and a family.

To fill Margot's shop in their small house requires scouring the surrounding countryside for pieces to sell. Sometimes, Margot wants to do this alone and encourages Jane to explore the town. On one of these trips, Jane notices an odd-shaped house surrounded by lawns covered with tangled, blossoming flowers. She also sees a woman walking very stiffly. With her small, shapeless body and beautiful white hair, the woman is very different from her own mother, who bleaches her hair and wears gaudy clothes. The second time she investigates she meets Harriet Farr, the child of the family, who invites her in to eat cake. The inside of the house, with its books and nineteenth century paintings, seems marvelous to Jane.

The two girls become fast friends, reading, exploring, and talking about books, sex, and life together. Margot is making friends also, so when Jane begins spending more time at the Farrs' home talking with Mrs. Farr, Margot does not appear to care.

Jane is fascinated with the Farrs' lifestyle. Unlike Jane's mother, Mrs. Farr cares about books and flowers. Mr. Farr, a lawyer, reads literature and acts in a courtly manner. The Farr home has many spaces where the two friends can be alone. Unlike her own world, the household seems calm, ideal. Although her mother has met Harriet and likes her, Jane senses that the parents would clash, so she does not introduce them. When her mother tells her some gossip about Mr. Farr having been in love with a much younger woman, Jane instantly puts the thought out of her mind. Once Jane observes a dinner table argument, but she prefers to forget that too.

As the summer continues, this viewpoint becomes harder to maintain. Once during a thunderstorm, when Jane expresses concern about her mother, she catches Mrs. Farr staring at her flowers, looking old and talking sadly of unrealized ambitions. When Mr. Farr announces he will be late for dinner, a shadow crosses her face. Her own mother has begun spending time with a man named Larry; only much later in life did Jane realize this was a result of jealousy.

Soon Jane's mother and father reconcile, and they leave North Carolina for San Francisco. For a while, the two girls write once a week, Jane telling of the wonders of the city, and Harriet writing about friends, bike rides, and books. In high school, their letters become more infrequent but, in the solitude of her room, Jane sometimes reenacts stormy adolescent scenes in the cool, calm manner of Harriet. When Jane goes to Stanford, the two girls lose touch.

Several years later, Jane hears that Emily has abruptly left her husband and gone to Washington, D.C., to become a librarian. Jane imagines the couple to be happier apart and is pleased. She has no direct contact with Harriet. She occasionally reads one of her poems and wants to write her but does not know how to approach her without being embarrassed by the things she wants to say. Later she learns that the couple has not been happier apart; that Mr. Farr has been drinking too much and has developed emphysema; and that Harriet travels a lot, has married several times, and has no children. When Mr. Farr becomes too ill to care for himself, Emily returns to care for him until he dies. She dies a few years later.

Jane finally writes to Harriet, in care of a poetry magazine. Months later a letter comes from Rome. Harriet recalls her parents' deaths but remarks that in the midst of it all, the image she remembered was of two ten-year-old girls on their bicycles. The image recalls her childhood, but the important thing about it was her parents' feeling for Jane. Jane was the one constant in their lives, the one element that they agreed on. When Jane was there, Harriet was not jealous; she thought that her parents liked her better with Jane than alone. Jane's presence brought harmony to the Farr family.

This revelation makes Jane, now in her thirties, examine her past and find new colors there. In a postscript to the story, she remarks that when she shows Harriet's letter to her husband, he says that Harriet sounds very much like her.

*Themes and Meanings*

Like much of Alice Adams's writing, "Roses, Rhododendron" focuses on the emotional lives of women who are trying to find their identity. Reliving her friendship with the Farr family enables Jane to examine these events from an adult perspective. Seeing them in this light, she can put away self-defeating attitudes and emerge as a woman who is capable of dealing with many satisfying roles in life.

At the end of the story, Jane's husband reads Harriet's letter and comments on how alike the two women sound. It is no wonder, as Jane has successfully submerged her personality to become like the Farrs. She spends most of her time that summer with the family, and after she and her mother move to California, she wishes Harriet were there to tell her what to do in stressful situations. She wishes she were Harriet, living in the family that she saw as perfect when she was ten years old.

Now, reading Harriet's letter as an adult, she realizes things were not as they seemed. Her presence had brought tranquillity to a home that, unknown to her, was far from peaceful and nurturing. Realizing the truth of these relationships empowers Jane to see herself as a stronger woman, ready to accept new challenges confidently.

Part of Jane's new strength comes from examining her role with the Farrs, but a crucial part results from looking at the complex relationships between mothers and daughters. After she first meets the Farrs, Jane comments that her own mother always chooses friends like herself, direct and honest. She, on the other hand, prides herself on choosing people who are mysterious. When she was ten, she needed these illusions and liked the Farrs for preserving the picture of civility and culture. As an adult, Jane realizes her own mother's feelings. This is also a maturing experience.

In an interview for *Contemporary Authors*, Adams noted that friendship was an important theme in her work. This story shows that several types of friendship are important: between girls of the same age, and between older and younger women. All help make a woman whole.

*Style and Technique*

"Roses, Rhododendron" has a simple plot line. It begins in the first paragraph with a tense situation: Jane's father has abandoned his family. The spirits tell Margot to take her belongings and her daughter and move. They follow this seemingly irrational plan, and the story unfolds. At the end, rather than a climax of action, the narrator slowly comes to realize what it all meant to her life. To add depth to this narrative, Adams writes with her characteristic understated language and adds the special technique of inserting her adult self into the story line using parentheses.

Adams uses only enough details to let the reader know there is emotion beneath the surface. In the scene where the Farrs quarrel, for example, she shows their reactions but does not detail the events that precede them. She mentions flowers frequently but does not describe colors and textures. The emotional undertones are implicit, which enhances the portrait of the Farr family, in which so much lies buried below the surface. Spare details also suit the character of Jane, who does not wish to look beyond appearances.

To comment on those things that a ten-year-old child would not realize, Adams inserts herself into the narrative with the use of parentheses. Adams also uses this technique to indicate places where Jane thinks something, but, in her attempt to be like the Farrs, does not want them to know. Sometimes, Adams inserts comments without the parentheses. The result is that the memory is richer because it is seen from several different points of view.

These techniques enrich Adams's themes by emphasizing what is important in a woman's life, the development that lies beneath the surface character. The undertones also enrich the symbolism of the two flowers, both of which are beautiful in different ways.

*Louise M. Stone*

# ROTHSCHILD'S FIDDLE

*Author:* Anton Chekhov (1860-1904)
*Type of plot:* Psychological
*Time of plot:* The 1890's
*Locale:* Western Russia
*First published:* "Skripka Rotshilda," 1894 (English translation, 1915)

> *Principal characters:*
> YAKOV IVANOV, the protagonist, an elderly, impoverished coffin
> maker
> MARTHA, his wife
> ROTHSCHILD, a Jewish village musician
> MAXIM NIKOLAICH, an ignorant but haughty doctor's assistant

*The Story*

The setting of "Rothschild's Fiddle" is a squalid little village where Yakov Ivanov, a Russian coffin maker, and Rothschild, an equally poor Jewish musician, both live. Yakov lives in a one-room hut, which contains his gloomy wares as well as his humble domestic possessions. Childless, the dour Yakov barely notices Martha, his downtrodden wife of fifty years. Yakov has an unexpected side to his character, for he is a gifted, if rude, violinist who is sometimes invited to join the local Jewish orchestra to play for weddings. Although the coffin maker needs the occasional money, he dislikes the Jewish musicians—especially the flutist Rothschild, who turns even the merriest songs into lugubrious plaints. Yakov abuses Rothschild and is once on the point of beating him. The quarrel ends Yakov's association with the orchestra, apart from rare occasions when one of the Jews cannot perform.

Yakov sees his life as an endless succession of "losses." Sundays and holidays when he cannot work represent losses; a wedding without music represents a loss; a rich man who inconsiderately dies and is buried out of town is another loss. Yakov keeps an account book of his losses, even calculating the interest he might have received on his lost opportunities. At night he arises from his sleepless bed and seeks relief by playing his violin.

One morning Martha feels ill but carries on with her chores while her husband plays his fiddle and gloomily calculates ever new and more distressing imaginary losses. That night the wife cries out that she is going to die. Her feverish face gives the impression that she looks forward to deliverance from her hard, loveless lot and Yakov's endless "losses." Horrified, the coffin maker takes her to a hospital, where the medical assistant shrugs her off as hopeless, refusing Yakov's pleas that he bleed her as he would a rich patient. Realizing the worst, Yakov takes his wife's measurements and begins work on a coffin, duly entering the loss in his account book—two rubles, forty kopecks. Before her death, the wife calls Yakov to her bedside and asks whether he remembers the baby with curly golden hair that God had given them fifty years before. The couple would take the child down to the river bank, sit under the willow, and sing. Yakov has no recollection of the dead child or the willow. That night, Martha dies, and Yakov arranges a miserly funeral, admiring the coffin as he takes final leave of his wife.

Yakov, feeling unwell as he walks home from the cemetery, reflects on his lifelong neglect of his wife in spite of her uncomplaining labor and help. At this point, a nervously bowing and scraping Rothschild approaches with a message from the Jewish orchestra leader, inviting Yakov to play for a wedding. The coffin maker once again abuses and threatens the cowering flute player, who flees pursued by a horde of small boys screaming "Jew, Jew!" Yakov now walks down by the river for the first time in many years, where he, too, is heckled by the village boys who address him by his nickname, "Old Man Bronze." Suddenly he comes on the willow and recalls the dead child. Yakov now falls into regretful reflection of his lost opportunities. Nothing waits ahead of him, and there are only losses behind. Now, however, Yakov's distress over his losses takes a new turn: "Why shouldn't men live so as to avoid all this waste and these losses?" He belatedly regrets his harsh treatment of his wife and the Jew: "If it were not for envy and anger [men] would get great profit from one another."

In the morning, seriously ill, Yakov returns to the "doctor." As the sick man walks home, he bitterly thinks that after his death he will "no longer have to eat and drink and pay taxes, neither would he offend people any more, and, as a man lies in his grave for hundreds of thousands of years, the sum of his profits would be immense." He concludes that life is a loss; death, a profit. Yakov is not sorry to die but regrets leaving behind his violin. At home he sits on the threshold and plays his violin with tears streaming down his face. Once again, a quivering Rothschild approaches Yakov on behalf of the orchestra director. This time, however, the Jew is greeted kindly. Yakov tells him that he is ill and continues to play. So plaintive is his song that Rothschild also begins to weep as he leaves. Later that day, when the village priest asks the dying man if there is any particular sin of which he wishes to repent, Yakov asks that his violin be given to Rothschild.

Time passes, and the townsfolk begin to wonder where Rothschild obtained the violin that he now plays instead of the flute. An even greater mystery is the source of the song he plays, which is so entrancingly sorrowful that wealthy merchants vie in having him come to their homes to play it over and over again.

*Themes and Meanings*

Anton Chekhov's major theme in this, as in many others of his works, is the isolation of the individual within himself and his often vain attempts to break out of his shell and establish meaningful contact with others. Yakov's anti-Semitism is but a particular example of this more general malaise. Yakov finally succeeds in reaching out to others and does so in the form of his music: first to his archenemy Rothschild through his death song and the gift of his violin, and then through Rothschild, who brings Yakov's harrowing melody to many others. Art is the means by which the two men, both deeply unattractive characters, surmount their isolation and manifest their shared humanity.

The theme of Yakov's losses is also important. "Losses" is the most frequently used word in the story, and through repetition it assumes symbolic meaning, referring to far more than Yakov's hypothetical financial setbacks. He is obsessed with his so-called losses. They have poisoned his life, and he has lost the capacity for love and simple pleasures (apart from his music). In fact, the death of his wife is the sole real loss that Yakov suffers, and it is only with this that he begins to reflect on his profitless, ill-spent life and his ill-treatment of his wife and Rothschild. This realization, especially in the face of his own imminent death, leads to his remorse and his final haunting melody. The final irony is that it is the Jew Rothschild rather than Yakov himself who profits and recoups the coffin maker's "losses."

*Style and Technique*

The story is told by an omniscient narrator the year after Yakov's death. Its formal structure is tripartite: the brief introduction that establishes the setting and the hero; the story itself, that is, the relationship between Yakov and Rothschild and the deaths of the wife and husband; and the ironic, bittersweet ending in which Rothschild plays Yakov's song. As in many Chekhov stories, a key event (Yakov's interaction with Rothschild) is repeated three times. The first two encounters are hostile, while the third depicts a reversal of the earlier ones. The last carries the story's message—the breaking down of the isolation of the two men through art and the establishment of their shared humanity.

The narrative technique through which Chekhov makes his thematic statement should be noticed. Superficially, Yakov and Rothschild seem very different: The coffin maker is big, strong, and aggressive, while Rothschild is gaunt, frail, and cowering; Yakov prefers merry songs, Rothschild, mournful ones; the Christian Yakov despises Rothschild the Jew. The narrative, however, poses a series of parallels that point to their essential sameness. Yakov is obsequious to the "educated" medical assistant, just as Rothschild is to Yakov. Also noteworthy are the parallel scenes in which the Jew fleeing from Yakov's fists is jeered by the village boys, who moments later jeer the bereaved Yakov. Both are "outsiders." The most important parallel scene, the one demonstrating their common humanity, is that in which the two men cry together as Yakov improvises his own death dirge. This evolving pattern ends in the identification of the former enemies, each of whom had lived in his own profitless prison of the self.

Chekhov's language is sometimes considered rather "flat," a feature of much realistic prose. On close inspection, however, Chekhov's language is not, in fact, "realistic" but rather evocative and impressionistic. The reader comes to know characters and their lives not through accumulated description but through the carefully chosen, evocative detail that suggests far more than it says. Similarly, the carefully elaborated formal structure contributes to the reader's sense of a meaning that goes far beyond the limits of the brief tale.

*D. Barton Johnson*

# ROUND BY ROUND

*Author:* Conrad Aiken (1889-1973)
*Type of plot:* Social realism
*Time of plot:* About 1935
*Locale:* A large Midwestern city
*First published:* 1935

> *Principal characters:*
> THE NARRATOR, a sports reporter for a large newspaper
> CUSH, an entertainment reviewer for the same newspaper

*The Story*

As the story opens, the narrator, a reporter, sits at his typewriter, composing an account of the title boxing match he has just watched, working from shorthand notes and drinking whiskey as he types. Cush, an entertainment reviewer for the newspaper, enters, drops his coat at his desk and asks the reporter how the fight went. The reporter replies that it was great but he "wasn't looking," and offers Cush a drink. Cush tells him that the new musical he attended that evening was exactly like all the others but adds that reviewers are not able to tell the truth about what the audience really goes to see anyway. He points out that both mayor and censor were there.

The reporter continues to read his notes and compose his story, remembering while doing so details that will not get into the account—such as the behavior of the fiancé of the champion, Zabriski. Cush, now working at his own typewriter, asks how the fight came out. The reporter tells him that there is a new champion, that the fight was a classic example of science over strength, but that he "wasn't there." Cush figures out that the reporter means that Ann, his girlfriend, has dropped him, not for the first time. He asks who she is now dating.

The reporter does not answer right away, turning instead to his notes, his copy, and his memories of the fight. Finally, he states that it was not only one man. Cush asks why he keeps after her and suggests that a chorus girl would be more faithful. The reporter answers that no one is faithful anymore; the psychologists have brainwashed everyone into believing that it is enough to be yourself. Ann is herself with everyone.

The reporter goes to the window to adjust the shade, but it flies out of his hand to the top of the roller. He looks down to a desolate alley forty feet below, only to conclude that jumping would do him no good. He does not want to die; he only wants Ann to be there with him to share this glimpse of modern life.

In the next section, the reporter returns to his whiskey and his story; again his account of the action mingles with his memories of the atmosphere. The story shows the challenger, Romero, to be taking command of the fight by outmaneuvering the champion. Meanwhile, the reporter sees again in his mind the hoodlums in the crowd, the actions of the seconds, the new warning buzzer, the forty-light canopy illuminating the ring, the two great overhead clocks. He wonders how much action he has missed while looking at the time. He sees that he has notes for every second of the fight, except for two rounds, for which he borrowed notes.

Cush complains again about the quality of current shows. The reporter offers to swap their next assignments and to throw Ann in for good measure. Cush asks where she is. The reporter replies that he does not know; the friend who was supposed to be covering for her missed the signals. He returns to his memory of the fight, especially of the byplay between the champion's girlfriend and four tough kids who harass him.

Suddenly he stops typing and glances up at a small photograph of the James family—the writer Henry, the philosopher William, and their sister Alice—sitting in an English garden. The picture strikes him because of the extraordinary integrity, the "profound and simple honesty" of their faces. They seem to him to be contemplating the truth of things in perfect serenity as they peer into and beyond the camera.

He returns to his typewriter, again combining an objective account of the fight with his subjective responses to the behavior of the crowd. Cush complains that no one seems to care anymore about keeping things as they belong. He asks the reporter for a ride home but learns that he is walking.

In the third section, both men continue working in silence. The reporter once more calls to mind the fiancé, a hard-bitten woman who remains true to her man, cheering him on to the end. The fight is now in the eleventh round. The reporter senses a mesmerizing, snakelike quality in the challenger's jab; he keeps fending off the clumsy rushes of the champion with the easy confidence of superior intelligence or planning. The fiancé's enthusiasm wanes, and the crowd begins to back Romero. He only has to keep boxing.

Cush interrupts his memories by asking if he has heard of a mutual acquaintance, whose drinking has finally led to a breakdown. The two men sympathize with his wife, who stayed by him to the end.

The reporter returns to the fight, now in the final round. The boxers slug it out toe-to-toe. Romero continues to block and make Zabriski miss, while scoring himself. The final round, and the fight, are his. Two images remain: Romero doing a knock-kneed dance of victory around the ring; Zabriski lying on a training table laconically commenting that he waited too long to make weight, that it would not happen again. His fiancé is still with him. The reporter hands his copy to Cush as the latter prepares to leave, and says that he is staying to write a letter.

In the fourth section, instead of writing immediately, he gets up and looks at the photograph again. What he has to tell Ann has something to do with that. He begins by saying that he is not going to write an ordinary letter, or argue as he has so often that he cannot accept her habit of casual flirtation. He senses a wide gulf between them; neither seems to hear what the other is saying. The rift deepens every time he sees her yield to the caresses of simple acquaintances. His feeling is not jealousy or prudery, as she has suggested; it is rather that he cannot divorce body and spirit as she tries to wedge them apart. For him, body and soul are integrated like two dancers; when they part, something fragments, and that fragmentation affects both. Body and soul united make love—and life—possible; separating them can produce only sainthood or evil, but not love. The photograph in front of him illustrates that kind of union, that integrity.

He breaks off in despair, knowing that he cannot explain these things to her. Either one feels them or one does not. Lacking that shared feeling, they are doomed to continue quarreling as they have, as the fighters are doomed to combat, and there will never be an end.

## Themes and Meanings

Conrad Aiken's story centers on human conflict and the possibility of cooperation, and it develops this focus on several levels of human interaction. To begin with there is the fight itself, the subject of the reporter's story. As he writes about it, he realizes that it is not a simple combat, not simply one man pitted against another, but an entire network of interlocking conflicts. There is, on the simplest level, the participation of the crowd, from those who go implicitly to see someone physically beaten, to those who side with one fighter or the other, to those who bait the loser, to the fiancé who stands by her man. There is also in the match more than mere physical competition: Will contends with will, intelligence with intelligence. Finally, the match is not over at the end; the fighters are not even particularly hostile to each other: Fighting is their business, and they immediately look ahead to the rematch. The conflict thus becomes self-perpetuating; further, it is peculiarly human.

Aiken brings this into contrast with three other elements in the story: the relationship between the reporter and his colleague Cush, the photograph of the James family, and the frustration of the reporter with his girlfriend. First, he and Cush work together in fellowship, sharing whiskey, problems, common interests, and common pursuits. Though their work could bring them into competition, they respect and help each other. The photograph deepens this sense of the possibility overcoming the limitations of the self. No conflict is apparent here; the figures are serene in repose, sympathetic to the pangs of existence, but somehow capable of transcending them and uniting with all humanity. This kind of peace is available only to those who enter imaginatively into the souls of others.

His conflict with his girlfriend does not have this kind of intuitive understanding. Because it lacks this, it parallels the physical combat of the fight; it has rounds and bouts, with temporary winners and losers, but it can never be resolved and will never end.

## Style and Technique

The most conspicuous characteristic of this story is the unconventional use of plot. The central interest lies in the relationship between the reporter and his girlfriend, but they do not occupy center stage, they do not interact, and the relationship does not change from beginning to end. What changes is his consciousness of the relationship, and this change is brought about by his experience of the fight and his appreciation of the photograph. Through them, he gains an understanding of the roles of body and soul in human conflict, but that understanding brings him no closer to her.

Structurally, the story could be termed cinematic. Aiken cuts irregularly from one level of action to another, often in the middle of a paragraph. This allows him to depict what is proceeding in the reporter's consciousness, to whom all these levels are present simultaneously. The opening of the story sets up this focus: The reporter states that it was a great fight, but he "wasn't there"; yet the details show that he saw every second of it, even that he saw some things without registering them distinctly, such as the reactions in the crowd. He means that his attention was on something else: His body was involved, but not his soul. This technique reinforces the major themes: the difficulty of integrating body and soul in any human endeavor and the difficulty of transcending the natural tendency of all men to conflict.

*James L. Livingston*

# ROYAL BEATINGS

*Author:* Alice Munro (1931-    )
*Type of plot:* Domestic realism
*Time of plot:* The 1930's
*Locale:* West Hanratty, Ontario, Canada
*First published:* 1977

> *Principal characters:*
> ROSE, a girl on the threshold of adolescence
> FLO, her stepmother
> HER FATHER, a furniture restorer

*The Story*

Rose, a girl nearing adolescence, lives with her father, her stepmother, and her younger half brother, Brian, in a small town in the Ottawa Valley of central Canada. Her father is a scrupulous furniture restorer who works in a shed behind the family's home and storefront. His earnings barely suffice to provide the most minimal of family needs. Their house in West Hanratty, a section of the town where the social structure "ran from factory workers and foundry workers down to large improvident families of casual bootleggers and prostitutes and unsuccessful thieves," is too cramped to provide any private space. The central action of the story takes place during the Depression, a period recalled as one of legendary poverty, when the clash between the aspirations of the members of Rose's family and the limits of their lives has created a condition of psychic tension that can be relieved only by an explosion of emotion that permits the family to temporarily overcome the frustrations inherent in their situation.

Rose's relationship with her stepmother has changed from a long initial truce to a continuously simmering conflict. Her father remains vaguely distant most of the time, an inward man whose poetic range of mind is not disclosed to Rose until after his death. Rose sees the inhabitants of Hanratty and West Hanratty as figures of foolishness, pretense, and casual violence; their antics are a means for Flo to support her own shaky sense of self-esteem through scornful dismissal. The absence of any satisfactory social relationships, the minimal resources available for even modest purchases, and the family's restricted living space compress Rose's family into a tightly wound, tension-ridden cluster of pulsating neuroses. Their anxieties and desires have been concentrated into a number of rituals devised to express their emotional needs and to alleviate the pressures of their deepest conflicts. The beating is prominent among these, a special event shaped into a dramatic exercise in which each person has an acknowledged role. In Rose's eyes, it has been exalted into an event that is both savage and splendid in an attempt to validate its importance and accept its unpleasant aspects.

Rose and Flo engage in an ongoing quarrel that escalates into a verbal battle in which each attacks areas of particular sensitivity. Goaded beyond endurance, Flo calls

Rose's father, who enters the arena from his workshed. His arrival raises the struggle to another level, the anticipation of a physical encounter arousing both trepidation and a curious kind of anticipatory excitement in everyone. Rapid interchanges of dialogue intensify the mood. The direct application of physical force is rendered with vivid language in an immediate present tense as Rose and her father seem to be caught in a flux of passion and confusion. Rose is driven into a frenzy of recrimination, Flo flutters about expressing concern, and Rose's father justifies his actions before lapsing into silence. The aftermath of the royal beating is revealed as an extraordinary state of calm for Rose, in which things take on a lovely simplicity. Flo tries to comfort Rose, and the whole family gathers for a dinner feeling a "convalescent indolence, not far off satisfaction." The ethos of strife has been transformed through a kind of catharsis. Rose's father, in a rare moment of expansive ease, tells the family about a sighting of the planet Venus. Flo performs an acrobatic feat. Brian, previously a silent spectator, cheers her on. In an unforeseen, but compelling and convincing, reversal, the episode ends with a current of happiness in the room following the release of enclosed psychic poisons in a torrent of wrath.

The story shifts abruptly four decades or so into the future. Rose, now living in Toronto, hears a centenarian, Hat Nettleton, interviewed on the radio. She realizes that he is one of three men who horsewhipped a town outcast years before her birth. This was one of Flo's anecdotes, and Rose realizes that Flo would have enjoyed hearing the interview. Flo, however, has been living in the same nursing facility as Nettleton for several years, completely removed from all social contact or conversation. The story closes with Rose in a reflective mood, her affectionate sympathy for Flo a strong contrast with her earlier animosity. Rose's perspective has widened considerably, and she has developed a much better understanding of Flo's behavior, and of her own.

## Themes and Meanings

"Royal Beatings" is the first story in Alice Munro's collection *The Beggar Maid: Stories of Flo and Rose* (1978). While each story is designed to stand as a single entity, the gradual accumulation of information about the two women and the continual intertwining of their lives achieve a novelistic scope. The effects of time's passage across decades of the characters' lives and the operations of memory in selecting details vital to a specific version of reality are two of Munro's essential concerns. "Royal Beatings" uses these motifs to show that a large part of a person's life often is hidden beyond what is immediately apparent to people who are close to them.

This story is anchored in Rose's consciousness and addresses a question Flo poses in a typical moment of anger: "Who do you think you are?" The query is supposed to keep Rose in her place, but as the query echoes through the stories in the collection and eventually becomes the title of the last story, it is evident that it is a guiding precept for Rose's exploration and establishment of a sense of self. This inquiry into the formative elements of personal identity is centered in the combative manner of communication that marks Flo and Rose's relationship—a mixture of taunting and sharing, probing and concealing, that implies an active dislike but which is actually a cover for fear and suppressed curiosity. Because a mood of contention dominates the story, those moments when the tension is eased are effectively emphasized by comparison. The dispersal of rancor after the beating is the prime example, but two other features are prominent as well. The radical shift at the conclusion when Nettleton is interviewed functions as a framing device, since he is introduced earlier in an extended anecdote that Flo tells Rose. Flo's pleasure in regaling Rose with local lore is evident, and a rough parallel is drawn between families and between two radically different types of beatings. Although no specific insights are stressed, the lack of information about Nettleton's motivation leads to fascinated speculation. Flo had conveyed to Rose her sense of the almost unfathomable dimensions of human possibility.

More significantly, the almost ephemeral picture of Rose's father suggests how incomplete one's understanding of a situation may be. Never named, he is a contributing agent as the administrator of the beating, but he engages Rose's imagination more profoundly when she hears him singing or reciting poetry at work. When she discovers his notebooks after his death, his reflections on natural phenomena and his intriguing inclusion of quotations ("All things are alive. Spinoza.") illuminate a hidden life, leading to the revelation that the person who spoke these words was not the person who spoke to her as her father. She is astonished by this perception, and it reinforces her wonder at the dimensions of human existence, a crucial factor in setting the narrative direction of the story and the entire sequence.

*Style and Technique*

Author Ted Solotaroff has described Munro as a maximalist who adds small details together to form "the narrative configuration of a life" and defines a character through "a mounting glow of implication" rather than through the flash of revelation familiar in short fiction. This technique works in accordance with Munro's conception of a world of multiple dimensions and expanding boundaries, where the immediate motivation for action is often apparently arbitrary. Consequently, "Royal Beatings" swings abruptly from one period of time to another, and the narrative focus shifts quickly from its location in an omniscient perspective to the viewpoint of either Rose or Flo, seeming to erase the barrier between an internal and an external depiction of character. Within this flexible frame, Munro uses vivid, explicit language in a style Solotaroff calls renovated realism and evokes an aura of immediacy with often pungent dialogue that energizes the narrative.

*Leon Lewis*

# RULES OF THE GAME

*Author:* Amy Tan (1952-    )
*Type of plot:* Psychological
*Time of plot:* The 1950's and 1960's
*Locale:* San Francisco
*First published:* 1986

> *Principal characters:*
> WAVERLY PLACE JONG, the narrator, a young chess prodigy
> LINDO JONG, her Chinese immigrant mother

*The Story*

Waverly Place Jong is a chess prodigy living in San Francisco's Chinatown with her Chinese immigrant parents. She is named after "Waverly Place," her family's address and, therefore, their claim to the United States. Waverly is diminutively nicknamed as "Meimei" (Chinese for "little sister"), whereas her two brothers have resonant, victorious names—Winston and Vincent.

Waverly and her mother, Lindo Jong, have an ongoing psychological battle, each surreptitiously trying to gain the upper hand. Although Waverly was born in the United States, her mother has instilled in her many Chinese rules of conduct. One important rule is that one must remain silent to win. The story's opening focuses on silence and on how controlling one's emotions endows one with a secret strength like the wind.

Once when shopping with her mother, the six-year-old Waverly longs for some salted plums. Because she fusses for them, her mother refuses to buy them. The next time, Waverly keeps her wants silent, and her mother rewards her with plums.

Later, Waverly sets a psychological ambush for her mother. As her hair is being combed painfully by Lindo, Waverly slyly asks her what Chinese torture is. Lindo knows that Waverly is challenging her pride in Chinese culture. Initially, Lindo deflects her daughter's question about the possibility of Chinese inhumanity, pointing out that Chinese people are good at business, medicine, and painting. Then Lindo's chauvinism overcomes her, and she adds, "We do torture. Best torture."

At a church Christmas party, the Jong children receive gifts, among which is a used chess set. At church, Lindo thanks the ladies, but at home, she sniffs proudly that they do not want it. Thus she socializes her children to exercise silence and power over their true feelings; even unwanted gifts must be acknowledged as exceeding what one deserves.

Watching her brothers play chess, Waverly becomes intrigued by the rules of the game. She does not understand these American rules, but she researches them in the library, learning the moves and the powers of each piece, and then easily defeats her brothers. When she stumbles on some old Chinese men playing chess in the park, she invites one, Lau Po, to play. He teaches her more rules and tactics. Waverly soon wins neighborhood exhibition games, and her mother begins to take pride in her, although she still modestly disclaims that it is luck.

When someone suggests that Waverly play at local chess tournaments, she is eager to participate but overpowers her desires and demurs, remembering the plums. Lindo lets Waverly play and win repeatedly. Now it is Lindo who wears a triumphant grin.

With Waverly's victories, Lindo changes the rules in the household. Contrary to Chinese gender roles, Waverly no longer does dishes. Proclaiming "Is new American rules," Lindo relegates such chores to her sons so that Waverly can expend her energies on chess. At nine years of age, Waverly becomes a national chess champion. Lindo is thrilled as the cover of *Life* magazine features her daughter, both challenging traditional male hegemony over chess and testifying that Chinese people can do anything better.

Sauntering through Chinatown, Lindo announces to everyone that her daughter is "Wave-ly Jong," the chess prodigy. To Lindo's Chinese thinking, Waverly's success is their family's success. To Waverly's more American view, her success is her individual accomplishment, and she resents Lindo's appropriating it. Miscommunication between mother and daughter ensues, with Lindo concluding from Waverly's reticence that she is ashamed of her mother, her family, and her race.

When Waverly requests less ostentation and more silence from Lindo, Lindo calls her stupid. Waverly angrily runs away from home for half a day but returns when she realizes that she cannot survive independent of her family. Lindo exercises her power and gives her daughter the silent treatment, pretending to ignore Waverly's existence.

Waverly retreats to her room and imagines her mother's eyes as two angry, black slits directing the black pieces of a chessboard and routing Waverly's white pieces. In this waking dream, Waverly feels herself wafted aloft by a wind, detached from her family, and she remembers Lindo's words, "Strongest wind cannot be seen." In her terrifying yet exhilarating impasse, Waverly understands that to be herself she must assert her individuality but that she cannot do so without isolating herself from her family. Her dilemma is her next move.

*Themes and Meanings*

"Rules of the Game" is one of the stories making up Amy Tan's *The Joy Luck Club* (1989). It is also Tan's first written story, originally entitled "Endgame" in manuscript. Although the story was originally published as an independent work, it also contains several thematic motifs of the book.

The central subject of "Rules of the Game" is power. Although pure power itself is immaculate and invisible, the effects of power can be seen manifested in a mother-daughter struggle, a male-female tug-of-war, a conflict between Asian and American values in an immigrant family, and the opposition between black and white in a chess game.

The mother-daughter struggle for psychological ascendancy between Lindo and Waverly is the most prominent manifestation of Tan's theme of power. Lindo wants Waverly to be dependent on her for the fulfillment of Waverly's wants (salted plums), her physical and psychological well-being (home and nurturing), and even her unique, defining mental power (her chess talent). If Waverly admits her dependence, she is her mother's creature. If Waverly succeeds in asserting her independence by claiming individual credit for her chess powers, she will be her own person. Implicit in this mother-daughter struggle is a conflict contrasting Asian values, which emphasize familial and communal honor, against American values, which reward individual achievement. Asians more readily attribute a person's achievement to familial and communal nurturing (hence Lindo's claims), whereas Americans more readily give this credit to an individual's own efforts and talents (hence Waverly's assertions).

The story also portrays a male-female rivalry between Waverly and her brothers. This rivalry also intersects with the contrast between Asian and American values. By Chinese rules, the big brothers, significantly named Winston and Victor, should be the main achievers of the family, whereas the feminine "little sister"—Waverly's diminutive Chinese nickname—should be merely a decorative background figure. Here, however, it is the young girl who appropriates the chess set originally intended for a brother and who achieves victory and fame through mastering the rules of a game long considered a male preserve.

*Style and Technique*

Tan employs an intricate and piquant irony to develop these themes. Irony especially surrounds Lindo. An immigrant, Lindo is a proud repository of traditional Chinese values, which she nostalgically proclaims as superior to the values of the United States. One of her tenets is that strong people should remain silent, a behavioral strategy she inherits from Sunzi's classic *Sunzi Bingfa* (probably 475-221 B.C.E.; *Sun Tzu: On the Art of War*, 1910); as Lindo indicates in another tale in *The Joy Luck Club*, her maiden name is Sun. Ironically, however, when Waverly is featured on the cover of *Life* magazine, Lindo cannot keep silent about her daughter's prowess and pridefully trumpets Waverly's fame all over Chinatown. By breaking her Chinese reserve of silent strength and betraying her weakness for her daughter, Lindo has ironically made herself vulnerable and also has become just another ostentatious American mother. This is but one of several delightful ironies informing "Rules of the Game."

An equally intricate stylistic device is Tan's use of the wind as a metaphor. The wind, symbolizing an invisible power that becomes perceptible only through its effects, fuses Asian and Western traditions of imagery. In Chinese tradition, for example, the wind is a powerful component of geomancy, the art or science of positioning oneself advantageously. (The Chinese term for geomancy is *feng shui*, which means "wind and water.") Similarly, in the rules of mah-jongg, the Chinese game that metaphorically structures *The Joy Luck Club*, each hand is begun by rolling dice to determine the wind's direction (the source of bonus points). In Western tradition, too, the wind is an archetypal image for power. Thus the Bible likens the Holy Spirit (the active principle of divinity) to the wind (John 3:8), while the atheist poet Percy Shelley uses wind as a metaphor for physical, political, and ideological power in his "Ode to the West Wind" (1820).

Tan's narrative prose and dialogue also deserve attention. Tan's narrative delights by its sparkling vivacity, its many-faceted turns of phrasing, and its wry wit that continually surprises. For example, the bathetic movement of the story's opening paragraph juxtaposes a mysterious invisible strength with the apparently mundane child's play of a board game. Tan's authentic depiction of immigrant Chinese speech is another of her stylistic accomplishments, which she has analyzed in her award-winning essay "Mother Tongue" (1990). For Lindo's dialogue, Tan captures the colorful patois of immigrant Chinese speech, resourceful and vivid; thus does Lindo announce a change in rules regarding dish-drying chores: "Is new American rules. . . . Meimei play, squeeze all her brains out for win chess. You [Victor and Winston] play, worth squeeze towel."

*Ka Ying Vu and C. L. Chua*

# SABOTEUR

*Author:* Ha Jin (1956-    )
*Type of plot:* Political
*Time of plot:* The late twentieth century
*Locale:* Muji, China
*First published:* 1996

> *Principal characters:*
> CHIU MUGUANG, a university professor
> A POLICE OFFICER FROM MUJI
> FENJIN, Chiu's former student

## The Story

"Saboteur" is told through the consciousness of Chiu Muguang, a university professor who is arrested and briefly kept in captivity, although the final paragraphs of the story are narrated from the point of view of Fenjin, Chiu's former student. In a brief epilogue, an unidentified narrator makes clear the motives for Chiu's strange behavior after his imprisonment.

As the story opens, Chiu and his new bride are having lunch on the last day of their honeymoon in the city of Muji, China. Chiu is looking forward to returning to his job in Harbin, especially because he is worried about having a relapse of hepatitis, a disease that left him debilitated several months earlier. As he and his bride finish their lunch, a police officer at a nearby table tosses tea on the couple. Chiu finds this action inexplicable and lodges a complaint. Instead of apologizing, the police officer arrests Chiu for disturbing the peace. Manhandled when he resists, Chiu is outraged, and as he departs with the police officer he asks his wife to contact someone at the university to bail him out of jail.

Like the officer in the restaurant, the officers at the police station are unmoved by Chiu's protests over what he believes has been a miscarriage of justice. They ignore his threats and toss him in a cell. Within hours, he is brought before the bureau chief, who possesses a thick dossier to support the police officer's claim that Chiu has been disruptive and disrespectful. Chiu is astounded when he learns he is charged with sabotage and that his status as a Communist Party member makes his crime worse. The bureau chief shows him several statements from eyewitnesses who support the police officer's side of the case, then asks Chiu to sign a confession. When Chiu refuses, he is dragged back to his cell.

As he lies in the cell, Chiu begins suffering what he is sure is a relapse of hepatitis. He appeals to one of the jailers for assistance, only to be told that he cannot get help on a weekend. Demoralized but resigned to his fate, Chiu spends a restless day in his cell, trying to remain calm to minimize the effects of the disease. Ironically, he realizes that he is not as bad off as he thought, and he places his hopes on being rescued by someone from the university.

Those hopes are dashed the following morning when Chiu hears noises from the courtyard outside the jail. Looking through his cell window, he sees a young man handcuffed to a tree. Chiu recognizes him as Fenjin, one of his former students, no doubt sent by university officials to rescue him; but Fenjin has instead been placed under control of the police. As Chiu watches, a police officer enters the courtyard and begins to torture Fenjin.

Chiu is hauled back before the bureau chief, who once again offers him a chance to sign a confession and be on his way. Now suffering acutely from hepatitis and realizing Fenjin will continue to be tortured until he consents to the chief's demand, Chiu agrees to sign a false statement acknowledging his crime.

On their release, Chiu and Fenjin meet outside the jail. Although Fenjin wants to depart immediately for Harbin, Chiu insists that the two eat and drink at several of the curbside stands in Muji. Ill with hepatitis, a contagious disease, Chiu moves from one of these places to the next, drinking tea and eating something at each. All the while, Chiu mutters curses against the police under his breath. Fenjin notices that his former teacher has become unpleasant.

The epilogue relates the news that, within a month after Chiu's visit to Muji, an unexplained epidemic of hepatitis broke out in the city.

*Themes and Meanings*

The first few paragraphs of "Saboteur" bring readers into a Kafkaesque world in which unprovoked action and nameless crimes place an individual in a situation over which he has no control and for which he has no rational explanation. On this level, Ha Jin's story is an existentialist tale in which the protagonist must strive to understand what seems to be a meaningless universe and take control over his own life. What may seem a macabre ending in which Chiu exacts poetic justice on the people who imprisoned him is, on the philosophical level, his attempt to assert his own importance in a world in which the individual is worth nothing.

There also is a political dimension to the story, and it is possible to read "Saboteur" as an indictment of communist Chinese society. The police arrest Chiu simply because they can; he is powerless to stop the action of men he calls hooligans, even though he is a member of the Communist Party. Ironically, Chiu believes in the communist dogma that all people are equal under the law; his experience teaches him the emptiness of that platitude. The authorities in the outer reaches of the country seem little concerned about any form of retribution they might suffer from national leaders; in their region, they are, in essence, petty kings.

Through this story Ha Jin demonstrates what happens too frequently when those in power deal ruthlessly with those under them. As he lies in jail, Chiu settles into his role as victim; although he never accepts his status completely, he quickly accommodates and even begins to be impressed with the ability of his captors to build a case against him. When he is released, however, instead of turning to higher authority to give him justice and reestablish the social order, he becomes a perpetrator of evil. His behavior toward the innocent citizens of Muji is as reprehensible as that of the police who had arrested him without cause.

### Style and Technique

Readers familiar with the literary tradition will see parallels between this story and the work of European writer Franz Kafka, especially *Der Prozess* (1925; *The Trial*, 1937), a novel in which a man is arrested and tried for a crime he did not commit. In Ha Jin's story, as in Kafka's work, the power of the state to deal summarily with its citizens is revealed as arbitrary and frightening. In "Saboteur," the individual who has been wronged is able to achieve some measure of revenge. In doing so, however, he merely stoops to the level of those who have perpetrated injustice on him; there is no sense that retribution is justified.

The central literary device used in "Saboteur" is irony. Readers sense from the beginning that actions and consequences are disconnected and arbitrary. The arrest of Chiu is ironic, because he has committed no crime. The willingness of the citizens of Muji to come forward to give testimony against a visitor to their city is ironic because they do not know him. The arrest and torture of Fenjin is ironic because he had come to Muji as Chiu's savior. Chiu's intent to infect the citizens of Muji with hepatitis is ironic because by doing so he has become like his captors, a person who inflicts punishment on the innocent simply because he can.

Ha Jin is particularly effective in conveying this irony because he uses a controlled, understated style of writing that relies on simple sentences to relate facts and conclusions. Seldom does he dwell on the emotions of his protagonist. The absurdity of the situation takes on an air of normalcy. The same kind of effect was created by Kurt Vonnegut in his *Slaughterhouse-Five: Or, The Children's Crusade, a Duty-Dance with Death* (1969), in which Vonnegut's narrator dismisses the horrors of the bombing of Dresden with the simple phrase "So it goes."

Another principal literary device used subtly by Jin is that of sickness as metaphor. Chiu's hepatitis is a symbol of the sickness of Communist China. It has invaded his body, and although at times it goes into remission, it returns with a vengeance when his body is placed under stress. So it is, the story suggests, with the country as a whole. China is suffering from an invidious disease—communism—that is eating away at its vitality. Given the right circumstances, the disease can break out into an epidemic, with disastrous consequences.

*Laurence W. Mazzeno*

# THE SAD FATE OF MR. FOX

*Author:* Joel Chandler Harris (1848-1908)
*Type of plot:* Animal tale
*Time of plot:* After the American Civil War
*Locale:* The Deep South
*First published:* 1880

> *Principal characters:*
> UNCLE REMUS, an aged black man and former slave, who tells
> the story
> MISS SALLY'S SEVEN-YEAR-OLD SON, an appreciative audience
> BRER FOX, the villain/victim in this story
> BRER RABBIT, the trickster-protagonist
> MISS FOX, the wife of Brer Fox
> TOBE, Brer Fox's son

*The Story*

"The Sad Fate of Mr. Fox," the last of Uncle Remus's tales in *Uncle Remus: His Songs and Sayings* (1880), marks the end of Mr. Fox, as well as the end of the book. It is, as Uncle Remus says, "de las'rower stumps, sho." For this reason, Uncle Remus is more serious when the evening storytelling session begins, and he states at the beginning that Brer Fox dies in this tale.

The focus of the tale, however, is, as usual, Brer Rabbit. Hoping to share Brer Fox's dinner, he tells Brer Fox that his wife is sick and his children are cold, but Brer Fox offers him only a piece of fire to take home. Frustrated, but not defeated, Brer Rabbit returns to Brer Fox under the pretense that the fire went out. When he asks the fox about the beef that he is cooking for dinner, the fox offers to show him where he, too, can get as much meat as he wants. The next morning, Brer Fox takes Brer Rabbit down by Miss Meadows's place, where a man keeps a special cow. When called by name, "Bookay," this cow will open her mouth and let the fox (and the rabbit) inside her body where they can cut away as much meat as they can carry.

Inside this magical cow, they begin to cut off pieces of beef, but Brer Fox warns Brer Rabbit not to cut the "haslett" (the edible viscera of an animal such as the heart and lungs). When Brer Rabbit hacks the haslett, the cow dies. Brer Rabbit hides in the gall, Brer Fox in the maul. The next morning, the owner of the cow, upset to discover his cow dead, cuts her open to see who or what killed her. Brer Rabbit jumps out of the gall and tells the man that the killer of the cow is hiding in the maul. Immediately the man takes a stick and begins to beat the stomach of the dead cow, killing the fox hiding there.

However, the death of his old enemy is not enough for Brer Rabbit. He asks the man for the head of Brer Fox, which he takes to Miss Fox, telling her that it is a good piece of beef but that she should not look at it until after she cooks and eats it. Her son, Tobe, curious and hungry, looks in the pot and tells his mother what he sees. The angry Miss Fox and her dogs trap Brer Rabbit in a hollow log. Unfortunately, she leaves Tobe to guard the rabbit while she goes to fetch the ax. Tobe is no match for the wily rabbit, who tricks him into going to the nearby stream for water. When Miss Fox tries to whip Tobe for being so stupid, he too runs off through the woods, where he meets Brer Rabbit. While they are talking, Miss Fox catches them both and declares she will kill the rabbit and whip her son.

This time Brer Rabbit has another suggestion: He urges her to grind off his nose with the grindstone so that he will not be able to smell after he is dead. Hopping up on the grindstone, the cooperative, clever rabbit suggests that Tobe can turn the handle while Miss Fox gets water for the stone. The gullible widow agrees, and the rabbit escapes again. At this point the story ends. The little boy asks if that is the last of Brer Rabbit. Uncle Remus now bows to oral tradition and tells the child that the truth is hard to determine. Some people, he says, claim that Brer Rabbit actually married Miss Fox; others say that the rabbits and the foxes became friends. Uncle Remus does not take a stand. Instead he carries the little boy piggyback up to the big house for bedtime. Readers of the Uncle Remus tales need not despair. *Nights with Uncle Remus*, published in 1883, contains seventy-one more stories in which both Brer Rabbit and Brer Fox figure prominently.

*Themes and Meanings*

The violence in this story is startling. In contrast to stories such as "The Wonderful Tar-Baby Story," "The Sad Fate of Mr. Fox" seems harsh and unexpected. The understatement of the word "sad" is gravely humorous, and the moral advice found in many of the other tales is reduced here to Phineas Taylor Barnum's epitaph for suckers: "There's one born every minute." Certainly one is appalled by the fate of Mr. Fox. Joel Chandler Harris's story, however, does not stop with the horror of the fox's head in his wife's stew pot. He goes on to detail the incredible stupidity of the widow and her son as they try in vain to capture the clever rabbit. What does this reveal about the characters and the worldview of Uncle Remus?

There is no doubt that it is the persona of the black slave, in the guise of the physically weak but clever rabbit, that escapes from the clutches of the more powerful, but slow-witted, foxes, which are obvious symbols of the dominating white man. Indeed, escape is not enough; Brer Rabbit seeks and finds revenge. However, the story does not celebrate death or revenge; it is a story of survival, the survival of the feisty spirit of Brer Rabbit. Although the main characters, Brer Fox and Brer Rabbit, seem to cooperate, there is no compromise. Even though they share the same beef, there is no honest connection or communion between them. Thus, Brer Rabbit has no qualms about betraying the fox. Revenge is sweet, no matter how horrible it may seem to the outsider. No matter how sad the fate of Mr. Fox may seem, this story is not tragic; the foolishness of the foxes is funny. Nor is the narrator a grim applauder of cruelty and trickery, for he himself would not do the terrible things that the characters do. He further distances himself from the reality of the story by suggesting that there are several optional conclusions for the irrepressible Brer Rabbit.

"The Sad Fate of Mr. Fox" reveals more clearly than some of the other tales the depth of anger that the slave felt against white society—a society made up of "foxes" and "wolves" who maintained the power, the money, and the status that could never be his. The moral of this fable may simply be a warning: In an unfair world, only the clever survive.

*Style and Technique*

Harris's attempt to reproduce the dialect in which he heard these stories told presents a literary hurdle for some readers. When read aloud, however, the story is clear and sensible. The oral nature of the story is also emphasized by the frame in which it is set: the old man telling stories to a young boy who asks questions at the beginning and end of the tale. The genres of the animal fable and the trickster tale, common in West African storytelling, are adapted to, and reflective of, the social experience and the anger of the African American slave. Because this anger is so violently expressed in this story, the double barrier of the dialect and the framework of the storytelling situation protects the reader from the horror of Mr. Fox's sad fate. Harris further tempers the effect by continuing to speculate on what eventually happened to Brer Rabbit and Widow Fox.

There are few realistic touches in this story; instead, the plot borrows from the supernatural as the rabbit and the fox climb into the mouth of the willing cow, Bookay, in order to cut away pieces of beef. This "unreality" also softens the implication of cannibalism in Brer Rabbit's revenge. Although humorous in presentation, "The Sad Fate of Mr. Fox" is a serious and rather grim tale for the end of the first published collection of Uncle Remus tales. The specter of malicious mischief out of control may explain why this story did not achieve the degree of popularity of others such as "The Wonderful Tar-Baby."

*Linda Humphrey*

# THE SAILOR-BOY'S TALE

*Author:* Isak Dinesen (Baroness Karen Blixen-Finecke, 1885-1962)
*Type of plot:* Fantasy
*Time of plot:* About 1865
*Locale:* Mediterranean Sea; Bodø, Norway
*First published:* "Skibsdrengens Fortælling," 1942 (English translation, 1942)

> *Principal characters:*
> SIMON, the protagonist, a young sailor
> NORA, a Norwegian girl
> IVAN, a Russian sailor
> SUNNIVA, an old Lapp woman with magical powers

*The Story*

While en route from Marseilles to Athens during a gale, the young sailor-boy Simon spots a bird that is stuck high in the rigging of his ship. Seeing that the bird is a peregrine falcon, the boy climbs up in order to free it. The ungrateful falcon rewards Simon for his kindness by hacking him in the thumb so hard that he bleeds, and the boy responds in kind by giving the bird a strong blow to its head.

Two years later Simon experiences the full consequences of this seemingly unimportant incident. He is now a crew member on another ship that is docked in northern Norway, in order to buy herring at Bodø, a thriving and gregarious market town. While on shore leave one evening, Simon meets a young girl named Nora, to whom he gives an orange in exchange for the promise of a kiss. The following night he goes ashore again in order to collect his payment. He ends up in the company of Russian sailors, however, and one of them, Ivan, tries to prevent him from going to meet Nora, saying that he wants Simon to stay with them so that they can show him a good time. Simon responds to Ivan's advances by stabbing him to death.

Simon proceeds to his meeting with Nora. Although she is uncomfortable with the realization that Simon has killed a man, she acknowledges that it was a necessity, especially because he would have otherwise been unable to come to her. After promising never to marry anyone else, Nora gives Simon the kiss that she owes him—an experience that Simon feels has a maturing effect on him. Nora cannot do anything to hide Simon from the Russians, however, because her father is the local parson.

Ivan's friends are now looking for his killer; Simon hides in the crowd at a dance in order to elude them. As he despairs of being able to save his life, an old pagan Lapp-woman named Sunniva appears, claims that Simon is her son, and tells him to come home with her. Sunniva lets Simon wipe his bloody hands on her skirt; as she hides him, she cuts her own thumb in order to explain the blood on her skirt to the Russians. They treat her with great respect, as Lapps are thought to have magical powers.

Sunniva reveals to Simon that she is the falcon that he once released during the storm in the Mediterranean. As a Lapp, she has the power of flight. She also tells him she likes his commitment to Nora, and that she will place a mark on his forehead that will make girls like him. She has the power to do this, she explains, because of her position in a great conspiracy of the females of the earth.

Sunniva then arranges safe passage for Simon back to his ship, which is to leave Bodø the following morning. She explains that she is helping him not only because she likes him, but also because of her sense of justice, for he deserved to be repaid for helping her when she was caught in the rigging when she was in the form of a falcon. In order completely to settle her accounts with Simon, she boxes his ear in return for the blow to her head that he once gave her.

*Themes and Meanings*

The two central themes of "The Sailor-Boy's Tale" are the relationship between men and women and the issue of justice. In order to outline her theory of justice, Isak Dinesen presents the reader with three interpersonal relationships, those between Simon and Nora, Ivan, and Sunniva.

The relationship between Simon and Ivan appears relatively simple. Ivan presents himself as Simon's friend and is accepted as such by Simon, but he must die because he is trying to prevent Simon from meeting Nora. The threatening homosexual overtones in Dinesen's description of Ivan appear to provide Simon with a justification for killing the man.

The story also shows that the essence of an intimate relationship is an exchange of value for value, symbolized by the kiss as payment for the orange given to Nora by Simon. It is in the relationship between Simon and Sunniva, however, that Dinesen most clearly spells out her concept of justice as the exchange of equal value. Because Simon once saved Sunniva's life—when she was in the form of a falcon—she is obligated to save him from Ivan's shipmates. While she was in the shape of the bird, she pecked so hard at Simon's thumb that it bled; it is thus only just that she wounds her own thumb in her effort to save him. Simon also gave her a blow to her head; that, too, must be repaid in order to balance the scales of justice. The story's concept of justice resembles that of the Old Testament's Mosaic code, which demanded neither more nor less than an eye for an eye and a tooth for a tooth.

Simon's relationship with Sunniva provides the vehicle through which a theory of the relationship between the sexes is made manifest, and his relationship with Nora offers a practical application of the theory. Simon is a young man who is willing to do absolutely anything in order to be with the woman he loves. Both Sunniva and Dinesen find that this is a very admirable quality, so Simon is rewarded for being a man of commitment. After Simon is presented as a heroic figure, however, it comes as a surprise when Sunniva tells him that it is the women of the world, not the men, who determine the outcome of events. Her claim that the women direct the lives of their sons, and, by extension, those of their husbands and fathers, is a most radical notion. This is especially so from the standpoint of Western patriarchy, the ideology of which frames Dinesen's activity as a writer.

*Style and Technique*

The most notable stylistic device used in this story is the Norwegian folklore motif of shape-shifting. According to a common old belief, some people had the power to change their physical appearance into that of such animals as bears, wolves, or, as in the case of Sunniva, birds. Sunniva's capacity for shape-shifting is crucial to the story; it gives the text its aura of mystery, presents a justification for her intervention into Simon's life at Bodø, and links the text's beginning to its end, thus giving the reader a sense of having encountered a highly structured whole.

The shape-shifting motif also provides a number of specific stylistic devices that Dinesen uses in order to tie the figure of the peregrine falcon to the character Sunniva. For example, both the falcon and Sunniva have yellow eyes. Also, when Sunniva moves her head, it jerks like that of a bird of prey. She also uses the phrase "little bird" as a term of endearment when speaking to Simon, thus suggesting that she is both a falcon and a person.

The shape-shifting motif also gives the story an air of mystery and unreality that is necessary for readers seriously to entertain the notion of a great matriarchal conspiracy of existence. Within a patriarchal culture, such an idea runs counter to received understanding; if it were presented in a more realistic story, it would be summarily dismissed by most readers. The fantasy aspects of the shape-shifting motif allow the author to present the subversive notion of a matriarchal conspiracy so that it may at least be considered, if not accepted as possible.

*Jan Sjåvik*

# SAILOR OFF THE *BREMEN*

*Author:* Irwin Shaw (1913-1984)
*Type of plot:* Social realism
*Time of plot:* The 1930's
*Locale:* New York City
*First published:* 1939

> *Principal characters:*
> ERNEST, an artist and a communist
> SALLY, his wife
> CHARLEY, his brother
> LUEGER, a steward on the liner *Bremen*
> PREMINGER, a communist deck officer

### The Story

Ernest, an artist, is beaten and disfigured (losing an eye and his front teeth) when he participates in a communist demonstration aboard the ocean liner *Bremen*. As the story opens, his friends and family gather in his kitchen to hear Preminger, a communist deck officer aboard the *Bremen* (and a witness to the incident), explain what happened. Ernest's brother, Charley, a college football player, decides to take revenge on Lueger, the German steward who beat Ernest. Ernest, however, despite his injuries, remains committed to the communist ideal and objects on the grounds that taking revenge on Lueger will serve no purpose.

Ernest is overruled by Charley and by his wife, Sally, and they tell him to leave the room while they plot against Lueger. They decide to lure him to the waiting Charley by using Sally as bait. She is to let him pick her up and to pretend to bring him home with her, and Charley is to ambush him in the street.

When the *Bremen* returns to New York City, Sally is briefed over and over on the plan. Lueger takes Sally to see a film and then is concerned only with reaching her apartment (she has told him she lives alone), but she stalls him with the offer of drinks to keep the original plan on schedule. She begins to have second thoughts about delivering Lueger and almost backs out completely because, even though she hates him, he is "a human being and thoughtless and unsuspecting and because her heart was softer than she had thought." Lueger chooses this moment, however, to hurt her, and she is strengthened in her resolve to carry out the plot. Lueger is taken completely by surprise, and Charley is extremely savage in his treatment of Lueger, almost killing him with his bare hands.

The last scene is tinged with irony, as Preminger, who identified Lueger as Ernest's assailant in the story's opening scene and later pointed out the steward to Charley, must make another identification, this time to the staff at the hospital where Lueger is taken and to the detective who is investigating the incident. In a masterpiece of dramatic irony, Preminger offers a pat explanation for Lueger's fate: "You must be very careful in a strange city."

## Themes and Meanings

Irwin Shaw was considered a very political writer, often with leftist overtones in his work, but in "Sailor Off the *Bremen*," his thrust is simply antifascist, not necessarily procommunist. He seems, instead, to point to a happy medium between the two political extremes as the ideal for political thought.

Fascism is made repulsive by its representative in the story, the Nazi Lueger. Preminger (a German communist, and thus diametrically opposed to the German Nazi Party) may be prejudiced, but the reader must concur with his judgment where Lueger is concerned. Preminger, in reporting Ernest's beating, observes that the other stewards charged with breaking up the demonstration at least "were human beings. [Lueger] is a member of the Nazi party." To further emphasize Lueger's repugnance, Shaw hints that the Nazi is also a sadist, particularly in the scenes in which he and Sally walk through the streets alone; he takes pleasure in hurting her, pinching her arm, and kissing her harshly. Lueger and, by representation, fascism are thus portrayed by Shaw as being evil and, as he attempted to warn in this story in 1939, the time of the story's appearance, dangerous.

Although fascism is bad, communism is not necessarily good, as the communists are seen as impotent to act against Lueger. It is Charley, the football player, the thoroughly American man (whose only philosophy, according to Ernest, is "Somebody knocks you down, you knock him down, everything is fine"), who takes matters into his own hands and acts while the communists can only talk. Only after he has taken the initiative do Ernest's communist friends follow him. Preminger even delineates the concern for party over person when, "as a party member," he agrees with Ernest that no point can be served by paying Lueger back for the loss of his eye, but "as a man" he advises Charley to "put Lueger on his back for at least six months." He cannot have personal thoughts if the party is uppermost in his mind, and only when he thinks for himself does he admit that a wrongdoer must be punished, that some sort of action must be taken.

The sympathy of the reader is clearly with Charley and Sally, the Americans who are not affiliated with either political extreme. Charley and Sally's concern is not some lofty ideological goal, but rather the simple human concern of seeing that justice is done—literally an eye for an eye in this case. Through this sympathy for the middle course, Shaw points at the necessity of taking violent action against fascism. However, also seems to say that neither fascism nor communism measures up to the standards of American democracy.

## Style and Technique

The most interesting aspect of Shaw's style in "Sailor Off the *Bremen*" is his construction of the story. The reader's attention must be concentrated on the violent confrontation between Charley and Lueger, between the United States and Germany, so rather than depicting the action that leads up to Ernest's beating, which would have robbed the story's climax of much of its novelty as the most active portion of the story, Shaw introduces it through Preminger in the kitchen-table discussion in the opening scene. The demonstration and the violence that follow it are reduced to expository elements that cannot rob the climax of the reader's full and undivided attention, and Shaw manages to place importance where he felt it most belonged, in the retribution against the Nazi Lueger.

*Greg T. Garrett*

# THE SAINT

*Author:* V. S. Pritchett (1900-1997)
*Type of plot:* Parody
*Time of plot:* 1917
*Locale:* An English market town
*First published:* 1940

> *Principal characters:*
> THE NARRATOR, a seventeen-year-old youth living with his aunt
> and uncle
> HIS UNCLE, a semisuccessful furniture maker and the leading
> member of an obscure religious sect
> HUBERT TIMBERLAKE, a Canadian minister who is visiting the
> narrator's uncle

## The Story

The unnamed narrator lives with his uncle, the proprietor of a small furniture-manufacturing business, in an English county market town. The uncle is a prominent lay member of the small Church of the Last Purification, of Toronto, Canada. The Purifiers believe that God created everything; that God, being good, could not have made evil; and that what appears to be evil is an illusion. "Don't let Error in" is a favorite slogan of the Purifiers: Do not believe in the reality of disease, misfortune, or death, for they are no more than illusions. Membership in the Purifiers brings scorn and persecution from its adherents' neighbors, but it also gives them the exhilaration of knowing that they alone know the Truth.

The narrator begins to doubt the Truth. If evil is an illusion, where did the illusion come from? He talks to his uncle, who simply repeats the Purifiers' stock phrases. At this juncture, the Reverend Hubert Timberlake, a leading minister from the Purification Church's headquarters in Toronto, comes to town. After giving an address on Sunday morning, he spends the afternoon with the narrator's family. Timberlake, who has been told of the narrator's wavering faith, proposes that the two of them go punting on the river after dinner. Timberlake insists on poling the punt, to show that he understands young people and that he is a regular guy.

All goes well until Timberlake, lecturing on how Error makes people dwell on sorrow, ignores the narrator's advice about the river's current and poles the punt through some willow trees. A tree branch catches him in the chest, lifts him off the punt, and leaves him clinging a yard above the water. Slowly, slowly he dips into the water; as he makes a futile reach for a higher branch, his shirt pulls out of his trousers, exposing flesh like a fatal flaw in a statue. At that instant, the narrator realizes that Timberlake does not have the answer to the question of the origin of evil, and that nobody has the final revelation about the meaning of life.

The narrator struggles to get Timberlake back into the boat. Concerned that the minister might catch cold, he suggests returning home, but Timberlake insists on proceeding, all the while pretending that nothing has happened. When they return to the uncle's house, Timberlake refuses either to change clothes or to sit by the fire. Sixteen years later, the narrator learns that Reverend Timberlake, who had become fat and jowly, died of heart disease at the age of fifty-seven.

*Themes and Meanings*

This short story, which helped establish V. S. Pritchett's reputation as a master of the form, is strongly autobiographical and makes up part of a larger working out of his relationship with his father. The same autobiographical themes appear in some of Pritchett's other works, most notably his 1951 novel, *Mr. Beluncle.*

Pritchett was born into a lower-middle-class family in Ipswich, an English market town; his father, Walter, was a self-centered man who exaggerated his own meager accomplishments as a traveling salesperson and manufacturer of fancy upholstery for furniture. As the father's fortunes fluctuated, the Pritchett family was supported by his Uncle Bugg, an Ipswich building contractor and pillar of the local Presbyterian church. After trying out several nonconformist denominations, Walter became a Christian Scientist. Founded in Boston, Massachusetts, by Mary Baker Eddy, Christian Science is based on the belief that God is completely good, all-powerful, and the basis of reality. That which is not like God, such as evil, disease, and misfortune, cannot exist in reality; they are only a distorted human perception of reality that can be dispelled through prayer and study.

"The Saint" clearly deals with this background. The Church of the Last Purification, of Toronto, Canada, is modeled on the Church of Christ, Scientist, of Boston, Massachusetts. Reverend Timberlake is thus similar to a Christian Science practitioner. The narrator's unnamed uncle is a combination of Walter Pritchett and Uncle Bugg. The narrator is Pritchett himself.

The narrator cannot reconcile the evidence of his own experience with his family's religious beliefs, which deny the reality of the world. Timberlake's attempt to resolve the conflict fails, however, because the minister's own belief system rests on the denial of material reality. Hence Timberlake dismisses the accident with the willows as "letting some Error in" and deals with it by refusing to change his clothes. The narrator concludes that Reverend Timberlake is a material being who denies both his own material humanity and the goodness of matter. "By no word did he acknowledge the disasters or the beauties of the world. If they were printed upon him, they were printed upon a husk." The glimpse sixteen years forward to Reverend Timberlake's death reinforces the sense of pretense and denial, for it was the material nature of disease, supposedly Error, that killed him.

Pritchett moves beyond this individual judgment to draw a more general conclusion about the nature of belief. Not only does Timberlake misunderstand the nature of evil, but Pritchett's narrator also becomes convinced that the final revelation of ultimate Truth has been vouchsafed to no one.

*Style and Technique*

Pritchett uses three images to make his points: the ape, the statue, and the miracle. The narrator describes his doubts as being like an ape following him around; at the end of the story, he comments that the ape that merely had followed him around had been inside eating out Reverend Timberlake's heart. The ape image, which Pritchett uses in other works, stands for the material, fleshly, and sexual nature of the human condition. People must come to terms with this condition, for they cannot deny it out of existence.

The second image is that of the statue. The slice of Timberlake's white underbelly, glimpsed when his shirt and trousers separate, reminds the narrator of a crack appearing along the belly of the statue of some Greek god. This recalls the loss of faith of the last pagans, as they see that their gods are nothing more than flawed pieces of marble. The narrator's glimpse reveals both Timberlake and his belief system as flawed. The statue image reappears when Timberlake and the narrator rest in a meadow filled with goldenrods. Timberlake's wet clothing is covered with golden pollen, making him look like the gilded statue of a saint.

The third image is that of the miracle, which occurs throughout the story. What the vulgar would call miracles occur among the little congregation of Purifiers routinely every day. Timberlake performs miracles, even, it is said, raising the dead. At the end, the doctor who inspects Timberlake's body remarks that it was a miracle he had lived as long as he had. Pritchett thus shows that talk of miracles can be meaningless cant in the mouths of true believers.

At times in the story, Pritchett uses humor to illustrate his points about cant. For example, the uncle boasts about how Timberlake has sacrificed an income of a thousand pounds a year as a successful insurance salesperson in order to serve the Truth, but then adds that Timberlake now makes fifteen hundred pounds as a Purification faith healer. Another example is when the narrator almost blurts out that Timberlake might catch his death of cold—not the thing to say to a faith healer who denies the reality of both sickness and death.

The scene that forms the story's centerpiece—Timberlake dangling from a branch like a round blue damson ripe and ready to fall, then slowly sinking into the river—is both funny and sad. Pritchett describes him as hanging tidy and dignified, blinking his chicken-pale eyelids and staring quietly at the sky; the narrator imagines that he is praying one of the Purifiers' scientific prayers. Will his faith triumph over matter? Will he walk on water? In other hands, this might have been a hilarious scene, but Pritchett's treatment emphasizes the sadness of it all. Timberlake is not so much a tragic figure, although there is some of that in him, as he is a small and inadequate one.

*D. G. Paz*

# SAINT AUGUSTINE'S PIGEON

*Author:* Evan S. Connell, Jr. (1924-      )
*Type of plot:* Satire
*Time of plot:* The early 1960's
*Locale:* New York City
*First published:* 1965

> *Principal characters:*
> KARL MUHLBACH, an executive with the Metropolitan Mutual
>     Insurance Company, a widower more than forty years old and
>     the father of two children
> MRS. GRUNTHE, his housekeeper, a guardian of domestic order
>     and virtue
> EULA CUNNINGHAM, a stout spinster intent on becoming the
>     second Mrs. Muhlbach
> ROUGE, a teenage girl whom Muhlbach meets in Washington
>     Square
> PUIG, Muhlbach's college roommate, a career officer in the
>     United States Navy

*The Story*

Karl Muhlbach decides, after reading a passage from Saint Augustine's *Confessiones* (397-400; *Confessions,* 1620) dealing with the tension between flesh and spirit, that the celibacy enforced by the death of his wife should end. Barely more than forty years old, Muhlbach rebels against his ordered, ascetic life, presided over by his housekeeper, Mrs. Grunthe, and decides to cross the river into Manhattan one Saturday evening in search of a mistress. His choice of that word is significant; it reveals how out of touch with the mores of his society Muhlbach has become.

The carefully structured life that Muhlbach leads, with dinner each night at eight and wine with it only on Sundays, stifles both body and soul. He silently assures Mrs. Grunthe that he intends this evening to go to Hell. Showering in preparation for the journey, Muhlbach admits that he looks "professorial" but hopes that his chances will be improved by the fact that he has plenty of money in his pockets. He is looking for a sophisticated woman, somebody uninhibited sexually. Muhlbach admits that what he wants is a companion as unlike himself as possible. With his children Donna and Otto safely occupied and Mrs. Grunthe prepared to mount guard over the home, Muhlbach takes the first step on his descent into the underworld by taking a subway ride to Manhattan.

Muhlbach is convinced that the type of woman for whom he is looking is not that represented by Eula Cunningham, who had called while he was in the shower. Eula confesses to thirty-two but reminds him of thirty-eight, and Muhlbach finds her too ordinary and domestic to tempt him. Getting off the subway, he thinks that he sees the profile of Blanche Baron, an elegant redhead whose husband has killed himself. The sight of her sparks his imagination, so Muhlbach telephones her apartment. The fact that a man answers the phone discomfits him a bit, but it also encourages him in his quest. If Blanche Baron can find a new companion, so can Karl Muhlbach. It is clear, however, that he has no strategy in mind to accomplish this purpose. Muhlbach is carried along the street by the crowd and ends up in a bar on Lexington Avenue that he has not visited for nearly a year. There he is eyed by a Hollywood actress whose name he cannot quite remember, but he recognizes that she has no real interest in him. Her glance suggests that he must content himself with somebody ordinary and unimaginative, such as Eula Cunningham.

Stung by this rejection, Muhlbach takes a bus to Washington Square to try his luck among the bohemians of Greenwich Village. He literally bumps into a teenage girl named Rouge, who takes him to a coffee shop called the Queen's Bishop. Both confused and attracted by her language, a mixture of French and contemporary English slang, Muhlbach accepts Rouge's challenge to play chess. He recognizes too late that she wants to win the game. He initially thinks that the hamster nibbling his trouser cuff is Rouge's foot expressing sexual interest. He takes the appearance of her friends Quinet and Meatbowl as a sign of acceptance. The shop manager brings four bowls of soup, and Muhlbach takes this as an indication that he has fit in at the Queen's Bishop—until the manager makes it clear that he is expected to pay for all the food. Muhlbach concludes that he is paying for intruding into a place where he does not belong. A passage from Saint Augustine's *Confessions* comes to his mind. It discusses serving one's fellows, seeing them as pilgrims like oneself, in order to live in God's sight.

Outside the coffee shop, Muhlbach feels a renewed sense of sexual deprivation, and it seems to him a kind of illness. "Yet the cure is absurdly simple," he thinks: "The body of a woman, that is all." Muhlbach takes a taxi to the Club Sahara, where exotic dancers with names such as Nila, Lisa, and Riva perform for patrons in need of fantasy. He finds these performers, especially Nila, attractive; they appeal to his imagination as much as to his sexual appetite. As time passes and he continues to drink, their attraction diminishes, so Muhlbach leaves the Club Sahara, meeting on the street his old college roommate, Puig, a career navy officer out on the prowl for a woman.

Puig does not have scruples about his behavior, nor does he worry about his dignity. As a result, when Muhlbach and he go to another bar, Puig finds a woman named Gertie who, despite her drunken claim that all men want is sex, leaves the bar with him. Muhlbach admits to himself that he would have shared her bed if he had been asked, and he recognizes how far toward Hell he has descended during this evening's journey. The driver of the taxi Muhlbach finds outside this bar, looking "like a messenger of God," takes him back uptown toward Times Square. Muhlbach recalls another passage from Saint Augustine, this one about the imperfectness of perception through the flesh, and finds its truth confirmed by the fact that his wallet is missing. Only by reassuming his identity as an insurance company executive and insisting that the desk clerk at the Tyler Plaza awaken the manager to authorize cashing a check does Muhlbach begin the upward journey back toward the world that he normally inhabits.

His night in the hotel is a painful one. Resolving to drown his lust in alcohol, Muhlbach goes to the cocktail lounge and makes a pass at a waitress named Carmen. His attempt to restore pride and self-confidence leads to a potentially violent confrontation with her boyfriend Porfirio, and Muhlbach recognizes, in Saint Augustine's words, that he has exceeded the limits of his own nature. The next morning, he sees Rouge and her companions Quinet and Meatbowl outside a bookstore across the street from the Tyler Plaza, and he hurries toward her, in a final attempt to make a connection with some woman, only to have a pigeon relieve itself on his hat. Rouge and her two friends laugh hysterically, and Muhlbach's illusions about himself come to an end.

*Themes and Meanings*

The pigeon, referred to in the title of the story, makes a final satiric comment on the self-deceiving romanticism of Muhlbach. His need for companionship, both physical and emotional, is so great that he finds the potential for passion in the most unlikely situations. Muhlbach admits that he is immature, even adolescent, in terms of his sexual fantasies. He is also unrealistic in his expectation that sophisticated women would find him attractive. References to his balding head, diffident manner, and awkwardness while making conversation suggest that Evan S. Connell, Jr., intends Muhlbach to appear like the title character of T. S. Eliot's "The Love Song of J. Alfred Prufrock."

The central thematic point of "Saint Augustine's Pigeon" arises from the juxtaposition of Muhlbach's conscious descent into the hell of New York City's nightlife and his unintentional ascent from this dark world by the assistance of Saint Augustine's *Confessions*. The satire to which Connell subjects Muhlbach depends on awareness of the aptness of the passages he quotes from the *Confessions*, and it further depends on recognition that Muhlbach misreads, at times deliberately, Saint Augustine's meaning. The confusion of body and soul that he experiences leads him to find justification in the *Confessions* for a conscious choice of sin, and it is only through the agency of the saint's pigeon that Muhlbach attains a truer insight. "I have spent one whole night attempting to distort the truth which was born in me," he concludes; "now I have learned."

The truth Muhlbach recognizes may be something as simple as the necessity of being true to one's own nature. Muhlbach, from the very start of the story, is an unlikely actor in the drama he imagines for himself. Recognition of the fact that he may have to content himself with Eula Cunningham would come hard, but it would confirm his acceptance of the truth conveyed by the pigeon's action. The message from Saint Augustine may also have something to do with Muhlbach's need to accept the loss of his wife, Joyce, whose illness and eventual death are the subject of an earlier story entitled "Arcturus," published in Connell's *The Anatomy Lesson and Other Stories* (1957).

Connell also treats Muhlbach as a character in two stories called "The Mountains of Guatemala" and "Otto and the Magi," both reprinted with "Saint Augustine's Pigeon" in *At the Crossroads* (1965), and in the novels *The Connoisseur* (1974) and *Double Honeymoon* (1976).

*Style and Technique*

The chief stylistic device at work is Connell's use, as the major structural pattern, of a variation on the descent into Hell common in epic literature. The journey takes place without the formal guide characteristic of some of the epic models, but Muhlbach's frequent quotations from the *Confessions* serve to cast Saint Augustine in that role. It is appropriate, therefore, in the light of his guide's long service in Africa, that Muhlbach goes to Club Sahara. It also makes sense that Rouge's name evokes the fires of Hell, that the taxi driver taking him away from Greenwich Village looks like an angelic messenger, and that the bird that brings the message of truth to Muhlbach is a pigeon or dove. Connell's details allow for a fairly thorough allegorical reading.

Nevertheless, as the limited third-person narrator makes clear, it is Muhlbach who sees the trip into New York City in these terms. He is the one, not Connell or the narrator, making these associations, for the journey occurs as much in his consciousness as in the actual city. As a result, the conclusions that Muhlbach reaches about himself at the end of the story seem to develop out of his personality and the situation rather than being imposed on him by the narrator or the author.

*Robert C. Petersen*

# SAINT MARIE

*Author:* Louise Erdrich (1954-    )
*Type of plot:* Wit and humor
*Time of plot:* 1934
*Locale:* North Dakota
*First published:* 1984

> *Principal characters:*
> MARIE LAZARRE, the narrator and protagonist, about fourteen
> years old at the time of the story
> SISTER LEOPOLDA, a demented nun, Marie's mentor and foe

## The Story

Marie Lazarre is reliving the day that she tried to join the nuns in the Convent of the Sacred Heart. Walking to the door, she considers her motives: to be respected, even revered, by the nuns, who look down on her because she is from the reservation (even though she does not "have that much Indian blood"), and to get away from "the bush" and into town. She also remembers the day Sister Leopolda, hearing the "Dark One" in the coat closet, hurled a long hooked pole through the closet door, then made the terrified Marie stand in the dark closet because the girl had smiled.

Sister Leopolda shows Marie in by the back door, then takes her to the larder and lets the girl see the rich food reserved for the priest. She feeds Marie goat cheese and talks to her while they mix and knead bread. Marie challenges the nun, asserting that she will inherit her keys to the larder, and Leopolda says that she can see the devil in Marie's soul. When a cup rolls under the stove, Leopolda makes Marie reach under with her arm rather than the poker to retrieve it. As the girl lies on the floor, the nun places her foot on Marie's neck, pouring boiling water on her back and shoulders to warm her heart with devotion.

As Marie eats cold mush, waits for the bread to rise, and listens to the nuns eating their sausage, she has a vision: She has been transformed into gold, her breasts tipped with diamonds, and she walks through panes of glass that Leopolda must swallow. Two French nuns enter the kitchen, ask if Marie belongs to Leopolda, and compliment the girl on her docility; they help rake coals into the oven. While the bread bakes, Leopolda takes Marie to her room and puts salve on the girl's back; Marie sees her vision again and tells Leopolda that it is the nun who is caught by the Dark One. When they return to the kitchen, Leopolda, fork and poker in hand, orders Marie to help take the bread out of the oven. When the nun opens the oven door, Marie tries to kick her into the hot oven, but the nun's outstretched poker causes her to rebound out. She turns and impales Marie's hand on the fork, then knocks her out with the poker.

About half an hour later, Marie awakens, lying on clean sheets on a couch. All the nuns, including Sister Leopolda, are kneeling in attitudes of reverence around her.

Marie lifts her bloody, bandaged hand and calls Leopolda to her in the voice of a saint. Leopolda says that she explained to the nuns that Marie had received the stigmata and then fainted. Marie laughs, then blesses Leopolda. However, seeing the emptiness and hunger for love underlying the nun's depravity, she cannot relish her triumph.

### Themes and Meanings

"Saint Marie," the second in the cycle of fourteen linked stories that make up Louise Erdrich's novel *Love Medicine* (1985), centers on the complex relations between Indians and non-Indians, a theme that runs throughout the book. Marie in this story and the next, "Wild Geese" (which takes place on the same day, as Marie leaves the convent), is a tough, intelligent, willful daughter of adversity. The nuns look down on her as "Indian," whereas her future husband, Nector Kashpaw, regards her as merely a "skinny white girl" from a family of drunken horse thieves. She is truly an orphan.

Marie Lazarre is engaged in an archetypal quest for a mother. Seeking a better home than that of her own impoverished family, she enters the convent as the protégé (though really, it is suggested, the slave) of Sister Leopolda. As if in a fairy tale, Sister Leopolda turns out to be a wicked stepmother: Like Cinderella, Marie must dress poorly (not like the other sisters), sleep behind the stove, and eat meager and coarse food. Worse yet, Sister Leopolda physically mistreats the girl, and when Marie attempts to thrust her tormentor into the oven, the witch rebounds and stabs Marie.

The central conflict resembles a legendary joust: Leopolda sees herself as fighting the devil for control of the girl's soul and insurance of her salvation, while Marie perceives that to be thus controlled is to perish. The contest is imaged in parodies of chivalric legend, first Leopolda's lance hurled at the devil in the closet, then hand-to-hand fencing with poker and fork—albeit both weapons are in Leopolda's hands, while Marie's hand triumphs through a wound. This wound gives the girl her final, bittersweet, triumph: Even as she relishes the comedy of Christian forgiveness that signifies her supposed saintliness, she recognizes in Leopolda the voracious hunger for love that makes the nun a fellow human rather than solely a devilish adversary.

Marie's battle with Sister Leopolda also encapsulates the inherent absurdity of assimilationist doctrines: the attempt to "kill the Indian in order to save the person." The contradictory aims of Christian colonizers have been to maintain the lowly status of the colonized peoples while claiming to elevate them as "brothers in Christ." It may be no accident that Sister Leopolda is named for the Belgian king who presided over one of the most oppressive colonial regime in Africa.

### Style and Technique

Marie Lazarre's narration is down-to-earth, laden with pungent metaphor and psychologically acute. In a manner reminiscent of Huckleberry Finn, she moves between the language of the unlettered country girl ("They don't want no holy witness to their fall") and the astuteness of the clinician: "Veils of love which was only hate petrified by longing—that was me." Both statements epitomize the story's multiple levels of meaning. The drunkards do not want the nuns to see them literally falling down outside the bar, nor, thinks Marie, do they want witnesses to their "fall from grace." The veils remind the reader of the nun's veil to which Marie aspires (to hide her origins?), but the veils are really stone, that frozen immobility of hate and longing that barricades and conceals the vulnerable and misused little girl.

Christian themes and allusions enrich the story. Sister Leopolda's hooks, first on the long oak window-opening pole and then on the poker, recall two biblical hooks: the shepherd's crook, adopted as a symbol of bishops' guidance and authority, and fishhooks, reminiscent of the New Testament passage in which the apostles are to become "fishers of men" and "catch" souls for Heaven. Marie compares herself in her naïve faith to a fish that has taken bait, and at the end of the story she squirms like a gaffed fish in her recognition of Sister Leopolda's pathetic hunger for love.

This comparison is one of many references to food and eating throughout the story. Further paralleling the comparison of fish's bait to the "lure" of faith is Marie's allusion to Indians who had eaten the smallpox-infected hat of a Jesuit; instead of receiving what they thought was healing power, they consumed infection. (There are many accounts of the "white man's gift" of smallpox; sometimes trade blankets have been deliberately infected, sometimes a box is the receptacle, and so on.) In "Saint Marie," the image is a central metaphor for relations between Sister Leopolda's Christianity and the powerless children she teaches. In a parody of the Sacrament of Holy Communion, which to believers imparts life and healing, the Indians swallow disease; Leopolda fasts herself gaunt but is herself consumed by madness, which Marie interprets as the devil possessing her.

Although Marie's and Leopolda's job ("the Lord's work," Leopolda says) is baking bread, Marie does not eat bread in any communion with the nuns; rather, the nun feeds the girl first stolen goat cheese (recalling the reference to Judgment Day and separation of the sheep from goats) and then cold mush. Marie's initiation into the Christian life of the convent also includes a blasphemous "baptism," as Sister Leopolda first pours scalding water over the girl and then rubs her back with salve. Marie's eventual triumph also begins with an image of eating, when she envisions Leopolda following her, swallowing the glass she walks through.

In addition to references to the Sacraments, traditional Christian iconography and familiar superstitious practices appear in the story. When Leopolda places her foot on Marie's neck, she is imitating a popular representation of the Virgin Mary in which the Madonna is shown to be standing with her foot on the neck of a serpent representing Satan. Related to this powerful Madonna is the woman clothed with the sun described in the book of Revelation, which pious art frequently identifies with the Virgin Mary, and which resembles Marie's vision of herself as transfigured in gold and diamonds. Finally, there is the stigmata: the belief that the bodies of certain holy individuals spontaneously reproduce the wounds of Christ. Marie, seeing that Sister Leopolda has used the appearance of stigmata to avoid having to admit that she stabbed the girl's hand, ironically colludes with Leopolda in deceiving the naïve nuns.

*Helen Jaskoski*

# SAINTS

*Author:* Denise Chávez (1948-      )
*Type of plot:* Sketch
*Time of plot:* The late twentieth century
*Locale:* United States
*First published:* 1992

> *Principal characters:*
> SOVEIDA, the narrator, who reminisces about her Catholic upbringing
> MAMÁ LUPITA, her grandmother, who urges her to become a nun

## The Story

Soveida is a young woman who has always identified with saints. She expounds on a list of the saints with whom she most identified when she was a girl in a Catholic school. Figuring large on her list are "the passive lay-down-their-life-and-die-rather-than-screw virgins." For example, she finds the story of Saint María Goretti especially compelling. María Goretti was a little girl who was raped and murdered; her story, the narrator notes, was the introduction to passion to the children at her school.

The narrator lists other saints of all shapes, sizes, and moods. There is Saint Sebastian, who introduced the girl to male beauty. There is Saint Theresa of Lisieux, another child saint, who provides the narrator with a sense of calmness and simplicity of spirit that the more desperate adult saints, who were more acquainted with sin, cannot. There also are saints who help people with lost causes or lost shoes.

Soveida also recalls a saint particular to her culture. A Mexican American, she describes with tender and merciless irony the position of San Martin de Porres in the household. This saint was the first African American man of whom she was ever aware. A saint of the outcast, the poor, and the marginalized, he is a favorite among Mexican Americans. The family's little old ladies keep his image in their bedrooms, where no men have visited for more than thirty years. On the other hand, it would be a scandal if a daughter should decide to marry an African American man.

There are practical saints who are summoned and dismissed in a sentence or two. San Isidrio helps farmers. Saint Christopher helps travelers. Saint Joseph, however, introduces a major theme of the story: the varieties of good-for-nothing men there are in the world, and the sufferings they put women through. People pray to Saint Joseph, Jesus's surrogate father, with their male-related problems. The words used to describe these male-related problems, not to mention the knowledge and the understanding of the problems themselves, are not those of the girl Soveida. The adult Soveida uses them with facility, however, and reveals that the source of her education was her grandmother, Mamá Lupita. Mamá Lupita's influence is strong, as is the influence of sexuality. Mamá Lupita seeks to save Soveida from men.

As a girl, Soveida uncritically accepts the parade of women saints who gladly let their breasts be torn off, their eyes plucked out, or their limbs cut off, rather than surrender to lust. Prayers, the adult Soveida narrates, rolled off the tongue of her younger self. The adult Soveida also notes how Saint Claire, a female equal of healthy, happy Saint Francis, is rarely mentioned. Saint Joan remains too aggressive even for the adult Soveida.

Mamá Lupita, who wants Soveida to become a nun, tells her of the horrible and incorrigible behavior of men—of their stink, of how, like monkeys, they cannot be trained in civilized behavior, of the little hairs they leave all over the bathtub, of their abysmal ignorance. She tells Soveida that she did not want to become a nun, but rather a priest. She hopes that someday women may become priests. Mamá Lupita points out how a friend of Soveida's mother, who became a nun, is happy and has no wrinkles on her face. Soveida's mother, on the other hand, has a face full of wrinkles because of the sexual infidelity of her husband, Soveida's father, who cannot keep "the little thing" where it belongs. Mamá Lupita points out that Soveida likes to read; as a nun, she would be able to read and not be bothered by a smelly man who wants sex. Mamá Lupita spins her arguments to the little girl in a hilarious mixture of apt metaphor, crude detail, and the occasional perfectly chosen Spanish word.

After Soveida decides to become a nun Mamá Lupita urges her to join an order as soon as possible. When Soveida starts school, however, she sees Manny Ordóñez and falls in love. Magdalene, the narrator points out, is the saint of "fallen women . . . something I imagined as a child I would never become."

*Themes and Meanings*

"Saints" is about the ironies of remembering and about affirming one's past. Rather than reject the teachings that she received from her religion and her grandmother, Soveida recalls them within the ironic context of her adult experience. She still identifies with saints. In accepting herself, Soveida accepts what has shaped her.

Another theme of the story—which is as overstated as Soveida's acceptance is understated—is sex. "Saints" is the story of one part of the education of a girl in the matters of sex and sex roles. Soveida learns from her grandmother that women should be allowed to be priests and that men are beastly. Her grandmother also supports Soveida's reading. In this sense, Soveida's grandmother is a feminist. She even argues that the prayers of nuns, more powerful than those of men, are "little by little . . . making God a nicer man." Mamá Lupita's arguments against priests—who, in her opinion, are all either homosexuals or womanizers—against Soveida's own father, and against men in general are perhaps inappropriate for the ears of a child. On the other hand, they provide a balance, especially in their realistic detail, to the messages about sex that Soveida is receiving at her Roman Catholic school. Soveida reads many hagiographies of female saints who would rather suffer terrible torture than lose their virginity. Presumably, she does not read of ordinary desire, or of women who exercise their sexuality without guilt or punishment; such concepts seem alien to her world.

Along with sex come sex roles. Men, Mamá Lupita tells Soveida, are typically born with one of three invisible signs on their foreheads: priest, married man, or jerk. Women, Soveida surmises, are also marked at birth, as woman, wife, mother, or martyr. Tellingly, men are not marked with the word "man." Mamá Lupita's being a woman kept her out of the priesthood; being born a man, however, does not assign one to a category. A woman may also become fallen, Soveida learns. She has as examples Saint Mary Magdalene and the shameless whores whose company her father seeks, her grandmother says. The story implies, however, that Soveida, as an adult, has become neither mother, martyr, saint, nun, nor fallen woman. Soveida, one may infer, has transcended the limitations of her education.

Finally, "Saints" is about saints. The narrator describes a variety of saints and their significance to her. Saints clearly play an important role in Soveida's mental life, including her adult life. Soveida also tells that Saint Dymphna, the saint of the mentally ill, is a particular favorite, but does not explain what, if any, experience she has had with mental illness or the mentally ill. She often describes saints in personal terms, such as "popular," "desperate," "aggressive," "dependable," and "pal." This familiarity is not without irony. Saints are important in Soveida's life, but her regard for them lacks the reverence, and has the humor, of one who no longer accepts the teachings of church and family with uncritical naïveté.

*Style and Technique*

"Saints" is told in the first person, and significant portions of it are direct quotations from Mamá Lupita. A critical element of the story's style and technique, therefore, is the use of voice. Every person, and every character in a story, has a way of speaking that tells a great deal about that person's background, habits of mind, education, and emotional state. Indeed, the way one speaks is perhaps what tells most about a person. A person's voice also tells more than what a person wishes to tell. For example, when Mamá Lupita denounces men, she does so with great verbal fluency and an eye for ugly detail. When she says that she wanted to be a priest herself, the reader can infer more. Clearly, she is an intelligent person who deeply resents the roles of housewife, mother, and martyr that, being a woman, she was obliged to accept.

Much of the story's humor comes from the narrator's or Mamá Lupita's choice of words. For example, the prim, grim, and churchy seriousness of the story of Saint María Goretti is undercut with Soveida's ironic wording. The man who raped the saint, for example, found the beginnings of his downfall reveling lasciviously in pictures of naked women he hid under his bed. Soveida clearly knows of the pleasures of purple prose; she has reveled in it since childhood.

*Eric Howard*

# SAM THE CAT

*Author:* Matthew Klam (1964-      )
*Type of plot:* Realism
*Time of plot:* The 1990's
*Locale:* An American city on the East Coast
*First published:* 2000

> *Principal characters:*
> SAM BEARDSON, the narrator, an advertising executive
> LOUISE, his girlfriend
> JOHN DRAKE, a housepainter and the lead singer in a band

*The Story*

"Sam the Cat," a story about a man's inability to understand why he is attracted to a man he sees at a party, begins with the narrator's extended meditation on his past girlfriends and his attitudes about love and sex. Sam Beardson has had girlfriends ever since he was in the second grade and will probably have one until he dies. He particularly recalls one girlfriend, Annie, a model wearing a leather motorcycle coat, whose picture he still has above his desk. He says that he would do anything to get her back and that he needs her to want him again. However, he knows that if she were to come back, he would not want to see her or listen to her voice on the telephone.

Sam has always wanted real love, loves being in love, and is in love with the love drug. His present girlfriend, Louise, is the only person he has ever truly loved. The real problem, he says, is that he loves women in general. He knows that if you give women a normal degree of fidelity, they will let you do whatever you want to them. He says if he were a girl he would have sex with ten guys a day, but then he says he would never want to be a girl, for they have the worst deal in history.

After this rambling five-page monologue about love and girlfriends, Sam describes going to a party with Louise and seeing a tall, skinny girl at the bar with sharp hipbones and an athlete's bottom. However, when he goes over to have a chat with her, he discovers that what he thought was a woman is really a man. Instead of being put off by this discovery, Sam becomes more and more obsessed with the man. He says that, in his mind, the man, whose name is John Drake, is sort of a woman. He does not understand his feelings, wondering if he went to sleep one night and woke up the next morning to find himself a homosexual.

Later at a cowboy bar, Sam sees the man again, singing for a band. Sam gets drunk with John and the band and wakes up the next morning hung over. He buys some flowers and takes them to John to apologize for his behavior, telling him that his ad agency needs a country band for an advertising campaign they are doing. He then goes to a men's boutique and buys new clothes as well as some hair gel and some cream to tone his skin. He puts on the cream, which makes him look as if he has a tan, and a lip mois-turizer that makes his lips a deeper red.

When Louise tells Sam he looks like Sinbad, Sam changes his clothes,. He is still wearing the lip gloss and the tanning cream when he goes to see John; however, he runs away before he meets him. When Sam calls John and asks him to come over for dinner, John wants to know if he is gay. Although Sam says he is not, John hangs up on him. The story ends with Sam wondering what all this has meant.

*Themes and Meanings*

"Sam the Cat" bears some similarity to Thomas Mann's classic novella *Der Tod in Venedig* (1912; *Death in Venice*, 1925). In Mann's story, the central figure Aschen-bach falls in love with a young boy named Tadzio and puts on makeup, just as Sam does. Neither story, however, is really about homosexuality. *Death in Venice* is about a man torn between the cold purity of artwork and the warm decaying flesh of a human body. "Sam the Cat" is about a man who becomes fixated on a man he initially thinks is a woman and who thus becomes a sort of woman for him. Mann's story is about love at its most paradoxically profound, whereas Matthew Klam's story is about de-sire as an obsession that human beings cannot control.

The most important theme in "Sam the Cat" centers on the relationship between Sam's attitude toward women and his obsession with John. Although Sam says he has always wanted real love, his definition of real love has nothing to do with commitment and everything to do with desire and the illusion of romance. He says he wants cut flowers, the finest champagne, and amazing parties with a see-through dance floor. What first attracted him to his former girlfriend Annie was her gorgeous long black hair; he was disillusioned to find out that the hair was a wig and that she was bald from a disease.

Sam says he loves women and that he loves being in love, even when he does not know with whom he is in love. However, at no time does he indicate that he likes a par-ticular woman for her individual self. When he discovers that the woman with the high, tight athlete's bottom at the bar is really a man, he actually has the perfect love object for his narcissistic self. Because Sam likes himself better than any woman he has ever met, his attraction to John, a man like himself, is inevitable, that is, as long as he does not define that attraction as homosexual. When Sam says that in his mind John was sort of a woman, he asks, "What do I want to say here?" What he wants to say is that John has none of the characteristics of women that Sam dislikes and all the characteristics of himself that he does like. Thus, it is inevitable that the story would end with Sam saying that he should marry himself and sail around the world with his cat as the mascot, for maybe out on the sea, he would come across something that he could understand.

*Style and Technique*

Voice is the key element in this story. Told in the first person, it is a classic dramatic monologue, for Sam reveals who he actually is even though he is not self-aware. The tone of the story is flip and brittle, rambling and self-oblivious, often going for the laugh with clever queries about his desire for love. For example, at one point, he asks if loyalty and trust are "Under a rock? Inside a chocolate-chip cookie?" Also, when he describes his fascination and sense of possession about his girlfriend's bottom, saying "That's mine. It's beautiful," he then asks what a woman's bottom can actually do for you: "Hide you from the police? Call up your boss when you don't feel well?"

Sam constantly moves back and forth between his scornful comments about women, such as saying he likes to see them bark for him, to self-deprecating remarks about himself, wondering why girls ever go out with him. When he feels sexually aroused by thoughts of John, he feels queasy with the weirdness of it and calls himself bad and naughty, a dirty kitty-cat.

The reader is never quite sure whether to be scornful of Sam's superficiality or to be sympathetic with his self-deprecation. The center of this reader indecision is, of course, Sam's feelings about John. On one hand, his attraction to John seems an obvious implication of his ambiguous feelings about women, for he is narcissistically drawn to someone who does not pose a threat to him. On the other hand, he seems genuinely concerned with understanding the meaning of this attraction. When he wears tanning cream and lip gloss, he insists it is not a sex thing, that rather it is a third thing he is trying to describe, perhaps a spiritual thing. This is as close as Sam comes to an understanding or identification with the idealism of Aschenbach in Mann's classic novella.

When Sam calls John for the last time and John asks if he is gay, Sam insists that he did not think of sex with him but just wants to hang around with him, the two of them sitting together, getting a video or something. He says, "I don't have to explain this. It's obvious how I felt." The problem is that it is not so obvious how Sam feels. He does not want a male lover nor simply a buddy but rather some combination of the two. The rambling, puzzled voice of Sam is what makes the story real and believable. It is not clear, nor is it important, whether Sam understands how to articulate the feelings he has for John. The story ends with the same tone of puzzlement that has persisted throughout, a tone that makes "Sam the Cat" a genuine exploration about a basic human mystery.

*Charles E. May*

# SAME PLACE, SAME THINGS

*Author:* Tim Gautreaux (1947-     )
*Type of plot:* Psychological
*Time of plot:* The 1930's
*Locale:* A farm in Louisiana
*First published:* 1991

> *Principal characters:*
> HARRY LINTEL, a traveling pump repairman and widower
> ADA, a recently widowed farmer's wife

## The Story

"Same Place, Same Things" is told in the third-person limited point of view from the perspective of traveling pump-and-well-repairman Harry Lintel. Harry first encounters Ada on her small farm outside a small town in Louisiana. Despite Harry's uneasiness with her, Ada sees Harry as her salvation from a life she finds dull and unsatisfactory. When Harry realizes how desperate for change Ada really is and how far she has gone in her quest to move on, he understands that he has reached a certain contentment in his own life, one that she will never know.

The story opens with Harry arriving at the farm of Ada and her husband. Harry is a pump repairman who can fix almost anything mechanical. A forty-four-year-old widower from Missouri, he has spent the last few years following droughts around the South as the lack of groundwater in farming communities causes electric well pumps to break with the strain and thus creates a need for his services. On meeting Ada, he is immediately struck by her need to engage him in conversation and her interest in his transient lifestyle. When Harry finally checks the pump, he finds Ada's husband lying sprawled next to the well, dead. He has apparently electrocuted himself while working on the pump. Uneasy with the situation, Harry asks Ada's neighbor to notify her of her husband's death while he calls the sheriff. Harry is surprised that Ada is not particularly grief-stricken by the news, but by the end of the day he is working on pumps at other farms.

The next day, Ada locates Harry working on a pump at a neighboring farm and brings him a lunch containing sandwiches. Conscious of the impropriety of being seen eating and fraternizing with a new widow whose husband has died of what seems to be a freak accident, he quickly finishes the lunch and hurries away. Ada is not easily discouraged and brings him a bottle of strawberry wine that evening while he is dining at the motel café. She leaves him with a kiss that night, and he begins to think about taking her with him on his travels until he falls asleep thinking about his days as a young husband and father. Ada again finds Harry as he works on a farmer's pump the next day, and over a glass of lemonade, she tells him that this is the third time she has been widowed; she tells him she is sick of seeing the same place and doing the same things all her life.

Something about the death of Ada's husband has bothered Harry all along, however, and after he leaves Ada, he drives back to her house. Examining the wiring of the pump, he realizes that the electricity to it could be switched on or off from inside the house. Harry recognizes what he has suspected all along: Ada has killed her husband by turning on the electricity to the pump as her husband worked with the wiring.

Harry avoids Ada as he works the parish for the next ten days, until finally he awakes to a rainy morning and leaves in his truck, looking for a new place to work. Stopping for lunch, he finds that Ada has hidden under the tarpaulin in back and means to travel with him. Harry tells her that he knows she has killed her husband and that she cannot come with him. Ada waits for Harry to turn his back and attacks him with one of his own wrenches. She steals his truck and equipment while he lies dazed in the parking lot. He comes to his senses, and in a moment of clarity he knows that, unlike him, she will never find peace.

## *Themes and Meanings*

Much of the meaning in "Same Place, Same Things" is revealed in the central metaphor of the story: Pumps destroy themselves trying to draw water out of wells that are going dry because of the severe drought. The drought in the story is not only a physical case of there not being enough water available for farmers: As Ada makes clear to Harry, she feels that her life has gone dry and that she is burning herself out like an exhausted pump engine as she tries to dredge a life worth living from the dry soil of her married existence. Isolated, lonely, frustrated, and bitter, Ada reminds the reader initially of writer John Steinbeck's farmwife protagonist Elisa Allen in his often-anthologized short story "The Chrysanthemums" (1938). Ada seems to feel that Harry, as a man who can fix pumps and wells gone dry, is in effect a rainmaker able to bring life-giving water to the parched earth. As such, he should be able to restore meaning and worth to her fruitless life as well. Again like Steinbeck's Elisa, Ada seems interested in Harry only because he is a man who travels and goes places. At no point is there any indication that she is interested in whoever or whatever he might actually be as a man. After all, she meets him on the day of her husband's death and within two days implies to him that she is interested in leaving with him.

When Ada visits Harry in the field and in the café, she brings him either food or drink each time, including sandwiches (which he finds rather dry), strawberry wine, and lemonade. In a sense, she is Eve trapped in a desolate Eden, desperate to escape, tempting Harry to partake of forbidden fruit. Harry is indeed tempted at first, but when Ada tells him that she has buried three husbands, he begins to comprehend that she will always seek out a bleak and miserable life despite herself.

When the reader first understands that Harry is a widower who follows droughts around the southeast, living in motor courts and motels, it seems as though his life must also be sad and lonely, as deserted and despairing in its way as Ada's. Although Harry's life is a transient quiet one, however, he is a bit of an existentialist. He lives each day for the small and simple joys the day itself brings, not expecting too much and taking pleasure in jobs well done and the freedom of the open road. The loss of his wife, an early tragedy that has shaped his life, has taught him that although life may seem as barren and austere as a desert, one can still find life-giving water if one knows how to look.

## Style and Technique

In his first book of short fiction, *Same Place, Same Things* (1996), Tim Gautreaux distinguished himself from other southern writers in a number of ways. His stories, including "Same Place, Same Things," are not concerned with members of the southern gentility or aristocracy, nor are they populated by the grotesques that appear in fiction by southern writers such as Flannery O'Connor and Erskine Caldwell. His stories instead focus on realistic characters dealing with realistic problems; even though Ada is a murderer (with possibly more than one victim), her needs and wishes are human and recognizable, as is Harry's basic decency.

"Same Place, Same Things" also demonstrates Gautreaux's sure hand with dialogue. Harry and Ada become living and breathing characters through their laconic and sparse spoken language; Gautreaux perfectly captures the idiom and vernacular of the deep South and the farm. The economical dialogue serves as a counterbalance to the poetic descriptions of the drought-ravaged Louisiana landscape.

In addition to the drought itself serving as a metaphor for lives barren and desolate, the pumps that Harry services serve as symbols for people's hope that somehow life will provide a change for the better. Although Harry does not become the willing accomplice to Ada's release from a life of drudgery, his affinity with machines and ability to fix any pump is still worthy of consideration. Harry is able to take a seemingly broken machine and repair it so that it may continue on indefinitely, just as he has taken the presumably shattered remnants of his past and forged a new life. Had Ada but learned to repair rather than destroy, perhaps she too would find that her life could be salvaged.

*Scott Yarbrough*

# SANATORIUM UNDER THE SIGN OF THE HOURGLASS

*Author:* Bruno Schulz (1892-1942)
*Type of plot:* Fantasy
*Time of plot:* 1937
*Locale:* A mythical town, suggestive of the narrator's small Polish hometown
*First published:* "Sanatorium pod klepsydrą," 1937 (English translation, 1978)

> *Principal characters:*
> JOSEPH, the narrator, a young man living in a dreamworld
> FATHER, Joseph's deceased father, who is kept alive in the
> dreamworld Sanatorium
> DR. GOTARD, the head of the Sanatorium

*The Story*

Joseph arrives by train in a small, strangely dark town to visit his father, who is staying at a hotel called the Sanatorium. From the beginning, however, the reality of everything is in question. The physical world itself is shaky, shifting, and fluid. The Sanatorium is run by Dr. Gotard, a difficult man to find. The only other visible member of the staff is a chambermaid, a hardly less elusive figure.

Joseph anxiously inquires whether his father is still alive. Dr. Gotard replies that from a certain perspective, his father is dead, and "This cannot be entirely remedied. That death throws a certain shadow on his existence here." Nevertheless, in the Sanatorium, they have put back the clock. "Here your father's death, the death that has already struck him in your country, has not occurred yet."

Guests of the Sanatorium sleep most of the time. No one suggests to them that they are, so to speak, dead. Time itself is confused by the perpetual darkness, in which it is difficult to distinguish between night and day. Thus the guests are kept, in a certain sense, alive. Dr. Gotard invites Joseph to stay in Father's room. There is only one bed in it, and Father is fast asleep, filling the room with "layers of snoring." Joseph climbs in with him and falls asleep too. In the morning, he wakes to see Father sitting up, drinking tea, and making plans for the day.

Joseph's father leaves briskly, telling Joseph to drop by later at a store that the old man has just opened in town. Left on his own, Joseph explores the town, struck by its remarkable resemblance to his own native city. He easily finds his father's new dry-goods shop. Already, a parcel has been delivered to Joseph there (as his father informs him disapprovingly). Instead of the pornographic book that Joseph had expected, a folding telescope has been substituted. As Joseph gazes through the telescope, he has the sensation of sitting in a limousine. The slight touch of a lever causes the now-enormous black telescope-limousine, with Joseph seated in it, to roll out the door. Everyone watches disapprovingly.

Joseph stays in the Sanatorium, losing all sense of time. Mysteriously, his mother appears once but cannot speak and remains out of reach. Living conditions steadily deteriorate. The room is never cleaned. The other guests and the staff seem to have left. Food is to be had only in town.

The very landscape grows darker, and the country is overrun by packs of dogs. At the Sanatorium itself, one enormous, vicious dog is kept on a chain.

One day war breaks out, to universal consternation. "A war not preceded by diplomatic activity? A war amid blissful peace?" The enemy is greeted by discontented townspeople who now come out in the open to terrorize their neighbors. "We noticed, in fact, a group of these activists, in black civilian clothing with white straps across their breasts, advancing in silence, their guns at the ready."

Joseph's father resolves to push through the mob to reach his store. He orders Joseph back to the Sanatorium. Joseph obeys him, he says, from "cowardice." When Joseph gets back to the Sanatorium, he must face the chained dog alone. He is terrified, but seeing the dog up close, he makes an astounding discovery.

> How great is the power of prejudice! How powerful the hold of fear! How blind had I been! It was not a dog, it was a man. A chained man, whom, by a simplifying metaphoric wholesale error, I had taken for a dog.

In fact, the creature actually is still a dog but in human shape. With his yellow, bony face and black beard, he might be taken for Dr. Gotard's elder brother, but he is a fanatic, "a tub-thumper, a vocal party member," and it was his passion and violence "that made him a hundred per cent dog." However, Joseph pities the dog, unchains him, and takes him back to his room in the Sanatorium. Meanwhile, he notices the glare of a fire over the town. He guesses that Father is "somewhere in the thick of a revolution or in a burning shop."

Joseph tricks the dog into staying locked in his room while he himself escapes. For a moment, he feels remorse at the danger that Father will face. Then he remembers: "Luckily, in fact, Father was no longer alive; he could not really be reached."

Leaving the dark and menacing town, Joseph boards the same train on which he came. He never leaves the train again, but rides it forever, turning into a pathetic beggar in a torn black hat.

*Themes and Meanings*

Initially, in view of the narrator's childlike personality and his tremendous dependence on his father, the story reads like a pure psychological exploration of a son's relationship to his father. The author is now an adult, but he is reaching back into childhood to recapture the essence of his feelings and need for his parent. The relationship is not one of pure mutual admiration. Father shows disapproval of the son's pornographic book order (which is magically turned into a telescope). Though the son loves his father, he ultimately does abandon him and only after the fact consoles himself with the thought that Father is, after all, dead. The son's guilt and fear at letting Father go even in death form the very foundation of the plot: The Sanatorium exists precisely in order to give dead people only a little more time to continue living.

However, the theme of a son's grief, guilt, and poor adjustment to his loss by no means exhausts the story's message. The outside world intrudes in the form of a war, "not preceded by diplomatic activity," in which discontented local people actively collaborate with the invaders. The black clothing worn by the inhabitants of this dreamworld after death acquires other than funereal significance. Those who collaborate with the enemy wear black clothing crossed with white straps. As they march through the streets carrying rifles, they flash "ironical dark looks" in which there is "a touch of superiority, a glimmer of malicious enjoyment." When this story appeared in 1937, such an image could only be a transparent and bold reference to Nazism.

More than bold, the story was prophetic. The Holocaust had not yet reached Poland in 1937, yet how uncannily Bruno Schulz describes the process of relentless circumscription, relinquishment, and slow death. Joseph's father, a dead man who has not yet died, has opened a tiny shop in this dream-ghetto (from which he will never escape). Joseph finds the old man's behavior strange, "yet what could one expect of Father, who was only half real, who lived a relative and conditional life, circumscribed by so many limitations!"

The name of the narrator, Joseph, was not chosen by chance, but is very much part of Schulz's traditions. The name harks back to the Old Testament's Joseph, the prophetic dreamer and seer.

*Style and Technique*

Schulz is a consciously symbolic writer. As he stated in another story, "Spring," "Most things are interconnected, most threads lead to the same reel." Any detail in the universe may be relevant to any puzzling question in the universe.

The most visible symbol in "Sanatorium Under the Sign of the Hourglass" is the color black. It is found everywhere: on the mysterious train, in clothing, leaves, beards, the telescope, and the eyes of the terrible dog. There is a crescendo of black, enhancing the impact of the last three scenes: the outbreak of war (the black uniforms), the unchaining of the dog-man (black eyes and beard), and Joseph's end (a beggar in a black hat). In a similar manner, other recurring images also help to unify the story's tone and structure.

Schulz also practices a technique of extended and vivid metaphor that is uniquely his, and he hints at his other craft (he was a painter and art teacher):

> I broke a twig from a roadside tree. The leaves were dark, almost black. It was a strangely charged blackness, deep and benevolent, like restful sleep. All the different shades of gray in the landscape derived from that one color. It was the color of a cloudy summer dusk in our part of the country, when the landscape has become saturated with water after a long period of rain and exudes a feeling of self-denial, a resigned and ultimate numbness that does not need the consolation of color.

*D. G. Nakeeb*

# THE SANDMAN

*Author:* E. T. A. Hoffmann (1776-1822)
*Type of plot:* Epistolary
*Time of plot:* The early nineteenth century
*Locale:* Germany
*First published:* "Der Sandmann," 1816 (English translation, 1844)

> *Principal characters:*
> NATHANAEL, a student at the University of G.
> CLARA, a distant cousin and Nathanael's fiancé
> LOTHAR, her brother
> COPPELIUS, a lawyer
> GIUSEPPE COPPOLA, a trader in barometers, eyeglasses, and
>     optical instruments
> SPALANZANI, a professor of physics
> OLIMPIA, Spalanzani's "daughter," a doll

*The Story*

In the first of the three letters that open the story, Nathanael writes Lothar, a distant cousin who lives with his sister Clara and Nathanael's mother, of the distress he has felt following the recent visit to his room by an instrument trader named Giuseppe Coppola. Nathanael is convinced that Coppola is the lawyer Coppelius, who was responsible for the death of Nathanael's father years earlier during his childhood. As a child, Nathanael believed Coppelius to be the Sandman, who, according to a nursemaid's fairy tale, threw sand into children's eyes when they did not want to go to bed, causing their eyes to spring bloodily out of their sockets. One evening Nathanael decided to investigate the Sandman's activities in his father's room and hid himself behind a curtain in his father's closet. When the Sandman entered the room and Nathanael discovered that it was Coppelius, an old lawyer who occasionally had dinner with the family and whom the children found ugly and repulsive, Nathanael was transfixed. As the two men worked on a steaming experiment, his father suddenly appeared to him to be Coppelius's satanic double. When Coppelius shouted "Eyes here, eyes here," Nathanael fell out of his hiding place onto the floor, whereupon Coppelius threatened to burn out his eyes, causing Nathanael to faint. A year or so later, during Coppelius's next visit, an explosion in the laboratory killed the father.

Nathanael has addressed the letter by mistake to his fiancé, Lothar's sister, Clara, who tries to reassure Nathanael in the story's second letter that all the horrible things he experienced existed only in his imagination and not in reality. She recommends that he forget all about Coppelius and Coppola and adds that by recognizing them as phantoms of his real self he will be free of their evil influence over him.

A somewhat more sober Nathanael tells Lothar in the third letter of his acquaintance with a new physics professor by the name of Spalanzani, who has known Coppola for years and claims that Coppola has left the city. Nathanael now doubts that Coppola and Coppelius are identical, yet insists that he cannot rid himself of the image of Coppelius's hideous bearing. He also mentions that on the way to Spalanzani's lecture he caught sight of the professor's daughter Olimpia, whom Spalanzani keeps locked in a glass cabinet behind closed curtains. Her eyes seemed to stare at him, though she appeared not to see him.

At this point, the narrator breaks in to say that he has prefaced his own narration with these three letters because he knows of no other beginning that could adequately reflect the ardent intensity of Nathanael's story. The narrator then continues with Nathanael's return home, where the coolly rational Clara again tries to dismiss Nathanael's demoniac visions as imaginary. The ill effect of Coppola's visit on Nathanael, however, is apparent to everyone. In a long, murky poem, he depicts how Coppelius was destroying their love. According to the poem, at their marriage Coppelius touched Clara's eyes, which sprang into Nathanael's chest "like bloody sparks," and then threw Nathanael into a rapidly turning circle of fire. When Clara tells him to destroy the poem, he responds by calling her a lifeless "automat" (automaton). Lothar arrives and in a heated exchange of insults challenges Nathanael to a duel, which ends, however, with apologies and a reconciliation.

Nathanael returns to G. and finds his apartment destroyed by fire. His new room is across from Professor Spalanzani's house, and he can see into the room where Olimpia remains seated motionless for hours; he is not, however, moved by her steadfast gaze toward him. Just as he is writing to Clara, Coppola appears at his door and pulls thousands of eyeglasses out of his pockets. Nathanael is overwhelmed by the flickering lenses, which seem like a thousand eyes staring at him. As Coppola lays more glasses on the table, "flaming glances" leap around and shoot "their blood-red rays into Nathanael's chest." Nathanael, however, calms down enough to persuade Coppola to remove the glasses and settles instead for a small telescope. Involuntarily he looks into Olimpia's room with the telescope. At first her eyes seem fixed and dead, but then they become more and more lively the closer he looks at them. Coppola demands his money and leaves, laughing loudly. In the next few days, Nathanael thinks only of Olimpia and sees her image everywhere except in her room, where the curtains have been closed.

Spalanzani gives a ball and concert in order to introduce his daughter to the public. Olimpia is beautifully dressed and has a wonderful figure, though her movement is a bit measured and stiff. She plays the piano with great skill and sings with a bright, though brittle, voice. Nathanael stands at the back of the room and uses his pocket telescope to see her better. He becomes inflamed with longing and yells out her name, to the consternation of those around him. When her concert ends, he races up to her to invite her to dance. Although her dancing is rather mechanical and his heated advances are met with cold and laconic responses, he falls so deeply in love with her that he is oblivious to the snickering of the young people behind his back or the end of the ball. Spalanzani is delighted with Nathanael's interest in his daughter and invites him back any time.

Nathanael now lives only for Olimpia and reads to her from his writings for hours in her room, while she sits passively staring him in the eye. Her only words are "ah, ah" and an occasional "good night, my beloved." One day Nathanael decides to go over and propose to her, but on the stairs to Spalanzani's study he hears a horrible banging, swearing, and arguing. It is the voices of Spalanzani and the dreaded Coppelius. Nathanael bursts into the room and sees Spalanzani and Coppola fighting over Olimpia's body. Coppola wrests her away, hits the professor with her, and runs off, laughing madly, with her on his shoulder. Nathanael notices that her face has no eyes, only empty sockets. Spalanzani implores Nathanael to run after Coppelius, who is stealing his best automat and ruining twenty years of work. A pair of bloody eyes lie on the floor. Spalanzani picks them up and throws them at Nathanael, who tries to strangle him but is restrained and taken to an insane asylum.

When Nathanael regains consciousness, he is in bed at home, with Clara, Lothar, and his mother standing nearby. Nathanael appears to be fully recovered from his bout of madness and is now quieter. The family is preparing to move to a new house, and Nathanael intends again to marry Clara. In town one day, the lovers decide to climb the tower of the city hall. Nathanael pulls out his telescope and by chance looks at Clara, whose eyes suddenly seem to spew fire. He leaps wildly at her and tries to kill her, but Lothar manages to get her away from Nathanael and back down to safety. Nathanael meanwhile begins racing around the gallery of the tower, screaming, "Turn, circle of fire." A crowd gathers below, and when Nathanael sees Coppelius within it, he leaps to his death. Several years later, people claim to have seen Clara and a new husband playing with their two lively young boys in front of a country house.

*Themes and Meanings*

"The Sandman," like all of E. T. A. Hoffmann's tales, deals with the unsettling disparity between the self and the external world. For Hoffmann there were three possibilities for facing the basic disharmony between internal and external reality: Like Nathanael, one may allow the inner visions and feelings to predominate, leading eventually to madness; like Clara, one may insist on the primary importance of everyday, factual reality; or, like the Romantic writer, one may accept this dualism and try to transcend it with ironic detachment.

Nathanael's early childhood experiences (the nursemaid's story of the Sandman, Coppelius's threat to his eyes, and his father's death) make him susceptible to the destructive workings of his imagination. His obsession with losing his eyes and his fear of the evil father-substitutes, Coppelius and Coppola, destroy his love for Clara and make him easy prey for Spalanzani's and Coppelius's suggestive manipulations. The pocket telescope further distorts his vision, for instead of bringing external objects nearer and into sharper focus, it only magnifies their effect on his soul.

In Olimpia he discovers a mirror of his involuntary emotional responses. His statement to a friend that "only in Olimpia's love do I find my own self again" is a telling expression of his latent narcissism. He fails to take seriously Clara's sensible advice and becomes very upset when she sharply criticizes his premonitory poem about Coppelius's destruction of their love. It is easier for him to retreat into his private world and converse with a mechanical doll than to develop an open, unselfish relationship with Clara.

Nevertheless, the narrator's and Hoffmann's sympathies lie with Nathanael, for he is the one who recognizes the deeper creative and destructive powers that are hidden behind everyday experience. Nathanael, however, fails both as a poet and as an individual because he is unable to communicate his dark and esoteric visions with the least bit of distance and objectivity. The persistent motif of eyes and seeing emphasizes all the more the tragedy of Nathanael's blindness to his own drives and desires.

*Style and Technique*

At the beginning of his tale, Hoffmann provides no stable base of objective reality with which to distinguish between Nathanael's delusions and actual events. The narrative perspective constantly shifts between impartial observation and empathetic closeness. Although the three opening letters give the tale a documentary quality, the narrator's humorous digression on his difficulties in telling the story leaves the reader in doubt as to how seriously to take Nathanael's anxious concerns. Furthermore, Clara's rational interpretation of Nathanael's stories is just as unsatisfactory an explanation of Coppelius's hold over him as Nathanael's own understanding of the childhood events.

In order to blur the boundary between appearance and reality, Hoffmann seems to want to disorient the reader. Thus, Coppola's true identity remains uncertain until the climactic fight between Spalanzani and Coppelius; Olimpia's dollhood, though hinted at, is not revealed earlier, for she is described solely from the perspective of Nathanael, for whom she is a more loving and deeply spiritual being than Clara; Coppelius's final "giant" appearance in the crowd in front of the city hall may or may not be a product of Nathanael's madness. The author and narrator play both sides of the story—the psychological and demoniac, realistic and fantastic—against each other, and in the end give neither more credence than the other.

*Peter West Nutting*

# A SANDSTONE FARMHOUSE

*Author:* John Updike (1932-    )
*Type of plot:* Psychological, autobiographical
*Time of plot:* The twentieth century
*Locale:* A farmhouse in Pennsylvania
*First published:* 1990

Principal characters:
JOEY, a man who inherits a farmhouse
HIS MOTHER

## The Story

When Joey's mother dies, Joey returns to the sandstone farmhouse built in 1812 in rural Pennsylvania in which she was born and died. Joey lived in the farmhouse from age thirteen until he graduated from high school. After he entered college, he lived mostly in New York City but returned periodically to the farmhouse to visit. His mother lived there alone during her last years, refusing to leave and, for a while, refusing to die because she felt that the farmhouse needed her. Joey, however, resented the move to the farmhouse in his early teens because he had to leave a house he loved, his friends, and the city life to which he was accustomed.

After his mother's funeral, Joey begins to empty the farmhouse in preparation for selling it. He removes all the furniture and all his mother's other possessions, many of which she had stored in the barn or left lying about the house, including stacks of canned cat food, old newspapers, and mail-order catalogues as well as collections of plastic grocery bags, string, and twine. He keeps only a few things from the time before the family moved to the farmhouse. One of Joey's former wives takes his mother's old dog. A man from the humane society traps the cats his mother fed and takes them away. Joey traps some of the mice and kills others with poison, throwing their bodies in the swamp near the house.

On Joey's final visit to clean the house, he finds a dead flying squirrel drowned in the toilet; it had apparently fallen in, desperately thirsty after ingesting rat poison. He remembers a pair of flying squirrels from the first summer he lived in the house. Later, as he lies in his bed in New York City, he feels that the house calls to him and needs him. He always had wanted to be in the center of the action, and he discovers that for him the action had really been back at the farmhouse.

## Themes and Meanings

Like many of John Updike's works, "A Sandstone Farmhouse" grew out of his own life and especially out of his relationship to a six-room sandstone farmhouse on an eighty-acre farm near Plowville, Pennsylvania. He lived there from 1945, when he was thirteen, until 1950, when he left to attend Harvard University. Before living in the farmhouse, the family lived in Shillington, Pennsylvania, eleven miles from the farmhouse. Updike's mother was born in the house and died there. Several of his novels, including *The Centaur* (1963) and *Of the Farm* (1965), and many of his short stories, including those collected in *Olinger Stories: A Selection* (1964), are in part based on his experiences in and around the sandstone farmhouse. The Joey Robinson in *Of the Farm* seems to be the same person as the Joey in "A Sandstone Farmhouse." The story won first prize in the O. Henry Prize Stories competition, appearing in *Prize Stories, 1991: The O. Henry Awards*, and was also included in *The Best American Short Stories, 1991*.

For most of his life, Joey resented his parents' buying the house in which his mother was born and making him move there from the town of Olinger, one of the fictitious names Updike uses for Shillington. In Olinger, Joey had friends and felt comfortable. He disliked the isolation of the house and the hard work involved in rebuilding parts of the house and adding on to it. Before his mother died, he resented her attachment to the house. He did not feel comfortable visiting the house and wanted his mother to move away. She, however, insisted that the house needed her, even though she was too old and sick to take care of it.

After her death, Joey decides to sell the farmhouse. He becomes obsessed with cleaning it, selling or destroying most of the things his mother kept in the house. In examining her old photographs before discarding them, he sees how happy she was during her childhood in the farmhouse. The only things that he keeps are those his family owned before moving to the farmhouse, that is, those objects from the time he considered himself to be happy. Thus, he tries to reject the farmhouse and all he thinks it represents in his life. It is as though Joey is fervently trying to erase all relation he might have had to the house, as though he is trying to erase the time he spent in the house and convert the house into an empty shell. He almost succeeds. The death of the flying squirrel, however, reminds him of his early days in the farmhouse and of the things he and other members of his family accomplished there. It produces in him the epiphany with which the story ends: his realization that he has been fruitlessly attempting to find real life away from the farmhouse. Now that the farmhouse, like Joey's life, is empty, he realizes that true life for him was to be found only in the farmhouse. Like his mother, he feels that the farmhouse needs him. It was, he feels, a kind of paradise that he has ignored for far too many years. Now his realization that the house needs him— and that he needs the house—probably comes too late.

Many of Updike's central characters are dislocated people, longing for a past that may never have existed. They are dissatisfied with their own lives in which they repeatedly experience broken marriages, grief, and the loss or death of loved ones. They recognize that people and things change, decay, and eventually die or deteriorate beyond recognition, and they often try to counter that recognition by immersing themselves in their present lives and work. Joey follows this general pattern, including three broken marriages; however, for him, the changes seem irrevocable. He learns that the center of his life—the escape from grief, dislocation, and longing—could have been the old farmhouse, but only after he destroys the last vestige of life in it.

*Style and Technique*

A large portion of "A Sandstone Farmhouse" involves a series of flashbacks about Joey's very ambiguous relationship to the farmhouse as it was before his mother's death as well as descriptions of his actions after her death. The story is written using a third-person limited narrative, with the consciousness being near to but not exactly the same as Joey's own consciousness.

The story begins with an account of his first glimpse of the house, his eventual move there, and his first summer there. It abruptly jumps to the death of his mother, more than forty years after the summer of 1946, when Joey moved to the farmhouse. It ends with Joey as inheritor of the house and his own final recognition that, for him, the house was where things were—and always had been—happening during his life. He sees his mother's buying the house where she was born and moving into it as an attempt on her part to return to what he thinks of as her own paradise, and he ends with the recognition that, unlike her, he cannot even attempt to return to that paradise, in part because it had never been a paradise for him; it could have been, but it never was. He also cannot return because he has robbed it of whatever life and memories could make it into a paradise for him.

In his works, Updike often begins with incidents based on his own life and then reworks them into fictive form. Joey is based on Updike. Many of the things Updike experienced Joey experiences; however, Updike reshapes those experiences into a work of art with a definite conclusion.

The flashbacks and descriptions of Joey's attempts to empty the farmhouse of all things that remind him of his life there correspond to his growing realization of the emptiness of his life. They all point toward the epiphany he has at the end of the story when he realizes that his whole life has been wasted; he realizes that he, who always wanted to be where the action was, was always looking in the wrong place. For him, the action always was at the farmhouse. Thus, the tone of nostalgia that permeates the short story is tempered with the realistic ending in which Joey discovers that his life has been empty, a kind of mockery of life, just as the farmhouse after Joey prepares it for sale is a mockery of the warm, living place it was for his mother and could have been for him.

*Richard Tuerk*

# SARAH COLE
## A Type of Love Story

*Author:* Russell Banks (1940-     )
*Type of plot:* Domestic realism
*Time of plot:* The late twentieth century
*Locale:* Concord, New Hampshire
*First published:* 1984

> *Principal characters:*
> RON, the narrator, a handsome professional man of about twenty-eight
> SARAH COLE, a friendly, homely woman of about thirty-eight

*The Story*

An unusually good-looking young man, Ron is quietly unwinding after work at Osgood's, a small upscale bar, where he is approached by Sarah Cole, the homeliest woman he has ever seen. Acting on a dare from her friends, Sarah introduces herself to Ron. As they converse over drinks, Ron finds himself becoming inexplicably attracted to the lumpish Sarah.

Two days later Ron and Sarah meet again at Osgood's. Though Ron has almost forgotten about their previous encounter, he once more finds himself inexplicably attracted to Sarah and tries to draw her out—to include her within his life. After they leave the bar together, Ron readily offers Sarah sympathy when she discovers that her car has been slightly dented in the parking lot, but they do not go home together. Ron finds himself the object of snickering scrutiny by other patrons of Osgood's as Sarah takes her leave of him.

After another encounter at Osgood's several weeks later, Ron invites Sarah to his apartment. There they discuss their mutual attraction and grow more comfortable in each other's presence. They admit that they would like to sleep together, but both recognize the real differences between them—in their lifestyles and appearances.

Some weeks later Ron remains obsessed with Sarah, though he has avoided seeing her. He unexpectedly meets her while running an errand on his bicycle. She invites him up to her apartment and suddenly takes the initiative by kissing him. Seeming perplexed and shaken by Sarah's impulsiveness, Ron silently leaves. The next morning Sarah appears at his apartment, where they are soon making love.

Over the next several weeks Ron and Sarah continue their uneasy affair. They never go out together, but instead meet at Ron's apartment, where they enjoy their lovemaking and learn more about each other. Tensions develop, however, when Sarah asks Ron to take her out in public with him. When Ron resists that suggestion, Sarah accuses him of being ashamed to be seen with her. He finally relents, and after enduring several miserable outings to bars or to Sarah's friend's houses, where Sarah often drinks to the point of incoherence, he becomes disgusted with the relationship. Sarah, who apparently wants something more from Ron, wishes for him to meet her children from her first marriage. When Ron hesitates, trying to come up with an excuse, Sarah senses a problem. They agree to meet to talk about it.

Ron informs Sarah that the relationship is over, and she briefly resists his wishes, pretending that it cannot be true. He finally forces her to leave his apartment and calls her a "disgusting, ugly bitch." As he speaks, Sarah becomes more beautiful to him with every mean word that he utters. She leaves, crying, and he feels as if he has killed her.

## Themes and Meanings

The subtitle to this short story—"A Type of Love Story"—should cause the reader to expect a problematic tale even before the narrative has begun. Russell Banks may be asking the reader to decide, along with his hesitant narrator, Ron, if this strange relationship in any way constitutes love. Certainly that seems to be one of the problems with which Ron continually wrestles, as throughout the story Banks allows his narrator to wander back and forth between a kind of single-minded intensity regarding his attraction to the homely Sarah, and an almost irritating indecisiveness concerning his own motivations.

By focusing his characterizations on two physically opposite types—the handsome Ron and the repugnant Sarah—Banks both questions and subverts the issue of physical attraction in a relationship. In a "typical" love story the idea of opposites attracting, then finding unexpected love, might surely be viewed as romantic; however, here Ron's continual questioning of his own motivations, coupled with Banks's constant realistic portrayal of the stark differences between Sarah and Ron, act to refocus this, in other ways, innocent picture of Ron's and Sarah's newfound love. As their relationship matures, then begins to unravel, the reader may feel the need to go beyond the issue of looks to find an answer to the characters' difficulties.

It may be easier to see how Sarah could be attracted to the younger and more handsome Ron, whose attraction to Sarah is as much a puzzle to him as it is to the reader. He is candid to the point of insensitivity when he describes his initial reactions to Sarah's homely appearance, and later, even as he finds himself attracted to her, he makes unflattering comments about her "dough-colored skin" and "thick, short body."

It is only after Ron and Sarah have been making love together for some time that the real differences between them start to surface. It becomes more and more clear that Ron and Sarah are simply from two different worlds. Sarah has a mundane job packaging copies of *TV Guide*, while Ron is clearly a professional man. She drives a wreck of a car while Ron drives a Datsun fastback. Sarah is "lugging two large bags of groceries" from the store on foot while Ron is collecting his starched shirts from the cleaners on his ten-speed racing bike. Ron's apartment is modern and located in the "heights." Sarah lives with her children in a "dark and cluttered" apartment in a "rough neighborhood."

The story's contrasting images continually amplify the mismatch between the lovers. As the story progresses, it becomes increasingly apparent that while Sarah moves from initial uneasiness to a kind of hesitant satisfaction in the relationship, Ron moves from uncomprehending physical attraction to disgust. What is more, Ron seems to be continually looking for reasons to deny his attraction to Sarah and justify his feelings of disgust. For this reason, the reader is more willing to sympathize with Sarah rather than Ron. However, Banks ultimately makes it difficult to sympathize completely with either.

*Style and Technique*

The several points of view through which "Sarah Cole" is related all belong to Ron. As the story begins he speaks conversationally in the first person. Later—and especially as Ron's part in the story becomes more painful to him—the voice becomes third person, with Ron commenting about himself as though he were a character. At first this shifting perspective might cause the reader to question Ron's reliability as a narrator, for one cannot escape the sense of Ron's scrupulous attempt to spare no important detail. He seems painstaking in his efforts to omit nothing, the bad or the good. Further complicating this question of reliability is the fact that he relates everything ten years after it has occurred. Also, he begins the story by revealing that Sarah is dead, which is not literally true. Ron only thinks of her as dead (in fact, thinks of himself as her killer) after he somewhat callously ejects her from his life.

Part of Banks's strategy would seem to be to allow the reader to work through Ron's problem of understanding this strange relationship along with Ron himself. The level of personal detail about Ron and Sarah, as well as the portrayal of their lives, is as meticulous as Ron is persistent in trying to understand the anxiety he feels over this failed romance. Though at first one might be suspicious of Ron's motivations and exercise caution regarding how much to trust this one-sided portrayal, the events unfold in a believable way. Both Sarah's and Ron's motivations make sense, and it would seem Banks has taken care to ensure that even though presented from Ron's point of view, this story appears an honest re-creation of events.

Though presented secondhand, so to speak, Sarah's "voice" is as genuine as Ron's. Ron's switches from first-person to third-person narration, instead of making the reader ultimately suspicious, add to the feelings of embarrassment and pain that Ron reveals force him to relate this story impersonally at times. Banks has allowed his narrator to question his own motivations by seeming to distance himself from what he does not trust himself to honestly relate, and thereby relate it as a disinterested and objective observer. The reader is given the bizarre task not only of analyzing and making sense of subjective as well as objective observations, but also of deciding on their veracity.

*George T. Novotny*

# SATURDAY NIGHT

*Author:* James T. Farrell (1904-1979)
*Type of plot:* Psychological
*Time of plot:* 1929
*Locale:* Chicago
*First published:* 1947

> *Principal characters:*
> JOSEPH "DOPEY" CARBERRY, an unemployed high school dropout
>     in his mid-twenties
> MICHAEL "MIKE" McGUIRE, his uncle
> ANNA McGUIRE, his aunt
> KATE CARBERRY, his sister
> PHIL GARRITY, the rebuffed suitor of Kate
> JACK KENNEDY and
> RED MURPHY, Dopey's and Phil's pals

## The Story

From a detached and rather cool third-person point of view, the reader observes Joseph "Dopey" Carberry shamble into the dining room of his Uncle Mike's and Aunt Anna's home and sit down to eat, only to begin yet another Saturday night of bickering and blathering with his relatives. Dopey and his two sisters have been living with their aunt and her brother since their father remarried. He is harangued by all assembled for his shiftlessness. His Aunt Anna directs the abuse: "We've helped him, fed him, clothed him, waited on him, coddled him, tried to point the right way out to him, but it's just not in his bones."

Dopey hardly listens; he silently laments his lack of "two bucks to lay on Red Pepper after Len had come around the corner with that hot tip," earlier in the day. He eventually offers some excuses and evasions for his lack of energy, and his aunt retorts, "Yes, I know what you want. A banker's job from twelve to one, with an hour for lunch." Given the brevity of the scene, there is more satire displayed than bathos, and the bigotry and corruption of their milieu are deftly sketched.

In the second scene (there are ten in all, matching the straightforward chronology of the evening), Uncle Mike counsels young Joe (who, after quitting high school, has had a number of jobs—one of which he describes as "a slave factory for dopes"—and a period of vagabondism) to change his ways, and Dopey tells him, "I'd like to go back to sea or else be a bookie." Through a ruse, Dopey then manages to borrow five dollars from his uncle.

Phil Garrity arrives in the fourth scene, looking like a "Big Shot," as Dopey's sister Kate tells him. "Why, Phil, you're all togged out like Joe College." Phil has just made a large amount of money "legit," playing the stock market with money from his La

Salle Street job, and has just purchased a new used car, a Lincoln. He is attracted to Kate but has not gone out with her for six months. He and Kate banter about dating, but Phil is not able to extract a commitment from her. He and Dopey go out for a night on the town and, through scenes five and six, the third-person point of view severs its attachment from Dopey and secures itself to Phil, who thenceforth assumes the position of protagonist. James T. Farrell manages this switch rather smoothly because it coincides with a change of location, from inside to outside.

Phil and Dopey drive to the corner of Sixty-third and Stony Island, where it is "bustling with Saturday-night activity, crowded with people, noisy with the traffic of automobiles and streetcars." They join a crowd outside a drugstore, and Phil muses on his lack of success with women, his hopes for marriage to Kate, and her lack of interest in him, wishing all the while that he could be "wild, carefree, dashing, romantic, brave, a guy who didn't care two hoots in hell for anything in the world."

After picking up some speakeasy gin, as well as another friend, Marty, they "put their liquor in their pockets and left to see Jack Kennedy." Kennedy's apartment, where "most of the space is taken up by a wide in-a-door bed, which was unmade," is full of the din of single young men recounting old times and former glories, their unsatisfying work, and lack of money. The dialogue is brisk and fresh throughout. Phil yearns for Kate and is sent out to buy more liquor.

After his return, Phil, Dopey, and Jack set off for the whorehouses of Twenty-second Street, and Red Murphy, another acquaintance of their big-city—yet excruciatingly tiny and parochial—world, staggers up to them as they are getting into Phil's new car. As Phil drives badly down the Midway, the essential realism of Farrell's style keeps this foreshadowing from being too heavy-handed when the remains of an earlier car wreck catch their eyes and they stop and survey the debris. "There's a lot of blood in one person. This blood might mean just one poor sonofabitch killed," Red comments.

The drunken men arrive at the Sour Apple on the near North Side, a tearoom and dance hall with a bohemian reputation. Phil hesitantly asks a young woman for a dance, and she "acted as if she had not heard him. He repeated it, humiliation eating inside of him." Rejected, he retreats into further reveries of Kate and unintentionally insults a husky lad by telling him that he "can't dance to the Notre Dame *Victory March*." A brawl commences. When the club's proprietor asks what started the fight, a denizen of the Sour Apple explains, "Four drunken Irishmen with liquor, four sober Irishmen with girls."

Unable to secure pickups at the Sour Apple, the four friends depart and find the brothels on Twenty-second Street closed by an unexpected police raid. They do manage to pick up four older women who are leaving a nearby dance hall. With Phil at the wheel, they drive out to the country fields. "Large shadows raked the road, and the car whipped on." After a few miles it smashes head-on into a Cadillac "going as swiftly as Phil's Lincoln."

Phil and one of the young women disentangle themselves from the wreckage, and Phil drags her, dazed and drunk, into the fields, where they are found later by the police with their britches down—an effective, if moralistic, yoking of sex and death. "You ought to swing for this, you sonofabitch," the cop tells Phil. The dead bodies of Jack and Dopey are pulled out of the car. The story ends with Phil left delirious and uncomprehending.

### Themes and Meanings

"Saturday Night" repeats many of Farrell's central concerns and subjects. His fictional world, the cosmology it describes, echoes, in many ways, the teaching that was instilled in him as a boy growing up in a Roman Catholic family and attending parochial schools on the South Side of Chicago in the early twentieth century. There is a sense of predestination and original sin with which all his characters come equipped, though Farrell's own attitude seems to be one of alternating cynicism toward and respectful anger at this worldview.

Dopey does not elicit much sympathy in Farrell's depiction; his death, though, is a consequence of his closest friendship, albeit a friendship of convenience and exploitation on Dopey's part. Phil is trapped in his own unrequited longings and sexual inexperience and ambivalence, the perpetual boyishness visited on most of Farrell's male characters, and he becomes the agent of destruction. Farrell has retained a good bit of the Catholic puritanism of his youth. Phil's sexual initiation is accomplished only at dire cost. Both society and Farrell disapprove of the boys' behavior.

Farrell reveals his own ambivalence as a left-wing social critic in "Saturday Night." The most amusing lines are given to Aunt Anna, a conservative scold, and to the habitue of the Sour Apple, Wolcroft, a self-proclaimed poet. In addition, Danny O'Neill, Farrell's closest counterpart in the O'Neill pentalogy of novels, is spoken of at Kennedy's apartment as a "cracked socialist" who "was trying to write books." The terrible fate of the young friends is presented not in the language of Marxist determinism (these young men all being sacrifices to alienated labor and the inexorable march of capitalism) but according to Farrell's own personal determinism, which he is exercising over the blockheads of his youth who did not appreciate the special young man whom they had in their midst. The Sour Apple, indeed: "Saturday Night" could be described as a mixture of sour grapes and bad apples.

### Style and Technique

James T. Farrell has never been praised as a stylist; in fact, he is often described as an undistinguished writer of prose. His power comes, as it does with many American writers, from sheer force and accumulation, the command and sweep of factual material that does not need or solicit strenuous interpretation (though the car crash could be viewed as an allegory for the stock-market crash to come). Farrell overwhelms the reader with the visceral, with what he describes, somewhat mockingly, in "Saturday Night," through the words of poet Wolcroft, as not just "realism. That's old-fashioned. My poetry, now, it's superrealist." Farrell's early naturalistic writing was in the mainstream and remained fashionable until that stream was thoroughly diverted and rechanneled after World War II.

Farrell, though he wrote many short stories, was not so much a master of the form as its earnest supplicant. The stories he wrote that were short enough became short stories instead of novels. Farrell had a novelist's skill at synthesizing but also the novelist's appetite for size, for the repetitive scene; the short story form does not profit from that sort of segmentation. Farrell's stories are often novels in miniature, rather than short stories in full bloom—although "Saturday Night" is one of his most effective, rich with humor, energy, and life, and not simply scenes from a novel writ small.

*William O'Rourke*

# SAVE THE REAPER

*Author:* Alice Munro (1931-    )
*Type of plot:* Domestic realism
*Time of plot:* A summer's day in 1998
*Locale:* Near Lake Huron, Ontario, Canada
*First published:* 1998

> *Principal characters:*
> Eve, a former actress and grandmother
> Sophie, her daughter
> Ian, Sophie's husband, an academic
> Philip, Sophie's son
> Daisy, Sophie and Ian's daughter
> Harold, a man who lives in a decrepit house
> The girl, a prostitute

## The Story

Eve, the central character of "Save the Reaper," has rented a house near a Lake Huron, Ontario, beach, which she had known as a child, in order to entice her married daughter Sophie and her children, Philip and Daisy, to visit. Eve has not seen the family in five years, for they live in California. Her daughter and the children arrive first. When Sophie goes to meet her husband's plane in Toronto, Eve takes her grandchildren Philip and Daisy for a drive to a nearby village to get ice cream.

Along the way, they play a tiresome game that involves imagining space aliens in other vehicles. When a truck they are trailing turns into a lane, Philip wants to follow it, but Eve decides to drive on. However, before she can do so, she sees the lane's gateposts: unusual constructions of whitewashed pebbles and colored glass. Eve suddenly remembers that once, when traveling with her mother in this area, she had seen a similar wall on which fascinating pictures were made of colored glass.

Eve turns into the lane, which is lined by large drooping pines, and follows the truck. She comes on a derelict barn surrounded by rusting machinery and a dilapidated house. The sight is mildly frightening. She would like to escape, but the truck is parked in such a way that she cannot turn around. She gets out of her car and asks the driver of the truck about the wall with colored glass. He persuades her to go into the house to meet someone named Harold, who may know something about the wall. She and the children go into the house.

The house is incredibly filthy, smelly, and messy. Four men are playing cards at a table and drinking whiskey; one of them, who is naked, is Harold. The truck driver asks Harold about the wall but gets only evasive answers. Eve now is frightened. Though she fears that she and the children will not be allowed to leave, she finds the door is unlocked and then that the truck driver has moved his truck. They escape down the long lane, but not before Eve catches a glimpse of a fragment of a whitewashed wall in which bits of glass are imbedded. She was right in remembering it from her childhood.

As she drives slowly along the lane, the youngest of the men from the card game opens the car door and jumps into the empty front seat. The man turns out to be a girl, a prostitute who wants to escape from a party that had turned too rough. The girl tells Eve that she left without being paid and asks Eve for money. Eve refuses. Then the girl makes a pass at Eve, and Eve feels a pang of desire. When she lets the girl out to hitch another ride, Eve gives her twenty dollars and impulsively tells her where she lives—in case the girl does not get a ride.

At home, Ian and Sophie are there. Eve tells them a censored version of the day's outing, and the family seems more harmonious than ever before. Eve knows her daughter, husband, and children will leave the next day. She wonders if the girl will come to see her after that and wonders what dangers will accompany such a visit.

*Themes and Meanings*

"Save the Reaper" initially seems to be an ordinary story about a dysfunctional family. As measured against the childhood Eve remembers, her family is not happy. Both she and her daughter have had illegitimate children, though her daughter is now married, happily it seems. However, even though she and her daughter were close when Sophie was growing up, Sophie's marriage has turned her away from her mother. They have not seen each other for five years. It is obvious to Eve that Sophie and the children have come only because Ian needed to be away at a library. Eve speculates that her daughter is desperate to leave. In addition, though Eve tries hard, she cannot really amuse the bratty young Philip. It is revealed that she disliked and made fun of her own mother and that she has not spoken to her brother in years.

Another theme is clear from the beginning of the story: Old ways are giving way to new ones. Alice Munro has stated that when she wrote this story she was aware of such changes in the lives of people of her generation. In this story, readers see not only the crumbling of the old and eccentric fence that had charmed Eve as a girl, but also changes in the village (a supermarket, high prices), in transport (airports, seat belts), and in the topics children talk about (space aliens). Eve seems to have adapted well to change, but the reader sympathizes when she seems to yearn for earlier and simpler days.

When Eve turns into the dark lane, the story turns as well. The sights she sees at Harold's house are ugly and nasty, sexually nasty. Eve thinks she and the children are in danger, and a reader is worried as well.

The real danger to Eve is different. Her past is revealed in bits and pieces. She has led an unconventional life. She seems to have been an itinerant (though not particularly successful) actress, playing roles all over Canada. She seems to have been sexually promiscuous, for Sophie was conceived when she and a married man from India coupled on a train between Calgary and Winnipeg. Now when the prostitute strokes her thigh, her comparatively placid middle age is rocked by her response. She remembers her sexual past and realizes she still wants love. Giving the prostitute her address is an implicit invitation. At the end of the story, Eve knows the danger she faces, for the prostitute is part of Harold's world. If she comes to Eve, she may bring other people and other dangers. At the story's end, Eve is ready.

## Style and Technique

"Save the Reaper" is a third-person, limited omniscience story. Readers, experiencing the story through Eve's mind as she reflects on the present and the past, get to know her well and sympathize with her. She comes across as a nice woman, genuinely hopeful, yet painfully sensitive to what others may be thinking. Occasionally Munro inserts some hurtful dialogue in parentheses, dialogue that the reader soon guesses is occurring in Eve's imagination. Eve is also painfully frank with herself about what is happening to her. At the end, she knows the danger she is in.

Events in the present proceed in an orderly time sequence but are frequently interrupted by Eve's memories, memories that slowly reveal the story's meaning. For example, Eve does not reflect on Sophie's conception until after the prostitute has made her pass.

As the story begins, it seems to be ordinarily realistic. The details of the car ride and of Philip's space alien game are conventionally banal. However, when Eve's imagination is stirred by the gatepost, the prose becomes surreal. Eve remembers the pictures made by the bits of glass: "Triangular Christmas trees and tropical-colored birds half as big as the trees, a fat horse with dinky legs and burning red eyes, curly blue rivers of unvarying width, like lengths of ribbon, a moon and drunken stars and fat sunflowers nodding over the roofs of houses." Eve's vivid imagination is at odds with what to this point has seemed to be her ordinary life. When she gets to the house, the surreal scene becomes gothic in its menacing intensity. The house is not only messy but also incredibly foul. The people inside not only are crude but also form a living tableau of particularly disgusting and dangerous examples of many of the deadly sins. Eve is forced to recognize a side of life she has put behind her, a side of her own past she had tried to set aside.

The story's title points to its one rich symbol. Just after she drops off the girl, Eve remembers a rhyme: "Only reapers, reaping early.... Save the reapers, reaping early." The story is full of reaping and potential reaping. Eve drives on though farmland with hay bales and fields of golden barley. When Eve returns home, Sophie and Ian have bought many ears of corn for dinner, newly picked corn that Eve will think about as she goes to sleep, wondering if the girl will visit. At first, the reapers seem to refer to the young prostitute: Save such early reapers, Eve asks. Ultimately, Eve may know that her prayer is for herself, a reaper as well.

*George Soule*

# SAY YES

*Author:* Tobias Wolff (1945-      )
*Type of plot:* Domestic realism
*Time of plot:* The early 1980's
*Locale:* An unspecified American suburb
*First published:* 1980

> *Principal characters:*
> THE HUSBAND, the unnamed protagonist
> ANN, his wife

*The Story*

On its surface, "Say Yes" concerns racism, specifically, opposition to interracial love and marriage. The unnamed protagonist and his wife, Ann, both white, discuss the subject. They quarrel, or at least disagree, and nothing is resolved except that they are really fighting about their own relationship.

Sitting in any kitchen in any house in the white suburbs of America, this typical middle-class couple are doing nothing more than talking while doing the dishes one night after dinner. Most of the two-thousand-word story is dialogue about this one topic: Can two people who are from different backgrounds love and understand each other completely and meaningfully?

The husband argues "no" and the wife argues "yes," but neither offers convincing arguments. The husband appeals to practicality, citing divorce statistics that show that such relationships are doomed to separation and failure. By contrast, Ann cites an abstract ideal of love, which would have it that if two people love each other they should be able to overcome such obstacles no matter what.

The tension builds as they snap and quip at each other, both being careful not to cross an unstated line over which they cannot retreat. In her nervousness, Ann cuts her thumb on a knife in the dirty dishwater. When she bleeds, her husband gives her every kind of attention in the forms of rubbing alcohol, bandages, and sympathy.

As the husband continues to dry the dishes, Ann resumes the argument, determined to make him agree with her. She forces speculation about what would have happened had she been a member of another race. He counters by arguing that in such a case they would have been from different social groups, would never have met, and therefore would never have fallen in love and married. Ann cannot accept this. She persists, attempting to get him to say that he would have loved her unconditionally, no matter what. She insists that this is the only possible way in which their relation can be meaningful, lasting, and pure.

On finishing the dishes, the husband notices blood on the kitchen linoleum from Ann's wound, which he now thinks that he has caused. He meticulously cleans up the stain, leaving the floor spotless. Needing to leave the kitchen, he performs the husbandly ritual of taking the trash out to the street. He breathes deeply, focuses on the traffic, and calms himself down. Two dogs fight over the garbage can in much the same way he and his wife had been fighting over the dishes.

He returns directly to a dark house, one in which Ann has already gone to bed—but not to sleep. After he undresses and gets in bed, they lie quietly but have no contact. Ann gets up from the bed and goes quietly into the silent house. He hears her movements and knows that his wife is a stranger, if not to herself then at least to him.

## Themes and Meanings

Ostensibly, the subject of this story is interracial love and marriage. To what extent can such relationships succeed? What bearing does race have on love? The two marital partners struggle with these issues from a "white" perspective; because both are white, they can only speculate. Each has a different viewpoint. The husband argues about practicality; the wife argues about love's conquering all.

Nothing is resolved because what is really going on is a marital power struggle. Which partner will subject the other to his or her will? As the story's title suggests, the husband feels that he is being emotionally coerced into just "saying yes." At the same time, he is just as determined to make the wife agree with him, primarily by discontinuing the conversation so that his wife goes to bed like a good girl, submissive to her husband's will and better judgment.

Viewed from this perspective, the story has little, perhaps nothing, to do with interracial love and marriage. Certainly, no questions are answered, and neither person offers any observations that go beyond stereotypes and banalities. The domestic power struggle, then, is the real problem. Interracial love is no more of an issue here than which end of the toothpaste tube is squeezed or whether the toilet seat should be left up or down.

Tobias Wolff's main point is that men and women, different genders, are as different as "races." People tend to identify with their own gender in more important ways than they do with their so-called racial markers. Men and women exist in different worlds; the barriers between them are much more difficult to overcome than those posed by racial differences, backgrounds, or milieus. The result is a hopeless entrapment in alienation from the other race—that is, the other gender. It is easier for blacks and whites to understand each other and have meaningful relationships—including love—than for men and women to do so.

From this perspective, the story is about the inevitable failure of male-female relationships. The husband here is not the stereotypical male chauvinist, nor is the wife a radical feminist. Both are thinking persons given to their own inclinations about the topic. The opening of the story emphasizes that the husband is helping with the dishes, and does so consciously in order to prove to his wife that he is not like other men, who define housework by gender. Similarly, the wife expresses her own "masculinity" by being assertive. Wolff is thus careful to negate gender stereotypes before introducing the conflict between his characters.

This hopeless alienation between members of the two genders is revealed at the end of the story. The husband is left alone in bed; his wife, now a stranger, seems to be moving silently out of his bedroom, his house, and his life. Assuredly, the problem is not interracial marriage; rather, it is intergender marriages, something inescapable in the institution of husband and wife.

### Style and Technique

Wolff conveys his story primarily through dialogue. Character, motivation, psychological perspective, and insight, as well as meaning, are revealed mainly through utterances of the characters. They talk in the terse, clipped sentences and fragments of sentences of those who have been married for a long time and have little need for words to communicate with each other. At the same time, because they take opposing viewpoints, some verbal conversation is necessary simply to further the conflict and increase the tension.

Like most couples who have been married a long time, each knows much of what the other will say. Toward that end the author, telling the story from an omniscient point of view, indicates that both characters know the effects of their own statements before they make them. Therefore, they willingly enter the argument—and they willfully keep it going to move it to their final separation at the end of the story, which is also the evident end of their relationship.

The setting of the story is the ordinary kitchen of a typical modern home. It has no distinctive characteristics because the author is writing about all such kitchens in all such houses, and about the inevitable breakdown of such relationships. The spotlessness of the linoleum and other fixtures recalls the sterility of Ernest Hemingway's "A Clean, Well-Lighted Place" (1933).

Wolff uses two obvious symbols. In cutting herself, Anne is offering sacrificial blood to the relationship. It falls on the floor (that is, the underpinning) of their home and relation. The husband succeeds in cleaning up the blood, but not in cleaning up the mess. When the husband takes out the trash and sees two dogs fight over it, the animals are reenacting what has just occurred in the kitchen. Human nature is animalistic. The selfishness of the dogs in refusing to share the garbage reflects the determination of the human couple to force each other to "say yes"—to agree to be submissive. The consequence of such conduct is invariably separation. The couple not only learn that they are strangers to each other, but that this has always been the case between men and women.

*Carl Singleton*

# A SCANDAL IN BOHEMIA

*Author:* Arthur Conan Doyle (1859-1930)
*Type of plot:* Mystery and detective
*Time of plot:* About 1888 or 1889
*Locale:* London, England
*First published:* 1891

*Principal characters:*
SHERLOCK HOLMES, the world's first consulting detective
DR. JOHN H. WATSON, his friend and biographer
IRENE ADLER, a beautiful young operatic soprano
WILHELM, KING OF BOHEMIA

*The Story*

Soon after his first marriage, Dr. John Watson leaves the Baker Street flat that he has shared with Sherlock Holmes and returns to private medical practice. In the course of his calls, he passes through Baker Street one day, sees Holmes pacing before the window, and on an impulse walks up to visit his friend. Holmes tells him that a client is expected that evening, one whose case may be interesting to Watson in his capacity as Holmes's chronicler. The client arrives, a huge man, richly and garishly dressed and wearing a mask. Holmes quickly penetrates the disguise, however, and identifies the man as King Wilhelm of Bohemia. The surprised king unmasks and tells Holmes why he has come.

It seems that some years earlier, the king fell in love with a young soprano named Irene Adler. The woman is not only beautiful but also possessive. The king's engagement to another woman, a princess, will soon be announced, and Irene Adler has sworn to stop the wedding. She threatens to publish a compromising photograph of her and the king, thereby creating a scandal that will lead the bride's family to call off the wedding. She refuses to sell the photograph to the king; twice, burglars have failed to find it in her house; her luggage has been searched without success; and on two occasions robbers have stopped her, but without finding the picture. The king lays the matter in Holmes's hands, begging for his help.

The next morning, Holmes disguises himself as a seedy-looking horse groom and goes to the neighborhood around Miss Adler's house to see what gossip he can pick up. There he not only learns that Miss Adler has an admirer, Godfrey Norton, but also becomes involved in an incident that amuses as well as enlightens him. He sees both Norton and Miss Adler set off in separate carriages for a nearby church. When he follows them there, the disguised Holmes is commandeered as a witness for their wedding. Now that Irene Adler is married, Holmes expects her to leave London at any moment. He must therefore act, and do it swiftly.

On the following day, Holmes again disguises himself, this time as a clergyman, and requests Watson's help for his scheme. They go to Adler's house separately. Once there, Watson sees Miss Adler arrive, and she is immediately beset by a crowd of loafers. Holmes, in disguise, comes to her aid, is attacked and apparently wounded by the crowd, and falls to the ground. He is carried into Adler's house and laid on a couch near a window where Watson can see him. On Holmes's signal, Watson throws a smoke bomb through the window, and the people on the street outside begin to cry "Fire!" After the tumult that follows, Holmes joins Watson outside, and on their walk back to Baker Street, he explains what has happened.

Reasoning that Miss Adler had the photograph well hidden somewhere in her house and that she would immediately go to it in an emergency, Holmes stage-managed the little scene outside her house to see where she would run in such a case. The plan worked, and now he knows where the photograph is hidden. On the morrow he plans to go to the house with the king and take the photograph while Miss Adler is not in the room. As Watson and Holmes pause at Holmes's door, a short, cloaked figure passes them on the street and wishes Holmes good evening.

The next morning, all goes as planned until Holmes and the king reach Adler's house. There, an old woman tells them that Miss Adler and her husband have left for their honeymoon and that she expected Holmes to arrive. Alarmed, the two men are shown into the drawing room. Holmes goes at once to the secret compartment that held the photograph but instead finds there a photograph of Miss Adler herself and a letter addressed to him.

The letter explains that she had been warned that the king might use an agent. After Holmes, dressed as a clergyman, was brought into her house, she began to have suspicions. She left the room, put on a disguise of her own as a man, and followed Holmes and Watson back to Baker Street. She says further that now that she loves a better man than the king—Godfrey Norton—the king need not worry any longer about their photograph: She will not hinder his marriage.

The astonished and relieved king thanks Holmes for his services and offers him a ring from his finger as reward. Holmes refuses, however, and asks for something else—the photograph of Irene Adler, which the king gives him.

*Themes and Meanings*

"A Scandal in Bohemia" was the first Sherlock Holmes short story that Arthur Conan Doyle published. Two earlier novels, *A Study in Scarlet* (1887) and *The Sign of Four* (1890), had already introduced the great detective to the public, but largely in the character of, as Watson says, "the most perfect reasoning and observing machine that the world has seen." A theme that runs throughout the Holmes stories is that reason is a trusted guide through the confusion of everyday life. As Holmes says to Watson, representative of the ordinary person, "You have not observed. And yet you have seen."

For those who both see and observe—such as Holmes—even an apparently meaningless detail speaks volumes—and the trained mind is a reliable guide. However, there is something mechanical about the way that Holmes is presented in the two long stories that introduced him, and Doyle both modifies his theme and amplifies the character of Holmes in "A Scandal in Bohemia."

The story's first sentence says of Irene Adler, "To Sherlock Holmes she is always *the* woman"; the last sentence is almost identical: It says that Holmes always refers to her "under the honorable title of *the* woman." In this story, if Sherlock Holmes is the intellect, Irene Adler is clearly the emotions. Watson emphasizes this interpretation by stating Holmes's aversion to all emotions as disruptive of the working of his mind, comparing a strong emotion in Holmes to a piece of grit in a delicate machine. Here again the reader sees the image of the machine used to describe Holmes. However, to make Holmes only a machine denies him his full humanity; he is indeed capable of powerful feelings, as the story shows.

"A Scandal in Bohemia" might loosely be called the most feminist of the Sherlock Holmes tales. Holmes is something of a misogynist in many of the stories, often scorning what he regards as a feminine tendency to emotionalize life. He frequently makes generalizations about women that seem glib from one who lacks everyday contact with them. That a woman could outreason Holmes, could see one step further than he has, and could anticipate his next move teaches him a lesson that he does not forget: As Watson says near the conclusion, "He used to make merry over the cleverness of women, but I have not heard him do it of late." Holmes has discovered humanity both in women and in himself.

### Style and Technique

"A Scandal in Bohemia" was Doyle's first attempt at a new literary form: a self-contained short story with a continuing character at the center of it. Although Holmes appeared twice before, it was in novels. The usefulness of a familiar character in a series of short stories is immediately obvious, once one considers it: In a short story, an author must either give a very sketchy portrait of the main characters or violate the dictum of Edgar Allan Poe that a short story must aim at producing a single effect without one wasted word. If the character is already known to the public from earlier stories, however, the author can begin with the plot at once. So effective was this technique, especially for the detective story, that many later authors followed the same practice, writing a series of stories about a detective—Nero Wolfe or Ellery Queen, for example.

The character of the detective was built up throughout the series, producing a much more lifelike character than would have been possible in a single story. "A Scandal in Bohemia" also introduced the structural pattern that Doyle was to use again and again in the Holmes stories. The mystery is first revealed at Holmes's apartment at Baker Street with the arrival of the client. Holmes demonstrates his powers, to the amazement of the client, by revealing something about the client that he has not yet been told. By this means, Holmes also gains the confidence and respect of his employer. Next, both Holmes and Watson journey at least once to another location; there Holmes acts mysteriously, but this time he does not explain. Finally, Holmes, Watson, and the other principals gather for a "revelation scene," in which both the mystery and Holmes's method are explained.

Doyle used all these elements over and over again, keeping the stories fresh by inserting new mysteries into this setting or by occasionally adding some detail about the character of Holmes or Watson. The technique was to make Doyle one of the most popular writers of his time on both sides of the Atlantic, and it was a technique first employed in "A Scandal in Bohemia."

*Walter E. Meyers*

# A SCANDALOUS WOMAN

*Author:* Edna O'Brien (1930-        )
*Type of plot:* Domestic realism
*Time of plot:* The 1930's or 1940's
*Locale:* Rural Ireland
*First published:* 1974

> *Principal characters:*
> EILY HOGAN, the teenage daughter of a farming family
> THE NARRATOR, her schoolfriend
> JACK, a young bank clerk in the village
> EILY'S FATHER

*The Story*

A grown woman recalls her friendship with Eily Hogan, and from the opening paragraph, the reader is alerted by her remark that she has been "connected" with Eily's life. At first, that connection takes the form of romantic admiration. The narrator sees Eily as a high-spirited person who brings excitement into their dull lives. Their childhood bond, based on play, soon becomes a bond of collusion when Eily begins a sexual relationship with a bank clerk. The narrator helps Eily to cover her tracks when she goes out into the woods to meet Jack, whom they call Romeo, and their shared sense of the danger and sinfulness of what they are doing colors the romantic glow with foreboding. Images of violence and guilt have been prominent from the beginning, even in their childhood games of hospital. This first phase ends in a triumphant scene in which the girls meet in a meadow and Eily produces a bottle of perfume. The narrator's most intense pleasure in their friendship is focused on this moment.

When the bank clerk ends the liaison rather brutally, the girls enter a new phase of their collusion. The narrator tries to calm Eily's suicidal thoughts, and together they visit a fortune-teller. This unpleasant and witchlike character encourages Eily to believe that the dream of Jack's return will come true. Overlooking the sinister note in the witch's words, "You'll end your days with him," they return home in joyful anticipation of a reunion with Jack. The joy is short-lived, for Eily's father comes on the lovers one evening. This insanely violent man imprisons Eily in a room, and the narrator's loyalty is tested as she must deny all knowledge of Eily's earlier meetings.

The bond between the girls is broken when it becomes apparent that Eily is pregnant, and the Hogan and Brady parents begin to coerce Jack to marry her. They succeed, but in the process, the narrator observes the destruction of Eily's joyous spirit. It appears that Jack is marrying Eily in hatred and frustration, and the narrator realizes that Eily and other women also are trapped victims of a crude male power structure.

In later years, the narrator's memories of her affection for Eily return, prompted by glimpses of her. Broken in spirit, she has become the mother of three children in four years, and as her husband prospers in business, she slides into a breakdown. Many years later, the narrator finds her functioning competently in her husband's business but without feeling or affection except for the narrator's child. Worse still, she has lost all memory of their joy together as girls. The story ends with an expression of the narrator's grief and anger at the destruction of women by her native countryside.

The "connection" of the narrator's life to this image of youthful vitality so brutally destroyed is not made clear, but it is implied that the narrator's sense of life has been overshadowed by these memories. The "spark" of joyous pleasure of which she became aware was extinguished for her also, and it is hinted that no later experience has given her the same intensity of pleasure or of love. She appears to have married a man who is indifferent to her feelings and lavishes his affections on his vintage car.

*Themes and Meanings*

The general theme is evident: A woman's capacity for finding joy and pleasure is destroyed at an early age by an environment in which all relationships are colored by the fear of punishment. This feminist theme takes on a local significance, however, in the Irish peasant setting with its closely knit family and community ties through which the intimidation of dogma and physical violence is transmitted.

The fathers in the story live close to the land, and the grim regime of hard physical work for long hours makes life a matter of joyless endurance. Their closeness to the animals that breed and are bought and sold influences their ways of thinking about sexual relationships and marriage. Taciturn and abusive, the men seem to control relationships by provoking fear and repression. Mothers cater to them, and daughters too, and the prominence of Catholic teaching seems to extend the power of the father into the social arena; the father's authority seems to have social and divine sanction. What the girls fear most, discovery, is connected with public disgrace and with a fear of final damnation. Sin and guilt are associated with disobedience, and so the girls are led to doubt their own feelings and impulses. Their pleasures and their innocent play are a self-defeating mixture of escape and submission and prayer. When the narrator is held down so that Eily's sister can pretend to be the doctor about to remove her female parts, the hopelessness and humiliation surface in the bewildered comment, "For some reason I always looked upward and backward." It is not surprising that Eily's craving for romantic adventure leads her to an indifferent exploiter who fits well into her father's code of behavior, even when he is being bullied into marriage.

The girls are trapped in another way: by their religious and literary education. Eily believes that "the god Cupid is on our side," and the narrator dramatizes herself as a Shakespearean heroine. Their favorite perfume, "Mischief," creates an atmosphere "of mystery and sanctity," and the sacred and the profane are again confused when the chapel is "better than the theatre," the "rosary beads . . . were as dazzling as necklaces," and the mission priest is imagined as a lover. The overactive imaginations of the girls veil the reality of their circumstances from them, even as imagination is their means of transcending the impoverishment of their environment.

It is only at the end of the story that the narrator acknowledges the prosaic tragedy that has overtaken Eily: Her youthful revolt has embedded her even more deeply in this environment that kills individual feeling and joy. The narrator wants the little luxury of re-creating in memory "the good old days," but Eily tells her that "they're all much of a muchness." Repression has flattened her affective life, killing even her memories.

### Style and Technique

The story is told in an apparently effortless, episodic recollection and then, suddenly, ends with a howl of despair at the destruction of the innocent joy that was re-created in the narrative: "I thought that ours indeed was a land of shame, a land of murder, and a land of strange, throttled, sacrificial women." The role of storyteller seems to remove the narrator from the category of "throttled" women, but the anger that issues directly here is present throughout under the calm surface. The style blends a wide-eyed innocence appropriate to the age of the schoolfriends with a bitter irony and a grotesque humor that are suited to the exposure of that horrific reality that the girls in their innocence do not consciously oppose. By entering fully into the girls' earlier experience, the narrator tells the story with a surprising acceptance of the horrific reality that is part of things as they are in the world.

Sometimes the irony is directed against the children's way of observing and of expressing themselves. "She would work like a horse to get to the main road before dark to see the passerby"; such a sentence captures the grim routine of the farm, which turns Eily into a workhorse, and also her craving for excitement or release. This is a typical, understated sentence, apparently factual but catching a raw quality of the life there. The next sentences deepen the insight that was dropped so casually: "She was swift as a colt. My father never stopped praising this quality of her and put it down to muscle." The humor of this innocent and ignorant commentary is prominent and heightens a grimmer irony that underlies it. The father's sense of an affective response to life's possibilities issues in animal images that are demeaning; when Eily is pregnant, he says she has "a porker in her."

Grotesque humor is again unintentional on the part of the narrator and serves to underline the pervasive violence and repression that are accepted as bland fact. The blandness and the horror are wonderfully captured in a sentence such as this: "As usual, my mother ate only the pope's nose, and served the men the breasts of chicken." At a turning point in the story, poignancy and comedy blend with the grotesque. Eily's secret pregnancy becomes public knowledge at a religious service attended by the entire community, and she is taken outside the church. The narrator's overly literary manner reports: "They bore her aloft as if she were a corpse on a litter." The narrator appears not to realize the irony of her metaphors.

The style in which Edna O'Brien reveals her world owes much to James Joyce's early fiction; in "Araby" and "The Boarding House," Joyce used a similar mixture of styles to convey the sinister ordinariness of a life that is a form of death. O'Brien adapts Joyce's style to her country world and gives it a nostalgic innocence and humor.

*Denis Sampson*

# THE SCAPEGOAT

*Author:* Paul Laurence Dunbar (1872-1906)
*Type of plot:* Sketch
*Time of plot:* About 1900
*Locale:* Cadgers, a fictional American city
*First published:* 1904

*Principal characters:*
  ROBINSON ASBURY, a leader in Cadgers's black community
  SILAS BINGO, his political rival
  ISAAC MORTON, a school principal, a political tool, and later a
    rival of Bingo
  JUDGE DAVIS, an old white judge, a loyal supporter of Asbury

*The Story*

The story opens with a brief survey of Robinson Asbury's rise from a bootblack to an owner of a barbershop-social club for blacks in the town of Cadgers. With this shop as a base, Asbury becomes politically visible and, with the patronage of party managers, the town's recognized black leader. Because Asbury has further ambitions, he studies law on the side and, with the help of Judge Davis, a white man and the only member of the political establishment with moral principles, is admitted to the bar. Rather than leave the black district and enter the elite class, Asbury opens up a law office next to his barbershop, declaring a loyalty to the black people who gave him his success.

At this point, Paul Laurence Dunbar introduces the antagonist, Silas Bingo, and the central conflict of the story. Bingo and Latchett, partners in a black law firm and envious of Asbury's rise to power, plot his downfall by creating a new faction within the political party, by gathering all the "best people" to their side, and by co-opting an innocent school principal, Isaac Morton, to be their figurehead. At the Emancipation Day celebration, during which the black leader Asbury heads a procession, the Bingo faction tries to compete with Asbury by organizing a counterprocession but fails. Asbury thus becomes the party's candidate in the next spring election. When Asbury wins the election, the defeated party cries fraud. In order to clear its name, the winning party searches for a scapegoat. Only Asbury himself has the prominence to ensure a complete purgation. Tried and convicted, he begins his revenge even before his sentence. He makes a public statement at the trial naming all the political leaders as being guilty of criminal acts—all but Judge Davis. Against his own conscience and wishes, Davis sentences his friend to one year in prison. Bingo had betrayed Asbury by joining forces with his accusers, and now he tries to capitalize on Asbury's absence, but his bid for popular support must contend with a scapegoat suddenly turned martyr.

The second part of the story treats Asbury's political life after his release from prison. Amid speculation over what he intends to do, Asbury turns his law office into a "news-and-cigar stand" and declares that he is no longer engaged in politics, a stance that pleases and convinces Bingo. As Emancipation Day once again approaches, Bingo, now the black leader, must face a faction headed by Isaac Morton, who resents being used earlier by Bingo. Although the contest for leadership is still close, Asbury visits Bingo to offer his support, but when the day of the procession comes, Bingo discovers that Asbury has tricked him and gained revenge for past betrayals. Behind the scenes, Asbury has turned practically the entire black community, including the leadership, against Bingo. Even his law partner, Latchett, abandons him. At the spring elections, everyone in the party organization who was in power when Asbury was convicted is defeated at the polls. Asbury has mobilized the entire black vote to defeat the party machine. Still, he declares to a reporter after the election is over, "'I am not in politics, sir.'"

## Themes and Meanings

The idea of a scapegoat has a long literary tradition and has taken various forms. Oedipus, though guilty of punishable crimes, is himself a victim whose suffering and exile purify the city of Thebes. Hamlet, who is a more innocent example, still must die for Denmark's corrupt state to be redeemed. Shirley Jackson's "The Lottery" offers a twentieth century version of the ancient ritual sacrifice. In all three works, the scapegoat dies or suffers excruciating pain. Dunbar's scapegoat is a sociopolitical figure, at least on the surface; Asbury has none of the deep, mythical, religious, or cultural significance that one attaches to these other examples, or to the goat that the Jewish high priest sent off into the wilderness. He neither dies nor suffers—at least Dunbar does not show the suffering. Instead he chooses to show Asbury's triumph, strength, and self-confidence.

Within the structure of the story, Asbury remains a scapegoat for only a few moments; afterward he is unquestionably and permanently a martyr. The martyr chooses his fate, and while Hamlet, too, makes such a choice toward the end of his play, Asbury is a martyr who remains alive and enjoys privately the fruits of victory. Dunbar creates a man willing to submit to social ostracism and even to self-exile from public honors. What he will not give up, however, are his principles and the power that derives from them. He consistently abides by the principle of democratic rule—one person, one vote; he remains loyal to the people; and most important, he does not define the best people according to wealth and status. Such a presentation of the scapegoat suggests an unexpected optimism in a black writer at the turn of the twentieth century: Goodness will out, even in politics; the truly good man will, in the end, receive his due. What he must be willing to sacrifice are vanity and material success.

Behind this political story, however, lies a hint of racial comment. The final statement in the story, "Cadgers had learned its lesson," may have implications beyond the political one that the will of the people must not be violated. Dunbar is speaking specifically to the black community as a political bloc capable of challenging white supremacy. His specific advice is to black leaders who use the people to get power, then abandon them, and perhaps even to white leaders who underestimate minorities. That Dunbar's story is a form of protest literature should be clear from the beginning. In his initial paragraphs Dunbar describes the demographics of American cities: with the "usual tendency [of blacks] to colonize, a tendency encouraged, and in fact compelled, by circumstances, they had gathered into one part of the town. Here in alleys, and streets as dirty and hardly wider, they thronged like ants." When Asbury goes into business for himself, he puts up "the significant sign, 'Equal Rights Barber-Shop.'" Together with this protest, however, Dunbar insists on a pragmatic deception in achieving ends. Isaac Morton begins his political career as "an innocent young man," whose "ideals . . . should never have been exposed to the air." He eventually becomes more adroit, and Asbury's own success relies on the principle of deception.

*Style and Technique*

As a black writer at the turn of the twentieth century, Dunbar had a problem, to some extent imposed on him by William Dean Howells—whether to write in dialect and meet certain expectations of a white audience, or to write in standard English, which he preferred, because he wanted to deal with "serious" issues. Although he could not see dialect as a medium for serious poetry or fiction, he did write numerous stories in the plantation tradition, concentrating on rural blacks. Most are pleasantly nostalgic (though even here he does reveal his concern with racial injustice in the South). His identification with the rural poor and his feeling for their plight are also in the urban tale "The Scapegoat," but well in the background. In the foreground are a language that is standard American English and an argument that is serious enough, perhaps, but mild-mannered and apparently innocuous.

It should not be surprising to find a black writer at that time, a writer anxious to succeed as a professional, choosing indirectness rather than an overtly revolutionary style. If he were to register a protest or assert any political ambition in the name of black people, he would do it subtly. If such thoughts are in "The Scapegoat" at all, they would be hidden. As with almost all black literature in America, not only with that of Dunbar's, there is an underlying irony, a second perspective that lies just beneath the surface. One is tempted to see it even in the name of the hero as a whimsical play on words: the man who is "black as a berry" and the living man who acts as though he were buried.

The story's title leads one to expect death or suffering, but instead one gets ultimate victory in this life: an ironic incongruity. Dunbar also uses verbal irony within the story. In one notable instance, as Asbury plots with Bingo, he actually plots against him. Asbury's language reveals one thing to Bingo and another to the careful reader: "I don't want to appear in this at all. All I want is revenge. You can have all the credit, but let me down my enemy." Although Bingo applies "enemy" and "revenge" to Isaac Morton, his opponent, Asbury is actually referring to Bingo himself.

However, the main ironies in the story lie in the incongruities of the story and the character of Asbury. The surface calm in Dunbar's tone and the quiet confidence of a man betrayed do not jibe with the realities of such a situation. The ultimate victory may be at a deeper cost after all. Asbury allows the public to see only what Dunbar himself allows the reader to see. In this short sketch of Cadgers's life, the real face of Asbury never appears from behind the mask. Dunbar remains true to the words in his most famous poem, "We wear the mask that grins and lies" (which is itself an ironic violation of the deception principle), by not permitting his audience to "be overwise." In "this debt" that Dunbar "pays to human guile," one wonders what "tortured soul" might have resided in that "news-and-cigar stand"; one wonders what resemblance there was between Asbury's hermitlike existence and Dunbar's own private thoughts. Perhaps the irony turns back on itself, and "The Scapegoat" turns out to be an acutely appropriate title.

*Thomas Banks*

# THE SCHARTZ-METTERKLUME METHOD

*Author:* Saki (Hector Hugh Munro, 1870-1916)
*Type of plot:* Fantasy
*Time of plot:* About 1910
*Locale:* The English countryside
*First published:* 1911

> *Principal characters:*
> LADY CARLOTTA, the protagonist who is mistaken for the
>     governess, Miss Hope
> MRS. QUABARL, a wealthy woman who wants to hire a governess
> MR. QUABARL, her husband
> CLAUDE,
> WILFRED,
> IRENE, and
> VIOLA, the Quabarls' children

*The Story*

   While traveling to visit a friend in the English countryside, Lady Carlotta steps out of her railway carriage as the train stops at a provincial station. She observes a carter abusing his overworked horse, intervenes on behalf of the beast, and misses her train. An "imposingly attired lady," Mrs. Quabarl, assumes that Lady Carlotta is her newly hired governess, Miss Hope, and imperiously whisks her off to the family mansion. Lady Carlotta says nothing to correct the misunderstanding. During the trip Mrs. Quabarl instructs her that she does not wish her children to be taught but rather to be made interested in their lessons, especially in history, in which she expects the children to be introduced to the life stories of real people. She also informs the supposed governess that French will be spoken several times a week at meals. When Lady Carlotta replies that she will instruct the children in French and Russian, Mrs. Quabarl begins losing control over her.

   At the family dinner Lady Carlotta not only drinks wine along with her new employers but also discusses various vintages and recommends a merchant to the dumbfounded Mr. Quabarl. She further confounds them by announcing that she teaches history by the "Schartz-Metterklume method," which the Quabarls agree to accept but clearly do not understand. The next morning Mrs. Quabarl discovers one daughter, Irene, sitting on the stairs and the other, Viola, covered by a wolfskin rug and perched on the window seat behind her. She is told that Irene is supposed to be Rome and Viola a she-wolf. Suddenly from the lawn comes angry screaming, and she observes her sons, Claude and Wilfred, dragging the lodgekeeper's small daughters toward the house. Lady Carlotta informs Mrs. Quabarl that the children are reenacting the rape of the Sabine women. Mrs. Quabarl fires Lady Carlotta and rescues the girls. As Lady

Carlotta walks toward the railway station, she tells her former employer that because of her interference her children will grow up thinking that the Sabine women escaped.

The story concludes with Lady Carlotta's country friend remarking to her late-arriving guest how tiresome it must have been to miss her train and spend the night with strangers. Lady Carlotta replies that it was not at all tiresome—for her.

## Themes and Meanings

The main purpose of this story is to deflate the pretensions of the overbearing Mrs. Quabarl by exposing her middle-class values and ignorance to the better informed and aristocratic behavior of Lady Carlotta. Such social satire was the stock in trade of Saki, who wrote dozens of such stories for fashionable periodicals such as the *Westminster Gazette*, in which this story first appeared. He attacked most of the institutions of his Edwardian era including Parliament, modern styles of dress and behavior, and various religious, political, and social beliefs.

The character of Mrs. Quabarl is a typical target for Saki's derision. Overbearing, pretentious, and newly rich, she cannot maintain her self-assurance when faced by the comfortable style and confidence that is bred into Lady Carlotta. In their confrontation Munro pits the traditional savoir faire of the aristocracy against the affectations of the newly arrived. There is really no contest, however, as autocrats are seldom a match for aristocrats in Saki's fictional world. Lady Carlotta knows more about how to carry off the lifestyle to which Mrs. and Mr. Quabarl aspire, and she refuses to be distracted by the trappings of their wealth, such as the Quabarls' fancy new car, in the assertion of her superiority. Quabarl Mansion might impress a real governess, but not Lady Carlotta, for whom such places appear false.

Like his fictional Quabarl children, Saki was educated with his brother and sister at home. His father often employed governesses, so he was familiar with the nature of the type. As A. J. Langguth, Saki's biographer, points out, the Munro children early had worked out a version of the "Schartz-Metterklume method" in their nursery by acting out history among themselves. Such an unconventional education may have worked in the confines of the eccentric and aristocratic Munro household; however, in the story such an unorthodox approach to the subject proves too radical for the more conventional Quabarls. Although they appear to have aristocratic aspirations, they remain middle class at heart and resist anything that might undermine their recently acquired social position. Saki develops that idea through their reactions to Lady Carlotta's fabricated educational program.

The fact that Lady Carlotta's history-teaching method has the obviously German-sounding name of "Schartz-Metterklume" adds to the satire. Throughout his life Saki was staunchly British and deeply suspicious of the effect that continental ideas were having on his native culture, so he frequently aimed his wit at foreign values.

## Style and Technique

Saki developed a "high" style in his prose and became famous for his ability to undercut the authority of his characters with well-chosen phrases that reveal subtle nuances of class or social position. For example, when Mrs. Quabarl becomes aware that Lady Carlotta is not impressed by her family's wealth, she reveals to the reader her social insecurity as well as her class pretensions. Lady Carlotta naturally does not notice the Quabarls' riches, as a real governess might, because she has grown up around similar trappings of wealth. Her discussion of wines at the dinner table further establishes her position and undermines that of her employers.

Lady Carlotta always thinks or speaks with a demeanor that reveals her confidence. On the other hand the Quabarls, through their hesitancy and confusion, expose their own lack of confidence. Even Lady Carlotta's quiet acquiescence at being swept up by Mrs. Quabarl from the railroad station reflects her absolute self-confidence. Nothing that she does or experiences can diminish her aristocratic bearing and class position. Mrs. Quabarl would be mortified to be mistaken for a governess because her own sense of self is based largely on surface appearances, not on internal assurance or birth. In "The Schartz-Metterklume Method," Saki makes the point that one may purchase a manor, but truly to have the manner, one must be born to it.

*Charles L. P. Silet*

# THE SCHREUDERSPITZE

*Author:* Mark Helprin (1947-    )
*Type of plot:* Fable
*Time of plot:* The twentieth century
*Locale:* Munich and the German Alps
*First published:* 1977

*Principal characters:*
WALLICH, the protagonist, a commercial photographer
WALLICH'S WIFE AND SON, both deceased
FRANZEN, another commercial photographer

## The Story

From its very first sentence ("In Munich are many men who look like weasels"),
"The Schreuderspitze" is pervaded by a sense of strangeness and mystery. As the story
opens, one of these weasel-like men, a commercial photographer named Franzen, is
rejoicing at the disappearance of Wallich, a rival photographer. Franzen regards
Wallich with a mixture of respect and scorn: Although Wallich is capable of taking
beautiful pictures, he lacks the drive that would make him successful. He probably
fled to South America or jumped off a bridge, Franzen suggests, because he was too
weak to face himself and understand "what sacrifices are required to survive and pros-
per. It is only in fairy tales that [the weak] rise to triumph." If that is so, "The
Schreuderspitze" is itself a fairy tale. Franzen disappears from the story; Wallich, the
protagonist, emerges triumphant, though not in a way that his earthbound rival would
be able to understand.

Wallich has disappeared to try to adjust to the death of his wife and son in an automobile accident. Only once before has he left Bavaria, on a weeklong honeymoon in
Paris, and even then he was homesick. Now he seeks a place where he can be alone,
yet where he will "have to undergo no savage adjustments." He finds it in the Alpine
village of Garmisch-Partenkirchen, close to the German border, which he is afraid to
cross. By the end of the story, a fable of mystical transformation, he will cross a border
more profound than any national boundary.

Wallich goes in October, and, in response to the railroad agent's warning about
snow, claims on the spur of the moment that he is a mountain climber. In fact, he has
always been poor at sports and "would close his eyes in fear when looking through
Swiss calendars." However, one may ask "why was he going to Garmisch-Partenkirchen anyway, if not for an ordeal through which to right himself?" That ordeal,
mad as it seems for one with neither talent nor experience, will be to attempt a five-
day ascent of the nearly vertical west face of the Schreuderspitze, the most imposing
peak in the area.

In the village he feels too awkward to eat in restaurants and so almost haphazardly begins to starve himself. He begins to exercise; at length the noise he makes gets him evicted from his hotel room, and he moves up the valley to the even smaller village of Altenburg-St. Peter—another significant stage in his journey. By the end of February, five months after his arrival, he is doing 250 push-ups four times a day, 150 of them on his fingertips; he runs for four hours every night, "sometimes in snow which had accumulated up to his knees." Meanwhile, he has been reading mountaineering manuals—determined to press on despite their graphic warnings against climbing without proper training—and ordering the finest equipment.

So far, his movement has been exclusively upward and outward, away from humanity. Now, in May, he sees his reflection in a shop window and finds that his face has grown hard and lean, lacking gentleness. He buys a radio and listens to music by Ludwig van Beethoven to bring himself back into balance, knowing that "unmitigated extremes are a great cause of failure." At the railway station, awaiting the arrival of a rope he has ordered, he encounters an attractive family—father, mother, two small daughters—which appeals to him greatly. At this point, just over halfway through the story, he begins to dream. The remainder of "The Schreuderspitze" consists largely of detailed depictions of his mysterious dreams.

At first, inspired apparently by the encounter at the station, the dreams unfold "like the chapters in a brilliant nineteenth century history." It is "as if the mountains and valleys were filled with loving families of which he was part." He dreams then of his wife, who embraces him and then parts from him. Then begin the dreams of climbing. He feels light and strong, "as if he had quickly evolved into a new kind of animal suited for breathtaking travel in the steep heights." In his dreams as in his waking life, he is becoming a new man.

Earlier, in a high meadow, he had fugitive glimpses of a boy whom he comes to believe is his dead son. He finds that in certain conditions of light he can see and sense miraculous things, hints of the world beyond. Again he dreams of climbing in the pure world of ice and reaches the summit of the Schreuderspitze. Meanwhile, down below, he has packed up his gear, readying himself to return to Munich without having attempted a physical ascent.

In a final dream Wallich finds himself again at the summit in a mighty storm. He sees that the mountain is far higher than he thought: "The Alps were to it not even foothills." He has a mystic vision of the world, with Munich at its center, "shining and pulsing like a living thing." He longs for the city now, and he returns to it ready to resume his work, having "found freedom from grief in the great and heart-swelling sight he had seen from the summit" of the Schreuderspitze. He realizes that soon enough he will be reunited with his wife and son in the world of light.

### Themes and Meanings

"The Schreuderspitze" is a quest story: the story of a man, wounded by the loss of his loved ones, who undertakes a physical and spiritual journey and returns triumphant, born anew. The weasel-like photographer, Franzen, who appears in the opening section, ironically is blind to everything except the requirements of commerce, and this tunnel vision enables him to get ahead in the world. Wallich, on the other hand, is less successful materially precisely because he has an eye for beauty, for the rich and grand possibilities depicted in fairy tales. It is this vision that saves him in his hour of need. It drives him up into the mountains where he can be alone and discover the meaning of life and death. The Schreuderspitze, as he prepares to climb it, has a perilous beauty for him, for, as the story makes clear, to attempt a physical ascent would be to die, despite all his valiant preparations. However, having lost his wife and son, he is more than half in love with death.

He is saved finally by his openness to the world of human life: the Beethoven symphonies to which he listens, the family on the platform. Thus, he is able to climb to the summit, the world of ice and pure radiant light, in his dreams (as a result of his arduous preparations), yet he is anchored to the world as a mountaineer is anchored by ropes and pitons. The journey is circular, as it must be. Franzen, who stands for all who neither think nor see, will never understand him. However, Wallich, an unassuming, not very successful little man to those who know him in Munich, is a true hero. Having stood at the border, seen the light, come so close to being reunited with his wife and son, he yet returns willingly to "struggle at his craft." In that he is most heroic of all.

## Style and Technique

"The Schreuderspitze" is not a realistic story, in the sense of depicting ordinary events in the waking lives of ordinary people, nor is it intended to be. Rather, it is a fable whose purpose is to compel belief in, or at least open the reader's mind to, extraordinary spiritual phenomena. A fable is not limited in subject matter as a realistic story is; it can contain, as this one does, the stuff of dreams.

Much is customarily taken for granted. Here, for example, there is no close-up psychological examination of Wallich's grief; it is simply a given. The fabulist has two methods of persuading the reader to believe in the strange events he or she depicts. One is the copious use of highly specific detail; the other, the use of a calm, authoritative, rather formal and distanced narrative voice.

The use of specific detail, although important throughout, is especially noteworthy in Mark Helprin's descriptions of Wallich's climbing dreams: "Anchoring two pitons into the rock as solidly as he could, he clipped an oval carabiner on the bottom piton, put a safety line on the top one, and lowered himself about sixty feet down the two ropes." This kind of sentence is common, and it serves an important thematic function. To the reader, as to Wallich himself, the ascent is absolutely real, even though Walllich never climbs the mountain in body. Thus, by the end, the distinction between spiritual and bodily ascent becomes insignificant. Wallich has climbed the Schreuderspitze in the only sense that matters.

The voice must be established at the beginning, as it is here, so that the reader will at once be inclined to trust the author and listen openly to whatever he has to say. "In Munich are many men who look like weasels," the first sentence of the story, is on the face of it a very odd statement. However, Helprin goes on to expand on it—the possible causes of such a phenomenon—as if it were a simple matter of fact, readily verifiable.

For the purposes of the story the statement becomes true, then, just as it is true later on that Wallich runs for four hours nightly through knee-deep snow (a feat beyond the strength of a world-class athlete), that high in the Alps he receives clear signals from a Berlin radio station, or (more crucially) that he has elaborate dreams that he remembers in perfect detail. There is no question of deceit between author and reader; the reader simply agrees to believe in order to be led, finally, to a profound and liberating idea about the nature of human life.

*Edwin Moses*

# SCHRÖDINGER'S CAT

*Author:* Ursula K. Le Guin (1929-    )
*Type of plot:* Science fiction
*Time of plot:* Probably the mid-twentieth century
*Locale:* Unspecified
*First published:* 1974

> *Principal characters:*
> THE NARRATOR, a writer and cat lover
> ROVER, a mailman who sounds like a dog
> A YELLOW CAT, which might have been Schrödinger's cat

*The Story*

The narrator, a writer who is never identified by gender or name, lives in a world that is absurd: When a couple says they are breaking up, they mean it literally—the woman becomes a disassembled collection of body parts, hopping across the floor, then a tangled bundle of nerves, while the man is reduced to pieces trotting around, bouncing and cheeping like chicks. A tremendous grief parallels the absurdity of the action. The narrator admits to a struggle with writer's block and complains of "Adam's Disease," a version of the Protestant work ethic curable only by total decapitation. There is a larger grief here, an unidentifiable longing for something that cannot be named. A musical note that keeps playing makes the narrator want to cry, but he or she does not know for what. With a stray cat asleep on his or her lap the grieving narrator dreams, hoping that somehow the cat will suggest what has been lost, what is being grieved for.

The most obvious cause of grief should be the distemper of the world, which is heating up at an unbearable rate. Stoves give off waves of heat even when they are turned off, water comes scalding from the cold-water tap; even forks and pencils are too hot to touch. Unbearable heat radiates from other people, whose kisses burn like branding irons. Rational inquiry has been unable to diagnose the source of the heat, which threatens to melt the world.

In the midst of this disorder, a knock at the door announces the mailman, whose monosyllabic "Yah," "Wow," and "How," so remind the writer of a dog that the writer promptly names him Rover. Rover drops a large knapsack on the floor. The narrator, who has fed the cat sardines, opens a can of pork and beans for Rover. When he sees the yellow cat calmly licking sardine oil off its whiskers, he growls, then recognizes that this particular cat belongs to the famous physicist, Erwin Schrödinger. Rover professes his delight, and reveals that the burden of his knapsack is a large box, with a gun attached. This and the cat are all that is necessary to complete Schrödinger's experiment.

The experiment involves putting the cat in the box and shutting the lid. After five seconds, the box will emit a photon. That photon will strike a half-silvered mirror, and either pass through or not pass through. If it gets through the mirror, the gun will shoot silently into the soundproof box. The viewer, Rover explains, cannot know whether the cat is dead or alive until the box is opened. Two possibilities, life and death, are reduced to one certainty when the box is opened.

The narrator is disturbed by the closed system of thinking that Rover has represented. "But why does opening the box and looking reduce the system back to one probability, either live cat or dead cat? Why don't we get included in the system when we lift the lid of the box?" Rover does not know, but he pleads for certainty. He needs to know for sure that God is playing dice with the world.

As the two argue over the morality of the experiment, the cat jumps in the box and flicks the lid closed with its tail, setting things in motion. The narrator and Rover wait in suspense, then lift the lid. The cat is not there.

The story ends with the house itself becoming a large box; the roof lifts off and lets in the light of the stars. The narrator finally identifies the note that brings such grief: "It is the note A, the one that drove the composer Schumann mad."

*Themes and Meanings*

Ursula K. Le Guin has long been fascinated by the notion that our world sees reality through a particularly dense set of glasses, fashioned by people who dote on reason as the only legitimate mode of expression, and who see themselves as the world's only true intelligence. "By climbing up into his head and shutting out every voice but his own, 'Civilized Man' has gone deaf," she notes in her introduction to a short story collection. "He hears only his own words making up the world."

In "Schrödinger's Cat," Le Guin takes on the reality humankind constructs by having both the narrator and the cat participate in a subversion of humanity's rational experiments. Rover makes the fatal mistake of believing that his own mind can encompass all the realities of the universe. He engages in a search for certainty, even if the only certainty available is the cold comfort of knowing that God plays dice with the world.

The story alludes to Erwin Schrödinger (1887-1961), a famous Austrian physicist who helped develop quantum mechanics and who wrote a mathematical equation that purported to represent the possibilities that can occur in a system. Because this equation was based on a mathematical rather than a visual model of the atom, Schrödinger was able to reduce the possibilities of the universe to a finite number. Albert Einstein admired Schrödinger's work, but said, "an inner voice tells me it is not yet the real thing."

Le Guin agrees with Einstein's assessment. The world is not a mathematical model, and so there are more than two outcomes possible as a result of Schrödinger's experiment; the cat proves that by disappearing. Rover and, by implication, the rest of the world, have forgotten that the ability rationally to understand the world is limited, because the world does not operate only within rational limits. Words can describe a portion of meaning, but they also restrict meaning, just as the box is a restrictive representation of the universe.

The sudden heat that afflicts the world of the story is caused by entropy, which is the measure of the degree of disorder in a system. The disorder represented by the woman who is literally coming to pieces and the heat that makes a kiss like a branding iron has reached critical dimensions. The narrator likens rational attempts to study and observe this breakdown to the desperate observations of a man being dragged down to Hell. "One wonders," the writer observes, "if hell would exist if he did not look at it." Is it possible that attempts to define and describe the universe create the very horrors from which people long to escape? At the very least, this story suggests that despite human efforts to contain the world in a neat little package of certainties, it escapes every attempt at interpretation.

When the lid lifts off the house, and the starlight floods in, the universe expands beyond its original, restricted definition. The note A, which may be seen as a metaphor for language itself, resonates with a clearer tone, signifying that the realm of understanding had expanded as well. Humans cannot rely on their own closed interpretations of reality, shutting off the different viewpoints of the cat, the narrator, and perhaps even those of plants and minerals, if they hope to find truth.

*Style and Technique*

The action of this story is simple, if disjointed. A reader who enters the narrative looking for the traditional line of connected events will be dismayed. In this story, no rational patterns appear—that is part of the writer's art, and her message. Nothing is what it seems, which is appropriate, as the story concerns breaking out of the certainties of life to explore undiscovered realms. Words refuse to obey the simple demands of the reader's expectations; they change meaning from one sentence to the next. Claiming at one point to have both a husband and a wife, the narrator confounds even our desire to know his or her gender.

Le Guin is in the delicate place of trying to describe a world that defies linguistic and rational meanings when the only tool available to her is the very words she wishes to discredit. Thus, she works by indirection, building a desire for certainty to a pitch almost as feverish as Rover's. She works with puns and with literal interpretations, making the reader's head spin in the effort to keep up. In doing so, she demonstrates just how subjective meaning can become, even when one stays within the linguistic and grammatical rules that govern writing.

Language, Le Guin suggests, must be reinvented to recognize and represent the diversity of viewpoints found throughout creation. As she notes in her introduction to *Buffalo Gals and Other Animal Presences* (1987), there must come a time "when the word is not sword, but shuttle," a time when meaning includes rather than closes off alternative perceptions. Her slippery language is a finely tuned technique for teaching how to do this.

*Susan E. Keegan*

# THE SCORPION

*Author:* Paul Bowles (1910-1999)
*Type of plot:* Fable
*Time of plot:* Unspecified
*Locale:* Unspecified
*First published:* 1945

> *Principal characters:*
> AN OLD WOMAN, who lives alone in a cave
> ONE OF HER SONS
> AN OLD MAN, a resident of a nearby village

*The Story*

An old woman lives in a tiny cave that was carved out of a cliff by her sons long ago. Her existence is animal-like. Neither happy nor unhappy, she does not have to argue with or share her meager existence with anyone else. She realizes that she will soon die and assumes that her sons, who now live far away in the town, have forgotten her.

Occasionally an old man from a nearby village passes by, always resting on a rock within sight of the entrance to the cave, but he never acknowledges the woman's existence. The old woman suspects that he does this to annoy her and plots ways to annoy him in return, but never acts on her ideas. The only other creatures the woman encounters are the occasional small animals that blunder into her cave but which she can never catch and the scorpions that live there, which she brushes off the walls with rags and smashes with her bare heel.

One day one of her sons appears. The day is becoming dark, and she is annoyed that her son's shadow darkens her tiny abode even more. When she reluctantly allows him to enter the cave, he tells her that she must come with him. The son refuses to let her postpone the trip a day, but does allow her to sleep while he waits outside.

The old woman dreams that she is in the large town her son plans to take her to. The bells of its churches ring all the time, and she thinks that the people in the streets might be her sons, although they are unable to respond to her. At nightfall, she finds herself at a house whose women rise to meet her, assuring her that she has a room there.

At this point in her dream, she becomes a little girl who is crying. Then she sees a scorpion crawling down from the ceiling. Because she has nothing to brush it away with, she uses her hand, but the scorpion nimbly grabs her fingers and refuses to be shaken off. When she realizes that it is not going to sting, she is overwhelmed with happiness. She lifts the scorpion to her lips, and it crawls into her mouth and down her throat and becomes hers.

The old woman wakes up and announces to her son that she is ready to go. As they set out, her son tells her that their destination is three days away, noticing, as he does so, her feeble condition. The old man sitting on his rock seems surprised to see them leaving. The son asks who the man is, but when the woman claims she does not know, her son responds that she is lying.

### Themes and Meanings

Appropriately enough for a story entitled "The Scorpion," the old woman's encounter with a scorpion in her dream constitutes the work's key episode. Although Paul Bowles makes it clear that this episode is part of a dream, the image of the creature's passage into the woman's mouth and down her throat is so horrifying that the reader may fail to appreciate the dreamlike, symbolic nature of the rest of the story.

Bowles's characters are unnamed and minimally described; they are referred to only as an "old woman," "one of her sons," and an "old man." In fact, they have little more personality than the scorpion itself. The setting is not specified, although one or two clues within the story, and knowledge of Bowles's travels and other writings, suggest that it may be set in Central America.

The old woman lives in a tiny, damp cave—a fairy-tale setting that symbolically suggests the individual psyche and the womb. Her son plans to take her on a journey of three days, a symbolically significant period of time traditionally used to indicate the passage from death to life, as in the story of Christ's Crucifixion and rebirth. Her guide will be her son, to whom she once gave the gift of life, and who will now lead her on an equally significant journey. As her dream further suggests, she will be reborn as a little girl.

Other themes concern sexual and generational antagonism, although these also are so understated that one is scarcely aware of them. The old woman often had had to argue with her sons to fetch wood for her oven, and she is clearly happy that she no longer has to share her food with them. In fact, she is not sure which son has come to visit her and looks for an identifying deformity of his hand. She is displeased that his shadow darkens her cave, and only her dream softens her attitude toward him. Significantly, the men she encounters in the street in her dream, who she thinks may be her sons, are unable to communicate with her. Once she reaches a house, however, there are other women, women who show her to a room—a comforting if unfamiliar equivalent of the cave she is about to abandon in her waking, conscious life.

The themes of generational and sexual antagonism are repeated and reinforced in the story's final scene: The old woman claims not to recognize the old man sitting on the stone, and her son accuses her of lying. However reassuring her dream may be in an ultimate sense, it has not negated the difficult facts of her existence.

"The Scorpion" may be read straightforwardly, as the story of an aged woman whose son has at long last returned home with the unwelcome news that she is no longer capable of living by herself. At this level, the woman's dream represents her coming to terms with a disorienting and frightening situation: She literally swallows her fears. At another level, the woman sets off on a far more significant journey, from the end of life to death—symbolized by the disquieting episode with the scorpion—to life again. Read with this meaning in mind, "The Scorpion" is no longer horrifying but deeply moving.

*Style and Technique*

Bowles has written that as he was reading a collection of translations of Native American texts, a desire came over him to create his own myths, composed from the point of view of a primitive, nonliterate mind. He wrote "The Scorpion," the most tangible result of his experiments, with no conscious control. According to Bowles's account, he simply recorded the words that came into his mind, allowing his subconscious free rein. These facts about its origin account in large part for the story's compelling symbolic content.

Bowles records his story with fablelike simplicity. His language is flat and unadorned, his sentence structure straightforward. Although one may sense significant psychological complexity beneath the story's surface, its characters and situations are presented in the simplest possible terms with the least possible elaboration. The reader is scarcely aware that a story is being told. As a result of this technique, "The Scorpion" seems, and indeed is, timeless. Its opening words, "An old woman lived in a cave," recall various fairy tales and such Mother Goose rhymes as "There was an old woman who lived in a shoe." These associations remove it from the world of the individual writer and place it in a universal context accessible, at least on a symbolic level, to every reader. They also serve to render the central episode of the scorpion even more disquieting.

In recording the genesis of "The Scorpion," Bowles has remarked that he initially hesitated to write fiction because he did not feel that he understood life. The techniques he employed in this story—the automatic writing with no conscious control, the adoption of the primitive point of view—were so successful that he continued producing short stories, most of which are set in Central America, North Africa, and South Asia. He has been recognized as one of the masters of the form in the twentieth century.

*Grove Koger*

# THE SCREAMERS

*Author:* Amiri Baraka (Everett LeRoi Jones, 1934-    )
*Type of plot:* Psychological
*Time of plot:* The 1960's
*Locale:* Newark, New Jersey
*First published:* 1967

> *Principal characters:*
> THE NARRATOR
> LYNN HOPE, a jazz saxophonist

## The Story

The narrator and other patrons are in a Newark nightclub, waiting for Lynn Hope and his musicians to begin playing. Most of the crowd are African Americans whom the narrator divides into two groups: "our camp," which includes those who have had some success, such as being light-skinned or lucky enough to have mothers who were social workers and fathers who were mail carriers, and "those niggers" of the lower class, who work in coin-operated laundries and beauty parlors. Lynn Hope and his men appeal to both groups, although the former cannot quite believe in the musician's greasy hipness.

When the musicians begin, their music becomes a backdrop for the men's efforts to meet women. The narrator wonders who he will get. His expectation that he will end up with a light-skinned girl who has fallen on bad times, or a disgraced white girl, illustrates his self-consciousness about his own middle-class status, and he muses that a wino's daughter would see him as part of that America that is oppressing her.

The narrator's essay on African American saxophonists as "honkers" defines the honk as "a repeated rhythmic figure, a screamed riff, pushed in its insistence past music." His recounting of the great "honkers" leads to a description of Big Jay, who "had set a social form for the poor," and whose earlier performance in the club has set the challenge for Lynn Hope to follow.

Hope tries to meet the challenge inside the club, but when he gets his riff, the crowd pushes him until he leaves the hall, marching at the head of the crowd into Belmont Avenue, stopping traffic with this secret communal expression and gathering an even larger crowd as he proceeds.

The march is peaceful until the police arrive with paddy wagons and fire hoses. They are met by the "Biggers," who are ready for a violent confrontation. The musicians, the narrator, and others in the crowd who are not ready for this kind of action, "broke our different ways, to save whatever it was each of us thought we loved."

## Themes and Meanings

*Tales*, Amiri Baraka's only published collection of short fiction, was published in 1967, two years after he left his white Jewish wife and his bohemian existence in

Greenwich Village, a move precipitated by the assassination of Malcolm X. In 1966, the year of his return to his hometown of Newark, Baraka says in an essay collection titled *Home: Social Essays* (1986), "I have been a lot of places in my time, and done a lot of things. . . . But one truth anyone reading these pieces ought to get is the sense of movement—the struggle, in myself, to understand where and who I am and to move with that understanding. . . . And these moves, most times unconscious . . . seem to me to have been always toward the thing I had coming into the world, with no sweat: my blackness."

It is not easy to maintain this sense of ethnic identity in the face of middle-class pressures, however, and the struggle to move toward it is a major theme in "The Screamers." The narrator and his camp must fight Baraka's fight because what should be natural has been distorted by the influence of white values and the resulting self-hatred that African Americans often feel.

This self-hatred is amply illustrated in the kinds of "girls" for whom the men search. The white girl, disgraced and with "halting speech, a humanity as paltry as her cotton dress," nevertheless has a line of men behind her, "stroking their erections, hoping for a picture to take down south," where those left behind will be impressed by the whiteness.

The narrator realizes that the men are also being judged by white standards of beauty when a light-skinned African American girl will not dance with him. A girl named Erselle rejects him because his hair is not straight enough. Those girls who are not light—and therefore not as desirable—are also out of reach, he imagines, ironically seeing him as "some stuck up boy with 'good' hair, and as a naked display of America, for I meant to her that same oppression."

The narrator mourns his inability to fit into African American society, blaming it on his upbringing: "My father never learned how to drink. Our house sat lonely and large on a half-Italian street, filled with important Negroes." Like the respectable ladies whose stiff arms keep them isolated from the black experience of the dance, the narrator is an observer, not a participant.

What is needed for the crowd to make its journey into blackness is black music—the vehicle for the nonverbal experience of the dance, a sensual and physical means of communication that gets past the white-influenced divisions in this black culture. "In this vat we sweated gladly for each other. And rubbed." It is an environment in which only "the wild or the very poor thrived," however, for "America had choked the rest, who could still sit for hours under popular songs, or be readied for citizenship by slightly Bohemian social workers."

The music also has the potential to be the voice for those searching for blackness. Unlike the English language and mainstream literature, it is not contaminated by white usage and values. This is especially true of the honk, which speaks the "hatred, frustration, secrecy and despair" of the people with "no compromise, no dreary sophistication, only the elegance of something too ugly to be described . . . diluted only at the agent's permission." Thus when Lynn tries to move the crowd, even the narrator responds, doing the one step he knows, while staying safely at the back of the hall.

The movement from the hall into the larger society represented by Belmont Avenue is a move out of safety, however. At first, this black community is able to shape outside society, stopping traffic as they scream at "the clear image of ourselves as we should always be." Society cannot allow this open communal assertiveness, and when the agents of control arrive, the community breaks up. The "Biggers who would not be bent" fight with knives, razors, coke bottles, aerials. Others, including the narrator, go their separate ways, still unable to give up whatever they thought they loved for the complete embrace of blackness.

*Style and Technique*

Two aspects of African American culture influence the style and technique of "The Screamers": oral tradition and music, especially jazz. The story is a tale told by an autobiographical narrator. The other characters, including Lynn Hope, exist for the reader only as described by the narrator. Baraka's use of present tense at the beginning of the tale shifts quickly to past tense, resulting in a more reflective, nostalgic tone.

In his autobiography, Baraka notes that the writers of the Black Arts movement were drenched in black music, even wanting their poetry to be black music. It is clear in "The Screamers" that African American music has revolutionary possibilities. One of those possibilities is transforming literary form by incorporating the rhythms, the musical form of jazz. Baraka does so in this tale, and the result is both poetic and musical.

Baraka's prose in "The Screamers" is rhythmic, with fragmented sentences and long series of phrases that are like jazz riffs, sometimes punctuated by single words or short phrases. He opens the story in this fashion: "Lynn Hope adjusts his turban under the swishing red green yellow shadow lights. Dots. Suede heaven raining, windows yawning cool summer air, and his musicians watch him grinning, quietly, or high with wine blotches on four-dollar shirts." This is a tale meant to be delivered in the oral tradition, by a storyteller-poet, an African griot.

The story is filled with images that the narrator observes: Lynn Hope's turban, "bright yellow stuck with a green stone," the musician's "red string conked hair," a girl with "carefully vaselined bow legs" and a filthy angora sweater. The narrator also catalogs dances (the Grind, the Rub, the Slow Drag) and dance places (Lloyd's, The Nitecap, The Hi-Spot, and Graham's), trying to include those aspects of African American culture from which he, a middle-class black, has been separated.

During the period when Baraka was writing *Tales*, he was also trying to develop an African American aesthetic, an alternative to Western literary tradition, which he had begun to find stifling and alienating. His cataloging of African American experience, imitating of the rhythms of jazz, bringing together the scream of the saxophone and the screams of the dancers in an assertive communal experience, exemplify his own artistic movement into blackness.

*Elsie Galbreath Haley*

# THE SCULPTOR'S FUNERAL

*Author:* Willa Cather (1873-1947)
*Type of plot:* Satire
*Time of plot:* The late nineteenth century
*Locale:* Sand City, a small Kansas town
*First published:* 1905

> *Principal characters:*
> HARVEY MERRICK, a sculptor
> JIM LAIRD, a local lawyer
> PHILIP PHELPS, a local banker
> HENRY STEAVENS, one of the sculptor's pupils
> ANNIE MERRICK, the sculptor's mother

*The Story*

Harvey Merrick, a distinguished sculptor, has died of tuberculosis at the age of forty. As the story opens, a group of townsfolk waits for the arrival of the night train that is bringing Merrick's body back from the East for burial in the small Kansas town where he grew up. The conversation among those waiting reveals the small-mindedness of their assessment of Merrick. When the train pulls in, Jim Laird, a local lawyer, drunk as usual but seemingly the only person who has a real purpose in being at the station, leads the group of waiting men to the express car. There they find Henry Steavens, a young apprentice of Merrick, who has traveled from the East with the coffin. Steavens, who worshiped his master, is stunned by the apparent lack of any connection or similarity between Merrick and the men who have come to collect the body. He watches them gaze with curiosity but without comprehension at the palm that lies across the coffin lid, a symbol of Merrick's distinction as an artist.

When the coffin reaches Merrick's home, his mother rushes out into the yard, screaming for her dead son. Steavens tries to see some evidence of kinship between her and his idol, but he is appalled by her look of violence and fierce passion, as well as by the power she wields over everyone around her. Steavens is equally appalled by the cheap vulgarity of taste that is everywhere apparent in the decor of the house and can scarcely believe that Merrick could ever have had any connection with this place. Despite her show of pious grief and decorous behavior, Mrs. Merrick stages a horrifying tantrum when her servant makes a small mistake, and it is evident that only this same servant, along with Mrs. Merrick's weak, worn-out husband, actually feels any sorrow for the dead man. Steavens's distress at the abysmal family situation finds an echo in the expression he sees on the dead sculptor's face, which looks "as though he were still guarding something precious and holy, which might even yet be wrested from him."

Steavens begins for the first time to see the full significance of Merrick's achievement. The sculptor's accomplishments now take on a near-miraculous aspect, especially when seen against the background of his dreadful family and the physically difficult and culturally impoverished life of this small frontier town. Steavens also begins to understand the connection between the tragedy of Merrick's personal life (that is, the sculptor's deep introversion and reluctance to be involved in personal relationships), and his past life as a boy in Sand City.

Steavens joins the group of watchers in the dining room, who are as dreadful a collection of small-town types as can ever have been gathered together into one room. Everything they say reveals their pettiness and sordid materialism. The banker Phelps, representative of the mean-spirited callousness of all the watchers, discusses usury law with another banker. To these men, Merrick was a failure, and they dismiss him contemptuously for his lack of material success, his straining of the family resources for the purpose of financing his education, his inability to deal with the practical aspects of farm life, and his effeminacy.

Just as Steavens is wondering how much more he can take, Jim Laird bursts into the room. Despite the fact that he is a drunkard, Laird is a strong and intelligent man, as well as a shrewd lawyer, and Steavens has already recognized the fact that he is the only person in Sand City who has any understanding or appreciation for Harvey Merrick. Laird launches into a bitter tirade against those assembled in the dining room and everything for which they stand. In this climactic moment of the story, Laird reveals his own stature as a human being as well as the vision of greatness that he and Merrick shared as young men. Merrick was able to achieve his vision, it is implied, only because he never returned to Sand City. Laird, on the other hand, who did return, found that the town did not want great men but only "successful rascals," which is what he became. Laird confesses that he had felt shamed at times by Merrick's success, but at other times proud that Merrick, at least, had escaped. The next day, Laird is too drunk to attend the funeral, and, in a final moment of irony, Willa Cather relates that he died the following year of a cold he caught in the Colorado mountains. One of Phelps's sons had been involved in criminal activity, and Laird had gone out to defend him, thereby upholding to the end his image of himself as a successful rascal. In what has clearly been his finest hour, Laird defends his old friend Harvey Merrick from the vicious attacks of Phelps and the others, but it is too late for him to salvage any kind of meaningful life for himself. Merrick's death, on the other hand, although it has tragically cut short a life of great achievement and promise, affirms the values for which that life stood, despite the failure of the people of Sand City to understand or cherish those values.

### Themes and Meanings

Many of Cather's early stories probe in a highly self-conscious manner the relationship between the artist and society. Despite her own statement that the world was tired of stories about artists, Cather returned to the subject over and over again, indicating clearly her passionate concern with it. In "The Sculptor's Funeral," the clash of values between Harvey Merrick, the artist figure, and the inhabitants of the frontier town to which he returns only in death, is absolute. Only by escaping to the East, representative of older, more civilized traditions and values, has Merrick been able to achieve artistic fulfillment, and even then the fulfillment is premised on a total sacrifice of self.

For Cather, the artist represents everything that is beautiful and noble in terms of human endeavor, and yet artistic achievement is seldom acknowledged or even recognized by ordinary people. In the case of Harvey Merrick, the ultimate irony lies in the failure of the artist's own family and fellow citizens to understand the value of his art. Life is too harsh and demanding in the primitive conditions engendered by pioneer society, to support anything except a crass materialism that blights any appreciation for the creative spirit. Although Cather came to believe later that she had been overly harsh in her condemnation of western society in this story, the intensity of her commitment to art and her desire to defend its value against the encroachment of vulgar materialism remained with her during her entire life.

*Style and Technique*

The deliberate choice of rendering the events of the story through the point of view of Steavens, Harvey Merrick's young apprentice, strongly colors the reader's response to those events. An unworldly young man whose chief characteristic is his admiration for the dead sculptor, Steavens looks on Merrick's family and the inhabitants of Sand City with such horror and scorn that they take on the aspects of caricature at times. There is no indication that Cather does not share the views of Steavens, but she does complicate matters with her portrayal of Jim Laird, who is by far the most interesting character in the story. The biting and to some degree simplistic satire on small-town life, the descriptive style that verges at times on the naturalistic, despite Cather's avowed distaste for this term, are qualified by the figure of Laird. Laird's physical appearance (he is large, redheaded, bearded) and vitality make a strong impression, and in one scene, in which he opens with one blow of his fist a window that Steavens has been unable to move, there is a suggestion that this strength is not simply physical. The speech he makes in response to the petty criticisms the townsfolk have leveled at Merrick, is a set piece that rather too clearly expresses the views of Cather herself. However, it is also a moving testimony to what remains noble and visionary in Laird. He is a lost soul, one who sees the truth but has not been able to follow it himself. Cather clearly intends the reader to view him sympathetically. The beauty of the prairie landscape, along with Cather's portrayal of Jim Laird, suggests the possibility of a less monolithic vision of pioneer life than the story, for the most part, offers, and one that would shape Cather's later work.

*Anne Thompson Lee*

# SEATON'S AUNT

*Author:* Walter de la Mare (1873-1956)
*Type of plot:* Horror
*Time of plot:* Around 1890 and 1900
*Locale:* Gummidge's preparatory boys' school in rural England, London, and Seaton's country home
*First published:* 1923

> *Principal characters:*
> WITHERS, the narrator, a British schoolboy of about twelve, later a young man
> ARTHUR SEATON, his schoolmate
> SEATON'S AUNT, actually his half-aunt and guardian
> ALICE OUTRAM, later Seaton's fiancé

*The Story*

Withers, the story's narrator and central consciousness, is first aware of Seaton as an unpopular schoolfellow at Gummidge's. Seaton has money, but he is unattractive and unskillful at games, and he is often the butt of practical jokes. Nevertheless, he manages to persuade Withers to spend the half-term holiday with him at his aunt's.

When they arrive, Seaton dawdles rather than entering the house directly, acting as if vaguely afraid of something. Finally they approach the house to find his aunt watching them ominously from an upper window as if brooding over them. When she meets them she mispronounces Withers's name but overwhelms him with attention, in marked contrast to her disdainful treatment of Seaton, of whom she says, "Dust we are, and dust we shall become." She presides over a lavish and sumptuous lunch, which she attacks with gusto, while Seaton merely nibbles. Taking Withers to a neatly appointed bedroom, she speaks slightingly of her nephew.

That afternoon, during which she pointedly ignores the boys, Seaton confesses uneasily that she sees and knows everything—that she is "in league with the devil." He adds that she is not his real aunt, that the estate is actually his. At tea she mocks him again, referring to him as "that creature." Later she deliberately prolongs a chess match with Withers, carefully avoiding mate while praising his play, and sweeping the board clear so that play cannot be resumed. She seems to be toying with him.

That night Seaton awakens Withers shortly after they retire. He hints that the house is full of ghosts, all at his aunt's command. He suggests further that his aunt was responsible for his mother's death and that she has the power to suck souls dry. He fears she intends that fate for him. Suddenly he freezes; he has sensed her eavesdropping at the door.

Believing that Seaton is simply trying to scare him, Withers bets that the aunt is still in bed. Seaton takes up the challenge, and the two set off. Noises in the house seem to reinforce Seaton's fears of ghosts, and when they reach the bedroom, after passing a labyrinth of shadowy corridors, the bed is empty. Worse, they hear her coming. They hide in a cupboard; through a crack they watch her enter. After what seems hours they manage to sneak out, but Seaton seems drained by the experience. Withers helps him back to his dingy, littered, uncomfortable bedroom, then hides underneath the bed-covers. The following morning, Withers finds it easy to believe that Seaton's aunt knows every word and movement that occurred.

On their return to school, Withers drops Seaton, who shortly thereafter leaves. Their next encounter takes place by chance several years later in London; Seaton announces that he has come to town to buy an engagement ring. He admits that he and his aunt have lost much money and that she has aged. He also implies that Withers continues to discount their boyhood experience and invites him to come down to meet his fiancé and confirm his earlier impressions. Withers reluctantly agrees.

Shortly afterward, Withers returns to find the place considerably run down. When pressed, Seaton states that he finds the deterioration fitting: humanity brings ruin in its wake. Withers rejects this philosophy. The two lunch, then play a desultory chess match, interrupted by the arrival of Alice Outram, Seaton's fiancé. The couple spend the rest of the afternoon discussing their future, but without animation, as if they sense futility in the face of an unseen destructive force.

They join Seaton's aunt for dinner; she seems older, but more massive and powerful than before. The meal itself is stupendous, though poor; her appetite remains voracious. She manages the table conversation brilliantly but directs implicit sarcasm at Seaton. Among other topics, she singles out marriage as a refuge for fools and evolution as a reservoir of degeneration, and she hints darkly at the "spiritual agencies" to which the truly superior have access. The two ladies withdraw.

Seaton confides that he fears leaving Alice alone with his aunt. When Withers attempts to downplay these fears by suggesting that the old lady's spite proceeds from feeling neglected, Seaton insists there are unseen forces and that his aunt makes use of them to gain control over others, fattening herself on their souls. When they rejoin the ladies, his aunt asks the betrothed couple to promenade in the moonlit garden while she plays the piano for Withers. Her playing is diabolic: First she inverts and parodies the romantic sentiments of the *Moonlight Sonata*, then transforms the simple hymn "A Few More Years Shall Roll" into a commentary on the bitterness and squalor of life. When she finishes, she speaks briefly on the beauty of darkness: "dark hair, dark eyes, dark cloud, dark night, dark vision, dark death, dark grave, dark DARK!" She suggests that she will not be lonely after Seaton's marriage because she will have her memories for company, and she hints at her awareness of everything said and done in the garden during her playing. Withers invites Seaton to join him in town before the wedding.

However, Withers loses touch with Seaton. That autumn, realizing that he must have missed the marriage, he rushes off to make amends. Once there, he finds himself reluctant to enter the house. The housekeeper tries to fend him off but finally admits him. Seaton's aunt seems to have faded in the interim. She tells him that Alice has gone to Yorkshire, and she is evasive about Seaton. She accuses her nephew of having spread lies about her; when Withers asks directly where he is, she stares him down, mumbles incoherently, and leaves.

Withers remains alone until it is dark. Finally resolving to depart, he finds his way to the front hall, where he makes out Seaton's aunt peering down from the landing. She calls for Arthur; then, recognizing Withers, says that he is disgusting and orders him out.

He runs from the house, not stopping until he reaches the village. There he asks the butcher if Mr. Seaton still lives with his aunt. The butcher's wife replies that he has been dead and buried these three months, just before he was to be married. Withers is stunned; finding no course of action, he leaves with the reflection that Seaton "had never been much better than 'buried' in my mind."

*Themes and Meanings*

Though ostensibly a subdued horror story of the vampire or diabolic possession variety, "Seaton's Aunt" is in many respects rather an inversion of the narrative of coming of age—a failed rite of passage. To that extent it traces the life of one who does not pass through boyhood through adolescence to maturity, and it focuses on some of the fears and perils of that passage.

At the beginning of the story, Seaton is the prototypical "odd boy," in-expert at all the skills that constitute social acceptance in boyhood. He is not good at games, does not mix well with others, and depends on his extra money to buy companionship. As Withers gets to know him better, he discovers further disadvantages. Seaton's parents are dead; his guardian aunt is unsympathetic at best; finally, as the reader learns at the outset, he has to leave school in semidisgrace. His very beginnings are clouded.

Further shadows appear in the peculiarities of his relations with his aunt. It is not only that she continually denigrates him—though that is significant, for nothing can grow if it is routinely stifled—but also that she is hostile to life in ways both real and symbolic. She takes delight in humiliating others, in strenuously asserting her own superiority; she toys with others, letting them live only because her own life is drawn out of theirs. She is more than the older generation suppressing the younger; she is the bloated ego glorying in the failure of others, the cannibal feeding on the young, in the process destroying life itself.

In this way she becomes the embodiment of many standard adolescent fears. She is the evil stepmother, who succeeds first in depriving Seaton of his childhood, then of his estate, then of his fiancé, and finally of his life. She controls evil forces, robbing others of their souls. In the end she becomes the spider to which Seaton has likened her, surrounded only by the desiccated husks of those on whom she has preyed and dismissing Withers (note the name) as a "dreadful creature" because she has no power over him.

*Style and Technique*

Walter de la Mare diffuses the real horrors of this rather horrible story by his choice of point of view and by a deliberate use of parallelism. Withers is presented as the commonplace "regular guy," both at school and in early manhood; thus he is both significantly different from Seaton and enough like him to sympathize distantly with his distress. From the beginning he sees Seaton as a failure, in the way that boys rate their schoolfellows as if gauging their chances of surviving adolescence. By all the signs, Seaton will not make it, and that causes Withers some discomfort. However, he cannot identify with Seaton, in the way of friends—Seaton is at first too unprepossessing, later too "sensitive," or "imaginative," or simply embarrassing, for that.

In this way, Withers—and the reader—are spared the full horror of Seaton's fate. He tells the story as if he were relating the curious story of someone else, of one of the others, those who are not quite like us. By the end, he comes close to accepting what happened as something predestined for those like Seaton—but not for him and, by inference, not for the reader. Thus he does not finally assent to Seaton's version of the events, with its overtones of evil spirits, diabolic possession, and occult influences; he remains free to believe that Seaton's aunt is merely conventionally rather than unconventionally evil—the parent who blights the child by indifference and hostility, the egotistical bully, rather than the demon who sucks souls. He leaves with the safe observation that Seaton had been buried all of his life.

*James L. Livingston*

# THE SECOND TREE FROM THE CORNER

*Author:* E. B. White (1899-1985)
*Type of plot:* Parable
*Time of plot:* The late 1940's
*Locale:* New York City
*First published:* 1947

> *Principal characters:*
> MR. TREXLER, a psychiatric patient
> THE DOCTOR, his psychiatrist

*The Story*

   Mr. Trexler, a New Yorker, is an unenthusiastic psychiatric patient. Plagued by what he claims are the dullest set of neurotic symptoms in the world, he suffers from dizziness, pains in the back of the neck, apprehension, tightness in the scalp, anger and anxiety over his inability to concentrate or work, pressure, tension, and gas in the stomach.

   Trexler's relationship with his doctor is uneasy from the start. The doctor's initial question, asking if he has ever had any bizarre thoughts, unnerves Trexler. As one who has had nothing but bizarre thoughts since he was a young boy, Trexler feels cornered. Unable to choose an appropriate bizarre thought to share, Trexler lies that he has never had them.

   After what seems to Trexler like an interminable length of time, the session draws to a close. The doctor shakes his hand and, with a smile, assures him there is nothing wrong with him: He is just scared. The doctor knows this because of the way that Trexler kept inching away from him in his chair when he asked him questions. Trexler politely feigns acceptance of this assessment and exits.

   Despite his ambivalence, Trexler continues to see the doctor. After several weeks, he notices that their time together takes on a pattern. Trexler begins by recounting his symptoms, which persist unabated, and the doctor listens attentively. The doctor then asks if he has found anything that brings relief. Trexler answers that a drink helps, and the doctor nods his understanding.

   Trexler's thoughts wander during these meetings. He gazes at the medical books on the office shelves and his eyes rest on a title, *The Genito-Urinary System*. He is suddenly gripped by the certainty that he has kidney stones.

   Along with his hypochondriacal musings, Trexler is beset by the tendency to put himself into the shoes of others. He finds himself mentally slipping into the doctor's chair and engaging in the proceedings from the other man's point of view. During one of these reversals, the doctor asks Trexler what he wants. Trexler replies that he does not know what he wants; probably nobody knows what they really want. Does the doctor know what he wants? The doctor assures him emphatically that he knows just what he wants: more money, more leisure, and a new wing for his vacation home.

Repelled by this pat response, Trexler resumes his role as patient for the rest of the visit. At the end, the doctor again assures him that nothing is wrong with him; he is only afraid and his fears are insubstantial.

Out on the street, it is dusk and Trexler is struck by the scene before him. The final rays of the sun play on the "brick and brownstone walls . . . giving the street scene a luminous and intoxicating splendor."

Walking along, Trexler continues to ponder the doctor's latest question to him. Immersed in the beauty of the early evening, he is suddenly aware that he knows what he wants, in fact, what all men want, only they don't always know it. Certainly the doctor doesn't; a new wing, indeed! What he longs for is both inexpressible and unattainable, and anyone who attempts to define it in a doctor's office will fall flat on his face.

Gazing up at a small tree rising out of the concrete sidewalk, aglow in the last light of day, Trexler declares out of his depths, "I want the second tree from the corner, just as it stands." Basking in the knowledge that no one can give and no one can take away, Trexler befriends his sickness. Having glimpsed "the flashy tail feathers of the bird courage," he is strengthened to face his fears and go on.

### Themes and Meanings

The longing for that which is both inexpressible and unattainable is a recurrent theme in the life and work of E. B. White. Despite his talent and success, White was beset with anxiety and lack of confidence throughout most of his life. As a young boy, he found joy and inner freedom each summer when his family left their home in Mt. Vernon, New York, for Maine, where he swam, fished, and canoed. As an adult living in New York City, White recaptured this joy by purchasing a farm in Maine, spending portions of the year there, and eventually retiring there. The barnyard of his farm in Maine provided a rhythm with which he was comfortable. His happy participation in the domain of geese, pigs, and chickens provided fodder for his literary life as well as strength for coping with his inner demons.

Toward the end of the 1940's, White consulted with a prominent New York psychiatrist for help with the same symptoms that plague Trexler in his story. "The Second Tree from the Corner" is, undoubtedly, White's own story. Just as Trexler finds courage to cope with his frailties through his appreciation of life's beauty, White seemed to find what he needed on his farm in rural Maine.

The natural world as the source of grace is a theme throughout much of White's work. It is the means of salvation for Wilbur the pig in *Charlotte's Web* (1952) and is embodied in the free and unobtainable Margalo, the bird for which Stuart quests in *Stuart Little* (1945). Although this theme permeates his work, sometimes subtly, sometimes not, perhaps nowhere is White clearer about what the natural world means to him than he is in "The Second Tree from the Corner."

What we all long for, according to White, is deeper than words and beyond possession, because it is the ability to appreciate the goodness of life through the natural world in the face of fear and death. In the story, Trexler's symptoms do not go away, but he is able to transcend them momentarily because he glimpses the fundamental benevolence of life.

*Style and Technique*

Although the narrative is not related in the first person, it is told from Trexler's point of view. By revealing Trexler's thoughts directly to the reader, White effectively characterizes him as convincingly neurotic. Trexler's paranoia is evident when, as the doctor questions him, he senses the doctor creeping toward him like a lizard toward a bug. Trexler freely projects his own fears onto a hapless man in the waiting room of the doctor's office, certain the man is terrified of dying of heart disease.

Privy to this hypochondria and his tendency to overly identify with others, the reader is immersed in the thoughts of a man who is clearly not well. This intimacy with Trexler makes his revelation all the more compelling. Sailing along with Trexler in the troubled seas of his mind, the reader experiences an epiphany, too, as Trexler's recognition of grace calms the waters, filling him with courage.

*Kim Dickson Rogers*

# THE SECRET INTEGRATION

*Author:* Thomas Pynchon (1937-     )
*Type of plot:* Psychological
*Time of plot:* The early 1960's
*Locale:* Mingeborough, Massachusetts, in the Berkshires
*First published:* 1964

> *Principal characters:*
> GROVER SNODD, a "boy genius"
> TIM SANTORA, his friend
> ETIENNE CHERDLU, another friend
> HOGAN SLOTHROP, a nine-year-old reformed alcoholic
> CARL BARRINGTON, their black friend
> MR. MCAFEE, a black musician

*The Story*

"The Secret Integration" takes place among a group of children living in Mingeborough, a small but growing Berkshire community. Led by Grover Snodd, "a boy genius with flaws," the group includes Tim Santora; Hogan Slothrop, at nine already a reformed alcoholic and a member of Alcoholics Anonymous (AA); Etienne Cherdlu, a notorious practical joker; and Carl Barrington, a child from a black family that has recently moved to town. In addition to dabbling with Grover's experiments and listening to the radio that he has built, the children spend time exploring the abandoned Gilded Age mansions around the town and working on "Operation Spartacus," the annual dry run for a projected anarchistic uprising.

The children of Berkshire find their projects disturbed, though, by two events. One, which takes place a year before the second, occurs when Hogan is called by AA to sit with Mr. McAfee, a black musician passing through town. Although Mr. McAfee recognizes that Hogan has been sent as a joke by white men who do not want to help a black man, the boy and his friends do their best. They sit through the night with the musician, listening to his anecdotes and trying to reach his girlfriend on the telephone. Eventually, though, the police come and take McAfee away. The children never learn what has happened to him, but they retaliate by staging a raid on the local train at night, using green lights and masks and costumes to scare the passengers .

The second event has been caused by the arrival in town of the Barringtons, Carl's parents. The white adults in town are fiercely opposed to any integration in their community, and Tim catches his mother making an anonymous threatening call to the black couple. The children are confused by these events and make vague plans to help the Barringtons, but their projects are cut short. Finding garbage dumped all over the Barringtons' lawn, the boys recognize trash from their own houses, and the Barringtons angrily send them away when they offer to help.

As the group walks home from this disturbing event, Carl offers to "lay low" for a while, and the other children agree that he should leave. It is only then that the reader discovers that Carl is not real, but is, rather, an imaginary friend whom these young people can no longer support. Tim, Grover, and Etienne then all head to the comfort of their homes and families and "dreams that could never again be entirely safe."

## Themes and Meanings

This story is overtly concerned with racism in American life, not only in itself but also as an example of how a society's dominant mores and ideologies seek to reproduce themselves in succeeding generations. The children of "The Secret Integration" are innocent in that they lack an understanding of the terms and behavior of the adult world. They recognize, though, that forces are at work that seek to modify and control their behavior and way of thinking. They know that something is being plotted against them at PTA meetings and dispatch Hogan to infiltrate the adult group (although he is thrown out). Grover keeps coming across Tom Swift books, which he is convinced are planted to indoctrinate him with a notion of how boy geniuses are supposed to behave and with the racism that Tom manifests in the book.

It is this threat from the adult world that has led the boys to create "Operation Spartacus," inspired by the Kirk Douglas film about an uprising of Roman gladiators. Although it is Grover who conceives of this "conspiracy," the others share his motivations: They find the adult world threatening in its blandness, conformity, and lack of purpose or surprise. The old Gilded Age estates are contrasted with a new housing development called "Northumberland Estates," which lacks not only the grandeur of the old mansions but also the hiding places and mysteries that surround them. The adults seem content to stay within their houses, sitting in front of their television sets, all tuned to the same channel despite the vague discontent about their lives and jobs that Grover senses.

Racism is seen as one more example of the blandness of white adult life, which seems opposed to any form of color; when Tim asks his father if they can have a color television, he is told that "black and white is good enough." The Barringtons represent the kind of difference and surprise that the town of Mingeborough seems determined to eradicate. Tim thinks of the imaginary Carl "as not only 'colored' himself, but somehow more deeply involved with all color." Racism, then, is portrayed as not merely an aberration within American culture but as a symptom of a larger malaise.

The children in the story represent hope for the future, but that hope has definite limits. First, the children are, after all, children, and they are limited in the scope of their knowledge. Tim does not understand the word "nigger," and Grover admits that the only integration of which he has ever heard is the mathematical term. More important, when these children have to choose between Carl and their families, between their vague vision of a better society and the safety and comforts of the present order, the families win. Still, with "dreams that could never again be safe," there is at least the hint that these children may remember some of what they have believed and learned.

*Style and Technique*

The great technical strength of "The Secret Integration" lies in the story's seeming simplicity. Although the characters of these children and their friends are sketched out in engaging detail, they lack the self-seriousness and artificiality of the characters in most of Thomas Pynchon's early works. Although clearly unusual by the standards of realistic fiction, they are still recognizable in behavior and thought as children and as individuals, plotting conspiracies at one moment and splashing in puddles the next.

Similarly, Pynchon's setting comes alive through his detailed descriptions of the landscape and its past. Combining aspects of his own Long Island home and the Berkshires as described in a regional guide put out in the 1930's, Pynchon gives a tangible presence to the story's surroundings. The descriptions of Tim riding a bicycle down a hill, of Mr. McAfee's hotel room, and of a lavish party hosted a century before in one of the mansions portend Pynchon's startling re-creation of World War II London in his 1973 novel *Gravity's Rainbow*. (The town of Mingeborough reappears in that book as well, as the boyhood home of the novel's main character, Tyrone Slothrop, who is the uncle of Hogan Slothrop in "The Secret Integration.")

As in much of his other fiction, Pynchon makes use of technology and science to provide images and metaphors. Here again, though, he does so more subtly than in such earlier works as "Entropy." The major metaphor in "The Secret Integration" is the term as it is understood by Grover, from mathematics. Drawing a graph for Tim, Grover sketches out a $y$-axis, an $x$-axis, and a curve and explains integration as theoretically infinite segments of $x$ that are drawn vertically on the graph. Although they look like the bars on a jail cell, Grover explains that they never fill in completely solidly, so that if someone "could make himself any size he wanted to be, he could always make himself skinny enough to get free."

Although integration is the mathematical opposite of differentiation, it is clear that racial integration is an admission and acceptance of difference. The mathematical model, though, also seems to suggest that no matter how much a society tries to impose its hegemony on individuals, there is always the possibility of escape, of getting out from behind the bars. It is that possibility with which Pynchon leaves the reader as the children return to the safety of their homes, which will not be as safe for them again as they once were.

*Donald F. Larsson*

# THE SECRET LIFE OF WALTER MITTY

*Author:* James Thurber (1894-1961)
*Type of plot:* Fantasy
*Time of plot:* The late 1930's
*Locale:* Waterbury, Connecticut
*First published:* 1939

*Principal characters:*
>WALTER MITTY, the protagonist, a middle-aged, henpecked
>husband who is unhappy with his life
>MRS. MITTY, his assertive and domineering middle-aged wife

*The Story*

Although Walter Mitty's daydream life has much exciting action, his waking life, as recounted in the story, is routine, uneventful, and, at a deep subconscious level, unsatisfying. In his waking life, Mitty motors on a wintry day with his wife into Waterbury for the regular weekly trip to shop and for Mrs. Mitty's visit to the beauty parlor. After dropping his wife off at the salon, Mitty drives around aimlessly for a brief time, then parks the car in a parking lot, purchases some overshoes at a shoe store, with some difficulty remembers to buy puppy biscuit, and goes to the hotel lobby where he always meets his wife. After a short time Mrs. Mitty appears, complaining to Mitty about the difficulty of finding him in the large chair where he has "hidden" himself, and then for a "minute" (actually much longer) leaves Mitty standing in front of a nearby drugstore while she goes to accomplish something she forgot. Interspersed with these events are Mitty's five daydreams or fantasies, which not only are induced by the events of his waking life but also affect them.

*Themes and Meanings*

James Thurber's expression through his characterization of the protagonist of the ineptitude, oppression, and disappointment nearly all human beings at some time feel in their lives in the real world (particularly in middle age) is so universally applicable that the name "Walter Mitty" has been canonized as a term in the English language denoting these ideas by inclusion in the *Webster's Third New International Dictionary* (2002) and *Merriam-Webster's Collegiate Dictionary: Tenth Edition* (1993).

The story's four main themes are the contrast between a human being's hopes for life and its actuality, the power of the mind or imagination, the conflict between the individual and authority, and the ascendancy of technology and materialism in the twentieth century. These themes are conveyed through the deflating disparity between Mitty's heroic ability and stature in his five daydreams and his hesitancy, servility, and ineptitude in real life. Mitty's first fantasy of captaining a hydroplane in a terrible ice storm is shot down, so to speak, by his domineering wife, who says that Mitty is driving the car too fast on the icy highway into town. Mitty's second fantasy, of being a published, world-renowned medical specialist and surgeon, is punctured by having been evoked by a double subordination, to his wife and to the family doctor; in subconscious reaction to his wife's patronizing attitude in her response to his highway driving—"It's one of your days. I wish you'd let Dr. Renshaw look you over"—the daydreaming Mitty becomes a medical authority, a commanding figure to whom Dr. Renshaw, in the fantasy, is obsequious.

In his third daydream, Mitty, the defendant in a murder trial, is yet in control in the courtroom, bravely exploding his attorney's alibi that Mitty's right arm was in a sling the night of the murder (Mitty boldly announces his expert ambidextrous marksmanship) and with youthful virility adroitly punching the chin of the district attorney, who has physically accosted Mitty's beautiful young beloved on her headlong rush to join Mitty on the witness stand. The immediately preceding scene, however, which stimulates the daydream, shows Mitty as manually incompetent (unable to park his car properly or remove tire chains), helplessly subordinate to both the parking attendant and the garage mechanic who removes the tire chains, and dimly and unhappily aware of being middle-aged in contrast to the cocky youths taking charge of his automobile.

To the more subtle domination of his wife's making him wait in the hotel lobby, Mitty's subconscious counters with the fourth fantasy of being a forceful, dauntless, and insouciant World War I British aviator. Finally, to the minor humiliations of being disregarded by his wife and told like a child to wait in front of the drugstore, his imagination replies with the last fantasy of Mitty's being the victim of a firing squad, physically under some restraint but still in control of the situation by his proud and disdainful bearing.

Beyond Mitty's subconscious search in his daydreams for power, freedom, and authority in his relations with people is a quest for mastery over technology, one of Thurber's perceptively prophetic themes in this 1939 story. In all daydreams except the last, Mitty can expertly manipulate some technological instrument, whose complexity is usually emphasized in the description of it: the hydroplane with its "row of complicated dials," the "huge, complicated" anaesthetizer with its "row of glistening dials," any firearm (and especially the Webley-Vickers 50.80), and the two-man bomber, which "Captain" Mitty can heroically pilot alone. A motif of the same sound emitted by the various machines in each of the fantasies, "pocketa-pocketa," emphasizes their technological presence.

Mitty seeks power and control over technology in daydreams because he is subject to it and to its controllers in real life, as exemplified by his various difficulties with his automobile. Even the more primitive technological device of the hotel's revolving door seems in conspiracy to mock or subordinate him, for as he leaves, it makes a "faintly derisive whistling sound." Besides its onomatopoeic aptness in conveying the sound of machinery, the "pocketa" motif may also suggest Mitty's feeling of confinement or restraint by technology, of enclosure as if in a pocket.

Mitty's feeling of oppressive enclosure in his life is expressed by the buildings of Waterbury "rising up" and "surrounding him" after his third fantasy, and the sergeant's remark "the box barrage is closing in" in the fourth fantasy as well as Mitty's echo, "things close in," when rudely jolted awake by his wife in the hotel lobby. The prevalent references to flying in his fantasies are not accidental, for they reflect Mitty's desires for escape and freedom; the magazine that he casually scans in the hotel lobby, which is the immediate cause of his fourth fantasy, has the appropriate title *Liberty*. In one sense, the overall pattern of Mitty's five fantasies is unhappy because their trend is toward an increasingly certain death of the fantasy protagonist, which suggests that Mitty's hope and the reader's for him are waning.

Near the story's conclusion, Mitty's wife, who perhaps could aid him, does not. In response to an unexpected though oblique assertiveness from her husband, she continues in her failure to achieve sympathetic understanding of what ails her spouse. Instead, she remains aligned with the oppressive forces of technology and materialism, failing to sense that her husband is not suffering from a physical or material ailment, and so does not need to see Dr. Renshaw or to have his temperature taken, her materialistic solutions proposed at the story's beginning and ending. Rather, with some pathos, Mitty remains alone, awaiting his daydream firing squad; he is "inscrutable," because no one around him recognizes his inner frustration and pain. However, his daydreams, paradoxically, do allow a measured triumph as well. In a sense he is a limited victor in his fantasies, but a victor, even in the last, which recalls a similar idea in Thurber's fable "The Moth and the Star"—that triumphs of the imagination have their own compelling reality.

## Style and Technique

One admirable component of the story is Thurber's keenly observed, often ironic, small detail of human action that reveals personality. Almost imperceptible is the detail of Mitty racing the car motor when told by his wife that he needs overshoes because he is no longer a young man—a response that suggests Mitty's furtive defiance. Another such detail is Mitty's reaction to a police officer's curt command "Pick it up, brother" at a traffic signal that has changed. Mitty first put on his gloves in the car as ordered by his wife, took them off when she was out of sight, but now puts them back on, suggesting that he equates the traffic officer with his wife as an authority figure, to whom he has been guiltily disobedient in the matter of his gloves. Though merely ordered to move on now that the traffic signal has turned green, Mitty (whose last name recalls the sort of gloves imposed on children) acts to rectify all misbehaviors. Mitty's subdued rebellion is also glimpsed in carrying his new overshoes out of the store in the box rather than wearing them, for which his wife later scolds him.

Still another unobtrusive detail is Mitty's going not to the first A & P grocery store available but to a smaller one farther up the street in his quest of puppy biscuit (a particularly unheroic task). Earlier, Mitty was embarrassed by a woman's laughter at his isolated utterance "puppy biscuit" on the street and thus wants to gain as much distance as possible from the site of his shame.

The story, as might be expected from one of America's premier humorists, is constantly amusing. Mitty continually misapplies melodramatic film clichés (from war films, courtroom dramas, and the like) in his fantasies, creating, for example, a comically exaggerated Englishman whose understatement in response to an explosive demolition of the room in which he is standing, "a bit of a near thing," is enjoyably ludicrous, as is the British "Captain" Mitty's attempt at carefree profundity: "We only live once . . . or do we?" Other amusing touches include the hydroplane commander's full-dress uniform in the midst of a storm and his nonsensical orders about a turret, Mitty's made-up medical jargon for his hospital fantasy, and marksman Mitty's incredibly exaggerated claim of how far he can accurately shoot (with any firearm) and mention of an impossible caliber.

However, the comic exaggeration—Mitty's fixing a complex machine with a fountain pen, being the only one on the East Coast who can make the repair, or having as his patient not only a millionaire banker (a point needlessly repeated in the fantasy except as a bolster to Mitty's ego) but a personal friend of President Roosevelt—like the other elements of humor in the story, has a serious point. At heart, all human beings need respect, dignity, and freedom. Walter Mitty is a comic Everyman.

*Norman Prinsky*

# THE SECRET LIVES OF DIETERS

*Author:* Perri Klass (1958-    )
*Type of plot:* Psychological
*Time of plot:* Unspecified; apparently the 1970's
*Locale:* San Francisco
*First published:* 1982

> *Principal characters:*
> POLLY, an artist who has been ill
> DONALD, her neighbor and coworker
> LOUISA, Donald's live-in girlfriend

## The Story

Polly, an artist, is home alone in her apartment, recovering from mononucleosis. Donald, who works with her at Ground Zero Graphics, has agreed to stop by her apartment regularly after work to bring her food and a few work assignments. Donald usually stays to visit and chat with Polly, telling her what he will be preparing for dinner for his girlfriend, Louisa, and himself, how their diets are going, and what is going on at work. He even begins to share with Polly the problems that are surfacing between him and Louisa. Donald is unaware that Polly has fallen in love with him, that she stares out of her window at his apartment, and that she has begun to tell herself stories every night about him and Louisa.

One night Donald brings Polly broth, bread, cottage cheese, and cheesecake. For himself and Louisa, he plans to broil red snapper with leeks, mushrooms, and spices. He envies Polly her cheesecake, and she wants to offer him a piece, but is afraid that he will resent her encouraging him to go off his diet.

Although Donald and Louisa have lived together for an unspecified length of time, Louisa has decided that they have become too much of a couple. She has no interest in marrying Donald; Donald's feelings on the subject are never specified. When pressed, Louisa admits that she wants to have an affair with Phillipe, a French teacher at the private high school at which she teaches English. In a desperate attempt to stop her, Donald offers to send off his portfolio and application to graduate school if she promises not to have the affair, to which Louisa agrees. To celebrate, Donald suggests that they go out for cheesecake, to which Louisa, reluctant but giggling, agrees.

Polly continues to obsess about Donald. She has had only one serious relationship in her life—with a strange computer programmer who ate frozen food without thawing it out. He moved to Boston but still calls her in the middle of the night. Polly assumed that when she fell in love again it would be with another man with a bizarre personality and is confused by her attraction to Donald. Still her obsession grows. She begins illustrating her nightly stories about Donald and Louisa in a special sketchbook. Phillipe eventually begins to appear in the illustrations, but Polly never includes herself. Her drawings are meticulously detailed, except that they show Louisa as heavier than she really is.

One night, Donald returns to his apartment and tells Louisa that he has been accepted into the fine arts program to which he applied. She gives him a hug and he kisses her, but suddenly stops and accuses her of having gone through with her intended affair. Admitting that this is so, she angrily leaves the room and starts washing dishes while he reminds her that he has kept his part of their bargain. Donald is determined to wait Louisa out, hoping that she will want to save their relationship. They continue their domestic arrangement, never mentioning Phillipe, but they have no emotional or sexual connection.

Two days before Polly is due to return to work, Donald brings her sausages, salad, and eclairs. She wonders if she will still love Donald after she returns to work, and if he could ever love her, or whether he will always associate her with sickness. When Donald tells her that he hopes to illustrate children's books after he gets his masters degree, she is disappointed; she would prefer to work on pornographic animated films herself.

Donald finally leaves Polly's apartment to go home and prepare a small steak with salad and green peas for himself and Louisa. Polly fills the final pages of her sketchbook with pictures of Louisa, now thin but graceless, packing to move out. That night, Louisa tells Donald she is planning to move in with Phillipe. Before packing, however, Louisa washes the dishes. Donald goes to the bedroom and stares despondently out the window in the direction of Polly's building, where she is drawing the scene that he has not yet described to her.

*Themes and Meanings*

"The Secret Lives of Dieters" uses its three characters to illustrate the changing nature of male-female relationships in the wake of the women's movement. Donald wants only to be with someone; Louisa wants only to be in control; Polly wants only someone whom she cannot have.

Donald illustrates both the positive and negative extremes of the sensitive new man who began to emerge in the media in the 1970's. On the one hand, he is a nurturer—he plans and cooks lovely low-calorie meals for Louisa and himself, he shops for foods that will tempt Polly to eat and thus build up her strength, and he hopes to illustrate children's books. On the negative side, Donald is a passive spectator of his own life— he has been unwilling to pursue the advanced degree that he needs to progress in his career until he is forced into it by Louisa, and he is unwilling to confront Louisa or make any demands on her, despite the fact that she is sexually involved with another man even as she continues to live with him. At the end of the story, Donald stares out the window, paralyzed with depression, realizing that he is now thin and on his way to graduate school but is alone.

Polly and Louisa present opposite images of women: Louisa is strong, psychologically and physically, an assertive woman who takes charge of her own life; she shows no emotion as she leaves the caring, responsible Donald and moves efficiently on to another man. Polly is weak and thin, living alone with her fantasies; she has never had a relationship with a man whom others would consider to be normal. Although she imagines herself to be in love with Donald, she not only does not pursue him, but she does not even include herself as an observer, much less a participant, in his life when she illustrates it nightly in her sketchbook. Unlike the no-nonsense Louisa, Polly has an almost witchlike quality about her, as she proceeds to draw intimate details of Donald and Louisa's life together with an eerie accuracy: Louisa examines her thinned-down self in the mirror, Polly draws such a scene in her sketchbook—did Donald describe this to her? Can she see Louisa from her window? Did she foresee—or even cause—Louisa's action?

The use of food as a symbol of connection between people is foretold by the title. As Donald tries to build up Polly's strength, he is also concentrating on slimming down both himself and Louisa, even after he discovers that Louisa is dieting to make herself more attractive to another man. As Polly's meals—like her fantasy life—grow richer and more flavorful, the meals that Donald fixes at home—like his domestic life—become ever more spartan.

*Style and Technique*

Many stories in Perri Klass's second collection *I Am Having an Adventure* (1986) concern girls or young women from conventional backgrounds who have wandered off to a faraway locale to have adventures. In this story, however, the protagonist never leaves her urban apartment, and adventures take place only in her own mind. The author uses flat, uninflected prose to lead the reader on a dreamy stroll through Polly's fantasies. Although the omniscient narrator refers at times to Donald's thoughts, and once to Louisa's, the largest part of the story is seen from Polly's perspective. In some paragraphs, the narrator switches from Donald's apartment to Polly's mind as if they were one, providing little distinction between reality and Polly's fantasies.

None of the characters is revealed directly, but only through the narrator's and Polly's observations. Although the characters seem like young professionals, their ages are never indicated, and there are few specific descriptions of their appearances or environment. One notable exception is a passage in which the narrator observes Polly's looks and apartment. Polly usually thinks of herself as a small, dark animal, but on this day she has braided her thick, dark hair into twenty-three tiny braids. "She is no longer a small furry animal, she is a spider. Her apartment is her lair, or her web, it is always dark, and there are mysterious things piled in the corners and complicated woven rope sculptures on the walls. . . . if Donald touches the furniture, he will stick to it." Using such simple but evocative speech, Klass ensnares her reader in the dark, mysterious lair of Polly's mind.

*Irene Struthers Rush*

# THE SECRET MIRACLE

*Author:* Jorge Luis Borges (1899-1986)
*Type of plot:* Antistory
*Time of plot:* 1939
*Locale:* Prague, Czechoslavakia
*First published:* "El milagro secreto," 1944 (English translation, 1954)

> *Principal characters:*
> JAROMIR HLADIK, an author of obscure scholarly works and an
> unfinished play
> JULIUS ROTHE, a Nazi official who decides his fate

*The Story*

An extract from the Koran that serves as prologue to the story hints at the miracle of the title. It tells of a person whom God has made die over the course of a hundred years. To this person, the time that has passed has been "a day, or part of a day."

The story itself begins on the night of March 14, 1939, in an apartment in Prague. It is the home of Jaromir Hladik, an author, whose principal works include an unfinished play and two scholarly volumes, one entitled *Vindication of Eternity*, the other a study of Jewish sources of the seventeenth century Christian mystic Jakob Boehme.

Hladik dreams of a centuries-long chess game whose opponents are two prominent families and whose forgotten prize is rumored to be infinite. The chessboard itself is set up in a secret tower. In his dream, Hladik is the first-born son of one of the families, and as he runs to make the next move, he realizes that he cannot remember the rules of the game. At this point, Hladik awakes to the sound of Nazi soldiers marching down his street.

Five days later, Hladik is arrested because of his Jewish blood and his inquiries into Jewish sources. Julius Rothe, the Nazi official who must decide Hladik's fate, is convinced of Hladik's importance from a catalogue listing. This listing was prepared by the publisher of Hladik's translation of the *Sepher Yezirah*, an early work of Jewish mysticism. Ignorant of the world of scholarship, and oblivious to the publisher's exaggeration of Hladik's reputation, Rothe condemns Hladik to death.

In prison, Hladik imagines all the possible details of his execution. On the night before he is to face a firing squad, he is distracted from his imaginings by the thought of his play, *The Enemies*. Anxious to redeem himself from his unsatisfactory literary career with this play, he asks God to grant him a year to complete it.

Just before dawn, Hladik dreams that he is hiding in a library. To the librarian's question regarding what he seeks, Hladik replies that he seeks God. The librarian responds that God is in one of the pages of one of the four hundred thousand books in the library, and that he himself has gone blind from searching for him. Someone returns an atlas to the librarian, who hands it to Hladik, after dismissing it as useless. Hladik opens the atlas at random and touches a letter. A voice tells him that his year has been granted. He awakens just before two soldiers enter his cell and order him to follow them to the courtyard. The soldiers are early. The squad must wait fourteen minutes, until it is precisely nine o'clock. At the appointed time, the sergeant gives the command, and the universe stands still. Hladik, paralyzed, reflects that if he were dead, his thoughts would have ended, which they have not. He falls asleep, and on waking, finds the world still immobile.

Hladik finally realizes that his secret miracle has been granted. Within the secrecy of his mind, a year will pass between the command to fire and his death. So, in his mind, he labors on his play. After adding the last finishing touch, gun blasts bring him down. Hladik dies at 9:02 in the morning.

*Themes and Meanings*

"I have always come to things after coming to books," Jorge Luis Borges has written. This insight suggests that the meaning of "The Secret Miracle" lies in the questionable primacy of literature. The protagonist, Jaromir Hladik, is a writer. The action of the story is propelled by his literary reputation; he is sentenced to death based on a misreading of his importance as an author. At the same time, Hladik's preoccupation is to be redeemed by one of his works.

The choice of religious terminology suggests the values that guide Hladik. He dreads death because it will prevent him from producing a work of art tailored to his strengths and weaknesses, that is, his verse play. He does not question his life as a morally responsible human being—he does not even reflect on the inherent value of the play to which he would devote himself. In his bargain with God, Hladik goes so far as to suggest that his redemption through his play would result in God's own justification.

The uses and creation of literature dominate the story. The Nazis deem it necessary to determine how dangerous certain works of literature may be and to eliminate their authors. Hladik's final minutes, whether two or however many a year comprises, are spent plotting out and revising his play. Much of the narrative is taken up with describing Hladik's works.

One of these is a translation of the *Sepher Yezirah*, "The Book of Creation," which invests the twenty-two letters of the Hebrew alphabet with cosmic significance. All beings are created and sustained by their connection to these letters, and everything that exists somehow contains them. Some believe that the text was used for magical purposes, based on the creative powers of the letters. Significantly, the vehicle through which the voice of God speaks to Hladik is a letter. The library that houses the book containing this letter may be interpreted as the meeting place between God and human beings. It is a place of revelation.

Just as these associations with God and the creation of the universe would appear to exalt literature, the story also works to undermine this view. The author who is its protagonist is evidently an incompetent one. His scholarship is described as "a product of mere application"; Hladik's translation of *Sepher Yezirah* is "characterized by negligence, fatigue, and conjecture."

Borges refuses to resolve these contradictions, just as he remains ambivalent regarding the actuality of the year granted Hladik. Literature, like dreaming, possibly like life itself, is both hallucination and reality. Quantum physics, with its uncertainty principle and its parallel universes, would seem to support Borges's view of the world as a web of time whose strands embrace every possibility.

The miracle of creation is, at heart, a secret. Can the human desire to emulate creation through literature ever be realized? Borges seems to agree that literature is a vain pursuit, and, winking, admits that he is compelled to pursue it. In his story, "Borges and Myself" (1957), the narrator bemoans his association with the writer Borges, to whom he attributes "a habit of falsification." The story ends with the confession, "Which of us is writing this page I don't know." Borges, it would seem, intends to sow seeds of doubt in his readers, reveling in the confounding thoughts they will produce.

*Style and Technique*

Reading "The Secret Miracle" can be compared to looking at an M. C. Escher drawing. Perception is not fixed, but in flux. Within the same frame, some figures walk upstairs, while others make their way downstairs. Even as one shifts focus to experience the work in one way, the mind is teased to view its opposite.

Similarly, Borges puzzles his reader with paradox. The story's context is historical: the Nazi occupation of Prague on March 15, 1939. However, dreams and daydreams predominate. A dream begins the story, and the plot turns on a dream. Precision of detail lends a sense of accuracy to the reporting of the story: The prisoner arrives at 8:44 in the morning at the courtyard where he will be executed; he is said to die at 9:02 A.M. Nevertheless, as the details accumulate, they begin to seem hyperreal, creating a sense of unreality. The perspective remains ever shifting.

As a master of irony, Borges relentlessly reverses expectations. Hladik hopes that his anticipation of the details of his execution will somehow prevent them from happening; instead, he is left fearing that they will prove prophetic. Envisioning a labyrinth of passageways, stairs, and connecting blocks on his way from his prison cell to the courtyard, Hladik instead is led down a single stairway. The dark humor that saturates the narrative intensifies the irony of Hladik's life and death. His sentencing itself is a joke, based on a misunderstanding of a falsification. Clearly, the narrator's characterization of Hladik's play as a tragicomedy of errors refers to his own story, as well.

In Hladik's play, the protagonist is revealed as someone else; the drama has never taken place. The play, indeed the story itself, is a circular delirium the protagonist lives and relives. The device of a story within a story adds another dimension of circularity, of wheels within wheels. The reader is left feeling dizzy, disoriented, and a bit thrilled, the mental equivalent of braving an amusement park ride.

*Amy Adelstein*

# THE SECRET ROOM

*Author:* Alain Robbe-Grillet (1922-    )
*Type of plot:* Surrealist
*Time of plot:* Unspecified
*Locale:* An underground room
*First published:* "Le Chambre secrete," 1962 (English translation, 1965)

> *Principal characters:*
> A NAKED WOMAN, chained to the floor and bleeding
> HER ASSAILANT, a man dressed in black

## The Story

A macabre scene unfolds before the reader like a motion picture in slow motion as a close shot of crimson streaks slowly pulls back from a small detail without context opened to reveal a broad shot of a vast room with massive columns and a great staircase shaped in a helix that rises up into the darkness. A silver incense burner issues out scrolls of smoke, providing partial context for a woman stretched out on the floor with blood streaming from a gruesome wound to one of her breasts. As from out of the corner of an eye, readers catch a glimpse of a man in black, flowing cape, a mere silhouette fleeing to the top of the stairs.

Switching from a distant shot to a close-up view of the woman, the narrator describes the shape of the woman's white, soft body, the colorful Oriental rug on which she is lying, and the purple color of the plush cushions that prop up her body. This secret chamber seems to stretch out for some distance, and its immensity suggests there are probably other strange and chilling scenes similar to this being enacted in other niches and passageways. The woman appears to light the room with her glowing white body.

Rewind. Now the scene seems to be played backward. The darkly dressed man is again at the foot of the steps and has taken his first step up the winding staircase. These steps narrow as they wind upward, leading to a temple or theater. As the mysterious man reaches the third step, he turns to look at the bound and helpless woman for the last time, his black, swirling cape revealing a red lining with intricate gold embroidery. He looks concerned and frightened, as if something unexpected will happen as his hand reaches for a balustrade that is not there. He looks at the woman chained in a cross-shaped configuration. She is fastened to the thick columns and floor by iron rings that are used to restrain animals. Her right arm and leg are obscured by the darkness, but the left arm and leg can be seen in the most minute detail. The chain has cut into her ankles and the rug is crumpled, apparently from her vigorous struggle.

The man looks at her face, upside down from his perspective. He notes her large eyes and her wide-open mouth, which appears to scream, but emits no sound. He is seen only in profile and appears to be happy. His cape with the gold embroidery blocks the view of the woman's wound from the reader, but the narrator takes care to describe the blood flowing from the wound across her body.

The scene rewinds again, moving closer to the actual attack. The man is now kneeling over the woman's body as she breathes more and more rapidly. Her head turns from side to side and her mouth twists open as he tears open the flesh of her breast. Her mouth opens wider, she struggles more violently, and is then silent.

Again temporal linearity is destroyed as the scene fast-forwards to the previous moment and the man is once again at the top of the stairs, about to enter a little doorway of light. The woman's color and the light emitted from her body begin to fade. The smoke from the burner straightens its wavy pattern as it rises toward the top of a canvas.

*Themes and Meanings*

The large room in which the story opens is reminiscent of a cathedral with its incense burner, large hall, and columns, and is a symbol of some Western institution. The woman bleeding on the floor represents the victimization of women in Western culture. This victimization takes place in the dark, secretly, and no one is to know about it, with the possible exception of other murderers and other victims in other rooms.

The layout of the room represents the ideas of the Great Chain of Being and its effects on women. The narrowing staircase represents the pyramidal hierarchy with God at the top, followed by angels, priests, men, and finally women and beasts. Only men ascend the staircase; the women stay at the bottom, chained like animals. It is clear that other mutilations could be going on in this sunken chamber because of its vastness. The repetitions of scenes are meant to demonstrate that this victimization is not only spatial, but temporal as well.

The man on the stairs turns to look back at the woman, presumably to feel empowered by the act he has just committed. This is shown most clearly when he looks at her with fear that something bad will happen and reaches for the balustrade that is not there. He symbolizes a search for the illusion of masculinity that is supposed to empower him; the missing balustrade symbolizes its absence.

When the woman opens her mouth to scream, both during the mutilation and as the man gazes back at her, no sound is heard. She symbolizes the voice that women in Western culture have yearned to have but have not. This empowers and pleases the man as he finally smiles down on her. As he does this, he views her upside down and does not make an attempt to see her from her own point of view.

The man's cape figures prominently in the story, as both a symbol of the Church and a shield behind which men can hide themselves as well as their acts. It is embroidered in gold on a red background much like a papal cloak, but black on the outside. Alain Robbe-Grillet uses this to show the reverse or negative side of the Church that is not often exposed in Western culture. The cape is used to block the view of the woman bleeding, but Robbe-Grillet shows what goes on behind the cape as it is blocking it. This moment encapsulates the whole story.

The woman who would be hidden by the cape lies chained in the shape of a cross to be sacrificed on the altar of the patriarchy. The man hopes this will show that her commitment to play the role of martyr is as unforced as the voluntary sacrifice made by Christ. This is a false symbolism on the man's part, because the woman is forced into this position and is given the disgraceful role of scapegoat rather than the revered role of messiah.

In the last line, smoke drifts from the incense burner in an oscillating pattern that smooths out to a straight line as it rises "vertically, toward the top of the canvas." The wild wavering of the smoke smoothing into a line demonstrates how the unfair treatment of women, that should so clearly be seen as askew, has come to be accepted as normal and correct. This final line is also Robbe-Grillet's way of saying that it is not only the Church that is guilty of perpetuating violence against women, but Western art itself.

*Style and Technique*

Robbe-Grillet uses surrealism to illustrate feelings about traditional gender relations. This is perhaps the best form in which to express such thoughts, as the topics and questions raised challenge the traditional way one thinks about the world. It is also more effective to present this conflict with shadowy characters in an unreal setting than to discuss it in a more realistic manner. The surreal context allows readers to step outside their own situations and look at the story from a perspective that had not been previously possible. Thus readers may empathize with a fictional character who may not be unlike a person from everyday life. Readers may then be equipped to apply this new perspective to their own situations.

Robbe-Grillet's writing is characterized by detailed descriptions. The story begins with the minute details of a flow of blood that, at first, seems to fill the entire picture. It is hard for the reader to tell what will happen next, because the setting is so unfamiliar.

When the unfamiliarity is established, Robbe-Grillet denaturalizes the view of the reader through a cinematic viewpoint. The reader is coerced into viewing the scene in the way the author has presented it. This cinematic technique is useful in demonstrating the author's assertion that the mutilations described happen in a temporal context as well as in a spatial one, a fact most clearly demonstrated as the story appears to rewind and play back, and also when the author reveals the same scenes from different vantage points.

*James Kurtzleben and Mary Rohrberger*

# THE SECRET SHARER

*Author:* Joseph Conrad (Jósef Teodor Konrad Nałęcz Korzeniowski, 1857-1924)
*Type of plot:* Coming of age
*Time of plot:* 1880
*Locale:* The Gulf of Siam
*First published:* 1912

> *Principal characters:*
> THE CAPTAIN, the narrator and protagonist, a young man in his
>    first command of a ship
> THE CHIEF MATE, an elderly, simple man
> THE SECOND MATE, a slothful, insolent young man
> LEGGATT, the first mate of the *Sephora*, a neighboring ship, who
>    has committed a murder
> ARCHBOLD, the captain of the *Sephora*, an obstinate man who
>    always goes by the rules

*The Story*

As the story opens, the young protagonist, having suddenly been given his first command of a ship, feels a stranger to the ship, to the crew, and to himself. Untested by the rigors and responsibilities of command, he wonders to himself "how far I should turn out faithful to that ideal conception of one's own personality every man sets up for himself secretly." He has not long to learn, for no sooner does he assume his duties as captain than he spies, one night while on watch, a young swimmer hanging onto the ship's rope ladder. He hauls the swimmer on board, only to learn that the young man is Leggatt, the former first mate of the *Sephora*, who has escaped after killing a sailor in an angry outburst at the sailor's ineptitude. His rescuer feels an immediate affinity with Leggatt, so much so that he hides him in his own cabin, at great personal risk. During his infrequent, whispered conversations with Leggatt, he learns that they both come from similar homes, have been graduated from the same naval school, and share the same values and outlook on life. Often the captain feels so great a kinship with his stowaway that he believes that they are doubles or even two halves of the same person.

In the second half of the story, the captain's complicity in Leggatt's escape deepens when the captain of the *Sephora* visits him to question him about the escaped man. In response to these questions, the young captain goes to great lengths to protect, hide, and lie about Leggatt. All this while, his officers and men are becoming distrustful of his odd, erratic, and agitated behavior, while Leggatt remains remarkably cool and self-possessed.

Finally, Leggatt suggests a plan to the young captain: He asks the captain to drop him off in the dead of night on one of the small nearby islands. The captain does so, at great risk to his ship and crew. This expedition is so hazardous that the ship nearly founders on the land. Desperately seeking an object by which to steer the ship, he spots in the water a white hat, the very hat he had given his secret visitor to protect him from the elements in his place of refuge. Satisfied that Leggatt has escaped and sure of his bearings, the captain successfully guides the ship away from land, certain of his ability to make the lonely decisions and to fulfill the individual responsibilities of command. He is satisfied as well that he has helped Leggatt to make a free decision about his own fate.

### Themes and Meanings

This story, like many of Joseph Conrad's tales, subjects a young, untested man to the rigors and responsibilities of leadership. Through a crisis, which tests him to the limit, he learns who he is and what he is capable of doing. Some men, such as Jim in *Lord Jim* (1900), fail this test, despite great promise and public favor. Others, such as the young captain of "The Secret Sharer," arouse the suspicion and criticism of others, yet, by taking full responsibility for their actions, they rise to the demands of their office and prove themselves fit adversaries of the sea, which relentlessly waits to claim them.

What distinguishes the young captain from Jim is his ability to recognize and accept the darker possibilities within his own soul, possibilities that he embraces in his admission of kinship with Leggatt. He understands that he, like Leggatt, is capable of murder. Were he in similar circumstances to those Leggatt described, burdened with a good-for-nothing sailor, hampering him from performing the one action that could save the ship in a gale, he, too, might have killed the man.

Recognizing as well that the murderer must be punished, he knows that he would demand, like Leggatt, to find punishment at the hands of his peer or peers—not a land-bound jury of tradesmen but a wellborn sailor like himself, who shares his background, education, and values. Thus, the captain willingly risks his ship and his men, in a questionable series of actions, in order to offer Leggatt the punishment of exile rather than of hanging. The captain has earned the right to make this difficult decision through full acceptance of responsibility for it: He thus claims for himself the unique privileges as well as the great burdens of command.

The tale celebrates the coming of age of a young man at his first command. It also tacitly posits an aristocratic code of behavior for the young captain, which repudiates the apparent democratic brotherhood of all naval officers. The tale maintains that the greatest commanders must be judged by different standards than those used for other officers, that such leaders are entitled to take greater risks because they are able to make finer choices.

### Style and Technique

This story shows Conrad's finest use of the doppelganger, or double, a symbolic figure who serves to show the true character of the protagonist by exhibiting the darker, more unsavory sides of his nature. Thus, Leggatt, who shares the middle-class background, naval training, morals, and assumptions of the young captain, forces the captain to admit that he, too, is a potential murderer and therefore less than the perfect hero that he originally hoped to be. In other words, Leggatt and the captain are alter egos, dark and light sides of the one self. In fact, the impression that the two of them together form a single complete person, both good and evil, is reinforced by the fact that only one of them has a name.

Conrad's style is also very rich in pictorial description. He masterfully uses setting to suggest the possibilities and meanings of human action: Thus, the water, like the green young captain, at the beginning of the story is remarkably calm. Similarly, the life-threatening gale during which Leggatt commits the murder suggests the psychological and moral turbulence of that episode in his life.

In addition, Conrad's narration emphasizes the larger moral and social issues that give dimension to what otherwise would be merely a fine tale of adventure and suspense. Accordingly, as the protagonist is assured of Leggatt's successful escape, he expresses satisfaction that "the secret sharer of my cabin and of my thoughts, as though he were my second self, had lowered himself into the water to take his punishment: a free man, a proud swimmer striking out for a new destiny."

Finally, Conrad suggests to the reader the magnitude and the justice of the young captain's decision by having him narrate this tale of his youth at a much later period of his life. Thus, his story gains distance and dimension.

*Carola M. Kaplan*

# SEE THE MOON?

*Author:* Donald Barthelme (1931-1989)
*Type of plot:* Antistory
*Time of plot:* About 1965
*Locale:* The narrator's house
*First published:* 1966

> *Principal characters:*
> THE UNNAMED NARRATOR, an eccentric intellectual
> SYLVIA, his first wife
> ANN, his current wife
> GREGORY, his seventeen-year-old son

*The Story*

The form of this story is that of a monologue in which the speaker's perceptions and revelations are the primary content. The speaker, or narrator, would seem to be confiding his deepest apprehensions and ambitions, along with much of his life history to an interlocutor of some sort, a visitor or friend, or perhaps even a psychiatrist, because the narrator's personality is, to say the least, odd. He claims to be conducting "very important lunar hostility studies," although his methods "may seem a touch light-minded. Have to do chiefly with folded paper airplanes." Indeed, he confesses to "a frightful illness of the mind, light-mindedness" while at another point he asserts that he is nevertheless "riotous with mental health."

To a literal-minded reader, the narrator may seem simply to be insane. In the world of this story, however, conventional standards of neither sanity nor fictional form have much relevance. The narrator's obsession with the moon and its possible negative influence implies inevitably the origins of the word "lunatic." The implication is more than likely ironic and intentional on the author's part, for if the narrator is a "lunatic," he is certainly a brilliant one whose provocative observations cannot be dismissed merely as the product of a deranged mind.

During the course of the disjointed, meandering narration, a coherent autobiography emerges, fragment by fragment. The narrator was, in the late 1940's, a very promising student at an unnamed university on the Gulf Coast. He was drafted into the United States Army on graduation, however, and sent to Korea. On his return to civilian life, he was hired by his alma mater as an assistant to its president with the primary responsibility of writing "poppycock, sometimes cockypap" for the president's speeches. He married Sylvia, and they had a son, Gregory. Within a few years he became disillusioned with his work at the university; rearing a child proved to be a further stress; he resigned from his job, and his marriage ended in divorce.

At the time of the story, Gregory is a freshman at Massachusetts Institute of Technology (MIT). Obsessed by his own quest for selfhood, Gregory makes frequent, unexpected telephone calls to his father with questions out of the blue such as "Why did I have to take those little pills?" or "What did my great-grandfather do?" The narrator has meanwhile remarried in middle age, and his current wife, Ann, is pregnant with a child whom they call Gog—a name whose apocalyptic associations seem, in this instance, bizarrely incongruous.

Although it is hard to say what the narrator at this point actually does for a living, a bohemian lifestyle is rather obviously implied. An eccentric freelancer, he devotes his "moonstruck" brilliance to various "little projects" such as the aforementioned lunar hostility studies and the equally eccentric pursuit of "cardinalogy"—a taxonomical study of cardinals of the Catholic Church, "about whom science knows nothing."

In the concluding section of the story, the narrator addresses his monologue to his unborn child. It appears now that the story also represents the father's concern for (and need to justify himself to) his offspring—as he says, "You see, Gog of mine, Gog o' my heart, I'm just trying to give you a little briefing here. I don't want you unpleasantly surprised." Thus, to help forestall "unpleasant surprises" in life for his new child, he has presented the truth (whatever that is) of the world as he knows it: the report of a traveler to someone beginning the journey. Beyond human understanding, though, there are realms of terror and fascination that no "reports of travelers" can describe. In the narrator's mind, the bright, austere face of the moon is equated with the threat and the allure of the unknown mysteries of life; in the climactic next-to-last line of the story, he voices the resolve to protect his child by making "sure no harsh moonlight falls on his new soft head."

*Themes and Meanings*

The narrator's autobiographical revelations bear a strong resemblance to the author's own life. Like his protagonist, Donald Barthelme was a brilliant student at a Gulf Coast university (the University of Houston) in the late 1940's and early 1950's, was drafted and served in Korea, returned to civilian life as a writer and editor for his alma mater, and by the early 1960's had moved to New York, staking his career on his unconventional, radically creative intellect and imagination. Given this sort of clear authorial presence in the story, as well as the quirky incisiveness of the narrator's commentary, the reader may reasonably enough identify the narrator with the author.

It is probably more accurate to think of the narrator as a persona, or character mask, through which the author speaks (and thus the "you" to whom the narrative is addressed is also the reader in addition to some hypothetical listener within the story). The effect of montage, or overlapped planes of meaning, is central to Barthelme's method and outlook. Nothing is ever quite literally itself in a Barthelme story, because, for the author, fact and illusion, appearance and reality are not absolute, mutually exclusive categories. Truth, if it can be known at all, must be approached obliquely through satire, irony, and ambiguity. Thus, the author leads the reader, like Alice through the looking glass, into a strange world of wacky events and imaginings, non sequiturs, and unsettling parody of contemporary society.

The thematically most significant aspect of the story lies in its application to the U.S. quest to reach the moon in the 1960's. Published in 1966, on the eve of the Apollo program, which led to the lunar landings three years later, the story raises fundamental questions about the nature of this quest—the motives involved; the unforeseen dangers and consequences to human society; the mythic dimension of the whole enterprise. Such concerns tend to be obscured within the community of technical expertise because of its preoccupation with method and quantitative judgment—not the "why" of things, but the "how." In this story, Gregory (the promising MIT student) clearly is identified with this community. However, his competence in arcane subjects such as "electron-spin-resonance spectroscopy" is ironically undercut by the naïveté and urgency of his personal quest for self-knowledge. The narrator, in contrast, knows that all mortals are fallible; that the truth is never quite as clear-cut as the scientific approach assumes; and that even the current technological quest for the moon is really an aspect of humankind's age-old fascination with the heavens. Thus, his "moonstruck" obsession with the moon may be more "sane" than is the scientist's linear, one-dimensional understanding of this momentous undertaking.

*Style and Technique*

A key to Barthelme's fictional approach lies in a statement that occurs twice in this story: "Fragments are the only forms I trust." If the term "montage" applies to Barthelme's overlapping planes of narrative perspective, then "collage" aptly describes the effect of his narrative style. His stories generally, and this one most assuredly, seem assembled from a jumble of unrelated materials: pedantic literary allusions, current events, scraps of scientific jargon, profound philosophical issues, trendy pop culture. Moreover, the tone of his writing oscillates freely from hysterically comic to sad, from whimsical to deadpan earnest.

Thus, to take but one significant example, the narrator calls his unborn child "Gog," using the name of the biblical monster and legendary English giant in a humorously ironic way. The sound of the name in turn prompts an allusion to the old sentimental tune "Peg o' My Heart." The parents' apprehensions about the impact the child will have on their lives leads to an extended, metaphorical comparison of the child to a battleship. Finally, the narrator's hopes for a bright, intelligent child who will mature into wisdom leads to a reference to Pallas Athena, the Greek goddess of wisdom, who according to myth leaped fully armed from her father Zeus's head ("in another month Gog leaps fully armed from the womb").

The zany collage style of the story reflects Barthelme's postmodernist sensibility. Like so many contemporary artists, Barthelme seeks to create a coherent vision of life yet profoundly mistrusts the conventional techniques of "serious" art. Thus, his kaleidoscopic manipulations of thought and language are central to his artistic purposes: Only by such unconventional means can a valid image of life in the contemporary world be presented. The narrator, in justifying his self-revelations, also would seem to be speaking for the author when he says, "It's my hope that these . . . souvenirs . . . will someday merge, blur—cohere is the word, maybe—into something meaningful."

*Charles Duncan*

# SENSE OF HUMOUR

*Author:* V. S. Pritchett (1900-1997)
*Type of plot:* Sketch
*Time of plot:* The 1930's
*Locale:* A small English town
*First published:* 1936

> *Principal characters:*
> ARTHUR HUMPHREY, the narrator, a traveling salesperson
> MURIEL MACFARLANE, a hotel clerk
> COLIN MITCHELL, her boyfriend, a local garage mechanic

*The Story*

Arthur Humphrey is a smooth-talking, plausible traveling sales representative in a new territory. He decides to stay in the new town over the weekend, planning to go to church on Sunday—"Presbyterians in the morning, Methodists in the evening"— hoping to impress the locals with his piety and teetotalism, so they will remember him when he solicits orders on Monday. Bored on a rainy Saturday afternoon, he flirts with Muriel MacFarlane, the hotel clerk. In the middle of their chat, Colin Mitchell, Muriel's boyfriend, pulls up in front of the hotel on a new, loud motorcycle. Colin, a not-very-bright mechanic at the local garage where Arthur keeps his company car, wants Muriel to come for a ride on his new motorcycle, but she is becoming interested in Arthur, who has a white-collar job, a smooth manner, and a real car. That evening, Muriel and Arthur go to the movies. Arthur quickly replaces Colin in Muriel's affections.

Thereafter, every Sunday, which is Muriel's day off, the two date. At first, Arthur rubs it in by making Colin pull the car out, fill its gas tank, and check its oil. Then he notices that they always see Colin on the road, roaring along on his motorcycle, cutting in and out of traffic. Arthur confronts Colin, who denies following them, claiming that he only goes to the places they go by accident. Anyway, Colin adds, you took my girlfriend from me.

Colin stops shadowing them until the Bank Holiday, a long weekend holiday at the end of summer. Arthur plans to take Muriel to meet his elderly parents, but Colin tries to ruin their plans by sabotaging his car. Arthur instead takes Muriel by train, furious at Colin's trickery and the cost of the train tickets.

Shortly after they arrive, Arthur tells his parents that he and Muriel are getting married. The conversation is interrupted by a telephone call for Muriel. Colin, who has followed them, is dead, killed because of his reckless motorcycle driving. Muriel goes to her guest room and lies on the bed, weeping and calling out Colin's name. Arthur sits by her side to comfort her and then lies down next to her. The two stroke each other's bodies and make love. The next day, Colin's body is brought to the house. Arthur and his father, who is semiretired from his undertaking business, fix the details of the funeral. Arthur will drive the hearse, saving Colin's mother some money. When Muriel hears about the plans, she wants to ride in back with Arthur and the body, partly to do her duty to Colin, partly to have the experience of riding in a hearse. That evening, Arthur goes to Muriel's room to convince her to return home by train, but she insists on going in the hearse. The two make love again, knowing that Colin's body is downstairs in the front room.

The next morning, Arthur and Muriel set off in the hearse with Colin's body. As they drive along in the well-sprung, smooth-running vehicle, its engine purring, passing through village market squares, bystanders raising their hats in respect, little boys running after the hearse, Muriel laughs. She and Arthur feel like royalty.

*Themes and Meanings*

"Sense of Humour" is based on V. S. Pritchett's experiences as a young author. In 1923, he was commissioned to write a series of articles on Ireland for the *Christian Science Monitor*. He spent the next year traveling around the island. In one town, Pritchett met a traveling sales representative who gave his girlfriend rides in his father's hearse. During this year in Ireland, Pritchett also met his first wife, Evelyn Maude Vigors, an actress. Pritchett has been reticent about his first marriage, which ended in divorce in September, 1936, three months after this short story was accepted for publication. It is not unreasonable to suggest that the character Muriel MacFarlane hints at his first wife.

The story's title refers to the stereotypical ethnic theme of the good-humored Irish. When they first chat, Muriel finds it hilarious that Arthur Humphrey's father is an undertaker. Seeing that her laughter offends Arthur, she says, "Don't mind me. . . . I'm Irish." "Oh, I see," the narrator replies. "That's it, is it? Got a sense of humour." Later, when he introduces her to his parents, his father remarks, "Oh, Irish! Got a sense of humour, eh?"

Although Muriel's sense of humor allows her to see some of the absurdities of the human experience, it does not affect her treatment of Colin Mitchell. Muriel really does not like him because she thinks he does not have a sense of humor, but he is the best that the small town she is in can offer. She goes out with him because her only alternative is to stay in the hotel on Sundays. However, she treats him offhandedly, and drops him as soon as Arthur turns up and shows an interest in her. She is a user of people. Muriel is also a chiseler in a small way: She accepts samples from the other traveling sales representatives; when they go to the movies, she tells Arthur to buy tickets for cheap seats, because they can sneak into the more expensive seats when the lights go down.

Pritchett's unflattering, candid, yet nonjudgmental portrait of Muriel is matched by that of Arthur. Arthur spots Muriel's tastes and caters to them, offering her better stockings than the ones she has on, and bringing her a present every time he visits her town. He tells her the gifts are mostly samples, which cost him nothing. Arthur also is concerned about calculations and mundane matters. While comforting Muriel on the first evening at his parents' house, he was planning how to introduce his firm's autumn line; not until they begin making love does he stop thinking about business. Several days later, on the way back in the hearse, Arthur worries that their lovemaking may have ruined his calculations. He had planned on waiting eighteen months to get married, by which time he would have saved eight hundred pounds—the equivalent of about two years' wages—but if Muriel becomes pregnant, they will have to get married at once.

The relationship of the two is ambiguous. Muriel rejects Colin because he has no sense of humor, yet she realizes after his death that Colin truly loved her. She wants Arthur because he offers her a way out of the town and the hotel, a move up to a more secure future. However, Arthur admits to himself that he had "never thought of her in that way, in what you might call the 'Colin' way." If that is the way of love, why does Arthur want to marry Muriel? The story takes an unexpected turn when Arthur tells his parents that he plans to marry Muriel; Pritchett never hints at Arthur's motives for the marriage.

Muriel's and Arthur's sexual values also are ambiguous. On their first date at the movies, Muriel makes clear that she is not sexually available, but she is receptive to Arthur's flirting and sexual innuendo. When the two do make love, they do so with no apparent guilt, unusual for their time, place, and class.

Pritchett uses the story to depict the values of the lower middle class in England between the world wars. His characters want the outward appearance of respectability—the appearance of churchgoing, the appearance of good taste in funeral appointments—but they count pennies and reckon up cost savings.

*Style and Technique*

Pritchett writes in a simple, spare style, telling the story from Arthur's point of view. Arthur sees, and clearly conveys, the unfolding of events, but he does not understand the deeper meaning of those events. He is only dimly aware of the ambiguities of his and Muriel's relationship, and not at all aware of the ironies and hypocrisies of his own behavior. However, Arthur's character is rounded and rises above caricature because of his questioning. Arthur tries to understand Colin's behavior; he honestly wants to know why Muriel rejects the mechanic, and he attempts to puzzle out the deeper meaning of his and Muriel's relationship.

Pritchett originally called this story "The Commercial Traveller," but the editor of the magazine *New Writing*, in which it first appeared, convinced him to change it to "Sense of Humour." This is a fitting title, because the story is marked by a quiet, understated, humorous view of human behavior. One of Pritchett's strongest talents as a writer is his ability to expose the comedic aspects of people's action without indulging in excessive mockery or crude caricature. He combines clear observation with a basic respect for others, to show the different layers of meaning in human behavior. Pritchett's subsequent work displays the same quiet humor, powers of observation, and respect for his characters.

*D. G. Paz*

# THE SENTINEL

*Author:* Arthur C. Clarke (1917-　　)
*Type of plot:* Science fiction
*Time of plot:* 1996-2016
*Locale:* The moon
*First published:* 1951

> *Principal characters:*
> WILSON, a geologist and veteran lunar explorer
> LOUIS GARNETT, his assistant

*The Story*

Wilson, a geologist, recalls his role twenty years earlier as leader of a lunar expedition to a massive plateau, the Mare Crisium, or Sea of Crisis. Although the name is portentous, initially the journey appears to be mundane. Wilson even laments that there is nothing hazardous or especially exciting about lunar exploration. It is, he claims, an uneventful routine.

Wilson's expedition is well equipped. Traveling from the main lunar base, some five hundred miles away, the crew is laden with heavy equipment, including overland tractors, rockets, and scientific sampling machinery. It appears they have little to fear from the unknown. They are in constant radio contact with their base and can survive for a month in their pressurized tractor cabins if there were an emergency.

The men live in relative comfort during their tour of duty on the moon. Short wave radio contact with earth provides ubiquitous music for the men as they dine on freshly cooked food. This particular expedition, however, soon deviates from the routine. While preparing his breakfast sausages, Wilson observes a glint of what appears to be a metal object on a far mountain bordering the plateau. Against unanimous dissent from his crew, Wilson and his assistant, Garnett, journey to investigate the object.

After scaling a ten-thousand-foot-high mountain at the edge of the plateau, Wilson discovers a small crystalline pyramid. He initially believes that it was created by an extinct, previously undiscovered, indigenous culture. The absence of any other artifacts, coupled with the presence of a sophisticated force-field surrounding the object, soon prove to him that the artifact's provenance is both extralunar and extraterrestrial.

Wilson describes the twenty-year process by which scientists seek to dismantle the artifact and ascertain its nature and function. When all methods prove ineffectual, the scientists resort to atomic energy, reducing the inscrutable object with its mysterious energy source to rubble. Its purpose never determined, the artifact, which had withstood natural destructive forces for millennia, is rendered inoperable by humans.

Wilson provides his interpretation of the significance of his discovery. The object, he believes, is a sentinel, one of millions planted throughout the universe by an unimaginably advanced race in order to watch over the promise of life. Wilson believes its destruction would signal its creators that sentient life had evolved from terran primordial soup, and had proved its fitness to survive by having ventured forth from its earthen cradle. Because the object's destruction will alert its creators to the probability of human intervention, humanity, according to Wilson, surely will not have long to wait for its first extraterrestrial contact.

*Themes and Meanings*

Written only a few years after the atomic bombs dropped on Hiroshima and Nagasaki ended World War II, Arthur C. Clarke's "The Sentinel" contains several themes that would become common in Cold War science fiction. Reflecting a shared dread that humanity might entirely destroy itself through nuclear war, many authors viewed the advent of a nuclear era as being a universal rite of passage for any civilization. While harnessing nuclear reactions was considered necessary for scientific advancement, it also provided a means for planetary self-annihilation. All civilizations advancing to the level of nuclear weapons, therefore, must learn to transcend their base instincts. Only after successfully accomplishing this rite of passage, thus assuring the continuation of planetary life, can a race begin a new phase of space exploration and alien contact.

A second theme, first encountered in "The Sentinel" and appearing throughout much of Clarke's later fiction, is the presence of a vastly superior civilization, one whose existence predates human civilization by unknown millennia. It is a patient race, observing the evolutionary development of more primitive species throughout the universe, presumably awaiting their maturation. Childlike humans, themselves only newly sentient, can only guess at the intention of the superior race, hoping it is benign rather than sinister. Even in their scientific investigations, humans are portrayed as childlike. When researchers cannot penetrate the protective force field, they resort to "the savage might of atomic power." In other words, like children, they break it.

In "The Sentinel," the intention of the superior race is unknown. Are they benevolent, or, because they are a very old race, will they be jealous of youth, as Wilson fears? The story closes forebodingly with humanity awaiting its first contact with the unknown advanced civilization.

"The Sentinel" contains the germ of an idea that would be further explored by Clarke and director Stanley Kubrick in the film *2001: A Space Odyssey* (1968), and in Clarke's novelization of the film that appeared in the same year. In *2001*, not only does the superior race observe human evolution, but it also intervenes, benevolently guiding humanity to new evolutionary heights. Appearing at crucial junctures in human history, the film's black obelisk, although vastly different from the small crystal pyramid of "The Sentinel," is reminiscent of that earlier alien artifact. The final visual image in *2001*, the human adult who turns into a fetus of a new super race through alien, god-like intervention is the ultimate expression of that metaphysical theme first suggested by "The Sentinel."

In *Against the Fall of Night* (1953) and *Childhood's End* (1953), considered by many to be two of his finest novels, Clarke further explores the theme of humanity awaiting guidance from an ancient extraterrestrial civilization. These novels continue a trend that began in "The Sentinel," and would become a trademark of Clarke's fiction.

## Style and Technique

Clarke, a scientist with degrees in physics and mathematics from King's College, England, usually incorporates in his fiction an optimistically advanced future based on steadily progressing scientific inventions. Nevertheless, the transcendence of human ingenuity in the form of science is merely the backdrop against which he presents his principal focus: the search for meaning and humanity's place within the universe.

Using simple language and foregoing mystical imagery, Clarke convincingly questions the future of humanity. The uncomplicated narrative of the seemingly routine lunar mission, and the contrasting complex metaphysical theme incorporated in the story, provide a striking juxtaposition. The combination of uncomplicated style and metaphysical musings typifies much of Clarke's fiction.

In "The Sentinel," characterization and dialogue are minimized. The reader is told virtually nothing about Wilson other than his name. Even that small fact must be deduced from an offhand comment made by a member of his team regarding Wilson's desire to climb the mountain on which the artifact stands: He calls it "Wilson's folly." From a passing reference to his exploits as a young man, the reader learns that Wilson is a veteran explorer. No other information is given. Even less is known about Garnett, the story's only other named character. Minimizing character development and dialogue emphasizes the central theme and the ominous mood of the story.

Unlike character and dialogue, however, setting is crucial. Clarke's predictions for the scientific advancements leading to the establishment of the moon base and exploration of the moon may appear overly optimistic in the late 1990's. Had the United States space program continued the rapid pace of its development in the 1950's and 1960's, however, Clarke's prediction likely would have been close to the mark. However, the chronology of space exploration is rendered insignificant against the backdrop of Clarke's setting, the moon itself. The details he provides firmly establish the nature of life on the moon. Although the chronology of "The Sentinel" may be off by some years, questions regarding the nature of humanity's place in the universe are timeless. The moon, symbolizing a step in humanity's evolution, is not only the starting point for further scientific advancement but also, perhaps, for further spiritual evolution.

*Mary E. Virginia*

# SERVANTS OF THE MAP

*Author:* Andrea Barrett (1955-    )
*Type of plot:* Historical, epistolary
*Time of plot:* 1863-1864
*Locale:* The Himalayan Mountains, Tibet
*First published:* 2000

> *Principal characters:*
> MAX VIGNE, a surveyor
> CLARA, his wife
> DIMA, a woman with whom he has an affair

*The Story*

"Servants of the Map" consists mostly of letters that Max Vigne, a young surveyor with a British mapping party in the Himalayan Mountains, writes to his wife, Clara, in England. However, there are many things that he does not describe to her—the hardships, the physical discomfort, the exhaustion, and the loneliness. Nor does he tell of his being mocked by the older, more experienced men, who laugh at his pale blond appearance, his books, and a trunk of letters that his wife has written and given to him before he left, each of which are to be opened on certain dates and special anniversaries. He does not tell Clara about finding the head of a man sticking out of a snow pack or about falling into a fissure himself, out of which he managed to dig with great effort. Other things he does not tell Clara are the stories he hears of massacres of women and children and other horrors of local tribal wars.

Bored and lonely, Max spends much of his time reading Joseph Hooker's *Himalayan Journals* (1854), Charles Darwin's *On the Origin of Species by Means of Natural Selection* (1859), and Asa Gray's *First Lessons in Botany and Vegetable Physiology* (1857). Max tells Clara that he increasingly gets confused by the many new experiences he is having and can make sense of them only by describing them to her. He also tells her that trying to maintain connection with her without touch changes him. Throughout Max's correspondence to Clara, he finds himself becoming a different person but unable to communicate the nature of that change to Clara.

Max writes to Clara about his encounter with a Doctor Chouteau, a French physician, who has traveled in the area widely, but to whom maps mean nothing. He also tells her about a correspondence he has had with Dr. Hooker, the author of *Himalayan Journals*. During the coldest part of the winter, when Max must stay in a village, he meets a woman named Dima, with whom he begins a sexual affair. For a long period he does not write to Clara or answer the letters that he receives from her. Finally he decides that he wants to stay on longer in Tibet after the survey ends, but he cannot write any of this to Clara. Instead he writes that he would like to start over again with her, in some new place where he can be his new self and live his new life.

## Themes and Meanings

The metaphor of the map in this story reflects Max's personal efforts to discover where he is and therefore who he is. This is complicated by the fact that he is in a wild area where he cannot find any context within which to locate himself. He is distant socially from the men with whom he works, and he is distant spatially from his wife, Clara. Moreover, because it takes so long for letters to get to him from Clara, his emotions lag far behind the events. For example, for him, it is as though his new daughter had just been born, although she is five months old. Moreover, the sensory data he is confronted with every day is a jumble in his mind until he writes them down, either in his journal or in letters to Clara. Although he considers himself a "servant of the map" that he and his companions are preparing, the map is in process, not an accomplished artifact.

Because everything Max experiences is translated into language, either in the letters or his journals, the writing process as a means of capturing and understanding reality is a large component of the theme of the story. However, because Max can scarcely recognize himself any longer, he finds it difficult to use language to make clear to Clara the "aberrant knots" of his character. One of the various results of this "living by writing" is that one's pleasures are seen in retrospect, not in the present, becoming acts of the imagination rather than events in the physical world. Moreover, Max feels he has heretofore been blind and that he is now learning to see, a process that becomes more important to him than anything else.

Max's past life seems to be disappearing as the story progresses. Ultimately he wants to tell Clara that everything has changed for him, that he is changed. However, he cannot, feeling that if his letters were meant to be a map of his mind, a way for her to follow his trail, then he has failed. This does not suggest a deficiency in Max's ability to communicate, but rather an inescapable characteristic of communicating by language. In her contributor's notes to *Prize Stories, 2001: The O. Henry Awards*, and *The Best American Short Stories, 2001*, Andrea Barrett says that as she wrote many drafts of the story she realized that its central theme had to do with the implications of communicating with one's beloved solely through letters over a long period of time. As Max says in one of his letters, which he later scratches out, "Trying to stay in touch without touch . . . changes us deeply, perhaps ever deforms us."

## Style and Technique

The basic narrative convention that Barrett uses in "Servants of the Map" is the form of the epistolary novel, popular in the eighteenth and the nineteenth centuries, in which the entire story is told by means of letters. However, Barrett departs from the pure epistolary novel by interspersing the letters Max sends to Clara with comments by an omniscient narrator, who expresses the feelings of loneliness, despair, and confusion that Max believes he cannot or should not tell Clara. Furthermore, by having Max frequently comment on the very limitations of trying to communicate his feelings by writing letters, the story becomes less an attempt to replicate the old epistolary fictional form and more a self-reflexive exploration of the nature of that form.

An implication of the writing process of which Max becomes aware is the reader's need to imagine what the writer can only hint at. Max asks Clara to imagine things he describes, for he says that when he tells her enough to let her imagine them clearly, he can imagine himself. Trying to discover the self through the act of writing thus becomes not only the central theme of the story but the central technique as well.

The fact that Max is writing to one that he loves makes the task even more difficult. For the writing process reminds him of the common lover cliché that "words cannot express" the way that one feels. In his letters, Max wants to communicate himself truly, but in letters there is always the danger of the recipient "reading between the lines" and misunderstanding. Thus, the writer must be more careful than if he were present with the loved one. Max wants to give Clara his truest self, everything he is thinking, seeing, feeling, but increasingly as he tries to do this he becomes more self-conscious and therefore uncertain about who that self really is. "How," he asks himself, "can he offer these aberrant knots of his character to Clara?"

At one point Max considers writing intimate about sexual fantasies to Clara, but decides he cannot, and then feels despair that Clara can never know who he is these days if he hides both his worries and his guilty pleasures. More and more Max learns that there are aspects of human experience that cannot be clearly mapped or easily recorded. Over and over, he thinks that his learning to "see" these subtle and complex aspects of experience is more important than anything else. More and more, he writes Clara saying he cannot tell her certain things, that he should not tell her certain things. As time passes and his self-consciousness about the limitations of language grows, he changes more and more, his past life seeming to disappear and his memories becoming jumbled, as if he were dissolving and turning into someone he does not recognize. Grappling with this loss of confidence in language, he finally stops writing to Clara altogether.

The metaphor of a "servant of the map" that holds the story together suggests that when Max loses confidence in his ability to map the mysterious terrain that identifies where and who he is, the resulting loss of self is positive rather than negative, for he realizes that there is something inherently limiting and even false in limiting the self by mapping.

*Charles E. May*

# SETTLED ON THE CRANBERRY COAST

*Author:* Michael Byers (1971-    )
*Type of plot:* Domestic realism
*Time of plot:* The 1990's
*Locale:* Various beach towns on the Washington State coast
*First published:* 1994

> *Principal characters:*
> EDDIE, a retired high school teacher and part-time carpenter
> JODIE, his sister, the principal of an elementary school
> ROSIE, a woman he knew in high school
> HANNAH, Rosie's six-year-old granddaughter

*The Story*

Affirming that it is never too late to find happiness, "Settled on the Cranberry Coast" is a mellow, unsentimental story about Eddie, a middle-aged, single high school history teacher who has just retired and who runs into Rosie, a single woman on whom he once had a crush. When Eddie and Rosie were in high school, they did not run in the same crowd. She is half Indian and hung around with rough guys who drove pickups and wore leather jackets. Eddie lost sight of her after high school. He went to college in the East and lived for a few years with a woman he thought he would marry before coming back to Washington State to teach. After his retirement, he advertises himself as a carpenter and plumber and gets a call from Rosie, now a park ranger, who has just bought a house that needs a lot of work.

When Eddie goes to Rosie's house, he meets Hannah, her six-year-old granddaughter, who she is raising after Rosie's daughter Carolyn abandoned her. Eddie goes to see his sister, Jodie, who is principal of the elementary school and gets angry with her when she asks if he has a problem with Carolyn leaving Hannah with Rosie. Rosie tells him about Carolyn, who was working on a California strawberry farm when she brought Hannah home and later moved to Mexico; she has not heard from her in more than a year. The only appearance in the story of the man who is Carolyn's father occurs when he shows up in a tractor to get his mail and urinates in Rosie's driveway.

Eddie's growing closeness to Hannah is evident when they go to a kite festival; he is envious that a man he knows can tease Hannah and talk to her easily. When Eddie's sister comes to visit and brings a bottle of wine and a twelve-pack of beer, Eddie, his sister, and Rosie begin to get slightly drunk. For the first time, Rosie talks openly about Carolyn, saying she is no longer a part of her life or Hannah's. "She is not even something I think about any more," Rosie says. "She's gone, gone, gone. And now here's Eddie."

Eddie spends the night on Rosie's sofa, and the next morning, when Hannah gets up, he asks her to go with him to a nearby town to buy some radiators for the house. On the drive, Eddie allows himself for the first time to think about marrying Rosie. Hannah goes to sleep, and Eddie carries her into the store while he buys the radiators. As the radiators are being loaded into his car, he stands under an overhang waiting for the rain to stop, holding Hannah, her head on his shoulder. He knows he is on the verge of something, and he just stands and waits, listening to her easy, settled breathing.

*Themes and Meanings*

The central thematic statement of "Settled on the Cranberry Coast" occurs when Rosie says that her daughter Carolyn is no longer part of "our lives," and Eddie can imagine moving in with Rosie and her granddaughter Hannah. He thinks "we don't live our lives so much as come to them, as different people and things collect mysteriously around us" and he feels as though he is coming to Rosie and Hannah, easing his way toward them. The story is largely about the mysterious way that people become who they are, not for any particular reason, but just because things happen that way. There is no particular reason, for example, that Eddie is past middle age and still single or that Rosie is responsible for bringing up her granddaughter. Things have simply happened that way.

It is an unexpected blessing that Eddie, who did not have a chance with Rosie when they were in high school, meets her again when he is retired and she is a grandmother and gets a "second chance" to have a relationship and become "Settled on the Cranberry Coast." The second chance for Eddie is also a second chance for Rosie, a woman who had an illegitimate child, who in turn had an illegitimate child, for whom Rosie is now responsible. Because of the presence of Hannah, Eddie finds himself in the position of easing his way into a ready-made family. Eddie has no experience with small children and therefore feels envious of the man at the kite festival who seems so comfortable teasing Hannah. However, Eddie discovers that childish teasing is not as important as genuine feeling; at the end of the story he feels completely at home with Hannah's head resting "perfectly round" on his shoulder as he stands listening to her "easy, settled breathing."

"Settled on the Cranberry Coast," an O. Henry Awards prize winner in 1995 and included in Michael Byers's first collection *The Coast of Good Intentions*, is typical of his work. In the tradition of such young writers as Ethan Canin and Christopher Tilghman who appeared in the late 1980's and early 1990's, Byers affirms, in a seemingly simple, matter-of-fact way, the solid unsentimental values of family, commitment, and hope for the future. Byers focuses primarily on men who, although certainly not simple, are simply trying hard to do their best. Like Eddie, the retired schoolteacher in "Settled on the Cranberry Coast," they are still looking hopefully to the future. As Eddie makes Rosie's house sturdier, their relationship grows as well, gradually affirming Eddie's opening sentence in the story: "This I know; our lives in these towns are slowly improving."

*Style and Technique*

The understanding, loving, and forgiving values in Byers's story are hard to resist, but they are also hard to present without either irony or sentimentality. Byers manages to avoid both, giving the reader characters who are neither perfect nor petulant, neither ironically bitter nor blissfully ignorant, but rather who are complex and believable human beings, simply doing their best, which, Byers seems to suggest, is simply the most human thing anyone can do.

Byers was only in his late twenties when his first collection of stories was published, but critics were so impressed with the technical accomplishment of his stories that they felt it would be patronizing to call him promising, for he had already arrived. He was highly praised for his ability to portray older adults and small children with convincing detail and to reveal character through carefully controlled dialogue.

The secret to the appeal and success of "Settled on the Cranberry Coast" is the straightforward, likable voice of the central character and narrator Eddie. He is presented as a man who makes no apologies for his life, does not complain, is proud of his work, and is straightforward in his dealings with others. Eddie is understanding and nonjudgmental. When one of his colleagues, a math teacher named Jack Patani, marries one of his students, Eddie says that because the girl adored him, gave him good conversation and a nice young body, "it's hard to argue with that." At the end of the story, when Eddie takes Rosie's granddaughter with him to pick up the radiators, he thinks of what Patani had told him, that he had married his student to give himself a few more good times. Eddie thinks the couple is still happy together, has had several nice years, and is looking for more. With a similar expectation, he allows himself to think for the first time about marrying Rosie.

Because Byers likes Eddie, the reader likes him also. He represents that hope in all people that no matter how old they are, life still holds out the promise of fulfillment. The style of "Settled on the Cranberry Coast" is as straightforward as the character of Eddie himself. Although it does make use of the extended metaphor of Eddie's repairing Rosie's house to reflect the possibility of his own life being regained, at no time does the story become self-consciously literary. The conclusion of the story, with Eddie standing waiting for the rain to stop, holding Hannah, creates a simple picture of a man who is happy to be on the verge of something, happy that it is never too late for a new beginning.

*Charles E. May*

# SEVEN FLOORS

*Author:* Dino Buzzati (Dino Buzzati Traverso, 1906-1972)
*Type of plot:* Fantasy
*Time of plot:* Unspecified
*Locale:* Italy
*First published:* "Sette piani," 1958 (English translation, 1965)

> *Principal characters:*
> GIOVANNI CORTE, a lawyer who is ill with an unnamed disease
> PROFESSOR DATI, the head of his hospital

## The Story

Giovanni Corte arrives at an unnamed sanatorium somewhere in Italy to be treated for a mild case of an unnamed disease. He is pleased by the appearance and amenities of the sanatorium building. It has seven floors, with a fine view from the upper floors, especially from the seventh floor where he is roomed. Unfortunately for those on the bottom floor there is no view at all except for the trees in front of the windows. In a conversation with his nurse, Corte learns that the seventh floor is for people like himself, those hardly ill at all. However, the lower floors are for people who are most ill. The first floor is only for those who are dying. Appalled but fascinated by this system, he looks down at the bottom floor and sees that most of its rooms have their venetian blinds pulled down. Now he discovers that the blinds are pulled down only when a patient has recently died.

After some days Corte is asked if he will, for the moment, give up his room to accommodate a new patient who is bringing her two children and needs more space. He agrees, but then is dismayed to discover that the only room available for him is on the sixth floor. Nevertheless, thinking he will soon be brought back to the seventh floor, he goes down to the sixth floor. Here the routine is different, for the patients are truly ill although not seriously so. Corte is assured that he belongs above, but he is made aware that something, after all, is wrong and perhaps he should stay here, where the doctors really know their business, as opposed to the less knowledgeable physicians above.

Suddenly the patients on the seventh and sixth floors are separated into two classes—those less ill and those more ill. By apparent bureaucratic mischance, Corte is placed among the more ill who are sent down to the fifth floor. He objects violently but finally agrees, because he suddenly lacks strength to continue protesting. On the fifth floor he develops an eczema that will not go away and that can only be treated by an apparatus located on the fourth floor. His doctor does say that Corte belongs on the fifth floor but that he must not tire himself by going up and down the stairs, and so he should go to the fourth floor. Corte reluctantly descends.

Soon Corte's fourth-floor doctor says that to cure his disease properly, Corte should go to the third floor, where he will get full treatment and at last get well. Once more he unwillingly descends. Shortly thereafter the third-floor staff goes on a two-week holiday; to be sure of his correct care Corte must go to the second floor. His stay on the second floor is "temporary," but when the nurses come to move him a week later he asks if the third-floor staff has come back early. No, he is to move to the first and last floor; his removal order has been signed by the head of the sanatorium, Professor Dati himself. A doctor assures Corte that there has been a mistake, but Professor Dati will be gone for some days, so Corte must go down. After he comes to the last floor, he suddenly becomes aware that the venetian blinds are closing.

## Themes and Meanings

Dino Buzzati's worldview has been likened to that of Franz Kafka. What they both reflect is a universe in which certainty has been lost, the absurd universe of modern humankind. Certainly Buzzati's world is strange and perhaps incomprehensible, filled with mystery and threat. His general intent is, however, clear enough in "Seven Floors." This is a kind of satire of organization. Because any organization is both human and universal, and because wherever there are human bureaucracies there is also fate, humans are caught up in both.

This story is a satire, but also something more than satire; it is a kind of allegory on individual lives as members of humanity and as beings in the universe. That is, it is a recognition of the conditions of human existence, of human refusal to accept those conditions, and of the pointlessness of individual refusal.

On an immediate level, Giovanni Corte is a victim of the hospital staff, continually tricked and manipulated in order to get him from one floor to another. This mirrors the outside social world in which people are victims of dishonesty, inefficiency, carelessness, and insensitivity. The hospital staff does not seem inefficient or careless, however, and they may not be entirely dishonest or insensitive. On the surface at least they are providing the treatment that seems best for Corte and they may be hiding the truth about his disease out of compassion. In short, they are simply other human beings. They thus may be victims of the system themselves, and perhaps even potential patients.

The hospital workers certainly do not control that system. The head of the hospital, Professor Dati, is said to plan everything that takes place. Nothing, indeed, seems to be left to chance; however, Dati is more than the head of the hospital. He is also a kind of god figure, the creator and ruler. Because Corte never actually sees Dati, one cannot be certain that Dati himself even exists. Perhaps, then, the planner as well as the plan do not exist, either. Perhaps no one has any idea of what the plan is and what it all means; perhaps the hospital staff are only blind functionaries.

One must add that all the people in the story are members of the middle classes; there is no plain statement about the economic organization of this society. There is certainly no mention of money. This is deliberate; to put any emphasis on money would make the story merely a criticism of the political and economic human world and thereby suggest a possible cure. Instead, Corte becomes a kind of Everyman, not just Economic Man.

Corte is all of humanity. His fate is everyone's, for human existence does not make sense. It is inescapable and death is its inevitable end.

## Style and Technique

"Seven Floors" is, on the immediate level, a simple, realistic tale. Nothing extraordinary happens. There is no careful development of character, not even of Corte's character, although this "lack" of character is what makes him Everyman. The story's language is straightforward, concrete, exact, and simple, with nothing fantastic suggested by metaphor or image. Such language emphasizes the actuality of the story; however, it is in the tension between its simple style and the simple but strangely odd story that the meaning of the work develops.

One notes first certain rather small matters, such as no one being given a name except Corte and Professor Dati, and the deliberate refusal to identify the disease treated at the sanatorium. These are, however, no small matters. Everything in the story is itself, but everything is also multi-symbolic. If allegory tends to limit the symbolic meanings of objects, one must say that "Seven Floors" is more than allegory. For example, the hospital building, with its seven floors, is an "actual" place, but the number seven is rich in mystical meanings. Corte's gradual descent to the first floor reverses the seven days of creation; it is a seven-floor descent ending with dissolution, not creation. If Corte's disease is a real disease, it obviously stands for much more. Doubtless, it represents life itself, life that closes, like the venetian blinds, with death.

The limited point of view of the story also emphasizes its themes. Everything is told from the point of view of Giovanni Corte and, in large part, the reader knows only what Corte learns and experiences. Occasionally an authorial voice enters, saying that Corte felt this or acted thus, as though reporting what impression he would make on an observer. Nevertheless, keeping the observation almost entirely on what Corte experiences emphasizes his aloneness, his separateness from everyone else in the sanatorium and his separateness from everyone else in the world, even though he is Everyman. He is truly alone, as all people are. It seems to be ironic that Corte knows almost from the beginning that the first floor is for those who are about to die, but this irony is Buzzati's emphasis on the fact that everyone is going to die, that although people are intellectually aware that they will die, emotionally, they do not think it will actually happen to them.

*L. L. Lee*

# SEVENTEEN SYLLABLES

*Author:* Hisaye Yamamoto (1921-    )
*Type of plot:* Domestic realism
*Time of plot:* The early twentieth century
*Locale:* Near Los Angeles, California
*First published:* 1949

> *Principal characters:*
> ROSIE, a teenage daughter of Japanese immigrant parents
> MRS. HAYASHI, her mother
> MR. HAYASHI, her father
> JESÚS, her classmate, the son of Mexican immigrants

*The Story*

The Hayashi family lives in a small farming community near Los Angeles. Mrs. Hayashi has begun to write haiku, but when she tries to share the joy of creating poetry with her daughter, Rosie is unable to appreciate her works because she cannot speak Japanese, her mother's native tongue. Mrs. Hayashi's English is no better than Rosie's Japanese. When Rosie wants to share a haiku poem that she has found in her mother's magazine, it is impossible for her to convey to her mother the meaning of the poem written in English and French. All Rosie does when shown her mother's poems is utter words of affirmation, instead of telling her mother that she does not fully understand them.

When Rosie's family visits the Hayanos, another Japanese immigrant family, her mother is absorbed in a discussion of haiku with Mr. Hayano. While Rosie enjoys herself with the four daughters of the family, who are named after the seasons in Japanese, Rosie's father is forced into conversation with Mrs. Hayano, who has mental problems. When he decides suddenly to leave the Hayanos' home without giving any signal to his wife, Rosie is puzzled and Mrs. Hayashi finally notices his irritation. On the way back to their house, Rosie feels angry toward her father because he denies her mother personal enjoyment, and she is angry toward her mother because she does not confront her husband's tyranny.

Paralleling her mother's devotion to writing, Rosie is engrossed in her attraction to Jesús, a son of Mexican workers, who attends the same high school that she does. One night, when Rosie's family has guests, she goes out of the house to meet Jesús, telling the family that she is going to the lavatory outside. That night he kisses her for the first time, and she cannot get him out of her thoughts.

About a month after Mrs. Hayashi starts writing, a man from the Japanese newspaper comes to the Hayashi residence to tell her that she has been awarded first prize in a haiku contest. He has brought an *ukiyo-e* picture as the prize. It is in the middle of the family's work on the farm, and the father grows impatient while waiting for his wife to return to work. His irritation toward her indulgence in poetry reaches the point of outrage. He breaks into the conversation and crushes his wife's prize.

When the man from the newspaper hastily leaves and Rosie approaches her mother, she seems rather calm. Although Rosie is reluctant to listen, her mother tells her of the circumstances surrounding her marriage to Rosie's father. She had fallen in love with a man whose high family status did not allow her to marry him. After abandoning their newborn child, she wrote to her aunt in the United States for help and came to the states for an arranged marriage with Rosie's father. The marriage was an alternative to suicide. Having finished the story, the mother kneels down and asks Rosie never to marry. Rosie wonders about the brother whom she has never seen, and thinks of Jésus, whom she adores. She agrees to her mother's request and then starts crying. Although the mother consoles her, Rosie feels that the consoling hands have come later than she thought.

*Themes and Meanings*

Focusing on the relationship between Rosie and her mother, the story illustrates the gap between Japanese immigrants and their American-born children. The gap is rooted not only in generations, but also in linguistic and cultural differences. As the title suggests, the linguistic difference is most evident in the story and is given a symbolic role. The gap between Rosie and her mother is compounded by cultural differences, as shown by the fact that Rosie fails to understand that her mother's behaviors were acquired in a Japanese cultural context.

Mrs. Hayashi apparently is not satisfied with her present situation and has sought to release her emotions by becoming a poet. She uses a pseudonym when she writes, and Rosie feels as if her mother is two different people. The motivation of the mother's writing is not explicitly discussed, however, indicating Rosie's disinterest in her mother's inner world.

Mrs. Hayashi's urge to write is born out of her suppression, which is primarily caused by her linguistic handicap in the immigrant land. Another major factor in her suppression is the submissiveness of women to men, embedded in the traditional Japanese culture. She seems to accept her role as a wife, although she tries to acquire her own world by indulging herself in writing poetry.

Her husband has the power to determine the welfare of the other members of the family, and his disapproval cuts off Mrs. Hayashi's creativity. When she is talking about poetry at the Hayanos' residence, her husband decides to leave for home without consulting her. Although his self-centered action upsets Rosie, Mrs. Hayashi remains calm and her frustration is not revealed. She does not get sympathy but only contempt from Rosie for her reaction. Mrs. Hayashi remains reserved, even when her husband's irritation has grown into outrage and he breaks the prize for her haiku poem.

The distance between Rosie and Mrs. Hayashi is inevitable, and no solution is suggested in the story. Rosie is unable to perceive her mother's deep feelings, especially when the mother kneels down to beg her not to marry. At the end of the story, their gap is confirmed with the perception of the mother's consoling hands. When Mrs. Hayashi consoles her crying daughter, Rosie feels that the mother's timing is a little too late.

*Style and Technique*

Haiku serves as the metaphor of the narrative technique employed in the story. Haiku is supposed to convey the packed emotion of poets while offering their observation of the outer world. It is for the reader to connect the inner and outer worlds. The poet is required to choose words carefully, as the poem may contain only seventeen syllables.

As haiku demands a reducing of words, this story intentionally holds back some information. Mrs. Hayano's insanity is simply narrated as a fact, but no accounts follow. Nor is the motivation for Mrs. Hayashi's writing explained. Apparently these episodes are related to the Japanese immigrants' dismay over their linguistic disadvantage.

The author uses haiku as the representation of the traditional Japanese culture, as well as of Mrs. Hayashi's packed emotions. Rosie's incapacity to appreciate her mother's haiku highlights the linguistic and cultural gap between them. Not understanding the language used in the mother's poems, Rosie does not decipher the mother's complex inner feelings or her need to write. The only emotion narrated in the story is Rosie's, and the contrast of Rosie's inner voice with the absence of her parents' voices shows that the story is narrated from her perspective. At the same time, the silence of Rosie's parents shows the strict self-control that their native culture has encouraged in them.

Hisaye Yamamoto's writing itself signifies the essence of haiku poetry. Yamamoto shows the gap between the first and second generations of Japanese Americans by sketching the Hayashi family concisely. Yamamoto, a Japanese American herself, is not foreign to the generational gap shown in the story. As emotions are condensed in haiku, Yamamoto puts all her emotion into a short story. She offers only a brief illustration of the Hayashi family, and seldom describes the characters' emotions.

*Yasuko Akiyama*

# THE SEVENTH TRUNK

*Author:* Heinrich Böll (1917-1985)
*Type of plot:* Antistory
*Time of plot:* The mid-twentieth century
*Locale:* Cologne, Germany
*First published:* "Warum ich kurze Prosa wie Jakob Maria Hermes und Heinrich Knecht schreibe," 1965 (English translation, 1966)

>*Principal characters:*
>THE UNNAMED NARRATOR
>JAKOB MARIA HERMES, the author of a short story that has fascinated the narrator for thirty-two years
>HEINRICH KNECHT, the author of a tract titled "The Secret of the Seventh Trunk, or How to Write Short Fiction"

*The Story*

The unnamed narrator of "The Seventh Trunk" is a writer who hopes to find or to create the perfect work of fiction. Early in his career, he thought that this goal had been achieved. He read in the *Bockelmunden Parish News* the first installment of what was supposed to be a two-part story by an author named Jakob Maria Hermes. Unfortunately, however, the publication went out of business, so the conclusion of Hermes's story never appeared.

The narrator gives only the briefest account of its plot: A nine-year-old girl is lured into joining a religious order that attends mass not once, but twice each Sunday. Although the narrator is unable to present the story exactly as he read it years earlier, he insists that it was the most nearly perfect work of fiction that he has ever read. Only one sentence struck him as flawed. On seeing the young girl, a nun of the order is said to be aware of her own "senselessness" (*Sinnlosigkeit*). The narrator says that the word seems ridiculous in its context and must have been a printer's error for "sensuality" (*Sinnlichkeit*). He draws this conclusion because, shortly before this, the same nun notices a spot of chocolate appearing on the young girl's blue dress. This image, the narrator concludes, must evoke feelings that the nun is powerless to suppress.

Curious as to how the story turned out, the narrator searches for information about the author in everything from writers' indexes to the Bockelmunden parish register. At last, he is forced to conclude that the name "Jakob Maria Hermes" must have been a pseudonym. He then begins to seek out Ferdinand Schmitz, a retired schoolmaster who was the last editor of the *Bockelmunden Parish News*. By a remarkable coincidence, Schmitz dies only a day or two before the narrator arrives in town. At the old man's funeral, the narrator is told by relatives that the entire archives of the *Bockelmunden Parish News*—perhaps half a dozen boxes of correspondence, records, and unpublished manuscripts—were burned during the final days of World War II. Left with no means of recovering the story's original ending, the narrator resolves to complete the story himself.

This task proves to be quite difficult. After thirty-two years of false starts, the narrator is still unable to come up with an ending that satisfies him. The reason, he concludes, is that for this story he is unable to open the "seventh trunk," which he regards as the secret to all successful fiction. This phrase is not his own; he has borrowed it from an obscure pamphlet, entitled "The Secret of the Seventh Trunk, or How to Write Short Fiction," that he acquired years earlier in Cologne. Although only a few pages long, "The Secret of the Seventh Trunk" is, the narrator says, the most important guide to writing that he has ever seen. Its author, Heinrich Knecht, compares the writing of a story to the opening of nested trunks, each of which contains something more compact but more valuable than the last.

Like Jakob Maria Hermes, Heinrich Knecht proves to be a mysterious individual. The cover of the pamphlet states that the work was printed at the corner of Teutoburg and Maternus streets in Cologne. When the narrator begins to look for this address, he discovers that Teutoburg and Maternus streets never actually meet. By extending their lengths on a map, he finds that the address listed on the pamphlet would have been in the middle of the Rhine River. Because the publisher's name is listed as "Ulrich Nellessen" and the meal at Ferdinand Schmitz's funeral had been catered by "Nellessen's Inn," the narrator speculates that "Hermes" and "Knecht" were both pseudonyms that Schmitz himself used in his various writings. Perhaps these two mysteries actually lead in the same direction.

The narrator then explains the image of writing fiction as opening a series of seven trunks. In the early stages of one's art, description tends to be excessive. Lavish details are provided so that readers may visualize every aspect of an object, such as a train station, a school, or a block of tenements. As artists become more skillful, they learn how little detail is really necessary. In other words, they have opened a smaller trunk. By paring the story down to its barest essentials, one finally arrives at the seventh trunk, the core of fiction in its highest and purest form.

Knecht's tract describes the sudden opening of the seventh trunk as being like a mouse leaping from a box. This image reminds the narrator of one of his great-grandmother's superstitions. She believed that if crusts of stale bread were bound together in a box, they would be transformed into a mouse. The narrator comments that this process of spontaneous generation is precisely what an author is seeking in the seventh trunk: By condensing a plot to its most vital elements, the perfect story should write itself, independent of the author's will. The narrator concludes with some despair that, even after thirty-two years, the bits of Hermes's story have not yet come to life in his imagination. For this reason, the ending to the story of the young girl in the blue dress cannot be told.

## Themes and Meanings

"The Seventh Trunk" is Heinrich Böll's attempt to provide, in a fictional form, a description of his own artistic process. As a member of the school of German authors and critics known as *Gruppe 47* (Group 47), Böll sought to purge his country's literary style of the complex clauses and linguistic density that had come to be associated with the Nazis and Prussian militarism. At the same time, he strove to simplify the plots of his stories as well. Building on few details and even fewer characters, Böll hoped to create stories that would spring spontaneously to life, rather like the mice leaping from the boxes described by his narrator's great-grandmother.

Although "The Seventh Trunk" is very brief, each detail in it is of great significance. Both the spot of brown chocolate on the young girl's dress and the one mistyped word in Hermes's short story are seemingly insignificant flaws that become focal points in the lives of people who notice them. Both Hermes's story and Knecht's pamphlet are lost in the same knapsack during the war. These two items are symbols of perfection, the illusions of a lost paradise that the narrator hopes to regain.

Perhaps the most important image in the story is that of boxes and their valuable contents. The cases containing the archives of the *Bockelmunden Parish News* that were burned at the end of the war, Knecht's theory of the seven trunks, and the cardboard box from which mice leap spontaneously, all are representations of fiction itself. Böll suggests that the truth that fiction contains is sometimes developed from the humblest of materials. All the author need do is to assemble the proper ingredients and allow them to come to life in the mind of the reader.

*Style and Technique*

"The Seventh Trunk" is an antistory or nonstory. In this type of fiction, the plot of the work itself is less important than the author's exploration of the creative process. "The Seventh Trunk" does not draw a clear boundary between where fiction ends and the author's own life begins. The narrative voice that Böll assumes in the story is largely indistinguishable from his own. Like Böll, the narrator of "The Seventh Trunk" grew up in Cologne, became a writer, and was captured by the enemy during World War II. It is difficult to determine, therefore, how much of the story resulted from the author's recollection and how much is his own invention. If it were presented as a nonfiction article, "The Seventh Trunk" would be almost indistinguishable from a rather routine reminiscence. Only the artfulness of the account itself, and the role of coincidence in the story, suggest that this is a work of fiction.

Böll's structure in "The Seventh Trunk" is a free flow of ideas. His description of his attempts to uncover, and later to write, the second half of Jakob Maria Hermes's short story leads him to summarize Knecht's account of the writing process. Knecht's image of the opening of nested trunks leads him, in turn, to recount his great-grandmother's superstition. This, too, Böll regards as a suitable metaphor for the writing of fiction. Like any narrator of fiction, Böll has selected a few details, brought them together, and allowed them to take on their own life.

*Jeffrey L. Buller*

# A SHAPE OF LIGHT

*Author:* William Goyen (Charles William Goyen, 1915-1983)
*Type of plot:* Coming of age
*Time of plot:* Long ago and many years later
*Locale:* There, in a southern town, and here, in a city
*First published:* 1952

> *Principal characters:*
> BONEY BENSON, a seeker after the mysterious shape of light
> ALLIE BENSON, his forsaken wife
> THE NARRATOR, a later seeker, and a shaper of the record of
> Boney's quest
> YOU, a counterpart of the narrator, "kite-maker and kite-flyer," to
> whom part of the story is addressed

## The Story

Boney Benson, a man obsessed with a singular quest, lived in a town where it was his job to flag the midnight trains with a red lantern. Wizened, scary, almost ghostlike in appearance, but gentle, he awakened the imagination of the town. The people would whisper his story, passing down what they knew to the younger generation. Some said he spent his days in the graveyard, sprawled on the earth over the place where Allie, his wife, and their unborn child lay buried. It was said that the baby murdered Allie, that in the last month of her pregnancy the child had risen in her body until it lodged beneath her heart and nested there, a kind of vampire, until Allie could not breathe.

Allie died in terror, fighting for air without knowing what was strangling her. It might have been her husband, for all she knew, for he often left her without warning, to pursue "a lighted shape, much like a scrap of light rising like a ghost from the ground." They might be sitting at the supper table when the powerful urge to follow the light would strike him, and then he would rise, go saddle his purple horse, King, and be off, to wander over the countryside all night long, until, at daybreak, the light vanished into the ground.

In a fit of conscience, Boney turned against himself and mutilated his body; he buried his severed member in the grave with his wife and child. It was said that the child was born in the grave and lived underground, like a mole, but rose each night in the shape of a ball of light. Mexicans who lived at the edge of the graveyard first saw the specter. Fishermen and campers also reported an eerie shape of floating light. When Boney heard about the haunting, he attempted to seal the light in the dirt with a slab of slate, holding it down with the weight of his body. Finding it impossible to contain the light, he began to wait in the graveyard each night, mounted on King, for the light to rise. Then he followed it wherever it led. Three young men, who went with Boney on one of his nightly journeys, reported having followed the shape of light to a field of grave-children, and beyond, through a phantasmagoric landscape riddled with nursing mothers, martyrs, hermits, "wings and limbs of a lost son falling from the sky," and lovers mating like strange insects. They followed Boney, who followed his light, into another country, where the wearied young men turned back, and Boney died. He was returned home and buried alongside Allie, but the destructive-creative light continued to rise for someone to give his life over to following it.

This skeleton of Boney Benson's tale can be pieced together from the two sections of "A Shape of Light": "The Record" and "The Message." However, to exhume a plot from William Goyen's poetic narrative hardly conveys the archetypal force of the story or its haunting effect. At the heart of "The Message," in a city, long after the life and death of Boney, his image surfaces from the past, through the retelling and fabulation of his tale, to claim the imagination of a "kite-maker and kite-flyer," addressed only as "you." This character replaces the narrator of "The Record" and seems at times to be both author and reader, or a figure for a type of messenger-message relationship, like that of writer and story.

Boney appears, "his face, swimming and dipping and bowing and rising and darting, looking down at you . . . his kite face . . . send up a message! You had built kite and kite had taken his message and delivered it. Now you must shape him, like kite, and send his message back to him." This writer's story attempts to give shape to something essentially inexpressible through the quest of Boney Benson and the appearance of the light. It seems to have been written, in part, to exorcise ghosts of memory that would overshadow the artist if the story could not be told. Not only the kite-maker but also the kite itself, the artist must look down and confront his mooring, the power holding the string, which is his own past: "You turned and called out, man now and no longer child, speaker now and no longer listener, asking man's question, crying man's cry. . . . Now Boney Benson was all your question and all your pain; and tell it." Out of grief and guilt, out of what has been forever lost to memory, out of the failure of language to communicate, the messenger must find the perfect vehicle for his message. The obsession of the kite-maker to shape a story out of the wreckage of memory and words parallels the seeker after the light who must surrender himself and live separate from the world in order to fulfill his quest.

*Themes and Meanings*

This complex story traces the ancient pattern of the journey in parallel narratives, one about the seeker, Boney Benson, and another interwoven narrative about the process of discovering truth through fiction-shaping. Partially, it is a traditional coming-of-age story, for the shift from listener to teller completes the artist's passage into manhood, and in the writing of the story he is able to shed the ghosts of his memory that threaten to strangle his power of expression. The figure of Boney, whose very name holds a foreboding of mortality, and the shape of light he must follow against reason reveal the story's true message.

Boney has been touched, poisoned, or made crazy by the light. Once he is converted to the light he no longer belongs to the world. He lives apart from the rest of the town. As a "follower" of the light, he must abandon everything else and look to the light alone for meaning in his life.

> He had to give himself wholly, unafraid, surrendered to it. He had to leave things behind . . . and this was his life, bearing, suffering the found-out meaning of what he was involved in, haunted by it, grieved by it, but possessing it—and watching it continue to grow, on and on, into deeper and larger meaning.

The Christian parallels both in pattern and in language are so strong that they become the real center of the story. In this light, the initiation pattern is subsumed into the conversion experience.

Just as there is no reasonable explanation for the events of Boney's life, there is no proof of God or of Jesus's life and Resurrection, except through faith. Jesus said, "I am the light of the world. Whoever follows me will never walk in darkness, but will have the light of life" (1 John 8:12). Boney's dedication to the light seems to predicate a post-Pentacostal world, when the Holy Ghost, set loose in the world as guide and comforter, has taken the place of Jesus the man and teacher, and conversion must be wholly a matter of faith in the unseen.

Another name for Jesus, found in the beginning of the Gospel of John, is the Word, the incarnate Word of God. It is these dual aspects of God, light and word, that Goyen's story about dual quests attempts to express, always aware in the telling of what words can never say. In the face of the inexplicable and inexpressible, words are ever more precious to bridge the dark silence between humankind and Creator.

The image of the kite-message, with its crossed sticks stretched over with fragile paper, becomes an emblem for Jesus. In the same way that this kite enables the artist to find his voice, the mystery aglow in the world illuminates the smallest details of "the frail eternal life of the ground." Some of Goyen's most impressive writing goes into descriptions of this natural wonderland, which needs only to be apprehended to be celebrated. Once illumined, one is made aware of the world's intimate beauty of design, evidenced in living forms, and once one has seen, one must tell it. Like Boney, who still sees and must follow the light where it leads, even after blinding himself to escape it, the converted will never be free of the force of that illumination. However, they, like the artist, do not wish to be apart from what defines them, even though they can never really be part of the world in the same way again.

## Style and Technique

Goyen's distinctive style permeates any other investigation into his fiction, be it for character, for plot, or for theme. The surface of his language is inescapable, seeming to envelop the reader in a lyrical web that can best be approached as a kind of spoken music, a cadenced, colloquial music put down in words from deep attention to the rhythms and repetitions of a regional, yet interior, voice. Goyen's voice, a blend of

Texan and Mexican and rural tongues, touched by the King James Bible and the Romance languages, cannot be located in the mapped world; his language charts its own place, becomes a world at times so heady that a single sentence tumbles through so many transfigurations of simile that anyone in search of a regular story would feel lost and perhaps even fatigued by the force and passion in the prose.

As in much of Goyen's fiction, someone in "A Shape of Light" struggles to listen, to comprehend, and then to set down for others a story essentially too complicated to be told. Much of the experience that seems worthy of being passed on is noncorporal, or spiritual, in nature and therefore doomed to find only partial expression in language. The effect of this visible effort is nearly magical; the complexity of overlapping texts, of records and messages, retellers and relisteners, brings to light what cannot otherwise be spoken. To simplify stylistically would be a lie in the face of the mystery. In this way, Goyen's voice embodies both a fictional territory all his own and a very intense struggle to make lasting shapes, to "tell it" against the destructive intrusions of time and death.

*Cathryn Hankla*

# THE SHAPE OF THE SWORD

*Author:* Jorge Luis Borges (1899-1986)
*Type of plot:* Mystery and detective
*Time of plot:* The early 1940's
*Locale:* Tacuarembó, Argentina, and Connaught, Ireland
*First published:* "La forma de la espada," 1944 (English translation, 1956)

> *Principal characters:*
> BORGES, the frame narrator
> THE ENGLISHMAN OF LA COLORADA, a reclusive ranch owner in
>    Argentina

*The Story*

The frame narrator, Borges, describes a lonely, mysterious Englishman who lives at La Colorada. His appearance is notable for the vicious scar that crosses his face in an arc—from his temple on one side to his cheek on the other. Borges has heard many rumors about the Englishman of La Colorada, but no one knows exactly where he came from or how he came by his scar.

One stormy night, the narrator finds himself unexpectedly stranded at La Colorada. After spending several hours drinking with the Englishman, he asks him about the scar. The Englishman changes color, then agrees to tell the narrator the story of the scar on the condition that he not belittle any of the infamous details of the story, nor minimize the scorn that it provokes in him.

The Englishman explains that he is actually Irish, and that in 1922, in Connaught, he belonged to a group of Republicans, Catholics, and romantics who were conspiring to help Ireland win independence from Great Britain. One evening their group was joined by a new comrade, John Vincent Moon, an arrogant, inexperienced, callow young man from Munster who talked glibly about Marxist theory. Later that evening, the Englishman and Moon were walking along the city streets, arguing about communism, when they were surprised by a sudden exchange of gunfire. A British soldier ran into the road and screamed at them to halt. The Englishman fled at first, then turned back to strike down the soldier and rescue Moon, who was not only paralyzed with fear, but who later cried when a stray bullet grazed his shoulder. The Englishman brought Moon to the strange, rambling, vacated country house where he had taken refuge, then made him tea and dressed his superficial wound. The next day, when he told Moon that their comrades expected them to join in the fighting, Moon complained of a fever and a shoulder spasm. The Englishman, realizing that Moon was an incurable coward, went on alone.

For nine days, the Englishman left the house at dawn and returned at dusk to participate in the increasingly violent battle between the Irish revolutionaries and the British army. Moon hid in the country house, nursed his wound, and read books on military strategy. On the tenth day, the Englishman returned to the house and overheard

Moon on the telephone, betraying him to the British for a price. Moon suggested that the British soldiers arrest him as he crossed the garden of the country house when he returned that evening. Furious, the Englishman pursued Moon down the house's staircases and through its labyrinthine corridors. He finally cornered Moon in the library, where he snatched down a scimitar mounted on the wall and used it to mark Moon's face "with a half-moon of blood."

At this point in his story, the Englishman pauses. The narrator asks him what happened to Moon. The Englishman answers that Moon turned in his comrade, took his Judas money from the British, and fled to Brazil. When the narrator, still unsatisfied, asks him to continue his story, the Englishman points to the scar on his face. Stammering, he explains that he himself is the traitorous John Vincent Moon, and he tells the narrator to despise him.

*Themes and Meanings*

"The Shape of the Sword" raises provocative questions about identity, betrayal, memory, and storytelling. Jorge Luis Borges was particularly haunted by these issues, and he explored them throughout his fiction. In this tale, before the Englishman reveals his true identity, he remarks that he felt as ashamed of John Vincent Moon's cowardice as if he himself were the coward. The Englishman goes on to articulate Borges's philosophy about the interdependence of all human experiences: "What one man does is something done, in some measure, by all men. . . . Perhaps Schopenhauer is right: I am all others, any man is all men, Shakespeare is in some way the wretched John Vincent Moon."

This idea is poignantly illustrated by Moon's actions and their effect on him. His betrayal of his comrade, which Borges specifically compares to Judas's betrayal of Jesus, ignores their common humanity, as well as the sacrifices that the other has already made on his behalf. Moon's intense guilt, years later, indicates that he himself has suffered for what he did to his comrade.

The narrative structure of "The Shape of the Sword" cleverly reinforces the idea that "what one man does is something done, in some measure, by all men." By telling his tale not from his own point of view, but from that of the man whom he betrayed, Moon affirms their commonality. Just as he plays the roles of both narrator and protagonist, so he also plays the roles of both traitor and hero. The narrator of "The Shape of the Sword" preserves this narrative device when he retells the story to the reader. As "The Englishman" concludes his tale by revealing that he is John Vincent Moon, the narrator concludes his story by revealing that he is actually Borges himself. The different levels of the story's narrative structure thus illustrate its theme. Through the story, the reader can vicariously experience the roles of both traitor and hero, narrator and protagonist.

*Style and Technique*

"The Shape of the Sword" is an elegantly constructed, self-reflexive story that asks profound questions about the nature of human identity. Borges was fascinated with the doubling of human consciousness, and with the complementary roles that can be played by a single man—themes that he also explores in his witty essay, "Borges and I," and in other stories, such as "Theme of the Traitor and Hero," "Death and the Compass," and "Three Versions of Judas."

"The Shape of the Sword," in particular, uses the literary device of the double to illustrate the multiplicity of human consciousness. A double is a literary character with an uncanny likeness to the protagonist; typically, the double represents a single aspect of the protagonist's character, such as the conscience or the unconscious. Stories featuring this device usually end, as "The Shape of the Sword" does, with a struggle between the protagonist and the double, and with the death of one of them. In "The Shape of the Sword," however, Borges elaborates on the psychological implications of this literary device. John Vincent Moon and the martyred Irish patriot are actually separate characters, but in telling his tale, the Englishman switches their identities. After his act of treachery, the Englishman apparently began to identify himself with the man whose death he caused.

Borges also emphasizes the theme of the double in the story's imagery and wordplay, beginning with its title. "The Shape of the Sword" refers simultaneously to the semicircular scar on the Englishman's face, the curved scimitars mounted on the wall in the library of the country house, and the form of the story itself—which reveals the identity of its main character only at the end. This shape, of course, is also that of a crescent moon. Although the narrator reveals at the beginning that the Englishman's name is of no importance, it turns out to be the key to the entire story. His last name, Moon, alludes to the half-moon shape of his scar. The half-moon suggests, in turn, that he is now only half Moon; the other half of his personality identifies with the man whom he betrayed.

The phases of the moon also recall the changeability of the protagonist, who has been described in ambivalent, ambiguous terms from the beginning. The narrator has heard rumors suggesting that, as a master, the Englishman is both cruel and fair, both timid and apprehensive. This dual nature is later confirmed by the tale that he tells the narrator. Even after he has revealed his true identity to the narrator, the Englishman remains a complicated and ambiguous figure. Has he redeemed himself through his suffering, or is he as cowardly and evasive as ever, because he denies his true nationality, and even pretends that he is someone he is not? By the end of Borges's brilliant little story, the reader knows the secret of the protagonist's mysterious scar, but that revelation only leads to more perplexing questions about the nature of human identity.

*Susan Elizabeth Sweeney*

# THE SHAWL

*Author:* Cynthia Ozick (1928-     )
*Type of plot:* Psychological
*Time of plot:* The early 1940's
*Locale:* A Nazi concentration camp
*First published:* 1980

> *Principal characters:*
> ROSA LUBLIN, a Polish Jewish prisoner of the Nazis
> MAGDA, her infant daughter
> STELLA, her niece, also a prisoner

*The Story*

Rosa, a Polish Jew who has been captured by the Nazis, desperately secures her baby, Magda, in a shawl, but Rosa's fourteen-year-old niece, Stella, covets that comfort. The three are part of a group of starving people who are being forced to march— presumably to a concentration camp. Rosa worries what might become of her child: If Magda is regarded as "Aryan," Rosa may give her away in a village. Because Rosa's body cannot supply the milk that would sustain Magda, Rosa considers the shawl that hides the baby to be magic. Magda seems to live by sucking it, and her breath smells of cinnamon and almonds.

Some time later, Magda, miraculously still alive, is old enough to walk, and she, Rosa, and Stella are in a concentration camp. Concealing Magda is more difficult now. Rosa even suspects that Stella might devour the infant or that another prisoner might inform on Rosa for concealing a child or steal and eat Magda. Magda is not stolen or eaten, however, but meets her death after Stella steals the shawl. Magda runs out of the barracks, into the light of the open space where the prisoners assemble for roll call. To Rosa's surprise, Magda is howling—revealing that she is not deaf but also dooming herself by drawing the authorities' attention to her. Rosa hesitates: should she first try to retrieve her child, or go first to get the shawl with which she hopes she will be able to conceal her?

Having decided that it would be futile to retrieve Magda without having a means to protect her, Rosa first looks for the shawl. She finds it covering the sleeping Stella. Rosa grabs the shawl and rushes outside, where she sometimes has heard lamenting voices in the electrified fence. There she sees Magda riding high on someone's shoulder. The person carrying Magda is a soldier, who hurls the child to her death against the fence. As horrifying as it is to watch the murder through Rosa's eyes and thoughts, the reader must also experience all that Rosa cannot do. She must bear the sight of the remains of her undernourished child at the foot of the fence, and do nothing. Rosa must listen to those haunting voices in the fence urging her to collect the body, and instead survive by refusing to reveal herself as the mother of a child who has been hidden. Rosa must endure the screams that fill her body and make no sound. To stifle her horror, she chooses the object that both Magda and Stella have craved. Rosa stuffs the magic shawl into her own mouth until she tastes "the cinnamon and almond depth of Magda's saliva" and drinks of it "until it dried."

## Themes and Meanings

Although Magda dies, "The Shawl" affirms the miracle of courage. Rosa doggedly conceals and sustains her child during the exhausting march and then under the horrible conditions in the camp. As agonizing as the final paragraph may seem, it emphasizes the steadfastness and fortitude that enable Rosa to survive the death of her child as well as her persecution by the Nazis.

Much can be learned from this brief story about the mass persecution of Jews and other Europeans that has become known as the Holocaust. In her autobiographical essay "Washington Square, 1946," Cynthia Ozick says that she "lived in the narrow throat of poetry" until she was "at last hammer-struck with the shock of Europe's skull, the bled planet of death camp and war." The early paragraphs of "The Shawl" evoke the exhaustion, starvation, and terror of prisoners forced from their homes by the Germans. One notices the infamous yellow stars that were sewn onto clothing to brand Jews. From Rosa's concern that her baby has blue eyes and blond hair, which may reveal Magda to be one of their babies, it appears that Rosa probably has been raped by her captors.

Later, the sunlit roll-call arena suggests the terrorizing tactics of the camp guards, and the "flowers" and "rain" of excrement and urine establish the disgusting conditions inside the prisoners' barracks. The electrified fence indicates the technologically efficient and impersonal means employed to confine captives. ("The Shawl" was inspired by a line about babies thrown against such fences in a history of Nazi Germany.) Finally, the "bitter fatty floating smoke that greased Rosa's skin" refers to the fact that concentration camps were usually death camps—holding facilities for those eventually gassed or burned alive in the ovens.

One may well ponder the ambivalent role of Rosa's imagination. On one hand, she feels like a "floating angel, alert and seeing everything." On the other, the "lamenting voices" in the fence offer advice that could be fatal to her. The first half of the story develops several options regarding Magda, while in the second, any influence over the child's welfare is taken from Rosa. By the end, speculating has not helped save her daughter, and Rosa must quickly find a means to sustain herself.

The source she finds—the magic shawl—deserves consideration. It hides Magda from danger and nourishes her when her mother's breasts go dry. It is so desirable that Stella steals it instead of stealing Magda, as Rosa had feared she might do. Although there is no indication of how much time passes during the story, the shawl has permitted Magda to live longer than expected. Critics have noted that the shawl resembles the Jewish prayer shawl. The taste of cinnamon and almonds confirms the religious and mystical nature of the shawl. Cinnamon and almonds are the contents of the spice box that Jews sniff during the ceremony at the end of the Sabbath, for unity and strength during the work and trials of the week ahead. It is likely that Ozick, to whom the traditions and meanings of the Jewish religion are real and vital, intends that Rosa's reliance on the shawl is not merely an act of personal strength, but testimony to the miraculous ways of God.

## Style and Technique

"The Shawl" remarkably applies lyrical language to the Holocaust. From the sixth sentence, in which Rosa calls herself "a walking cradle," Ozick repeatedly uses metaphor to convey the intensity of her perceptions. Her language is also precise. The series of images at the start of a sentence about Rosa's milkless breasts—"The duct-crevice extinct, a dead volcano, blind eye, chill hole"—shows Rosa struggling to say exactly what she means. This sentence also illustrates the compression of which Ozick is capable. She squeezes into a dozen words what some writers would extend through several sentences. In her essay "The Seam of the Snail," Ozick describes herself as a "pinched perfectionist" who scrupulously reworks each sentence until it is "comely and muscular." Perfectionism, however, is not the entire explanation. Often devoting her art to religious purposes, Ozick fashions sentences as though they were ritual. Such an endeavor cannot be taken lightly, especially when writing about the Holocaust, which some thinkers have declared beyond the limits of art, as least the art of persons who were not victims.

"The Shawl" seems to exist outside of time, a quality appropriate to a story designed not merely to document the horrors of the Holocaust, but to convey the mind of a person trapped in that "place without pity." It is fascinating to reread the fourth and fifth paragraphs and try to determine when the narrative arrives in the camp, but there is no explicit transition. Likewise, what appears all along to be a story about horror turns into a miracle of survival. One realizes that in lacking a specific chronology and definite location, the story is as whole, magical, and mystical as the shawl for which it is named.

*Jay Paul*

# SHE IS BEAUTIFUL IN HER WHOLE BEING

*Author:* N. Scott Momaday (1934-    )
*Type of plot:* Adventure
*Time of plot:* The mid-twentieth century
*Locale:* Navajo Indian Reservation in northeastern Arizona
*First published:* 1989

> *Principal characters:*
> SET, a young Native American man
> GREY, his lover
> LELA, her mother
> NANIBAH, a young girl

*The Story*

It is summer in Lukachukai, a town in northeastern Arizona's Navajo Reservation. Set and Grey have recently begun living together in a hogan near Lela's house, where the family eats and visits together daily. Almost as soon as Set and Grey entered Grey's family life, Set saw that Grey had "assumed an attitude of deep propriety, dignity," and that she had effortlessly returned to the Navajo habits, dress, styles, and language of her mother's people.

In awe of this woman whom he loves, Set marvels at how swiftly Grey has been transformed before his eyes from a beautiful girl into a beautiful woman, with experience, purpose, and grace. Moreover, she has retained her sense of humor and her ability to love and communicate fully with Set. She is truly, as her mother, Lela, says, "beautiful in her whole being."

By the end of the first paragraph it is clear that Grey belongs to Set, and he to her. The only problem is that Grey is "whole" in her being, while Set is not. A young man of Kiowa ancestry, Set has lived outside the Navajo world all of his life. Furthermore, he was apparently raised without a family of his own, in orphanages on the fringes of society. Because of his fragmented family background, he remains incomplete. In the Navajo language he is *daats'i*, a person alone—an orphan in every way.

At first feeling almost boyish in Grey's presence, Set gradually enters her world, the world, and begins to see, as for the first time, the stars, the night, the dawn, and the land spreading out around him. During the summer, he runs each morning and throughout the day in order to breathe in new life from the entire world. As he gains in strength, his creative spirit emerges. Drawing on earlier artistic training, he creates simple but strong paintings. He listens to the natural music of the wind and thunder, and the birds and coyotes, and to the Navajo words of Grey, Lela, and the others. Through those sounds and rhythms he begins to understand both the Navajo language and the Navajo world. A young Navajo girl, Nanibah (Grey's younger sister, cousin, or niece; the exact relationship is uncertain), warms quickly to Set and adopts him.

Nearly a year of preparation passes before Set can declare to Lela that he wishes to marry her daughter. It is the same moment that he realizes this fact himself. The burden of his apartness, the burden of the *daats'i*, endures, however. It is a burden that Set must shed, if he can.

As the seasons approach full circle, spring quickens the mountain world of the Navajo. Puppies play by the house, butterflies flutter in the air, and rock formations shimmer in the heat. The entire world lives. With each day, Set learns and grows ever stronger, ever more a part of the living and whole world. Exercising, painting, watching, and talking all make him more complete. Grey's love nourishes him. Lela's cooking feeds him. The sweat lodge purifies him. Finally, when he is fully ready, he enters into the current of the wind, of water running, of shadows extending, of sounds rising up and falling away, and joins the world of the Navajo. He has become whole in his being.

*Themes and Meanings*

N. Scott Momaday's choice of setting is important. Navajos traditionally believe that mountains are powerful places for healing ceremonies, and they believe that the Lukachukai Mountains are the most powerful mountains of all. Lukachukai therefore is the ideal setting for the protagonist's year-long healing ritual.

More important, Set's healing ritual is an adventure of life and love, a celebration of what it means to be a part of—as opposed to apart from—the world. Paradoxically, Set becomes whole only as he becomes part of the world. His story is thus also an initiation ceremony, one in which the naturally and elementally pure forces of nature and love sustain and perpetuate life.

Throughout the story, the basic conflict hinges on whether Set, the outsider, can become part of the whole world to which Grey and her family already belong. This conflict stems not so much from Set's non-Navajo origins, but from the knowledge that his past isolation from any type of unified or family-oriented society may interfere with his healing and joining process. The reader immediately sees that Grey is "beautiful in her whole being." The question remains as to whether Set can also become beautiful in his "whole being."

Lela describes Set's situation succinctly with a Navajo metaphor, telling him, "The bear stands against you"; that is, something powerful and spiritually or physically dangerous threatens his health or plans. Set recognizes the threat, but he also knows that within himself rises a force capable of meeting and defeating the bear: His name, *Set*, means bear in Kiowa. The bear and he are thus one; he is the bear. (At first he feels like a mere "boy bear," a *Set-talee*.)

The array of names with which Set refers to himself as he begins to enter the Navajo world (Set-talee, Tsoai-talee, boy bear, rock-tree boy) introduces a significant autobiographical element into the story. *Tsoai-talee*, which means "rock-tree boy" in Kiowa, is the author's actual Kiowa name. However, another autobiographical note is the fact that Momaday's mother, a Native American of non-Kiowa ancestry, was herself initially treated as an outsider among the Momaday family.

The Kiowa, like the Navajo (and perhaps most societies), also believe that the names people have greatly influence their lives. Names do more than simply describe people, with many societies allowing or requiring their members to adopt new names to signify changes in social status or role. Examples abound, even in English-speaking cultures, in which most people gradually acquire capitalized titles such as Mister, Ms, Miss, Missus, Doctor, Captain, Sir, Madam, or Judge. Although naming patterns may themselves change, marriage remains one of those occasions on which new names are commonly chosen. In Set's quest, however, naming plays but a minor role in the overall process of becoming whole.

As Set becomes whole, largely because of Grey's love—the force that has brought him to Lukachukai—he becomes part of the whole to which the bear, Grey, Lela, and everything and everyone else belongs. All comes together as a unified whole, with the union of Set and Grey in marriage a metaphor for the unified Navajo world. The story thus stands as a passionate and profound metaphor for one life, two lives, and all life together.

*Style and Technique*

Momaday's language is precise and well controlled, yet figuratively expansive and inventive. His mastery is evident throughout. For example, a simple oxymoron physically describes Grey as at once "soft and firm," effectively combining a range of male-female sensual imagery. The use of chiasmus at the center of the story represents the story's balance point and shows Set engaged in life and nearing oneness: "His life was in motion; in motion was his life." The theme of life as motion in "She Is Beautiful in Her Whole Being" echoes a message in Momaday's *House Made of Dawn* (1968), his Pulitzer Prize-winning novel about a young man attempting to find himself in, and join himself to, the living, moving world.

Set's passage to oneness of being is also a literary allegory for life itself. Life cannot be complete—nor can it continue—either in isolation or without love. Love leads one out of isolation, out of the self alone, and into family and society, where love and life and beauty become, in an ideally complete world, one unified whole.

"She Is Beautiful in Her Whole Being" is a perfect love adventure, one culminating in a marriage of parts that are each complete but which together constitute an ideal whole. As the firestick is ceremonially consumed, so too are both Set and Grey joined as one. They become one whole, both beautiful in their whole being.

*William Matta*

# THE SHE-WOLF

*Author:* Giovanni Verga (1840-1922)
*Type of plot:* Verism
*Time of plot:* The late 1800's
*Locale:* A rural Sicilian community
*First published:* "La lupa," 1880 (English translation, 1896)

> *Principal characters:*
> GIUSEPPINA, the She-wolf and protagonist
> MARICCHIA (diminutive of Maria), her daughter
> NANNI, a young local man

*The Story*

The villagers have given Giuseppina the nickname "the She-wolf" "because she never had enough—of anything. The women made the sign of the Cross when they saw her pass," and even the parish priest lost his soul for her. Maricchia, her daughter, bemoans her own fate: No one would want the daughter of such a woman as his wife, even though her dowry and landholdings are the match of any young woman in the town.

When Nanni, a young man of the village, returns from his compulsory military service, the She-wolf falls desperately in love with him. Much older than he, with the telltale pallor of malaria on her face, she nevertheless presents an imposing and handsome figure that belies her age, with piercing, black eyes and lips that devour men with their intense color. Her passion for Nanni, however, is thwarted. Nanni will have the daughter, not the mother, and so he tells her, directly and laughingly. A few months later, she offers Maricchia to him; the dowry is discussed, and the She-wolf tells him to come at Christmastime to arrange the marriage.

Maricchia is repelled at the sight of Nanni when she first sees him, oily and dirty after his labors, but her mother imperiously forces her to marry him, threatening to kill her if she does not. After some years have passed, Maricchia is occupied with her children, while the She-wolf, almost destroyed by her continuing passion for Nanni, seems to have lost her energy and will. Nanni, now quite satisfied with his life, laughs in her face when she looks at him, while Maricchia, who has grown to love her husband intensely, reviles her mother, "her eyes burning with tears and jealousy, like a young she-wolf herself." The She-wolf continues to visit Nanni in the fields. He chases her away again and again, yet, she returns, like an ill-treated dog, only to be chased away again. Finally, however, Nanni falls prey to the She-wolf. Maricchia senses what is happening, and even threatens to make her own humiliation public by reporting the situation to the police. This she does eventually, but the She-wolf refuses to give up the corner of the house that she has reserved for herself with the married couple.

A short time later, Nanni almost dies after being kicked in the chest by a mule. The parish priest refuses to give him the Final Sacraments unless the She-wolf leaves the house. He recovers, performs an act of public penance, and again begs the She-wolf to leave him alone, this time threatening to kill her if she comes to him again. "Kill me, then," she responds, "for it makes no difference to me; without you I have no desire to live." This chilling rejoinder immediately precedes the final paragraph, in which she does, indeed, seek out Nanni one final time as he is working the soil of a vineyard. As she approaches him, devouring him with her black eyes, a mass of red poppies in her hands, Nanni leaves off his work, picks up his ax and watches her draw nearer, cursing her soul in a stammering voice as the She-wolf comes toward him.

*Themes and Meanings*

The She-wolf is dominated by a single, overriding passion that ultimately destroys her and those closest to her, yet it is a passion that remains true to its own nature throughout, giving her an exalted role in what might otherwise be an undistinguished rustic domestic drama. Nanni stammers out his final curse; he is unable to cry out with the same strength of resolve that characterizes the sure, determined movement of the woman who faces him. Does he kill her? The author does not say, because ultimately it is not important. What is important is that the She-wolf has no power over the forces that have brought her to this point, nor can Nanni resist her. They are both victims of a tragedy that is played out over and over again in every age and in all socioeconomic circumstances. There are crucial differences, however, between the two: The She-wolf is as proud in her strength as she is unswerving in her purpose; Nanni's weakness is as inevitable and inexorable as is the She-wolf's obsession.

Adhering to the Verist canon of impersonality, Giovanni Verga insisted that the work of art must rise spontaneously, naturally: It should appear "to have made itself," the hand of the author never seeming to interfere. It must be a human document, direct, unadorned, plunging directly into "the necessary development of passions and facts leading to the denouement, which is thus rendered less unforeseen, less dramatic, perhaps, but not less fatal." This briefest among Verga's greatest short stories gives full credence to his doctrine. This simple peasant woman, perhaps his finest creation, expresses both the power and the vital force of a cultural entity that had been denied a voice in Italian literature before the 1800's, before Verga.

The She-wolf, transformed by her passion, establishes a terrible superiority of isolation over the common tenor of communal life that levitates against her. Its structures, its mores, and its punishments are fixed; thus, the outcome of the story will be fatal, whatever form that fatality may take. The She-wolf plays out her tragic drama in every gesture and every linear action that she initiates. She is the parched fields under a blazing summer sun, the desire of the new plant for life in a harsh terrain. Although she knows that she is a sinner and accepts her fate, she is, at the same time, an awesome, albeit oblique, example of integrity, of purity.

Deterministic in every detail, the story moves immediately to the level of the deepest implications of desire and despair, to those places in the heart where differences of class and status have no meaning. The violent truth of the She-wolf's tortured soul takes her beyond the specific Sicilian setting to achieve the stature of the Greek heroines who have reappeared in every succeeding epoch, beyond the consolations of religion, beyond plaint.

In the introduction to another story from the collection in which "The She-Wolf" first appeared, "Gramigna's Mistress," Verga asks the question: "Shall we ever reach such perfection in the study of passions that it will become useless to continue in this study of the inner man?" His answer is that of the artist who captures a reality and presents it in the form of a modern myth, remaining true to his theory of the human document, enhancing it with the subtlety of his art.

## Style and Technique

Identifying as much as possible with his characters, Verga entered their world through the cadence of a language as closely mimetic of their speech as can be achieved without actually using Sicilian dialect. He explained the genesis and effectiveness of this technique following his chance discovery of a ship captain's log, written in the abrupt and truncated manner of one little practiced in the art of writing, with the day's events recorded and chronicled in a straightforward and rough-hewn language, asyntactic but effective—a language, in short, consonant with the individual's thoughts and ability to express those thoughts. As a logical extension of this pattern, dialogue predominates over description, and where description is necessary, it springs directly from the characters' perception, the narrator himself taking on the identity of a character in the story, an anonymous fellow villager. This identity is heightened, and the factual reality of the events underlined, through the specific use of proverbs or proverbial statements that recapitulate every pattern of behavior, every expression of feeling, in a traditional and formulaic saying.

Only the She-wolf ventures out "in those hours between nones and vespers, when no good woman goes roving around." To express her feeling for Nanni, the She-wolf uses an old Sicilian simile: "It's you I want. You who are as beautiful as the sun, and sweet as honey." After Maricchia and Nanni are married and the She-wolf is sick with longing, "the people were saying that when the devil gets old, he becomes a hermit."

The brief descriptions focus on the inclement contrasts that dominate both the landscape and human passions. The cold winds of January are no harsher than the August sirocco, the thirsty and immense fields no more mournful than the howling dogs at night in the vast, dark countryside. Nor will the She-wolf sate her thirst while working next to Nanni in the fields, for she does not want to leave his side even for a minute.

There is no intervention on the part of the author. The narrator is part of a dialogue that involves the characters and the reader equally. At moments, this dialogue becomes an interior monologue, penetrating primitive needs and becoming the voice of a primordial world, conforming dramatically to the nature of that world.

*I. T. Olken*

# THE SHERIFF'S CHILDREN

*Author:* Charles Waddell Chesnutt (1858-1932)
*Type of plot:* Social realism
*Time of plot:* The late nineteenth century
*Locale:* A county seat in rural North Carolina
*First published:* 1899

> *Principal characters:*
> COLONEL CAMPBELL, the protagonist, a county sheriff
> POLLY CAMPBELL, his daughter
> TOM, his illegitimate mulatto son

*The Story*

An unfamiliar event, the murder of an old Civil War veteran, has roused a placid North Carolina village. Within twenty-four hours, the sheriff and his posse have captured a suspect, a young mulatto, who is unknown to any of them. Disappointed that the preliminary hearing will not take place for another week, a crowd gathers around a whisky jug and plans to lynch the suspect, but Sheriff Campbell, an educated and socially prominent man, is tipped off and proceeds to hold the mob at bay.

After their initial retreat, the sheriff takes up a position in the prisoner's cell as the best position for keeping an eye on the mob. He removes the handcuffs and fetters from his prisoner to give the man a chance in case his protector is killed, although he feels nothing but "contempt and loathing" for the suspect. When a gunshot from the nearby woods whistles through the window and distracts the sheriff, the prisoner seizes a revolver that the law officer, armed with a shotgun, has left on a nearby bench. As the sheriff lays aside his shotgun, the prisoner, regarded as too cowardly and lacking in initiative to pose a threat, takes the sheriff prisoner.

Although he insists that he did not kill the old war veteran but merely stole a coat from him, the young man knows that he has no better chance with a jury than with the mob, and so he forces the sheriff to unlock the cell and front doors and prepares to kill him. When the sheriff exclaims, "You would not kill the man to whom you owe your own life," the prisoner informs him that he has spoken more truth than he realizes, for the young man is the sheriff's own son Tom by one of his slaves from prewar days. Campbell sold the mother and son south to a rice plantation in Alabama. "You gave me a white man's spirit, and you made me a slave, and crushed it out," his son censures him.

He promises not to kill his father if the latter will promise to delay attempts to recapture him until the following morning; when the sheriff hesitates, Tom raises his arm to fire only to have the weapon shot out of his hand by Polly, the sheriff's daughter, who has silently entered the jail during the confrontation. The sheriff binds the wound, tells his son that he will have the doctor attend him more thoroughly in the morning, locks him back up, and goes home to examine his conscience. Rejecting the idea of allowing Tom to escape as incompatible with his duty, he decides to devote all of his energies to securing an acquittal. On his return to the jail in the morning, he discovers that Tom has torn the bandage off his wound and bled to death during the night.

### Themes and Meanings

In some ways, Charles Waddell Chesnutt's fiction anticipates that of William Faulkner and other later southern writers. He immediately establishes the pervasiveness of the Civil War even among southerners who lived far from the principal action. In a simpler way than Faulkner, he presents the evil that continues to flow from slavery and particularly from miscegenation under the slave system. Furthermore, Chesnutt depicts the conflict between educated but guilt-ridden southern leaders and a citizenship generally marked by ignorance and insensitivity to the claims of the law.

However, Chesnutt's purposes in this and other stories of "the color line" are quite different from those of Faulkner. As a black who had grown to manhood and trained for the law during Reconstruction, Chesnutt felt keenly the failure of that program and the blighting of the hopes of the immense majority of less fortunate blacks after the earlier promise of the Emancipation Proclamation. Tom is intelligent and well educated but has turned into a petty criminal facing the prospect of hanging for stealing a coat, and he is desperate enough to kill his father. His fate is not that of a typical freed plantation hand in a segregated society but that of a man who has no place in society, a man who has learned enough to interpret his situation and feel the full bitterness of unfulfilled human aspirations.

The author also wishes to explore the conscience of the ruling class. From the time he first appears in the story, the focus is on the sheriff. He represents statutory law in its conflict with lynch law; in addition, he must endure the inner conflict between the claims of duty and those of blood. Tom has brought forcibly back to him the fact that instead of freeing his son, as he might have done, he pursued the expedient course of selling him into the Deep South.

The sheriff is fundamentally a decent man, prejudiced but determined to carry out his duty at the risk not only of his popularity but also of his life. He hopes to establish his son's innocence of the murder charge and then find some way to atone for his past injustice, which he recognizes as a sin against his son, society, and God. Chesnutt leaves the reader to surmise the thoughts of Tom, who is unaware of his father's resolve and who would probably be unable to believe in it or in its efficacy even had he known. It is easy to see, however, that Tom reaches the very pit of despair before his death.

The author has created a vivid picture of a man's past moral failing returning to haunt his later life. Unless his resolution to make amends is itself his salvation, the evil he has done is irreversible. He—not the mindless, would-be lynchers—is the measure of justice available to black citizens in a society unwilling to take the risks involved in acknowledging its moral responsibility to secure the full liberty of its newly enfranchised citizens.

*Style and Technique*

Chesnutt aimed to counter the sentimental version of slavery so popular in fiction of the late nineteenth century. Sensing the unwillingness or inability of white America to come to terms either with the historical reality of slavery or with the failure of Reconstruction, he attempted to show the harsh reality of both pre- and post-Civil War society. His description of his mythical county has almost a documentary quality. His use of Sheriff Campbell as protagonist shows how easy it was for even a conscientious man to acknowledge his past irresponsibility. By depicting him as assuming an ingrained inferiority in his prisoner, Chesnutt exemplifies the attitude that institutionalized second-class citizenship for blacks from the late 1870's until long after the author's death.

The title of the story is clever. Although only one child is introduced early in "The Sheriff's Children," the author establishes that Sheriff Campbell had been one of the few people in the region to own numerous slaves before the war, and thereby hints at the significance of the title. The sheriff survives his ordeal because one of his children disarms the other. Chesnutt does not develop the character of the quietly resourceful daughter very amply, however, and he does not permit her father to reveal to her the prisoner's identity. Because of his decision to confine the moral conflict to the father, he establishes no relationship between the children.

The author reveals the sheriff's chief failing to be a lack of imagination. Unable to imagine a black fugitive enterprising and daring enough to appropriate an unguarded revolver in the midst of the threat from the mob outside, he exposes himself to capture. The same lack of moral imagination creates the very possibility of such a predicament, for although his stated motives for selling Tom and his mother were a quarrel with her and temporary financial difficulties, a man such as Campbell would be more likely to anticipate embarrassment from a freed slave or a favored one on his own property than to expect any threat from a boy banished to a rice paddy. Once he determines to make amends, he cannot grasp the state of mind of the recaptured son after all his hopes of escape have faded, and thus the son's act of self-destruction surprises him completely.

In arranging this ironic retribution on the father, Chesnutt did not provide Tom with a plausible motive for returning to his native region. The fact of the son developing into an articulate and thoughtful young man, while unlikely, has the virtue of illustrating the bitter truth that even a black man of considerable attainments might well wind up a vagabond and outlaw. However, the author does not make clear why Tom, if he returned to make a claim on his father, would go elsewhere first and steal a coat. Unless Tom's motive was simple retaliation—and there is nothing in the story to suggest that it is—or moral suasion, it is difficult to see why he came back to North Carolina at all. The reader may also wonder why the author, having decided to give Tom's half-sister an important role, did not involve her in the horror of the family situation.

Despite these problems, the story holds the reader's interest with its frank portrayal of the conflict within the sheriff and its tense struggle of sheriff versus mob and sheriff versus prisoner. The author presents the sheriff in an evenhanded way and understands white society, even to its paradoxical tendency to choose the best person in it to lead and then to resist that leadership. He knows that the black man, on the other hand, remains a mystery to the best of white men in such a society; thus the reader sees Tom only as his father sees him. Nevertheless, the reader can sense the anguish in Tom. It is doubtful that any white writer in 1899 could have presented the struggle within a white father such as Sheriff Campbell and the embitterment of a black son such as Tom as powerfully as Chesnutt does in this story.

*Robert P. Ellis*

# SHIFTING

*Author:* Ann Beattie (1947-    )
*Type of plot:* Domestic realism
*Time of plot:* 1972
*Locale:* Philadelphia
*First published:* 1977

> *Principal characters:*
> NATALIE, a young married woman
> LARRY, her husband, a graduate student in chemistry
> MICHAEL, a sixteen-year-old boy who teaches Natalie how to
>     drive a stick-shift automobile
> ANDY, Larry's friend, a wounded Vietnam veteran

*The Story*

The relationship of Larry, a graduate student, and his wife, Natalie, began when they were ten years old. They dated through college and married at the end of Larry's first semester in graduate school. The emotionless tone in which this long period of time is recounted suggests that the relationship continued more out of habit than feeling. The two seem to have very different personalities and interests.

Larry is the ultimate planner. He plans their marriage to take place after his examinations; he teaches, attends classes, visits his friend Andy, a paraplegic Vietnam veteran, and his parents, cleans his car, and plays basketball in the gym—all on schedule. It is Larry who decides the couple will not have a baby until he has finished his master of arts degree.

Although Natalie seems to be passively complying with Larry's regimen, she is actually an imaginative, impulsive, and intuitive person. She senses that Larry's parents, especially his mother, do not approve of her because she does not center her life around him. Her greatest pleasure is to visit an art museum that contains a fascinating modern sculpture of intertwined figures. When Larry requests that she photograph their furniture for insurance purposes, she experiments with photographing parts of her own body. This incident illustrates her husband's need for control over his life, and her own growing need to express her identity.

When Natalie inherits a 1965 Volvo from her uncle, Larry decides she should sell the car so that they can take a vacation with the money, and at first, Natalie agrees. Larry also points out that Natalie cannot drive a vehicle with a stick shift. Larry's emphasis on Natalie's lack of mechanical ability has undermined her confidence in the past, but now she determines to keep the car and learn to use the stick shift without telling her husband.

Choosing Michael, the sixteen-year-old boy who delivers her elderly neighbor's paper, to teach her how to drive the stick-shift Volvo gives Natalie a non-threatening teacher. When the lessons are concluded, the fact that their employer-employee relationship has changed to a personal one is highlighted when Michael leaves the money for the lessons in the car. Although he cannot appreciate Natalie's adult feelings, his obvious admiration provides an emotional stepping stone for a change in her life.

Buoyed by this support of her person and identity, Natalie views her total body naked in a mirror and decides that the touch of her body is like the touch of the sculpture in the museum. This sense of her physical and emotional wholeness implicitly expresses the shift or change in her life. The concluding sentence—"This was in 1972, in Philadelphia"—indicates that this is a retrospective narrative of the protagonist's life, which has changed radically since that time.

*Themes and Meanings*

Life is dynamic; ongoing movement marks either the development of the personality or its deterioration. Unfortunately, society often stresses external goals and relationships so much that little attention is paid to internal needs. Such neglect results in spiritual paralysis, unhappiness, and isolation. "Shifting" presents the lives of several characters as examples of these different attitudes toward life and different accommodations of lifestyles to the tensions between internal and external pressures.

Larry represents those who replace internal development with external movement. The narrative recounts his courtship of Natalie, his attendance at high school and a local college, a transfer to a more prestigious college, his marriage, and his current attendance at graduate school. He expects that they will have no children and that Natalie will support his plans by keeping their apartment clean, shopping, and cooking. From society's vantage point and his, Larry's life is a carefully planned and executed success.

Larry's parents represent a failed relationship in which the spouses seek personal fulfillment outside themselves. Ironically, Larry's mother is so obsessed with what she sees as her daughter-in-law's lack of commitment to her son, she does not realize she has failed her own husband, who dedicates himself to his hobbies in order to avoid her. Larry's father seems to need to validate his identity by taking photographs of himself working at his hobbies—building model boats and fixing clocks. Larry's parents have found alternative activities to accommodate the void in their personal development and in their relationship to each other.

The narration of the events in Natalie's life prior to the opening of the story suggests an almost decisionless downhill movement. At the opening of the story, she has arrived at a standstill in her life. Each day has its scheduled activity centering around her husband's personal, physical, and career needs. Natalie's only emotional outlet is to go to the art museum.

Natalie's ability to perceive the emptiness in the lives of these people who maintain an external facade of concord marks the beginning of her slowly executed rebellion against the stasis. She is aware of the difference between her aesthetic appreciation and that of her husband and his family. She invites Larry and, later, his mother to visit the art museum and view her favorite sculpture. Larry looks past it to gaze at a Francis

Bacon painting. His mother does not even notice the sculpture; she spends the time chatting about her son's need for vitamins. Natalie connects her identity with appreciation of the statue when she complains that Larry "could have shifted his eyes a little and seen the sculpture and her standing and staring." When Natalie observes the inability of Larry and his parents to shift the stasis of their emotional development, she is implicitly preparing to shift her own life.

### Style and Technique

To express a theme of spiritual paralysis, Ann Beattie uses flat prose that produces a low-key tone. The primerlike syntax of the first sentence—"The woman's name was Natalie, and the man's name was Larry"—matches that of the concluding one—"This was in 1972, in Philadelphia." The narrative summary of the protagonists' lives up to the events of the story is as unemotional as their lives are.

The title, "Shifting," and its use as a motif throughout the story, is appropriate because the word indicates a change from the ordinary position, a change occurring after a significant period of time. The title identifies the almost accidental nature of the catalyst that initiates Natalie's breaking out of her paralysis: inheriting a car with a stick shift. Her desire to learn how to drive this car becomes a move toward separating her life from her husband's because she conceals her driving lessons from him. Although she frequently stalls in her driving attempts, she foresees her independence in her freedom to drive to the museum and to vote. Learning to shift becomes the external sign of Natalie's control over her own life.

The ability to shift—to move positively in the dynamism of life—is identified with Natalie's aesthetic ideal: the ability of an Alexander Calder mobile to be free to shift its position. The wholeness comprising these shifting fragments perhaps helps Natalie to work with the fragments of her life.

Emphasis on fragments can distract the viewer's attention from the whole. For example, Andy's fragmented body renders him impotent to get on with his life. When Larry asks his wife to photograph their furniture to validate any future insurance claims, Natalie resents his emphasizing material values over the personal value of her time. She shifts from photographing pieces of their furniture to shooting fragments of her body. Later, she moves from looking at fragments of her body to viewing her entire naked body in the mirror. When she sees and feels the wholeness of her body and equates the experience with the wholeness of the sculpture she admires, she has filled the void in her life. Although Natalie says she could not handle the radical shift that occurred in Andy's wartime experience, each decision to act independently is moving her toward a radical shift. The protagonist's name, Natalie, which means "new born," underscores the radical shift that is occurring in her life: the protagonist's growing understanding of her identity as she shifts out of her spiritual paralysis.

*Agnes A. Shields*

# SHILOH

*Author:* Bobbie Ann Mason (1940-      )
*Type of plot:* Domestic realism
*Time of plot:* The 1970's
*Locale:* Kentucky
*First published:* 1980

> *Principal characters:*
> > LEROY MOFFITT, a truck driver
> > NORMA JEAN, his wife
> > MABEL BEASLEY, his mother-in-law

*The Story*

Leroy Moffitt watches his wife, Norma Jean, building up her pectorals by lifting dumbbells. After injuring his leg in a tractor-trailer accident, he does not want to make any more long hauls. Considering what to do next, he builds things from craft kits, including a miniature log cabin. Leroy notices that Norma Jean often seems disappointed to find him at home when she returns from work. He wonders if it reminds her of their marriage before he went on the road and of their son, Randy, who died of sudden infant death syndrome. They have never talked about Randy's death, but Leroy now thinks that one of them should mention it. Realizing that he and Norma Jean barely know each other, he wants to start fresh and create a new marriage. The cabin he constructed with ice cream sticks gives him an idea—to build Norma Jean a full-scale log house from a kit.

When Leroy goes to buy marijuana from Stevie Hamilton, a doctor's son, he notices that subdivisions are "spreading across Kentucky like an oil slick." He wonders where all the farmers have gone, and he thinks about Randy. If he had lived, he would be about Stevie's age. When Leroy gets home, Norma Jean's mother, Mabel Beasley, is there. She visits frequently, making sure that Norma Jean is keeping up with her housework. Mabel urges them to visit the Civil War battleground at Shiloh, Tennessee. After Mabel leaves, Norma Jean rereads Leroy a list of jobs he can do, while she goose-steps through the kitchen, wearing ankle weights.

One day Leroy comes home to find Norma Jean crying because her mother has caught her smoking. When Mabel arrives the next day, she tells them about a baby killed by a dog while its mother was in the next room. Reminded of Randy, Norma Jean thinks Mabel is getting revenge on her for smoking. Leroy realizes something is happening. Norma Jean has been going to night school. After completing her body-building course, she has enrolled in an adult-education course in composition. When Leroy confides in Mabel about his marriage, she advises him to take Norma Jean on a second honeymoon to Shiloh. When Norma Jean comes home, she responds to the idea rudely. Mabel chides her for using bad language.

Norma Jean eventually agrees to go to Shiloh with Leroy. While they are having a picnic near the cemetery for the Union dead, she tells Leroy that she wants to leave him. Realizing that his plan to build her a log cabin is foolish, Leroy knows that he must think of something else, quickly. Norma Jean walks to the edge of a bluff overlooking the Tennessee River, then turns and waves her arms. Leroy does not know whether she is beckoning to him or doing chest exercises.

## Themes and Meanings

When Leroy asks Norma Jean if her behavior is a result of the women's movement, she tells him not to be silly. Ironically, Norma Jean has been affected more than she knows by feminist ideas and images of women in the media. Leroy compares her to the television character Wonder Woman. Influenced by advertising, she eats "Body Buddies" cereal. Although Norma Jean does not begin lifting weights until after she observes Leroy's physical therapy, she has seen articles about bodybuilding in magazines sold at the drugstore where she works. She identifies with the film star Marilyn Monroe, whose real name was also Norma Jean. Like many women influenced by feminism, she is taking night courses and planning to leave her husband.

Leroy has also been influenced by the media. One of his pastimes is needlepoint, a practice popularized for men by media coverage when football player Rosey Grier begins doing it. Influenced by television, Leroy makes a Star Trek pillow cover, and he tries to remember if it was on Phil Donahue's show where he heard that losing a child generally destroys a marriage. Leroy is becoming aware that he should not believe everything that he sees on television or reads. When Randy died suddenly, Leroy was told that it just happens sometimes. Leroy observes that now scientists believe crib death is caused by a virus. Nobody knows anything, he thinks.

Norma Jean's identification with Marilyn Monroe has ominous implications. Monroe, whose early life was like Norma Jean's, died at the age of thirty-six from an overdose of sleeping pills, possibly a suicide. She exemplified the classic show-business tragedy. Before they go to Shiloh, Norma Jean tells Leroy that his name means "the king." This identifies Leroy with Elvis Presley, who was also from a small southern town. Elvis rose to fame and fortune, only to die at age forty-two of health problems complicated by his reliance on drugs. Leroy sometimes used speed on the road, smokes marijuana, and asks Stevie Hamilton what other drugs he has. With those references, Bobbie Ann Mason suggests the potential destructiveness of twentieth century mass culture. Norma Jean also tells Leroy that her name comes from the Normans, who were invaders. This connects to the story's title and relates Norma Jean to the North, Leroy to the South, in the Civil War.

At Shiloh, Confederate forces ambushed Union troops on April 6, 1862, pushing back the lines of the invading army. The next day Union forces retook the lost ground, pushing the Confederate troops back to Corinth, Tennessee. Neither army won this battle, in which approximately ten thousand men were killed on each side. Leroy ambushed Norma Jean when he came home after his accident. When Mason describes Norma Jean marching through the kitchen doing goose steps, she implies that she has become a soldier in the army of mass culture. Her counterattack on Leroy occurs when she says she wants to leave him. The end of the marriage represents the death of the family in twentieth century society, and of the future, represented by Randy. The baby died in the backseat of their car, while Leroy and Norma Jean watched *Doctor Strangelove* (1963) at the drive-in—a film about the end of civilization.

*Style and Technique*

Mason writes "Shiloh" in a realistic style into which she weaves symbolic images and references. By paralleling Norma Jean and Leroy with the North and South in the Civil War—and, further, by linking this conflict with the mutual annihilation of the West and the East imagined in *Doctor Strangelove*—Mason approaches allegory. The word "civil" can refer to marriage as well as to the war between the states, which is also ironic. Mason's references to Monroe and Presley, to songs such as "Sunshine Superman," and to films such as *Doctor Strangelove*, provide a commentary on the characters and incidents of the story. All of these references communicate Mason's view of the direction taken by history since the defeat of agrarianism in the Civil War.

Mason also uses patterns of imagery to communicate her theme. Images of death are dominant. Death from industrial pollution is linked to the subdivisions spreading "like an oil slick." Leroy relates this to the disappearance of the farmers, another kind of death. He compares the new, white-columned brick house of Stevie Hamilton's father to a funeral parlor. At Shiloh, he thinks the cemetery of the Union dead, with its white markers, looks like a subdivision site. Norma Jean walks through this cemetery following a brick path. The word "brick" echoes its use in the description of Dr. Hamilton's house. This suggests to the reader where Norma Jean will end up if she leaves Leroy—in the subdivisions.

With another set of images, Mason offers hope. After flying past scenery for fifteen years on the road, Leroy describes his rig as "a gigantic bird that has come home to roost." To roost is to sleep. Later, watching birds at the feeder close their wings, then fall, he thinks of Norma Jean, who closes her eyes when they are in bed. However, Leroy also thinks he and Norma Jean are waking from a dream together, and the birds he watches spread their wings to catch themselves after they fall. This foreshadows the ending when Norma Jean stands at the edge of the bluff—about to fall?—and waves her arms at Leroy. Consciousness of their predicament in the twentieth century United States may save them. Still, the sky is "the color of the dust ruffle Mabel made for their bed," under which Leroy said they could hide things.

Mason also alludes to the Christian myth of the Fall. She describes the path Norma Jean follows at the end of the story as serpentine, suggesting the snake in Eden. Norma Jean will fall if she continues to accept the values of a civilization that seeks absolute power over nature. Another Christian reference provides an answer. The log cabin Leroy made with ice cream sticks reminds him of a rustic Nativity scene. Leroy, Norma Jean, and the world need a rebirth of love.

*James Green*

# SHOEMAKER ARNOLD

*Author:* Earl Lovelace (1935-    )
*Type of plot:* Social realism
*Time of plot:* A New Year's Eve during the 1950's
*Locale:* A rural village in Trinidad
*First published:* 1982

> *Principal characters:*
> ARNOLD, a fifty-year-old shop owner
> NORBERT, a twenty-nine-year-old employee in Arnold's shop
> OLD MAN MOSES, a solitary charcoal burner
> BRITTO, the owner of a bar

## The Story

The third-person omniscient narrator of this brief tale opens the story with a compressed exposition of Arnold's character and background. The shoemaker is a proud man, recognized by the villagers for his "undefeated stubbornness," his "unrelenting cantankerousness," and his "readiness for confrontation." No one contests his freely expressed opinions; he is master of his world, the shoemaker's shop. So difficult to live with is Arnold that, years before, his wife and three children "had moved not only out of his house but out of the village." Maintaining his solitary pride, Arnold refuses to accept even his own sexual needs, admiring but resisting village girls in a "testing relationship of antagonism and desire." Young men in the village fare no better; his apprentices never satisfy him, and they can seldom tolerate him long enough to learn the trade.

The village is shocked, then, when Arnold hires—and retains—Norbert, who is a drifter, drinker, and gambler. He disappears from the shop for weeks at a time, but Arnold always takes him back, albeit with a severe scolding. He steals money, providing his friends with free shoes and drinking sprees. In short, Norbert is "so indisputably in the wrong" that he is "exactly the sort of person that one did not expect Arnold to tolerate for more than five minutes." This puzzling about-face in Arnold's attitude leads the villagers to believe that Arnold wishes to demonstrate "one of his rare qualities, compassion." Whenever Arnold welcomes Norbert back to his shop, Arnold basks in a self-congratulatory "idea of his own goodness," feeling that no one in the world is "more generous a man than he."

Norbert, however, does have redeeming qualities beyond those of his zest for spontaneous revelry. He works hard when he works. Having left the shop for a piece of ice two weeks before Christmas, Norbert did not return for three weeks; yet on New Year's Eve, when others would not have bothered to return, Norbert is back and "working like a machine to get people's shoes ready." Arnold admires Norbert for being "faithful," for returning on "Old Year's Day" to finish repairs due before New

Year's Day. He does not scold him, deciding that Norbert "shows appreciation" for him. Appreciation, Arnold thinks ironically, is all too rare an attribute among people.

As Arnold contemplates Norbert's appreciation while looking down the street from his shop's door, he sees Old Man Moses, the charcoal burner, dozing on a donkey cart with a small boy riding in back as it meanders up into the bush. Realizing that it will soon rain, Arnold complains to Norbert that Moses should not be getting soaked but should be feasting with his family for the New Year: "That is how we living. Like beast." Ignoring Arnold's outrage in his metaphor of people as orphans, Norbert responds only briefly, saying, "Maybe he want to go up in the bush" in order to protect his coals from burning down into powder; yet Arnold ignores the suggestion that Moses may be doing what he wants to do. As an analogue for Arnold and Norbert, Moses and the boy evoke Arnold's impulse to order the world around him; his own loneliness, his fear of solitary aging, and his foreboding "sense of the approaching new year." He tells Norbert that "the world have to check up on itself," oblivious to the irony that he must examine his own life, and he introduces the subject of Norbert's recent unexplained absence.

In the conversation that follows, Arnold's deep cynicism becomes apparent. He fears both a useless life and a living death, bemoaning his own drinking and justifying his habitual lecturing: "What else to do but drink and waste and die. That is why I talk." Norbert contributes only his blunt remark, "We dying," again and again, to Arnold's question, "You think we living?" When Arnold learns how much older he is than Norbert and considers Norbert's "condition," his despair that "life really mash you up" disturbs Norbert to the point that he reminds Arnold that they have three more pairs of shoes to finish, Arnold having thrown down the pair that he was fixing. Arnold's genuine concern for Norbert—and for himself—is broken abruptly when two girls arrive to pick up Synto's shoes.

Arnold responds harshly to the girls as he demands that they enter the shop while waiting for him to finish. With Synto's niece is a girl "who reminded him of rain and moss and leaves." Distracted by her alluring presence and aware of his own gruff manner, Arnold asks, "You fraid me?" Hoping that he sounds tough, Arnold is not surprised when the girl confesses that she is afraid, "A little." Norbert is shocked at Arnold's next gesture: He offers her a chair, "dusting it too." A peaceful, calm ambience fills the shop as he repairs the shoes for the waiting girls. In further kindness, Arnold carefully wraps the shoes in a newspaper that he had been saving to read. When the girl thanks him as she is leaving, her voice "made something inside him ache"; she leaves behind the "breathlessness" of "the scent of moss and aloes and leaves" as "if all his work was finished." Then Arnold offers to buy Norbert "a nip," returning Norbert's earlier offer.

When Norbert returns with the rum, Arnold's usual tough mask of self-righteousness has fallen completely. His longing for intimacy, his desire for community, and his need for renewal have led him to comprehend "how he could leave everything just so and go" as Norbert had done. Arnold tells Norbert, "I dying too," admitting that perhaps he does frighten people.

When they close the shop that evening, Arnold and Norbert go to Britto's bar. There they share in the revelry with Britto, his family, and his friends. As Norbert sings along with the band's traditional songs, Arnold wishes "he could cry." Later, after singing, drinking, eating, and dancing, Norbert draws Arnold's attention as he opens another bottle of rum; hesitating before he drinks, Norbert looks at Arnold and says, "Let me dead." Arnold, thinking about the girl in the shop, believes that if she were "sitting there beside him he would be glad to dead too." Arnold, perhaps for the first time in his life, acknowledges the joy in living.

*Themes and Meanings*

Earl Lovelace offers in "Shoemaker Arnold" a character study in which personal identity is reconciled with the spirit of place, in the sense of both nature and culture. Arnold's consciously fashioned identity consists primarily of self-sufficient, tough masculinity. Seeking self-respect just to survive in a poverty-ridden rural village, Arnold has held the world at bay with his frightening mask, but he has done so at the cost of alienating much of the community, including his own family. His incessant talking achieves little authentic dialogue; consequently, the very expression in which genuine intimacy is grounded further isolates him: He has tolerated no voices other than his own. As the mask of self-sufficiency drops in order for Arnold to understand Norbert's spontaneity and as the mask of masculinity falls in order for him to show kindness to the girls, Arnold discovers his own neediness. With the masks removed, Arnold can then participate fully in the community's life and joy, which he does at Britto's celebration.

With Arnold's reconciliation of his own social needs also comes his acceptance of the consoling power of nature and sexuality. Although nature here is not transcendent, it does offer the renewal of rain and green leaves, metaphors for the regenerative power of the young girls as well as that of Norbert. Despite a fallen nature in the figure of Norbert and the fecund island world, the death present in this world is still capable of renewing life just as Norbert attempts to show Arnold that Moses's life, apparently beastly, may be a choice to tend his coal—heat for cooking and warmth out of dead trees. Arnold seems to fear weakness, aging, and death, but, in actuality, he fears the strength and youth of life itself. Ironically, when Britto greets him as a "man now," thinking that he acknowledges Arnold's tough image, he greets an Arnold who is discovering that masculinity consists of intimacy and compassion rather than unconscious fears.

Norbert's theft in generosities to friends, his penchant for leaving spontaneously with friends, his prodigal returns to the coarse Arnold, and his "appreciation" for Arnold all embody the "faith" of the people in one another. Even amid Norbert's awareness that "we are dying," he gives himself to a faith in the life of the community. It is this faith that Arnold embraces when he realizes that Norbert leaves work for "something deeper, a call," not merely "a good time." That faith is the freedom of spirit within both nature and culture: It is Arnold's salvation from the desperation of his loneliness and the alienation of his neediness.

*Style and Technique*

Lovelace's story succeeds in his capacity for compact but complex characterization. Arnold and Norbert come fully alive through descriptive exposition and dialect: They sound like a crusty, aging shoemaker and his carefree assistant. The dialogue is rapid; Arnold displays his propensity for outraged rambling, and Norbert delights in what he suspects may be a profound idea, that one must accept death in order to live completely. West Indian rural English echoes throughout sentence fragments without subjects and patois variants of subject verb agreement. Even the closing sentences' use of the noun dead instead of the verb die (first in Norbert's final remark and again in the narrator's assumption of Arnold's sensibility) helps unify characterization with theme. As the narrative voice develops, the point of view and the use of dialect in the narration mingle increasingly with that of the characters' dialogue: A community of characters and narrator results, and the omniscience of the narrator is no longer detached but found now among the characters.

To complicate the characterization further, Lovelace reverses roles for Arnold and Norbert. This reversal occurs when Arnold's cynical despair causes him to throw down his shoes while Norbert works on, reminding him of the remaining repairs. The reversal unifies theme with character development; by exchanging their customary roles of diligence and indifference, Arnold and Norbert complement each other in a microcosm of community. When the girls enter, Arnold continues the reversal in his attention to them, enlarging the metaphor for the community to include an implicit sexual (hence, natural) basis. The reversal proceeds when Arnold buys the rum, and, by the time they reach Britto's celebration, both enter fully into that yet larger community, one founded on family and tradition. Subsequently, the reversal strengthens the renewal of both men, a renewal symbolized by New Year's Eve and the scent of aloes (a plant with healing properties). In the closing moment of the final scene, Arnold and Norbert stand out in relief, whole individuals yet intimate members of a vital community.

*Michael Loudon*

# SHORT FRIDAY

*Author:* Isaac Bashevis Singer (1904-1991)
*Type of plot:* Fable
*Time of plot:* Unspecified
*Locale:* The village of Lapschitz
*First published:* "Der Kurtser Fraytik," 1945 (English translation, 1964)

>        *Principal characters:*
>            SHMUL-LEIBELE, a simple but devout tailor
>            SHOSHE, his pious wife

## The Story

Shmul-Leibele is a simpleton, unsuccessful but honest in his trade. Although he is not scholarly, he is expert at following the basic tenets of his religion. His wife, Shoshe, is a meticulous homemaker and more competent in her trade than her husband in his. Together they create a life, a marriage, and a home devoted to the observance of Jewish ritual and customs.

The couple's commitment to making and keeping the Sabbath is unequivocal. A recognition of the day on which God rested after completing the Creation, the Sabbath represents the culmination of the devout couple's daily spiritual strivings. Shmul-Leibele ceases work at noon every Friday, takes a ritual bath, and aids in the temple's preparation for the Sabbath prayers. Shoshe purchases special foods to cook and prepares herself and her home in royal fashion. Both attempt to create an earthly paradise in which to experience, as best they can, the divine presence.

On one winter Friday, the shortest Friday of the year, the couple's preparatory rituals begin in customary manner, but the elements of nature effect change. A severe snowstorm hampers movement outside and makes it difficult to distinguish day from night. The rooster's morning crow is not heard and the couple arise late. Shmul-Leibele decides not to work his half-day, spending the day instead at the bathhouse and in study.

When he returns home, however, the candles that announce the Sabbath's official arrival are lit and the home, as usual, sparkles with a spiritual essence. Shoshe is dressed beautifully, adorned with her wedding necklace and a polished wedding band. Despite the physical manifestations of winter, to Shmul-Leibele the experience is particularly enchanting. He leaves for the synagogue, where his prayers seem assuredly to transcend his earthly lips and find an audience with God's ears.

After temple, Shmul-Leibele tries to hurry home to Shoshe, anxious that some ill may have befallen her. Instead, she greets him looking radiant; their home sparkles with a Sabbath glow and the scents from the Sabbath meal are alluring. Having fulfilled the ritual obligations to partake of their dinner, the couple intersperse their meal with Sabbath hymns, chants, and prayer. Finally, exhaustion overcomes Shmul-Leibele, who falls quickly asleep, with Shoshe following shortly thereafter.

Sometime later, Shmul-Leibele awakens, eager to satisfy his physical desires for his wife. After fulfilling the proper observations regarding marital sex (that his wife has attended the ritual bath signaling her preparedness for sexual relations; that he speak first of his love for her and his hope that their mating may produce an offspring), the couple consummates the sexual act. Despite Shoshe's warning that something may be burning in the oven and that the flue is closed, they fall immediately asleep.

Both awaken from dreams of death and burial. Shmul-Leibele believes he has had a terrible nightmare but alters his perceptions on hearing that Shoshe has had the same experience. They realize that they cannot either move or hear sounds, and come to understand that they have died, perhaps by asphyxiation. First with a sense of alarm and then with pious acceptance, the couple prepares to greet the angel of God who will come to lead them into paradise.

*Themes and Meanings*

This is a story about a love and marriage, a life and death, enhanced and embraced by spirituality. Here the daily laws, rituals, and customs of Judaism provide two simple and ordinary people the opportunity to rise above the mundane trappings of the physical world and to sanctify their humble lives.

A portrait of simple but beautiful piety, "Short Friday" examines the role of faith and religion in one's life. All aspects of life are included: Shmul-Leibele and Shoshe apply their beliefs to their work, their marriage, their sexual relationship, and ultimately their death.

A slow and sloppy tailor, Shmul-Leibele uses only the strongest thread, the finest materials, and returns scraps to his clients. Shoshe not only keeps a proper home but also acquires additional money from outside sources. Having married each other for their serious and pious natures, the couple achieves a love so great that not even their inability to bear children (one of God's commandments) threatens their future together.

Shmul-Leibele remembers the Law even during moments of great passion for Shoshe. Aware that the sexual act is intended for procreation, he nevertheless permits himself to experience pleasure from caressing and exploring Shoshe's physical beauty. "The great saints also loved their wives," he maintains, planning to attend the ritual bath the following morning in recognition of any transgression. For Shoshe, Shmul-Leibele's praise of her worth each Sabbath is truly God's blessing: "Here am I, a simple woman, an orphan, and yet God has chosen to bless me with a devoted husband who praises me in the holy tongue."

As the couple allow no aspect of life to pass without an attempt to render it holy, so do they embrace their sudden death. Despite Shoshe's initial alarm and confusion ("We went to sleep hale and hearty. . . . We were still young people. . . . We arranged a proper Sabbath."), and encouraged by Shmul-Leibele's acceptance of their fate ("Yes, Shoshe, praised be the true Judge! We are in God's hands."), the couple recall their final act of devotion as they prepare to give accounts of themselves to the angel of God.

The contrasts and parallels between the physical and spiritual worlds dominate the story. An examination of the story's title itself suggests one such link: In the physical realm, it is on the shortest Friday of the year, when daylight fades rapidly, that the couple's life also ends. Concurrently, it is on their holiest day of the week, the Sabbath, which begins on Friday evening and ends the following night, that Shmul-Leibele and Shoshe are called on to make a new beginning together.

This Friday is particularly dark, cold, and foreboding, whereas the Sabbath glow permeates the auras of Shmul-Leibele and his wife. In their home, the physical warmth from Shoshe's oven and the spiritual warmth of the Sabbath combine to bring a sense of beauty, calm, and peace to an otherwise harsh existence. Ironically, it is Shmul-Leibele's love of warmth that causes both his neglect of Shoshe's warning that there is food still in the oven and, finally, his death.

A story that seeks to define even its readers' faith, the appeal of "Short Friday" is the comprehension of universal themes linked by a common spiritual thread. One is encouraged to study and understand how to achieve meaning in life; how to approach death; how to prioritize opportunity and experience; how to create and recognize the spiritual dimensions of the physical world; how to consider religious teachings for a morally uplifting life.

*Style and Technique*

The style of "Short Friday" is that of the fable or folktale. The language is simple and direct; the natural and the supernatural (the couple's awareness after their death) are treated on the same plane.

A significant example of the story's fabulistic style is the use of foreshadowing to prepare for the couple's fate. On the Friday of their death, a portrait is painted of an exceptionally cold and bleak day in which darkness and daylight are indistinguishable. As the evening and the beginning of the Sabbath approach, the sky grows clear and a full moon arises. Clearly, this Friday is marked by divine intervention; the town and the heavens have merged and the couple's home is at the mercy of God. What is perhaps being suggested is that, ultimately, all return to God.

It is noted that Shmul-Leibele loves warmth, and for this he pays a dear price. In another allusion to fire, at the bathhouse Shmul-Leibele uses a willow broom against his skin "until his skin glowed red."

Premonitions of death and danger are present as well throughout the story within the context of the couple's marriage. After Sabbath services, Shmul-Leibele hastens home because he worries that Shoshe may be in trouble. The couple speak often of their fate should one die before the other. It is clearly a dreadful thought for Shmul-Leibele: "God forbid! I would simply perish from sorrow. They would bury us both on the same day." He need not have feared, for in death as in life they are united.

*Shelly Usen*

# THE SHORT HAPPY LIFE OF FRANCIS MACOMBER

*Author:* Ernest Hemingway (1899-1961)
*Type of plot:* Coming of age
*Time of plot:* The 1920's
*Locale:* Africa
*First published:* 1936

> *Principal characters:*
> FRANCIS MACOMBER, a wealthy American sportsman
> MARGOT MACOMBER, his beautiful wife
> ROBERT WILSON, a white hunter

*The Story*

While on safari in Africa with Robert Wilson, a professional hunter and guide, Francis Macomber shows cowardice in the face of a charging lion. The story opens at noon as Macomber, his wife, and Robert Wilson are having a drink before lunch. The atmosphere is tense, though Wilson and the African porters try to act as if everything were normal. Macomber is very upset because of his earlier behavior, while Margot, his wife, ranges in her reaction from tears to merciless criticism. As Macomber tries to apologize for his failure, Wilson becomes increasingly impatient, not so much because of the events of the morning but because Macomber insists on talking about them. The final insult to Wilson comes when Macomber asks for reassurance that he will not talk about the incident when they return to civilization. Just as he has decided to break any social contact with Macomber for the remainder of the safari, the latter apologizes in such forthright terms for not understanding the custom of not talking about failures that Wilson cannot simply dismiss him. As their conversation ends, Wilson suggests that Macomber might make up his failure with the lion when they hunt buffalo the next morning.

That night, Macomber is haunted by memories of the lion hunt as he relives it in his mind. After having listened to the lion roar and cough all night, Macomber is unnerved the next morning, even before they start out for the hunt. Not knowing, as an old Somali proverb says, that "a brave man is always frightened" when he sees a lion's track, hears him roar, or confronts him, Macomber loses confidence in himself. When they go after the lion, Macomber is nervous to the point of being reluctant to leave the car in which they are traveling to take his shot. Ordered out by Wilson because it is unsporting to shoot from the vehicle, Macomber shoots badly, wounding the animal, which retreats into the bush.

Macomber does not want to pursue the lion into the dangerous bush, and even suggests that they simply leave him. Wilson, the professional, is shocked at this suggestion, but he does tell Macomber that he need not go in after the wounded animal if he does not wish to do so. Macomber, though frightened, does want to go, so together they enter the tall grass. Hearing them coming, the lion charges. "They had just moved into the grass when Macomber heard the blood-choked coughing grunt, and saw the swishing rush in the grass. The next thing he knew he was running; running wildly, in panic in the open, running toward the stream." Wilson kills the lion, and Macomber senses the contempt of the hunter and the gun bearers. Most contemptuous is Margot Macomber, who witnessed the entire scene from her place in the car. As they await the gun bearers, who are skinning the lion, Macomber attempts to take her hand, but she draws it away. Then, "while they sat there his wife had reached forward and put her hand on Wilson's shoulder. He turned and she had leaned forward over the low seat and kissed him on the mouth."

Macomber believes that his wife is through with him, but in a short sketch of their marriage, Hemingway points out that these two are inextricably bonded. Macomber is so very wealthy that his wife will never leave him. Though she is still very beautiful, Margot "was not a great enough beauty any more . . . to be able to leave him and better herself and she knew it and he knew it." She knows that he is not successful with other women, so she does not worry about him leaving her either. "All in all they were known as a comparatively happily married couple, one of those whose disruption is often rumored but never occurs." On the night of the lion hunt, Macomber awakens and realizes that Margot has left their tent to sleep with Robert Wilson. He confronts her on her return, insisting that she had promised not to be unfaithful if they made this trip. She blames him, saying that he spoiled the trip by the lion episode.

After an awkward breakfast the following morning, they go in search of buffalo. Three bulls are discovered and chase is given in the car. As the buffalo are overtaken, Macomber seems to lose his fear. He shoots well and drops all three bulls with only minor help from Wilson. However, as they are celebrating their luck, a gun bearer brings news that the first of the three bulls that they shot has got up and made its way into the bush. "Then it's going to be just like the lion," Margot says, but Wilson answers, "It's not going to be a damned bit like the lion." Macomber "expected the feeling he had had about the lion to come back but it did not. For the first time in his life he really felt wholly without fear." Macomber is transformed by this experience, and it is a different man who follows Wilson into the bush after the buffalo.

Macomber is eager to go in after the bull, even urging Wilson to action before he is ready. As they wait, Macomber tells Wilson, "You know, I don't think I'd ever be afraid of anything again," and proposes that they might go after another lion because, "after all, what can they do to you?"

> "That's it," said Wilson, "Worst one can do is kill you. How does it go? Shakespeare. Damned good. See if I can remember. Oh, damned good. Used to quote it to myself at one time. Let's see. 'By my troth, I care not; a man can die but once; we owe God a death and let it go which way it will he that dies this year is quit for the next.' Damned fine, eh?"
>
> He was very embarrassed, having brought out this thing he had lived by, but he had seen men come of age before and it always moved him. It was not a matter of their twenty-first birthday.

As Wilson and Macomber move into the bush, the bull charges. Macomber and Wilson both shoot, and Macomber can see fragments fly as his bullets bounce harmlessly on the boss of the large horns. He stands his ground in the face of the charge, calmly firing until "he felt a sudden white-hot, blinding flash explode inside his head and that was all he ever felt." Margot Macomber had shot at the buffalo to protect her husband, and the bullet had struck him in the head.

The ending of the story is only slightly ambiguous. Though Wilson reiterates several times that the shooting was accidental, the reader comes away with little doubt that Margot has shot her husband deliberately. "That was a pretty thing to do," he says to her, then adds, "he would have left you too." The story ends as Margot begs Wilson to stop his accusations.

*Themes and Meanings*

"The Short Happy Life of Francis Macomber" includes several of Ernest Hemingway's important themes and introduces characters typical of his work. This is a story of a man's coming of age, but it also presents something of Hemingway's attitude toward "the code" for which he is famous, his views on women, and the value he placed on the life of action. Each of the main characters can illustrate one of these themes.

Robert Wilson, the white hunter, is an archetypal Hemingway hero. He lives a life of action—a manly life—that is governed by a code that he never states, but which is his standard for judging his own as well as others' behavior. Sportsmanship, courage, and "grace under pressure" are the hallmarks of Wilson's behavior. His professionalism is more than simply an attitude; it is a philosophy that governs his life. To him, it is morally unthinkable that he might leave a dangerously wounded animal in the bush, talk about his clients behind their backs, or otherwise violate the unspoken contracts of his trade. His philosophy, however, is expressed in action, not words, and he is suspicious of those who, like Macomber, ruin an experience by too much talk. He respects men who, like himself, can face danger courageously, certain that death is less to be feared than a coward's life.

Francis Macomber is described as one of "the great American boy-men," the sort of men who are likely to remain immature throughout their lives. Untested under pressure, he "had probably been afraid all his life" until the buffalo hunt. In the buffalo hunt, things happen so fast that he does not have time for fear to manifest itself, and he is transformed by the event. As Wilson puts it, Macomber would "be a damn fire eater now. . . . More of a change than any loss of virginity. Fear gone like an operation. Something else grew in its place. Main thing a man had. Made him into a man. Women knew it too. No bloody fear." The title of the story refers to those few minutes between the time Macomber shoots the three buffalo and the moment Margot's bullet crashes into his brain when he does savor life fully as a man.

Margot Macomber is perhaps the least attractive of Hemingway's women characters, many of whom share characteristics with her. She is spoiled, selfish, domineering, and castrating on the one hand, insecure and frightened on the other. Such women are able to control weak men, as Macomber was at the beginning of the story, but cannot work their wiles on the strong. Wilson takes her casually in his tent partly because he shares her contempt for her husband. After Macomber's death, however, it is he who reminds her that she would have been left had she not killed him. The relationship between Macomber and Margot is based on their mutual weaknesses, and could not have survived his maturity. Knowing this, Margot kills him as a perverse act of self-preservation.

*Style and Technique*

Hemingway is the best-known stylist in modern American literature, and this story is an excellent example of his method. Understatement is the best term to characterize his writing. Using simple, declarative sentences, he avoids elaborate description, allowing exact physical details to suggest the settings, backgrounds, and implications of his stories. The reader is never told, for example, that Robert Wilson is British, but careful examination of his dialogue reveals his origins. Similarly, in the opening passages of the story, only the words "pretending that nothing had happened" alert the reader to anything out of the ordinary, yet by the time the reader learns that Macomber had been a coward, it comes as no surprise. Through slight intonations of dialogue and description, Hemingway has "shown" its effects before he "tells" about Macomber's failure.

Hemingway rarely uses symbols overtly, yet subtly they are embedded in the story. Wilson's admiration of the beasts he hunts, usually expressed in such terse lines as "damned fine lion" or "hell of a good bull," suggest that these animals embody the qualities that he, and Hemingway, admire most: courage, strength, honesty, and grace under pressure. Ritual is important, too, in Hemingway's work, and is most emphasized in the hunt itself, which brings out the best in man and animal. In other ways as well, small rituals bring order into the story and structure life into a meaningful whole.

Finally, attention should be paid to Wilson's speech when he says, "Doesn't do to talk too much about all this. Talk the whole thing away. No pleasure in anything if you mouth it up too much." Hemingway shares this basic distrust of language, especially abstract language, so he allows as nearly as possible the action of the story to speak for itself. In "The Short Happy Life of Francis Macomber," his technique succeeds in heightening the power of the story.

*William E. Grant*

# THE SHOT

*Author:* Alexander Pushkin (1799-1837)
*Type of plot:* Sketch
*Time of plot:* About 1815, 1821, and 1826
*Locale:* The fictitious villages of N—— and R—— in Russia
*First published:* "Vystrel," 1831 (English translation, 1875)

> *Principal characters:*
> IVAN PETROVICH BELKIN, the compiler
> LIEUTENANT-COLONEL I. L. P, the narrator
> SILVIO, a former officer in the Russian hussars
> R—— a lieutenant in the infantry
> COUNT B—— a former officer in the hussars
> MASHA, his wife

*The Story*

This double story-within-a-story is presented by Ivan Petrovich Belkin, a gregarious but even-tempered army officer who committed to paper much of what others had told him before his untimely death. The first of his tales, which was related to him by Lieutenant-Colonel I. L. P., takes place among the garrison stationed in the village of N——. At the outset, so the story goes, all present in the garrison are awed and mystified by one Silvio; generous without any thought of recompense, he has retired at an early age from the hussars and exists on an uncertain income. His skill at pistol shooting has taken on nearly legendary proportions. It is said that he can take a loaded pistol and shoot a fly dead from across a room. Already rumors are current that he is troubled by some past dueling incident.

More enigmatic is Silvio's curt dismissal of an episode that the others consider to be manifestly grounds for a duel. During a game of cards, another officer, Lieutenant R——, twice challenges Silvio's scorekeeping, and thus, his reckoning of the money stakes; after two silent rebuffs, he hurls a candlestick at their host. In a cold fury, Silvio demands that he leave. The others expect a formal test of honor and are greatly surprised when Silvio later accepts a slight apology.

One day Silvio receives a letter and immediately begins to pack his possessions. He holds a final dinner for the regiment, and afterward he requests the narrator to stay behind. Pallid, preoccupied, but with devilish coolness, Silvio remarks on the general puzzlement when he did not duel with the unruly officer. Then he informs his guest that six years before, he had fought another hussar, who was also left alive. He shows the narrator a red cap from his previous regiment, with a bullet hole above the forehead.

Embarking on his story, Silvio recounts how he was stationed in a garrison town on the frontier; among his comrades he enjoyed an unrivaled reputation for gallantry, drinking capacity, and dueling skill. A newcomer to the regiment, Count B——, from a well-born family, outdid Silvio in cleverness and was more successful with the ladies. At a formal ball, Silvio sought out his rival and whispered an insult into his ear. When the count slapped his face, a duel was arranged for the following dawn. At the appointed place, his opponent, calmly eating cherries, put the first shot through Silvio's cap. Perturbed beyond measure by the other's nonchalant impudence, Silvio elected not to continue. He has now received an announcement of the other's betrothal to a young and beautiful lady in Moscow.

Following the telling of Silvio's story, five years pass. The narrator has moved to R——, another country village. A nobleman has purchased an estate in the area, and when the narrator comes calling, he is struck by the opulent furnishings. His attention is drawn to a painting of a Swiss scene, with two bullet holes in it right against each other. When the conversation turns to pistol shooting, the narrator lets slip Silvio's name; Count B——, for it is he, is thunderstruck. He completes the story of the interrupted duel. Quite unexpectedly, Silvio appeared at the estate, dusty from a long ride, and demanded of the count the shot he had not taken before. Then, unwilling to fire on an unarmed man, Silvio proposed that they draw lots; with a diabolical smile that the count shall never forget, he announced that, as before, his opponent had the first shot.

Unnerved, the count sent his bullet into the picture. Silvio took aim just as Masha, the count's wife, entered the room. Wildly he proclaimed the entire confrontation a joke—just as the original duel and the count's errant shot had been in jest. Then, taking heed of the count's visible consternation, he paused for a moment and pronounced himself satisfied; he measurably struck fear into his adversary, and that will always remain on the count's conscience. As Masha fell into a faint, Silvio turned to go; then, at the doorway, he drew back his pistol and almost effortlessly sent a second bullet into the picture beside the first shot. The narrator has also heard somewhere that, on the outbreak of the Greek revolution, Silvio commanded a detachment of volunteers and was killed in action against Ottoman forces.

*Themes and Meanings*

The modern reader is at first taken aback at the melodramatic quality of this story; the narrative as it unfolds also seems to a great extent to depend on coincidence. There is, however, a clear though indirectly stated thematic intent. Certain virtues of the military officer—stoicism, indifference to danger, and an unyielding sense of personal honor—are first set forth and then called into question where they appear to excess. At the outset, Silvio appears to be the embodiment of this heroic, valorous type, the more so for the aura of mystery that enshrouds much of his past. With calm and controlled dignity, he dismisses the offending officer from their game of cards; yet he does not, as many would have, pursue the matter to a formal duel. The narrator is even more astonished when he learns that Silvio's conscience is troubled, not by a victim of his extraordinary skill, but by memories of the effrontery of an opponent who ridiculed the fears most men inwardly suffer when dueling.

The count's story casts the issue in a different light. Although there is still the image of Silvio as mercurial and diabolically impulsive, marriage and the passage of time have tempered the count's carefree fatalism. Thus, he was betrayed by his visible agitation when, six years later, Silvio came to finish the duel. That the count had no interest in continuing indicates the degree to which his new station in life has instilled in him responsibility and a greater value for life and security.

The grounds, or indeed pretexts, mentioned here for dueling seem slight if not altogether frivolous. The narrator suggests that only the young can take them seriously. Silvio seems to acknowledge that some grievances are transitory when he refuses to challenge another officer over a disputed score in a card game; he confesses to the narrator that, when he originally insulted the count, his calculated provocation was intended explicitly to incite the other man to a challenge and a formal test of honor. The actual outcome of the duel was of little consequence; what seemed to matter was that each man was able to face imminent death with apparent indifference. Indeed, this open and feckless disregard for personal safety appears to be even more highly esteemed than marksmanship; neither of the parties seemed intent on actually wounding or killing his opponent. The two duels in part seem to have taken place within each participant, who in each case put his own presence of mind and coolness under fire to the test and then evidently abjured the practice. Indeed Silvio, though he pursued the count six years after their suspended duel, eventually enlisted his energies in a larger cause and died fighting for the liberation of Greece.

*Style and Technique*

This work derives much of its impact from the way in which it is told, and notably from the author's ability to fuse several points of view and to join tales from periods years apart into a single narrative with its own internal logic. The style, while often richly descriptive and evocative, is terse, and the mannerisms of the two duelists who tell their own tales blend imperceptibly with the narrator's anecdotal approach. Each episode arouses the narrator's, and the reader's, attention and points the way for the unfolding story of Silvio's duel in two parts with the count. The incident of the duel that was never fought, with Lieutenant R——, prods Silvio into revealing details of the unsettled confrontation from his past. A chance conversation about marksmanship, commenced just as the narrator realizes Count B——'s identity, then leads to the story about the second half of Silvio's duel.

Characterization heightens the reader's interest, for the tale hangs above all on the qualities of reckless valor often displayed in dueling. Silvio is depicted as taciturn and moody; at one juncture the narrator describes him as conjuring up images of the diabolical. Similar imagery is used when the count discusses Silvio' challenge to him; whether the satisfaction he has ultimately obtained has tempered Silvio is left unstated. His dark and brooding qualities are offset by the more outgoing traits of the narrator, and by the count's balanced maturity, which during the years since his first duel has come as a result of ripening experience. Eventually for him dueling stories become merely examples of youthful ardor carried to extremes.

*J. R. Broadus*

# MASTERPLOTS II

## SHORT STORY SERIES
### REVISED EDITION

# TITLE INDEX

# TITLE INDEX

# TITLE INDEX